THE CAMBRIDGE HISTORY OF IRAN

IN EIGHT VOLUMES

Volume 1

THE CAMBRIDGE
HISTORY OF
IRAN

Volume I

THE LAND OF IRAN

edited by

W.B.FISHER
Professor of Geography, University of Durham

CAMBRIDGE
AT THE UNIVERSITY PRESS
1968

Published by the Syndics of the Cambridge University Press
Bentley House, 200 Euston Road, London, N.W. 1
American Branch: 32 East 57th Street, New York, N.Y. 10022

© Cambridge University Press 1968

Library of Congress Catalogue Card Number: 67-12845

Standard Book Number: 521 06935 1

Printed in Great Britain
at the University Printing House, Cambridge
(Brooke Crutchley, University Printer)

BOARD OF EDITORS

GENERAL EDITOR'S PREFACE

"Considering the immense number of books which have been written about Persia", observed E. G. Browne in 1902, "it is strange that so few attempts should hitherto have been made to set forth in a comprehensive yet comparatively concise and summary form the history of that ancient and most interesting kingdom." It was partly in order to remedy this defect that Browne embarked upon his greatest work, *A Literary History of Persia*. Yet despite the many virtues of that splendid opus, and the writings of Sir Percy Sykes and others in the meanwhile, J. H. Iliffe could still write in 1953, "The neglect which has engulfed Persia and Persian history is the more remarkable when the range and splendour of her achievements are considered".

When I undertook to edit a volume of essays on Persian culture and civilization, *The Legacy of Persia*, my purpose was to produce a volume of moderate size which would adumbrate, and little more, the contributions made by the Iranian people in the various fields of human endeavour, in a form acceptable to the general public. That book fulfilled and continues to fulfil its limited aim. But the experience gained during that by no means light labour more than ever made me realize the justice of Browne's and Iliffe's words, and stimulated the ambition to create something more substantial.

During the years when His Excellency Qods Nakhai was Ambassador of Iran in London, I discussed with him on a number of occasions the desirability of having a full-length work on the history and cultural achievements of his country; and naturally (for His Excellency is after all a Persian, and therefore both poet and artist, and lover of poetry and art) our discussions disclosed an admirable unanimity of opinion. At this juncture I was reminded of the remark of the Second Merchant to Angelo in *A Comedy of Errors*: "I am bound for Persia, and want guilders for my voyage." To my intense gratification, His Excellency was soon able to convey to me the offer of a most handsome subsidy from the National Iranian Oil Company towards the costs of compiling and publishing a large-scale History of Iran. The Syndics of the Cambridge University Press, being informed of this offer, speedily matched it by a like generous undertaking; and so the idea of a *Cambridge History of Iran* was born.

The next step was to constitute a Board of Editors. I was very fortunate, and immediately secured the consent of a number of eminent scholars to join with me in setting up a Board. The Board at its first meeting agreed upon a plan of work, and the Syndics accepted their recommendation that the enterprise should be completed in eight volumes of some 500 pages each. Each individual volume was to be planned by a Volume Editor; and here again the scholars invited to undertake this arduous task, involving correspondence with many authorities of many lands who would (it was hoped) write the respective chapters, accepted the call with encouraging celerity.

The entire enterprise has prospered so remarkably—a model, one dares say, of international co-operation—that now in 1968 this first volume of the eight is published; to be followed immediately by the fifth. The scheme (to quote from the Notes for Contributors) is as follows:

Volume I	Physical and Economic Geography; Anthropology and Demography; Flora and Fauna.
Volume II	Prehistory; the Archaeological Periods; Iran in relation to the Ancient World.
Volume III	The Seleucid, Parthian and Sasanid Periods.
Volume IV	The Period from the Arab Invasion to the Saljuqs
Volume V	The Saljuq and Mongol Periods.
Volume VI	The Timurid and Safavid Periods.
Volume VII	The Eighteenth Century to the Present.
Volume VIII	Bibliography; Notes on Folklore; Survey of Research; Indices.

Volumes II–VII are classified according to major events and dynasties in Iranian history for convenience only: the series is not intended to be simply a history of Iran. It is intended to be a survey of the culture which has flourished in the Iranian region, and this culture's contribution to the civilization of the world. In addition to history, the religious, philosophical, political, economic, scientific and artistic elements in Iranian civilization will be described, with a measure of emphasis on the geographical and ecological factors that have contributed to this civilization's special character.

Volume I (as now presented) will be a demographical and geographical study forming a compendium of information about Iran (physically speaking) not hitherto collected concisely and accessibly in a single work. Inevitably, so rapid is the course of modern developments, particularly in regard to land reform and oil technology, judgments reached in certain chapters will have been overtaken by events. Whereas, therefore, the remaining volumes have been entrusted to the editorship of specialists in the human history and culture of Iran, the editor appointed for this first volume is a distinguished geographer of the Middle East.

When the reader thus surveys the majestic panorama of the history of Iran, disclosing a continuous civilization of nearly three millennia, he cannot fail to wonder at the persistent integrity of that culture. Though the broad lands of Iran have been ravaged not seldom by foreign invaders, and from time to time held in captivity by alien rulers, the indigenous rulers and people of Iran have never lost faith in the high destiny of their nation. Ideas from abroad, if proven valuable by the test of years, have been readily, indeed eagerly *iranized*, to accumulate an ever richer inheritance. Physical disasters—the destruction of beautiful cities and the slaughter of their inhabitants—have served often as a challenge and a spur to national revival. Throughout all these centuries of turbulence the Iranian people have remained true to themselves and their most prized ideals.

The Board of Editors desire to express their hearty thanks to all those who have made possible the realization of their plan: first, to His Excellency Qods Nakhai and the Directors of the National Iranian Oil Company; next, to the many scholars who have agreed to participate in this undertaking; finally, to the Syndics of Cambridge University Press, the Secretary of the Press, and his staff.

It may be taken as a happy augury, not only for the success of this enterprise, but for the prosperity of other like tasks in which Great Britain in the reign of Queen Elizabeth II joins hands with Iran, that this work has been begun and, God willing, will be completed during the reign of His Imperial Majesty the Shahanshah, Mohammad Reza Pahlavi.

A. J. ARBERRY

Cambridge
January 1968

CONTENTS

CONTENTS

PART 2: THE PEOPLE

PART 3: ECONOMIC LIFE

PART 4: CONCLUSION

PLATES

VOLUME EDITOR'S PREFACE

It would be normal to expect that in approaching the study of a region so extensive, isolated, and incompletely known as is Iran, there would be much convenience in having at hand some kind of atlas or gazeteer to which reference could be made regarding location and distribution. This is in one aspect the basic function of a volume that appears as chronologically the earliest in a series entitled *The Cambridge History of Iran*: to set the physical stage for the human events that have unrolled their remarkable pattern over so long a period; and to render in some degree comprehensible the varied natural elements that together produce the overall physical environment of Iran. In this way it is hoped that volume I will in certain measure furnish support and function as a companion for the remainder of the series.

Yet the influence of natural environmental factors goes far beyond that of merely providing an unmoved backcloth against which the human drama takes place. A highly significant trend in modern geographical studies has been to demonstrate that the natural setting exerts pressures and influences of widely differing kinds. This topic is developed at length as the final contribution to the present volume: here, the writer wishes merely to state his opinion that in some cases these environmental influences are of limited effect, whilst in others they could be held to amount to control. It is the thesis of volume I that the natural elements of location, geological structure, physiography, and climate would appear to shape in distinct and recognizable ways the course of human activity, on a global and also on a regional scale. Even in a highly evolved and sophisticated society of long standing, where the apparent influences of environment would seem to have been diminished or possibly removed by human progress and activity, the proposition still holds, as the present writer believes—though in subtler and more indirect ways. To whatever degree the ingenuity of man may seek to obscure or vary the situation, there is really no way round such hard facts as, for instance, that Switzerland has been for long more easily defensible than Belgium; that petroleum is present in larger quantity and exploited more cheaply in Iran than in Italy; or that the climate of California attracts a greater volume of human settlement than that of Qatar or Labrador. R. H. Tawney saw the rise of capitalism as the effect of particular opportunities for resource-use in the special environmental and human situation of Western Europe. Marx and Lenin, whilst denying the total control of physical environment over human will, ascribed the driving force of history basically to material situations and distributions; and from certain points of view the ideas of Rostow on "take-off" imply at least close involvement with environmental conditions.

Moreover, a civilization or culture never occurs in total isolation: Heyerdahl demonstrated that even the remotest islands of the largest ocean in the world could have been touched by influences originating hundreds of miles away. Just as man is not in himself an island, any study of a community must consider the problems of relations to out-side territories and their inhabitants. Some peoples may be held to be fortunate in having had fairly well-defined, defensible, and endowed regions in which to live, whilst others have had to struggle with ungrateful, constricted, or amorphous territories.

Iran offers the picture of sharp identity as a geographical unit that derives from overall similarities based on highly varied and often harsh natural conditions at local level. The concept of a mosaic often occurs in reference to Iran, since whilst the smaller, regional, pieces tend to be markedly different, in totality a clear and recognizable pattern emerges at national level. Because of the character of Iranian geography, its inhabitants have experienced considerable vicissitude, and elucidation of the complex relationships involved between terrain and people is a principal aim of the present volume.

As C. S. Lewis recognized in his *New Ignorance and New Learning*,[1] part at least of the forces or abstractions which bear the names "destiny" or "fate" can be resolved into influences of a natural kind that derive from the physiographical environment. Such a situation appears also to have been apparent to many of the early savants of Iran—the astrologer–astronomer–mathematicians who were conscious of a cosmological control that often to them appeared more concrete than anything implied in the expressions destiny and fate. This aware-ness appears to have led to a search for a means of escape, in personal terms, from the sub-firmamental pattern of existence imposed by the natural conditions of Iran. Much of the content of Iranian poetry, though expressed in a different idiom, could be regarded as deep yearning for escape from the realities of human existence as confined and rounded by inexorable realities of the physical environment. Such

[1] C. S. Lewis, *English Literature in the Sixteenth Century* (Oxford, 1954), pp. 1–65.

limitations and controls imposed by cosmology we now translate in terms of climate, physiology, resources, and territorial location; but the continuity of thought and similarity of concept are there.

In this volume treatment of the general topic of the land and people in Iran has been of necessity selective. Besides the inevitable limitation imposed by space, there are gaps in knowledge and understanding concerning certain regions and topics. The problem has obtruded, sometimes critically, as to whether it would be justifiable to risk a statement made in broad general terms, in order to give a reasonable overall appreciation; or whether, because of variation in quantity and reliability of data, to confine the writing to those topics which could be held to have a secure factual basis. One other difficulty, normal in works of this kind, is the barrier of language. To find experts in specialized fields adept in the one, two, or even three Oriental language families current in parts of Iran may be asking over-much. Lack of objective data, the sheer physical obstacles to extensive field investigation, and paucity of resources—human and financial—reduce further the available source material.

Knowledge in more detail of the upper atmospheric conditions over Iran, where extensive exchange of air-mass and energy takes place as two sharply dissimilar temperature contrasts develop seasonally, would greatly strengthen our appreciation of the varied weather conditions that affect the country. Similarly, we so far lack certain human data that would allow closer analysis of sociological situations among the populations of the country, though the situation is changing.

Mention has been made of difficulties and omissions. There has also been valuable and sustained assistance, both at a personal level, and from institutions. Certain contributors to this volume have been able to work in Iran thanks to interest from the Rockefeller Trustees, who generously supported proposals made from a relatively unknown university department. This initial interest was continued in a most timely way by the Hayter scheme which allowed further activities from Durham within the Middle East.

Travel in Iran is not always wholly straightforward, and the British Institute for Persian Studies, through its Director, Mr D. Stronach and Deputy Director, Mr B. Spooner, provided a welcoming and secure base from which field visits could be organized.

Grateful acknowledgment and thanks are also offered to the following organizations and individuals for the use (in whole or part) of reports, field material and learned articles made available to this volume either by private communication or general publication: the American Association of Petroleum Geologists, Tulsa, Oklahoma, and the *AAPG Bulletin*, vol. XLII, no. 12, 1958 (P. E. Kent), and special publication, *Habitat of Oil* (1958) (N. L. Falcon); E. J. Brill, Ltd., Leiden, *Proc. 3rd World Petr. Cong.*, 1951; the British Petroleum Co. Ltd., London, for geological folder relating to S.W. Iran, 1956; the Geographical Association, Sheffield; *Geologische Jahrbuch*, vol. LI, Hanover, 1962 (R. Huckreide, M. Kursten, H. Venzlaff); the Institute of Petroleum, London, *Journal*, vol. XXX, 1944 (N. L. Falcon); Knapp Verlag, Halle/ Düsseldorf; Laboratoire de Géographie Physique et de Géologie Dynamique, Paris, *Révue*, vol. VII, 1934 (A. Rivière); National Iranian Oil Co., Tehrān, Geological Map of Iran, 1959; Schweiz. Mineralogische u. Petrographische Gesellschaft, Basel, *Schweiz. Min. Petr. Mitt.* vol. XLII, 1962 (A. Gansser and H. Huber).

My colleagues in Durham have been willing to tolerate a certain remoteness and ineffectuality on my part when local interests were for a time superseded by Iranian preoccupations. To Professor H. Bowen Jones especially I owe much in that he has afforded advice, support, and material and intellectual sustenance during a period of stress in part at least related to the accordion-like expansions, halts, and contractions that now seem normal in British University life. Mr D. L. Dent and Mr R. G. Hartley have given much assistance in the preparation of maps and diagrams; and the whole process of writing owes a great deal to energy, helpfulness, and concern from Miss S. J. Pennington (now Mrs M. Billingham). Miss J. A. Brown, Dr J. I. Clarke and Dr D. F. Darwent have kindly allowed the use of some of their own work on Iranian cities. The task of functioning as Volume Editor was greatly lightened by the initiative, vision, and courtesy afforded by the General Editor, Professor A. J. Arberry, and I am glad especially to express my obligations to the Editorial Secretary of the Series, Mr P. W. Avery, for friendly comment, sustained interest, and unfailing understanding and welcome. Lastly, I also wish to record my deep appreciation of the hospitality regularly extended on frequent occasions over the past few years by King's College, Cambridge.

W. B. FISHER

Durham, January 1968

UNITS OF MEASUREMENT

Use of units, whether metric or otherwise, has proved to be an awkward matter, the more so as Britain is currently edging towards wider employment of the metric system. The solution adopted throughout this volume is to regard the various systems as wholly interchangeable; and rather than give an equivalent alongside, which might unduly encumber the text, a particular system as used by an individual author has been preserved. Conversion tables to be found on pp. 765–6 will, it is hoped, allow such equivalents as may be wanted to be readily obtained.

W. B. F.

PART I

THE LAND

CHAPTER I

PHYSICAL GEOGRAPHY

The present Iranian state covers an area of some 628,000 square miles (1,648,000 sq. km) and extends between latitude 25° and 40° N., and longitude 44° and 63° E. More than six times the size of Great Britain and approximately three times the size of France, which is the largest country in Western Europe, Iran has a frontier that has been estimated at 2,750 miles in total length, of which over half is sea coast, with 400 miles lying along the southern Caspian shore, and the remainder (1,100 miles) comprising the northern parts of the Gulf of Oman and Persian Gulf. From the extreme north-west to south-east—at approximately the frontier with Turkey and the U.S.S.R., close to Mt Ararat, as far as the Baluchistan border just east of Chāhbahār[1]—is a total distance of 1,450 miles; whilst an opposite diagonal, so to speak, from Bushire (Būshahr) to the Soviet frontier north-east of Mashhad, would measure 830 miles.

Physically, Iran consists of a complex of mountain chains enclosing a series of interior basins that lie at altitudes of 1,000 to 4,000 ft above sea-level. These mountain ranges rise steeply from sea-level on the north and on the south, and equally abruptly from the very flat and extremely low-lying plain of Mesopotamia to the west. Eastward, and also in the extreme north-west, the highlands extend beyond Iran in the form of largely continuous and uninterrupted features: in the first area they are prolonged as the massifs of Afghanistan and Baluchistan (West Pakistan), and in the north-west as the plateau uplands of Russian Azerbaijan and eastern Asia Minor.

Most of the frontiers of Iran were delimited between 1800 and 1914, and in disposition show considerable correlation with local features of topography. For the greater part they tend to follow watersheds or riverlines, the break of slope between plain or plateau, and mountain ranges, or else they are related to areas of low human occupancy such as marsh, swamp, or arid desert. Included within the boundaries of Iran are a few, but remarkably small, expanses of lowland: mostly in

---

[1] So on modern Persian maps, but Chāhbār is an established variant, see V. Minorsky: Ḥudūd al-ʿĀlam (London, 1937), p. 373.

Fig. 2. Iran: political. *Ostans* (provinces) numbered: 1 Central (Tehrān), 2 Gīlān, 3 East Āzarbāïjān, 4 West Āzarbāïjān, 5 Kurdistān–Kirmānshāh, 6 Khūzistān–Luristān, 7 Iṣfahān–Yazd, 8 Fārs–Banander, 9 Kirmān, 10 Balūchistān–Sīstān, 11 Khurāsān, 12 Māzandarān–Gurgān.

the province of Khūzistān (which in terms of topography and geomorphology could be held to be part of the Mesopotamian plain), and also fronting the coasts of the Persian Gulf and the Caspian Sea. However, the width of these lowland strips is well under fifty miles, and often less than ten miles. Iran is therefore overwhelmingly an area of pronounced relief, with mountains a dominant element. The average height of the land surface of Iran can be regarded as being over 3,000 ft above sea-level—a feature repeated only in relatively few countries of the world, such as Spain, where the average is 2,000 ft, or again in Turkey, Mexico, Tibet, and Bolivia.

In terms of physical geography, Iran comprises the western and larger portion of a more extensive mountain zone that extends from

4

eastern Asia Minor and the Caucasus as far as the plains of the Punjab. This entire upland is in fact spoken of by some writers as the Iranian plateau, despite the fact that politically it includes most of the state of Afghanistan and a large part of the territory of West Pakistan. Further, the term "plateau" is applied in a general way, by several American and English writers, to the whole upland mass; whereas French and German geographers, notably Derruau, Bobek, and Scharlau (as will be noted later in this volume) tend to restrict the term to the inner central basins of the Iranian state, and hence speak of the surrounding highland ring as a distinctive and somewhat separate mountain zone. In the view of the present writer there are no strong grounds for extending the connotation of "Iranian plateau" to include upland areas of Afghanistan and West Pakistan. Because of its political implications the term could be seriously misleading, and there is no clear physical unity within the wider zone thus denoted. In fact, the existence of a series of north–south-running ridges and divides tends to separate the southern desert basins of Iran from the Helmand lowland; and these ridges, although narrow and not especially imposing, nevertheless afford a reasonably precise basis for division. One could therefore speak with validity in purely physical terms of an Iranian upland zone that would correspond closely to the existing political unit. Any merit deriving from a strictly physiographical application of the term "plateau" regardless of national division is dubious and slight when set against the considerable political disadvantage inherent in it. Use of the term "Iranian plateau" will therefore, throughout the rest of this volume, be restricted to the upland area actually territorially within the boundaries of the present state of Iran. The matter of "plateau" generally, inclusive or exclusive of the surrounding mountain ring, is more difficult. A reasonable approach would seem to be to try to make clear in an individual context whether the writer implies only the interior basins or not, and this will be attempted whenever possible. Even though the single expression is neater, differing interpretations by individual contributors to this volume make necessary some detailed indication of what is meant.

In general form Iran has been likened to a bowl, with a high outer rim surrounding an irregular and lower, but not low-lying, interior. The rim is formed by various groups of mountain chains, some of which, especially in the west and north, are not only high and bold but also extensive in ground area; whilst those of the south and east are

5

narrower, lower in general height, more interrupted by lowland basins, and therefore less of a barrier. In the east, however, climatic effects— chiefly aridity, with the accumulation of sand and rock debris—re- inforce the diminished importance of relief: hence the concept of a physiographical "rim" to Iran can be maintained.

Most developed of all the mountain ranges of Iran is the Zagros system. This extends from north-west to south-east, defining as it were the principal "grain" of much of Iran, and occupying the entire western part of the country—about one half of the total area. Diverging from the northern Zagros in an easterly direction are the Tālish and Alburz chains, which, though narrower, are equally high and also relatively unbroken. The open side, so to speak, of this angle between the south-east-running Zagros and east-trending Alburz is closed to a partial degree, as we have already noted, by more scattered highland massifs—and there is no single collective name that can be applied to this group of irregularly disposed and detached ranges. "Eastern Highlands of Iran" is a makeshift used by some writers, but is open to the obvious objection that it would appear to denote a major and continuous system comparable with the Zagros and Alburz.

The remaining major physical units forming Iran are (i) the interior basins contained within the surrounding mountain rim; and (ii) small expanses of lowland, coastal and riverine, located on the outer peri- phery of this rim. It is scarcely appropriate to refer to the interior as a single extensive basin, but better as a complex of several hollows or drainage sumps lying at varying altitudes, and delimited by irregular but sometimes imposing topographical divides which in certain in- stances become considerable mountain ranges.

Since mountains make up much of the scenery of Iran, there are two types of topography: that of the mountains themselves, or else a juxtaposition of remarkably flat stretches with upland ranges. Over much of the inner Iran, and again on the extreme outer parts, one has the impression of flats and levels, sometimes wide and extensive, sometimes restricted, but almost always limited at short or long dis- tance by an abrupt mountain wall.

When we examine the general geographical aspects of Iran, it is convenient to proceed on the basis of the major physical units discussed above, even though these are of considerable size. We can therefore arrive at four major divisions of the country: the Zagros system, including small outer plains (chiefly the Khūzistān region), which are

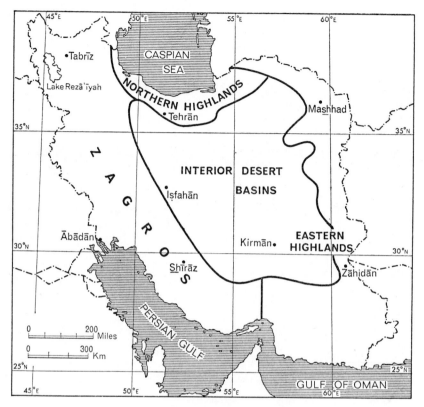

Fig. 3. Iran: physiographic units.

part of the Mesopotamian and Persian Gulf lowlands; the Alburz and associated Caspian plain; the eastern and south-eastern upland rim; and the interior. Within this broad framework more local and sub-regional contrasts can be drawn; and whilst in a few instances precise demarcation between the major units is far from straightforward, for the most part the scheme adopted in the succeeding pages allows easy breakdown into units of distinct geographical significance.

THE ZAGROS REGION

As a single major physical region, the Zagros could be said to dominate the entire western portion of Iran, for it comprises some of the most imposing fold structure and clusters of high peaks to be found not only in Iran but within the whole of the Middle East. In terms of structure and

7

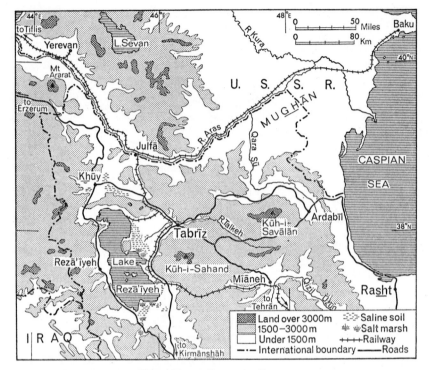

Fig. 4. The north-western Zagros.

hence topography it shows considerable variation, and two distinct
sub-regions may be recognized: a north-western section extending from
the Turkish–Russian frontier broadly as far as the zone Qazvīn–
Hamadān–Kirmānshāh; and the remainder, beginning at the latter line
and extending as far as Bandar 'Abbās and Hurmuz on the Strait of
Oman. The name "Zagros" tends to be restricted, in fact, to this latter
portion; but in the writer's view the name could better apply to the
upland as a whole, and a case could even be made for regarding the
Zagros system as continuing through the Makrān towards the Pakistan
frontier.

The north-west

The north-western Zagros may be described as roughly rectangular
in disposition, and it consists of a series of massive structures, chiefly
of Upper Cretaceous, Miocene, and Plio-Pleistocene geological age,
which have been much disturbed—partly by folding on a relatively

8

restricted scale, but more especially by fracturing followed by differential warping. A further effect resulting from fracturing and dislocation of the rock series has been the rise of magma on a considerable scale, so that much of the land surface is now formed by extruded igneous material.

The general topographical effect is consequently that of a series of irregular tablelands, which lie at an average altitude of 5,000 to 6,000 ft over much of the area; greater heights tending to occur in the extreme north and west, where average elevation could be said to be between 7,000 and 9,000 ft. The plateau surfaces also exhibit a general tilt that produces lower elevations mainly towards the south and east of this sub-region; and the overall effect of a "stair" topography is further emphasized by fault-scarps, which define a number of fault-valleys and downthrow basins. One such major fault-structure is the Aras valley, which consists of a sequence of rifts or fault-troughs that later became joined as a single valley by the effect of river erosion. Consequently the Aras valley has alternate open and narrow sections—a gorge just below Julfā, for instance, contrasting sharply with much flatter and broader stretches above and below.

Largest of the downthrow basins is that of the Rezā'īyeh (Urumīyeh) system, from which there is no drainage outlet; and other basins of similar structure but smaller extent are the lowland around <u>Kh</u>uy, the upper basin of the Qareh Sū river around Ardabīl, and the associated tributary valley of the Ahar lying north-east of Tabrīz.

Another element of much significance, and very often with striking topographical effects, is the superposition of large volcanic cones upon the high plateau surfaces. The best-developed but by no means the only examples produce the peaks of Savalan (14,000 ft), Sahand (12,138 ft) and Ararat (16,946 ft)—this last being just outside Persian territory. Dislocation and readjustment of the rock series in this area have by no means ceased, and the region is thus subject to a considerable number of earthquakes. Especially vulnerable is the city of Tabrīz, where building styles minimize the effects of earth tremors: one, or only a few storeys, and light construction unless on a massive rock foundation.

This liability to earthquake devastation is characteristic of much of Iran, and of the north and west especially. Figure 5 shows the local effects of one major tremor that took place in 1964.

The final major influence in the evolution of landscape in the north-western Zagros has been erosion due to rivers. Because of its con-

9

siderable altitude, rainfall is distinctly heavier over much of the plateau, with as much as 35 to 40 in. in parts of the extreme west; and the effect of this is augmented by the sharply seasonal onset, which concentrates the erosive effects into a short period. As a result, a number of deeply incised streams have cut considerable, often gorge-like valleys in less resistant strata. Effects due to heightened erosion are best exemplified in the north and west, towards the frontiers with Turkey and Iraq. Here the plateau is at its most developed, with maximum elevation produced by tilt; and the presence of numerous strong streams dropping rapidly towards the Iraqi lowlands gives rise to majestically contrasting scenery: enormous domes and jagged peaks, sombre defiles or dizzy gorges, and tenuous but well-defined valleys and flats, often grassy or wooded. Farther to the east and south, still within this northern zone of the Zagros, conditions take on more the character of an irregular, rolling plateau, broken by occasionally higher summits and a few deeper basins or river valleys. Certain of these valleys, especially towards Qazvin and Hamadān, are synclinal, i.e. the results of surface folding rather than of faulting and downthrow; and as we have already noted, crustal folding on a restricted scale is by no means entirely absent, even in the extreme north.

However, the predominant appearance of the north-western Zagros is one of tabular arrangement rather than intense folding: this differentiates the region strongly from its neighbour the central Zagros lying farther south-east. Routes within this sub-region must follow relatively tortuous valleys, or cross plateau surfaces at high altitudes and subsequently find a precarious way to lower levels across steep scarps.

Drainage in this area is complex. The tectonic trough of the Aras has a number of subsidiary downthrow basins opening off it, and in consequence there is a well-developed pattern of feeder tributaries flowing partly in relatively broad, flat-floored valleys, where the stream meanders or even splits into distributaries; and partly in constricted gorges, where the banks are close and the flow is swift. Equally important is the aretic (closed) system draining to Lake Rezā'īyeh. Of a total area of some 20,000 square miles, this drainage basin is defined on the east by the massifs culminating in Mt Sahand. Some thirty to forty miles west of the lake shore lies a series of major mountain crests that give rise to a watershed now adopted as the frontier with Iraq, and from this watershed the headwaters of the Great and

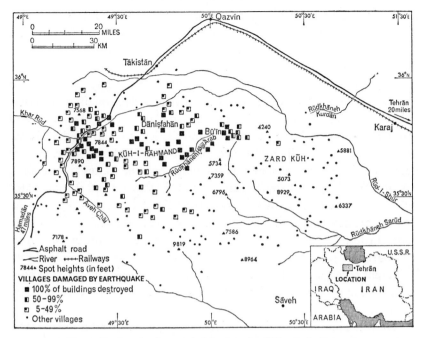

Fig. 5. Earthquake damage in March 1964. (After J. A. Brown.)

the Lesser Zāb plunge westward to join the main Tigris–Euphrates system. On the east, the Qizil Uzūn has cut backwards to produce an intricate, involuted drainage pattern that ultimately finds its way eastward to join the Safīd Rūd in a breach through the Alburz system. In general, then, the north-western Zagros has a complex pattern of markedly radial drainage, with a large central basin—that of Lake Rezā'iyeh—from which there is no outlet.

Lying in a depression produced mainly by tectonic action rather than by water erosion, Lake Rezā'iyeh is a shallow sheet of water lying at 4,250 ft above sea level and measuring very approximately ninety miles by thirty. It is without steep retaining banks close to the present shore, and is consequently liable to much fluctuation in surface area. During the spring season, and following especially heavy winter rains, it can be as much as fifteen to twenty feet deep but it shrinks to as little as four to six feet in certain places after a pronounced dry period. The streams feeding it, particularly those from the east, have cut into layers of gypsum and other minerals. Much of the territory round Lake Rezā'iyeh consists basically of limestone series, with extensive igneous intrusions. The episodic and relatively low rainfall (about 12 to 13 in.) leads to a marked grading of surface soil and rock deposits. Towards the higher ground, and away from the lake, deposits are relatively coarse, and soils more open and thus better drained. The content of soluble minerals in the rock layers near the surface is distinctly higher than in some other areas, with gypsum and volcanic beds providing considerable quantities of salts that have now accumulated in the lake waters and in the soils surrounding the lake. Salinity is less than in the Dead Sea, but there is a markedly higher proportion of sodium carbonate. Except at times of very high water (usually late spring), the shores are occupied by an expanse of salty sterile mud; and as the streams and subsoil water are also saline for some distance away from the lake, the shores are for the most part empty and desolate, with only a very few halophytic plants and shrubs. Of interest to the geographer are the remains of numerous topographic benches, strandlines, and deltaic deposits, which indicate different levels and oscillations of the water-surface, and provide considerable evidence, as yet far from fully worked out, on earlier climatic phases.

Despite a number of substantial handicaps, which in addition to water salinity also include a difficult topography, heat and cold, and a disturbed political background, human settlement is here more extensive than in many other parts of Iran. The north-western Zagros ranks as one of the most densely peopled areas of the country. As we have noted, great altitude in certain parts results in a distinctly higher rainfall, and this, together with the recent phases of vulcanicity, has given rise to a somewhat deeper and more fertile soil in a number of localities. Hence at lower levels, where there is shelter from the bitter winter winds and soil has accumulated as small deltas or flats, cultivation occurs on a scale greater than in many other parts of Iran—the Caspian lowlands excepted. At higher altitudes, on the plateau surface, the climate is often too cold and water too scanty (because of percolation into a porous substratum) to produce anything more than a thin vegetational cover of short grass and low scrub, which is frequently broken by expanses of bare rugged rock. Towards the frontier with Iraq, great height and relative remoteness have still preserved a native woodland, which continues to flourish in certain spots. This is most likely a relic of earlier, wetter times, and once cleared rarely regenerates naturally, since the small depth of soil in which it grows is rapidly eroded off.

Two somewhat different ways of life have thus come into existence in this north-western region: pastoralism in the higher parts, and cultivation, mostly of a settled kind, in the more favoured, lower-lying areas. Sheep and goats, with some cattle and a few horses or even camels, are reared by herders, who tend for the most part to be sedentary and have some attachment, at least for a portion of the year, to the cultivated areas at lower levels. But nomadism still exists, particularly towards the west, where Kurdish shepherds continue to migrate seasonally, sometimes across frontiers into Iraq and Turkey (not, of course, into the U.S.S.R.) and on a smaller scale in the Mughān steppe zones of the north-east. It is an interesting reflexion of the significance of pastoralism in north-west Iran that the Qarā Qoyūnlū (Black Sheep) Türkmen, who ruled Iran during the fifteenth century, made Tabrīz their national capital.

Cultivation follows the general Iranian pattern, with cereals (wheat, barley, and some maize) the basic crops, and a wide range of fruit and vegetables. Mediterranean fruits—vine, almond, and apricot especially—grow very well in the more favoured parts of this region; and cotton, tobacco, opium, and oil seeds are also important. Villages tend to cluster near water-courses, where a few willow, poplar, or walnut trees dominate the smaller but more numerous fruit trees and orchards. Chief areas of cultivation are (1) those parts of the middle and higher Rezā'īyeh basin away from the saline areas: especially the valley of the Ajī Chāi leading to Tabrīz; (2) parts of the Qizil Uzūn lowlands, particularly round Miāneh and along a tributary valley, that of the Zanjān river; (3) the Qareh Sū valley round Ardabīl; and (4) the Khuy basin and adjacent parts of the Aras near Julfā.

This north-western section of the Zagros has importance as the focus of major routes. Besides containing a number of ancient east–west routes linking the Aegean, Asia Minor, Central Asia, and India, the region is now on the principal lines of communication between Iran and the Soviet Union. In consequence, there have long been considerable external trading interests, and the local products of the region—wool, leather, and dried fruits—have found commercial outlets in other countries. This nodal position where the more ancient east–west routes intersect the newer north–south lines (now of growing significance), explains why Tabrīz has at several periods functioned as the capital of a wide territory, which has sometimes included not only Iran but even lands beyond. Trading of an international character, as well as a fundamental strategic importance, has added important extra elements to its two basic economic activities of herding and cultivation.

Tabrīz

Tabrīz, in the present century at least, has ranked as the second city of Iran, though now approached more closely in population size by Mashhad and Iṣfahān. Its name has been held to refer to the thermal springs which are numerous in the locality; or, as the name in modern Persian indicates, to its good air ("fever-dispelling"). Tabrīz may date from early Sasanid times (c. third or fourth century A.D.) or, more likely, from the seventh century A.D. At several periods it has functioned as a national capital, notably under Tīmūr, under the "Black Sheep" Türkmen (c. 1450), and in the sixteenth century under the earlier Safavids. However, its greatest importance may have been under the Īl-Khāns of the late fourteenth and early fifteenth centuries, when it was the chief city of a state that extended as far as the Nile valley and Central Asia. Recurrent warfare and earthquakes have destroyed much of the medieval part of the city, so that only two older monuments survive, the Arg or Citadel, which is a reconstructed medieval mosque, and the Blue Mosque (c. 1450). Consequently the city has distinctly less of the architectural beauty and appeal of, for instance, Iṣfahān, Shīrāz, or even Mashhad.

Placed in the extreme north-west of Iran, in the open countryside from which relatively easy routes reach the Caspian central lowlands, Russia, eastern Anatolia, and the Black Sea coastlands, Tabrīz has developed considerably over the last century and a half as a military centre. By no means surprising in view of its location, it has been occupied since 1800, once by Turks and several times by Russians, the last of these occasions being as recently as 1947–8. Changes in the disposition of frontiers during the first part of the nineteenth century made Tabrīz in effect an important salient commanding the approaches from the vital north-west towards central and southern Iran. This continuing strategic position was recognized by inclusion of Tabrīz in the Central Treaty Organization radar chain.

Parallel to its military and strategic significance, it has importance as an exchange centre, since it handles a good deal of the trade involving countries to the north and west of Iran. Carpets, agricultural and pastoral products (especially dried fruit), Caspian fish, and machinery

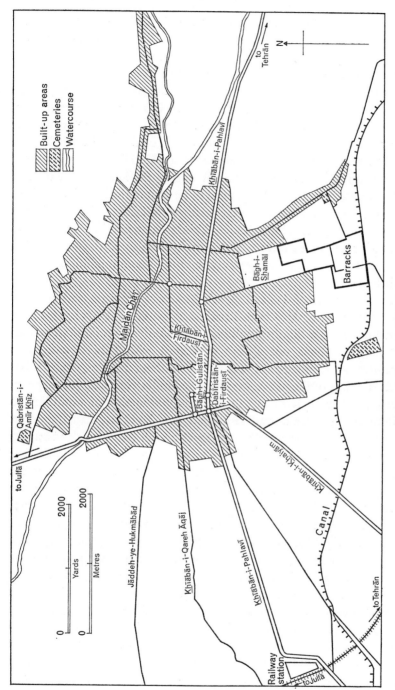

Fig. 6. The city of Tabrīz.

from Europe are marketed, either via Russia or the Black Sea ports of Turkey. It is noteworthy that Tabrīz was linked to Russia by the eighty-two mile extension of the Russian system through Tiflis and Julfā long before Tehrān had a major railway.

As the regional market and administrative centre for one of the most densely populated parts of Iran, Tabrīz also has important local trading and manufacturing interests, especially in carpets and to a lesser degree in leather. But with the diminution of commercial links through Russia after about 1945, following the "Iron Curtain" policy of Stalin, the expansion of Tabrīz, prominent during the later nineteenth and early twentieth centuries, has tended somewhat to slacken. Faced with a shift of commercial interest to the southern oilfields, and the rapid rise of Tehrān as an economic leader, Tabrīz has tended of late to hold something of an ex-centric situation in Iranian affairs—a position exacerbated by its virtual exclusion from Iranian political control during 1942–8.

As the capital of Persian Āzarbāijān, with cultural and political links that continue into both Russia and Turkey, Tabrīz has for long been known as a highly "politically minded" town, with advanced and radical groups not always in accord with Pahlavī nationalist sentiment as expressed in Tehrān. For these reasons, Tabrīz has received fewer of the new state-supported industries than, for example, Iṣfahān, S̲h̲īrāz, or Kirmāns̲h̲āh. Recent construction of a rail link to Tehrān and the main Iranian system has, however, had important results, and it is now possible to travel by rail (with break of gauge) through Tabrīz to Moscow and Western Europe. For the increasing number of tourists arriving by car from Europe, Tabrīz remains the point of entry to Iran, and this, whilst adding to or reviving the traditional functions and anxieties of the responsible foreign agencies, at the same time augments the commercial activities of the city.

Tabrīz is also characterized by a relative absence of good water. The many mineral springs and solid deposits associated with the near-by volcanic complex of Mt Sahand render much of the surface water brackish, and supplies are brought by qanāt (aqueduct) at considerable trouble from relatively few and distant sources. Hence there are few of the gardens, fountains, and shady corners that tend to be found in some other Iranian cities; and owing to the extensive use of dark volcanic tuff as building material and the restriction of height owing to tectonic disturbances, the town has a somewhat sombre appearance.

The main Zagros

At a narrow zone which could be very summarily defined as coinciding with the line of the highway from Qazvīn to Hamadān and then south-west towards Kirmānshāh, the nature of the Zagros uplands begins to change markedly. For about 750 miles from north-west to south-east, and over an extent of 200 to 250 miles in width, there occurs the principal development of the Zagros system, with well-defined and highly characteristic features. Chief of these are the remarkable fold structures which for the most part are alined from north-west to south-east, and arranged in a distinctly regular pattern as a sequence of elevated domes or hogs' backs. These are of varying length but of very similar trend and alinement. In the north, that is, from Hamadān–Kirmānshāh as far as the region of Bushire, the folds are extremely regular, straight in form and parallel in strike, and relatively tightly packed together. Farther south they open out, becoming less densely grouped, and from being straight they take on more of an arcuate or cuspate shape, so that the overall trend changes, with several major variations in direction.

Towards the east, where the Zagros folds abut on the resistant blocks that form the inner plateau of Iran, a greater degree of dislocation has produced imbrication of structures, and a considerable area of overthrusting—that is, an elaboration of nappes rather than simple folds. The implications of this difference are of course greatest for the geologist, but in influencing topography the effects are also of much interest. The eastern margins of the central Zagros tend to be higher, more rugged in appearance, and of a more complex trend. On the west, the folds are on the whole lower in altitude and less compressed together, so that many authorities describe this as a distinctive zone of minor foothills forming, as it were, a transition from the imposing ridges of the central and eastern parts of Zagros to the plains of Iraq and the Persian Gulf coast.

A further remarkable physiographical element is the pattern of drainage. In the north, relatively heavy precipitation gives rise to numerous and well-developed rivers; and these have cut valleys of an extremely varied and intricate nature. In some instances the rivers weave a tortuous way round the ends of ridges or elongated domes, gradually dropping westward towards the Tigris and Persian Gulf, and producing a "trellis pattern" of drainage. But other streams appear to avoid broad and open valleys produced by folding, and cut across mountain ridges at some of their highest and most intractable parts by means of enormously deep but narrow gorges. These clefts (or *tangs*) are sometimes straight, but can as well be markedly looped, like gigantic meanders. Excellent examples of this last are to be noted on the Saidmarreh river (known lower in its course as the Karkheh) below Kirmānshāh and at Shāh Maḥmūd. Yet, having crossed by tangs several imposing ridges, the river then turns abruptly to the south-east, being deflected by one ridge that it has not breached: the Kabīr Kūh.

The origin of the tangs themselves has usually hitherto been ascribed to cross-faulting, and the intricate drainage network could also have been influenced by rapid erosion along these lines of what was initially crustal weakness; in certain cases this has resulted in a "capture" or diversion of the streams. But in other instances there would seem to be no evidence either of faulting or of capture, and there then remains the question of possible antecedent drainage, that is, a previously existing pattern of streams flowing over lower relief, which was later gradually uplifted at a sufficiently slow rate to permit the streams to cut down at a rate that allowed them to retain their original "line". This problem is examined at length by T. M. Oberlander in a contribution to the present volume.

Farther to the south, rainfall is progressively smaller in total amount and more sporadic, so perennial streams and rivers become less and less a feature. Most tend to be seasonal, or flow for a short distance only to end in closed basins or by total loss into the ground. Even the Karkheh, which is in its upper reaches an imposing stream, no longer achieves as it did in earlier geological time a full junction with the Kārūn, but disperses its waters in sands and swamps between Ahvāz and Al-ʿAmara.

The main Zagros area exhibits much variety in scenery and opportunities for human utilization. In the extreme north-west the folds stand very high and abruptly above the Mesopotamian plain farther to the west; but, equally, they are in process of heavy erosion by powerful streams that make up the catchments of the Lesser Zāb and Sīrvān (Diyala) rivers. This region, together with adjoining districts that form the south-west watershed of the Rezāʾīyeh basin, is known as Persian Kurdistān. Adequate, sometimes abundant, rainfall and a considerable swing of temperature—from bitterly cold winters, especially on the higher parts, to marked summer heat—result in a distinct zonation of vegetation. Though massive expanses of bare rock or gorge greatly reduce the effective soil cover, there still remains an appreciable extent

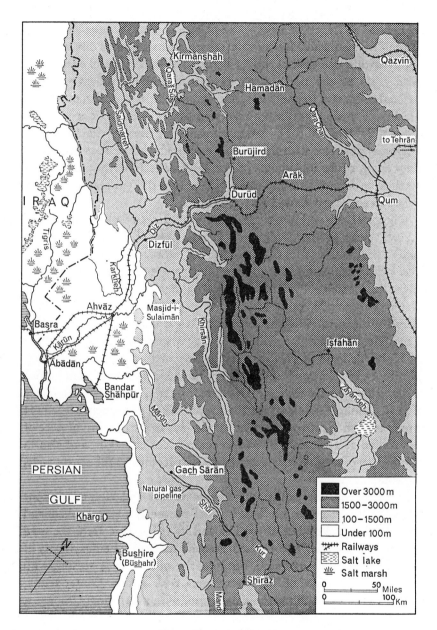

Fig. 7. The central Zagros.

of woodland, which gives way to an alpine pasture on the higher levels. Patches of alluvium also occur, and these support regular cropping. Hence "transhumant" movement (i.e. a restricted human displacement largely within one district, but at differing altitudes) is still a feature in these areas of the north-west; and some semi-nomadism—that is, seasonal migration to another, quite separate region—is also prevalent. But in the main, human activity centres on permanent stone-built villages, tightly built for defence, with some of the inhabitants making temporary absences with their flocks and herds during summer. Many if not most, of the inhabitants of Persian Kurdistān have some kind of attachment at least to a particular village site, though seasonal move-ment still remains a distinctive feature.

Transhumance and nomadism are also features of the northern and western areas of the Saidmarreh basin. Here marked regularity in folding produces a series of open synclinal valleys that are almost high-level plains, which carry a good natural grassland. Bounded by giant ridges that occasionally reach 12,000 to 14,000 ft above sea-level, many of these mountain valleys remained extremely isolated until very recently, and were visited only by nomads and transhumants. A further cause of isolation was the difficulty of the lower parts, where, on leaving the high synclinal valleys, the rivers then began to cut defiles and gorges. Of recent years, however, the situation has greatly changed, and human settlement is on a much larger scale than formerly. Beginning as a policy of Rezā Shāh to "stabilize" nomadic pastoralists, permanent settlement is now extending more of its own accord, due to the new importance of this region as a routeway between central Iraq and Iran, and also in response to oilfield development in near-by regions to the north, west, and south-east.

In sharp contrast to the long grassy valleys and high continuous ridges of the Saidmarreh basin, relief is much more broken and accidented in the region of the Diz and its tributaries. Here the total overall width of the Zagros system is much reduced by embayments of lowland penetrating eastward, but intensity of folding is greater, with resulting dislocation of the component rock strata. Consequently, jagged rough outlines are more common, with sheer mountain walls, bare rock faces, and constricted tortuous valleys. Landslides are a frequent phenomenon, and soil cover much less extensive than in the two areas previously discussed. With such physical conditions, human occupation tends to occur as small isolated groups of settled farmers, to some extent cultivators, but mainly pastoralists. A clan organization based on small unitary groups in the same locality is also a feature. Down to the very recent past the Diz area was a difficult one, with few rewarding or attractive parts, and this led to the classic response of attempting to enhance a bare living wrung from an unfriendly environment by exactions on neighbours and travellers. With its re-entrant of lowland extending the Mesopotamian plain, the Diz "waist" provides the most direct route from the head of the Persian Gulf to the region of Tehrān; though its intrinsic difficulties both topographically and in human terms retarded any major expansion of communications until the last few decades. Traditional routes tended to avoid the Diz area and swing away to the north or the south. Moreover, the importance of the Persian Gulf towns is largely due to oil developments, and hence is not of long standing, so that routes via central Iraq and Baghdad tended until very recently to be far more important than any links direct from the shores of the Gulf.

A first stage in the shift of influence which began to end the isolation of turbulent local groups under petty chieftains came with the building of the Trans-Iranian Railway. Here directness of route more than compensated for the difficulties of construction in a tangled mountainous territory, and the line was accordingly built along the line of the Diz direct to Qum and Tehrān, even though this involved considerable initial cost and later difficulties in operation. More than one quarter of the line through the Zagros is in tunnel, and between Shāhpasand and Durūd there are thirty miles of tunnel in eighty-three miles of track. The Diz river is crossed nine times, and there are curves and spiral tunnels, with at one spot two miles of line to cover a direct distance of 328 yd.

Today, the whole district is considerably less remote than it was. Nevertheless, away from the railway, settlement is still relatively sparse, and pastoralism remains a principal way of life in many areas. But over the last twenty or so years small patches of cultivation have appeared, especially in the upper valley of the Diz, south-east of Burūjird, where there is a broader valley floor and fertile alluvial deposits.

The Kārūn and its tributaries flow at times, like the Diz, in deep gorges—one in fact is 8,000 ft deep. Yet in comparison with its northern neighbour, the Kārūn has a more open valley with alluvial flats of fair size and distinctly easier accessibility. There is a greater variety in natural conditions, with a range from high, alpine-type pasture and some remnants of woodland, down to scattered alluvial benches with meadowland and fertile grassy valley bottoms. Such an environment fosters a wide range of human response: semi-nomadic or transhumant pastoralism, and settled cultivation of barley, wheat, vegetables, and fruit. Some of the more sheltered valleys with a southern aspect are warm enough in summer to allow cultivation of rice. Human groups too are varied: in the west live groups of Kurds and Lurs, with a few Armenians still, and towards the east numerous Bakhtiārī and a few Qashghā'ī. As compared with the Diz region, greater accessibility and openness for travel have made the Kārūn basin an easier routeway through the central Zagros; and with the rising importance of the ports on the Persian Gulf, along with the Kārūn's proximity to the major oilfield zones, the area has lost a good deal of its formerly wild character. More even than the Diz basin, the Kārūn region has been rapidly drawn into currents of modern development, and older tribal ways are very much in decline. With new opportunities for employment in and around the oilfields, part of the local population that once exacted tolls from travellers and skirmished over grazing rights is now either employed directly by the oil industry, or is able to grow agricultural produce for the expanded number of residents; moreover there are other opportunities to gain quick employment far outside the area itself.

Distinctly less affected by this evolution are communities living immediately south-east of the the Kārūn basin, in the region traversed by the upper Khirsān, Mehrān, and Zuhreh rivers. With deeply entrenched and often turbulent rivers that produce steep-sided valleys, wild crags, pinnacles, and frequent gorges, this region affords distinctly less upland pasture than the Kārūn basin; whilst the cultivable parts are fewer, more scattered, and often sharply isolated as tiny terraces, benches, or valley flats hemmed in closely by towering heights and steep cliff faces. Remoteness and isolation are emphasized still more by the broken and intricate relief, and the area to some extent remains one of tribal strongholds, with clan leaders and a tradition of resistance to central government. This attitude dies hard; and despite nearness to an important regional capital (Shīrāz) on the east, and a large and growing oilfield (Gach Sārān) to the north-east, it has still been feasible for local Qashghā'ī tribesmen to maintain a serious and sustained military campaign against the forces of the Imperial government. During 1962–3 movement and travel in this region were greatly restricted by what was described in Tehrān as local banditry and turbulence, and by the Qashghā'ī as a major insurrectional and dissident movement.

Shīrāz

The largest town of this southern region of the Zagros system is Shīrāz, which as a continuously inhabited site may date from Sasanid times or even somewhat earlier. Reliable records, however, go back only as far as the early Islamic period.

The city lies among the major Zagros chains, within the confines of a tectonically produced mountain basin, at an altitude of about 5,000 ft. Some eighty miles long and in places as much as fifteen miles wide, the basin declines greatly in width at its northern end, and Shīrāz lies actually within one mile of an abrupt hill slope. Contrasts in relief are intensified by marked flatness of the basin floor, which is due to extensive infilling by outwash from the near-by slopes. Shīrāz is located within the shallow crook of a river-course that drains south-eastward to Lake Māhalū, but this watercourse remains dry for the greater part of the year. The central position of the city within the southern Zagros area, and in a relatively fertile and productive local zone, has made it a natural exchange centre between local cultivators and pastoralists living in the surrounding hill ranges—Qashghā'ī and Khamseh especially. Its command of routes crossing to various regions of inner Iran, as well as to the southern coastlands, fostered its growth in early times as an administrative and military centre of a wide territory, and it functions now as the capital of Fārs province. Much the same general geographical features existed in early times, hence we find Shīrāz as the successor of two far older cities sited broadly in the same area, with the same strategic and economic functions: the Achaemenid royal cities of Persepolis and Parsagadae some thirty-five and eighty-five miles, respectively, north of Shīrāz. Among the most splendid days of Shīrāz were those in the eighteenth century A.D., when under the Zand dynasty (1750–94) it functioned as the national capital of most of Iran, Khurāsān excluded.

Like almost all Iranian cities, Shīrāz has experienced great vicissitudes. No fewer than ten major earthquakes have probably occurred since the tenth century A.D., in addition to many minor tremors. Floods, famine, epidemics, sieges, and locust plagues have also affected Shīrāz, though the city's population escaped large-scale massacre by the Mongols. Tīmūr did not repeat the destruction of 70,000 inhabitants, as happened at Iṣfahān. British and Dutch trading rivalry within the Persian Gulf area was an inhibiting factor during the

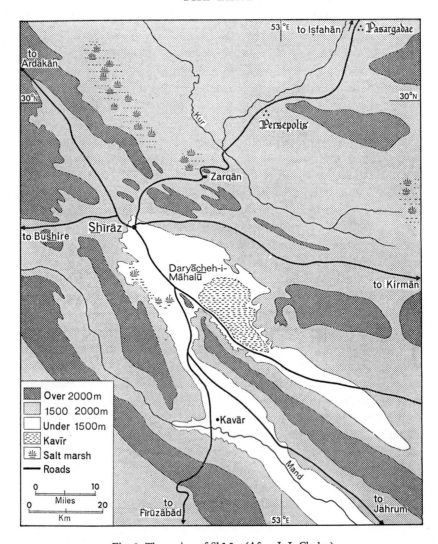

Fig. 8. The region of Sh̲īrāz. (After J. I. Clarke.)

seventeenth and eighteenth centuries, but the city began once again to develop and expand during the nineteenth and twentieth centuries. It is now one of the most important in Iran, ranking sixth in order of population, which in 1965 was estimated at 175,000.

Sh̲īrāz today comprises two distinct parts: an old city once tightly hemmed in by a defensive wall, now extended by the accretion of modern developments, chiefly on the south and west (fig. 101, p. 440). Within the old city, recently cut through by a number of wide modern avenues, lay the Jewish quarter of the "Mehalla", but this tends nowadays to be occupied only by poorer Jews. Less well endowed than Iṣfahān with splendid public buildings of the Middle Ages and later periods, Shīrāz nevertheless has an impressive and very agreable impact on the visitor. It was long famous for its gardens, most of which have now disappeared; and a number of buildings of the medieval and Safavid periods remain, as a reminder on a small scale of Iṣfahān and Mashhad. Shīrāz is also famous as the centre of Iranian poetry, due in large part, but by no means entirely, to the fact that Sa'dī and Ḥāfiẓ were born in the city.

Besides its highly important activities of commercial exchange and its function as an administrative centre, Shīrāz has some significance as a manufacturing town. There are several medium-sized textile mills producing cotton yarn and cloth; two cottonseed-oil plants; and a number of food-processing factories. Glass-making is a traditional craft, and there are the usual brickworks and small potteries common to almost all Iranian cities. As transport costs are high and clay relatively abundant, it is cheaper to manufacture locally rather than import the finished clay products. Bazaar crafts still flourish—inlay work (*Khatam*) especially—together with light engineering and motor-repair shops. Another traditional occupation in Shīrāz is wine-making: the heavy *Khulār* wines, somewhat resembling sherry, have long been esteemed in Iran, and some have even suggested that the name "sherry" derives from Shīrāz rather than from Jerez de la Frontera in Spain. This in the writer's view is not likely.

A large cement plant is located some ten miles west of the city, and fertilizers and sugar are produced at Marvdasht, thirty miles to the north. Further developments of this kind are in prospect now that Shīrāz itself and both the former areas are supplied with natural gas by pipeline from the Gach Sārān oilfield (constructed 1963).

Despite the developments just listed, Shīrāz underwent a period of economic difficulty beginning in the 1930s. Construction of the Trans-Iranian Railway farther to the west somewhat eclipsed Shīrāz and its outlet Bushire in favour of the newer terminals, Bandar Shāpūr and Khurramshahr; and other inhibiting circumstances have been the differences between the central government and the Qashghā'ī and Khamseh tribes, referred to above. There is also the general tendency, with more centralized and pervasive government activities, for the regional centres of Iran to decline somewhat in power and influence as compared to the rapidly growing metropolitan city. As a result, there has been a marked human emigration from Shīrāz over the last few decades.

But a favourable factor is the undoubted appeal of Shīrāz as a tourist centre. With a pleasant climate, striking historical monuments, and easier communications, the visitors flooding in from many part of the world are starting to show interest in such sites as Persepolis and Parsagadae, as well as in Shīrāz and its neighbour Iṣfahān. Moreover, Shīrāz with its large population (*c.* 175,000) is now without rivals in point of size within its region; and although the southern Zagros, of which it is effectively the regional capital, is distinctly less populated than the northern and central parts, there would seem to be more villages scattered around and tributary to Shīrāz than elsewhere in the southern part of the Zagros area. Oilfield development in reasonably close proximity is another useful feature.

The southern Zagros

The parts of the Zagros range lying immediately south-east of the Kārūn basin and of the area just described, show the beginnings of major differences, which become so marked farther to the south and east as to justify recognition of this area as one whose features are in many respects quite distinct from those of the Zagros. Between the Zagros proper and this south-eastern region there could be said to exist a transition zone, which is here defined as extending over about 250 miles between the Kārūn basin and Bandar ʿAbbās, with a breadth that is at least 150 miles. As regards rock type and structure, connexion with the north and west remains very clear: there is still an overwhelming predominance of N.W.–S.E. alined ridges composed of Upper Mesozoic (chiefly Cretaceous) and Lower Tertiary series (Miocene especially). But towards the south the ridges become more widely spaced—almost as fingers of upland within a plateau rather than serried ranks of ridges and valleys. Considerable deposits of recent sediments and wind-deposited sands begin to appear on the lower ground, which is still synclinal in structure. Moreover, an alteration of trend in the folds is apparent—towards the south there is increasingly a west–east pattern. A further element that differentiates this part of the Zagros is the occurrence of salt plugs and domes on a considerable scale, though

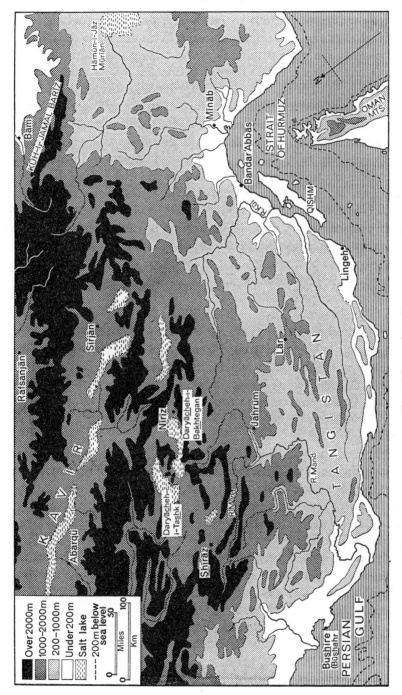

Fig. 9. The southern Zagros.

27

here we are concerned not so much with their geological interest as with the effects on landscape and land utilization (fig. 10, p. 31).

However, the most striking factor separating this southern Zagros area from the others is that of climate. Rainfall is very much lower as compared with the regions of the Zagros so far described, with consequently major changes in the nature of topography and in human responses. Besides a reduction in overall amount, rainfall tends to be distinctly more unreliable and sporadic in onset, with a tendency to heavy but short falls, and irregularity both in season and from year to year. One important result of this is that material eroded by stream and river action, although considerable in amount—even greater sometimes than in wetter areas, owing to the sudden and heavy onset— is not transported far, since the streams are not always perennial. Consequently there has been a good deal of local infilling of the synclinal valley bottoms by sheet deposits of recent geological age, which produce the somewhat more regular and rolling topography mentioned in the previous paragraph.

As regards human activities, the emphasis shifts towards conservation and a much more careful use of water. One begins to encounter practices that are less widespread farther north and west in the Zagros, but increasingly commonplace in the interior and east of Iran: irrigation systems dominating the layout of cultivated areas, with ditches fed by springs. Qanāts, too, are important; and in areas of lower altitude, where temperatures can be very high, covered tanks and pools (*birkāt*) are increasingly used.

With a distinctly warmer and drier climate, the crops produced show a change in character. Millet tends to assume enhanced importance, and wheat and rye diminish or entirely disappear. There is, however, much cultivation of barley, which is tolerant of greater aridity; and maize and some rice are produced where water supplies allow (irrigation here is essential). The date begins to bear really eatable fruit, and the longer, hotter summer is deleterious to certain other species of fruit and vegetables, so that unless specially protected (e.g. by palm fronds or hedges) there is less cultivation of plants such as the tomato and artichoke. An aspect towards the mid-day sun, and the closed-in, sheltered sites, which in the north are usually a major advantage for agriculture, here turn into liabilities, as summer conditions become harsh and even barely tolerable.

This intermediate or transition area is made up of three major catchment basins: from north-west to south-east, respectively, those of the Shāhpūr, Mand, and Shūr rivers. The Shāhpūr basin, like its northern neighbours, consists of a section of the main Zagros folds alined from north-west to south-east, and on the western flank there is an abrupt drop to an almost level coastal plain fronting the Persian Gulf. As compared with the Kārūn region farther north, relief outlines are distinctly reduced in altitude and generally rounder in form, with far less of the rugged landscape that characterizes the central Zagros.

The main valley of the Shāhpūr offers a route from the coast at Bushire to Shīrāz, and this is now followed by a major road. With oil development taking place in this region there is once again an increasingly familiar pattern of human evolution—what was once a remote, difficult area is now pierced by a route of increasing commercial and political importance, and new sites and settlements are appearing in zones once used mainly as tribal grazing grounds. Extremely recent features are the construction of a gas pipeline from the oilfield at Gach Sārān to Shīrāz and beyond, and the growth of Khārg island as a major loading terminal for crude oil from the same field, which is one of the most important and fastest developing fields in Iran. This growth of activity along the road inland via the Shāhpūr valley is in a sense a revival rather than a totally new activity, since the routeway is extremely ancient, and is in fact marked by remains of extensive human occupation—at Persepolis and Parsagadae, where there are still important Sasanid rock reliefs.

Climate plays a dominating part in the physiography of the Mand basin. One of the largest basins within Iran, since it extends over some 20,000 square miles, it has at the present time a relatively poorly developed flow of water. This is a result of reduced precipitation over the higher hills as compared with conditions farther north, giving a pronounced dearth of winter snowfall and hence of extensive water-seepage into porous rock strata; and evaporation on a considerable scale.

The entire basin is clearly an area where major land forms were developed fundamentally at an earlier, pluvial period, and are now in process of alteration towards semi-arid or fully arid forms of a very different kind. The upper valleys of the Mand and its tributaries are broad and open, and show accumulation of debris transported from adjacent hill slopes or deposited by wind action; whilst the lower parts, adjoining the Persian Gulf, have streams deeply slotted into the surface, with little lateral erosion, so that patterns of settlement and lines of communication differ markedly between the coastal zones and the higher interior. In the mountain valleys of this latter area there is reasonably good winter pasture, and here are the winter quarters of the Qashghā'ī tribes; to an increasing extent some of these tribes also cultivate either seasonally, or more permanently, on the lower valley floors and sides. The Qashghā'ī tend to move northward in summer to the edge of the Shīrāz basin and surrounding hills.

The lower areas farther to the south and west are known as Tangistān; and it is significant that here the Zagros highlands rise immediately from the Persian Gulf: there is no intervening coastal plain. Ridges front much of the coast in parallel ranks, producing a closed coastline devoid of indentations that could serve as harbours; and the small size of rivers and their deeply indented valleys greatly reduce the possibilities of irrigated agriculture and the occurrence of natural pasture. Poor in resources, without major routes that could assist development, Tangistān has only scanty and small settlements that produce dates, a little millet and barley, and vegetables. The inhabitants live self-sufficient lives away from the country's main currents of activity, in which they do not share. This makes them a somewhat "difficult" people, but one that is apparently still left to an individual way of life. Gradually, however, the attraction of work elsewhere is leading to a growing volume of migration, and though Tangistān is still not greatly affected directly, there is an indirect and growing influence from other near-by, rapidly altering areas.

Eastwards again, fronting the re-entrant of the Gulf of Hurmuz, is a physiographically distinctive region whose relief is much influenced by the presence of numerous salt domes or plugs that have erupted from considerable depths through overlying strata. Further, the trend of the ridges making up the Zagros swings progressively towards the east from west–east to S.W.–N.E. The salt plugs are thought to be of Cambrian age (G. M. Lees) and occur as almost circular masses with somewhat rounded tops. As a semi-plastic substance, the salt has been forced through overlying rock formations and some plugs now stand at heights of 2,000 to 4,000 ft above the surface, appearing as pinkish-white or yellowish masses. In certain instances the rise of rock-salt has been accompanied by igneous activity that has been in part contemporaneous with the extrusion of salt. In other cases magma has risen along lines of fracture and weakness originally opened up by

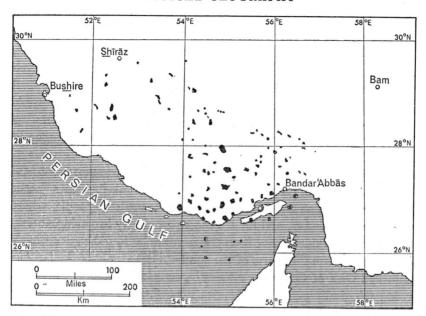

Fig. 10. The distribution of salt plugs in the southern Zagros (G. M. Lees).

movement of the rock-salt. Plugs and domes of this kind may therefore include bands or irregular veins of igneous and metamorphic material which is of darker colour than the salt; and a large plug may have been preserved against subaerial erosion by a capping of such material. The salt itself has little if any commercial value, and the extra salinity imparted by drainage from the areas where plugs occur is a considerable disadvantage—Rūdshūr (or *Rūd-i-Shūr*) means "Salt River"—but the igneous and associated metamorphic veins are exploited in a few localities for sulphur, pigments, and oxide of iron. In some places an original salt plug may have been eroded away so that the rocks have fallen back into the solution hollow, producing a chaotic local landscape of jumbled rock strata and irregular topographic outlines.

The remarkable change in trend of the Zagros folding that produces the enormous embayment situated in the region of Bandar 'Abbās, together with the related extension of Oman so far northward in the form of a spur reaching well beyond the "normal" line of the Iranian coast, have many points of interest. Such a major interruption of the predominant trends in the Zagros system raises questions of considerable geological and geophysical import which are outside the

31

scope of this present chapter; but several points of a geographical kind are relevant. In the first place, the sudden change in direction of the present-day coastline, which now runs north-eastward from Lingeh, means that, in sharp contrast to the area west and north of Lingeh (including Tangistān), the component ridges of the Zagros are alined at right angles to the coast, which is consequently much more accessible and "open", with better harbours. A number of coastal settlements have thus grown up, with distinctly larger numbers of people than in the area farther west.

Also, the constriction of the Persian Gulf to its narrowest point here has favoured migration by Iranians at various periods into the adjacent territories of Oman and Muscat. These movements of people, whilst very small in number, and for the most part chiefly involving sailors, fishermen, and traders, have been one factor in leading the government of Iran to declare that parts of the southern coastlands of the Persian Gulf and Gulf of Oman are ethnically, economically, politically, and even geologically part of the Iranian state. For long these nationalist claims remained a minor affair, but following political changes in Arabia during 1967–8 and a greater feeling of strength and self-confidence in Tehrān, they have recently been revived as a significant issue.

Lastly, the swing of the Zagros ridges north-east and then their continuation south-east greatly reduce the effective width of the mountain barrier, and give rise to a narrow "waist" that allows easier access to the southern interior of Iran. Until very recently geographical difficulties, such as physical and climatic inhospitality, and the poverty and lack of people in the south made this corridor of little real value, and travellers were very few indeed. Now, however, with plans for developing the interior of Iran, the enhanced strategic importance of the south and east as a link with Pakistan (reflected in the activities of the Central Treaty Organization), also the strong possibilities of new exploitation in the centre of Iran—have both led to proposals to develop Bandar 'Abbās and its region as a major port outlet. This will give much more direct access to Mashhad and eastern Iran, as compared with existing routes through Ābādān, Khurramshahr, and Tehrān. In round figures, the journey direct from Bandar 'Abbās through Kirmān to Mashhad could eliminate 600 to 700 miles from the 1,600 miles involved in the route via Ābādān and Tehrān. Road construction now in progress is gradually bringing about some change in the present economy, which can be summarized as hitherto extremely meagre subsistence agriculture with some pastoralism. At present, goats are a mainstay, with a very few sheep and camels, and there is cultivation of dates, millet, and vegetables in the few favoured localities where water is fresh or can be brought by qanāt.

Khūzistān

Situated on the south-western flanks of the central Zagros, in the region of the lower Kārūn river as it makes its way towards the Persian Gulf, lies the single largest expanse of true lowland within the Iranian state. This riverine area, roughly triangular in shape, is defined by the N.E.– S.W. ridge of the Zagros, by the eastern coast of the head of the Persian Gulf, and by the Irano-Iraqi frontier. No more than 120 to 150 miles across in its widest part, the region is really in physical terms a segment of the great valley of Mesopotamia. Yet whilst it is only the alinement of the modern frontier that brings this lowland within the Iranian state, it could be argued that much, if not most, of the Mesopotamian valley in this area is the gift of the Kārūn and Karkheh rivers: a platform built out by the deposition of sediments eroded from the Zagros mountains, and hence an extension of the Iranian plateau. Whatever view one takes of this sort of reasoning, it is wholly valid to assert that the Kārūn lowland provides an extremely valuable façade to the western Zagros, and a route of entry from the Persian Gulf to the interior of Iran that is of rapidly growing importance.

From sea-level in the south for a distance of about seventy-five miles the surface is extremely low-lying and flat, with a rise in elevation in some parts of little more than one in. per mile. Large expanses are covered by marsh, some of which, close to the coast, is salt mangrove swamp, while most of the rest is freshwater marsh produced in one of two ways: either by impeded or indeterminate river drainage; or else by the rise of the tide in the Persian Gulf, which further impedes surface flow of river water out towards the sea, and in places actually reverses this for a few hours twice a day.

At Ahvāz the river breaks though the very first foothills of the Zagros system by means of a series of rapids, and this break of slope could be said from most points of view to mark the limit of the Mesopotamian lowlands. But farther north-east beyond these outer ridges, physiography remains still relatively flat and low-lying as compared with the main Zagros farther east still. Hence one might regard the lowland as extending in the form of an embayment farther up the Kārūn (Āb-i-Diz) river for another fifty to eighty miles.

As elsewhere in the region of the western Zagros, the transition from extremely flat, almost featureless, and low-lying plain to hill ridge and then mountain is remarkably abrupt, but especially so in the Kārūn area. Didalus Sicarus first commented on the sharp topographical contrast, or "ladder", formed by the Zagros massifs overhanging, as it were, the humid riverine and coastal lowland.

Such a clear dichotomy in land forms is to be explained by the contrasts in geological origin. The Zagros is a massive and complex upfold; the lowlands immediately on its western flank are a zone of downwarping, or geosynclinal that has been partially infilled by sediments which were brought down mostly from the Zagros but also from the plateau of Asia Minor by the Tigris–Euphrates and Kārūn–Karkheh river systems. The more detailed process that has resulted in the present physiography is less certain. At the beginning of the present century De Morgan postulated that in relatively recent geological times (c. 10,000 to 5,000 B.C.) the shoreline of the head of the Persian Gulf lay much farther to the north-west, in approximately the region of modern Baghdad. The four rivers Euphrates, Tigris, Kārūn, and Karkheh all entered the sea by separate and distinct mouths. As the last two were swifter, owing to more rapid descent from the highland, they tended to carry proportionally more sediment than the larger Euphrates and Tigris. Gradually then a delta was built out southward across the Persian Gulf, thus reducing the area to the north into a lake and then into a marsh; sediments from the Euphrates and Tigris filled up the intervening portion. This process, according to De Morgan, implies a south-eastward creep of the coastline forming the head of the Persian Gulf.

De Morgan's views were current for many years, and are still held by some to be valid; but in 1952 G. M. Lees and N. L. Falcon advanced a different explanation. According to them, the Gulf lowlands represent a slow and irregular downwarping of the surface under the increasing weight of sediments as these are brought down by the four rivers. Irregular subsidence of the whole area would produce intermittent flooding of the land surface, followed by persistence of marshy conditions. One important piece of evidence in support of the idea of downwarping is the rate of accumulation of river sediment. The known rate of accumulation is such that present-day lakes and marshes could not

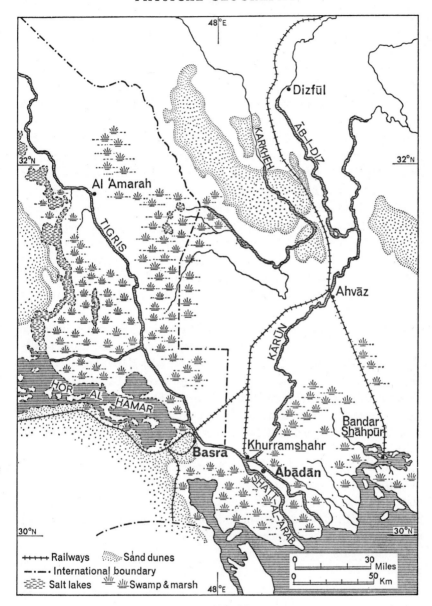

Fig. 11. Khūzistān.

long survive unless there were subsidence: if the surface remained stable, a land surface would build up fairly rapidly. Moreover, to the north-west of the present coastline, sediments laid down since the Pliocene are of freshwater type, whilst to the south-east they are of marine origin. This strongly suggests that the coastline at the head of the Persian Gulf has remained in more or less its present position since the Pliocene, and that therefore there is no "creep". Other evidence adduced by Lees and Falcon goes far to substantiate the idea of a permanent coastline, and in the present writer's view it is difficult to sustain the ideas first enunciated by De Morgan. However, further investigation may be necessary before a final verdict can be given.

The lowland area, which forms a large part of the Iranian province of Khūzistān, has considerable potential for agricultural development. Of late years, following the construction of river barrages, availability of irrigation water in the regions adjacent to the foothills has allowed the spread of cultivation, especially of cereals and sugar (cane and beet). But in certain areas the soil can be very prone to salinity if too much water is applied; and especial care is necessary, not only in the amount used, but also in the kind of crop raised. Provision for rapid drainage of the lower soil is a further essential, but expensive, matter. Close to the Shaṭṭ-al-'Arab, which is the stream formed by the junction of the Euphrates and Tigris, there is a zone of date groves. These extend for a distance of about one mile inland from the Shaṭṭ and the twice-daily rise of the tide, alluded to above (p. 33), ponds back the river water and produces a wholly natural but nonetheless valuable watering of the palm groves.

Most of the rest of the territory is marsh and swamp, diversified by occasional dune-like drier areas. Salinity remains a problem, and the waters of the Kārūn and Karkheh spread out by small distributary channels and thus fail to reach the main drainage flow (the Shaṭṭ-al-'Arab) as single important and recognizable streams.

Of late years, the region has taken on a greater importance as a principal gateway by sea to and from Iran. Difficulties of a shallow sea, shifting coastline, and a marshy interior that is liable, at least near the rivers, to extensive seasonal floods—all these once made the area unattractive, and communications tended to be either farther north through Baghdad and Asia Minor, or farther south through such places as Jāsk and Bushire. Except in ancient times lower Khūzistān had few important towns before the present century, though Ahvāz has always held importance as a river-crossing point. However, with the growth of the oilfields and the development of modern dredging methods, these obstacles in the natural environment have diminished, and over the last fifty years there have grown up a number of sizable modern towns. Bandar Shāpūr, chosen in 1928–32 by Rezā Shāh as the southern terminal of the Trans-Iranian Railway, was sited well to the east, partly to avoid difficulties with silting from the Shaṭṭ-al-'Arab, and partly to avoid the political problems arising from the location of the national frontier, which does not run down the centre of the waterway, as is usual, but along the eastern bank. Although there has been some development, it cannot be said that Bandar Shāpūr has grown to primacy among the Gulf ports. By far the bulk of economic activity remains concentrated close to the Shaṭṭ-al-'Arab, where two much more important Iranian ports are sited at Ābādān and Khurramshahr.

Ābādān was developed as a refining centre by the former Anglo-Iranian Oil Company, and until nationalization it dealt only with incoming and outgoing cargo for the oil company. The petroleum installations were for long the most extensive in the world, and besides handling almost all the output from the Khūzistān fields, Ābādān came to function as a considerable port, with ship-chandling on a large scale. But the development of oilfields other than in Khūzistān, the growth of alternative outlets for petroleum—for example, the terminal at Khārg Island—and the decline in production of the older oilfields, such as Masjid-i-Sulaimān, have meant a decline in the dominance of Ābādān. Proportionally it handles less of the Iranian output of oil, though in absolute terms its importance remains, and its activities continue to grow. As a new town devoted entirely to the industries of oil and shipping, it presents an appearance totally different from that of other Iranian cities, among which it now ranks fifth in order of size.

A short distance away is the riverine port of Khurramshahr. Until recently it handled general cargo for Iran, complementing the activities of the port of Ābādān. Now it is involved in the general expansion of commerce along the Shaṭṭ-al-'Arab, and the division of function is much less than in earlier days. Both Khurramshahr and Ābādān have a rail link through Ahvāz to the main Iranian system, and there is also a roundabout and somewhat intermittent connexion to Basra. Khurramshahr is more "traditional" in appearance and activities, with distinctly less of the modern industrial skyline that characterizes Ābādān.

Inland, one town, Ahvāz, centralizes communications, and performs the function of a regional capital. Its command of routes through the first foothills of the Zagros, as well as the necessity of a portage for shipping on the Kārūn river (because of rapids at this zone of break-through by the river), have made it a natural trans-shipment point; and like its neighbours it has shared in the developments caused by oil exploitation. For long, no more than a compulsory staging post for river traffic (though its historical tradition goes back to the time of Alexander the Great), and with hardly the best reputation for amenity, Ahvāz has nevertheless grown rapidly as a traffic centre and as the outlet for a developing agricultural area.

THE NORTHERN HIGHLANDS OF IRAN: ALBURZ AND TĀLISH SYSTEMS

Viewed on a small-scale topographical map, the Alburz appears hardly more than a minor spur diverging eastwards from the main mountain massifs of north-west Iran, and completing in a somewhat diminished way the rim of upland that frames the central regions of Iran. In fact, the Alburz extends as a shallow arc or, better, a boomerang-shaped mass of upland, from the Russian frontier at Āstārā over a length of some 600 miles as far as Jājarm in the east, where at least topographi-cally, if not geologically, it appears to dwindle and partially die out. Though narrow, with a maximum width of only eighty miles and an average of under sixty miles, it is unusually high, including as it does Iran's greatest peak, Mt Damāvand (18,955 ft), which lies approxi-mately in the centre of the entire chain, some forty miles to the north-east of Tehrān. It may be noted that Damāvand is higher than any summit to the west of it in Asia or in Europe.

Because of its restricted width, the Alburz is extremely steep. This is especially true of the northern slopes, since these rise directly from the coastal plain of the Caspian, which lies at or just below sea-level. On the southern, interior side, the great altitude of the inner plateau reduces the relative differences of level; but even here the Alburz for much of its length provides a striking panorama of sheer and rugged slopes abruptly dominating a nearly level plain. Viewed from either side, the mountains appear as an almost continuous wall, pierced but not broken by a few narrow defiles; whilst to the south the land surface drops more gradually by shallow terraces and low bluffs to the flat wastes of *kavīr*.

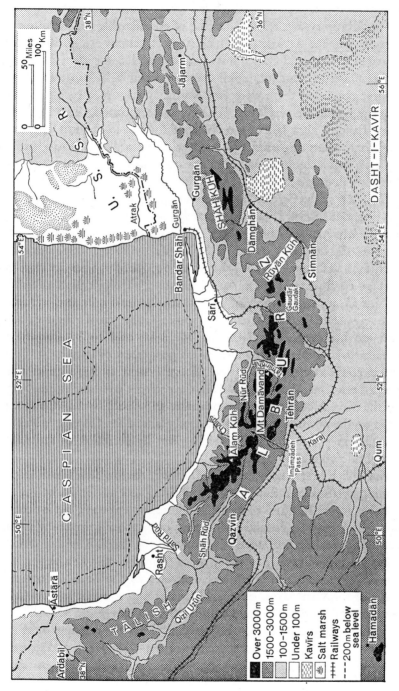

Fig. 12. The northern highlands of Iran.

The Alburz system offers a number of considerable problems to the investigator, not the least of which is its structural origin. From the degree of folding and dislocation in the Alburz it is apparent that there has been intense mountain-building activity; and E. B. Bailey and L. C. King suggest that there were two distinct phases of this, one in the Late Cretaceous or very early Tertiary, and a second in Late Miocene times. Bailey's view is that a number of rock series, mainly Old Red Sandstone, were displaced and overthrust towards the north, hence implying that a significant amount of earth movement originated from the south, in the zone of the Central Plateau.

This view of the Central Plateau, as an area in active, though sporadic movement northward, is not acceptable to certain other geologists, notably Rivière, who preferred a more orthodox interpretation that involves displacement towards the south by forces originating in Northern and Central Asia. It is beyond the scope of this present chapter to offer comment on these varied attempts at elucidation of what remains an unsolved problem, but one may at least note that within a relatively narrow zone of territory, opposing concepts of a fundamental kind are involved. This situation could be said to be frequently characteristic in relation to much of the geography of Iran.

It is convenient to discuss the Alburz system as made up of two unequal portions: the Tālish hills in the extreme west and north-west, and the main Alburz massifs in the centre and east. Fronting the entire range on the north is the narrow coastal plain of the Caspian, which is presently in process of slow building out by accretion of sediment brought down mainly by rivers.

The Tālish hills consist overall of a long, narrow hog's-back ridge running north-west and south-east, and rising to a maximum height of just over 10,000 ft. Much of the surface lies above 7,000 ft, but is deeply scored by narrow defiles and ravines formed by short, torrential streams that plunge mainly north-eastward towards the Caspian, whose shores lie no more than twenty to thirty miles from the crest-line. A smaller number of streams run south and westward to the broader lowland valley of the Qizil Ūzun river, which is in part a major longitudinal trough running parallel to and within the main axis of the Alburz.

Even here, however, the land surface is far from being open or uniform. An extensive gorge occurs on the Qizil Ūzun at Darband (=defile), where the river flows for over a mile in a cleft no more than 100 yd wide.

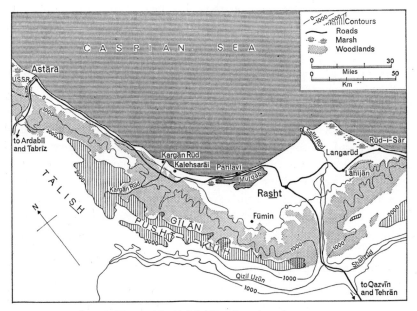

Fig. 13. The Tālish hills of northern Iran.

Lying close to the Caspian Sea, the Tālish hills have a heavy rainfall without a really dry season; but the seasonal variations are considerable, especially in the foothill regions, where autumn and then, lower down still, spring are the wettest periods. On the higher slopes, however, this distinction tends to disappear, and rainfall is persistent in most months. These conditions give rise to a thick vegetation cover, which in association with the broken nature of the mountain flanks, makes penetration on the whole very difficult: as a result, many of the higher parts remain remote and relatively unknown. There are, however, a number of crossing-points including one relatively easy route through Herowābād (Hirābād) to the Caspian coast at Siāhchial. Human settlement is largely restricted to the broader valleys, on small flats of more or less level ground eroded or deposited as outwash by streams. Villages here practise mixed agriculture, with cereals (especially wheat and some barley and maize) grown alongside or below fruit trees. Patches of meadow are also common, whilst a few grazing areas are usually maintained on the higher slopes above the villages. In common with most of the central and western Caspian plain, the abundance and luxuriance of natural vegetation as compared with the rest of Iran are a

41

most striking feature; and on these northern Tālish slopes the proliferation of small fields with a profusion of fruit and grain, boundary
hedges, and water-courses lined by willow and alder suggest broad
parallels with the *bocage* country of north-western France.

The largest of these cultivated expanses is that of the Kargan Rūd,
which has "captured" a number of smaller streams and eroded a basin
distinctly larger than most others in the region. Farther towards the
coast, the heavier and sometimes water-logged soil, the frequent water-
courses, and dense vegetation, with a greater predominance of liana
species, offer more serious obstacles to human occupation. Here, too,
malaria has been another drawback.

On the south-east the Tālish system comes to an end in the narrow
flexure of the Gīlān Pusht-i-Kūh (not to be confused with a ridge of the
same name in Khūzistān), which attains a height of approximately
10,000 ft. A large stream, the Safīd Rūd, has cut back through this upfold, or anticline, and acquired two important headwater tributaries,
the Qizil Ūzun and Shāhrūd, which, as we have noted, flow in a longitudinal structural trough (a syncline) that succeeds the upfold farther
to the south. Increased erosive power from this enlarged river has produced a wider valley, which separates the Tālish hills from the main
Alburz system lying farther east.

The river itself flows at times in a narrow gorge or defile cut below
the level of the main valley and hence difficult to traverse; but the gap as
a whole provides a major route from Tehrān and Qazvīn to the
Caspian lowlands, and is responsible for the location of Rasht, which
commands its northern entry.

Immediately east of the Safīd Rūd gap the same geological features
continue for a time largely unaltered, but after about twenty-five miles
the simple pattern of ridge and trough composed of a restricted range
of rock types begins to change. The mountain system broadens and
rises in altitude; rock series are much more varied and structure more
complex, with shatter-belts and zones of dislocation. A further, significant result is a considerable development of vulcanicity. Superimposed on the general level of the mountain ranges are a number of
volcanic cones, the two largest of which are Damāvand and Ālam
Kūh (15,500 ft).

Two major chains of unequal height can be distinguished, separated
by the valley of the Shāhrūd. The northern chain culminates in two large
peaks Ālam Kūh and Avān Kūh (14,811 ft), and is drained by a series

of small consequent streams, chief of which is the Alāmūt. The southern ridge, about twenty miles away, is distinctly narrower and lower in altitude. Between them, the Shahrūd flows in a valley which for the most part is exceedingly broken and accidented. The oscillations to which the whole region has been and still is subjected—in conjunction with a heavy and distinctly seasonal rainfall, including prolonged winter snowfall acting upon a range of varied rock series—have given rise to impressive erosion features: stupendous gorges with sheer slopes, bevelled terrace-flats, suites of benches, incised meanders on the courses of streams, and gravel outwash fans where mountain torrents enter the main river. Scenery along most of this northern chain is extremely striking, but most imposing of all is probably the side valley of the Alāmūt, which starts just below the two summits of Ālam Kūh. The eastern Ālam Kūh is the higher (15,910 ft) and in places has almost vertical walls up to 3,000 ft in height.

Around the summits of the Ālam Kūh occur a number of small icefields, described by C. P. Peguy. The largest development of these is towards the north-east of the massif, where three permanent tongues of ice converge to form a glacier some four and a half miles in length. This terminates at a height of just under 12,400 ft above sea level. About two thirds of the ice surface is entirely covered by rock debris, and there are even recognizable lateral, median, and terminal moraines. Other icefields may occur to the south and west of the main crests, but these, if they exist as permanent features, are of much smaller size. At least part of the main glacier appears to be in movement, being fed by regular snowfall. Other parts are stationary and without clear evidence of any adjoining snowfield. Because of this, Peguy suggests that the glacier may be fed (at least in large part) by irregular avalanches from the higher parts of the Ālam Kūh, which are steep and show cirque- or cliff-formation here and there. Such conditions would allow creep of the glacier below the normal limit of permanent ice. Other, less likely, possibilities are that the glaciers are maintained from exceptional snowfall at longer intervals—of five to ten years (this has been demonstrated for other regions of the world); or that there could be a sublimation process by which the icefield maintains itself directly from snowfall.

The Shahrūd becomes increasingly entrenched below main valley level as it flows westwards to join the Qizil Uzūn at Manjīl, hence its valley above this confluence offers relatively little inducement to settlement.

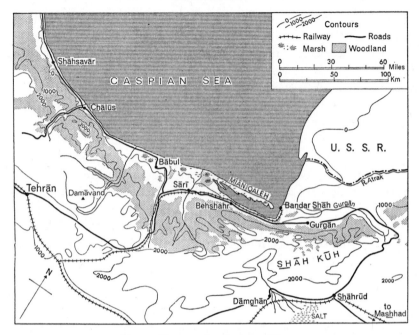

Fig. 14. The central and eastern Alburz.

Towards its source, however, the valley becomes rather more open, though higher in altitude; and here there are small villages, sited usually on terraces or on alluvial deposits near the side tributaries. Cereals, usually wheat with some rice, are grown, together with fruit— vines, peaches, etc.—and vegetables and nuts. There is some breeding of sheep, goats, and pack animals. Because of its topographical difficulty, due especially to the slotted nature of the main river, much of the valley remained for a long time remote and little visited. A number of tracks usable by animals cross the region in a north–south direction: the chief of these is the Ṭāmir Khān pass at 11,500 ft, which usually remains open throughout the winter. With increasing use of motor transport and the opening of good roads farther to the east and west, these tracks are less used, and are more and more the preserve of nomads, local traders and smugglers.

The centre and the most extensively developed portion of the Alburz complex may be said to begin east of the line from Karaj to the Chālūs river. Three main ridges can be discerned, with what appear as irregular plateau surfaces between; and the dominating feature is the large volcanic cone of Mt Damāvand in the centre of the entire system. The peak is very recent in origin, having grown up mostly during the Late Pliocene and Early Quaternary, and outflows from it have deflected and impounded a number of local streams, thus producing the small lake Lār. Now its sides have become deeply scored by erosion channels; but the symmetry remains and is even enhanced by this weathering. Isolation from other peaks, a continuous snow cover, and its large size make Damāvand by far the most striking feature of the Alburz panorama, which is itself very remarkable.

Damāvand has been formed for the most part by flows of andesite, together with material exploded from the crater. There is no scoria cone, and the crater itself is distinctly small. Activity is in its last phase, being mainly characterized by what are known as fumaroles and mofettes— the emission of gases and small quantities of highly sulphurous materials that now occur as irregular deposits as far down as 15,750 ft below the summit. Beside the andesitic flows, which are the predominant feature and appear to make up most of the structure of the volcano, there are intercalated bands of limestone, mud flows, and breccias. The local presence of conglomerates laid down under conditions of heavier and at times torrential rainfall, together with other physical evidence, suggests that there were one or more phases of definitely colder climate, with temporary increases in precipitation. Owing to the great extent of the lava flows, cultivable land, even round the outer base of the volcano, is greatly restricted, occurring in small patches rather than wide expanses.

A permanent glacier exists, according to Derruau, at the upper end of the Ta'alluh valley; and there are a number of persistent, possibly permanent, snowfields, some in the crater itself, in parts sheltered from direct heating by the sun. The glacier is about two km in length and ends at a height of 16,730 ft in a series of ice-falls and crags that drop abruptly to a hollow known as the Valley of Hell. Unlike the glacier of Ālam Kūh, the surface here is not covered by rock debris; and other significant differences in mode of occurrence and deposition patterns emphasize the location of Damāvand on the inner, drier parts of the Alburz, as compared with Ālam Kūh in the distinctly wetter northern slopes of the range.

Within the overall pattern of ridge, peak, and undulating upland occur a number of valleys: some hardly more than defiles, some broader and with relatively flat floors, and others more in the form of a basin, with a downstream rim that is breached by an emergent stream. Certain, but by no means all, of the more open valleys have deposits of soil large enough for cultivation of cereals, fruit, and vegetables; whilst the poplar, so characteristic of parts of upland Iran, occurs here only in scattered groups. The variety in rock exposure can be striking: a few parts are dark and shaly, not unlike an industrial slag-heap; others show dazzling expanses of bare limestone pavement, or abrupt crags developed on more resistant strata. Here and there more rounded slopes carry a light natural vegetational growth of grass, scrub, and occasional trees.

Drainage from this central part of the Alburz is mainly by short consequent streams flowing either north to the Caspian, or south towards the interior of Iran, but the Harāz river has developed a number of longitudinal tributaries such as the Rūd-i-Nūr and Rūd-i-Lār. In several localities two streams flowing respectively north and south have cut back towards each other sufficiently to reduce the intervening mountain barrier to a pass or divide, hence providing a route through the mountain chain. Three such passes ocur. The first is at the head of the Chālūs valley, from which two alternative routes can be followed: one by the Karaj valley and the other more directly towards Tehrān. A short distance east of Tehrān the Imāmzādeh Pass (8,700 ft), lying just west of Mt Damāvand, provides a second major route; whilst the Gaudār Gaudak col (6,620 ft), still farther east from Tehrān, is sufficiently wide and shallow to be used by the northern branch of the Trans-Iranian Railway as an approach to Bandar Shāh on the Caspian shores.

Settlement in the Alburz has several distinctive aspects. The lowest interior slopes immediately north of Tehrān were once occupied as isolated summer resorts; but now, almost incorporated in the outer suburbs of the city, they have a permanent, largely commuting population that has brought the city limits well onto the first foothills of the mountain chain. Generally speaking, settlement in the higher parts of the Alburz is in the form of hamlets or small clusters of houses grouped alongside a few fields; but there is now a tendency for single habitations to grow up, especially along the new motor roads. In many parts still, however, because of steepness and barrenness, there is no human habitation whatever (this was until lately particularly true of parts of the Imāmzādeh route).

East of the Gaudār Gaudak pass the Alburz declines gradually in height and displays more irregularity in trend. The main upfolds reach only 10,000 ft, with two ridges, the Kūh-i-Nizvā, and Kūh-i-Shāh continuing the overall pattern of an arc by trending respectively east-north-east and north-east. A third ridge, the Rūyān Kūh, trends N.N.W.–S.S.E., thus interrupting the general symmetry and acting as a divide between two large embayments of lowland. In the westernmost of these lies the district of Jamnān, and in the eastern, Dāmghān. A fourth route crosses the Alburz range from Shāhrūd to Gurgān; then east of this the extreme eastern limit of the Alburz system is attained. From here east-wards altitude declines, and the folds die out into an area of rolling high plateau, in the centre of which lies Jājarm. This zone of broken plateau (it cannot be described as lowland since it is several thousand feet above sea-level) acts as a watershed between, on the one hand, the Gurgān and Atrak rivers, which flow separately northwards to the Caspian; and, on the other, the less clearly defined drainage system that trends southward towards the kavīrs of the interior.

The Caspian lowlands

From Āstārā in the west to Ḥasan Qulī Beg in the east there extends a low-lying plain, some 400 miles in overall length but extremely variable in width. Occasionally, less than one mile separates the sea coast from the first foothills of the Alburz system, but over much of its extent the plain attains a width of fifteen to twenty miles; and in the extreme east, between the Atrak and Gurgān rivers, it opens out farther into the broad Türkmen lowlands.

The Caspian Sea is at present some eighty-five ft below mean sea-level, and is slowly shrinking in size, with an average annual fall in level of about eight in. The precise rate of fall depends mainly upon inflow from the Volga river, its principal feeder, which, like others in the same region, has been much influenced by climatic fluctuation. Within relatively recent geological time there have been many oscil-lations, both major and minor.

As a result, old shorelines are strongly indicated by the presence of topographical flats and benches, marine erosion phenomena such as stacks and caves, lines of marine dunes, and ancient cliffs with pebble beds at the base. These are frequently visible in many parts, occurring as far south as the first Alburz slopes and the Türkmen steppes. Such obvious fluctuations of the sea level provide much material for specula-tion upon climatic and topographical changes in historic and pre-historic times. Full delimitation and correlation of the Caspian strand-lines have not so far been achieved, and many problems still remain to engage the attention of future researchers. Besides the evidence of differing climatic phases, pluvial and arid, the interrelations of topography, rock structure, and archaeology are also of considerable interest.

The Caspian Sea has no real tides, but *seiches* (temporary local rises in level) occur sporadically, mainly as the result of sustained wind action. Currents of a definite kind exist, mainly from west to east as regards the Iranian shore. Though lacking an outlet, the Caspian is far less saline than other enclosed water surfaces in the Middle East, such as the Dead Sea and Lake Rezā'īyeh, and less saline even than the open oceans. Its salt content is only thirty-seven per cent of the average of the major oceans, and twenty to twenty-five per cent of that prevailing in the Mediterranean and Red Seas.

As it is produced by shrinkage of the water surface, the present coastline of the southern Caspian is one of emergence: that is, it appears generally straight or only very slightly curved, without extensive cliffs or prominent headlands. It is also characterized by a succession, first of coastal sand dunes, spits, and bars; then inland, behind these, a low-lying expanse of brackish lagoons or freshwater marsh; third, a slightly higher and generally drier terrace zone; and finally, a piedmont zone marking the beginning of the Alburz foothills. The dunes close to the present coast may attain heights of thirty to sixty ft and they carry a vegetation of coarse grasses, bushes, and scrub: fairly abundant in the extreme west where annual rainfall is much greater, and thinning out markedly in the east, to merge into the general steppe and sub-arid flora of the Türkmen plains. The marsh-lagoon area has a heavy cover of reeds, sedges, and aquatic plants, again especially dense towards the west; whilst the natural climax vegetation of the higher plain and foothills is the Hyrcanian forest, which is special to the area. However, clearing has taken place over the centuries, particularly during the last fifty years, so that paddyfields and other cultivated zones now predominate in many parts, and the forest has retreated or even in some places totally disappeared.

Administratively the Caspian lowlands comprise three provinces: Gīlān in the west, with Rasht as its political capital and communications centre; Māzandarān in the centre, with a number of smaller towns (chief of which is Sārī); while Gurgān to the east has one large urban unit as its capital, which was once known as Astarābād and is now renamed Gurgān city. These territorial divisions reflect real geographical differences, and it is convenient to discuss the whole area on this tripartite basis.

Gīlān can be said to consist essentially of the lowlands of the Safīd Rūd, which has built out a delta north-eastward into the Caspian and hence extended the width of the plain to about twenty miles. In common with other deltaic areas, the river itself divides into several distributary channels that are frequently shifting; and towards the seaward side are a number of lagoons partially enclosed by developing sand spits. One of these lagoons (*murdāb*), lying on the western flank of the delta, is about twenty miles long and five miles wide, and on its northern fringing spit lies the port of Pahlavī (Enzeli). Gīlān is said to mean mud, and for this the extremely rainy climate and large volume of the Safīd Rūd are primarily responsible. It can easily be appreciated why Gīlān has a heavy rainfall, for it is situated, as it were, within an angle between the Tālish–Zagros and the eastward-trending Alburz systems; moreover it is close to two large water-surfaces and is in a zone followed by eastward-moving depressions originating from Europe and the Mediterranean. Besides this, however, its low altitude compared with that of most of the rest of Iran, and the sudden descent of air masses from the mountains to west and south, which induces a degree of *adiabatic warming*—these together produce high average temperatures. The overall effect is often described as that of a hothouse: steamy heat, with luxurious vegetation of a subtropical kind, allowing the cultivation of crops usually restricted to monsoon regions of the world. By careful management it is possible to maintain a system of almost continuous cropping without seasonal break, since at no time of the year are climatic conditions totally inimical to growth. But such a régime also produces monotony and some degree of enervation in the people, who are very liable to malaria. Nevertheless, Gīlān is by far one of the most densely peopled areas of Iran, with average figures of thirty persons per square kilometre (1960 Census) and approximately one sixth of the total population of Iran. This relatively dense cluster of people shows no sign of diminution; rather, as more and more areas are cleared of virgin forest, there are increased opportunities for settlement, greatly welcomed by those living as semi-nomads in the adjacent Alburz regions or farther away still within central Iran.

Beside rice plantations, which are of great importance, sugar, cotton, tobacco, maize, tea, citrus fruit, and other cereals and vegetables are grown on an increasing scale; and there are extensive mulberry groves which support silkworms. Rice-growing has its greatest development, as would be expected, on the marshy lowlands at or near sea-level, with the other crops located on slightly higher ground. Thus the countryside has a distinctive appearance: houses are relatively well made and of wood, with high-pitched shingle roofs. Many buildings, especially barns and storehouses, are raised on short piles to avoid flooding and contact with damp ground, and village sites tend to cluster on patches of higher ground. A great change has come about over the past few decades by the construction of all-weather roads, replacing tracks that were notoriously difficult. Because of this, much of the lagoon and marsh zone to the north and west of Rasht has been reclaimed as paddy land, and in some places cultivation now extends over the entire zone between the coastal lagoons and the Tālish foothills.

Farther to the north and west the Caspian plain narrows considerably until in the extreme north it is sometimes less than one mile wide. The same general succession occurs, however, with first coastal dunes and then a once-continuous forest cover that reaches almost down to the sea and is now in process of clearance. For many years communications in the lowlands were difficult, owing to the fact that numerous small streams cross the zone; but there is a long-established route across the Tālish hills linking Tabrīz to the Caspian shores via Ardabīl; and another route runs parallel to the coast from Rasht to the frontier town of Āstārā. Here a small stream forms the actual boundary, so that the northern bank is Russian and the southern is Iranian territory.

Āstārā once had some importance as a port, but it has been badly affected by the recession of the Caspian, so that steamers can now approach no nearer than two to three miles, and commerce has virtually ceased. The town retains some importance mainly as a frontier post.

With the construction of all-weather roads, Rasht on the other hand has developed considerably, and is now by far the largest town of the Caspian provinces. Besides its function as a regional agricultural market and capital, it handles a substantial part of the trans-Caspian trade through its outport at Pahlavī (Enzeli). Tradition is important here: having had an earlier start in this Russian trade Rasht tends to maintain its leading position through geographical inertia. Efforts by Rezā Shāh in the 1930s to develop alternative ports farther to the east, in Gurgān, proved largely unsuccessful, owing to the rapid silting of the harbours and the poverty of the hinterland. Thus despite the absence of a rail link to the rest of Iran, Gīlān and its capital Rasht remain by far the most active regions of the Caspian lowlands. In appearance Rasht offers certain contrasts to most other Iranian cities. There are no flat roofs; instead, heavy rainfall dictates a more sharply pitched and strongly tiled roof, covering also a low verandah on which some household activities can take place. Timber is very largely employed in building, and consequently the houses somewhat resemble those of old Istanbul, or of some of the Russian or Indian cities rather than those of the remainder of Iran.

Besides Rasht, mention may also be made of a few other but very small market centres such as Fūman and Lāhījān; a number of tiny ports or roadsteads, such as Kargan Rūd, Siāhchiāl, and Rūd-i-Sar, comprise the rest of the urban centres of Gīlān.

The boundary between Gīlān and Māzandarān is marked by a narrowing of the coastal lowland: from an average of five miles near Rūd-i-Sar, it almost disappears some seventeen miles to the east, where forest-clothed hill spurs practically reach the sea. West Māzandarān consists of a number of enclaves originally enlarged from the forest and hill slopes; the largest of these, the Tunikābun lowland, has Khurramābād and Shāhsavār as its centres. Another similar but rather smaller area is that of the lower Chālūs valley; and in both areas cereals (including rice), citrus fruit, and vegetables are cultivated on a relatively intensive scale. The two regions are among the most densely populated on the entire Caspian coast, and hence in the whole of Iran. The Chālūs area has taken on much importance by furnishing the shortest route from Tehrān to the Caspian; and with the opening of a good motor road there is markedly increased activity, due to tourism and the demands for market produce now reaching out from Tehrān.

Another marked narrowing of the plain occurs east of the Chālūs, with woodland and scrub somewhat thicker—though again much clearing has taken place over the last thirty to forty years. Many small streams descend directly as seasonal torrents from the central Alburz massifs, and here greater height results in higher rainfall, which is to some extent reflected in the number and size of these local streams. Farther east still, from the vicinity of Maḥmūdābād, there is a greater width of plain due to the presence of several larger rivers. One, the Harāz, has a developed upper course that reaches back into the longitudinal valleys of the inner Alburz; and because of its larger volume and more regular flow, it breaks up, like the Safīd Rūd, into a number of distributaries towards its mouth. Once more most of the lowland is given over to rice- and fruit-growing, and irrigation ditches are an increasingly prominent feature, since annual rainfall over the lowland begins to decline somewhat sharply eastward. Farther east still, however, the Bābol river becomes incised into its bed some ten to thirty ft below the level of the surrounding plain. Direct irrigation by full flow is consequently no longer possible, and rice-growing, which demands much water, tends to be replaced by the cultivation of other cereals, fruit, cotton, and flax. The area of eastern Māzandarān was at one time much more developed and prosperous, and it enjoyed the interest of the Safavid monarchs, of whom several monuments remain —notably at Āmul and at Sārī, the latter being the present regional capital. Rezā Shāh also stimulated some development. There is still a certain amount of fishing, and a small port trade concerned chiefly with the export of cereals.

Gurgān is definitely much more of a transition zone towards Central Asian conditions. Unlike the coastline in much of Māzandarān, which is generally straight and without indentations, Gurgān has prominent lagoon forms. The dunes backing the coast of Māzandarān continue as a large east-running sand spit, the Mīān Qaleh, which almost encloses a sheet of water some 350 square miles in extent to form Astarābād Bay. Over thirty-five miles long and scrub-covered, the Mīān Qaleh was for long a royal hunting preserve, and still remains thinly peopled and in part quite uninhabited. Rapid deposition of silt is taking place, so that Asterābād Bay is shrinking. Another salient feature, the abrupt northward swing of the coast, tends to be maintained rather than obliterated by this active and selective marine deposition. Partly because of the inhospitable and difficult nature of the coastlands, human activities are more developed towards the interior, on the piedmont and foothills. Deposits of loess brought in by wind action during the Quaternary and later periods are found on an increasing scale eastward along the base of the foothills and in the middle reaches of the Gurgān river valley. Overall, the climate is distinctly semi-arid; but on the hills there is greater soil fertility and slightly heavier rainfall, so that most of the towns and villages are to be found on the loess-covered hill slopes.

From the angle of Astarābād Bay which forms the south-eastern corner of the Caspian Sea, there is a rapid transition into semi-arid and then fully arid steppe conditions. The Gurgān river crosses this region and has frequently changed its course, so that there are a number of former channels, some ancient, others recent. Once again, as in eastern Māzandarān, the principal streams tend to flow in beds cut below the general plain-level to a depth of ten to twenty ft; consequently the landscape differs markedly from that of the centre and west of the Caspian plain. Here in the extreme east, the prevailing impression is of a generally level steppe, broken only by artificial mounds (*tepes*), representing older settlement sites, and by sudden gullied water-courses Aridity is now marked, hence the vegetation consists merely of scanty grassland and thorn scrub, freshest in spring, dried up in summer, and sometimes lightly snow-covered for extensive periods in winter.

The Gurgān steppe would seem to have experienced local but marked oscillation of climatic conditions, and also human vicissitudes. Certain Classical and early Arab writers (notably Strabo and Ibn Khaldūn) speak of it as an extremely fertile and productive region, with cereals, fruit, and tree crops, especially vines and figs. Türkmen invasions caused regression; and pastoralism, particularly horse-breeding, became the principal way of life after the early Middle Ages. Many ancient irrigation works decayed irreparably, and settlements fell into ruins now recognizable only as *tepes*. Today, however, with greater political stability and the ending of Türkmen incursions, there are prospects for a revival of cultivation; and over the last few years settlement schemes have been undertaken as a deliberate policy by government and other agencies. According to these plans, peasants are brought in fairly small groups from other parts of Iran, and are settled on Crown holdings that are then made over on long- or short-term agreements to the new occupiers. In some cases a co-operative exploitation scheme is part of the settlement process; in others, peasants are left to arrange their own marketing. Redistribution of Crown estates in the north-east was one of the earlier phases of the general scheme for land reform undertaken by the present Shāh.

In terms of human geography the Alburz region presents many features of distinct interest. As has already been noted, the highest parts—that is, the terraces on the sides of the ridges, and their adjacent longitudinal or transverse valleys—have attracted settlement which in many instances is permanent rather than seasonal. In these localities fertile and cultivable patches allow agriculture based on winter wheat, spring barley, lucerne, fruit, and vegetables. On the southern, inner slopes of the Alburz, rainfall is much reduced, consequently patterns of cultivation alter. Where rainfall is just sufficient for plant growth, crops may be grown extensively only one year in two or three, the intervening seasons being used for the folding of animals on fallow ground. In this way much-needed fertilizer is made available for cultivation. Where rainfall is insufficient, irrigation may be possible on a very small scale, even in the higher mountain valleys, using streams that rise elsewhere; and stock is grazed outside the village for part of the year, then brought onto the fields usually in autumn after harvest, as was the custom in mediaeval Europe. In certain districts, therefore, the distinction between irrigated areas and rainfall cultivation is rendered clearer by the field patterns: irrigated areas need not be enclosed, and thus they extend as open field, with water-channels or large stones indicating boundaries; temporary fencing may appear at the appropriate season of fallow grazing, but not always, since shepherds sometimes remain with their animals all day. The rainfall-cultivation areas tend to have more permanently enclosed fields, with permanent pasture. It is noteworthy that crop yields in these areas of the Alburz are relatively high.

The limits of effective land utilization have been pushed to greater altitudes by the custom of summer pasturing, or what is termed trans-humance. Many villages still have subsidiary settlements used during May until August or September by groups from the permanent villages below. These summer pastures can lie at considerable distances—up to ten or twenty-five km—away from the parent village, and it was formerly the custom for whole family groups to migrate. Tents are now mainly used; but at one time, according to several observers, rough but more permanent habitations were made, and there was even a certain amount of cultivation, chiefly of barley and wheat, along with the cutting of planted and wild forage. Summer transhumance is now greatly declining; and De Planhol cites the case of Pulūr, where a summer pasturage at 7,400 ft altitude was formerly used by thirty families and now only by five. Animals cannot usually survive the normal Alburz winter even at middle altitudes unless some form of stabling is available; and besides the usual wooden sheds for this pur-pose, solution caverns in limestone or soft volcanic outcrops lend themselves to the hollowing out of semi-underground shelters.

Another fluctuating, but far from insignificant aid to existence in these high mountain villages used to be the presence of trading routes that followed the north–south gaps across the Alburz. Along these routes, rice, wood, salt, fish, and textiles from the Caspian plains (especially Māzandarān) were carried southward for sale in southern and western Iran, stimulating a return traffic of manufactured articles and animal products. Location on one or more of these routes could prove most rewarding, and in the late eighteenth and nineteenth centuries a growing volume of north–south trade enhanced living standards in some communities favoured by their geographical location, notably Lārījān in the upper Harāz valley. Because of this the mountain regions came to attain a position of semi-independence with considerable political autonomy.

Complementary to summer transhumance was a winter migration from the higher valleys to centres on the coastal plains of the Caspian. Agricultural life, especially at higher altitudes, tends to be sharply seasonal, but as we have seen, climatic conditions on the Caspian lowlands allowed activity all the year round. There was consequently some intermittent demand there for labourers, craftsmen, porters, and domestics at all seasons. Those mountain-dwellers who were landless or without stock tended often to spend at least part of the year in such temporary pursuits, and one could therefore speak of a fully developed system of vertical migration: upward to summer pastures and then downward to the Caspian lowlands during winter. (Some similarity will be noted with conditions formerly prevailing in parts of the Alps of Switzerland and France.)

Of recent years, however, this movement has greatly declined. The growth of towns, especially Tehrān, has induced migration of a more permanent kind. It is highly significant that many upland villages no longer maintain their summer pastures, which are to an increasing extent either totally abandoned, or else made over to nomadic pastoralists, sometimes for a kind of rent, sometimes as a "token of friendship"—depending on the relative strength and aggressiveness of the two groups. Cultivation, too, is tending to decline in the higher and more marginal parts. Terrace walls, as elsewhere in parts of the Middle East, are more and more in decay, and several investigators suggest that the upper limit of sustained cultivation has fallen by some 250 m (820 ft) over the last half-century, from an average of 2,500 m (8,200 ft) to 2,250 m (7,400 ft). Abandoned fields are no unusual sight in most of the region.

The piedmont areas of the southern Alburz are drier but not totally arid, and hence have offered special inducement to settlers. Sheltered from the keenest of the northerly winds, that can sweep for a time out of the Siberian plains and make winters particularly severe, the piedmont also has expanses of outwash silt and gravels that provide fertile, well-drained soils. Irrigation is possible in many localities—given sufficient initiative and effort—from the many short streams that descend the inner slopes of the Alburz; and also from the relatively widespread water-bearing layers below ground level, which allow the building of qanāts. The wide extent of qanāt-building around Tehrān indicates how frequently water can be tapped below ground.

Thus in human terms the southern Alburz foothills and piedmont had originally two aspects: the better-watered spots were cultivated by a sedentary population; while other parts were put to temporary use, for winter shelter and pasture (*qishlāq*), by pastoral nomads. It would seem that Tehrān's modern significance originated in its being a qishlāq for Qājār nomads who had long maintained the habit of wintering in the Varāmīn district. On gaining political ascendency over Iran during the eighteenth century, the Qājārs developed into a national capital what had served them initially as a combination of qishlāq, trading post, and centre of rule. According to De Planhol, intermingling of Turkī place-names with Iranian forms is a frequent characteristic of the southern piedmont, especially towards the east, and important evidence of the dual role played in earlier times.[1]

Further evidence regarding the composite patterns of origin comes from settlement morphology. For the sedentary population there was the perennial difficulty of defence against nomadic marauders, who tended nearly always to have the initiative; and this gave rise to settlement types dominated by needs of defence. (East and west of Tehrān there were many such settlements.) Dwellings were closely grouped in rough quadrilateral form, with numerous *qal'ehs* (forts). These were whole villages constructed to have blind outward-facing walls, sited round a central defensive tower and a structure—either a kind of peel or an interior compound—into which animals could be driven temporarily for safety. Further, there were extensive qanāts, from which a village could sustain itself and its animals against investment or a siege of several weeks. Thus there grew up on the southern Alburz piedmont a vigorous sedentary population that could hold its own, broadly speaking, against the menace of nomadic invasion; and a certain stability or *modus vivendi* developed, in strong contrast to conditions on the eastern Caspian plain (Gurgān), where nomads were normally stronger.

---

[1] Following the practice elsewhere in this chapter, there ought here to be consideration of Tehrān as a major city. Tehrān is, however, discussed in chapter 13, pp. 445–61.

When, however, Qājār rule brought to an end in this area the immemorial conflict between cultivator and pastoralist, a further phase of evolution began. Progressive landlords found themselves able to extend irrigation; and so over the last century and a half peasant agriculture gradually outgrew the old defensible and highly nucleated villages, incorporating new territory on a basis of extra irrigation developed by wealthier and more forward-looking proprietors. The more inconvenient settlements came to be abandoned, and have by now often fallen in ruins; or else the central refuge for animals became built over. At the same time new villages, to a certain extent daughter-colonies, have grown up on more open and more rewarding sites formerly unused because they were less defensible.

During the reign of Rezā Shāh, a significant number of these settlements passed into control of the Crown and found themselves somewhat unduly favoured, compared with non-Crown territory, in such matters as water rights, development capital, and the provision of amenities. This could lead to the expansion of cultivation into geographically unsuitable sites, but it also made possible unscrupulous manipulation of the irrigation pattern. The individual cultivator had, and still has, to stand up for his rights in the matter of irrigation, otherwise the due amount of water fails somehow to materialize. Water in Iran, like liberty generally, is purchased partly by eternal vigilance; and with an energetic despotic monarch as co-landlord, the weaker proprietors found their share in irrigation sharply diminished.

Within the last twenty years, an opposite situation has developed. The abdication of Rezā Shāh led to an increase of power for the landlords, who are now able to divert back to their own holdings the water once shared with Crown estates. Hence one may now see certain Crown villages in process of desiccation and regression to pasture, owing to the diversion of irrigation water. A further turn has been given to this long drawn-out conflict by the recent redistribution of Crown lands to peasant-holders. These people now have another and equally direct cause for grievance, over and above the general one of former social injustice, for their new holdings can be discriminated against by landlords over the matter of water supply.

The tenacity and ultimately successful establishment of a cultivating peasantry in this southern piedmont have had repercussions on the nomadic pastoralists, who have been increasingly compelled to base their annual circuits on the lower ground lying between the cultivated piedmont—with its springs, streams, and underground water—and the interior salt basins of the extreme south. Here aridity becomes very much more marked, and streams dwindle to intermittent flow, become saline, or lie in channels cut deeply below the general surface in a way that inhibits irrigation. So long as the number of animals is not too large, herding can be carried on, but there are definite limitations to this activity.

With the stabilization and expansion of cultivation in the piedmont zones, especially round Tehrān and Karaj, pastoralists have been driven to extend their annual migration farther and farther south, towards the heart of the central Lūṭ, in order to make use of very inferior and short-lived flushes of pasture that follow sporadic rainfall. It has been suggested by some observers that the nomads now cover as much as 2,000 km (nearly 1,300 miles) in a single annual cycle. While possible for a limited number of individuals, this seems hardly credible for tribal units as a whole, since it would involve about forty km per week, or between three and four miles daily, without respite. What is certain, however, is that some tribal units now send their animals far to the south in charge of a few shepherds, whilst the remainder of the group stays in the north, close to the piedmont or adjacent plains, living in tents or semi-permanent villages. The development of irrigation works such as those on the Karaj river, together with rising land prices and the spread of urbanism, have all greatly reduced the pasture lands in the southern Alburz region, and sedentarization of nomads is proceeding at a fairly rapid rate. At the beginning of the present century Sven Hedin commented on the importance of the Varāmīn plain and the region of Simnān farther east as centres of pastoral nomadism. Now, though far from negligible in total numbers, the nomads are far less in evidence, and their influence on the general life of the region is in marked decline. Many, possibly a majority, have become semi-sedentary with a wide range of auxiliary pursuits involving cultivation; in many cases transhumance has replaced full nomadism.

A different evolution of human occupation has taken place on the northern slopes of the Alburz. Here physical conditions, chiefly climatic, led to the formation of heavier soils, especially towards the zone of junction between piedmont and plain; and the consequent development of a heavy forest cover. The earlier, indigenous populations seem to have lived a patriarchal life; with pastoralism a principal element, and exactions on travellers and local trade an important supplement. But the predatory and turbulent habits of the Gīlakīs, continuing from Classical times down to the eighteenth century A.D., ultimately led the Qājār rulers in Tehrān to bring in numbers of Kujāvand Kurds from the Ardalān region. This colonization began on a significant scale towards the end of the eighteenth century.

Following the addition of population, the Caspian plain—especially the central part—was, as we have noted, gradually cleared of forest and transformed from jungle and swampy wasteland into a vast agricultural open field with holdings delimited by hedges and coppices, and build- ings (barns and store houses chiefly) raised on wooden piles or large boulders (*kuppas*). As late as 1936 Bobek could write of the forest edge that it often lay within sight of the Caspian Sea, marking usually the southward termination of the coastal lowland and the beginning of the Alburz foothills. At higher altitudes a system had grown up of mixed pastoralism and cultivation, with large flocks and herds transhumant between summer *yaīlāqs* in the mountains, winter quarters on the Caspian plain, and intermediate, home quarters on the lower hill slopes.

Since 1930–40, however, considerable changes have occurred. The construction of motorable all-weather roads, parallel with the rapid growth of Tehrān, created a two-way economic movement: the herders and farmers of the northern Alburz developed a taste for small luxuries such as tea, sugar, better clothes, and fuel oil, for which they could pay by sending charcoal for sale in Tehrān and other northern towns. At first, charcoal-burning became a widespread and locally valuable extra pursuit, engaging many individuals. But much of the forest has by now been cleared, at least in its more accessible parts within the zone 4,300 to 6,600 ft above sea-level, and few or no reserves remain. Emigra- tion has increasingly become the only remaining course, and at the present time there is a steady exodus, chiefly westward to the lower Safīd Rūd valley and Māzandarān, where development of intensive agriculture almost on the plantation system absorbs much human labour. Some migrants are also attracted eastward to Gurgān, where cultivation based on irrigation is also extending (though on a much more limited scale) and could expand further.

There is considerable resemblance between the human geography of the Alburz area and conditions in coastal Syria and Lebanon. In the latter a mountainous terrain with an exceptionally well-watered sea- ward side was sufficiently high and rugged to afford isolation and defensive points, yet not too irregular as to inhibit the accumulation of a soil layer that could offer cultivable patches. Such an environment could support small human groups who were willing or desirous to accept remoteness and a frugal mountain life as the price of relative security from raids and political oppression. With stronger overall rule in both areas after the eighteenth century, political and economic conditions were gradually ameliorated, and population numbers began to increase. One further crucial factor was the rapid growth of large cities on the very periphery of the mountain: Beirut, Tripoli, and Damascus in the Levant, Tehrān, Rasht, and Tabrīz in Iran; and the first effect of such urban growth was to foster a rapidly developing market for local resources. Later, however, and especially in the Alburz, the important resource of woodland became largely worked out; also, a growing disparity emerged between "the mountain" and "the town" in regard to amenities and living standards. The more civil security became assured, the greater the disparity. Hence in both areas, the Alburz and the western Levant, the uplands have declined in population over the last few decades. The "mountain", with its traditional values and ways of life, is losing its old meaning. Arduous work in maintaining cultivation terraces, or in shifting quarters up and down hillsides following animals at pasture, might be accepted when there was a risk of oppression or attack from outside, sometimes by marauders from a distance, sometimes from townspeople—landlords, armies, and officials. Now, when these towns have lost their former menace and taken on new glitter and attraction because of their opportunities and modernity, the disparities become harder to bear. In the words of De Planhol, "Whilst the forest becomes increasingly eroded away, Tehrān reaches out to alter human conditions".

EASTERN AND SOUTH-EASTERN IRAN

In marked contrast to the north and west, where the defining highland ring is broad, high, and extremely regular in structural pattern, the east and south-east of Iran consist of a number of upland massifs separated by topographical expanses of differing width and lower but varied altitudes. These uplands are distinctly irregular in disposition, trend, and physiography; whilst the intervening areas are plains only in a limited sense, for though most have a flat or rolling surface, some are open and others more basin-like. All stand at an altitude of at least 3000 ft above sea-level.

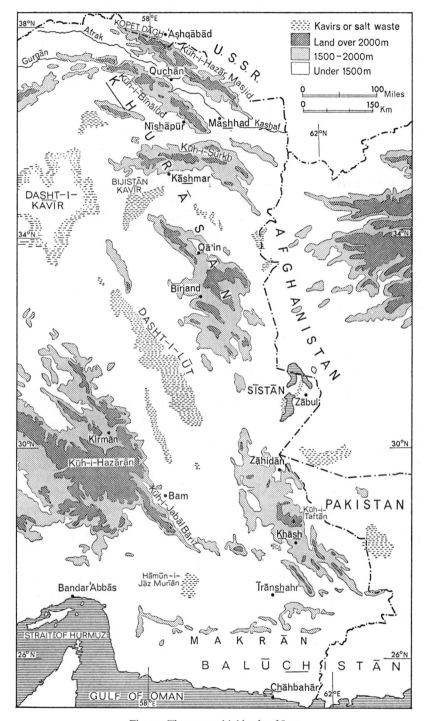

Fig. 15. The eastern highlands of Iran.

It is convenient in the present instance to define eastern Iran as beginning at the watershed between the Gurgān and Atrak rivers; from there it extends as far south as the southern border of the Sīstān basin (in the latitude of approximately 30° N.) through the ranges that form the Makrān and define the Jāz Murīān basin as far as the Gulf of Hurmuz, to the west of which the main Zagros can be said to begin.

The region so delimited extends over 800 miles from north to south, and its east–west spread varies from as little as fifty miles to on average about two hundred. It embraces land forms of many kinds, from peaks crowned by near-permanent snow, jagged and rounded crests, abrupt gorges and wide valleys, to extensive flats and drainage swamps. Much, but by no means all, of Iran's frontiers are on the eastern flanks of the massifs, where these drop to the low plains of Russian Central Asia or to the extensive inland drainage basins that lie farther south, in Afghanistan. Thus an encircling upland rim remains the predominating geographical feature, even though the more broken nature of the mountain chains—their scattered and irregular disposition, and the extent of intervening lower land—makes this part less rim-like and hence easier of access, than anywhere else in Iran. Climate, however, reinforces the obstacles set by rugged terrain; and so, despite the only moderately developed topographical barrier, this eastern region of Iran still restricts human movement and effectively isolates the interior. Three distinctive sub-regions make up the eastern segment of Iran: Khurāsān in the north; next, a complex of upland massifs sometimes termed collectively the Qā'in and Bīrjand highlands (for want of a better name) and associated with them the lowland basin of Sīstān and its western defining ridges; then lastly, the hill ranges of Persian Balūchistān and the Makrān, with their associated ranges that join onto them to form the extreme south-eastern angle of the Iranian highland rim.

Khurāsān

Khurāsān is distinguished by the presence of mountain ranges that show much more symmetry and regularity, at least in alinement and disposition, than do those of the Sīstān area immediately south. A predominating trend can be discerned from north-east to south-west; but in addition, there are flexures which link to this clear and well-defined pattern, the differently alined Alburz ridges. These flexures dovetail as it were into the main N.E.–S.W.-trending Alburz folds at a short distance farther west (fig. 16). Hence the entire mountain system

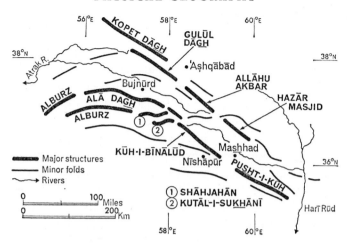

Fig. 16. North-east Iran; structure. (In part, after Scharlau.)

of Khurāsān consists of fold-structures that occur as successive ridges, for the most part in ranks, with local names. In the east, towards the Russian frontier, there are two main lines of ridges: one close to or partly within Russian territory, and another some forty to fifty miles to the south-west. Between these two nearly parallel lines there lies a trough zone, hardly to be described as a lowland, as its floor is at 3,000 to 4,000 ft altitude. In the opinion of Scharlau, these near-parallel sets of summits represent a merging of two major, large-scale structural arcs. The north-easternmost line, composed successively of the Kopet Dāgh, Gulūl Dāgh, Allāhu Akbar, and Hazār Masjid ranges, represents a continuation of the Caucasus system; whilst the more southerly line, made up by the Kūh-i-'Alī Dāgh (Ālādāgh), Kūh-i-Bīnālūd, and Pusht-i-Kūh ridges, is more properly a part or even continuation of the Alburz group of folds. It would seem that two structural arcs that in their western parts are widely divergent here merge together; and one might see in this a similarity with the Tālish hills joining the main Alburz range. But here the position is complicated by the existence of cross-folds or minor flexures exemplified in the hills north of Bujnūrd, and, more extensively, south of Quchān. These minor ridges would not seem to accord in trend with the northern line of major hills, which Scharlau terms the "Türkmenian range", but may represent an imbrication of the easternmost Alburz folds with the dominant Türkmenian trend.

63

It will thus be apparent that this northern part of the eastern rim has a structural pattern of distinct complexity; and writers on the geology of the region have offered somewhat varying interpretations of the conditions as now observed. Especial difficulty arises over the ultimate relationships of the various high ranges within Khurāsān to the Pamir, Hindu Kush, and inner ranges of Afghanistan and the Himalaya—a matter that is, however, beyond the scope of present discussion. Enough has been said perhaps to indicate why in the present work, the highlands of Khurāsān are not treated simply as an eastward continuation of the main Alburz, but as a partly separate physical region. Lithologically the predominant series of the main Alburz—Lower Jurassic and Cretaceous—continue uninterruptedly to form the main massifs of Khurāsān; but in terms of structure and climate, and hence in human response, there is a perceptible difference between the two regions.

Where the two systems come together and front each other, as in the area of Bujnūrd–Quchān–Mashhad, there is a zone of considerable crustal disturbance, as would be inferred from the earlier discussion of the general tectonic origin of the region. Faulting and downthrow have produced a long narrow trough or rift occupied by the Atrak and Kashaf rivers, and further dislocation has allowed intrusion by igneous rocks to the south of Mashhad, and extensive metamorphism to the west. The low divide that serves as a watershed between the upper course of the Atrek and Kashaf rivers is thought by Scharlau to be a small upfold, rather than a residual feature produced by river erosion or by downfaulting of adjacent rock structures.

The whole area is still one of marked crustal instability, especially in the neighbourhood of the trough itself. The town of Quchān experienced four violent earthquakes during the nineteenth century alone, the last of these (in 1893) so severe that the entire town was re-sited some eight miles to the east.

The Kopet Dāgh range, which is entirely in Soviet territory, and the associated folds known as the Gulūl-Dāgh, which curve westward and are partly in Iran, form together a fairly regular mass that rises steeply from the Türkmen plains to the east and north and attains a maximum height of over 9000 ft. Faulting and downthrow on the southwest side have tilted the whole structure, giving it something of the appearance of a dissected block or plateau, with a steep, narrow, north-east-facing side, and a rather gentler but more irregular south-

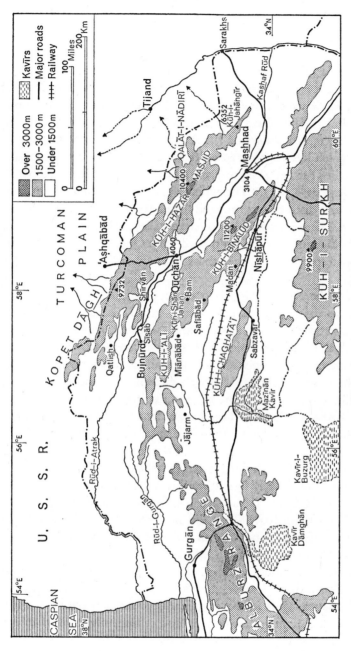

Fig. 17. North-east Iran: Khurāsān.

western aspect towards the Atrak valley. This difference is well illustrated by the variety in drainage pattern. To the north and east are short,
straight streams coursing directly from high ground to the Türkmen
plain, but to the south-west there is a more developed network, with
a number of subsequent transverse tributaries joining the Atrak.
These minor valleys have generally been eroded out in less resistant
strata, and in some places deep narrow gorges have been formed, mainly
but by no means wholly on the Atrak side. Above the general plateau
level, which lies at about 6,000 ft are a number of rounded summits
that attain a further 2,000 to 3,000 ft; the highest of them, Kopet Dāgh
itself, reaches 9,732 ft. The whole zone of the Kopet Dāgh massifs,
however, is distinctly less rugged than a recital of these altitudes might
suggest. There are a number of steep valleys and gorges where movement is difficult, but the main road from Quchān to 'Ashqābād is not
unduly steep or broken, even though it must rise to 7,000 ft to cross the
range.

Where the Kopet Dāgh is open to penetration by moist winds—
that is, to the north and north-west—rainfall occurs on a scale sufficient to produce a good flush of grass annually, and also to support a
fairly thick scrub vegetation with small clusters of trees such as alder,
oak, juniper, and hornbeam: an alternation, but basically a continuation, of the vegetation pattern characteristic of the eastern Caspian
foothills. Opportunities for irrigation cultivation occur in certain of
these northern valleys, and on alluvial fans that flank the outer scarps.
Here are communities of settled farmers raising cereals, citrus and
deciduous fruit and vegetables, while the villages are marked by walnut
and poplar trees. Until fairly recently such settlements tended to be in
the rather higher and less accessible valleys, in order to avoid the
menace of Türkmen raids from the Caspian littoral and farther east;
but of late there has been a distinct spread of settlement to lower
altitudes. The earlier population tended to be Kurdish in origin, as a
result of "planting" by Shāh 'Abbās.

Towards the south, rain-shadow effects begin to be apparent.
Vegetation is more sparse, and human occupation more precarious
and restricted. Thus in the middle Atrak valley, pasture is distinctly
less abundant, cultivation poorer, and settlements fewer than farther
north. The importance of the Atrak valley as a line of communication,
however, has led to the growth of a number of towns which function
as small markets, exchanging their local agricultural items for pastoral

produce and a few manufactured goods brought in from outside. Chief of these towns are Bujnūrd and Quchān, others are Qatlish, Shirvān, and Sīsāb.

Some 300 miles in overall extent, and forty miles in width, the Kopet Dāgh range may be said to end in a series of cols and open expanses that break the continuity of the main ridges due north of Quchān. This interruption provides a relatively high but easy route from Quchān to 'Ashqābād (Poltarsk): immediately south-eastward the summits once more become higher, and are known as the Allāhu Akbar. A minor break occurs when the system is penetrated by smaller transverse folds related to the Alburz massifs, then the south-easterly trend continues under the name of Hazār Masjid.

In these last two massifs contrasts in relief are somewhat greater than in the Kopet Dāgh. Summits are slightly higher (the maximum attains 10,400 ft), and erosion effects are more prominent. A number of longitudinal valleys break up the major massifs, and are fairly accessible and open. But streams descending directly from the sides of the ridges have cut extremely narrow and steep-sided gorges, and their openings are often marked by outwash sheets of ungraded scree—boulders, pebbles, gravel, and silt. The most interesting effect of enhanced erosion under subtropical and arid conditions is seen at Qal'at-i-Nādirī. This is a detached plateau fragment, oval shaped and trending N.W.–S.E. with its major axis about twenty miles in extent and its width some six miles. The entire structure is defined by cliffs that rise 700 to 1,000 ft and are broken only by a few tortuous paths. Morphologically a real "Lost World", the Qalāt was a traditional strong-point in the defence of north-east Iran, but now it is almost uninhabited.

As will be seen from fig. 17, the mountain chains that serve to define the Atrak–Kashaf trough on its southern side are somewhat more irregular in trend, and again slightly higher than their northern counterparts. The chains are predominantly of Jurassic age—a further contrast to conditions in the north, where Cretaceous series are better developed—and their main topographical component in the north-west is the Kūh-i-'Alī. This extensive upland is mostly over 8,000 ft, with a sharp fault-defined scarp series forming one side of the Atrak valley, and more irregular northern and western aspects. Once more, as in the Kopet Dāgh and Gulūl Dāgh, the areas closer to the Caspian are better watered, and consequently have a cover of scrub, even woodland, with important pasture flushes in spring. Farther to the south and west aridity becomes more marked, vegetation is thinner, and narrower gullies replace the wider valleys characteristic of the wetter north.

To the west and south of Quchān the mountain ranges take on a slightly more complex pattern because of the presence of minor structures that trend more directly east–west, cutting across the floor of the Atrak valley and continuing directly towards the Alburz as the Kūh-i-Shāh Jahān and the Kūh-i-Jaghatāi. This has the effect of producing minor structural "knots", rather than, as in the north, a simpler longitudinal arrangement of ridge and valley. Dominating the area farther south and east is the Kūh-i-Bīnālūd, eighty miles long and fifty broad—altogether the most imposing mountain system of Khurāsān. Of an average height that just exceeds 10,000 ft, with summits a thousand or two feet higher, it appears to dominate low-lands lying both on the east (the basin of Mashhad) and also the west (the plain of Nīshāpūr). This effect is heightened by the steepness of the lower slopes, especially towards the south. The higher parts tend mostly to consist of karstic plateau levels—empty and arid except in spring, when there is short-lived pasture and nomads arrive with their animals. Lower down, between 4,000 and 6,000 ft, and particularly towards the north-east, irrigated agriculture is developed in the narrow valleys where water is available. Some of these valleys appear as oases in a generally dry countryside, with cereals and vegetables sown beneath fruit trees and shrubs. Most observers are impressed by the marked alteration in conditions between the sun-drenched and monoto-nous clay or silt plain, with its occasional brick walls, and the verdant lower-hill scenery only a short distance away. One recent traveller summed this up as an overwhelming local contrast in geographical environment.

Chief town of the south is Nīshāpūr, the birthplace of ʿUmar Khayyām. The name of the town derives from King Shāhpūr I, a Sasanian monarch (A.D. 240–71) who founded it as a centre of trade and fire-worship. Lying within a tectonic zone and on the Türkmen and Central Asian frontier, Nīshāpūr has undergone many human and physical vicissitudes: destruction by earthquake on several occasions, devastation and massacre, but has also enjoyed an intermittent import-ance as a trading centre and a place of education and learning. Ibn Baṭṭūṭa described Nīshāpūr as a "Little Damascus". Besides commanding routes across the Kūh-i-Bīnālūd, north to Quchān and north-east to Mashhad, it functions as a market for agricultural and pastoral products, and also for turquoise obtained mainly from the western flanks of the hills, especially round Ma'dan. Construction of the rail link to Tehrān, which swings round the end of the Kūh-i-Bīnālūd and approaches Mashhad from the south, has been a further stimulus; but the extensive ruins of earlier settlement indicate that not only Nīshāpūr itself, but the whole region, was once far more populous and productive. Some revival is currently taking place, with cotton an increasingly important crop. Other villages and smaller towns are located on the piedmont or closer to the main slopes of the Kūh-i-Bīnālūd and Kūh-i-'Alī, often in association with springs, or where there are irrigation prospects from streams and qanāts. Southward begin the salt basins and deserts of the interior: hence this more heavily peopled and cultivated zone, which extends as an arc south and west of the mountain chains, could be regarded as a minor replica of the Fertile Crescent of Syria–Iraq. Chief centres, closely influenced by the availability of water, are Nīshāpūr, Sabzavār, Sulṭānābād, Ṣafīābād, Bam, Miānābād, and Jājarm; but apart from the first, none is now very large. One locally unfortunate feature is the outcropping of gypsum and rock-salt, especially north of the Juvain river, which greatly increases the salinity of ground water in these districts.

Mashhad

Mashhad is a successor to Ṭūs, a more ancient city that lay some fifteen miles to the north-west. In earlier days the region of Khurāsān had a much wider sphere of influence, which extended often as far as Herāt, Marv, and Sīstān, and was dominated by two urban centres, Nīshāpūr and Ṭūs. The latter is known certainly to have been important as early as the fourth century B.C. In A.D. 809 'Alī Rezā, the 8th Imām of the Shī'a died (some say he was killed) a short distance away from Ṭūs, at the site of what is now Mashhad ("the place of martyrdom") which hence became a centre of Shī'a pilgrimage.

After destruction of Ṭūs by Mongols in 1220, survivors resettled in Mashhad, and water supplies were diverted there. In this way the tomb of 'Alī Rezā and a few associated buildings became the nucleus of a town that gained markedly in importance. Location near or on relatively easy routes from northern Iran into Central Asia, Afghanistan, and the South-East via Sīstān and the Helmand basin gave it importance as a caravan- and trading-point. Lack of rainfall involved extensive dependence on qanāt or spring irrigation, so that Mashhad never attained the opulence of, say, Iṣfahān, Damascus, or Aleppo; and almost down to our own day it has suffered first from Mongol and later from nomadic raids. Nevertheless there has been a significant volume of commerce in spices, dyestuffs, pastoral products, carpets, and silk, with chandling for caravans that provided a market for foodstuffs and animal products from the local area.

Religious associations seem, however, to have contributed in greatest measure to the development of Mashhad. Despite its distinctly excentral relation to the rest of Iran, it was made an object of special solicitude in the seventeenth century by Shāh 'Abbās the Great: one may see in this a possible desire to buttress the secular power by association with religion, as well as a quest for economic advantages to be gained from having pilgrimage centres in one's own realm. During the nineteenth and early twentieth centuries the shāhs found it convenient to emphasize Mashhad's significance, as a strong Shī'a centre, again possibly in part for the same reasons, but also, more certainly, in order to develop a centre of Iranian national feeling and culture in a territory increasingly exposed to encroachment from outside.

The present-day city[1] consists of two quite distinct segments: an older nucleus dominated by a group of religious monuments, and a recent expansion towards the south and west, with wider streets, better private dwellings, shops, and a few hotels. In the ancient centre are the religious buildings of the Imām's tomb, and mosques and a madrasah, with extensive graveyards close by. Burial close to the mausoleum of Imam 'Alī Rezā was and is still highly sought after, and high grave-rents are paid—an important element in the general economic position of the city. Radiating from the religious area are numerous streets and alleys (kūchehs) lined mainly by narrow, single-storey shops and dwell-ings, and hemmed in originally by the city wall, which was rebuilt successively with an enlarged perimeter. Another important feature in the old part of Mashhad are the numerous caravanserai, which here take the form of a courtyard flanked by two-storey buildings—the lower for store and supplies, the upper for humans—and approached by a narrow tunnel-like entrance. Alterations by Rezā Shāh within the last thirty-five years have resulted in a broad ring-road, virtually

---

[1] A plan of Mashhad is given in chapter 13, p. 439.

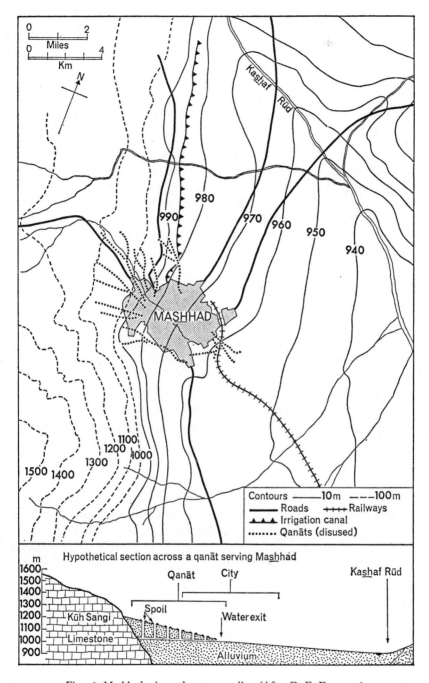

Fig. 18. Mashhad: site and water supplies. (After D. F. Darwent.)

turning the ecclesiastical nucleus into a closely defined "island", and also restricting burying-space because so much of the centre has been opened up to currents of trade and commerce by motor. Many pilgrims engage in temporary or part-time trading in order to finance their journey.

Enhanced economic activity in the centre of Mashhad during the last ten to twenty years has displaced poorer inhabitants from the centre to new houses on the north and east sides. At the same time, the richer quarters alluded to above are taking shape almost as a detached town to the south and west, in response to the pull of new roads and the railway station, which is a recent addition to the city. This tendency to segregation by class structure, not normal in traditional Middle Eastern cities, is one of the most obvious evidences of Westernization, here in Mashhad as elsewhere.

These changes have come about as the result of extensive migration into Mashhad. A population estimate of 1947 gave 147,000 as the population of the city, and the 1956 Census showed 248,000. Estimates for 1965 were about 300,000. It is believed that much of this increase is due to movement in from rural areas, not only within Khurāsān, but including Sīstān and Balūchistān. One contributory factor is the diversion of water eastward by the Helmand river scheme, and another the general withdrawal from conditions of life on large landed estates. An accompanying phenomenon, related also to Mashhad's status as a pilgrim centre, is the number of professional beggars: one observer in 1963 put this at 6,000, not including families.

Still retaining its function as a pilgrim centre, and now more open to communication with the rest of Iran, Mashhad has become the undisputed capital city of eastern Iran. Trading and cultural contacts with regions farther east persist, though on a reduced scale, despite the hardening of frontiers over the last thirty years. In human terms, Mashhad is now one of the most colourful of Iranian cities, with an unusual mixture of religious, Central Asian, and nomadic dress, along-side more normal "Western" styles. Tourist bric-a-brac, an index both of improving communications and debased general taste, is becoming a principal item of trade in the centre; but the title of Mashhadī, indicating that a person has made the pilgrimage (*ziārat*) to the tomb of the martyred 8th Imām of the Shī'a, is still respected in Iran.

Qā'in and Bīrjand highlands

South of the Mashhad basin the topographical pattern again becomes more complicated, with a bunching of fold-structures that are of different size and display varied trends. Between these uplands, which have been rather awkwardly termed "the highlands of Qā'in and Bīrjand" lie irregular plains and drainage basins. First in order southward, and the highest of the hill features, is the Kūh-i-Surkh, which is an upfold of Eocene with some Miocene strata extending over 150 miles to reach a maximum height of 9,900 ft. Its northern aspect, towards the Nīshāpūr plain, is only moderately steep but relatively unbroken: the southern flanks, overlooking Kāshmar and Turbat-i-Haidarī (or Haydarīyeh), are more rugged and deeply eroded, with sinuous valleys and gorges occupied by intermittent streams that drain southward to the Bijistān Kavīr (Kavīr-i-Namak). Eastward the Kūh-i-Surkh broadens into an undulating tableland of 6,500 to 8,000 ft altitude, with a largely barren surface partly occupied by minor undulations and irregular folds. Southward it is succeeded by a more developed ridge, the Kūh-i-Bīzak, which is simpler in structure and narrower, but of the same general height and thus quite prominent. This feature acts as a major watershed between, on the one hand, streams flowing west or south into the interior basins of Iran, and, on the other, the system of the Harī Rūd and Kashaf Rūd. In the angle formed between the two latter streams occur further ridges which, whilst less imposing in extent and altitude than their western neighbours, nevertheless exhibit clearly the same N.W.–S.E. structural trend dominant in Khurāsān farther north. Finally, the Kūh-i-Khwāf runs from the region just north of Turbat-i-Haydarīyeh as far as the Afghan frontier. Attaining a maximum height of about 8,000 ft, it has a few springs and seasonal streams that support a very small settled population of cultivators, and somewhat larger numbers of nomadic herders and occasional outlaws.

Between these ridges and mountain massifs are expanses of lower, flatter land, sometimes occupied in their sumps by *kavīr* or by monotonous gravel and sandy plains. The lowest levels of all, which lie eastward towards the Afghan border, can be at no more than 2,000 to 2,500 ft above sea-level; but average altitude is more of the order of 4,000 to 5,000 ft. It is at such intermediate altitudes that the few villages or towns tend to occur. The lowest parts are saline, bare and dusty for much of the year, or with a sharply seasonal and limited water flow that may suddenly grow into a devastating flash-flood; whilst the upper parts, closer to the highlands and hence not without a seasonal flush of vegetation, are on the whole climatically difficult: bare and wind-swept, arid in summer and snow-covered during winter. Apart from the few towns mentioned, permanent settlement is largely restricted to small cultivable patches clustered around streams, where these leave the uplands and are entrenched in gorges that offer some shelter from wind, dust, and snow, or provide a reasonably accessible water supply.

The area lying between the Kūh-i-Bīnālūd and the Kūh-i-Surkh furnishes a good example of the sort of geographical contrasts that occur in these eastern boundary districts of Iran. Close to the mountain chains, as these decline northward to overlook the wedge-shaped lowland in which lies Nīshāpūr, there occur many small villages of fair size. Lower down, on the more open piedmont, these settlements become smaller and fewer, taking on more definitely the character of oases. Passing through some of the lower-lying ones is the main line of communication between Iran and Central Asia via Afghanistan. At lower levels still, streams become saline and increasingly intermittent in flow. Sandy steppe with loose dunes and *namak* become the predominant features, with settlement extremely sparse.

South of the Kūh-i-Surkh massif and the associated ridges of the Kūh-i-Bīzak and the Kūh-i-Khvāf, there lies yet another extensive open region: hardly a lowland, since much of it lies above 3,000 ft, yet in comparison with higher zones to the north-north-east and south a distinctly less broken terrain. There is an irregular water-parting which divides streams draining westward to the Bījistān Kavīr (Kavīr-i-Namak) from those draining east and south towards the Namaksar-i-Khvāf, a salt lake, which is partly in Afghanistan. However, there are also a number of small swamps with local drainage, hence we can best describe this zone as one of ill-developed and indeterminate drainage patterns. Chief towns are Bījistān and Jūymand, which lie on the piedmont in the extreme south-west of the area, away from the saline lowlands.

Highland is once again a major feature farther south, where it develops on a moderately large scale as a series of interlocking fold-structures over an area about 150 miles from east to west, and about 200 miles from north to south. This is the Bīrjand–Qā'in highland region. In its northern parts, alinement of component mountain ridges

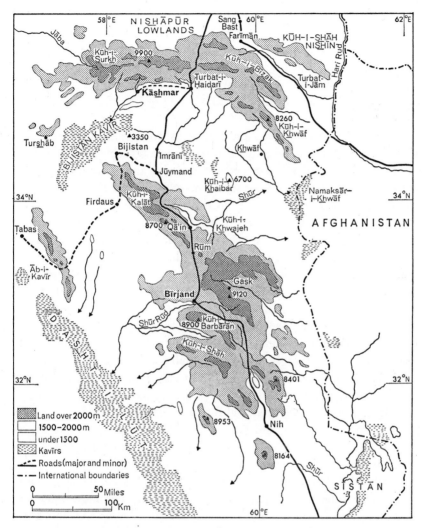

Fig. 19. The Qā'in–Bīrjand highlands.

is mainly N.N.W.–S.S.E., but farther south, that is, in the area of the Kūh-i-Shāh Nishīn, the trend is more W.N.W.–E.S.E., indicative of the markedly differential stresses and earth movements to which much of eastern Iran has been subjected. Among the highest summits of this Bīrjand complex is the Kūh-i-Khwājeh Shā'z, which attains a height of over 9,000 ft and overhangs a flat plain to the east on which there are a number of salt marshes and drainage sumps. At a short distance

75

away, and in fact alined through these and other swamps and water surfaces, is the political frontier with Afghanistan.

Between the mountain spurs and ridges are open rolling plains, sometimes eroded further into definite valleys where streams may flow, usually only seasonally. The town of Bīrjand, largest in the area, lies in such a broad valley, with the dried-out bed of its river, the Shāhrūd, serving as a roadway for most of the year.

Because of the continued prevalence of salt swamp or loose sand dunes in many of the lower-lying areas, human settlement tends still to be largely confined to intermediate altitudes and shallow slopes, at altitudes above 4,000 ft. Thorn scrub and other halophytic or xerophytic vegetal complexes dominate in most of the lower parts, but at least in some parts they give way at about 4,000 ft altitude to a more luxuriant cover of grasses, deciduous trees such as mulberry, and even willow and poplar. Here too cultivation occurs in small areas, with crops of wheat, barley, fruit, and opium. Terracing is possible in some localities, and the prevalence of vines, figs, and other Mediterranean fruits reminds us that this region still has affinities to the north as well as to the south. This is because the Bīrjand region is more open to northerly climatic influences. Winters can be bitterly cold, and although days are hot during summer, night temperatures fall considerably. Strong winds are a difficulty, especially in the south of the region towards Neh, where north-westerlies may persist for days during summer.

The largest towns are Qā'in and Bīrjand. The former produces opium, cereals, and root crops, and on the relatively abundant pasture of the uplands numbers of camels, sheep, and goats are reared. Bīrjand, somewhat more extensive, has a carpet industry along with the production of vegetable dyes from plants, some of which grow wild in the neighbourhood while others are cultivated on a small scale. The immediate surroundings are distinctly more fertile, due to a better soil and more abundant water supply. These in turn are caused by the fairly close presence of a number of high mountain ridges: the Kūh-i-Bagrāband (8,900 ft) to the south-east, and the Kūh-i-Mūminābād (9,100 ft) to the east, both of which attract and retain a snowfall somewhat heavier than that on the lower hills.

Sīstān

Southward the mountain mass dwindles to a single ridge or neck that lies between Neh and Nuṣratābād. East of this ridge lies a more developed lowland zone or basin. This is the Helmand basin or Sīstān, famous to Iranians as the reputed home of two legendary heroes, Rustam and Kai, but now divided politically, the larger area of the basin being in Afghan teritory. The Sīstān lowland, oval in shape, is a complex downthrow zone, with an especially steep boundary on its western side formed by the narrow ridge. Farther east, in its Afghan portion, the basin is more developed but also irregular in form, with the north-eastern rim made up by the Hindu Kush ranges, which rise to over 16,000 ft. Lowest levels within the Sīstān basin (1,540 ft only) occur in the extreme south-west, and this consequently means that the largest area of permanent water surface occurs within Iran. Thus, despite the fact that the Helmand basin as a whole (defined in terms of total catchment) covers 135,140 square miles (350,000 sq. km), little more than one tenth is Iranian. But the areas adjacent to permanent water, which are the more easily irrigable ones, lie largely within Persian territory. In fact, the principal water sheet of the Sīstān basin—that of the Hāmūn-i-Helmand (Hīrmand)—constitutes the largest single expanse of fresh water within the Iranian plateau, and this gives it special significance as a region of possible future development.

The major faults that define that western margins of the Helmand basin run almost due north–south, indicating tectonic affinities with regions farther east in Asia, rather than with the west of Iran. The floor of the depression exhibits three suites or layers of material that represent stages in the gradual desiccation of a vast enclosed sea, which was cut off from the Tethys during Late Tertiary times as the result of the upthrusting of folds that now form the present mountain ring surrounding the basin. Oldest and lowest-lying of the deposits is known as the Gobi or Siwalik Formation, and it consists of layers of green and red clays, sandstones, and conglomerates. This formation, of Late Pliocene age, has been greatly disturbed by local differential warping—uplift of the adjacent mountain massifs and downthrow of the lowland basin—hence it is enclosed at a marked angle towards the foothills of the rift zones. Above the Gobi series occur first Pleistocene sands and clays, which developed as shoreline benches and were then progressively eroded by streams draining into what was then a rapidly shrinking water surface. Finally, there are very extensive sheets of pebbles and smaller fragments lying closer to the hill slopes. Towards the lowest parts of the basin silts, clays, and mud predominate, and these form the present-day margins of the actual watersurface. Wind transport and erosion, acting selectively upon the various formations, have also produced vast areas of loose and shifting sand dunes.

The river system is of considerable interest. On the west, only a few strictly seasonal torrents plunge for a few days each year down the steep western flanks of the Helmand basin; and main water sources lie to the east, where the boundary rim is higher and more developed, and thus precipitation is not only more abundant, but also better spread, because of the peristence of snowfall into late spring. Main feeder stream is the Helmand (Hīrmand) river, which divides into two major and several minor distributaries just at the Irano-Afghan frontier. These streams produce a sheet of water which fluctuates considerably in area, not only seasonally but also very much from one year to another. The precise extent of the lake is conditioned first by the extreme flatness of the land surface (nowhere is the lake more than thirty-five ft deep); second, by the open nature of the surrounding territory, where there are few or no retaining features; and third, by the highly variable and inconstant nature of precipitation over the surrounding catchment areas. In May, the lake is usually at its maximum size, and it then covers over 1,158 square miles, extending across the Afghan frontier towards the north-east. Slower replenishment due to a decline in inflow, together with outflow through the S̲h̲alaq Rūd into the Gaud-i-Zirreh; and, above all, intense evaporation due to "the Wind of 120 Days" that begins to blow during this season—these reduce the lake to three separate, permanent water sheets: the Hāmūn-i-Helmand proper, the Hāmūn-i-Ṣābarī in the north, and the Hāmūn-i-Puzāk (the second lying partly, and the last entirely, within Afghan territory). All but ten per cent of the annual flow of the Helmand river occurs between February and June, and three quarters of the total between mid-March and the end of May.

The feeder waters of the Helmand are highly charged with sediment and dissolved solids, and in spring at least they appear very turbid, with up to eight grammes per litre of silt in suspension. Much of this material is first deposited over the floor of the basin, and is later transported, sorted, and redeposited by wind action. One estimate suggests that of the 1,200 square miles of lake area at the high-water period, 450 square miles dry out each year for a period long enough to develop cane-brake vegetation and a grass cover sufficient for animal pasture; 300 square miles turn to swamp, and the remainder (some 450 square miles) remain as lake. The waters of the lake itself are far clearer than those of

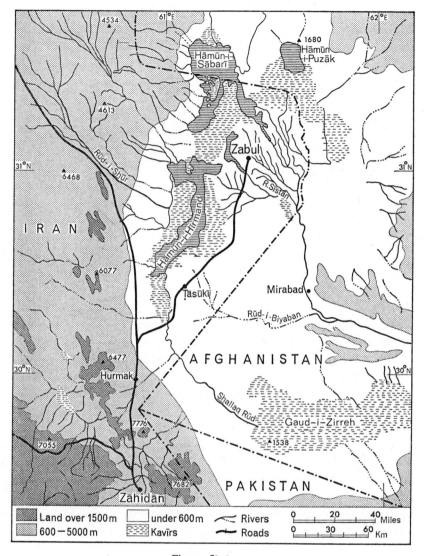

Fig. 20. Sīstān.

the rivers. Moreover the lake is fresh and does not become brackish. This is because for a large part of the year there is natural drainage outward from the lake system to the south-east via the Shalaq Rūd to the swamp known as the Gaud-i-Zirreh. Changes in level are small, only of the order of sixty to seventy ft or less, so that as the level of the main lake falls, outward drainage ceases and the Gaud-i-Zirreh waters become rather more brackish. But this short and seasonal flow is sufficient to prevent the elaboration of salt deposits within the main Helmand water surfaces—a remarkably delicate balance which in geomorphological terms is a highly temporary though fortunate circumstance.

Mention has been made of the Wind of 120 Days, which is especially vigorous and pervasive in Sīstān. It develops during most but not quite all of the days from May to October, rising in the morning as a hot blast from the north-west that is laden with dust and therefore thick and hazy. Usually, too, the wind is strong enough to carry sand particles that act as a highly efficient abrasive. Vegetation can be stripped of leaves, bushes and trees distorted, smaller plants crushed, and the growing layer of plants eroded away. In addition there is damage to buildings, which are in time deeply etched; lighter soil is stripped away, and, as already mentioned, there is intense evaporation from water surfaces.

Of the land devoted to regular cultivation rather than pasture, fifty to sixty per cent tends to be under winter crops, that is, harvested in May or early June. Here the climate, and particularly the wind, is a controlling factor. Almost all of the remainder tends to be left as fallow, apart from a very small summer cultivation, which amounts to no more than five per cent of the total area. Wheat occupies seventy per cent of the winter-crop area, with a good deal of barley and some beans and fodder crops: lucerne and clover. Sorghum, cotton, and vegetables (but especially melons), and a little millet are the summer crops. The cotton supplies only a small local demand, and is insufficient to form an item of trade. A very few trees exist, but it is surprising that there are few or no wind-breaks to protect trees and crops. Overall, standards of life suggest decline over the last thirty years, a process recently accelerated by the increasing diversion and use of Helmand waters within Afghanistan. Sīstān was once famous as a wheat-exporting area, and this continued in a small way down to the early years of the present century. Now, production may even be insufficient for the scanty population. A major limiting factor is of course the difficulty over regulation of the river water. Iran stands to benefit most, as she owns the lower, flatter parts where water naturally collects and can therefore be most economically used for irrigation. Afghanistan, on the other hand, controls both the river headwaters and the drainage sump of the Gaud-i-Zirreh—an intricate problem of geopolitics. At present, as we have noted, Afghanistan is developing irrigation schemes which are not only somewhat costly, but also much to the detriment of Persian Sīstān. Here is a challenge: Sīstān, as its past history alone shows, has distinct prospects for future improvement, given technical and international collaboration. Its geographical isolation in a remote corner, together with the fact that traffic routes by-pass it to the north and south (partly because of the disposition of frontier lines), are major handicaps. Yet Sīstān is one of the rare areas of the region that is endowed with supplies of fresh water: thus its potential for development is high, and this should serve to overcome the political difficulties that now exist. Indeed, Sīstān epitomizes many similar problems confronting Iran: how to secure political action to make superior use of undoubted environmental opportunities.

Persian Balūchistān and the Makrān

Within a zone (summarily defined, as lying east of a dividing line that would run from the Bandar 'Abbās–Mīnāb area fronting the Gulf of Hurmuz to the north of Zāhidān) there occurs a geographical unit sufficiently distinctive to justify separate recognition as the third sub-area forming part of the eastern and southern upland rim of Iran. In terms of geological structure, physiography, and climate, this south-east corner of Iran shows a certain individuality compared with its immediately northern neighbour, the Bīrjand–Qā'in upland mass, and a marked deviation from the main Zagros system adjoining it on the west. The great ridges comprising the Zagros undergo sudden and marked diminution both in height and in width; and, as we have seen above, they are obviously much broken into as a massive feature by the foundering of extensive areas to form the Strait of Hurmuz and Gulf of Oman. From its massive simplicity as a single and unified mass, the Zagros declines into two smaller formations: first, the system of ridges forming the coastal ranges and interior hills of the Makrān which continue with an east–west disposition as far as Afghanistan, and second, a widely diverging fold structure, that of the high, single anticline fronting the Qaṭar and Oman shores on the southern coasts of the Gulf of Oman.

Here we have an intermediate zone structurally, where the well-defined Zagros folds characterized by one simple line of trend become interlocked with formations best developed farther east in Afghanistan and Pakistan. Structural trends, rock character, and style of folding

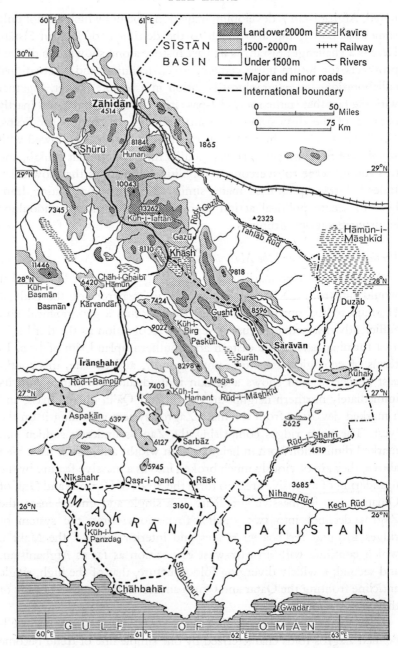

Fig. 21. South-east Iran.

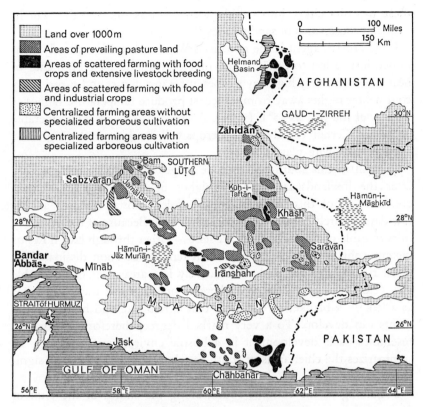

Fig. 22. Land utilization in south-east Iran.

tend to be different in these formations. The extreme south-east of Iran is itself characterized by very tight folding of the rock series in many varying directions, by considerable distortion of the surface by massive warping, and lastly, though extremely important, by much volcanic outpouring that has been on a scale large enough to give rise to major land forms. Structures shattered by intense and tangential folding, by vertical displacement or the upwelling of lava, are further degraded by the strongly erosive effects due to climate. These last effects are severe in places, and even violent. Hence topography is of a very complex nature, with vestigial structural features often obscured, at least in part, by lava flows, or by the development of extensive detrital layers, which have been either river-aggraded and deposited, or laid down in the form of lacustrine deposits. Further action due to temperature changes and above all to strong seasonal winds transforms these deposits either into pebbly wastes or, as one traveller put it, "squalid successions of sandy dunes".

Chief erosive agent is the notorious Wind of 120 Days already mentioned in relation to Sīstān. Lack of cloud results in a high rate of heat exchange: very high day temperatures in summer and surprisingly cold winter nights away from the coast produce temperature ranges as wide over the year as 40° C (72° F). Altitude also makes a considerable difference. Certain cereal and fruit crops will not grow in the higher or even intermediate plateau levels.

Rainfall in this south-eastern zone ranges only from one to six in. over the lowlands to distinctly higher figures over the mountain crests. Most of this tends to fall as violent downpours on a very few days, entirely between October and April. Because of the generally impermeable character of the rock series—either through lava flows or metamorphism—the effects of rainfall tend to be soon dissipated by rapid runoff; and it is only in relatively few areas, where permeable series exist on a larger scale (or where accumulation of water can occur as a lens in a blanket of detritus), that agriculture and human settlements can develop. To a very marked degree, therefore, cultivation resembles oasis development in a hostile environment, and Fig. 22 summarizes the chief areas of south-east Iran where there is any significant agriculture.

Beginning in the extreme south, along the shores of the Gulf of Oman and proceeding northward, we may first note the special characteristics of the Persian Makrān. This region is adjacent to the coast and comprises the zone between the Strait of Hurmuz and the frontier of West Pakistan. In its extreme western part, fronting the strait, the Makrān consists of a series of small ridges alined in a generally north–south pattern: an indication of the extent of tectonic disturbance that has formed the strait. Here is no minor downwarping and drowning, but a major interruption to a strongly established trend of folding. With the "grain" of relief running parallel to the coast, as in the south-east Zagros (p. 32 above), few settlements of any importance exist, in some contrast to conditions on the north and west sides of the strait. Relief is still closely concordant with structure—that is to say, anticlines form the ridges, with synclinal valleys between—and altitudes rise fairly rapidly inland to a series of crests that reach 3,000 to 6,000 ft within about fifty miles of the coast. Just west of Jāsk the ridges take on once more an east–west trend interrupted by the Strait of Hurmuz, and this continues as the dominating pattern as far as the eastern frontier.

Near the coast the rock series consist of Eocene and Miocene shales, conglomerates, marls, sandstones, and limestones. These are not strongly resistant even to the greatly reduced erosive power of the streams, and individual anticlines are small in longitudinal extent. Consequently the river pattern is smaller. Many valleys run directly in from the coast and merely skirt the edges of the folds, with extremely broad lower sections. There is therefore much less of the intricate trellis type of drainage that characterizes the Zagros, and access from the sea is easier, though in fact little utilized. Greater exposure of shales and dark-brown sandstones produces a sombre, often repelling landscape; and the action of erosion agents, here greatly developed, gives rise to pediments, isolated buttes and massifs on a small scale, and fantastically eroded pillars or rock formations. As previously noted there has been oscillation of the whole surface, and phases of down-warping and later uplift have produced prominent suites of terraces and flats, with deposition of silts, both freshwater and marine, on the benches thus formed. Further reflecting the marked crustal instability are numerous mud volcanoes in the extreme south-east (Plate 5).

Towards the north the character of the Makrān changes somewhat, owing to the occurrence of what is termed "Coloured Mélange". This wild mixture of igneous and sedimentary rocks of Cretaceous age has greater resistance than the coastal series and hence forms the major relief features: a group of ridges reaching 6,000 to 7,000 ft that define the northern edge of the Makrān and the rim of the Jāz Murīān depression. The northern Makrān is distinctly irregular in its topography, with folds rising from a broken upland mass that is about 3,000 ft above sea-level. One major col at Nashk (2,800 ft) gives access to the Jāz Murīān region. Overall, the landscape in this area is once more distinctly repelling: very irregular and accidented in places, due to its mode of origin, with dark-coloured rocks (often basalts) pre-dominating.

As compared with the Zagros, the Persian Makrān offers far less inducement to human settlement. A greater proportion of impermeable rocks means that springs and seepages are fewer, qanāts difficult or even impossible to construct; and the sporadic rainfall quickly disperses to the sea, often as flash-flood that can cover a valley floor to a width of up to a mile with sand and debris. Furthermore, even when perennial flows of water do exist, the amount of cultivable flat land close to such water supplies may be extremely limited.

Most agricultural development has occurred round Mīnāb, where there are two small but perennial streams, and the volume of water justifies the use of motor pumps. Dates, cereals, and a wide variety of subtropical and tropical crops, including citrus and mangos, are cultivated; and parts are even lightly wooded—rare indeed for the Makrān. Farther east, expanses of flat, soil-covered land are not numerous, and so where these occur in proximity to water, intensive cultivation takes place, with rice as a staple. Wheat, barley, millet, and sorghum are also produced, there is some growing of vegetables and lucerne; and dates are important.

In the regions nearest to the coast there can be a further geographical complication. Some slight summer rainfall occurs here, and relatively extensive areas of fairly flat ground are covered by fertile alluvial soils. Cultivation of a fairly wide range of crops becomes possible, but there are two major and opposing hazards. Rainfall in the coastal region and over the hills to the north is extremely capricious in onset and distribution. Thus in one year extreme drought may prevail, followed a short period later by extensive and equally disastrous flooding. Both catastrophes are of frequent occurrence. Hence it is hardly surprising that to Italian observers in 1957 the Makrān gave an overall impression of deterioration, of which the main symptoms were lack of maintenance of the irrigation system—canals and qanāts—together with a considerable human emigration. Goats and some sheep and cattle are maintained, either close to the irrigated areas or on higher pastures farther inland. In these latter, pasture may often be rather better, but inaccessibility is a great handicap, and the quality of the animals is low. The largest settlements are Mīnāb, Jāsk, Gwadar, and Chāhbahār, but none is very large, and the fact that three are on the coast indicates the relative poverty of the land.

North of the Makrān and its immediate neighbour to the north-west, the Jāz Murīān depression, is an irregular upland area dominated by the Kūh-i-Taftān range. The predominant trend discernible within the general mass of ridges and depressions is N.W.–S.E. but there are a number of exceptions to this general effect, with east–west and north–south alined structures present in some places. A narrow but imposing mountain chain is that of the Kūh-i-Basmān, which runs east–west to link the uplands of eastern Iran to the Zagros chains far to

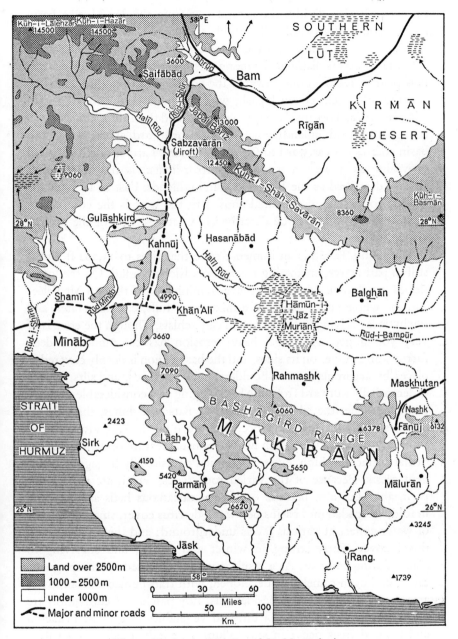

Fig. 23. The Iranian Makrān and Jāz Muriān basin.

the west. It also divides the central Lūṭ from the Jāz Muriān basin farther south. Eastward still, another mountain chain, the Kūh-i-Sultān, serves as a link with the mountains of Pakistan–Baluchistan.

Some observers distinguish among this spread of ridge and mountain two plateau regions, one towards the north, located around Zāhidān, and the other centred on K͟hāsh, with the mass of the Kūh-i-Taftān lying between. Together these two plateaus and the Taftān range form a triangular-shaped upland which tapers northward as the great Lūṭ basin encroaches eastward to form a boundary. Farther north still, and providing as it were a magnified mirror-image, is the upland area already described as the Bīrjand–Qā'in highlands. East of this lies the lowland of Sīstān, also treated above; to the west is the complex of interior basins that will be described in a later section of the present article.

The Kūh-i-Taftān is an immense cone that rises to 13,262 ft and is still in part active, emanating gas and occasionally mud. On the lower slopes is a "spine" or pillar of lava, reminiscent of that on Mt Pelée; and the whole area consists of a mixture of tuffs, conglomerates, and trachytic lavas lying above marl and clay schists. Though the cone is of very young geological age, heavy erosion has cut numerous deep furrows and gullies on its sides, and the base region is deeply covered in places by accumulations of boulders, pebbles, sands, and silts (in that order radially outward from the base). Lying at a considerable distance from the cone, the silts now appear as flats and dunes, the original furrows and valleys having been heavily infilled. This gives rise to "buried topography", which has the unusual feature of gently sloping or flat surfaces at high levels, diversified occasionally by jagged emergent crests. Because of the varied rock types, which are mostly impermeable, but also because occasional calcareous beds are arranged in folds or eroded into basins below the detritus cover, small quantities of water collect at various levels underground; and there is a vegetational cover, fairly strong in winter and spring, and surviving in places during summer. As a result, pastoralism based on sheep, goats, cattle, and even camels has developed, with transhumance from lower areas on a seasonal basis. Besides this, tiny patches of cultivation are found, with wheat, barley, fruit, and vegetables as staples. Pistachio and almond trees occur in small clumps or individually, as a native (i.e. wild) species, especially on the northern and north-eastern sides of the Taftān massif. There is some haphazard collection of the nuts, but the trees are in no way "cultivated"—rather, they suffer from the depredations of animals. Towards the west and the borders of the Lūt, particularly below altitudes of 4,000 ft, which over much of eastern Iran is a critical level, the vegetation becomes markedly xerophilous.

South of the Taftān crests there are a number of larger hollows or valleys cut into the plateau surface, and one of these, the plain of Khāsh, is of some interest. The "plain" or, better, broad valley, extensively infilled by detritus, stands at an altitude of over 4,000 ft and is defined by upland ridges that are partly igneous and partly of limestone. Due to elevation and the permeability of some rock series, this valley is relatively cool in summer and as compared with neighbouring areas, has a rather better, dependable water supply. Soil is present to some depth, with an alternation of silts, sands, and occasional clays. Here, in an area of about 1,000 hectares (an indication of relative importance), is to be found an "island" of distinctly advanced agriculture, with a developed system of mixed farming. Wheat, barley, and lucerne are the chief products; there are also vegetables and tree crops (apricots, apples, vines, pistachios, and pomegranates), together with trees deliberately fostered for shade. With animals kept close to the fields, either stall-fed or on rotation pasture, dung is collected and used for fertilizer—a rare practice elsewhere in south-east Iran. The fertility of this small but favoured area has drawn immigrant cultivators from other regions, especially western Iran, which in turn fosters a higher level of methods and techniques. Altogether, the tiny Khāsh district represents one of the best possibilities for agricultural development in this southern part of Iran.

North of the Taftān is a variegated upland zone broken by ridges that attain 6,000 to 8,000 ft. Extensive flatter areas have evolved, again due to infilling of older relief forms by pebbles, sands, and silts. This is the Zāhidān plateau, a region of extensive igneous and metamorphic outcrops thickly covered on their lower flanks by outwash fans, dune deposits, and scree. Human settlement is restricted to the lower parts: the valley flats, or, more particularly, detritus cones developed in association with these, represent the best opportunities available. One such open site, where several streams fed from almost permanent snowcaps converge to provide superior possibilities of irrigation, carries the settlement of Lādīz; another, on a somewhat larger scale again, is the site of Zāhidān itself. Owing to high relief and the intercalation of porous and impermeable rock strata below a covering of detritus, there is some retention of water and thus an opportunity for irrigation by qanāt. Cultivation of cereals, chiefly wheat and barley, is carried on at lower levels, with much fruit-growing (especially dates and citrus). Lucerne is also produced on a scale sufficient to support animals, and in a few localities there is even irrigation to provide fodder and pasture for animals, which can be kept as part of a mixed farming economy. The higher and unirrigated slopes are given over to semi-nomadic herders who have sheep and goats. These peoples still live in tents and exist principally on a diet of curds, yoghourt, and small amounts of cereals.

Zāhidān has some importance as the largest agricultural "oasis" of the region, and also as a route centre. It is an approach to Pakistan and India, and it stands at the terminus of a railway that was built by the British during the First World War as an extension of the Indian system. It is also at the crossing of this east–west route with a north–south line from Chāhbahār towards Mashhad; and with the enhanced strategic importance of southern and eastern Iran during the last twenty years, Zāhidān has grown slightly, though in absolute terms its importance still remains small.

Northward again of the Zāhidān plateau, as we have already seen, the highland ring contracts to a single ridge and plateau of a maximum height of 6,000 to 8,000 ft and only fifty to sixty miles in width. Here there is hardly any settled agriculture, the higher parts being given over to seasonal grazing by nomadic herders of sheep and goats, and the lower parts (on the western side at least) rapidly changing to salt steppe or scrub as the basin of the Lūt is reached.

THE CENTRAL DESERT BASINS

The highland rim surrounding and demarcating Iran encloses a central area of irregular shape and composed of a number of inland basins. Some of these are very large, others small, but all have one common feature: a lack of any outward drainage to the sea. Moreover, although they are generally areas of subdued relief, with extensive flats and terraces the dominating feature, topography is far from uniform. Much of the central area lies at an altitude of about 3,000 ft above sea-level, but there are a few regions where the lowest basins are only 1,000 ft or even a little less in elevation. Between the basins occur topographical divides of varying character. Certain of these are highly developed

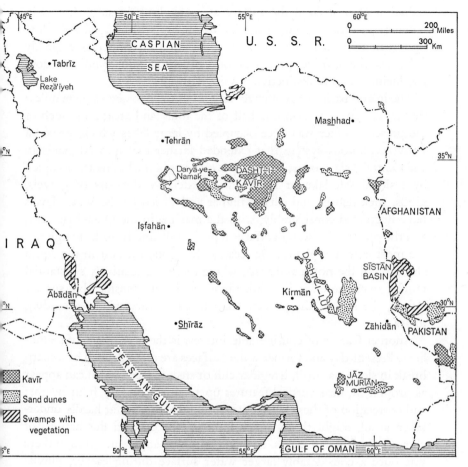

Fig. 24. Distribution of kavīr, swamp and sand dunes. (After N.I.O.C., 1957.)

mountain chains attaining heights of 8,000 to 10,000 ft; others are lines of isolated hummocks, and others again low cols of indeterminate relief.

Being shut off to a considerable extent—though not quite totally—from the influences of damp, maritime air masses, this interior area experiences only low amounts of rainfall, which are on average between one and six in. annually, with an incidence sharply confined to the six winter months. Summers are often almost cloudless, consequently temperatures are very high during the day. But again because of the lack of cloud, the elevation, and the dryness of the air, there is rapid radiation of heat from the surface at night, both in summer and in winter; this leads to temperature extremes, with surprisingly low figures in winter. This wide diurnal variation in temperature greatly enhances the erosive processes of exfoliation and wind abrasion, producing a highly distinctive physiography.

The inland basins of Iran cover an area of over 300,000 square miles: that is, rather more than one half of the total land area; and much of the present surface was once occupied by large lakes which formed a fairly continuous system that extended farther east into Afghanistan and Central Asia. Today, only the lowest parts of the basins are occupied by residual salt lake or marsh, with extensive deposits of gravels, sands, rock debris, and silts at higher and varied levels. Water levels have fluctuated considerably, with the maxima in the Quaternary era; and the present-day water surfaces represent distinctly arid, though not the most extreme, phases. Desiccation has gone furthest in the south and east: in the north and west, where there is a relatively substantial rainfall over the encircling hill ranges and thus considerable surface inflow, the size of the present lakes tends to vary widely according to season.

Another feature of considerable interest is the occurrence of strand-lines. Present-day and former water surfaces are often defined by a sharp break in slope—a small, irregular cliff or steeper face, which can appear as prominent, near-vertical features up to thirty or fifty ft in height; and correlation of these levels by careful mapping, so far hardly undertaken at all, might throw much light on the detailed fluctuations of climate. One overall fact is, however, strongly apparent. Though there was once a considerably larger water surface during earlier, pluvial periods, the erosive power of the streams even then proved insufficient to cut outflow channels through the outer mountain massifs to reach the sea. In Asia Minor, where a somewhat similar geomorphological pattern prevailed, the greater part of the interior basins, once water-filled, are now drained by powerful streams that have cut deep ravines through to the sea. It could therefore be inferred that Iran's rainfall in the Quaternary period (if not also in the Later Tertiary) was not outstandingly greater than it is now. There certainly are high-level cols through which drainage could once have taken place; but during the epochs of diminishing rainfall, no major drainage system maintained itself sufficiently to cut down its channels at a rate necessary to ensure continued drainage of the interior. The zone of closed, aretic flow is therefore extensive, and in fact covers the whole of the interior. It may one day be possible to arrive at a fuller understanding of the evolution of drainage in central Iran; but at present, in the absence of detailed local geomorphological studies and topographical surveys, the many interesting problems posed by the inner desert basins remain largely for investigation.

Physical features in the arid central basins of Iran are extremely diverse, and many have individual Persian names, of which a few may be cited here. *Lūt* is a broad term, referring to the desert basins generally but most often applied to the extensive arid areas of the south and east. *Dasht* is relatively firm and dry desert, composed of generally small and compacted rock fragments: pebbles, flints, or, most often, silts. Salt in efflorescence is not normally present in dasht to any considerable extent, and hence when subjected to rainfall, dasht drains relatively quickly and remains fairly firm. *Rīg* (or *reg*) refers to finer deposits, usually of sand, which may be in regular dune formation or irregularly deposited as a variable sheet. The dunes are of course controlled largely by local winds, especially in the east, where they are often extremely mobile, taking up "classic" forms like those displayed in north Africa and inner Arabia, though on a somewhat smaller scale: dunes of several hundred feet in height and over one hundred miles in length are not found. *Namak* is a salt lake, which can occur either as an open sheet of water, or with relatively uncomplicated salt crust (i.e. without much intermixture of silt, mud, and colloidal compounds). *Kavīr* denotes an expanse of slime or mud, viscous rather than free-flowing, with frequent salt efflorescence or continuous thick layers at the surface. A feature of both namak and kavīr is the formation of polygonal plates of salt crust on the surface. These develop as the water below is evaporated, and since in growing they begin to impinge on one another each plate tends to become arched upward. Sometimes the centre of the plate lifts off above the water surface, giving a hummocky appearance to the crust; at other times it is the edges that rise, and the plates then take on the appearance of concave cusps like an ice-floe; or again, angular segments may break off and litter the surface with irregular sharp fragments.

Below the salt surface of a kavīr, which can be from one to about ten cm thick, occurs an expanse of salty viscous mud or slime. The water in this mass is replenished from drainage channels, or *shatt*, where viscosity is much less. These shatt, or streams of ooze, are usually fairly narrow but deep—hence they form a considerable danger to animals and humans attempting to cross the surface, since they can be sufficiently extensive to engulf a whole group of people. The cover of hard saline crust can be continuous above them, thus giving absolutely no indication whatever at the surface of the presence of such channels, which remain liquid even in summer. Dry firm desert, confronted by energy and sufficient supplies, can be crossed; but the kavīrs of central Iran remained largely unexplored until the visits of Dr and Mrs A. Gabriel in the 1930s. One method of travel is to follow as far as possible the tracks of larger wild animals, but these are not by any means always found.

In a region of such marked aridity, the presence of relatively large water bodies is something of an anomaly. Analysis of the kavīr shows a considerable amount of deliquescent salts, especially magnesium chloride. It would appear that moisture is extracted from the atmosphere to a significant degree by these substances, despite a generally low atmospheric humidity. There could also be a process of attraction of lower ground water by the deliquescent layers lying above, and thus a slow but pervasive "creep" and accumulation of soil water from a considerable distance. Much more investigation is necessary, however, before the many questions relating to the character and mode of origin of kavīr are fully explained. One associated matter that could be important is the possible extraction of minerals on a commercially valuable scale. Very much larger in extent than the Dead Sea, and endowed with the potential for using solar energy as a fuel in extraction processes, the kavīrs of Iran could one day come to have a greater economic importance than at present.

One further point is the distribution of mineral deposits in the form of a giant "ring" or aureole. This regular arrangement of salts, almost amounting to stratification, is highly characteristic of central Iran, though it has also been observed in other parts of southern and western Asia, especially in Turkestan, south-western Siberia, and Anatolia.

At the lowest levels—that is, on basin floors and bottom-lands— calcium, magnesium, and sodium chlorides are found. On the next level, and often in a well-defined succession, there tend to be sulphates of these three elements; while carbonates (with calcium carbonate especially widespread) form an upper layer that impinges on tablelands and plateaus. This phenomenon, approaching but not totally reaching regularity in occurrence, has special significance, not only for studies of soil improvement and land utilization, but also for possible commercial exploitation of the basin deposits.

The northern group of basins lies immediately to the south of the Alburz mountain ranges and can be regarded as comprising one large basin, the Kavīr-i-Buzurg, or Great Kavīr, with a number of smaller sumps and basins ringing it to the north, east, and south. The British Admiralty Handbook of 1944 distinguishes up to ten such small, separate kavīr areas, and shows the Kavīr-i-Buzurg as a continuous expanse covering over 200 miles in an east–west direction; and it is more than forty miles wide in certain parts. The A.I.O.C. geological map of 1959 is more conservative in its delineation of the area occupied by kavīr; on the same map the central parts of the Kavīr-i-Buzurg are interrupted by outcrops of Miocene strata, in the form of ridges that have a definite trend generally N.E.–S.W., and also by a more irregular outcrop of igneous and metamorphic series east and west of Durūd. There is also shown a swarm of salt domes in the area lying about forty miles south-south-east of Simnān.

The three small western basins—that of Masīleh, and two closer to Qum—are visible from the main road joining Tehrān to Qum and the south; and there is a considerable expanse of open salty water, which tends to fluctuate in area seasonally because it is fed from streams that rise in the relatively well-watered uplands of the north-western Zagros. Fringing this towards the interior is the real kavīr, together with small belts of sand dunes.

The Kavīr-i-Buzurg, on the other hand, receives far less perennial and direct, open drainage. Shaṭṭ are however more common, especially in the north-eastern parts, and the actual margins of the kavīr zone vary considerably. In some districts, for example, the south-western part, high spurs tightly enclose the saline area, producing the impression of a salt sea or gulf between bold headlands. Towards the north and west, where the kavīr reaches to within six miles of Tehrān, there is a much more gradual descent from the Alburz foothill terraces to the kavīr surface, which lies at an altitude of about 3,000 ft above sea-level. The Kavīr-i-Buzurg in its north-eastern parts is much less known, and the upland zone referred to above (and mainly composed of igneous rock) separates the main kavīr from the minor kavīrs of Simnān and Dāmghān. Communications swing north and eastward, keeping close within the piedmont of the inner Alburz and avoiding on their southern flank vast stretches of salt steppe, loose dune, and kavīr. These expanses

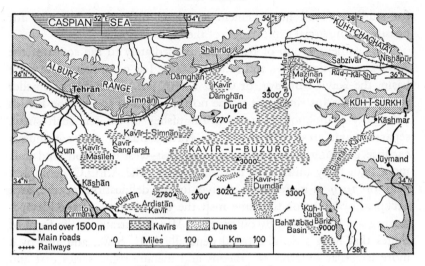

Fig. 25. The Great Kavīr region.

are diversified by residual land forms: bare eroded ridges; occasional peaks and crests which stand at 2,000 to 3,000 ft above kavīr level (i.e. summits attaining 5,000 to 6,000 ft above sea-level); and isolated columns of especially resistant rock. These last, similar in appearance to coastal stacks, and emerging usually as spectacular isolated features from a level waste of white salt crust or dark kavīr, reinforce the overall impression of a vast sea and rugged coastline.

The kavīrs fringing the Kavīr-i-Buzurg on the north and east, though much smaller in size, can be equally difficult and dangerous for human beings; because lying closer to the heavier-watered Alburz they have a number of drainage feeds, which, though sometimes open, are more often in the form of *shaṭṭ*. One curious feature is the *Sang farsh* (rock-carpet) kavīr, so named because of a causeway of stones that crosses it, thus affording a more direct route between Simnān and Kirmān. Some fifteen to eighteen miles long, and up to fifteen to forty ft in width, the causeway represents a prodigious expenditure of human labour, since all the stones had to be brought from a distance.

In the south-east of Iran, and extending between latitudes 29°–32° N. and around 58°–59° E. longitude, is the Southern Lūṭ, one of the most extensive and unusual natural features of Iran. Three major mountain systems, the southern Zagros, the ring of uplands between Afghanistan and Iran, and the interior complex of ridges lying east of Kirmān, converge gradually, leaving an extensive basin in the middle. This is the Southern Lūṭ, a deep, oval-shaped hollow that is defined strikingly by high hills; and in its lowest part it drops to less than 1,000 ft above sea-level—the least elevated area of central Iran.

On the west, a defining edge to this basin is provided by a series of hills that trend mainly N.N.W.–S.S.E., reaching altitudes in a few localities of over 10,000 ft. Main component ridges are the Kūh-i-Sagūch located east of Kirmān, and the Kūh-i-Jamal-Bāriz[1] to the south of Bam. A much narrower but very clearly defined saddle, continuing the line of the Kūh-i-Jamal-Bāriz into the Kūh-i-Basmān, serves to separate the Southern Lūṭ from the basin of the Jāz Muriān farther south; and then the Taftān massifs, which attain 13,000 ft in maximum height, complete the surrounding mountain ring on the north side. The Lūṭ therefore appears as an unusually strongly defined and deeply hollowed feature in a distinctly mountainous part of the interior plateau of Iran. Contrasts between the low-lying, doubly interior hollow, so to speak, and the abrupt retaining ring are very marked.

The basin is not uniformly hollow. Its deepest part is a long narrow sump occupied by salt water (namaksār), which lies closer to the western walls immediately east of Shāhdād (Khahis) and Kashīt, with a more gradual slope towards the eastern side. This expanse of open water, which covers an area approximately one hundred miles by fifteen, is fed by numerous streams flowing mainly from the Kūh-i-Sigah, and on the upper courses of these streams is a limited amount of human settlement. East of the namaksār is a heavily eroded area, the Shahr-i-Lūṭ.

The present namaksār would appear to be the remnant of a far larger sheet of water that once extended farther eastward. Now, because of the considerable drop in level—the present-day surface of the namaksār is only 800 ft above sea-level—as well as the relatively wide expanses between the edge of the actual salt lake and the mountain rim to the east, there has been much erosion of the surface, part of which is covered by soft silts. The primary agent in this erosive process was fluvial: small streams cutting deep troughs and gorges, and depositing the eroded material as deltas and fans on the lowest parts of their course. But with continued shrinkage of the water surface, wind erosion

---

[1] According to Sykes, the name Jamal Bāriz is erroneous. It should be Jabal Bāriz. Jabal = Mountain; P. M. Sykes, *Ten Thousand Miles in Persia or Eight Years in Iran* (London, 1902), p. 145. Cf. *Times Atlas*. Ed.

became more and more active: not only were the lighter and dried-out surface deposits directly removed but the acquired sand content greatly increased the abrasive power of local winds. East of the namaksār, therefore, lies a zone of intense denudation, with a maze of defiles and entrenched channels enlarged and altered by wind erosion and sand-blast. This is the Shahr-i-Lūt, a region that gives from a distance the strong impression of ruined cities or buildings (Shahr = a town). There is a strongly discernible trend in the general erosion pattern, with the widest troughs running for the most part parallel to the axis of the namaksār (i.e. N.N.W–S.S.E.). Close to the salt lake are expanses of true, viscous kavīr, with some shatt, but both are on a distinctly smaller scale than in the basin of the Great Kavīr farther to the north.

The extreme east of the Shahr-i-Lūt depression is covered by extensive sand dunes: forming the largest single expanse of loose sand within Iran, they occupy a zone of about 135 miles in length. Because of extreme susceptibility to the action of strong local winds, which are in turn a function of wide temperature contrasts, the dunes are very mobile, and their confused pattern is markedly different from that of the great formations of the Sahara and Rub' al-Khālī. Strong winds, often accompanied by blowing dust, are thus a major disadvantage in the basin. As altitude gradually rises towards the eastern rim, a very slight annual rainfall begins to occur, and there is also a certain limited amount of soakage from the higher crests farther east. Consequently, there can be a scanty vegetation of scrub and even grass on the more easterly parts of the Lūt, chiefly in the form of a winter flush.

On the western side, in the narrow zone between the northern side of the namaksār and the high, defining mountain ridges, there is distinctly more surface and subsurface water, derived chiefly from intermittent streams that course down the steep mountain slopes. They are fed by the more abundant precipitation, which is partly retained as a snow-cap over the higher crests. Some of this water remains at or near the surface, but by far the greater part is absorbed underground and can then be tapped for irrigation in favourable localities by wells and qanāts. Varied crops of wheat, millet, dates, fruit, and vegetables are raised in the few local areas where water is available; and consequently there are a few attractive and densely peopled spots in this area of otherwise extremely sparse human settlement.

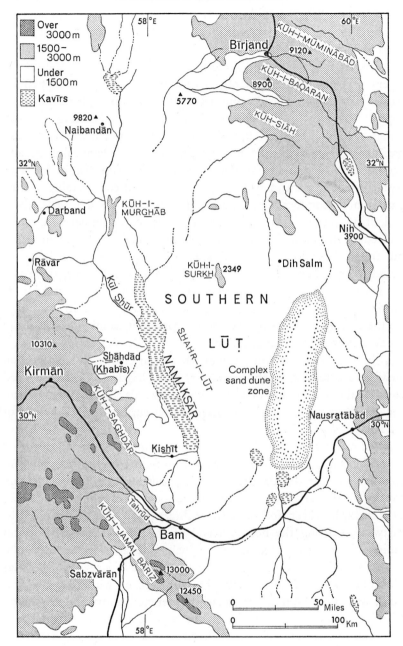

Fig. 26. The Southern Lūṭ.

Largest of these "oasis" zones occurs round Bam, in the upper part of the Tahrūd ("river bottom") valley. Here the massive, stratified detrital deposits show much variation in physical size and composition, ranging from boulders and scree to sands and limy silts. Within the layers occur significant quantities of water that can be tapped by qanāt. These reach considerable size: the town of Bam, for instance, is supplied mainly by one such qanāt that is ten miles long and terminates in a well 250 ft deep, whilst farther to the north-west is another qanāt some twenty-six miles in length. Lying at a moderate altitude, and sheltered by surrounding mountain ranges, the Bam district has temperate winters, a warm spring and autumn, and considerable diurnal variation in summer temperatures. Besides the usual cereals, dates and citrus fruit are also grown, and there are two commercial crops—unusual in this part of Iran—namely, henna and sugar beet. Clumps of nut trees, pistachio and almond, survive as wild specimens, but with pressure on water resources by growing flocks and herds, there is a tendency for the pastoralists to encroach on this tree-covered land to its detriment. Where water supplies allow, plots are also cultivated high up the mountain slopes by temporary workers who migrate seasonally from the lower areas around Bam.

Other market centres of a somewhat similar character, though even smaller, are Kashīt, Shāhdād, Rāvar, and Darband. These are sited towards the outer edges of alluvial flats, towards the hill zones, where the first outcrops of solid rock sustain a near-surface flow or seepage of water.

Most major routes avoid the Lūt and swing well to the north or south. This is especially the case with the important route from Kirmān to Zāhidān near the Pakistan frontier, which diverges considerably southward through Bam, keeping to the southern rim of the Lūt basin. One track, however, follows a more direct route from Kirmān north-eastward, skirting the northern end of the namaksār, but it is too difficult for extensive use. Hence the Shahr-i-Lūt remains in general the most forbidding, and consequently the emptiest, large-scale geographical unit within Iran. Extreme heat in summer, windiness, blowing sand, and topographical irregularity, over and above the handicaps of aridity and salinity, make it comparable in human terms with the Empty Quarter (Rub' al-Khālī) of Arabia—a negative, intractable area.

The principal settlement in this south-eastern region is Kirmān, a town lying at an altitude of 5,650 ft on an open plain that is bounded to the north by the wastes of the Lūṭ and increasingly hemmed in southward by the N.W.–S.E.-alined ranges of the main Zagros, which here attain 13,000 ft. The extremes of climate experienced in the interior desert basins are well exemplified by conditions at Kirmān. Rainfall averages 5·4 in. annually and occurs almost entirely between October and March, with the summer totally arid. The average diurnal range of temperature amounts to more than 30° F at all seasons: thus the notional July average of 81° F means in effect an average daily maximum approaching 100° F; and a January average of 45° F means frost occurring on most nights.

Kirmān

Kirmān province is the Caramania of the ancient geographers, and the town probably existed as a settlement in Sasanian times. By the time of Marco Polo's visit in 1271 it had become an emporium for traders from the Persian Gulf, Khurāsān, and Central Asia; and its own products, such as harnesses, armour, and turquoise jewellery, were well known. Over succeeding centuries, however, its remote position made it an easy prey. The city was sacked by Tīmūr, by Afghans on several occasions, by Nādir Shāh, and lastly in 1794 by Agha Muḥammad Qājār, who pillaged Kirmān province for three months, putting thousands to death and blinding or enslaving many others.

During the nineteenth century the town was rebuilt on a new site slightly to the north-west of the old town. More than a century passed before the city could be said to have recovered, but over the last sixty years its population has grown by some fifty per cent, totalling 62,157 in 1956. Industry has expanded once more, and the town has been able to acquire and develop the features of a strong provincial capital. Today Kirmān is a town in transition. Its walls and gates were removed in the 1930s, but the ruins of the walls can still be traced among the houses, and the names of the gates are remembered as street names. Attached to the walls in the west was the *Arg* or citadel. As in many Persian towns this has evolved into a centre of modern administration with offices of government departments, a branch of the national bank, and a large school and hospital—all in modern buildings. Most of the modern building in Kirmān has taken place in the western sector, and elsewhere the town remains largely within the line of the wall or on the site of ancient suburbs.

The street pattern of Kirmān consists largely of a maze of narrow, unpaved, and irregular lanes running between high, featureless mud walls. Superimposed on this are wide asphalt avenues, straight and tree-lined, created in the 1930s and '40s. These sometimes follow the lines of the old walls, but also cut boldly through the town. Still, only in the west is there anything approaching a network of modern streets, and not all of these are yet surfaced or complete.

The main street of the old town was the Vakīl Bāzār, leading from the Friday Mosque to the Maidān (square), which was formerly outside the Arg. This bāzār is still mostly arched with brick vaults, and lined with shops and caravansera. The square has been planted with a garden, and the former arcades around it replaced with shops, restaurants, and a cinema.

Most of the housing in Kirmān is of the old courtyard type, centring on a yard with a pool and small garden. A prominent feature of the Kirmān skyline are the "bād-gīrs" or wind-towers. Like a chimney in reverse, they ventilate rooms below, which are often subterraneous refuges against the heat of summer.

Outside the town large areas are given over to gardens, both for recreation and for producing fruit and vegetables, irrigated by qanāts which are among the longest in Persia. To the west are the brickfields fuelled by rather poor local coal.

Industry in Kirmān was until recently largely on a craft basis. Now, modernization of plant and further industrialization are a feature. There are a significant number of modern establishments, mainly textile mills and brickworks. The most important activity, in the value of the product and the numbers employed, still remains carpet-weaving. Kirmān carpets are world-famous for quality and design, and materials are still mostly local in origin. Work is done either in the home or in small workshops in the bāzār, with carpet "factories" being yet larger workshops where conditions are slightly more modern.

Many in Kirmān are engaged in administration and clerical work, which illustrates the importance of the town as a centre of provincial government; and large numbers are also in the armed forces. Kirmān has come to perform the functions of regional service centre throughout a tributary area that includes not only Kirmān province, but Persian Balūchistān, within which it is the only urban centre of any considerable size.

Further basins of closed drainage occur singly or in series along the

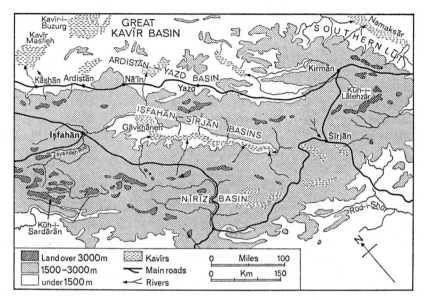

Fig. 27. The interior basins of the central Zagros.

eastern flanks of the Zagros range, where this system abuts on the central plateau. Hollows are enclosed between high, narrow ridges that trend mainly N.W.–S.E., as we have noted earlier, and lie no more than thirty to forty miles apart. Consequently the basins themselves are long and relatively narrow, and alined for the most part in two groups. The first of these groups, extending generally south from Ardistān, Nā'īn, and Yazd, almost as far as Kirmān, has small but fairly numerous expanses both of kavīr and sand. Irregularities of relief produce drainage by an intricate complex of flowing but short streams without consistent direction. Despite their small size, some of the kavīrs are still incompletely surveyed, but it can be said that most occur at an altitude of about 3,000 ft, accordant therefore with the Great Kavīr of the northern interior rather than with the water surfaces of the Southern Lūṭ.

A second cluster of salt basins lies farther south-west, beginning south-east of Iṣfahān, in the lowest part of the Iṣfahān plain, and extending as far as the Jāz Murīān basin. A small salt lake with some kavīr, fringed by areas of sand dunes, marks the termination of the Zāyandeh Rūd, the river that supplies Iṣfahān. The lake lies in a region known as Gāvkhāneh. Farther south-east, somewhat larger kavīrs occur east of Alūrkūh and west of Sīrjān; but these, especially the latter, are extremely shallow and dry out considerably during summer, leaving an expanse of salt crust. Despite the proximity of reasonably well-watered mountain ridges, shaṭṭ are much less numerous than in most kavīr districts of Iran—absent, in fact, over many areas. All the basins of this second group stand at a distinctly higher elevation than the rest, previously described. The lower Zāyandeh Rūd basin lies at 4,850 ft above sea-level, whilst the others are at altitudes of over 5,000 ft.

Iṣfahān

Located in the fertile upper valley of the Zāyandeh Rūd, where non-brackish water is available both from the river itself and from wells in the porous subsoil, is the city of Iṣfahān, fourth largest in Iran after Tehrān, Tabrīz, and Mashhad. The city lies at an altitude of approximately 5,000 ft, with the Bakhtīārī ranges of the Zagros to south and west, and the beginnings of the central desert basins on the east. Iṣfahān is within a "marchland" (the change from mountain to interior desert), and it owes its principal importance to a command of routes—southward from Tehrān, Qum, and the north along the margin of the desert basins; and south-westward through the Zagros system to the head of the Persian Gulf and the lowlands of Mesopotamia. Its name, "troop assembly point", indicates one of its main functions, and its long historical past is a further sign of its nodal position.

Iṣfahān can be traced back to Achaemenid times, when it was known as "Gabal". Some authorities associate it with a colony of Jews, said to have been exiled to the area by Nebuchadnezzar in about 690 B.C. Under the name "Jay" it appears as a garrison town of the Sasanid period, and in early Arab times it consisted of twin settlements: Yahūdieh or "Jewish town", partly on the site of the present Jewish quarter in the north-east of Iṣfahān; and Shahristān (Jay), the site of which is marked today by a small village two miles downstream of the city. Iṣfahān was walled as one unit in the tenth century under the Buyid dynasty, and early in the succeeding century it fell to the Seljuk Turks. From this period date some of the earliest monuments still existing, which include the Sarībān, Chehel Dukhtarān, and Masjid 'Alī minarets, along with parts of the Friday Mosque.

Iṣfahān was overrun by Chingiz Khān in 1235, with little destruction; but at the time of the city's second Mongol investment by a conqueror from Central Asia, in the early fourteenth century, the inhabitants first

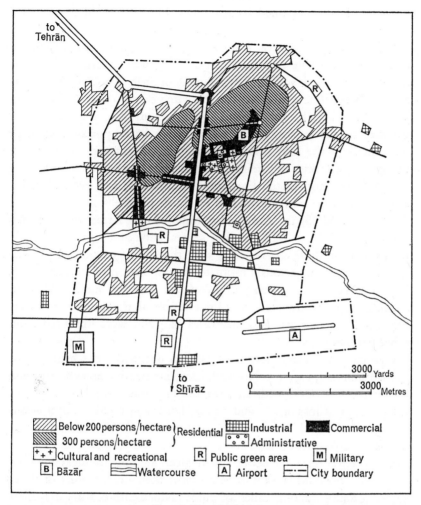

Fig. 28. Plan of Iṣfahān.

made terms with Tīmūr and later rose against him. Some 70,000 Isfahanis were massacred on this occasion, but, like the descendants of Chingiz earlier, the Timurid dynasty ultimately became converts to Shīʻa Islam and patrons of the arts, thus adding to the architectural wealth of Iṣfahān.

During medieval times the city functioned as a regional administrative capital and internationally known centre of trade and industry, with occasional periods as capital of a local dynasty. Under the Safavids, however, Iṣfahān attained its maximum importance. Sh̲āh 'Abbās I moved his capital in 1591 from Qazvīn to Iṣfahān, which rapidly became the administrative, commercial, and cultural centre of strong, extensive, and stable empire. Much building was undertaken, and the nucleus of Iṣfahān is still the Royal Square of Sh̲āh 'Abbās, or Maidān-i-Sh̲āh, where stone goal-posts for the game of polo may still be seen. The Masjid-i-Sh̲āh, the Masjid-i-Sh̲aikh̲ Luṭfullah, the Alā Qāpū gateway to the Palace, and the impressive bāzār portals still mark the centres of the four sides. Craftsmen from Iran and Europe were brought in; factories of foreign merchants encouraged, including those of the British and Dutch East India Companies; and even Christian religious houses were allowed to establish themselves. South of the Zāyandeh Rūd, Sh̲āh 'Abbās also founded the Armenian Christian community of New Julfā, settling several thousand families, forcibly removed from Julfā in Armenia, with the aim of encouraging trade. European visitors variously estimate the population of Iṣfahān at this period as between 700,000 and 1,000,000. The surrounding district, although highly cultivated, could not supply all the produce necessary for this large number, and quantities of grain were imported from other parts of Iran.

Gradually the magnificence of Iṣfahān declined: its Christian and Jewish minorities were persecuted, its rulers became less effective and commerce less developed. In 1722 the city was sacked by Afghans, there was great loss of life, and a period of anarchy and disruption was inaugurated. At the end of the century the Qājār dynasty, which restored stable government, chose Tehrān as a capital city, and Iṣfahān experienced continuing decay and neglect. During the next hundred years the city could be said to be no more than a community of about 50,000 existing among miles of ruins. Nineteenth-century travellers describe the empty bāzārs and caravansera, the diminution of trade, and the general atmosphere of despair, mitigated occasionally and only temporarily under a few enlightened and progressive governors. By the beginning of the present century, the historical monuments seemed largely beyond repair.

Modern growth in Iṣfahān dates from the regime of Rezā Sh̲āh. In 1920 there was no up-to-date manufacturing plant, but fifteen years later there were five large textile factories with modern German equipment and German managers. Textiles have always been the basis of Iranian industry, but now one half of the national textile output is from

Iṣfahān. There are currently twenty-five spinning and weaving mills using electric power mainly generated from oil; altogether they employ 18–20,000 workers, while six of them have over 1,000 workers each. Local raw wool comes from Kirmān, Khurāsān, and Khūzistān, and cotton from the northern provinces. In addition, merino wool is imported from Australia and materials for artificial fibres from Germany, Italy, and Switzerland. Besides the modern industry there are also 25,000 hand-looms in Iṣfahān and district, these have survived by producing special types of cloth cheaply for sale in the villages.

Other modern industries include flour-milling, cement- and brick-making, paper, vegetable oil, and matches; but none approach the textile industry in importance to the economic life of Iṣfahān.

Also since the 1930s there have been general improvements such as road-widening and -surfacing, the building of hospitals and schools, and the use of electricity. At present a modern water-supply system is being installed, but there is no sewage system. The historic buildings have been completely and expertly repaired, with the side-effect of reviving the local tile-making crafts, which, along with hand textile-printing and -engraving on silver and copper, had been almost defunct until recently. Much has been done to encourage tourism by building hotels, by the improvement of road and air services (Iṣfahān has no railway), and by publicity.

Most of the ruins have been cleared and new suburbs built, especially to the south and west, although, in the older parts of town, conditions are poor and unhygienic. Such districts are characterized by the narrow, twisting and unpaved alleys of old Iṣfahān, where the houses are all of the courtyard type: rooms facing inward to a paved court with a pool and small garden, showing nothing to the exterior but a bare wall of mud or mud brick. Mosques, baths, and small local bāzārs are scattered through this area, all built of the same materials and giving the same monotonous aspect. In the newer areas the houses are mainly of fired brick, often of two storeys, standing on the north side of a walled garden which varies in size with the wealth of the occupants. Here the streets are wider, suitable for motor traffic, usually surfaced and bordered with trees and a channel for water. New avenues are however being driven through the old town, indiscriminately destroying all in their path, yet opening all parts to modern circulation. The main shopping street is the Chahār Bāgh of Shāh 'Abbās, and the bāzar survives more as a wholesale market. The impression of verdure expressed by travellers throughout the centuries can still be felt today. Iṣfahān resembles a forest when seen from afar, with mosques and minarets still the only features to emerge from its gardens and avenues.

These abundant gardens, together with the sixteenth- and seventeenth-century monuments (which include two famous bridges across the Zāyandeh Rūd), have led to such comments as *nisf-i-jahān* ("Isfahan is half the world"); while a Scottish traveller declared it to be "one of the rarer places of the world, like Athens or Rome". But perhaps inevitably, there are various less appreciative and even scurrilous references to the inhabitants, which can be summed in the words "Only man is vile". Like Mashhad, this city had in the earlier part of the present century a reputation for being a somewhat reactionary centre of Muslim fanaticism, and there was some opposition here to the policies of Rezā Shāh.

Now, with the growth of economic activities and the commercial importance first of the Tehrān area and second of the oilfield regions of the south-western Zagros, Iṣfahān, located approximately half-way between the two on a major route, and possessing its own traditional activities, has begun to grow once more at a substantial rate. In 1930 it had 120,000 inhabitants; in 1940, 180,000; and in 1956, 254,000.

The last of the major inland basins of Iran is that of the Jāz Murīān, which in certain respects, especially in its structure, is a continuation and elaboration of the Ardistān–Yazd and Sīrjān troughs. It is however much larger as a basin, and its presence effectively narrows the Makrān mountain ranges to about one half of their normal width. The Jāz Murīān basin as a whole covers some 25,000 to 30,000 square miles extending over 200 miles in a generally east–west direction, and forty-five miles on average from north to south. A narrow but often steep and rugged upland zone separates it on its northern side from the Southern Lūṭ depression; and this mountain complex, whilst reaching peaks of over 10,000 ft—and even 12,000 ft—is pierced by a number of cols and passes, some of which are under 2,000 ft above sea-level. The southern edge is extensively defined by the succession of ridges that form a south-east continuation of the Zagros range through the Makrān, as far as Balūchistān.

The Jāz Murīān basin is thus a broad oval, deeply covered in silts and other lacustrine deposits laid down mainly during the Pliocene and Quaternary periods. At the lowest level is a sheet of namaksār fed by two major streams: the Rūd-i-Halīl on the west, and the Rūd-i-Bampūr on the east. Slopes are on the whole gentle, so that the water surface alters considerably between wet and dry seasons—and in many years it entirely disappears for some weeks. The two streams have cut small gullies in the soft alluvial deposits, producing some variation in terrain. Erosion by smaller streams draining towards the water surface from north and south, together with the presence of detached rock masses and small crests which protrude through the generally level basin floor in the west, have further diversified the topography. As one leaves the lowest levels of the Jāz Muriān basin, extensive flats and terraces come to dominate the landscape. Most of these are due to erosion, or else mark the location of old strand-lines; but some others are the result of lava flows, which, by producing high-level plateau surfaces and by infilling hollows, have tended to subdue relief rather than accentuate it. Infilling also by detritus has sometimes been to a depth of nearly 1,000 ft.

As would be expected from these general physical conditions, the region close to the lake itself is largely uninhabited; but away from the saline areas, limited cultivation becomes possible and human settlement occurs. Salt scrub and sand dune give place to patches of better soil that can support grass. In certain localities non-brackish water can be obtained, either from the higher courses of streams or, less often, by sinking deep wells through the loose surface deposits overlying an impermeable rock basin that acts as a catchment and reservoir. Then the bare, almost lunar, landscape changes to one with clusters of trees, a small dark grove or two, and tiny cultivated fields. Areas of cultivation occur in the middle and upper reaches of the Rūd-i-Bampūr, especially around Īrānshahr. The river here tends to be absorbed into porous detrital deposits (Quaternary and Recent), reappearing irregularly as springs and seepages lower down its valley towards Bampūr. Qanāts are thus much used, especially as surface flow presents some curious and intractable features. Seasonal fluctuation in level is considerable; and the crude methods of water control (e.g. often by temporary earth and brushwood dams that are altered annually) result in: (a) excessive quantities of water on some plots, which thus become eroded by flood-water; (b) a tortuous, wasteful channel system from which evaporation is very high, amounting often to over fifty per cent, and (c) a concentration on rice-growing in the over-irrigated areas as the best possible use of a swampy terrain—all this in a region with an enormous overall deficit in water supplies. Moreover the reconstruction of the dams year by year is a tremendous cost in human labour, which for one small area alone was estimated (in 1958) to amount to 3,700 man-days annually.

Other crops grown as staples in most parts are date-palms, with wheat, barley, sorghum, and millet. Vegetables are also important, and some citrus fruit is produced. In sharp contrast to conditions in areas such as Bam and Khāsh, not very far away, agricultural methods are generally poor and extremely primitive, with yields therefore very low. Cotton was tried a few years ago and proved a failure.

Some animals are kept: cattle of the zebu type, sheep, goats, and camels, and there is summer migration to mountain pastures on the rim of the depression. Again, yields from animal husbandry seem to be below those found farther east, e.g. in Sīstān.

At the extreme north-western end of the Jāz Muriān basin, cultivation is also carried on along the middle reaches of the Rūd-i-Halīl and its tributary the Rūd-i-Shūr, especially where these two merge, in the area of Jīruft [Sabzavārān]. In some parts the river channels are deeply entrenched in soft deposits; elsewhere they are braided and highly irregular from year to year: nevertheless, cotton alternates as a summer crop, with winter cereals and some oil seeds. Development within the upper Rūd-i-Halīl is aided by the distinctly heavier rainfall (up to 15 in. annually over the high Jamāl Bāriz and Kūh-i-Shāh Sarāvān ranges, which results in a more sustained and regular flow in the streams, and provides upland pasture that is used by relatively important numbers of animals. Most of the pastoralists tending them live permanently in the high mountains and bring their herds down to the plains near the rivers for a limited time during winter.

Despite the present limited level of economic development, this upper zone of the north-western Jāz Muriān basin appears to offer one of the best potentials among all areas in south-eastern Iran for future human expansion and material progress. This is because it has a greater amount of water than the other areas, a good soil, and an open topography. Such a region, however, being relatively small in size and confined to only a limited part of the basin, is in considerable contrast to the rest. Overall, south-east Iran is intrinsically poor in natural resources; it lies somewhat away from the main route-ways; and it tends to have as neighbours expanses of equally difficult or unattractive country.

CHAPTER 2

GEOLOGY

INTRODUCTION

Information regarding the geology of Iran is somewhat uneven. Many have contributed to make up the present sum of knowledge. Pioneers of the 1850s, like Loftus, and others of the late nineteenth century, like Blandford and Stahl, have been followed in this century by a number of geologists grouped around such leaders as De Böckh, Lees, and Gansser; while the few lone individuals have included Schröder, Rivière, and Furon. Until 1938 the geological surveys were done from the ground entirely but after that year aerial photographs became available as an additional tool. A few efforts to sink bore-holes were made during the nineteenth century, but "modern" drilling commenced only in the first decade of the twentieth century. This and geophysics, which has been evolving since the 1920s, have provided further aids to the interpretation of the geology. Part of the geological research carried out in Iran can be conveniently illustrated by maps, whose preparation is facilitated by the excellent exposures found in most of Iran and particularly in the mountains. Good reconnaissance maps are now available for much of the country, and there are also sheets in some detail designed to meet particular economic or academic needs.

Much stratigraphical detail has accumulated from special regions, but parts of Iran have barely been reconnoitred. As in most countries, the old formations are sparingly exposed and where they do crop out are liable to have experienced rough treatment, such as metamorphism, dyke-intrusion, and destructive jointing, which the younger beds may have escaped. Faulting and folding have also introduced uncertainties. The younger beds are widely distributed, and in undisturbed areas gradual facies variation can be followed. On the other hand, some young formations appear to have suffered widespread metamorphism around certain intrusions, and the parts subject to tight local folding have proved perplexing unless intermediate sections providing critical transitions happen to have been studied.

The stratigraphical column in Iran contains samples of all the systems, from Pre-Cambrian to Quaternary; and from the beginning

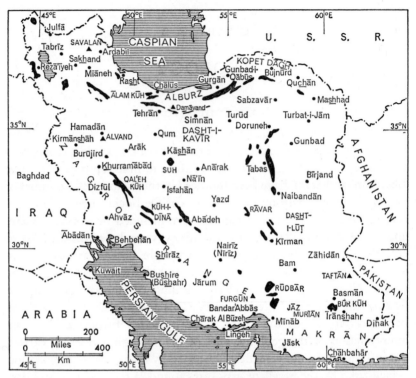

Fig. 29. Sketch-map of Iran showing main place-names in chapter 2, and also
pre-Cambrian and Palaeozoic exposures.

of the Palaeozoic onwards, diagnostic fossils are sometimes abundant.
At the present time vegetation is sufficient to embarrass geological
observations only in the Alburz mountains, where it produces and
preserves thick soil. Alluvium covers most of the basins with internal
drainage and hides the Tertiary and older beds within them.

STRATIGRAPHY

Pre-Cambrian

A case can now be made for Pre-Cambrian rocks being exposed
near Ālam Kūh in the Alburz mountains. Schist, marble, and hornfels
—all intruded by batholiths of granite in the slopes of Ālam Kūh—
are overlain unconformably by more than 1,500 ft of yellow-brown,
fine-grained dolomites interbedded with red sandy shales; both are
probably Cambrian because they in turn underlie reddish quartzites

and sandy shales containing *Cruziana*, a fossil marking a Cambro-Ordovician group. The *Cruziana* beds in turn are overlain conformably by shales containing Ordovician fossils. It is therefore argued that a Pre-Cambrian age may be reasonably assigned to the schist–marble–hornfels group (Gansser and Huber, 1962).

Metamorphic and associated igneous rocks occur on the flanks of the Alburz near Rasht in the west and near Gurgān in the east. In both places they lie below Devonian sandstones, which cover them un-conformably. They are therefore pre-Devonian, and since unmeta-morphosed Lower Ordovician and Cambro-Ordovician strata occur in Ālam Kūh, the age of the metamorphic rocks in other parts of the Alburz is likely to be Pre-Cambrian also. The unmetamorphosed strata include thinbedded, dark, foetid limestones and, red micaceous shales. They overlie shales and dolomites associated with epidiorites, which may all be Pre-Cambrian too.

In the eastern part of central Iran a suite of metamorphic rocks occurs north and east of Bāfq. These consist of garnet-micaschists, quartzites, and marbles and they are cut by granitic intrusions. At one point they crop out within two miles of Lower Cambrian sediments. They are accepted as Pre-Cambrian in age.

Unmetamorphosed sandstones, micaceous sandstones, and slates have been seen at two places about eighty miles south-east of Bāfq. In the one, sixty miles north-west of Kirmān, the old rocks are faulted against fossiliferous Cambrian sediments. In the other, fifteen miles west-north-west of Kirmān, similar micaceous sandstones and slates are covered unconformably by strata that include some from the upper part of the Lower Cambrian. The formation beneath is therefore Pre-Cambrian (Huckriede, Kürsten and Venzlaff, 1962).

Farther south, on the western side of the Jāz Muriān at Rūdbār, several square miles of hornblendic and epidotic schist are exposed, interbedded with phyllites and contorted, coarsely crystallized marble. This series was worn down to a plane, as if by marine denudation, before Jurassic time, for fossiliferous sandstones and shales, both con-taining Liassic ammonites, rest with low dips upon the truncated schist complex. This dates the schists as older than Lias. But it may be relevant to mention that unmetamorphosed Silurian sediments are known in Kūh-i-Furgūn [Kūh-i-Fārghān], about sixty miles to the west, and also at Būr Kūh, 110 miles to the east on the north side of the Jāz Muriān. The Rūdbār metamorphic rocks, definitely pre-Jurassic, lie in an area where the Silurian shales are themselves unaltered, which is also the condition of the Cambrian in the nearest exposures. Pre-Cambrian age cannot be ruled out here, therefore, and may even be probable.

Cambrian

Loftus in 1851 and Blanford in 1872 found fossils in Iran which were then regarded as Silurian but which may be older. In 1924 Lees found trilobites in dark shales associated with dolomites, amongst blocks brought up by the salt in the Al Būzeh salt dome, north-east of Lingeh, and this definitely established the presence of Cambrian in south-west Iran. Several salt domes later yielded blocks of shales with Cambrian trilobites; and in 1937 Bobek described a series in the Alburz containing *Cruziana* as well as Ordovician trilobites.

A thick series of red sandstones, black dolomite, gypsum, and acid volcanic rocks is known in eastern central Iran at several places north and west of Kirmān. The upper part of the series is interbedded with fossiliferous limestones, showing that this part of the series begins high in the Lower Cambrian and extends to the Upper Cambrian (Huckriede *et al.* 1962). Large areas of Cambrian are known in the Zagros mountains south-west of Iṣfahān, where the exposed sequence is nearly 7,000 ft thick. An upper fossiliferous part rests conformably on a lower unfossiliferous part that is shaly below and sandy above. Low in the shales occur beds of coarsely crystalline, leached, foetid, black dolomites. The shales are mostly red in colour with green streaks and blotches, but some are chocolate-coloured. An occasional bed of gypsum was observed, and friable, pink-coloured silt or sand containing specular haematite crystals appears to be associated with groups of salt springs. The higher horizons of the shales tend to be micaceous. The shaly member is about 1,700 ft thick and the sandy part 2,000 ft. Some of the sandstones are false-bedded. Towards the top grits and conglomerates are interbedded with the sandstones and contain cobbles of vein quartz, porphyritic andesite, and dark chert. Most of the sandstones are red but some are purplish, and throughout the series thin beds of white sandstone recur.

In a section near Rāvar, north of Kirmān, about 2,000 ft of purple sandstone have a capping of white sandstone followed by 450 ft of red shales. Beds of fossiliferous Middle Cambrian limestones overlie these shales, succeeded by about 1,500 ft of shale, sandstone, and platy dolomites. Where gypsum occurs in the Cambrian sequence it is unstable and liable to be squeezed out, as it were a salt plug. In the Zagros mountains, however, the Upper Cambrian increases to 3,700 ft and there olive-green colours are dominant in the shales and light brown or pale yellow in the interbedded thin sandstones. *Billingsella* is found at several horizons, and high in the series thin bands contain abundant *Lingulae*. Trilobites have also been found. Thin mottled limestones devoid of fossils, together with other beds full of dolomitic concretions, are also present.

Blocks of many different types of rocks have been brought up, along with the large masses of red shale, gypsum, and salt, the latter forming the core of many salt domes. The rocks include gneiss, schist, epidiorite, felsite, and a variety of acid and basic igneous rocks; there are also limestone and shale, in which Middle and Upper Cambrian trilobites and brachiopods have been determined. This heterogeneous assemblage of rocks scattered over the skirts of most salt domes is known collectively as the "Hurmuz series". As mentioned above, salt plugs in the Kirmān district contain similar material, also referred to as Hurmuz.

Ordovician

Bobek in 1937 first reported that red and violet limestones, interbedded with a series of sandstones and red and green shales, contained Ordovician fossils. They occur near Hazār Cham in Ālam Kūh, near the Takht-i-Sulaimān range west of the Chālūs river in the Alburz mountains. Lower strata contain *Cruzania furcifera* (d'Orb), and higher horizons visited by Gansser produced a trilobite collection dated as Lower to Middle Ordovician.[1]

Farther south in central Iran, in the Kirmān district, sandstones over 400 ft thick are covered by dark dolomites about 1,500 ft thick. Thin shales and limestones interbedded with sandstones are locally fossiliferous. The fauna, including orthids and conodonts, have been studied and recognized as belonging to Arenig and higher horizons of the Ordovician. There are also graptolites. Certain brachiopods have a Silurian aspect. The combined Ordovician and Silurian, mainly in a sandy facies, are about 600 ft thick (Huckriede *et al.* 1962).

Other beds which may possibly be Ordovician make the lowest

[1] W. O. Dietrich, *Zentralbl. f. Min. Geol. u. Pal.*, Abt. B. (1937), pp. 401–4. *Cruzania furcifera* (d'Orb.), worm tubes; *Symphysurus palpebrosus* (Dalm). *Orthis praetor* (Cowper Reed), *Eoorthis* cf. *christianae* (Kjerulf), in A. Gansser and H. Huber (1962). *Illaenus* sp., *Asaphus* sp., *Sinocystis* sp., and *Orthoceras*.

horizon seen at Furgūn. The beds are thin quartzites with intercalated greenish micaceous shales showing vague worm tracks, but no determinate fossils have been found.

Silurian

Dark shales about 200 ft thick crop out on the lower slopes of Kūh-i-Furgūn, forty-five miles north of Bandar 'Abbās, and have yielded Lower Valentian graptolites according to Elles (1930). Some 200 miles farther east, north of the Jāz Muriān, lies Būr Kūh, and in it thin sandstones interbedded with greenish shales are exposed. They are associated with sandy limestones and platy marls, with red shales above them. Fragments of trilobites, orthocerids, and brachiopods collected here were reported by Douglas as "possibly" Silurian.

Devonian

Beds of the Devonian system are thick and extensive in northern Iran, much thinner in the central part, and either very thin or absent in the south. Approximately 9,500 ft of sediments underlie the Permo-Carboniferous rocks in the central Alburz, but they are not all necessarily Devonian, for it was in these parts that Bobek found the Ordovician shales mentioned above. Three lithological groups can be recognized. A sandy group comes at the top, along with conglomerates, some beds of red shale, and lenses of dolomite and limestone which contain Upper Devonian fossils. It totals about 4,000 ft in thickness. The group below it contains light-coloured dolomites about 1,700 ft thick. The basal 4,000 ft include sandstones containing occasional limestones and hard red, green, and purple siltstones in which some Ordovician may be included. The location of the base is uncertain on account of disturbance and lack of fossils.

In central Iran near Ṭabas, a series of red beds at Murād, twelve miles west-north-west of Kirmān, lies unconformably upon folded Cambrian. Green shales with sandstones are interbedded with fossiliferous Upper Devonian limestones (Flugel, 1961). The same series has also been found near Suh, as well as north and west-south-west of Kirmān (De Böckh et al. 1929).

Spirifers have been found in a series of shales and calcareous sandstones at Kūh-i-Furgūn and are thought to be Upper Devonian.

Permo-Carboniferous

The term Permo-Carboniferous is more convenient than precise; the upper and lower boundaries both tend to be indefinite. Lower Carboniferous (Dinantian) is developed in the Alburz mountains but is missing or not identified in the Zagros. Upper Carboniferous or Lower Permian sandstones are thick in the Alburz and thin in the Zagros. In both regions Permian limestones are extensive, but these are thinner in central Iran and mingled with red beds carrying small deposits of gypsum. The lower limestone series is about 4,000 ft thick in the Alburz; the sandstone series, much of it false-bedded, about 3,000 ft thick, and the upper limestone series about 2,000 ft thick. In central Iran, at Rāvar, 500 ft of reddish false-bedded sandstones below are covered by about 700 ft of beds consisting of fossiliferous limestones and some dolomite and oolite, with interbedded red shales and sandstones and some gypsum. Farther east at Būr Kūh, on the north of Jāz Muriān in Balūchistān, at least 2,500 ft of Permian limestone are exposed, and this matches the limestone series extending in variable thickness along the Zagros Arc. North-east of Dizfūl it reaches a maximum of 3,500 ft and is fossiliferous.

The underlying white sandstone in the same district increases from an average thickness of about fifty ft to as much as 1,600 ft and it includes massive yellow sandstone, false-bedded sandstone, brown shales, and clay-pebble beds. *Sigillaria persica* (Seward, 1932) occurs in abundance very locally. Permo-Carboniferous beds are known in many other localities including Suh, north of Iṣfahān, and on the Russian and Turkish frontiers north and west of Lake Rezā'īyeh. Whilst the Lower Carboniferous lies upon Devonian sandstones in the Alburz, there is a gap in the Zagros where the Upper Carboniferous and Permian sandstones rest upon Cambrian shales. Consequently weathering and local movement without folding took place in part of Palaeozoic time.

Trias

Rocks of the Trias have been found in many parts of Iran, although they are probably absent from the south-east. Like the Permo-Carboniferous before it, most of the Trias is limy but with some interbedded sulphates. Trias is exposed in the north-west near the frontiers of Turkey and Russia: in the west and central Alburz mountains, along the ranges running north and south for 300 miles between Dasht-i-

Kavīr ("the Great Salt Desert") on the west, and the Da<u>sh</u>t-i-Lūṭ on the east. It is found wherever erosion is deep along the Zagros mountains between Furgūn, north of Bandar 'Abbās, and the Iraqi frontier along the Sīrvān river.

In north-west Iran and Āzarbāījān, the sequence includes 1,000 ft of thin-bedded limestones with *Pseudomonotis*, passing up into 500 ft of marls. These are capped in turn by 3,000 ft of dark- and light-grey limestones upon which volcanic rocks follow. In the Alburz mountains 300 ft of greenish-grey shales at the base are followed by nearly 5,000 ft of light- and dark-coloured limestones and interbedded marls. Gypsum and gypsiferous marls follow, with lavas above them. The exposures in central and eastern Iran reveal a sandstone at the base, with 300 ft of brick-red platy marls containing *Pseudomonotis* above. Then come 1,500 ft of well-bedded limestones and dolomites passing upward into 3,000 ft of shales with limestones and sandstone ribs of Upper Trias.

A transition from marl through gypsum to limestone has been recognized in the Naiband district (Stöcklin, 1961), where the different facies run in strips north-west and south-east. The fauna of the Alpine Trias occur here within a few miles of the fauna formerly described only from Oman and Timor. Whether the faunal break is due to change of facies or to tectonic causes is not known, but the former would seem more likely. A bed of bauxite occurs near the top of the Trias in a wide district east and south-east of Kirmān. The Trias seems to be absent in Balū<u>ch</u>istān.

In the Zagros mountains the thickness of the Trias varies from about 2,000 to 4,000 ft. *Pseudomonotis* occurs abundantly near the base of a series consisting of thin-bedded limestones and marls. There is a tendency for limestone to pass laterally into gypsum along the south-western edge of the region in Iraq and Arabia. Calcareous Trias is exposed in a belt of strongly folded country lying south-east of Iṣfahān near Abādeh.

Jurassic

Exposures of Jurassic rocks are widely scattered through Iran and occur almost everywhere except in the south-east. The formation is absent or not known in much of Balū<u>ch</u>istān and the Jāz Muriān. Elsewhere three different facies occur. One is a landward deposit, carbonaceous, with fossil-plants and coals; another is dominantly calcareous with "*Lithiotis*" and ammonites; and the third is siliceous with poorly preserved radiolaria contained in red cherts, sometimes associated with green eruptive rocks including serpentine and pillow lava. The first two appear together, the carbonaceous below and the calcareous above, throughout the Alburz mountains and the adjoining country to the south. The chert–volcanic group appears patchily along a line running from Kurdistān in the north-west to Balūchistān in the south-east. South-west of this the Jurassic is mainly calcareous, but anhydrite fingers in towards the south-west. It is sometimes difficult to draw a line between Triassic and Jurassic in parts of the Zagros range, for dark, unfossiliferous dolomites pass down into fossiliferous Triassic and up into fossiliferous Jurassic. Not only do Jurassic salt and gypsum occur in the adjoining countries of Iraq and Saudi Arabia but salt and anhydrite beds of this age are exposed north of Kirmān not far from Rāvar.

The coaly group of the Jurassic is disconformable upon a floor that exposes some Triassic and some Palaeozoic rocks; while in the east, near Mashhad, there is schist. The formation varies in thickness from about 1,500 ft to about 10,000 ft. Several lenticular beds of coal occur and have been worked for many years north of Tehrān and elsewhere at Zirāb, Gulandarūd, and Gājisun in the central Alburz. Identified fossil-plants are mainly Liassic. The calcareous formation overlying it is sparingly fossiliferous except in the south-east near Kirmān, where a cephalopod limestone is full of Lower and Middle Jurassic ammonites. Interbedded lavas also ocur. The limestone alone reaches a thickness of 1,600 ft and the volcanics are somewhat thicker. The sequence includes more Upper than Middle Jurassic rocks. Southward, in central Iran, the calcareous formation becomes more argillaceous and locally arenaceous. Here the Lias is marine, some limy and some muddy. Near Yazd a column 6,000 ft thick comprises shales, sandstones, grits, and conglomerates, and amongst them a few thin limestone bands persist. In the Kirmān district the carbonaceous facies is present, but here the coals in the Lias are lenticular. The Lias is covered by sandy marine limestones which interfinger with higher coal lenses, and the distribution of both indicates a neighbouring shoreline, shallow sea or land emergent. Similar conditions occurred in the western part of the Jāz Muriān, where grits, sandstones, and shales with Liassic ammonites rest upon the schist.

The western part of central Iran, from near Hamadān to the east of

Yazd, is occupied by a complex of phyllites with thin ribs of quartzite. This metamorphic belt is interpreted by Baier (1938) to be altered shaly Jurassic sediments, the metamorphism having happened before Middle Cretaceous times. The zone with the cherts and volcanic rocks comes next on the south-west. The failure to recognize any marker beds in strata that are strongly folded makes it almost impossible to determine their thickness. Probably this varies greatly in amount, but in some sections the chert formation may be as much as a few thousand feet thick. Nor has the thickness of the accompanying serpentines and lavas been reliably estimated.

In the broad belt of the Zagros mountains, which lie to the south-west, the Jurassic is calcareous and from 1,500 to 2,500 ft in thickness. Dark dolomitic limestones crowded with "*Lithiotis*" often occur near the base. The formation passes up into a light-coloured oolite and massive limestones. *Diplopora* and *Valvulina* are amongst the rather infrequent fossils. A shaly and bituminous patch is developed near Kirmānshāh, but south-eastward the more limy beds are less bituminous.

The Cretaceous[1]

A range of mountains alined north-west and south-east through central Iran in late Jurassic time had much to do with the present distribution of the Cretaceous in the land. Exposures are often plentiful. A land, perhaps a plateau, lay to the north, and a sea filled a deep trough to the south-west. The Lower Cretaceous is often present but thin in the Alburz mountains. Middle and Upper Cretaceous occur in the mountain flanks and usually start with conglomerates which pass upwards into marls and limestones with some interbedded lavas. The aggregate thickness amounts to 4,000 ft. The lowest Cretaceous at any point in central Iran is usually a conglomerate resting upon folded pre-Cretaceous. The Middle Cretaceous limestones contain *Orbitolinas*, and are followed by Upper Cretaceous rudist limestones with some red marl and gypsum intercalated between them (Stöcklin, 1961). Other sections have been described in which red cherts and lavas are interbedded with the marl. Such a mixed formation, called by Gansser (1955) the "Coloured Mélange", is also found in Balūchistān, where the beds are often disturbed and contain large blocks of foreign materials as in

[1] The Cretaceous in much of Iran can be divided conveniently into three. The Lower includes stages below the Albian; the Middle the Albian to the Turonian, and the Upper the Senonian to the Danian.

the Alpine Wildflysch. Along a line from Kirmānshāh to Nairīz [Nīrīz] red chert and pillow lavas occur, the former similar in appearance to the siliceous Jurassic. This red radiolarite may have been brought in by thrusting, but the field evidence that some of the chert is in place and belongs to the Upper Cretaceous seems convincing. A great mass of calcareous Cretaceous is involved in the Zagros mountains, where the Jurassic and Cretaceous appear to be conformable.

The Lower Cretaceous is conglomeratic, sandy, and silty on the north-east, but over most of the Zagros it is limestone and dolomitic limestone overlain by bituminous, phosphatic marls and shales passing up into *Orbitolina* and rudist reef-limestones of the Middle Cretaceous. Similar beds continue for more than 800 miles north-west and south-east; and they form a slab about 150 miles across, over which distance they thicken from about 1,000 ft near the edge (say near Behbehān) to 9,000 ft in the centre (fifty miles to the north-east), dwindling again to 1,000 ft at a distance of seventy miles to the north-east (Falcon, 1958). The Upper Cretaceous is present as marl and marly limestone about 1,000 ft thick in the south-western mountains near Behbehān, but about seventy miles north-eastward it gradually changes to a succession of siltstones and thin sandstones, which thicken to 7,000 ft, with the occurrence of rudist-rich reefs and conglomerates. The Lower, Middle, and Upper Cretaceous together make up nearly 15,000 ft, but the first two are thickest thirty miles south-west of the maximum thickness found in the Upper Cretaceous. Thus the basin moved during the Cretaceous and was filled with limestone in the Lower and Middle Cretaceous, whilst it collected debris, including much detrital chert, during the Upper Cretaceous.

Eocene

The Eocene in Iran is a system showing diversities in facies and thickness. Northward it was deposited in a shallow sea from which land emerged, but southward there was mainly open sea: conditions similar to or an extension of those which set in during the Upper Cretaceous. In northern and central Iran lavas and tuffs were copiously emitted from central vents, and probably there were also fissure eruptions. Minor intrusions—dykes, sills, and plugs—were also emplaced during and after the Eocene. A thick accumulation (up to about 10,000 ft) of tuffs, marls, silts, and sandstones, with some lavas, is described from the southern Alburz.

Eocene deposits rest upon a varied basement exposing strata from Devonian up to Upper Cretaceous. Angular unconformities and accumulations of conglomerate are known in the north-east of the Zagros, for instance near K̲h̲urramābād, but a few miles to the south-west is a gradual conformable passage from Upper Cretaceous to Eocene. The presence of the Eocene can usually be detected by the fossil evidence. It is not always possible to separate the Eocene from the Oligocene—especially where, as on the southern flanks of the Alburz mountains, they both constitute the "Green beds", which are largely composed of chloritic and radiolarian tuffs. By contrast, no fossiliferous Eocene strata have been determined on the Caspian slopes of the range.

The existence of a ridge here in Eocene times is emphasized by the occurrence of a wedge-shaped body of basal conglomerate on the south, which thickens in a few miles from zero to 5000 ft. In the eastern Alburz mountains the Eocene is represented by red-coloured volcanic rocks intercalated with red beds carrying lenses of gypsum.

About 100 miles south of the Alburz the Eocene is 7,000 ft thick and made up of a mixture of ashes, lavas, sandstones, marls, and some limestones. The nummulites represent both Middle and Upper Eocene. For another 100 miles southward a gap exists where Eocene has not been found. It may have existed at an earlier time, but if so it has all been removed by erosion.

However, on the northern frontiers of the Zagros mountains Eocene again appears, this time as flysch and conglomerates. At its thickest the Eocene flysch lies south-west of the thickest Upper Cretaceous, and it gives way south-westward to a belt where nummulitic limestones build up a formation about 2,000 ft thick. The sheet is thirty miles wide in the north-west and nearly 100 miles across in the south-east, where it interfingers locally with lenticular beds of gypsum towards the base. These lenses unite to form a bed more than 500 ft thick in Lāristān, about 100 miles west-north-west of Bandar 'Abbās. On the south-western side the great sheet of nummulitic limestone rapidly changes and gives way to marls and shales. This has been traced from the Iraqi frontier to the Strait of Hurmuz.

The Upper Eocene, lying in a strip along the Zagros mountains near Kirmāns̲h̲āh, consists of a series of red beds, sandstones, marls, and thin limestones. By contrast, far to the south-east in Persian Balūc̲h̲istān it is represented by another large deposit of flysch. The zone is complex since deposits lithologically similar but of different ages seem to have been laid down one after the other, during intervals from Lower to Upper Eocene. Igneous rocks are found commonly in the Eocene around the Jāz Muriān, where pillow lavas are numerous in the flysch. Eocene flysch containing volcanic rocks also covers much of the area between Dasht-i-Lūt and the Pakistani–Afghan frontier.

Oligocene and Lower Miocene

It is convenient to treat much of the Oligocene and Lower Miocene as a single group—a group of much economic importance, because most of the oil so far won from Iran was trapped and stored in the Asmari Limestone. Many aspects of its appearance, fauna, and composition have been studied and described (Thomas, 1960). The formation is distributed over most of Iran, from the north-western borders with the U.S.S.R. and Turkey to the shores of the Indian Ocean. It is absent along the Alburz mountains and from the plateau forming the eastern highlands of Iran overlooking western Afghanistan.

Over the large area it covers it is mainly an open-sea type of sediment, but shallow-water, fore-reef, reef, and back-reef conditions have also been identified. The back-reef deposit may be lagoonal and contain anhydrite, which is sometimes intercalated with the limestone. In much of central and south-western Iran the Asmari Limestone is conformable upon the Eocene below; but near Khurramābād, towards the north-eastern strip of the Zagros mountains, the Asmari rests with angular unconformity upon the Eocene.

In central Iran south of Tehrān a basin is filled with beds of the Lower Red formation. Red silts and marls with bodies of rock-salt and anhydrite, together with very local andesitic volcanic rocks, reach a thickness of 3,500 ft. Folding and erosion were followed by a marine transgression, resulting in extensive deposits of limestone, sandstones, and marls, whose thickness varies from about 7,000 ft downward. Marls predominate in the inner and thicker sections, and limestones are found towards the margins, where the column is thinner. The southern slopes of the Alburz mountains may be taken as a type-section. As the mountain is approached, thick marls pass into limestones only one third as thick, and these have a selvedge of coarse conglomerate wedging out over Eocene volcanics. Occasional plugs of quartz diorite pierce the sediments of this age in the south of central Iran.

An isopach map of the Oligocene–Lower Miocene formation in the Qum district emphasizes the unevenness of the original floor and indicates that a trough over 3,000 ft deep runs for 150 miles in a north-west and south-east direction (Furrer and Soder, 1955). There is a gap in the evidence in part of central Iran, but it is known that the thickness of sediments in the south of central Iran is of the same order as the thickness along the north-eastern margin of the Zagros mountains. Although there is no record of positive evidence across a terrain nearly 100 miles wide, marine beds akin to one another are found on both sides of the gap. Their lithology and fauna make is possible to suppose that the deposits north and south may belong to a series of beds laid down in different parts of the same sea.

The thickness of the Oligocene–Lower Miocene within the Zagros mountains shows that here, too, there were basins, their long axes orientated north-west and south-east, containing strata as much as 2,500 ft thick. Composed mainly of limestones, these strata commence about sixty miles north-east of the shore of the Persian Gulf, but become marly and enclose some thin anhydrite lenses on the south-western side. More massive limestones occur in the north-east; marls develop in the south-west. The change of facies takes place within a short distance.

Changes are also displayed along the trend of the Gulf where the Asmari Limestone is mapped. An upper Asmari Limestone continues for 500 miles, thinning north-westward. It lies upon bedded anhydrite in the north-west, but in the south-east it lies upon a Lower Asmari Limestone from which it is separated locally by lenses of anhydrite and a thin conglomerate. After continuing as a limestone body for 700 miles, it passes laterally into marls south of Bandar ʻAbbās. It is A. N. Thomas's opinion (1950), based upon very extensive palaeontological and field studies, that the Asmari Limestone may include the Oligocene, the Burdigalian, and part of the Helvetian stages in the Miocene. (See also Falcon, 1958; and Lees, 1953.)

Miocene–Pliocene

After the deposition of the Asmari Limestone, conditions changed over most of Iran: the open sea gave way to shallow inland waters, perhaps straits, gulfs, and lagoons, in which red beds were laid down with accompanying evaporites until they covered a still greater area than the Asmari Limestone had done. In central Iran a series of anhydrite deposits interbedded with red salty marls, siltstones, and occasional lenses of rock-salt, has been proved by drilling, although none of this sequence is seen at the surface; there are also some thin ribs of fossiliferous Lower Miocene limestone. The upper part of the formation contains more red beds, principally red silt and marlstone, and less evaporite; and in all, the formation is approximately 6,000 ft thick. Then two fossiliferous calcareous sandstones occur, which act as markers and are conveniently coloured green. Still another 10,000 ft of marls, silts, sandstones, and calcareous sandstones are present above the green marker horizons. There is a change in colour as the entire series is followed upward. The strata are red near the bottom and pass through greys to an upper cream-coloured part. Changes occur gradually within the basin, but towards its edges the percentage of sandstone increases and banks of conglomerate appear. Still younger conglomerates overlap the edges of this Upper Red formation.

A somewhat similar kind of change occurs in the Zagros ranges. The Lower Fars commences with a persistent bed of anhydrite 100 ft thick resting upon the Asmari Limestone. The anhydrite is followed by alternations of evaporites, marls, and sandstones, whilst several thin fossiliferous limestones are intercalated near the base. Drilling has disclosed that much rock-salt is present at depth, and that the disturbed complex of which it forms a part is thick in the synclines although it is sometimes completely eliminated over the anticlines. This salty group is known as Stage 1 in the oilfield region of Masjid-i-Sulaimān. Most geologists agree that it has been much affected by flow, which may have caused the observed rapid variations in thickness. Its average thickness is estimated at about 4,500 ft (O'Brien, 1957). Stage 2 above it is more regular, and it contains a succession of red and grey marls with interbedded gypsum in outcrops and anhydrites in boreholes at depth. This together with Stage 3—a group of grey marls, shelly limestones, and anhydrite—makes up about 1,500 ft. Although these saline deposits do vary along the strike, becoming more sandy to the north-west and more salty and gypsiferous for a distance to the southeast, detailed correlations have been achieved, in some of the oilfield country, notably near Gach Sārān.

In the region adjoining the Persian Gulf the Lower Fars is covered by a series of grey marls; while calcareous sandstones and algal reefs form the Middle Fars, a salt-water formation that passes laterally northwestward into terrestial red beds which cannot be distinguished

lithologically from the Upper Fars. The Upper Fars, with or without
the determinable Middle Fars, provides the cover for the Lower Fars
in the frontier district between Iran and Iraq. South-eastward from the
oilfields the Middle Fars facies continues as a shallow-water marine
formation along the Iranian side of the Persian Gulf. The Middle Fars
in this direction is divisible into two parts: the lower part starts with
a pebbly grit at the base but is followed upward by greenish marls and
interbedded, often coralline, limestone; the latter develops locally into
reefs, one forming a bed 2,500 ft thick. The upper part is largely brown
sandstone and reddish silt, with fossils all but confined to shell beds
consisting of banks of *Cardium* and oysters. Although some strata
abound in both micro- and macro-fossils, the two groups are vaguely
called Mio-Pliocene. In one locality their combined thickness reaches
9,000 ft. They are overlain by unconformable conglomerates, which
occur as bodies 2,000 ft or more thick.

The Upper Fars occurs as a series of red beds conspicuous in most of
the foothill country. The group includes false-bedded red sandstones;
red mudstones, and marls with selenite veins; rare, thin, freshwater
limestone, and very rare tuffs. The formation is taken to be between
3,000 and 4,500 ft thick, but both the top and bottom are indefinite.
The basal part is usually a transition from grey beds of the Middle
Fars type to red ones of the Upper Fars. On top the Upper Fars passes
into the Lower Bakhtiāri beds, the presence of red chert pebbles in the
sandstones being the sign of transition. Grey marls found about the
middle of the Upper Fars serve as a marker bed. A few oysters have been
noted, and *Chara* "seeds" are the other fossils. Near Behbehān an
early reconnaissance revealed nearly 10,000 ft of red beds, then referred
to Upper Fars, these may include some Bakhtiāri. Being mainly terrestial, however, the beds cannot be firmly equated with the Upper
arenaceous beds of the Bandar 'Abbās area.

The Bakhtiāri formation is developed above the Upper Fars in the
foothills of south-western Iran. The limits are arbitary—it may be as
much as 16,000 ft thick. The base in any section is taken where pebbles
of red and yellow chert first appear in the red sandstones. These pebbles
become abundant upward and form beds; still higher the pebble beds
include pebbles of Asmari Limestone and gypsum along with the chert;
and on top, pebbles of Cretaceous limestone are also found. The Upper
Fars and Lower Bakhtiāri at Āghā Jārī do not display any clear
unconformity throughout a section nearly 10,000 ft thick; but in many

other districts false bedding, which seems to point to roving distributaries, has been found along with unconformity and overlap, which both mark contemporaneous movements (De Böckh *et al.* 1929). The age of the Upper Fars and Lower Bakhtīārī is thought to be between Upper Miocene and Pliocene, because *Hipparion* has been found in both the Upper Fars and in the Bakhtīārī (Ion *et al.* 1951). Opinions on the age of the *Hipparion* range from Tortonian to Pontian.

The Upper Bakhtīārī is a massive conglomerate with boulders from Cretaceous to Asmari Limestone; in many sections it transgresses the Lower Bakhtīārī. It may occur in unconnected patches that are sometimes related to the mouth of an old, much-incised river channel. Sometimes it appears to be the relics of an immense sheet of gravel that once filled the synclinal valleys, where all that survives is an axial remnant. This sheet, however, now forms an upstanding peak in the foothills, indicating the large scale of Pleistocene denudation.

GEOMORPHOLOGY

A high percentage of the surface of Iran is made up of naked, folded rocks, which vary in competence and in the degree of jointing and induration; some possess bright and contrasting colours which affect the landscape. It is often possible to link closely the existing land forms with the structures. This is true in nearly all the mountain ranges, where little soil has accumulated or much vegetation grown. Only along the south-western fringe of Iran, or within the basins of central drainage or near the south-eastern part of the Caspian Sea, are structures effectively hidden by recent accumulations of detritus. The Zagros Arc exhibits magnificently expressive topography everywhere throughout a belt 200 miles wide, which runs along much of south-west Iran. Here the crust is made up essentially of sedimentary rocks without volcanics. Over the rest of Iran, a belt 600 miles across at its widest, the task of controlling the topography is shared by igneous and sedimentary rocks alike. Throughout much of Iran large deposits of salt and anhydrite, both buried at various horizons, have probably contributed to lubrication, which has had two effects on the landscape: not only has it helped to form shapely folds, but lubrication has certainly led to the emplacement of large numbers of salt domes, or salt plugs, which make a great show over a number of areas, particularly in central and south-western Iran. The salt domes are all the more impressive

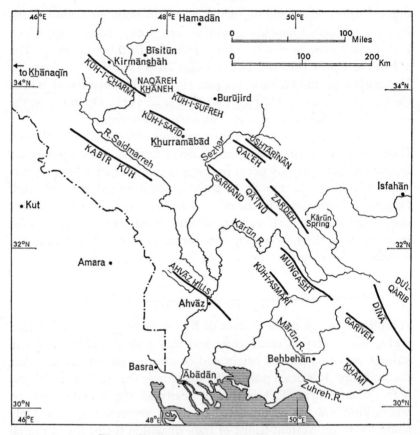

Fig. 30. Sketch-map of part of the Zagros ranges.

because the rainfall in southern and central Iran is very low. As a result, the salt that has been erupted is slowly and sparingly dissolved, and it remains exposed, contributing surprisingly coloured, exotic hills.

The mountain ranges in Iran are directly related to the direction of the axes of the folds and to the competence of the rocks exposed. The majority of the folds are oriented north-west and south-east, but the Alburz mountains in the north, rising from the southern shores of the Caspian Sea, introduce elements with curving outcrops which follow a trend approximately east–west. South of the eastern units of the Alburz range, some structures are preserved in a nearly north–south alinement. These continue for 200 miles towards the south before they bend round again and the mountains once more run north-west and

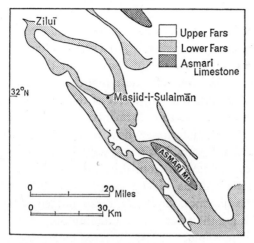

Fig. 31. Sketch-map of Masjid-i-Sulaimān and Asmārī mountain.
(After C. A. E. O'Brien, "Tectonic Problems of S.W. Iran", *Inter. Geol. Congress Report*, xviii Session, 1948.)

south-east. The fold-axes in the southernmost province of Iran, the Makrān, trend east and west from near the Strait of Hurmuz to the frontier with Pakistan; but because the rocks are not robust but incompetent, as a result, rather low saw-toothed, jagged hills are produced instead of more mountains.

An introduction to the geomorphology of the country can be made by journeying across it, preferably not too fast, from south-west to north-east. Starting then from the Shaṭṭ al-ʿArab near Ābādān and crossing an occasionally flooded alluvial plain for seventy miles, never far from the meanders of the Kārūn river, we come to a series of low isolated ridges of brown sandstone, the Ahvāz [Ahwaz] hills. These are alined north-west and south-east, and are dipping north-east. After another forty miles of plain we reach a mass of hills alined as before, made up of ridges of red sandstone or of browner conglomerates. Then contorted beds of white gypsum and grey, green, and red marls are brought up to the surface and colour the landscape accordingly. The surface, if we ignore minor irregularities, makes a nearly horizontal plain—as if some viscous fluid had welled out and slopped over at its edges, though in the main it assumed a state of imperfect hydrostatic repose after flow had stopped. Such wastes of gypsum occupy areas surrounded by sheets of red sandstones and piles of brown conglomerate. From this untidy jumble of coloured

9

beds a long isolated dome of grey limestone emerges and forms a shapely mountain, Kūh-i-Asmārī. It is followed, after a dozen miles of gypsum and marls to the north-east, by a series of long limestone domes, still magnificent although partly denuded in the course of erosion. Layer after layer has been removed: first the red sandstone, then the gypsum, and after that one or several of the nested limestone sheets. Since many massive limestone formations occur one over the other, the depth of erosion determines how much of the column is visible in any particular structure. It is now known, from geological and geophysical surveys as well as from drilling, that several domes do not reach the surface but lie hidden below the complicated jumble of gypsum and sandstones. Some of these hidden, evaporite-covered limestone folds are the reservoirs containing oil.

Limestone domes, more or less dissected by erosion but often forming high mountains, occur one after the other for another sixty miles to the north-east. Not all the domes are of the same dimensions. Rather, a large one may lie capriciously amongst its lesser neighbours. It may be near an edge of the chain; it may be near the middle. Faults to the north-east break some folds and create high cliffs that reveal a great thickness of strata. Kūh-i-Dīnā is like this, and another noteworthy example is far to the south-east, north of Bandar 'Abbās at Furgūn.

After this traverse of about 200 miles across the plains, foothills, and mountains of the Zagros arc, we pass out of the large whale-back mountains and enter less regular country. What may once have been smooth limestone domes have lost their regular contours, and their surfaces appear rough and knobbly, broken up by small movements along sets of intersecting joints. Besides the derelict domes, a traverse farther north-westward would lead us over diverse rock types (including, for the first time, igneous rocks). There are, for example, schists, peridotite, serpentines, and red cherts or radiolarites, pillow lavas and sage-grey flysch, none tough enough to make imposing and enduring mountains. This is also a zone broken by faulting, which can be detected in the tremendous cliffs of Bīsitūn, or in the superb crags of Kūh-i-Nagara Khāna, forty miles north-west of Burūjird. Some faults can only be inferred from a strip of crushing; and others, evident from aerial photographs, affect even Recent outwash fans.

As we proceed north-east again, the road runs through a jumble of hills over granite hummocks and smooth hills of phyllite to a pass through gently folded limestone beds, and down towards the Arāk plain. This is surrounded by isolated mountains. No longer are they dome-shaped but seem to be cliff-bounded fragments of limestones, residue of a once extensive sheet. No longer are there deep river gorges: instead, drainage is collected by shallow channels in the alluvium. The Iṣfahān basin 150 miles to the south-east is similar to the Arāk; and from each a pass some sixty miles to the north-east leads through lava- and ash-hills to the next basin, oriented north-west and south-east, from which long, low domes rise—low, that is, in comparison with the mountain-forming domes of the Zagros.

The hills near Qum are typical structure-controlled features; and between Qum and Tehrān some dark lava patches, still maintaining a north-west alinement, stand out above the general level of the exposed red marls and silts. These marls and silts are extensively covered by the salty mud of this central depression, one of the several salt lakes fringed by dark slime passing out into salt desert. So long as the desert east-south-east of Tehrān was imperfectly explored, the extent of the area under mud was exaggerated. Air reconnaissance has since shown that much more of the desert, previously thought of as alluvium, is country of low relief exposing red beds interbedded with grey and white sandstones. This assemblage is thick and intricately folded. About 150 miles east-south-east of Tehrān many salt domes puncture the strata and stand up as low, white circular hills, some of them strongly etched as a result of wind erosion (Gansser, 1960).

Near Tehrān terraces flank the basin flats and act as foothills to the Alburz mountains. The southern slopes of the mountains rise steeply, and although the gullies cut into them uncover very complicated folding, the structures do not often result in an expressive topography. When viewed from their tops, the Alburz look like part of an old peneplain, whose continuation was cut off abruptly, as if a block had been lifted up above the general level. The grassy slopes high up give way gradually to the barren lands of central Iran below and to the south. On the northern side the grassy upland yields to woodlands, and forests clothe the mountain slopes down to the Caspian Sea. Near the Caspian, terraces are again locally prominent. But near Bābo Sar, for instance, the lower skirts of the range reveal the presence of folded structures, partly in stream sections and partly through the physiography.

During the account of this traverse across Iran it has been remarked that many of the land forms encountered are structurally controlled. A few features result from accumulation, but many more result from differential erosion. The relation between the stream patterns and rock structures provides clear evidence regarding some stages in the evolution of landscapes. Normal rainfall, say between 25 and 40 in. per year, now obtains in the north-west and declines eastward and south-eastward to small amounts, probably under 5 in. per year. The northern slopes of the Alburz mountains experience heavy rains, more than 40 in. per year. Masses of confluent fans, now dry or poorly watered, point to earlier times when much more rain fell each year and runoff was an active transport agent.

Six large volcanoes of the central-vent type have been active during relatively recent times, yielding ash and lava cones that are still "diagrammatically" preserved. Ararat, Savalan, and Sahand are in the north-west. Damāvand (18,955 ft) stands by itself overlooking the rolling pastures of the high Alburz range within sight of the capital city. Basmān and Taftān are located far off in the remote south-east, the latter trim and youthful, the former more aged. Gently warped lava fields remain as they were erupted in the neighbourhood, and occasionally a volcanic plug like Mīl-i-Farhād is encountered. There are also two small shapely cones on the fault-trace east of Rāvar. (Although it is not volcanic, one of the few pits on the earth's surface thought to have been excavated by the fall of a meteorite is described from the desert north of Kūh-i-Basmān.)

Other features properly produced by air-borne materials include sand dunes. They tend to gather around the south-eastern or eastern sectors of some of the basins that have central drainage, such as the Dasht-i-Kavīr, the Dasht-i-Lūt, and the Jāz Muriān. Besides fixed dunes, barchans commonly occur. Individual dunes may reach a height of 600 ft above the silty floor of the basin. Sand is also piled against the eastern or south-eastern rocky walls that divide basin from basin, affording the only convenient or practicable gangway between them: routes negotiable even by reluctant camels.

Many of the basins do, at some time, contain pools or lakes around their lowest central part. Fine silt and mud are washed down, accumulate, and compact. Terraces at several levels, preserved on the sides of certain depressions far above any present flood level, seem to have required the accumulation of immensely larger bodies of water than there are now. Wind- and water-carried silts and banded clays, both laid down in a basin's centre in the later days of desiccation, have been attacked by destructive winds which have worn gullies and produced extraordinary scenery resembling ruined tenements or palaces, known by local tradition as _Shahr-i-Lūt_, the "Cities of Luṭ". (Along the Green river basin in Wyoming a similar kind of erosion has produced similar scenery, referred to as the "Cathedral Cliffs".)

Most of the basins with central drainage retain local vestiges of terraces, which are water-borne and -sorted deposits. Some are fans; some are shoreline beaches. Terraces of particular agricultural importance to Tabrīz surround Lake Reẕā'īyeh, where they reach a height of nearly 300 ft above the level of the present lake. Confluent gravel fans, which form the plinth upon which Tehrān stands, slope gently southward. Examples could be multiplied but one more will suffice: an array of confluent fans spreads westward from the foot of the Zindān range and overwhelms the eastern prongs of the Zagros mountains.

"Fossil" fans are particularly well displayed on the southern side of Kūh-i-Shu about eighty miles west of Bandar 'Abbās. They appear to have been produced by torrents long since dry, which once flowed high above the present drainage level. The water was sufficiently turbulent to carry a huge load of very coarse gravel through the mountain gorges, and then to drop it immediately at the mouth. These fans now form conglomerate mountains, themselves cut by narrow gullies concordant with the present episodic drainage system.

On a smaller scale are the terraces resulting from accidents within the mountains. Many a valley after being cut through by a stream has then been blocked by a landslide. As an example, terraces at three levels have resulted from the damming of the Saidmarreh river system by a large landslip that occurred in sub-Recent but pre-historic times. Lakes were held up behind three lobes of the slide, which to this day preserves ponds within the limits of the fan of debris (Harrison and Falcon, 1936). Terraces on a much larger scale stand along the southern slopes of the Dasht-i-Lūt depression, where five terraces can be seen at heights not less than 600 ft above the central sump. The formation of such features within areas of internal drainage seems to have required a filling and emptying of individual basins, possibly as a result of alternating wet and dry periods in the distant past. However, raised-beaches with river terraces to match are well preserved near the Indian Ocean, especially along the Makrān coast, and these cannot be attributed to differences in climate; they would have required changes of sea-level as much as 350 ft above the present level.

Another land form due to accumulation is the mud volcano. A few examples are known along the Makrān coast. One, forty-five miles north-west of Jāsk, erupts a liquid mud that has produced a gentle cone on the coast. Another, formed by a more viscous mud, has a steep-sided cone at Napag (Kūh-i-Panak), 130 miles east of Jāsk. Two other mud volcanoes have been described close to the Russian frontier north and north-east respectively of Bandar Shāh, the Caspian terminus of the Trans-Iranian Railway (Gansser, 1960). They form circular depressions like craters rather than cones. One of these is more than a quarter of a mile in diameter.

Wherever there is or has been adequate rainfall in Iran, the scenery usually shows the effect of differential erosion. This means that the ruins of pitching anticlines are weathered out as nests of concentric domes with scarp- and dip-slope amphitheatres round the ends, whilst the complementary synclines weather out as steep-sided elevations in which the more massive strata form cliffs. These are the basic components of the landscape, at least in the Zagros arc. The cores of the anticlines tend to be worn down, the centres of the synclines to resist erosion in the orthodox Davisian style. Because of its attitude, whereby it can withstand erosion preferentially, the youngest stratum forms the axis of a synclinal fold may be left as the capping of a peak. The scenery requires the presence of groups of strata, alternately strong and weak, the massive beds being tough and the thin-bedded ones soft or at least offering little resistance to weathering. Anticlines and synclines are crowded together in the Zagros mountains and are superbly exposed, but in parts of central Iran similar rock structures are partially buried under the deposits of alluvium, which tend to accumulate in the synclinal saddles. Such burial implies that synclines, after they were formed, had their centres removed by erosion, which provided a surface on which accumulation could take place.

As far south as the head of the Persian Gulf, rivers are at present perennial and many of them cross some anticlinal structures in narrow gorges. Some cross at the very crest of a dome and cut through it, making a slit of a valley known as a *tang* sometimes 5,000 ft or more deep. The Saidmarreh river will serve as an example. Here run-off from the watershed finds its way down fairly wide gravel-filled channels and gathers into a quiet river, meandering over the meadows near Kirmānshāh. A few miles south-east of the town it turns south and cuts through the narrow dome formed by Kūh-i-Charmī, making its incision near the crest of the dome, not at its plunging end. As it flows south it crosses three more folds, thus making a gorge through each, and then it flows into more open country south-westward. Farther on it crosses three more domes before reaching the broad syncline along the north-eastern flank of Kabīr Kūh. Here it changes direction from south-west to south-east, and for about 100 miles the river keeps close to the synclinal axis. Then it turns suddenly and flows south-south-west across Kabīr Kūh, but not at the lowest point where the limestone now makes the present pitching end of the mountain. At a higher level, and ten miles north-west of the present Asmari Limestone nose, it flows through a notch in the limestone sheath.

Along most of its course the river appears to have acted capriciously, incising some domes and skirting others. Water, unless in a pipe, can only flow downhill. Therefore the original surface on which the drainage was initiated could not have shown any expression of the structures now laid bare—apart from a pre-historic Kabīr Kūh. Two possible explanations seem to exist. Either none of the structures, except Kabīr Kūh, had formed when the embryonic drainage was set going, and these have all developed subsequently; or else the structures now seen did exist below, but the surface had been levelled off, so that they did not show at all. In the second case the structures would have become etched out as drainage dug down; the rise of the exhumed structures into mountains could then have been assisted by the erosion of the material that once buried them. The result, seen now, is that the rivers in the Zagros mountains rise in relatively mild rolling country and collect in shallow valleys. Ensconced in gorges, the rivers traverse the mountains (whose height far exceeds that of the rivers' source) and emerge on the edge of the Mesopotamian plains, across which they meander. A differential uplift of the mountain belt would probably explain this behaviour.

Farther south-eastward the rainfall is less, but episodic rivers, which infrequently carry running water, still manage to dispose of some runoff to the Persian Gulf in extraordinarily wet years. These rivers drain a basin as much as 150 miles wide. They too have valleys containing deep defiles, which are, however, less stark and abrupt than those in the wet north-west. The main difference is that the low ground here is much more extensively covered by alluvium. The amount of dissection must have reached 7,000 ft around Kūh-i-Furgūn. Much of the erosion must have been accomplished here when rainfall was abundant and episodic floods occurred, as so much of the eroded material has been carried away. This happened before the burying of the low ground under alluvium (Falcon, 1961).

On the other side of the Zagros mountains, beyond the watershed, the rainfall is now generally lower. The same pattern prevails here as in the Zagros: namely, the rainfall is higher in the north-west and lower to the south-east. Most of the runoff goes into one of the few inland basins, although drainage from northern Iran falls into the Caspian Sea (which is itself in such a basin), carried there either by the river Aras along the frontier between Iran and Russia, or by the Safīd Rūd, which breaks through the Alburz ranges near Ra<u>sh</u>t. The northernmost basin, near Tabrīz, has enough rainfall to nourish a perennial but salt lake, Lake Rezā'īyeh, formerly called Urmīyeh. In the other basins a large expanse of silt surrounds an episodic salt lake which may dry up into a salt desert in the summer. On the north-eastern side of the Zagros, where schists crop out, rolling hills with smooth slopes develop and rise above the alluvium; but where there is limestone, as for instance near Iṣfahān, crag-bound masses stand up 2,000 ft and more above the surrounding alluvial plains. In some of these the limestone lies flat and is undisturbed, but in others it has been folded. All these hills are relics of a sheet that was once more extensive.

Where the volcanic rocks come in, as they do to the north-east of a line from Tabrīz to Sīrjān, the variety of bedded rocks in the column increases; and besides limestones, sandstones, and shales, there are also lavas, ashes, and sills—all folded gently together in a series of open folds. This mixture of strata, some tough, some friable, has led to the production of a series of domes and troughs. The resulting features in the landscape are picked out in the harder rocks. Some of the domes in the basins are still large structures—they can be as much as forty miles long and six miles across, standing 2,000 or 3,000 ft above the surrounding country—but they lack the bold aspect which marks structures built up of the massive limestone facies in the Zagros.

The folding is slight along a part of the Safīd Rūd valley below Miāneh in the north of Iran. The strata here are mainly loosely consolidated and consist of alternating red and white sands, silts, shales, and marls. They are in one of the wetter parts of Iran, and erosion has produced in them the myriad of gullies and ridges characteristic of "badland" topography. Badlands are not common in Iran; another, though remote area occurs in the south-east near the Makrān coast, where Mio-Pliocene clays, silts, and sandstones are interbedded and slightly warped. The rainfall here is low, but heavy rainstorms break out occasionally and have resulted in the excavation of badlands somewhat west of Chāhbahār.

The physiography of eastern Iran is closely influenced by the structures. Domes, monoclines, and synclines are expressive as far as the western edge of Dasht-i-Lūt, and an alternation of strong and weak sequences emphasizes the dependence of the land forms upon structure. A sheaf of folds fans out to the north of Kirmān, the axes running north-west to the west of the terrain and north to the east of it. Some regular domes preserved by resistant beds make prominent mountains on the west, and in some places the monoclinal structure on the eastern side has led to the production of a line of scarps facing east. The orientation of the folds north of Ṭabas changes from north and south to north-east and south-west. Farther on this swings to nearly east and west. The twisting continues east of Doruneh until eventually the ranges moulded on the structures curve still further, so that the fold-axes run west-north-west and east-south-east right on to the Afghan frontier.

Within this curving ridge and scarp feature which runs from the south-western edge of the Dasht-i-Lūt to the frontier near Turbat-i-Shaikh Jām, there is a large area measuring 450 miles in a north–south direction and 200 miles from east to west. Bīrjand stands near the centre, surrounded mostly by low nondescript hills rising above low-lying bands of alluvium. A dome of older limestone occasionally appears through the multitude of low sandstone ridges. Although the stature of the individual ridges may be small, high points on the plateau stand 7,000 ft above the adjoining marsh-filled sumps of the Sīstān and Afghan borders.

The south-eastern end of the Dasht-i-Lūt is a waste of low hills whose grain runs north-north-west and whose rocks are flysch. Flysch is a formation made up mainly of alternating ribs of sandstone and shales and, in this district, scattered interbedded lavas. The region is overlooked by the large cone of the active volcano Kūh-i-Taftān. Occasional limestone reefs lie amongst the prevailing arenaceous and argillaceous beds and weather out to make an elevated chain. At about lat. 27° N., due east of the centre of the Jāz Muriān, the strike of the flysch changes from north-north-west to east and west. The many tight little folds predominating in the territory of Iranian Balūchistān inland from the Makrān coast tend to assume this direction. The greater part of this province is made up of an abundance of sage-grey ridges littered with coarse and fine detritus. These nearly parallel ridges produce a kind of secondary ornament superimposed on a rather even surface which rises from the coast of the Gulf of Oman to a maximum elevation of about 7,000 ft; this occurs between seventy and eighty miles from the Arabian Sea to form the divide between the drainage falling to the Indian Ocean and that destined for the Jāz Muriān.

The drab landscape of the south-eastern Dasht-i-Lūṭ is diversified by the sporadic occurrence of rocky spines, which may project 1,000 ft above the average height of the surface. When the spikes are formed of sandstone they have a fang-like shape, produced it would seem by a process of crushing. Many of the spines are coloured according to the rock type, some being mauve, pink, brown, grey-green, black, or white. They are often associated with a zone or strip of coloured rocks folded or faulted in between the prevailing expanses of sage-coloured flysch.

For a distance of about thirty-five miles from the coast, the flysch surface is patchily covered by great cakes of sandstone lying nearly flat or in slightly dish-shaped bodies. Individual examples stand as ovals thirty miles long and ten miles across. They rise as much as 4,000 ft above the folded floor where the flysch is exposed. They are usually rimmed all round by cliffs, and one mass may be separated from its neighbours by a passage a few miles wide.

Throughout the inland Makrān occasional flows of pillow lavas are found in the flysch; and green serpentine wedges whose surfaces are polished and striated—slickensided in fact—occur from place to place: indeed their colour as well as their form are a conspicuous part of the landscape.

The drainage in the Makrān is episodic. It may be several years before a particular water-course carries water to a basin or the sea, and when it does the fluid it transports is a foaming mud: for the alternation of the hot sun by day and the cold air by night in winter helps to disintegrate the poorly consolidated rocks, and leaves them loose-grained and riddled with open joints, ready to form sludge when the rain falls heavily. The erosion that a single storm can effect is tremendous.

The drainage is often incised, and the larger streams crossing the Makrān pass through valleys that are over 3,000 ft deep. As already alluded to (p. 136 above), a combination of circumstances has resulted in the formation of a large area of "badlands" near Bīr, 110 miles east of Jāsk and west of Chahbahār. Patches of raised beach up to 350 ft above the present sea level are well preserved near the coast, and they are matched by extensive stream terraces or bevelled benches farther inland.

The only part of Iran in which land forms do not appear to be closely related to the structure is in the central Alburz, where there is heavy well-distributed rainfall, and lush vegetation flourishes on the northern slopes. Apart from the well-preserved young cone of Damāvand, which is not in keeping with the rest of the landscape, the rolling upland surface of the range seems to have developed without direct dependence upon the underlying structure.

The scenery suggests that peneplanation has taken place, but this could not have developed on a strip only twenty to thirty miles wide. It is surmised, therefore, that this strip is an upthrown remnant of what was once a much broader region of topographical maturity. The southern slopes of the Alburz yield exposures of Mesozoic and Kainozoic strata folded and faulted in great complexity. But the ultimate effect seems to be that of an upthrusting of the northern block. Part of the great slab of thick and nearly horizontal Palaeozoic strata is seen in the Chālūs chasm, but it is hidden for the most part under the wooded Caspian slopes, where evidence is often difficult to see. Therefore it remains a guess that in the area near the Caspian Sea this slab has been faulted. It would be difficult to rebut this hypothesis— and it would be still more difficult actually to demonstrate the faults. However, the high plateau of the Alburz remains as evidence of very recent uplift, even though the attacks of headwater erosion at the present time are rapidly destroying the plateau.

Salt has been abundantly distributed over much of Iran at various times, in the Cambrian, Jurassic, and Tertiary. Because of their association with thick sediments in a region of suitable folding, the salt and anhydrite and associated marl have been moved away from their original sedimentary beds and some 300 salt-plugs have formed in Iran. Most of these occur in districts with low rainfall, so that the soluble salt enjoys an unusual permanence at the surface. Consequently salt domes make an imposing contribution to the geomorphology. A salt plug is essentially a cylinder of salt, gypsum, red and grey gypsiferous shales, and marls, from half a mile to four miles in diameter which either pierces whatever sediments lie above the original salt deposit, or else tilts them up into, ideally, a circular hill. The top of the cylinder may assume various irregular forms in response to the shape of

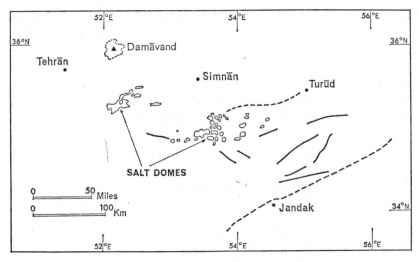

Fig. 32. Sketch-map of part of central Iran, showing salt domes. (After Gansser, 1955.)

the hole in the cover rocks through which the salt has been squeezed. Assembled around and upon the salt dome are masses or blocks, boulders or pebbles, of a variety of metamorphic, igneous, and sedimentary rocks—all debris created by the salt as it travelled to the surface and carried up rocks from below. Specular haematite crystals are also normally present (see p. 114 above). This whole haphazard collection is called the Hurmuz series.

In central Iran, east-south-east of Tehrān, the Tertiary salt pierces soft, apparently plastic interbedded Miocene gypsiferous marls, shales, and thin sandstones, and the salt itself forms low domes which rise to about 300 ft above the surrounding country. Each dome has a conspicuous jacket of white gypsum around it, against which the surrounding beds were dragged up and from which they dip steeply away. A few salt domes produced by the movement of Jurassic salt have been described north of Kirmān (Stöcklin, 1961). In one of these the salt lies between harder and faulted Cretaceous rocks, and it appears now as an oval mass, with the crest of the dome rising nearly 700 ft above its outer edge. A few of the plugs in eastern central Iran are made of Cambrian salt, which pierces Cretaceous, Eocene, or later limestone structures at the surface.

When the salt plug rises above the crest of its limestone dome, as happens in southern Iran, it may form a boss of salt and gypsum like an inverted cup. In some cups a little of the salt may have flowed down like wax from a candle and covered a part of the limestone girdle. If the limestone dome has been pierced away from its axis, so that the top of the salt plug is unsupported on one side, it may appear as if a tongue of salt has flowed down like a salt glacier. Most salt glaciers

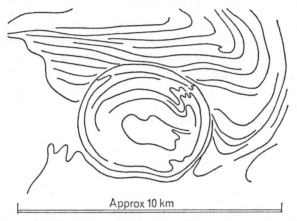

Approx 10 km

Fig. 33. Sketch of a salt dome in central Iran, south of Simnān, seen as though from above. The effect of the intrusion is to distort the surrounding red gypsum shales as if they were semi-viscous. (After Gansser, 1960.)

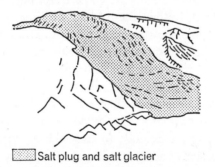

Salt plug and salt glacier

Fig. 34. Sketch of a salt dome and salt glacier. (After Kent, 1958.)

are short and their gradient steep, but rarely the salt mass appears to have been very mobile and flowed down a gentle slope; whilst the salt and gypsum mixture viewed from the air exhibits a series of gaping concentric fissures which are convex outward, reminiscent of the crevasses associated with ice falls. The salt may be white or grey, girdled by a ring of mingled and disturbed, even contorted, salt, gypsum, and red beds. It may contain sporadic fragments of volcanic rocks, which then add dark and often upstanding features to the landscape. Cases are known in which the exposed top of the salt plug has been dissolved away, leaving the empty "throat" of the intrusion available for inspection: this is a red-stained circular cliff terminating the limestones that were dragged upward when the salt came through (Harrison, 1930). Whatever the variations of this exposure, irregular shapes and curious details of structure are underlined by an assemblage of vivid colours. Black and white, red and grey and pink, purple, green, and rusty-brown, all occur together—and the whole is spangled with glittering crystals of specular haematite.

STRUCTURE

As we have seen, Iran is a country in which outlines of structure are often reflected by the physiography. It is fairly easy, therefore, to select regions of Iran suitable for description. The country as a whole can be regarded as an irregular figure contained by seven roughly rectilinear sides. The long northern one, although sinuous, runs nearly east and west; it includes the Alburz system and the Kopet Dāgh hills. The second is a short side keeping nearly north and parallel to the south western shores of the Caspian Sea. The third side, running approximately east and west, follows the frontier with the U.S.S.R. along the Araxes and cross-cuts the structural pattern. The fourth follows the crest of the Kurdish mountains and holds nearly south along the strike to the frontier with Iraq. The fifth side is the longest. It maintains generally a south-east course concordant with the structures forming the Zagros arc to the mouth of the Persian Gulf. The sixth side starts at the Strait of Hurmuz, runs east as do the structures, and is short. It is left to the long eastern side to close the figure as it runs nearly north from the eastern end of the Jāz Murīān to the Afghan frontier along the Harī Rūd east of Mashhad. The structures along this line are concordant in the south but transverse towards the north.

The main structure-lines in Iran are the units of the Alburz system in the north and the Zagros chain in the south-west. The "foredeep" of the Alburz skirts the south of the Alburz range and is a broken-down area closely connected with the chain. The "Complex belt" along the north-eastern flank of the Zagros and the "Volcanic belt" to the north-east of the Complex belt adhere closely to the direction of the Zagros. As a result of the divergence of the two principal ranges, a

Fig. 35. Sketch-map showing the structural elements of Iran
described in chapter 2.

widening gap develops between them east of Tehrān. This is filled by
two masses: the western one named the Ṭabas wedge, in which the
strike-lines fan out between north-west and north; and the eastern
named the East Iranian quadrangle, where Eocene strata are widespread but dip and strike vary intricately. The Makrān in the south-
east is an outlying district in which the strike is generally east and west.

The structures to be discussed in Iran are then as follows:

1. The Alburz system.
2. The Alburz foredeep.
3. The Ṭabas wedge.
4. The East Iranian quadrangle.

5. The Volcanic belt.
6. The Complex belt.
7. The zone of normal folding.
8. The Makrān.

The Alburz system

The term "Alburz system" is introduced to cover much more than
the Alburz mountains, though these are an important fraction of the

143

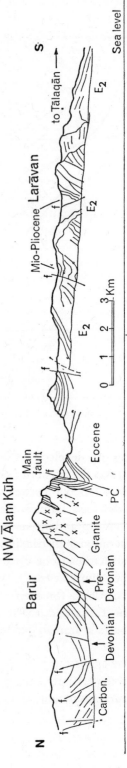

Fig. 36. Section across the Alburz mountains, with gently folded northern flank steeply faulted, a very disturbed old central complex thrust south over a synclinal area occupied by Jurassic and Tertiary green beds. (After Gansser and Huber, 1962.)

whole. The system comprises the ranges, about 800 miles long and up to sixty miles wide, which cross Iran and pass eastward into the Paropamisus and the Hindu Kush in Afghanistan. The western two thirds around the coast of the Caspian Sea are concave northward, from Rasht to Gunbad-i-Qābūs. The eastern third is convex northward, as if forming a salient from which to view the Türkmen plains of Russia. Subdivisions of the system include from west to east: the Tālish hills lying west of Rasht; the Alburz mountains rising south-east of Rasht and plunging west of Damāvand; the Gurgān hills rising east of Damāvand and declining to the pass near Jājarm; and still farther east the group of structures forming Kopet Dāgh and including the Quchān and Mashhad mountains. Other lesser ranges occur to the east between these and the Afghan frontier, which is marked by the bed of the Harī Rūd.

The Tālish hills, trending north-west and south-east, are made up of moderately folded Cretaceous and Jurassic sediments, and a much-faulted core exposed near Rasht contains pre-Devonian as well as thick Devonian and later Palaeozoic rocks. This core is regarded as a faulted anticlinorium which plunges south-eastward beneath a sheath of Jurassic and Cretaceous marls, and is obscured fortuitously on the north-west by a blanket of young volcanics.

The next mass of old rocks rises eastward from below the cover of Mesozoic rocks to constitute the Alburz mountains proper, with its glaciated summit of Ālam Kūh near Takht-i-Sulaimān. The basement here consists of strongly folded and faulted pre-Cambro-Ordovician schists, intruded by a granitic massif within a broad axial region where unconformable, gently dipping Palaeozoic beds lie on top (Gansser and Huber, 1962). Rivière (1934) believes that the schists were disturbed by low-angle thrusts over which the upper beds had been moved to the north. For stratigraphic reasons the late E. J. White thought this interpretation doubtful. Like Gansser he accepted the main breaks as steep reversed faults dipping south on the north side and north on the south side of the range. If this is so, the range is due to uplift between two advancing wedges.

Though strongly folded, the syncline on the southern flank is comparatively simple by comparison with the pinched, thrust, and crushed anticlines along the southern skirts of the range a little north of the latitude of Tehrān. Bailey *et al.* (1948) made the point that the folding is the result of two phases of compression, one about the beginning of, and one late in, the Tertiary. Whilst favouring thrusting to the north, he did not press his interpretation against that of Rivière, whose sections suggest overthrusting towards the south on the southern flanks of the Alburz. The high volcanic cone of Damāvand is situated near the eastern plunge of the Alburz, and just beyond it the strike changes to east-north-east.

The Gurgān hills exhibit a complex structure (Stöcklin, 1962). They are about 150 miles long and embody three structures, each involving an old rock: phyllite, schist, and epidiorite, respectively. An eroded massif of pre-Devonian lies in the north, and two long domes nearly

Fig. 37. Section across the Alburz with flat-faulted palaeozoics in the northern part, and a very disturbed syncline of green beds and schuppen of Jurassic on the southern side. (After Rivière, 1934.)

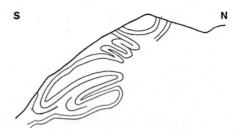

Fig. 38. Section in the "green beds" exposed on the southern steeply faulted flank of the Alburz. (After Rivière, 1934.)

parallel to each other crop out farther south. Above the unconformity, Devonian and Carboniferous, mainly limestones and shales are covered by dolomitic limestones passing up into Jurassic plant beds. Some marls and limestones of the Upper Cretaceous follow on; and synclines contain Miocene within them. The whole area is cut up by a series of reversed strike-faults which dip steeply southward, thrusting Devonian sandstones onto Tertiary beds; much of the northern massif is covered by Quaternary deposits, but there is also evidence of pre-Devonian folding. Some of the strike-faults in the Caspian region are still active, and it continues to be a district subject to earthquakes. The faults have topographical expression. The component structures plunge eastward and the Palaeozoic strata disappear below a cover of Jurassic plant beds and limestones, which maintain their east-north-easterly trend.

The axial direction in the region changes near the longitude of Jājarm and swings to about east-south-east, which is maintained as far as the frontier, a distance of nearly 300 miles. Geographically this area can be divided into two mountain chains with a broad valley between them. The Kopet Dāgh chain consists in the main of Cretaceous strata, limestones, and calcareous sandstones, folded into domes of the Jura type which comprise the north-eastern ranges. At the south-eastern end of the chain, older rocks form an anticlinorium, while Upper Jurassic limestones and Lower Jurassic plant beds crop out above a core of Palaeozoic rocks exposed near to the Afghan frontier.

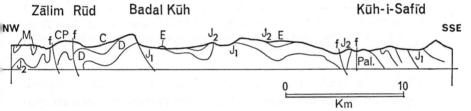

Fig. 39. Section across the Eastern Alburz near Gurgān, showing three broken folds in the Palaeozoic, a Palaeozoic massif steeply thrust to the north, and Mesozoic and Tertiary beds in Jura-type folds further south. (After Stocklin, 1962.)

The valley from Bujnūrd to Quchān and Mashhad is an earthquake zone where movement is still active along strike-faults; the alluvium-covered valley floor lies about 6,000 ft below the summits of the adjoining mountains. To the south-west Kūh-i-'Ālī, a fold comprising Jurassic with a core of Palaeozoic rocks, leads eastward to Kūh-i-Bīnālūd, a massif consisting of granite-intruded schists. This massif is covered at both ends by an unconformable capping of a little Lower and more Upper Jurassic.

The foredeep of the Alburz

A relatively low area lies along the southern side of the Alburz system, starting near Tehrān and continuing to the frontier with Afghanistan, near Turbat-i-Shaikh Jām. About half the area is covered by salt flats. The other half includes a diversified northern part in which rather long, narrow bodies of Cretaceous and Tertiary crop out, their trend being in general compatible with the strike in the adjoining

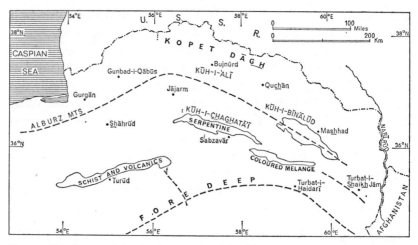

Fig. 40. Sketch-map of the foredeep south of the Alburz mountains and Kopet Dāgh, showing the serpentine lens of Kūh-i-Chaghatā'ī and the change in trend between Gurgān, Sabzavār and Turbat-i-Shaikh Jām.

Alburz. The southern part is characterized by the presence of thick Upper Tertiary. In this "foredeep" there are two incongruous components. One, a strip of schists with volcanic rocks, is about 120 miles long and up to ten miles across, running roughly east-north-east and centred on Turūd. The other exotic occurrence, Kūh-i-Chaghatā'ī, is about 100 miles long and up to fifteen miles across. Running nearly east–west, this mass of serpentine is in contact on its northern side with Eocene volcanic rocks, mostly tuffs; while fragments of Upper Cretaceous are associated with it near its western extremity. The mass of peridotite makes a bulge, convex to the north, near Sabzavār. Along the same line but farther east the map shows the Coloured Mélange, an assemblage of shales, thin limestone, ashes, and vesicular lavas, a grouping frequently encountered in the Middle East near emplacements of serpentine.

Faults are numerous in the vicinity, and the region is regarded as a much-faulted block lying between the high Alburz on the north and the broken-down area to the south, which was flooded by an Oligocene sea from the south-west. The faults are mostly strike-faults but some cross-faults are present: one, for instance, is seventy-five miles east of Turūd, where the fault-trace trends north-north-west. In this northern complex there has been minor fracturing without much foundering. Strong foundering did occur in the south of the basin, south-west of Turūd, where the Upper Tertiary filling is estimated at about 25,000 ft. Red beds, evaporites, limestones, sandstones, and conglomerates have accumulated within a depression more than 300 miles long and eighty miles across. The presence of such a large hole seems to justify the use of the descriptive term "foredeep".

Most of the folds within the foredeep are regular and affect the Upper Tertiary; their axes lie east by south in the west near Tehrān, but east-north-east in the centre. The regularity of the folds is interrupted by an amazing cluster of thirty-four salt domes inserted amongst these Upper Tertiary strata around a point seventy-five miles south of Simnān (see fig. 8, above). This intrusion of salt has distorted the Upper Tertiary strata in a way that suggests they might have been able to flow viscously away from the plugs. Another crowded group of salt domes has broken through similar red beds about fifty miles south-east of Tehrān. It is noteworthy that igneous rocks are absent from the southern part of this terrain and from its eastern extension as far as Doruneh. Eocene volcanic rocks are again recorded forty miles east of Doruneh, and they continue towards Afghanistan.

As mentioned above, a north-west to south-east crossfault lies seventy-five miles east of Turūd. The Upper Red formation appears sporadically above the alluvium to the south-west of it, but north-east of it Lower and Upper Cretaceous and Eocene are exposed in a series of anticlines orientated east-north-east in the west and east by south farther to the east. A long dome near Turbat-i-Shaikh Jām exposes a Palaeozoic core—but apparently in all this lowland foredeep the Jurassic, so abundant to the north, is absent. The intense folding and faulting affecting the strata near Tehrān no longer obtain in this eastern prolongation, where structures are less disturbed.

The Ṭabas wedge

A wedge-shaped block consisting largely of Jurassic beds stands out conspicuously on the coloured geological map of Iran. It is situated between the diverging elements formed on the north by the sinuous Alburz system together with its foredeep; and on the south by the long, nearly straight belt of volcanic rocks running from near Tabrīz in the north-west to Bam in the south-east. This block is shaped like an isosceles triangle with its equal sides each 400 miles long and its base 250 miles across. One of the longer sides runs north from Bam through Naiband and on to a point near Doruneh. The other long side, going north-west from Bam past Kirmān, is deflected somewhat towards the

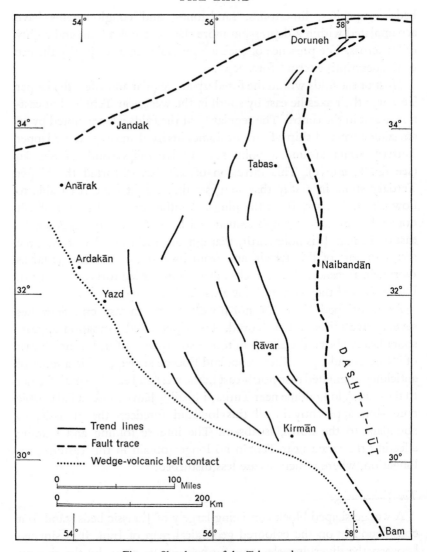

Fig. 41. Sketch-map of the Ṭabas wedge.

south-west before reaching Anārak. The short side, the base, is rather ragged but trends roughly west-south-west from near Doruneh to Anārak. Within the eastern part of the block the strike-lines run nearly north and south, and a set of faults affecting the southern part of the wedge has the same orientation. In the western part the strike varies between north-north-west and north-west.

A large area of granite-intruded metamorphic rocks appears to the north-west, and in this neighbourhood patches of Lower Cretaceous rest unconformably on the schists. Over the rest of the wedge a folded packet of strata consisting of Cambrian to Cretaceous is preserved, with sandy shales and calcareous sandstones of the Jurassic covering much of the region. The underlying Trias is present as a mixture of light and dark dolomitic limestone in the west, but it contains intercalations of red beds in the east. The Upper Palaeozoic below is exposed in a similar dolomitic limestone facies; the Lower Palaeozoic contains interbedded dolomite, gypsum, and some red sandstones. Any of these formations are likely to crop out along the east rim of the wedge, close to the fault that is alined north–south near Naiband. This brings the Palaeozoic and Lower Mesozoic strata on the west of the fault into proximity with the Eocene—the sandstones, shales, thin limestones, ashes, and lavas—occurring east of the fault. Other extensive outcrops of Cambrian are displayed along a line of marked disturbance running north-north-west from a point about twenty-five miles north of Kirmān and passing through Kūhbanān and Būuhuābād (Huckriede et al. 1962). Whilst no great vertical movement seems to have taken place, this zone of disturbance has been traced for more than 120 miles. West of the fracture zone the Pre-Cambrian is exposed in an unmetamorphosed facies north-west of Kirmān.

The strikes prevailing within the Ṭabas wedge start in the south and trend north-north-west. Gradually they become northerly, from the latitude of Bāfq, until in the latitude of Gunbad [Gumbad], the strike alters to north-north-east. It suffers stronger deflexion farther northward and becomes east-north-east south of Doruneh. It is the effect which might have been expected if a tectonic unit like the Alburz had moved eastward, dragging the northern extremity of the Ṭabas wedge along and imposing upon it the deflexion described from north-north-west through north to east-north-east. The observed strike in the Jurassic also changes direction along the south-western margin, where it turns from north to north-west.

In a series of facies maps Stöcklin has demonstrated that evaporites of four ages occur respectively in four different basins situated one above the other: in Lower Cambrian, in Upper Palaeozoic together with Lower Trias, in the Upper Jurassic, and at the base of the Middle Cretaceous. He has suggested that the lowest gypsiferous suite has taken part in the formation of two salt domes near Rāvar, and that

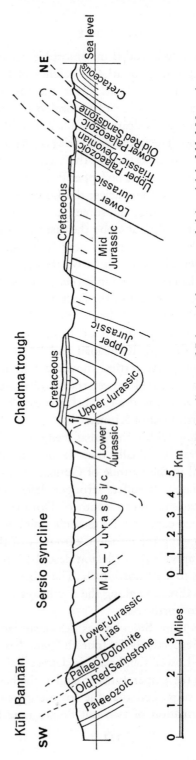

Fig. 42. Section across part of the Tabas wedge, showing glimpses of Palaeozoic basement underlying tightly folded Mesozoics up to Lower Cretaceous. The Upper Cretaceous was laid down unconformably on top and remains unfolded. (After Huckriede, Kürsten and Venzlaff, 1962.)

several others have been produced from the Jurassic evaporites (Stöcklin, 1961).

About thirty miles east of Rāvar two small, recently formed volcanoes stand astride the main fault zone, as if this had determined the place of eruption. Most of the country inside the Ṭabas wedge is relatively high, so that topographically the unit can be regarded as an elevated block, with a downfaulted area to the east of it containing the Dasht-i-Lūṭ. The possibility of a dextral tear-fault alined nearly east-north-east and west-south-west through Doruneh cannot be ruled out.

The East Iranian quadrangle

The area that lies east of the Ṭabas wedge is roughly rectangular in shape, nearly 400 miles long from north to south and about 200 miles wide. Topographically it forms a tilted block sloping gently towards the south-south-west, where the floor of the depression is little more than 1,500 ft above sea-level. The eastern edge of the block is elevated, and most of that country stands above 5,000 ft, with ranges like Kūh-i-Mūminābād, thirty miles east of Bīrjand, exceeding 9,000 ft above sea-level. The low south-western part, Dasht-i-Lūṭ, is 150 miles long from north and south and 120 miles across. Its floor is covered with horizontally bedded alluvium partly eroded into curious shapes by the wind, which is also responsible for the transport of sand to build up some enormous dunes along the eastern side: these are reported to stand as much as 700 ft above the desert floor.

Near the edge of the desert, beyond the locus of such superficial deposits, most of the strata exposed are Eocene: mainly a tuffaceous variety in the north, with some flysch and lenses of reef-limestone, while Eocene towards the south contains less ash. Complex structural conditions obtain to the north-west of Gunbad, at Bijistān, where a Cretaceous dome fifty miles long runs nearly east-north-east. It is approximately parallel to, and twenty-five miles from, the structures along the north-eastern part of the Ṭabas wedge. Only twenty-five miles to the south-east of this anticline another long Cretaceous dome emerges from an expanse of Eocene, and its axis runs south-east at right angles to the Bijistān fold. A long, faulted Jurassic structure forks like a prong eastward from it, starting some ten miles south-west of Gunbad.

The relationships among these various structures are not clear, though the Bijistān dome seems to follow the grain of the north-eastern part of the Ṭabas wedge. The structure starting south of Gunbad, although it adheres to the average trend of many structures in Iran, is not in harmony here either with the folds in the Eocene or with any in the northern part of the Ṭabas wedge. However, a south-easterly trend is persistent and reappears in a Cretaceous dome some forty miles long and lying to the east of Bīrjand. The dome is more in accord with the trend of the Eocene beds in this eastern part of the region.

The plentiful outcrops of Eocene seem to occur in a structure that bends round and produces a pattern something like a fish-hook. In the west, adjoining the faulted eastern edge of the Ṭabas wedge, the average strike of the Eocene is about east by north. Farther east, starting from near Bīrjand and going towards the Afghan frontier, the strike turns from east-south-east, through south-east, to become south-south-east at the frontier. Just north of Bīrjand the strike runs approximately east–west for fifty miles, but a few local changes in strike complicate the details of the hook-shaped design.

Continuous exposures in the highlands along the eastern side of the Dasht-i-Lūṭ—through Eocene flysch and Upper Cretaceous sandstones, shales, reef-limestones, with some lavas and ashes—are maintained southwards to the neighbourhood of Zāhidān; the strike keeps predominantly south-south-east. South of Zāhidān a suite of scattered intrusions comprising granites and gabbros has caused mild metamorphism extending across country for some fifty miles along and across the strike. Faulting is clearly developed north by east along the south-eastern edge of the Dasht-i-Lūṭ, whilst between it and the frontier the Eocene flysch and Upper Cretaceous limestones continue to strike south-south-east. It is within this folded country that the volcano Taftān (13,034 ft) has erupted and built up its cones. The strike runs consistently between north-north-west and north-west as far as Dehak on the Pakistan border, and along a line west of Dehak to Īrānshahr. Then it changes abruptly to an east–west direction, presumably on account of a massif exposed north of the Jāz Murīān. This strike prevails throughout much of the Makrān district.

The country, forming highlands from north of Neh to the south of Zāhidān, falls away steeply to lowlands dotted with several lakes and plains in the south-west of Afghanistan and in Sīstān. The change takes place along a line that runs approximately north and south as far south as Zāhidān; here the line curves gradually and assumes a south-south-east direction from Kūh-i-Taftān southward. This may coincide with a

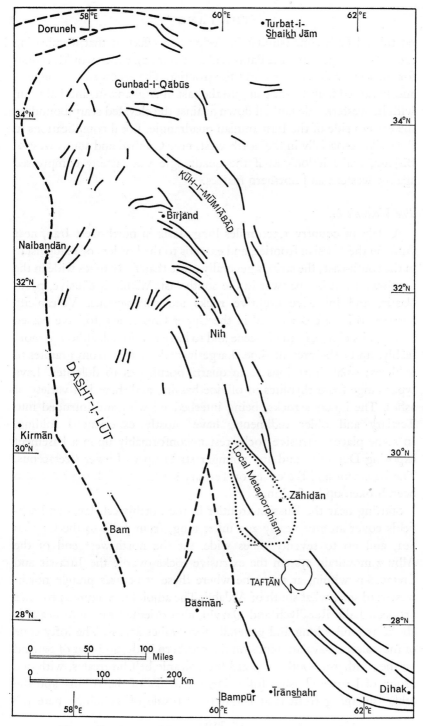

Fig. 43. Sketch-map of the East Iranian quadrangle and Dasht-i-Lūṭ.

postulated fault zone (similar in design and effect to that terminating the Ṭabas wedge along the Bam–Naibandān zone), which would account for the row of depressions near the frontier. The arrangement suggests another tilted fault-block rising to the east in Afghanistan and Pakistan, with its western side faulted down against the elevated scarp bounding the eastern side of the East Iranian quadrangle. Local complications in the strike, especially in the north-west, near Gunbad and south-west of Bīrjand, make it look as if the quadrangle was latterly compressed against western and northern masses.

The Volcanic belt

A strip of country 1,200 miles long starts in north-west Iran, near Julfā on the Russian frontier, and extends to the borders of Balūchistān in the south-east; the strip is generally more than forty miles wide in the north-west but is narrower in the south-east. Within it effusive, pyroclastic, and intrusive eruptive rocks are conspicuous. Vulcanicity appears to have commenced in the Upper Cretaceous, to have passed through its climax in the Eocene and to have continued, although more feebly, up to the present time. Large intrusions vary from granites to gabbros; small intrusions from quartz porphyries to dolerites. Lava types range from rhyolites to olivine basalts, and there is a variety of ashes. The igneous rocks, being interbedded with and intruded into Tertiary and older sediments, have mostly experienced folding. In some places extrusive rocks rest unconformably upon a basement exposing Devonian and any younger strata up to Lower Cretaceous. The basement and the cover of Tertiary strata after folding have also been broken up by faulting.

Starting near the Russian frontier in the north-west, lava- and ash-fields cover an area nearly 200 miles long, from Julfā to the Caspian Sea, and up to seventy miles wide. At the north-west end of the Alburz mountain system the extrusive rocks overlie the Jurassic and Cretaceous within, at the zone where these structures plunge north-westward somewhat south of Ardabīl. The adjoining volcanic province between Lake Rezā'īyeh and Qazvīn, also oriented east-south-east, is about 250 miles long and generally forty miles across. The lofty cone of the volcano Savalan stands on the northern body, and that of Sahand on the southern. South-eastward the volcanic belt bifurcates, with one group of lavas and ashes following the flanks of the Alburz and the other diverging from it at about the latitude of Tehrān, where the foredeep is postulated between the two. One more extensive lava field, over 100 miles long and about forty miles wide, lies forty miles west of the capital. The country along the road between Arāk and Tehrān is typical of the south-western region, where the belt is narrower. A series of strata, including Oligocene to Miocene limestones, red beds, ashes, lavas, and sills, is rather gently folded. The igneous sheets in the succession often control the topography and cap the low hills that stand among expanses of silt plains, salt marshes, and sand dunes.

North of Iṣfahān the basement, containing tightly folded Mesozoic and Palaeozoic beds, is capped by patches of lava and associated Tertiary sediments, with small granite intrusions breaking through them. Similar conditions obtain in the sector between Kāshān and Kirmān, but this region is cut by a group of north-north-west and south-south-east cross-faults. A small graben close to Nā'īn, eighty miles east of Iṣfahān, has been produced by two of these faults. One is situated fifty miles west of Nā'īn, and the other is just east of it. Between them lavas are preserved, whilst the basement predominates in the shoulders on either side. Farther south-east other lava fields— e.g. the one south of Anār, another north-west of Bam, and another south-west of Bam alternate with parts of the volcanic terrain in which ashes predominate. The belt ends at a large knot where a complex (eighty miles long and forty across) of lavas, ashes, and intrusives forms the skirts of the somewhat broken-down volcanic cone of Kūh-i-Basmān.

Large intrusions, each more than ten miles long, occur in several places along the belt. Two masses are exposed east of Julfā, at forty and eighty miles respectively. A neighbouring mass is situated sixty miles east of Tabrīz. A granite massif forms the mountain Shīr Kūh (13,315 ft) about thirty miles south-east of Yazd. It is also present in Kūh-i-Lālehzār (14,300 ft) eighty miles west of Bam. The longest stock in the whole belt is some sixty miles long; it carries the watershed between Dasht-i-Lūt and the Jāz Murīān, and it forms Jābal (Jamāl) Bāriz, a mountain chain forty miles south of Bam. Still another granite is intruded a further forty miles to the south-east, twenty miles south of Kāh-i-Basmān. Mention has been made in the paragraphs on eastern Iran (pp. 153–4 above) of a plutonic complex, occupying a triangular area 100 miles long and sixty miles across, which contains a suite from granite to gabbro. This complex runs across country northwest and south-east, close to Zāhidān and about sixty miles north-north-east of Kūh-i-Basmān. Granite also appears along the south-western flank of the Jāz Murīān, eighty miles south of Jābal Bāriz. The relationship between the granites north and south of the Jāz Murīān basin is unknown because they are separated by an expanse of alluvium.

The colours used on the geological map of Iran (1959) make this Volcanic belt stand out as the major feature it is. The flood of extrusive rocks broke out along this strip, which is presumably a line of weakness rather than one of faulting. A fundamental change takes place along it: there are eugeosynclinal conditions in the north-east, where vulcanicity accompanies a deposition of poorly sorted sediments, mainly mixtures of clays and sandstones; and miogeosynclinal conditions prevail in the south-west, where volcanics do not appear and the well-sorted sediments include many limestones and light-coloured sandstones.

The Complex belt

The strip of country that adjoins the Volcanic belt on its south-western side is about 100 miles wide and is complicated both stratigraphically and structurally. Here it will be called the Complex belt and be considered in three parts. The Iṣfahān–Sīrjān depression occupies nearly one third of its width and keeps along the north-eastern flank. The solid geology and structures of the depression are much obscured by deposits of silt and salt marsh. The rest of the belt is fairly well exposed, except at each end, and presents an assemblage in which folded and faulted sediments of different metamorphic grades are found associated with subordinate amounts of eruptive rocks sporadically distributed. A narrow, inconstant strip following the south-western margin is particularly disturbed. This is part of the zone of nappes (De Böckh *et al.* 1929).

The north-western termination of the belt is partially hidden by extensive Pliocene shales, marls, and tuffs, by the later lake terraces, and by Recent tuffs and lavas. But occasional gaps in the cover disclose the presence of schists below, with Carboniferous and Permian limestones and dolomites resting unconformably upon them—evidence that these schists are apparently pre-Carboniferous. The country west of Lake Rezā'īyeh is a complex of schists and of Palaeozoic and Mesozoic rocks, with Upper Cretaceous and Tertiary strata unconformable upon the earlier Mesozoics and older formations. The country to the south, along the Turkish, Iraqi, and Iranian frontiers, is made up of Upper Cretaceous sandstones, shales, and thin limestones. The map of this region is too generalized to be effectively interpreted; but it is known that the higher slices of thrust-faults mapped in Iraq exhibit movement from north-east to south-west (Mitchell-Thomé, 1960; Naqib, 1960).

Partial or inadequate exposures towards the south-eastern extremity result from the presence of an extensive sheet of silt that fills much of the Jāz Muriān basin and hides a large area of solid rock. Outcrops around its western edge reveal granites, lavas, schists, and sediments, along with folds, unconformities, and faults. The belt ends a few miles east of Īrānshahr, plunging beneath a mantle of sandstones and shales to form a Tertiary flysch.

In the region between these obscured terminations—i.e. from the mountainous district north of Hamadān to the environs of Sīrjān 700 miles away—the complex belt can be more satisfactorily studied. Here it is tightly folded, the axes of the folds tending to show a rather regular strike. Near Hamadān at the north-western end, sericitic and chloritic schists are developed within a tract 200 miles long and up to forty miles wide. Granite emerges sporadically and may have been in part responsible for the metamorphism. Alvand, the mountain overlooking Hamadān, is a topographic expression of the largest granite intrusion. The hills north-east of Burūjird, sixty miles south-east of Hamadān, contain the next largest body, and other granite stocks of smaller size have been mapped across country for fifty miles south-east of Burūjird.

Beyond the granites the grade of metamorphism is said to fall off, so that a variety of schists and phyllites merge laterally into a succession of shales and sandstones. A few thin limestones and coals have been regarded as akin to the Lower Jurassic plant-bearing coaly beds of the Alburz mountains. Baier (1938) and Gansser (1955) both refer to a transition from schists to all but unaltered, though strongly folded, sediments. Folded Jurassic shales and sandstones occupy much of the belt for the next 350 miles to the south-east, and they are intricately interfolded and faulted with fossiliferous Triassic and Permian limestones, dolomites, and shales—near Abādeh, for instance. In some places they have been followed along the strike for 150 miles but they are confined here to a strip about ten miles wide lying south-east of Shāhriza.

Lower Cretaceous conglomerates and sandstones accumulated on the south-western side of this fold-belt, with silts and marlstones replacing them farther to the south-west until they in turn pass laterally into limestones. Middle Cretaceous limestone later transgressed across the already folded Lower Cretaceous silts and sandstones towards the north-east. This may account for the masses of Cretaceous limestone found as outliers resting unconformably on folded arenaceous strata of the Lower Cretaceous. Such is the evidence left by a late Jurassic or early Cretaceous orogeny just outside or on the extreme north-eastern edge of the Zagros arc.

Disturbed Mesozoic rocks folded prior to the Middle Cretaceous continue into the neighbourhood of Nairīz [Nīrīz]. Beyond Nairīz the relation between the unaltered sediments and the complex of slates, schists, and epidiorites is not clear. The junction lies near the assumed prolongation of a fault-system running south-south-east from Nā'īn. This may be no more than a coincidence, for the continuity of the fault across an alluvium-filled depression can rarely be detected from the air and so may be no more than conjecture. In the south-eastern part of the complex, exposures of Permo-Carboniferous occur not far from Sīrjān (De Bockh et al. 1929), and open up the possibility that the meta-morphic rocks of the district may be old—at least older than Carboni-ferous.

Farther east gently dipping sandstones and shales containing Liassic ammonites rest unconformably on a planed surface across contorted schists and amphibolites. These schists in Jīruft are therefore certainly pre-Jurassic; probably pre-Carboniferous, and possibly pre-Devonian. It is tempting to hazard a guess that the schists are old and may be of an age with the schists in north-western Iran. If these speculations are valid, they mean that the schists in the north-west and south-east are old; and if Baier is correct, those in the Hamadān area may be younger, having been affected by local post-Jurassic metamorphism. Mention may also be made here of the development of a very young meta-morphism which was active in Tertiary times: near Zāhidān some of the Eocene flysch around a group of large intrusions was changed into schists and phyllites (geological map of Iran, 1959).

The south-western zone of the Complex belt corresponds to the zone of nappes described in *The Structure of Asia* (De Böckh et al. 1929). The nappes are sheets of strata, sometimes extremely disturbed by crumpling, shearing, and jointing. One nappe may contain rock types that are quite different to those of a neighbour; fragments of one nappe may have broken off and become wrapped up in or interspersed with rocks of another. The usual relationship, in which one packet of rocks lies deposited on another, is not common among these sheets. Rather, the position of one nappe in regard to another is unnatural, for they are folded tightly together with little or much distortion, splintering, inter-wedging, and movement. Nappes sometimes appear to be overriding by carriage, or underlying because of the downward plunging of inclined and recumbent folds. Sometimes the folds have broken into slivers, and a sequence of flakes, scales, imbrics, or *schuppen* (= lens-shaped blocks resulting from shearing under high pressure) inter-finger. Sometimes the nappe is a composite affair, partly recumbent structures or overfolds, and partly flakes or schuppen. Special com-plications result from local collapse, which may take place when contorted and thrust masses are piled up one upon the other, making a pile too steep for equilibrium; thus the folds and slices may fall off or glide down. A nappe may have travelled a long distance, perhaps tens

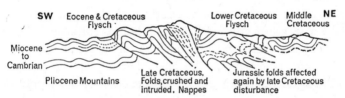

Fig. 44. Diagram showing sequence of mountain building from Jurassic to Pliocene times in central and south-west Iran. Scale about 20 miles to an inch. (After N. L. Falcon, *J. Inst. Petr.* vol. xxx, 1944.)

of miles, from the site of its origin to reach its present position. It may have overridden structural obstacles, or it may have rammed another nappe and abutted against it.

The country to the south-west is essentially made up of folded lime-stone, whereas the nappes driven towards or over the limestones include radiolarite: that is, thin-bedded red cherts containing radiolaria. In addition there is a massive peridotite, a volcanic rock rich in olivine; and the Coloured Mélange (Gansser, 1955), consisting of green shales and siltstones, of brown sandstones, serpentine (or altered peridotite), black pillow lavas, amygdaloidal and epidotic lavas, and of limestones in the form of thin ribs or fragments of reefs. In other places a nappe may be flysch, a useful term denoting a series of irregular alternations of shales and siltstones with ribs of sandstone and, rarely, a small per-centage of very local conglomerate or reef-limestone. The limestones provide a variety of colours, such as white, black, grey, yellow, and pink. Another nappe might consist of one rock type only, such as radiolarite, or perhaps peridotite, but others are composed of a variety of rocks occurring together sheared, jointed, or slickensided. Nappes of different sorts may lie one behind the other, or they may be arranged *en échelon*. In many nappes there is a bed of a rock liable to give way under strain and develop into a lubricant over which masses of tougher rocks may more easily slide.

Starting in the north-west from the Iraqi frontier close to Sulaimania, radiolarite forms the edge of the Complex belt for 120 miles and continues to do so for nearly fifty miles beyond Kirmānshāh. Calcite-veined and crushed Cretaceous limestones are stacked as a pile of recumbent synclines, forming the massive crags of Bīsitūn. They stand to the north-east of the radiolarite nappe. Lenses of peridotite and serpentine are found behind the radiolarite intermittently, marking a zone traceable for 150 miles along the strike.

Where the red cherts from Kurdistān end, their place in the front is taken by a series of crushed limestone humps for approximately 450 miles. They are untidy features such as might result from a smooth normal dome being ruined by later shearing and crushing. These are followed farther south-east by another sheet of red cherts. But this is in an unexpected alinement, for instead of being near the zone of the crushed limestone humps, the cherts are found nearly forty miles to the south-west of them. Patches of what was probably once a continuous radiolarite sheet have been discovered over a distance of 100 miles along the strike. Washington Grey (1950) has described the region and discussed the occurrence and its implications. He regards it as a far-travelled thrust-sheet, and submits that the red-bedded chert sheet overrides Upper Cretaceous limestone. The radiolarite was itself covered by a still higher Cretaceous stage before folding took place. Since then weathering has worn through the radiolarite layer and exposed a dome of Upper Cretaceous limestone below. Other interpretations may possibly be preferred; e.g. the limestone and the chert might be in stratigraphical and not tectonic relation.

Farther north-east a range littered with boulders and debris marks the front of another nappe. This consists of Coloured Mélange, containing pieces of sheared and calcite-veined dark limestones, white crystalline limestones, tooth-shaped fragments of sandstone and grits, thin-bedded siliceous brown limestones, red and green indurated shale, and purple marls. Characteristic scenery results, with many coloured fangs or spines made up of the more resistant rocks, upstanding above a plain of drab shales (see p. 161 above). Small spikes standing a few feet high exist close to large ones several hundred feet high. Gansser (1959) has drawn attention to the presence of such confused conglomerations, always associated with masses of slickensided serpentine, and recalls that such assemblages of about the same age are strung out across the mountain arcs of two continents from the Alps to the Himalayas.

A nappe of Coloured Mélange is developed around the metamorphic massif east of Nairīz, where gneiss, schist, marble, and epidiorite are reported. Presumably it is on this metamorphic basement that the Permo-Carboniferous twelve miles south-west of Sīrjān (at Saīdābād) rests (De Böckh et al. 1929).

The nappe front runs south-east from Nairīz for 100 miles. Beyond a patch of alluvium, alternations of Coloured Mélange and serpentine are alined approximately parallel to the nappe front. Then the direction of the front changes to about east-south-east, which is maintained for some eighty miles as far as Pūr, a village sixty-five miles north-north-east of Bandar 'Abbās. Over this part lenses of serpentine and associated formations tend to be alined north-north-east. The structure is complicated by many faults and some unconformities.

The nappe front suddenly alters direction near Pūr and turns south, twisting to south-south-east after twenty-eight miles, then proceeding in this direction for at least fifty miles more. The flysch that lies immediately east of the nappe front is trending parallel to it. From beyond the distant Ruwāndiz in northern Iraq (Naqīb, 1960) to Kirmānshāh and from there to Pūr, all movements along the belt have resulted in the carriage of nappes more or less from north-east to south-west; but from Pūr southward the thrust-masses are carried forward towards the west. For the fifty miles west-north-west of Pūr the nappe front is well exposed. Numerous schuppen occur to the north of the nappe front, giving lens-shaped outcrops of flysch, Middle Cretaceous limestone, Coloured Mélange, basic igneous rocks, serpentine, indurated shales simulating schists, and rounded blocks of quartzitic sandstones.

Twelve miles due north of Pūr, slivers of serpentine, lenses of schist, and interposed masses of Coloured Mélange, all with a nearly east–west alinement, are thrust against a narrow body of flysch that lies to the south; farther south a splinter of Coloured Mélange is caught in and carried into contact with brown Mio-Pliocene sandstones of the normal zone across the last few miles of the frontal fault. This complex of

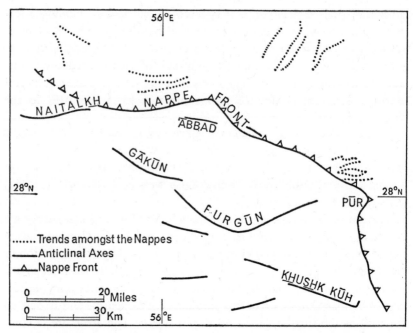

Fig. 45. Sketch-map of the nappe front between Naitalkh and Khushk Kūh,
showing the trend of some structures exposed within the nappe zone.

polished, striated, and sheared lenses is pierced by a cylindrical plug or
pipe of fresh uncrushed peridotite, which was presumably emplaced
after the Mio-Pliocene.

On the south-western side of the Complex belt anticlines and domes
of "Jura type" are developed, but those which lie in the crook of the
lower thrust-fault just west of Pūr show more faulting and distortion
than usual. Thrust-faulting affects the southern flanks of the domes, but
faults also appear in the core of the folds. Nearest to the nappe front
and south of it one surviving anticline, 'Ābbad, is sheared out along
its southern flank; moreover, oblique faults alined north-east and south-
west cross the dome. Three large domes apparently disturbed by their
proximity to the nappe front are Naitalkh, Kūh-i-Gāhkum (Gākūn), and
Furgūn. Each has a sheath, complete or partial, of massive Eocene
limestone; and each has a comparatively undisturbed northern limb, and
a broken one on the south. The westernmost dome, Naitalkh, runs
east and west, and although pierced by two salt plugs it is broken only
by a steep reversed fault along its southern side. The next, Gāhkum, is

oriented east-south-east, and its southern flank, too, is sliced by a reversed fault, which brings Carboniferous against Eocene limestones; other complications are caused by small tear-faults. A salt plug just to the south of the axis remains circular in plan and appears to be un-distorted—therefore it is an event later than the folding. Lastly, Furgūn is a fold in which the axis is sharply bent. It trends east-south-east in the west and curves round to lie east-north-east in the east. Not only does a thrust-fault break the southern flank, but the core is ruptured by a normal fault that brings the Trias into contact with the Lower Palaeozoic. After the thrust dies out eastward, prongs of lime-stone with their cover of Mio-Pliocene silts and sandstones plunge farther eastward apparently undisturbed by the proximity of the thrusted Eocene flysch of the Zindān range.

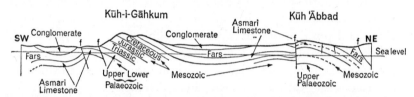

Fig. 46. Section across Kūh-i-Gāhkum, 'Ābbad and the Nappe Front with reverse faults affecting them. (After British Petroleum, 1956.)

It is noteworthy that in this neighbourhood west of the Zindān range, whilst some of these Zagros folds in Mio-Pliocene seem to be undisturbed, the older dome of Khushk Kūh has experienced a sharp turn at its eastern end. It is a fold exposing Lower Cretaceous and is thrust-faulted on its southern flank, which runs parallel to the axis, or nearly east and west, for some miles. At its eastern end the dome suddenly turns north and plunges downward. The turn is in the same direction as that in Furgūn but is more sudden. This deformity is close to the line of the Zindān front.

The change in behaviour exhibited by these folds—what are at first long, straight structures become notably bent—is what might happen if a fairly uniform sheet of sediments that is moving and folding up rather regularly south-west or southward is impeded by an up-lifted block of basement. Such a mass may exist along a line from the north of Oman to the region of Pūr. Another factor affecting the situation could be the ending of the Cambrian salt. This is thought of as extending along most of the Zagros, but the salt domes end on the west of the Oman–Pūr line. Where the salt is present there is a lubricant; where it is absent increased friction can be expected. This would cause dragging and a twist in the strike.

The conjectured Oman–Pūr block would also provide a reason for the change in strike in the western Makrān near the eastern side of the Strait of Hurmuz. The regional movement in the Makrān is southward, which has produced a general east–west alinement. Near the Strait the strike turns sharply to become north by west. It looks as if the moving sheet was halted by the Oman–Pūr obstruction. The zone running north of the Oman peninsula has been referred to in literature as part of the Oman line (Schröder, 1944).

The zone of normal folding

A zone of normal folding occupies most of the Zagros mountains and their foothills. It is an area in which long periods of quiet existed during the deposition of a thick packet of limestones, amongst which occasional bodies of limy clays were intercalated. Below these calcareous strata come sandstones and shales, which in turn lie upon a formation that includes salt, calcium sulphate, and dolomite. This whole assemblage of deposits covers a large area, and when subjected to lateral pressure it has reacted by folding in a rather regular pattern, with the folds assuming the shape of long domes. Near the north-eastern edge, however, some of the domes have broken and their north-eastern limbs have been thrust up towards the south-west, exposing the lowest horizons seen in the region. The faults are collected into two main groups, which trend obliquely to the alinement of the domes and run north-north-west. The fault-systems are each about 100 miles long, and they are disposed *en échelon* approximately thirty miles apart.

Above the great slab of limestone a further complication ensues in the foothills. Here, now covered by a variably thick mantle of sandstones and conglomerates, a deposit of mixed salt and gypsum was laid down; and it later suffered intense distortion in the course of regional folding. The types of folds produced in the gypsum and its accompanying marls and silts seem to have required the property of plastic flow in the strata. The folds are pinched, puckered, and contorted, and are utterly unlike the round-topped, smooth, and wave-shaped folds encountered in the limestones below.

The basal or Cambrian salt, deep down below the bottom of the limestone, has helped to lubricate interformational movement during

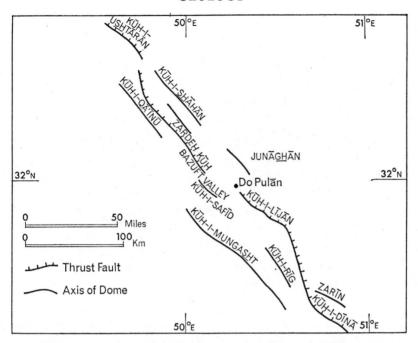

Fig. 47. Sketch-map of two major thrust faults in the north-eastern Zagros, one holding south-east from Kūh-i-Uṣhtārān to Zardeh Kūh, and another from Do Pulān to Kūh-i-Dīnā.

the epochs of folding, and to cope with readjustments among the thick or massive beds. But in doing so it has itself been folded and moved, and then, in suitable places, has burst through the overlying beds (locally some 20,000 ft thick) to form salt domes. Their abundance in the south-east of the Persian Gulf suggests that the salt formation was particularly thick under the Bandar 'Abbās district.

The map of the zone of normal folding is not a parallel-sided figure, but is formed of two bulges connected by a narrow part, looking much like half a dumb-bell. This pattern is conspicuous, particularly on any coloured geological map of south-west Iran. The north-westerly bulge, between 100 and 120 miles wide, continues south-eastward for 200 miles from the Sīrvān river, the frontier of Iran and Iraq. Its south-western flank is held up by three great, long domes lying close together and arranged nearly parallel to one another. They are Kabīr Kūh, Kūh-i-Qal'eh, and Kūh-i-Anarān. The first two are each more than 100 miles long, up to ten miles wide, and with an amplitude of about four miles from crest to trough. All three domes plunge south-

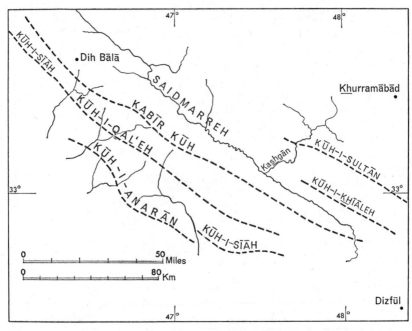

Fig. 48. Sketch-map of the Kabīr Kūh, the largest individual anticline in the
Zagros arc. It is over 100 miles long.

east near Dizfūl, thus accounting for the north-western bulge, to
terminate towards the south-east. The interior part of the bulge is less
mountainous than the south-western border. This central area exposes
well-rounded, comparatively gentle folds in a series of limestones and
thick detrital beds—beds which weather away easily, for they are made
of silts, sandstones, and marls of Upper Cretaceous and Eocene ages.
The few limestone reefs present are local but sometimes massive
phenomena, and by weathering out as they do in Luristān they form
unexpected mountains in the north-east, rising on the flank instead of
on the axis of a dome.

A conglomerate occurs locally as part of the flysch near Khurramābād, and in this district sections exposing upturned Eocene
flysch are overlain by nearly flat Asmari Limestone: satisfactory
evidence that folding and some erosion took place here between the
Eocene and Oligocene. These disturbances were severe in the north-
east, but they appear to fade away and cannot be identified south-
westward. The north-eastern conglomerates thin and give out, and
sands and then silts occur before marls come in. Thus the angular

unconformity displayed to the north-east disappears south-westward, where conditions of sedimentation appear to have changed little from Middle Cretaceous to Asmari Limestone times.

The north-eastern edge of the bulge still contains thick flysch, but the principal mountains depend upon the presence of two great domes of Middle Cretaceous limestones. These are Kūh-i-Charmī on the north-west and Kūh-i-Safīd plunging near Khurramābād on the south-east. It was observed that the Saidmarreh river cuts its valley across Kūh-i-Charmī at a place where the crest of its dome stands high above the

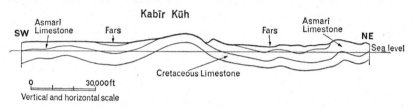

Fig. 49. Section across the Kabīr Kūh and its neighbours, showing diagrammatic symmetrical folding. (After British Petroleum, 1956.)

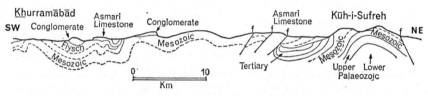

Fig. 50. Section from Khurramābād to Kūh-i-Sufreh. (After British Petroleum, 1956.)

surrounding country (see pp. 134–5 above), which can only be explained if the drainage was inaugurated on a surface unaffected at that time by the north-west and south-east ridges now in control. Radiolarite and serpentine of the Complex belt have been thrust against the north-east side of the Charmī fold as far east as the turn of the Kashgān river, but farther to the south-east, near Burūjird, the nappes are not clearly developed. Instead a deeply incised limestone dome displays its Permian core in Kūh-i-Sufreh, at the eastern end of Kūh-i-Chichil Naulakān, thus providing a first glimpse of the older rocks that become more generally exposed farther south-east.

Where the bulge ends the width of the exposed limestone terrain becomes restricted and continues as a narrow strip as far as Būshahr [Bushire], a distance of 280 miles. Structures within it can be grouped into three divisions. The first, along the north-east side, varies in width from ten miles in the north-west to nearly thirty miles at one place in the south-east. The whole sedimentary sequence of south-western Iran, from Cambrian to Miocene, is exposed in it in bold folds, many of them broken by thrust-faults dipping north-eastward. The second group of structures is found in the centre, where massive Cretaceous limestones are worn into shapes dictated by structure, providing expressive topography and still retaining a few relics in some of the synclines of younger formations now mainly swept away. This strip is forty-five miles wide. The third structure-type, up to seventy miles wide, embraces the south-western country and is expressed in foothills. Surface wastes of gypsum, red beds, and conglomerates overlie concealed domes of limestone. It is these which contain the oilfields.

The first division provides a foretaste of the fusulinid limestones in the core of Kūh-i-Sufreh near Burūjird. These strata, with the sandy and shaly Cambrian below, appear again forty miles to the south-east in a series *en échelon* of thrust-faulted folds. Together they form a range running south-south-east for 150 miles from Durūd on the Sehzar river to Kūh-i-Girreh. In most of the folds a massive Jurassic or Cretaceous limestone makes the high ridge on the north-eastern side of the fold, whereas the Palaeozoic formations crop out along the lower skirts of the mountains, in the valleys on their south-western side, and under an escarpment that may stand as much as 7,000 ft above the valley floor. Kūh-i-Ushtārān, Kūh-i-Vānizān, and Zardeh Kūh conform to this pattern. Exposures of the Lower Palaeozoic cover a large area around Qal'eh Kūh, where outcrops are ten miles wide and extend for many miles along the strike. The folds affecting these old strata are relatively gentle, but are broken occasionally by steep reversed faults, some of which bring the Lower Palaeozoic rocks against much younger formations on the south-western side. Thus Cambrian is found faulted against Mio-Pliocene, for instance, which is still preserved in one of the adjoining synclines.

Zardeh Kūh is an example of such a faulted fold. It is nearly fifty miles long. Along the major thrust the Cambrian is brought into contact with the Upper Fārs, and still younger, Bakhtīārī conglomerates, which are Pliocene, have been overridden after folding. Subordinate folds on the north-eastern side of Zardeh Kūh have suffered faulting, so that the northern flank is imbricated. This patch of imbrics ends at Kūh-i-Girreh, where the second line of Palaeozoic exposures starts about twenty miles farther east. Kūh-i-Sabzū stands near its northern end. This is a synclinal mountain that is underthrust by masses whose fault-planes dip towards one another. It is as if the structure had been raised by two wedges being driven together from opposite sides. Cambrian on the south-western side rides over Cretaceous by thrusting and Permian on the north-eastern side rides over Cretaceous.

The most imposing feature of the south-eastern Palaeozoic zone is Kūh-i-Dīnā, which runs south-south-east for eighty miles, with

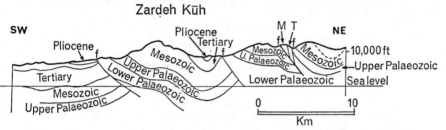

Fig. 51. Section across the Zardeh Kūh, showing an essentially synclinal fold uplifted to the south-west as a result of moving in the same direction. (After British Petroleum, 1956.)

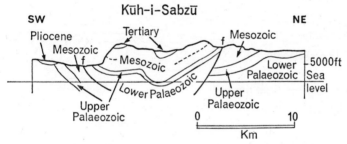

Fig. 52. Section across the Kūh-i-Sabzū. The mountain appears to have been lifted upon faults inclined towards one another. (After British Petroleum, 1956.)

Cretaceous limestone along the mountain top and the Cambrian sequence about one mile thick exposed below on the south-western slopes. Three ridges on its back are oriented nearly south-east and north-west, but unlike the subordinate folds on the north-east of Zardeh Kūh they have not broken under compression: they remain corrugations not imbrics.

The second strip exhibits groups of open folds controlled by the massive Cretaceous limestones but still with some residue of higher formations left in small patches in synclines in the north-west. South-eastward the percentage of country covered by younger formations is larger. Some of the domes retain a complete sheath of Eocene lime-stone—even Asmari Limestone may occasionally assume this cover-role. The folds are tighter in the north-west than in the south-east, which accords with the widening of the division southward. The unit is marked off from the Palaeozoic strip by long synclines, such as the one occupying the main valley of the Bazuft river, or the lowland including Khāneh Mīrzā under the brow of Kūh-i-Dīnā.

The dominating massive anticline in the north-west, drained by the Sehzar river, forms the great mountain Kūh-i-Qā'īnū. Its suite of

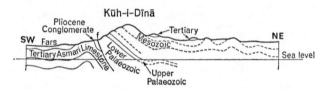

Fig. 53. Section across the Kūh-i-Dīnā and its wrinkled north-eastern flank. The palaeozoics are carried south-west by thrusting on to Pliocene conglomerates. (After British Petroleum, 1956.)

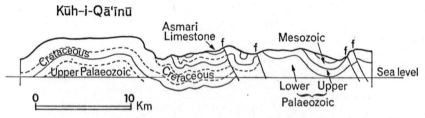

Fig. 54. Section across Kūh-i-Qā'īnū, in which a wide flat-topped anticline is preserved. (After British Petroleum, 1956.)

supporting folds gives the whole region the aspect of an anticlinorium, whose crest, south-west of Qal'eh Kūh, is developed in the Palaeozoic division. South-east of the plunging end of Kūh-i-Qā'īnū, the width from the Palaeozoic edge to the mountain front is still about thirty miles, but when Kūh-i-Mungasht rises *en échelon* to the south, the strip widens to sixty miles; see fault-zone map: fig. 47, p. 167 above. Mungasht is a much greater fold than its neighbours. Its long oval outcrop of Lower Cretaceous is gashed in two places by streams which have cut down into the Trias. After being the giant feature for forty miles, Kūh-i-Mungasht plunges and the country becomes fairly evenly corrugated. Most of the folds run to a type, yet are cut across by rivers in a capricious fashion. But domes standing high above their fellows continue to appear sporadically and may even rise close to the south-western edge. Kūh-i-Bingistān and Kūh-i-Khāmī are examples.

In general the limestone domes become less imposing south-eastward along a zone running nearly north-east of Būshahr. It is here that the narrow strip, the connecting link between the two bulges, comes to its end. Faulting is not conspicuous. Rocks younger than Cretaceous are more in evidence south-eastward, where several synclines retain large areas of Miocene beds within them.

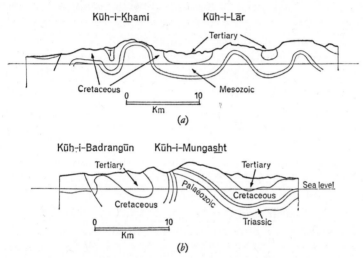

Fig. 55. (*a*) Section across the Kūh-i-Khāmī and Kūh-i-Lār. These large anticlines are the features off which the upper formations have slipped, giving collapse structures. (*b*) The section across Kūh-i-Mungasht shows a structure with a steep south-westerly limb so often seen where thrust faulting has broken an asymmetrical fold. (After British Petroleum, 1956.)

It was in this part of the Zagros mountains that the overturned gravity-collapse structures were first recognized on the north-eastern flanks of Kūh-i-Khāmī. Other fine examples of such curious folds have been noted from a few other localities in the Zagros chain, one in Kūh-i-Sahand near the Sehzar river, and another west of Kāzarūn near Naudān.

The third division contains the foothills between the edge of the present-day alluvium and the mountain front. It is about fifty miles across, but outlying ridges emerge from the alluvial plains near Ahvāz as much as 100 miles south-west of the mountain front. The style of the folds is less regular than in the limestone country to the north-east; this is one result of the compression upon the varied stratigraphical column, whose beds of low mechanical strength overlie the strong, competent Asmari Limestone. The base of the post-Asmari sediments consists of the mobile Lower Fars, made up of salt, gypsum, anhydrite, red and grey marls and silts, with some thin limestone ribs. The Middle Fars above it, a succession of fossiliferous marls, reef-limestones, and calcareous sandstones, is rather more robust—more so than the Upper Fars, a formation of alternating red sandstones, siltstones, and marls. Next come the Bakhtiārī beds made up of pebbly sandstones ultimately passing into bodies of competent brown conglomerates on top. The Lower Fars varies in original as well as present thickness, because it tends to be fugitive under unequal pressure. Thus the amount of salt in any drill-hole is peculiarly unpredictable. Flexures in the Upper Fars generally maintain the north-west and south-east regional orientation, but by Zagros standards the folds are narrow and do not reflect comparable structures below.

Sheets of contorted gypsum and marl sometimes protrude from the south-western side of a sandstone fold, as if they had flowed out as a paste. They are bounded by faults, and each mass forms a plateau that is nearly level overall: etched upon each plain is a shallow drainage pattern, a local affair, and there are many swallow-holes. The surfaces of neighbouring evaporite bodies do not stand at any constant level, but each one seems to be independent. The complicated contortions seen at the surface on such an extrusion are matched by innumerable wrinkles underground, where in one case they have been traced by drilling to a depth of two miles. On the other hand, in some drill-holes the gypsiferous Lower Fars is greatly attenuated and the Upper Fars comes close to the Asmari Limestone. Wherever present, the marl-gypsum–salt assemblage tends to lie disharmonically folded with respect to the Middle or Upper Fars.

Depositional unconformities as well as tectonic ones occur in the Upper Fars and the Bakhtiārī conglomerates. The latter, being firmly cemented, are durable and resist weathering better than the Upper Fars, and therefore they form the few peaks upstanding amongst the foot-hills. The Lower Fars beds are economically important because the plastic evaporite deposits provide an all but impermeable cover for the limestone domes below, thereby sealing in the liquid hydrocarbons in the oilfields. The gaseous constituents enjoy much greater mobility and are not so securely trapped, so that there tends to be some leakage.

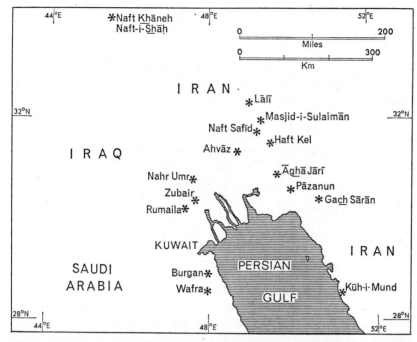

Fig. 56. Sketch-map of the oilfield province around the Persian Gulf. From Naft-i-Shāh and Naft Khāneh in the north to Masjid-i-Sulaimān, the first discovered field in the centre, and on to the exhausted field of Kūh-i-Mund in the south. (After Falcon, 1958.)

The escaping gas reacts with the gypsum above a gas dome and contaminates it with smelly sulphur-compounds, the product being known as "sour gypsum". Sour gypsum has often proved to be a reliable indicator of petroleum below. At times in the past, when the search for oil was proving difficult, and complicated evidence due to disharmonic folding was befogging the interpreters, the presence of sour gypsum in a wilderness of Lower Fars might have foretold with a reasonable accuracy the presence of an oilfield.

The oil and gas fields so far developed in south-western Iran are all contained in buried domes of limestone; nine of them are in Asmari Limestone, and one of the nine has a separate reservoir in the Cretaceous limestone. The fields are: Naft-i-Shāh, Lālī, Masjid-i-Sulaimān, Naft Safīd, Haft Kel, Āghā Jārī, Pāzanun, Gach Sārān, Ahvāz, and Khārg. The shapes of the various structures are known and recorded by the contours developed from bore-hole evidence and geophysical techniques. The surface of the ground above them has also been

175

geologically mapped; but apart from the clue given by the distribution of sour gypsum, it is doubtful whether the surface evidence alone could have led to the detection of the underground dome in the case of Lālī, Masjid-i-Sulaimān, or Naft Safīd. For Haft Kel and Gach Sārān there are rather difficult clues, whilst Naft-i-Shāh, Āghā Jārī, Pāzanun, and Ahvāz all yield reasonably good evidence on the surface.

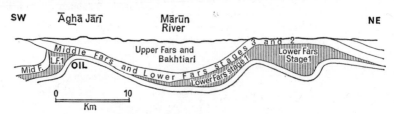

Fig. 57. Section through Āghā Jārī oilfield showing the thickening of Lower Fars Stage 1 from the Mārūn river north-eastwards. (After Ion, Elder and Pedder, 1951.)

The second bulge, situated east and south-east of the Bushire–Kāzarūn line, extends for 400 miles and ends against the Zindān range near Mīnāb. At its widest part it is 160 miles across, but it dwindles eastward as the axial direction of the constituent domes changes from north-north-west near Bushire to east-north-east near Bandar ʿAbbās. The bulge asserts itself where a series of folds, alined north-north-west, rise southward from the Bushire embayment. Kūh-i-Mund is an example. Standing by itself along the coast, it rises from sea level to 2,750 ft, is nearly ten miles wide and about sixty miles long, and exposes post-Asmari formations. Kūh-i-Khūrmūj, Kūh-i-Sīāh, and Kūh-i-Gīsākān lie inland and keep nearly parallel to it. In each of the four folds Cretaceous limestone is exposed at the core. Farther inland the domes are wide and gentle and may be covered entirely by Eocene or Asmari Limestone, or even by a veneer of Fars.

A score of contiguous domes, each with some Cretaceous limestone exposed, form a curving bulwark that guards the coast of the Persian Gulf from Bushire to Chārak. On the landward side the array of folds is still maintained, but the domes are less deeply eroded and most are not uncovered below the Eocene, although the Cretaceous limestone does crop out in folds south of Shīrāz and in one fold near Jahrūm, 100 miles north of the seashore. Eocene or Asmari Limestone are the feature-forming elements in many of the domes, whilst the Fars is preserved in the broad synclinal areas between the domes. North-eastward,

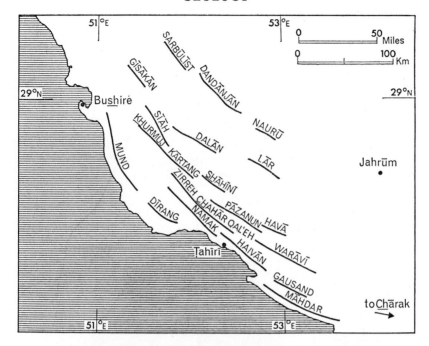

Fig. 58. Sketch-map of the Persian Gulf coast south-east of Bushire.

between Shīrāz and Nairīz, Cretaceous limestone is also frequently exposed. Upper Cretaceous is thick to the north of Shīrāz in the neighbourhood of Persepolis, but is strongly jointed and appears to have been involved in Late Cretaceous folding.

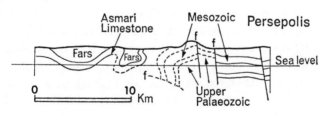

Fig. 59. Section across the Persepolis terrain, where faulting is conspicuous. (After British Petroleum, 1956.)

Longitude 54° passes close by Chārak and Lār. Several domes along this meridian lie with their axes running nearly east and west; and Eocene limestone is the formation now mainly in control at the surface. A degree farther east the domed axes are trending east-north-east, and

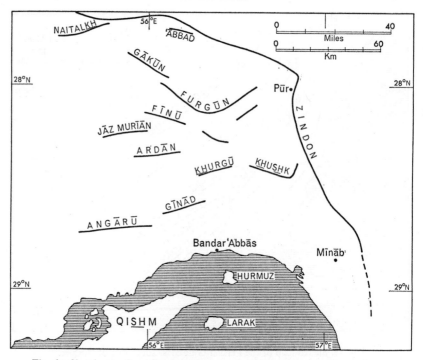

Fig. 60. Sketch-map from Bandar ʿAbbās to the Zindon range to the north-east
and to Angārū to the west.

bending occurs within the length of an individual fold. Kūh-i-Furgūn
is both twisted and faulted. Over a distance of twenty-five miles its
plan looks like a half-moon which is concave northward, as if the fold,
following a south-easterly course from the north-west, had been
disturbed by having its eastern half dragged northward—a process
applied with less drastic effect to the eastern part of the terrain.

The most easterly dome in the Zagros arc, Khushk Kūh, has had
similar treatment. After the structure has maintained a trend a little
south of east for fifteen miles, its eastern end is suddenly turned north,
the curving axis being concave to the north also. Synclines on the north
and east of these two folds, Furgūn and Khushk Kūh, are those overridden respectively by the serpentine nappe in the north and the
flysch nappe in the east (see p. 164 above).

Near Bandar ʿAbbās adjacent domes attain quite different heights.
Kūh-i-Gīnau, for instance, stands as a great mountain high above its
neighbours Kūh-i-Angārū and Kūh-i-Khūrgū. The predominantly

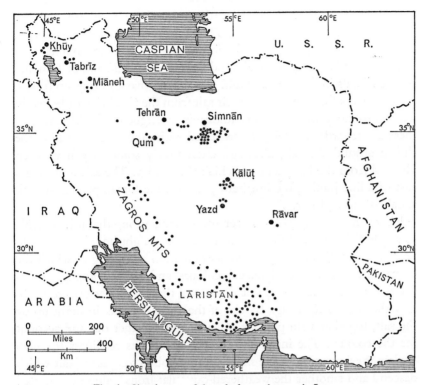

Fig. 61. Sketch-map of the salt domes known in Iran.

calcareous facies running on rather consistently throughout the Zagros arc terminates, apparently abruptly, along the western front of the Zindān range. Large smooth domes, the characteristic folds in massive competent limestones, do not emerge anywhere to the east in Iranian Balūchistān, a province of thin-bedded incompetent rocks which provide little or no expression of structure in the topography.

In south-western Iran salt-domes are widely scattered over the southern parts of the zone of normal folding. The main concentration is found on both sides of a line from Lār to Bandar ʿAbbās, although a few are encountered farther north within the catchment of the Kārūn river. Most of them can be attributed to the restlessness of Cambrian salt trying to escape from pressure. However, one small saltplug near Masjid-i-Sulaimān at Ambāl is built wholly with Miocene salt, from thick Lower Fars. In the south-eastern bulge saltdomes have pierced the long anticlines near Bushire. Five other salt domes stand close to

179

a straight line oriented north-north-west, whose northern end lies thirty miles south-west of Shīrāz. Then for nearly 100 miles to the east, as far as Jūyum [Juivūn], salt domes are uncommon; but east of Jūyum, near long. 54°, they abound both on the mainland of Iran and on the islands in the Persian Gulf. Several salt masses bring up fossils, which proves that they derive their salt from the Cambrian or below it. They also carry blocks of metamorphic and igneous rocks. Most of these are regarded as being interbedded with other rocks forming the sheath around the salt, although alternatively some may have been plucked from the basement on which the salt lay. The salt domes end east of a line joining the northern point on the Oman peninsula with Lārak Island and Pūr.

There are so many plugs—over 100—in this group that it is possible to suggest that several lie close to the same straight line; but it would be rash to say there is any obvious orientation according to which the domes are distributed. Unusual colours and curious topographical features characterize some salt domes; of these, salt glaciers are probably the most surprising. Blocks of the various rocks brought up by the salt, together with pockets of haematite, weather out and account for the colours. The instability of the salt and its readiness to creep explain the formation of the small, steeply poised tongues of salt which descend and smother the weathered-out "flat-irons" along the fretted edges of the surrounding limestones. Salt glaciers assuming a much gentler slope develop exceptionally where part of the limestone girdle is deeply breached. The course of these, as in their ice counterparts, is usually broken by a succession of concentric crevasses beautifully displayed in photographs from the air as has already been noted (p. 141).

Reviews incorporating new evidence from the salt domes in Iran, based on field-work and aerial photographs, have been produced by Gansser (1960) and Kent (1958); and O'Brien (1957) has discussed the role of the igneous rocks found in so many salt domes. For several years it has been accepted that the mechanism which generates the upward rising of the salt dome is the load of heavy sediments pressing upon the mobile salt, which has a relatively lower specific weight. This theory is now challenged, and some prefer to believe that heat from the associated igneous rocks, which are regarded as injected, set the salt moving. Accumulated evidence confirms the contention that salt domes have been injected at several different times. Some moved first in the Cretaceous and some are moving at present. The salt domes are oriented along lines running north-north-west (for instance, south-west of S̲h̲īrāz) and east-north-east (as in the district west of Bandar 'Abbās)—and the significance of this alinement is not known; but it has been thought possible for movements along buried faults to determine the positions at which some salt plugs were initiated.

The Makrān remains to be reviewed. It lies between the Strait of Hurmuz on the west and the borders of Pakistan on the east. This block is nearly 400 miles long in the north and 280 miles in the south, with an average breadth of about 100 miles. Nearly all the sediments at the surface are incompetent. Flysch of Eocene and Oligocene age predominates, but strips of Coloured Mélange are interfolded with the flysch in the north, while remains of Mio-Pliocene grits are abundant in the south. Farther north patches of pillow lavas with wisps and lenses of serpentine occur. No massive formation is found in the region to give robust folds which might weather out boldly as domes. Instead the incompetent formations are disturbed by numerous small sharp folds, many of which have broken and are faulted. Striated surfaces abound, and the lens-shaped blocks called schuppen (see p. 161 above) are produced from any of the harder beds like sandstones and lavas. The schuppen stand out locally as rocky fangs.

The very disturbed strips that may include bodies of serpentine alternate with others, which, whilst still strongly folded, are more orderly. The saw-tooth folds of the north and centre contrast with the quiet oval basins of younger grits situated farther south, which contain massive beds dipping gently towards a centre and bounded on their margins by cliffs. Each oval "cake" stands up as a mountain mass which may reach 4,000 ft in height, with slabs of grit resting upon disturbed silts and sandstones. Perhaps some of this disturbance was caused by movement of the silts away from the load formed by the patches of eroded grit: at any rate the effect is similar to that of a "valley bulge" (Hollingworth, 1944), with the low central cliffs in the gritstones also resulting from this movement by the silts as they have come under pressure. Many of the basins are as long as they are wide. The axes trend more or less east and west, and this is also the orientation of the tight folds in the north, to the east of long. 58°, about the position of Jāsk. At about this longitude, too, the trend changes. Some fifty miles inland it curves quietly from east and west to north-west and south-east, but makes a sharp bend nearer the coast, where it turns abruptly from east and west to north-north-west and south-south-east—a trend that is held as far north as Pūr at the northern end of the Zindān range nearly 160 miles away.

THE STRUCTURAL HISTORY OF IRAN

Much of Iran provides an example of what Kober thought of as a two-sided orogen. A lowland is situated on each side of the orogen from which mountain chains arise, and between these chains is a region of basins and ranges of lower hills. The Russian platform lies to the north of Iran, with the curving chain forming the Alburz mountains south of it. Central Iran, consisting of basins with subordinate chains, has a complicated history. The Zagros range skirts its south-western side for 800 miles and beyond the Zagros are the plains of Iraq or Mesopotamia, the growing delta of the Euphrates and Tigris, and the Persian Gulf. These elements forming the west of the region have features of structural history in common. Most of the information about the Alburz and the Iranian basin region comes from the research of Gansser and his team, enhanced by recent valuable summaries added by Stöcklin and his collaborators in 1964. The description of geological events in the Zagros mountains has been discussed by British Petroleum Company geologists in the last few years. Supplementary evidence about the eastern part of the central Iranian basin was published in Germany by Huckriede and his associates in 1962.

The earliest part of the story refers to the presence of an unconformity between the schists and green shales below, and a sequence above of red beds and dark dolomites which pass upward with apparent conformity into fossiliferous Cambrian. This has been noted at places scattered along the Alburz and in the basin to the south: at Ālam Kūh in the central Alburz; at Zanjān in the west; at Dāmghān in the east (350 miles from Zanjān), and at Saghand, some 220 miles south of Dāmghān. The beds immediately overlying the unconformity are certainly lower than Middle Cambrian, and they may perhaps precede Lower Cambrian and be pre-Cambrian. This widespread unconformity indicates a tectonic break, which, following Stille's nomenclature, is placed tentatively in the Assyntic period of the Pre-Cambrian era between 1,300 million and 600 million years B.P.[1] After this disturbance more than 600 million years ago in the pre-Cambrian, no further diastrophism was apparent in northern and central Iran until the

[1] Before Present—much used nowadays.

Jurassic. On the other hand, there is evidence that vertical movements did occur, causing gaps in the Devonian sequence and in the Permian sediments. Stöcklin concludes his review (1964) by stating that "stable platform conditions were created in pre-Cambrian time and persisted through the entire Palaeozoic era". Palaeozoic strata are also exposed in the Zagros mountains, but even in the deepest valleys do not reach any unconformable basement, such as schists. The lowest rocks exposed consist of dark dolomites and red beds, together with a series of olive-coloured shales and brown silty sandstones. There is, however, some conglomerate, and also pebbles of vein quartz and andesite.

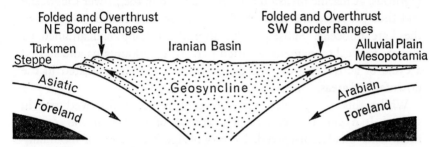

Fig. 62. Diagram of the Iranian orogen. (After A. Holmes, *Principles of Physical Geology*, 1944.)

Here too in the Zagros mountains there are gaps in the sequence of sediments overlying the Cambrian, but there are no angular unconformities within any of the Palaeozoic systems. The stable conditions visualized by Stöcklin for the centre and north hold also in the south-west.

The Jurassic in Central Iran is a mixture of shales, sandstones, limestones, and coals. It was folded and somewhat eroded before the transgression of the Middle Cretaceous limestone. In a strongly disturbed zone along the south-western side of the Iranian basin, where it adjoins the Zagros mountains, there is a body of metamorphic rocks. Baier (1938) has suggested that because their lithology is not unlike that which would have resulted from an alteration of the Jurassic assemblage, these metamorphic rocks may themselves be Jurassic in age. On the other hand, rocks that are similar to those in Baier's sequence are known to crop out along a line of hills to the north-west of Kirmān, and Huckriede has shown these to be Pre-Cambrian. In the Zagros mountains the Jurassic follows the Triassic without perceptible unconformity or much change in the type of facies. There is some un-conformity in the Alburz between the Jurassic and Trias.

When Gansser published the evidence from northern and central Iran, he described a number of episodes showing that central Iran was unstable after Middle Cretaceous times. Orogenesis, followed by up-lift, occurred before the Middle Cretaceous, and both coincided with widespread vulcanicity. It is also about this time, just before or in the Maestrichtian, that some of the large bodies of peridotite and serpentine were emplaced and faulting occurred. Folding again took place in the Lower Eocene, and before the Middle Eocene vulcanicity was again vigorous. A marine invasion flooded the basin in the Lower Oligocene and thus preceded the main Alpine orogeny, assigned by Gansser to the Late Pliocene. Subsequently, after the folding had attained its climax, vertical movements uplifted parts of the mountains and started a cycle of active erosion, the debris from which accumulated in the downfaulted areas.

Whilst this complicated programme was being followed out in central Iran and farther east, the course of events in the Zagros mountains was less involved. Here two vigorous pulses of mountain-building occurred. The first commenced in the Upper Cretaceous and continued into the Eocene. This was concentrated in the north-eastern part of the present range and was sufficient to erect a chain of mountains which soon suffered erosion; their ruins and stumps were subsequently covered by the Lower Miocene limestone. This angular unconformity was produced before the major upheaval in Gansser's Pliocene and the British Petroleum geologists' Mio-Pliocene. It was this, the second stage of mountain-building, which bent the strata into the folds dis-played at the present day in the Zagros mountains. Bailey (1948) summed up the position in the Alburz by saying that there were two important movements there, one late in the Cretaceous and the other late in the Miocene. Later uplift has affected parts of both ranges, Alburz and Zagros.

In the Zagros it has been established that the main orogenic uplift (as distinct from the folding), which must have been contemporaneous with the formation of the present Persian Gulf depression, has an amplitude of 40,000 ft in the Bakhtiārī mountain area, decreasing to the north-east and south-west. The way in which the great limestone folds of the Zagros have been exhumed and incised—for instance, by the Kārūn river in the Bakhtiārī mountains—can only be explained if the main river system was initiated before the present succession of north-west and south-east folds had a surface expression. It is clear also, from the thick Pliocene deposits in the Zagros foothills and the coastal area, that the main uplift took place concurrently with the folding.

The two-sided orogen so clearly represented in western Iran does not continue uninterruptedly throughout eastern Iran, but is truncated by the Oman line. This line, referred to by most authors who have dealt with the geology and structure of Iran as a whole, starts from the point of Oman, Rā's Musandam, and runs north to Pūr, seventy miles north-east of Bandar 'Abbās, where in Iran it is conspicuous on account of the Zindān range. The whole geological aspect on the west side of this range is different from that on the eastern side as far as Pūr. Here onwards the anticlines and the usual sedimentary column of the Zagros disappear and Eocene flysch with pillow lavas, associated with serpentine, come in. These beds are not folded into major anticlines, but the structure is more fault-controlled, and zigzag folds are common. Thrust-faulting is evident, bodies of flysch having been carried westward, over-riding the Mio-Pliocene at the extreme south-east end of the Zagros mountains; whilst the flysch itself is overridden by schist of pre-Liassic age. The thrusts occurred very late, presumably in Pliocene times. The effect and indeed the existence of the Oman line farther north are not obvious, although the faulting along a north to south feature on the west of the Dasht-i-Lūt, together with the regional strike in this area, form a northern extension of the trend. Beyond, towards Doruneh, the surface geology shows no sign of the trend continuing.

To summarize: after a turbulent start in the pre-Cambrian, there was a long quiet period until the Jurassic. Movements began in central Iran in the Jurassic and reached a climax in the Upper Cretaceous, when some folding took place with vulcanicity, north-east of the Zagros mountains. Volcanoes remained active through much of the Eocene. Then with some breaking down through faulting—which is important in central Iran—folding increased to a maximum in Pliocene or Mio-Pliocene, when the Zagros range was formed. During this folding, vertical movements also took place and erosion uncovered the folds and produced the mountain scenery of the present day.

CHAPTER 3

GEOMORPHOLOGY

The variety and nature of morphological forms in the upland mass that forms Iran are closely determined by the prevailing climate. Just as this climate can be called an orographically conditioned variant of the general climatic type characteristic of the arid belt of the Old World, so the surface forms occurring within Iran can be characterized in an analogous manner. Climatic and geomorphological provinces can be said largely to coincide.

The massif of Iran rises generally within the Alpine orogenic zone of Eurasia. Together with its surrounding frame of mountain ranges, this massif separates the Saharan–Arabian portion of the arid zone of the northern hemisphere from its Turanian–Central Asian counterpart; and in addition, it divides the desert regions of the subtropics (deserts which have formed because of their location in relation to the tradewinds) from the dry areas of the temperate zone, which may be said to owe their aridity to an extreme continental position. The Iranian upland is subjected simultaneously to "westerly" weather conditions in the north and to effects of the monsoon in the south. The mountain ranges rise sharply from their foreland, which greatly facilitates condensation from the air masses associated with the Mediterranean, Caspian, and subtropical oceanic areas; but the resulting precipitation occurs consistently and in quantity only on the outer flanks to the west and north. The atmospheric circulation carries further moisture inland to the more sheltered highland zones, producing rainfall on the lee, or the inward-facing, slopes. This explains the extension of precipitation to the mountainous areas in the east and south of Iran. A further characteristic of the rainfall distribution pattern is the general decrease of precipitation from west to east. As this is also coupled with a decrease in altitude from north-west to south-east within the interior basin of Iran, the number of dry months increases correspondingly: an important index of growing aridity in this direction. Further, there is a diminution of rainfall within the interior of Iran from north to south. As a result there are strikingly distinctive climatic–morphological areas, culminating in the desert basin of S̲h̲āhdād, which lies in the extreme south-east of the country.

Disposition of relief therefore conditions the contrast between the rainy outer flanks, and the sub-arid to almost completely rainless inner basin regions. But it also controls the hydrological pattern of Iran, which is characterized by similarly sharp contrasts and delimited by the alinement of water-partings.

As regards geomorphology, the watersheds are significant first because of their course, and also because of the specific effects they produce within the general pattern of relief. Though they are only one element in the general scheme of a river basin or group of basins with a similar geomorphological history, the watersheds are the most outstanding and immediately visible demonstration of the surface forms that can be produced by fluvial erosion. Their formation within the general relief is in each case the result of denudation acting as far back as the edge of the drainage system itself. Such a process depends basically on the volume of water transported, and especially on the total amount of rainfall within the catchment area and the seasonal distribution of this fall.

Along the summits of the Zagros mountains and uplands of Makrān runs a "first-order" water-parting. This separates drainage to the Persian Gulf and Gulf of Oman (i.e. to the Indian Ocean) from the "*endoreic*" or interior, closed drainage systems of inner Iran. Another watershed, which is of considerable significance in the drainage pattern of inner Iran, defines drainage to the Caspian Sea. Its disposition and alinement reveals that the Caspian catchment is by no means restricted to the northern slopes of the Tālish and Alburz mountains: it overlaps well into the inner plateau of Iran by an embayment stretching in a southerly direction. Hence for a relatively short distance within the north-western Zagros, this second watershed coincides with the main oceanic–endoreic water-parting already alluded to. Over the rest of its course it can be considered a "second-order" watershed, for as a continental interior divide it separates the Caspian drainage from that of interior Iran, from which there is no outward drainage. (See fig. 87, p. 270.)

The inner plateau of Iran may be regarded as divided hydrographically into two parts, by the southerly prolongation of the Caspian drainage system into the Qizil Uzūn–Safīd Rūd areas. On the west is the drainage basin of Lake Rezā'īyeh (Urūmīyeh), formed in a relatively straightforward, uniform manner, and characterized by perennially flowing streams. Possibly at an earlier period (Pleistocene?) this drainage system had an outlet to the Caspian Sea.

In contrast, the remaining region of inner Iran, from which there is no drainage outlet, is not only considerably larger in area but is also composed of a number of quite separate basins laying at different altitudes. These may be considered collectively under the heading of *desert basins of the inner Iranian plateau*, and classified according to the degree of alteration in landscape which occurs between the centre of each basin and its periphery. The central parts comprise the desert grouped round the Great Kavīr and the basin of Shāhdād (Southern Lūt). Next occurs an "inner" ring of bordering desert, which in the south is separated from the Zagros foothills only by the relatively low ridges of the Kūh-i-Rūd hills; whilst in the north-east it overlaps on to the mountainous terrain of Khurāsān. The "outer" zone is formed by various closed basins which are "inserted" so to speak, into the Zagros massifs and are distributed longitudinally within the trend of the mountain ridges. In the north, on the other hand, the steep fall of the Alburz sets a sharp limit to the number of basins; but this steepness varies eastward, where the main Alburz chains radiate as a fan and interlock with the ridges of the north-east hill country. Here the interior desert basins appear as a mosaic of "inserted" pieces.

The eastern border of the interior basin zone is formed by a third-order watershed, which extends across the mountains of southern and eastern Iran, and which also separates Iranian drainage from that of Afghanistan and Pakistan. Within the Iranian frontier these interior basins include: the regions forming a part of the Sīstān lowlands; the catchment system oriented towards the Harī Rūd; and finally, the tongue of lowland round Sarakhs, which to the south-west is a prolongation of the desert basins of Central Asia. Despite their actual location, these border regions belong morphologically to the Iranian upland.

This hydrographic boundary terminates in the great longitudinal valley of north-east Iran—the Khurāsān rift. This is drained northward by the Atrak river to the Caspian Sea, and southward by the Kashaf Rūd to the Harī Rūd. The Mashhad basin, which also forms part of the region, is connected with the inner desert zone by the low pass of Sharīfābād.

The close relationship between climatic and hydromorphological zones within the Iranian plateau is still more enhanced by considering the regional variety of morphological forms within the same fundamental scheme of hydrographic division.

Surface features on the Iranian plateau show clearly the effects of earth movement of relatively recent geological age, especially the process of downwarping in the region of the Caspian Sea, as well as various phases of orogenic uplift in the mountain ring that forms the outer border of Iran. But apart from earth tremors, which still occur throughout Iran, and despite volcanic activity in Mt Damāvand and Kūh-i-Taftān, which are not totally extinct, major activity apparently ceased with the transition from Pliocene to Pleistocene; so that since that time the basic agency responsible for the evolution of relief has been subaerial erosion. Water and wind are therefore the decisive physical factors in the formation of the present detailed landscapes of the Iranian plateau: this is shown by geomorphological evidence and by the nature of tectonic evolution.

The wetter, outer flanks of the Iranian mountains are consistently furrowed by deeply cut valleys; in the mountain forelands great alluvial fans were deposited and wide deltas built up. The rivers largest in volume (if not in length) are found in that part of the catchment area of the Caspian Sea where rainfall occurs all the year round. But most of the northern slopes of the Alburz chain are drained only by short streams that drop steeply. Consequently, in the region of the southern Caspian uplands there is very little lateral extension of the valleys by river erosion: their stage of development may be regarded as one of extreme youthfulness. The valley of the Hazār river does extend, it is true, east of Damāvand through the central mountain massifs, so that the highest summit lies outside the line of the main watershed; but only the Safīd Rūd ("White river"), which forms the lower course of the Qizil Uzūn and rises in the wetter mountains of Kurdistān, manages to break through the whole range—and this only by an extremely steep gorge.

The courses of these rivers developed largely under the influence of relatively recent tectonic processes. Because of these, the erosive power of the rivers was rejuvenated, and the effective catchment area of the Qizil Uzūn was enlarged to include a large segment of the interior plateau, which as a result now drains to the Caspian Sea. Outwash and deposition of sediments derived from erosion of the northern uplands have built up the level of the Caspian coastal plain. Only a few centuries ago this was totally marshy and inundated, but it is now almost entirely under cultivation, with a coastline diversified only by the *haffs* or sand-spits of the Safīd Rūd, Gurgān, and Atrak rivers.

Effects produced by shrinkage of the Caspian Sea itself are apparent as geomorphological features in the east, particularly in the Atrak valley. Here the Atrak has been able to unite into one system, by means of capture, a series of small basins grouped linearly within the faulted zone of the Khurāsān rift valley; but it has not yet made tributary the small aretic basin which forms a water-parting with the Kashūf Rūd. Erosion by the Atrak is apparently no longer sufficient to act as a major influence upon the physiological evolution of the Khurāsān rift valley. Its pebble-strewn floor and mighty scree deposits close to the valley flanks bear impressive witness to the fact that aridity increases with distance from the Caspian Sea. Furthermore, throughout the entire Alburz the Caspian watershed can be established as a sharp morphological divide between the northern slopes, which are broken by erosion ravines, and the bare slopes of the southern declivity, where there are only furrows cut by melt-water in spring.

From a corresponding complex of effects arises the morphological picture of the southern bordering massifs. From the structural point of view, the Zagros range is made up of several distinct mountain chains running in a N.W.–S.E. direction; arranged *en échelon* as a major arc beyond the Armenian upland mass, they enclose the inner plateau of Iran. As the primary element in this structural pattern, the Zagros chains include a system of longitudinal valleys and basins. The most important of these, the basins of Iṣfahān and Saidābād, lie within the inner chains and always form independent hydrographic units. By contrast, longitudinal valleys lying among the outer chains are usually broken into by cross-valleys. These "break-through channels" (e.g. that of the Kārūn into the Āb-i-Diz) were formed by faulting related to the general dislocation that gave rise to the contrasting relief zones of the Zagros to the east and the plains of Mesopotamia and basin of Khūzistān in the west.

The rivers of the Zagros area that have the greatest elaboration of course and volume of water are located, significantly, in the rainier north-west and west; whilst the more arid upland landscapes of the south have no major drainage worthy of mention.

Because of a generally insufficient and seasonally fluctuating volume of water, the erosive effects of most rivers in the Zagros area are now small. But within certain limited areas greater amounts of rainfall occur sporadically over a relatively short time, transporting eroded material and causing major landslides, which can block the rivers. Such damming of streams by landslips is by no means unknown in the Alburz region, but it becomes especially frequent in the Zagros chains and has been repeatedly observed down to the present day. A landslide in the Saidmarreh valley (Karkheh) near Dizfūl, which would appear to have occurred in prehistoric times, is possibly the greatest of its kind in the eastern hemisphere.

Hence the regions of most active geomorphological change as the result of river action would seem to be confined to the outer flanks of the Zagros range. But erosion also has a crucial influence on the morphology of the inner basins, with relatively large, if short-lived, falls of rain still producing some effect, especially in the north-west. Much of the runoff here, however, is increasingly maintained by melting snow from the higher parts of the mountain ring; and a consequent decrease of fluvial erosion processes from north-west towards the south-east is indicated by the more abundant sand- and pebble-cover of the basin floors in the latter area.

Transition to the arid climatic regime characteristic of inner Iran takes place more gradually in the Zagros than in the Alburz, and therefore the sequence of changes in land forms from the outer to the inner zones of the central basin is demonstrated much more clearly in the Zagros. Diminution of the effects due to water flow can be considered the prime reason for the greater variety of regional morphological forms that is apparent as one passes from the outer margins towards the interior of the Iranian central plateau.

Of the morphological forms present within the interior of Iran, the "sump" or kavīr structures would seem to be unique in that they possess no exact counterparts in any other region of the world (Gabriel). Two kinds of kavīr are involved—those fed by direct rainfall, and those maintained by underground seepage. In the slightly less arid areas of the north the expanses of kavīr are mainly moist; whilst in the distinctly drier south the kavīr is harder and without the extensive water surfaces that characterize the north. These southern basins, fed primarily by ground water, are today largely dried out. In the most arid parts of the south, comprising the interior districts of the Shāhdād basin, the kavīr landscapes of the residual lakes Namakzar-i-Shāhdād and Shūrgiz-Hāmūn show the almost completed final phase of drying out. The ground-water sumps came into existence at an earlier, markedly pluvial period, and now represent various advanced stages in the general drying-out process. They therefore provide important evidence of the effect of climatic fluctuation upon the evolution of land forms, as will now be examined in more detail.

During the earliest months of the year many parts of the inner basins are under water, mainly as a consequence of runoff from winter precipitation occurring over the border ranges that define inner Iran. Part of the north-eastern segment of the Dasht-i-Kavīr may be under water during the entire year. A dense network of valleys around the Dasht-i-Kavīr, together with recently formed talus that is now covered by rainwater runnels or worked over by drainage furrows, point unmistakably to the valleys' recent formation as the result of episodic falls of rain, which occur almost always as instability showers. Although denudation by wind plays a subordinate part, the transport of windborne material must in no way be overlooked or underestimated. This view, which emphatically contradicts an opinion widely held at present, is fully substantiated by, amongst other things, the existence of dunes on the southern margins of Dasht-i-Kavīr. And in the interior of the Shāhdād basin (Southern Lūt), morphological features produced by water action become fewer and fewer, and aeolian forces occupy unmistakably first place among the influences which have moulded the surface land forms.

Impressive proof of the effects due to wind action occurs in the arid areas round Shāhdād. In this region there have developed the *qal'āt* ("desert villages") through deposition of so-called "lake silt"; there are also "desert towns" (*Shahr-i-Lūt*), which have been built up from more strongly consolidated deposits and appear to consist of several storeys. But most of all the "boulevards" of the *kalut* landscape, extending over about sixty miles present a remarkable, almost unique, example of wind erosion on a grand scale. The existence of many residual (or deflexion) geomorphological forms, produced by the blowing away of sand or dust, indicates the importance of wind action as the formative agent. Hollows, "pans", furrows, and "blind" valleys without drainage outlet are further effects of wind erosion; while Sīstān's notorious Wind of 120 Days hollows out small basins arranged in rows.

These views on geomorphological evolution, put forward as the result of research by Gabriel and Startil-Sauer, have been supported by the aerial photographs of Bobek, who has also definitely established that the extensive hollows and small-scale basin structures of the Southern Lūt and Sīstān were scooped out by wind action. Complementary, as it were, to the areas of deflation in the interior deserts are extensive

1   Lake Rezā'īyeh, with S͟hāhī Island.

2   The Zagros in the region of Kāshān.

3 (*a*) The central Zagros in winter.

3 (*b*) The north-eastern Alburz, in the region of the railway from Tehrān to Bandar S͟hāh.

4 (*a*) Duplicated faulting in the region of Bīsitūn.

4 (*b*) The Gākūn region of southern Iran, showing a salt dome in the centre, with the axial part of a large syncline forming a distant mountain.

5   (a) A mud volcano of the viscous type.

5   (b) The cone of a mud volcano of the fluid type.

6 Photograph of Tang-i-Tāsar, in the Zagros, an ideal tang formation.

7 (a) A waste of "badlands" in the eastern Makrān.

7 (b) Wrinkled flysch at Kūh-i-Nārān in the eastern Makrān.

8 (*a*) Pillow lava in the flysch at Āb-i-Rāzī (Makrān region).

8 (*b*) The Kūh-i-Girīveh, near Pul-i-Kul in the Zagros Mountains: a mountain
preserved by an eroded syncline.

9 (*a*) A quartz porphyry plug called Mīl-i-Farhād extruded through
Tertiary sediments in the Makrān.

9 (*b*) "Schuppen" structures produced by strong shearing of beds of uneven
competence, at Sartap in the coastal Makrān.

10 (a) The north-east side of the Zagros Range at Du'l Qarīb, where upper limbs of folds have been thrust to the south-west and a vestige of the volcanic belt is exposed.

10 (b) Karaj town and the Alburz Range, looking northwards.

11   Mount Damāvand, Alburz Range.

12   (*a*) Outskirts of Iṣfahān: irrigation cultivation.

12   (*b*) Irrigated cultivation near Iṣfahān, showing a qanāt (centre foreground).

13   (a) Junction of the Sha<u>tt</u> al-'Arab, and the Kārūn River in the upper Gulf area above Ābādān.

13   (b) Gurgān (Māzandarān) showing typical house-type.

14   An ancient qanāt on the outskirts of Tehrān, now partially overrun
by suburban expansion.

15 (a) Deforestation on the northern Alburz slopes, Māzandarān province.

15 (b) Tehrān: a modern quarter.

16   The Royal Mosque at Iṣfahān, built by S̲h̲āh ʿAbbās I.

regions of accumulation, whose surrounding zones include extensively piled-up dunes, best developed in the southern portions. A special problem, however, would seem to present itself in the basin of Shāhdād, where a considerable accumulation of sand occurs, not in the south, but for the most part in the east. Here there are dark-coloured sands of an earlier period—these are to some extent differentiated by the partial occurrence of vegetational forms—which represent something completely different from the markedly restricted and definitely more recent lighter-coloured sands characteristic of the southern part of this basin. Since forms originating in remoter times can often be recognized in the inner desert basins, the question arises of the nature of the climate at these earlier periods.

As already mentioned, the kavīr zones have for long been regarded as evidence of a markedly wetter climate at an earlier geological period, for they seem to be the vestiges of once-extensive residual lakes, or possibly even the last stage in the drying up of one vast water surface that once included the whole region of the interior basins. But such a view of the effects produced by a pluvial phase in climate within the interior of Iran can definitely not be upheld, since the central desert areas never completely disappeared. What should be assumed is a contraction of arid areas during pluvial times, like that postulated for the Saharan desert belt. Bobek cannot accept this line of thought, since he rejects the assumption that there were one or more pluvial phases extending over the whole upland of Iran: however, the way seems to be opening towards some reconciliation of these opposing viewpoints.

Detailed studies of river terraces in the Kūh-i-Bīnālūd range of the north-eastern mountainous rim, as well as their dating and correlation with the numerous terraces occurring elsewhere in the hills surrounding the Iranian plateau, seem to affirm the existence of pluvial periods during the Pleistocene. On the basis of observations made and conclusions derived from these, it is possible to form an idea of the extent of regional variation in climate that occurred over the Iranian plateau during pluvial epochs. Basically there would seem to have existed, even during the cold or pluvial phases of the Pleistocene, a climatic zonation that corresponds broadly to modern conditions—i.e. there was a contrast between the cooler and damper surrounding hills, and the warmer, drier inner plateau. Hence increased rainfall occurred only on the hills, whereas the climate of the interior did not undergo any marked change, remaining apparently arid as before, though milder in its general characteristics.

Yet decisive morphological changes did in fact result from regional variation in climatic regime during the pluvial phases. Besides the formation of glaciers on the highest parts of the mountains, which led to the elaboration of surrounding glacial and periglacial zones, the greater rainfall over the entire mountain ring brought an increase in erosive activity and a consequent deepening of the valleys. The direct effects of increased precipitation during colder periods were confined to the mountainous zones; but since the overall flow of water from the mountains was increased, the ultimate effects reached far into the drier interior basins, which had relatively little rain and no emergent drainage. Therefore pluvial phases in the border mountain ranges of Iran always provoked a corresponding rise in river-flow in the interior— it was a time of higher river- and water-levels—and in this way large areas of the central inner basins became as it were drawn into a Pleistocene drainage pattern.

During pluvial phases there was additional outwash from the mountains, and the increased transportation power of the rivers, resulting from their greater volume, led to the accumulation of fluviatile material in the residual lakes within the desert basins. Whilst this was deposited with a force that is still partially observable today, there also occurred the removal of deposits that had formed on the valley bottoms on the upper courses of the streams. These deposits were a feature of drier phases, when the rivers' transportation power was insufficient to carry outwash very far into the foreland. Consequently, during arid intervals of the Pleistocene the accumulation of rock debris and pebbles was restricted to the bordering mountain ring and its valley floors, whilst deflation (removal of lighter deposits, such as silt and sand, by wind action) was then prevalent in the desert basins.

In conclusion, it can be seen that extended research within the Iranian massif might follow two related methods of approach: a specifically regional approach, linked with a consideration of the differences produced on surface morphology by overall fluctuations of climate. This research, whilst serving merely as a general preliminary view, could nevertheless offer a tenable first basis for further correlations. Geomorphological investigation thus has the task of elucidating and demonstrating on a regional basis the ebb and flow of process— glacial, periglacial, pluvial, fluviatile, and arid—which has produced the variety of land forms in Iran.

CHAPTER 4

THE ORIGIN OF THE ZAGROS
DEFILES

While the westward-flowing streams of the Zagros mountains provide some of the world's most impressive canyon scenery, they also present an extremely perplexing problem of drainage genesis. Transverse streams that seem unrelated to their geologic environment are rather characteristic of great mountain systems, but seldom are drainage anomalies as pronounced as they are among the great petrified waves of the Zagros, whose scanty vegetation and structural simplicity make every disharmony between structure and surface form conspicuous in the landscape. While the individual mountain ranges of this region are sundered indiscriminately by transverse streams that seem heedless of their presence, the morphology of the ranges in many cases exactly duplicates their tectonic structure. Thus we are presented in the Zagros with an unusual situation: the major land forms are structural, while the drainage lines, both major and minor, appear to disregard the geological environment altogether.

The disharmony between the drainage and the deformational pattern in the Zagros is manifested in the profound gorges, or *tangs*, which breach range after range in the youngest portion of the mountain system—a zone of powerful but rather simple anticlinal and synclinal deformation. The most typical tangs are extremely constricted slot-like defiles, 1,000 to 5,000 ft in depth, which split anticlinal mountains at any point from their culminations to their plunging extremities. The walls of such gorges rise perpendicularly from the rushing waters to heights of 200 to 1,000 ft or more, before falling back at slightly less precipitous angles; thus they bespeak strong recent incision by the streams flowing westward out of the Zagros. The configuration of the tangs has always interested travellers in the highlands, for the facing walls of a great number of the gorges are jagged and interlocking, giving the mountains the appearance of having been torn apart in some violent convulsion of the earth. Indeed, the first Western geologist to describe the Zagros surmised that the tangs were "due to the tension of the cooling mass at right angles to the axis of the chains in which they occur."[1] To many subsequent observers, direct tectonic movements of a more conventional nature have seemed the most satisfactory explanation of the tangs. These interpretations are based upon such morphological evidence as the sheerness of the tang walls, their fresh angular appearance, and the occasional "fit" of opposite faces.

In truth, the morphology of the tangs presents no real geomorphic problem. All of the transverse gorges cleave extremely youthful mountain ranges composed of limestone or calcareous conglomerate: materials susceptible to fluvial trenching and solution, but affected to a minimum degree by the more common processes of slope reduction. The effects on the same materials of a longer period of weathering, possibly under more humid conditions, may be seen in the older portions of the highland, which have not been subjected to strong post-Pliocene uplift and stream incision. In such areas the tangs are V-shaped and lack the slot-like lower storey that is an integral feature of canyons in the more unstable zones. Morphological analogues to the most constricted of the Zagros defiles may be seen in other parts of the world where the scenery is developed upon calcareous rocks upheaved during the later phases of the Alpine Revolution; the Dinaric ranges of Yugoslavia are an outstanding example.

Although the origin of tang morphology should no longer be in question, the drainage pattern in the strongly grained Zagros highland does present a genuine physiographic enigma: one all too common in mountain systems of a similar type, and one which can seldom be explained in a truly satisfactory manner. The genesis of drainage that runs transverse to fold-structures, although one of the more ubiquitous problems of geomorphology, has most often been attacked deductively. This constraint has been imposed by complexities of tectonic development and erosional history that are so monumental, even in the younger orogenic systems, that it is impossible to reconstruct with any degree of confidence the critical physiographic conditions prevailing during the earlier stages of orogenesis when drainage systems were being formed. Accordingly, anomalous drainage lines are usually dismissed as a heritage of some antecedant tectonic environment; as the result of superposition by unconformable cover-masses of which no traces remain; or as a product of headward stream extension under circumstances that are defined vaguely, if they are defined at all. The number

[1] W. K. Loftus, "On the Geology of the Turko-Persian Frontier, and of the Districts Adjoining", *Quarterly Journal of the Geological Society, London*, vol. XI (1855), p. 282.

of instances in which the operation of any of these processes can be proved conclusively are few indeed.

The uniqueness of the Zagros lies in the presence here of an exaggerated drainage anomaly that does not lend itself to explanation by these traditional hypotheses of transverse stream development, but which is singularly susceptible to the type of geomorphic analysis that can establish its origin beyond doubt. Fundamental to such an analysis is the possibility of reconstructing the former landscapes of those areas in which drainage anomalies presently occur. The tectonic and physiographic youth and simplicity of the Zagros allow us to make such reconstructions, for in this highland large areas still display the rarely seen initial physiographic conditions associated with strong deformational movements. Moreover, this area presents us with a matchless sequence of erosional landscapes illustrating each successive stage in the evolution of a thorough discordance between stream pattern and tectonic structure.

THE SETTING

The vast majority of the drainage anomalies and the most spectacular tangs in the Zagros are found in the zone of powerful but simple folding along the south-western (outer) margin of the highland. Nowhere on earth have large tectonic structures been formed more recently than here. At the same time this zone exhibits as great a discordance between drainage and geological structure as has been discovered in any mountain complex regardless of age or character. Recent investigation in the central portion of the Zagros (fig. 63) has revealed that in an area of 25,000 square miles large and small streams have effected some 300 full transections of anticlinal structures.[1] All significant drainage lines in this region incorporate important transverse components; and, as fig. 64 indicates, some of the trunk streams are discordant to structure almost throughout.

The major physiographic contrasts in the outer Zagros depend upon the tectonic development of the fold-system subsequent to the main Late Pliocene compression. Areas that remain unaffected by post-Pliocene uplift preserve intact anticlines with cleanly stripped cara-

[1] T. M. Oberlander, *The Zagros Streams* (Syracuse University Press, 1965). The area studied consisted of the mountain catchments of the Karkheh, Dīz, Kārūn, Jarrāhī, and Hīndīān [Hindījān] rivers. The simply folded zone, in which most drainage anomalies occur, comprises only about half of the total area of these watersheds.

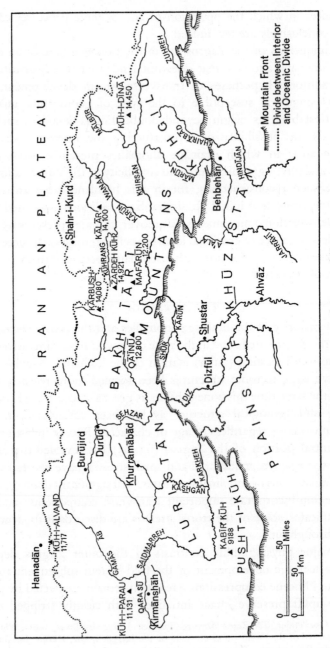

Fig. 63. Location map of the central Zagros.

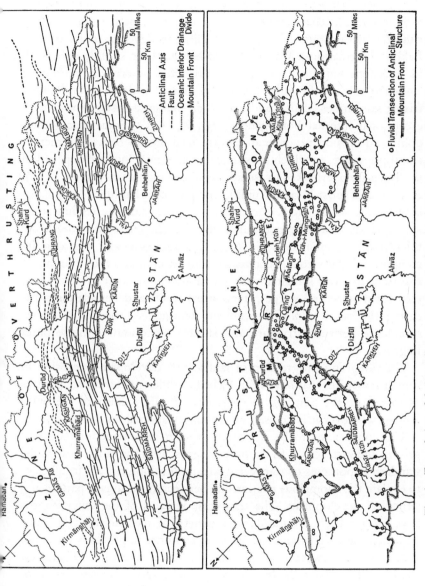

Fig. 64. *Top*, relation of drainage lines to structure in the central Zagros. *Bottom*, distribution of anticlinal transections in the central Zagros.

199

paces of the Oligocene–Miocene Asmari Limestone, well known as the producing horizon in the oilfields of south-western Iran. (fig. 65, *BB'* and *EE'*). These arches rise as much as 2,000 ft from synclines cluttered with Upper Miocene and Pliocene deposits (the Fars and Bakhtiari formations). Where the fold-belt has been slightly upheaved, its limestone anticlines are partially unroofed by erosion, producing lenticular subsequent valleys excavated in a great depth of underlying friable sandstones, shales, and marls—an immense flysch deposit with exceptional internal homogeneity (fig. 65, *AA'*). Somewhat greater uplift and erosion produce an inverse relationship between structure and topography, in which anastomosing anticlinal lowlands opened in the flysch are overlooked by isolated synclinal mountains (fig. 65, *AA'*). A centre of post-Pliocene uplift, such as the Ba<u>kh</u>tīārī mountains between the Sehzar and Kārūn rivers, is a sea of sharp-crested limestone anticlines that have been exhumed by denudation from beneath the thick flysch accumulation (fig. 65, *CC'*). The ranges of this area are composed of Mesozoic (Cenomanian) limestones, and they commonly rise 5,000 ft above synclinal valleys that are compressed so tightly that they form structural gorges. Thus great uplift and denudation post-dating the main folding movements re-establish the initial correspondence between structure and surface configuration in the outer Zagros.

The foregoing progression of landscapes, developed by erosion in similar structures that have been arched to different elevations, permits us to restore the past and to project the future scenery of the outer Zagros wherever it is crossed by seemingly anomalous drainage lines.

The conclusions to be drawn from such reconstructions are surprising and instructive. In the outer Zagros, as in the range as a whole, standard hypotheses of transverse stream development are insufficient to explain the anomalous relationship between the drainage pattern and structural development. The transverse streams of the outer Zagros have clearly been produced by a variety of mechanisms, the most important of which seems to have escaped notice in previous studies of disharmonies between drainage and geological structure. Of greatest significance, perhaps, is the discovery that a particular association of structure and lithology in the outer Zagros inevitably gives rise to drainage transverse to the orogenic system, producing wholesale transection of anticlinal structures and an astonishing number of gorges of the type hitherto attributed to regional drainage antecendence

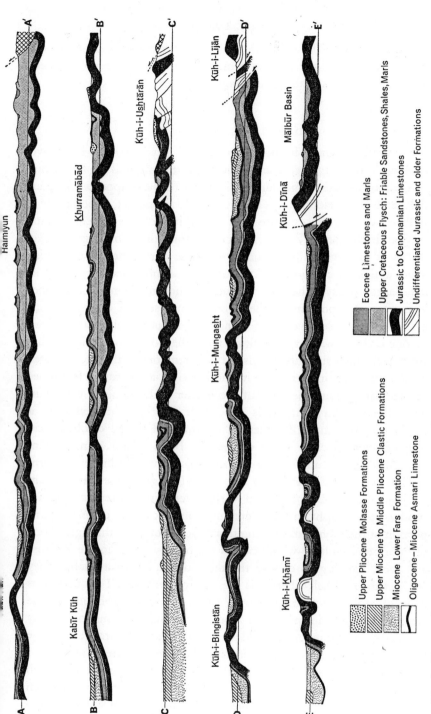

Haimyun

A'

Kabīr Kūh

Khurramābād

B'

Kūh-i-Ushtārān

C'

Kūh-i-Bingistān

Kūh-i-Mungasht

Kūh-i-Lijān

D'

Kūh-i-Khāmī

Kūh-i-Dīnā

Mālbūr Basin

E'

A

B

C

D

E

Eocene Limestones and Marls

Upper Cretaceous Flysch: Friable Sandstones, Shales, Marls

Jurassic to Cenomanian Limestones

Undifferentiated Jurassic and older Formations

Upper Pliocene Molasse Formations

Upper Miocene to Middle Pliocene Clastic Formations

Miocene Lower Fars Formation

Oligocene–Miocene Asmari Limestone

Fig. 65. Cross-sections through representative portions of the fold zone of the central Zagros. Length of each section approximately 76 miles. The horizontal and vertical scales are equal. The horizontal line represents sea level.

201

or superposition. The requisite geological environment is one of the most ubiquitous in the Tertiary mountain systems of the globe, where unexplained drainage anomalies abound.

DRAINAGE ANOMALIES

The drainage anomaly in the central Zagros may be resolved into two distinct problems: the courses of the trunk streams, and the behaviour of their tributaries, large and small. Each of these appears to be an independent development. The tributary drainage net, superficially a trellis-system, produces more than two thirds of the anticlinal transections in the central Zagros, and creates some of the most spectacular defiles in the region. The majority of these gorges breach otherwise intact anticlines composed of the uppermost limestones deposited in the Zagros geosyncline: the Oligocene–Miocene Asmari Limestone. Transverse components of the tributary net seldom extend twenty miles across the strike of the folding, and are ordinarily characterized by one or more 90° turns resulting from their deflexion by individual anticlines. Many such diversions are only temporary; the streams later breach the deflecting structure in another right-angle turn a few miles downstream, where the crest of the barrier is declining in elevation. Thus the tributary pattern is one of transection and deflexion, a bewildering mélange of structural control and fluvial disobedience. The principal streams south of the Diz Basin—the Kārūn, Mārūn, Khairābād, and Zuhreh rivers—share this general tributary pattern.

The five trunk streams of the central Zagros, the Saidmarreh, Kashgān, Sehzar, Bakhtīārī, and Kārūn rivers, rise in a region of rather subdued topography in the overthrust complex of the older (eastern) portion of the highland. Leaving this region they twist through a zone of imbricated faulting which carries the highest peaks in the Zagros; and then, seeming to choose the most difficult path available, they transect the fold-belt where it is most fully developed. They cross this zone of violent deformation by a series of zig-zags oblique to the structural trend, in profound gorges cleaving swarms of closely jammed anticlinal ranges of hard Mesozoic limestones—ranges that the streams appear to seek out. Where these belligerent torrents are turned into synclinal paths, it is only so that they may approach and breach an anticline nearer to its culmination. They consistently ignore open structural paths around fold-noses and through natural spillways, and often turn away when continuation of their previous line threatens to bring them free of a mountain group. Thus the major drainage lines of the central Zagros display a conspicuously rhomboidal pattern that largely coincides with the pattern of transverse structural culminations produced by adjacent sheaves of resurrected *en échelon* folds.

The drainage anomalies of the central Zagros cannot be attributed to regional drainage antecedent to superposition by an unconformable cover-mass. The pattern of course deflexions and structural control at the boundaries of the adjacent tectonic divisions of the highland indicate that the drainage of each successively younger zone is autogenous. The major structural complexes appear to have arisen from a marine environment as island archipelagos, precluding antecedent transverse drainage. A lack of summit accordance, and of any trace of regional erosion surfaces in the portions of the highland characterized by drainage anomalies, both frustrate any attempt to attribute the transverse drainage to superposition from some type of "surface". Local unconformable cover-masses of orogenic deposits, which would seem to be possible sources of drainage anomalies, are found to have been laid down by former synclinal streams perpendicular to those now transecting them.

THE TRIBUTARIES

The question of drainage anomalies created by streams extending less than twenty miles across the strike of the folding is best resolved by observing processes that affect the landscape of the outer Zagros at present. Drainage anomalies of this type are being initiated today. Most of them involve either local drainage antecedence or local stream superposition from disharmonically folded orogenic deposits.

Above the Asmari Limestone, the final layer of limestones deposited in the Zagros geosyncline, several thousand feet of marls and evaporites collected throughout the Later Miocene. This formation, the rainbow-hued Lower Fars series, behaved as an incompetent mass during the Pliocene folding, sagging off the developing anticlines and accumulating in the deepening synclines of the western half of the fold-belt. The intricate deformation of this material bears no relation to that of the underlying limestones, which are folded into relatively simple anticlines and synclines with local amplitudes of 5,000 to 20,000 ft. Sands and gravels (the Upper Fars and Bakhtiārī formations) were distributed over the surface of the Lower Fars accumulation by streams running off the emerging relief. Eventually this drainage was super-imposed upon limestone anticlinal crests that were developing under the plastic Lower Fars mass without permanent surface expression. Thus streams rising on slightly higher limestone anticlines could be superimposed upon coeval folds of lesser elevation that were more deeply buried under the disharmonically folded cover of clastic sediments. Such drainage would have been antecedent, not to the formation of these arches, but to their exhumation. The resulting drainage pattern is consequent upon the pattern of larger anticlines; and it is disharmonic to ridges only slightly inferior in size, as well as to the more recently exhumed plunging termini of the larger folds themselves.

Exhumation of limestone anticlines and superposition of drainage from their clastic cover are a continuing process, and can be witnessed today on the north-east side of the lower Saidmarreh valley, where the crests of a number of arches are being uncovered and incised by inter-mittent streams superimposed from the Lower Fars mass. In the area of Behbehān, table mountains composed of the Fars mass capped by Pliocene gravels stand 3,000 ft above the current base of erosion, and as much as 1,000 ft above adjacent limestone anticlines that are breached by undeviating transverse streams, including the through-flowing Mārūn, Khairābād, and Zuhreh rivers.

Local drainage antecedence, unassisted by superposition, has also been an important source of transverse gorges in the tributary stream network of the central Zagros. The anticlinal structures of the fold zone were clearly not all thrown up simultaneously. Certain arches dominate the fold zone, being both higher and longitudinally more persistent than their neighbours. Among these are Kabīr Kūh, Kūh-i-Mungasht, and Kūh-i-Mafārūn. Such structures are more complex and much more severely denuded than somewhat smaller adjacent anticlines, and it can be shown stratigraphically that they pre-date the inferior arches, some having been expressed as submarine ridges as early as Eocene time. Lesser anticlines in the vicinity of these snow-capped primary ranges are highly segmented by transverse streams that originate in deep canyons within the primary ranges. The transecting streams are un-questionably antecedent to the formation of the secondary ranges, which they breach without deviating from their original paths off the flanks of the great arches. By effecting transections of secondary anticlines in some regions, superposition from clastic formations may have supplemented local drainage antecedence; but numerous tangs attributable to such transection are found in areas that were never covered by a great depth of the disharmonically folded Lower Fars series.

Stream superposition from the Lower Fars series, together with local drainage antecedence, account for about half of the anticlinal transections in the central Zagros. Another fifteen per cent of the drainage anomalies in the region are attributable to headward extension of consequent gullies. Transections resulting from headward gullying by autogenetic streams are facilitated, first, by the rapid erosion of the flysch mass interposed between the resistant Asmari and Cenomanian limestones; and second, by disparate elevations of adjacent synclinal troughs in the fold zone. The latter condition allows lateral tributaries of deep synclines to extend across anticlinal axes, eventually undercutting the synclines on the far sides of such arches. Incipient captures by headward-extending gullies are rife among the narrow, strongly dissected anticlines of the Kūhgīlūyeh area south of the Kārūn river.

THE TRUNK STREAMS

The Kārūn river incorporates several reaches that became discordant because disharmonically folded orogenic deposits were superposed upon them; but only the terminal reaches of the other great through-flowing streams of the central Zagros may be explained in terms of the processes mentioned above.

Though the physiographic environments of the trunk streams north-west of the Kārūn bear little resemblance to one another at present, the courses of all of these streams, as well as those of their major tributaries, have identical structural environments. In the fold-belt they all follow transverse culminations—these being created by local *en échelon* fold-patterns. Two of the streams, the Sehzar (Diz) and its affluent the Bakhtīārī (Zalīkī, Darreh Qīyād), each flow about sixty miles through a continuous series of awesome chasms, 3,000 to 8,000 ft in depth. These gorges sunder lofty anticlinal ranges resurrected on Mesozoic limestones after a long period of relief inversion. The middle Saidmarreh river, by contrast, traverses a series of open lowlands overlooked by isolated synclinal ranges. The fourth stream, the Kashgān, is the key to the evolution of transverse drainage in this area. It is channelled through six barely contiguous axial basins in unroofed anticlines that originally had carapaces of the Asmari Limestone. Each of the four through-flowing streams of the area thus links several series of major anticlinal structures that are tangent laterally with *en échelon* dispositions. These anticlines are either unroofed negative forms, or positive features resurrected, by the exposure of deep resistant layers. All are undergoing or have passed through a period of relief inversion.

The different landscapes crossed by these individual through-flowing streams are models of progressive stages in the development of a seemingly anomalous transverse drainage; in fact, this drainage is the inevitable result of normal erosion in the given structural–lithological environment. The essential features of this environment are: dense *en échelon* folding with local variability in the level of synclinal troughs; and a stratigraphic succession including an accumulation of several thousand feet of erodible flysch deposits interposed between more durable limestones. To geologists this combination of circumstances is rather common throughout the Alpine system from Morocco to Assam —an area in which seemingly inexplicable transverse streams are almost without number.

ORIGIN OF THE TRUNK STREAMS

The principal through-flowing streams of the Zagros north-west of the Kārūn river appear to have originated during a period of relief inversion in the Zagros. As shown by their location with relation to local geological structures and present and past lithological outcrops, these streams were initiated as subsequent streams that followed exposures of weak rocks extending *across* the deformational strike. *En échelon* folding determined the location of the transverse streams by lifting easily eroded materials (under the Asmari Limestone cap-rock) to high elevations in zones oblique to the general structural trend. Several thousand feet of easily eroded flysch underlay the limestone envelopes of the folds, and this facilitated the rapid excavation of axial basins in *en échelon*, whale-backed anticlines, which were undergoing normal erosion by consequent runoff. The close packing of the folds, their *en échelon* dispositions, and variations in the elevations of the synclines to which axial-basin runoff was tributary, all meant that axial basins tributary to lower synclines could expand laterally to undercut adjacent higher synclines. Thus separate tiers of anticlinal basins were merged, creating compound subsequent basins extending diagonally across the fold-belt. Transverse subsequent lowlands of this type may be seen in the basin of the Karkheh river today. These large hollows of non-resistant flysch deposits are overlooked on either side by cuspate limestone hog-backs, which are constantly in retreat as a result of spring-line sapping at their base. Where the thickness of the soft materials has exceeded the amplitude of the folding, extensive subsequent basins composed of many lateral anticlinal structures were gradually occupied by through-flowing drainage systems, whose extension was completed before denudation could expose the hard Mesozoic limestones underlying the flysch accumulation.

The Kashgān river (Karkheh basin), a stream whose extension has only recently been completed in this manner, links oval subsequent basins that look like beads on a string. The Saidmarreh river (Karkheh basin) illustrates a more advanced development, in which the separate anticlinal basins have almost lost their identity in compound subsequent lowlands. The Sehzar and Bakhtīārī rivers (Diz Basin) developed in the same manner. Their present spectacular entrenchment in swarms of anticlinal mountain ranges is the result of post-Pliocene uplift of some 6,000 ft in the Bakhtīārī mountains between the Kashgān and Mārūn rivers. This massive uplift superposed the transverse subsequent Sehzar and Bakhtīārī rivers upon the strongly folded and resistant Mesozoic limestones that underlay the transverse flysch lowlands. Figure 66 summarizes the evolution of the resulting drainage anomaly.

Broad uplift of the regions crossed by the Saidmarreh and the Kashgān rivers would produce spectacular drainage anomalies similar to those of the Bakhtīārī mountains, for these streams are at present suspended, in their medium of flysch materials, exactly over the Mesozoic limestone crests of the major anticlinal clusters north-west of those transected by the Sehzar. In the floors of four separate anticlinal valleys, the Saidmarreh and Kashgān rivers have already exhumed the crests of Mesozoic limestone arches (as in fig. 66). The streams were sufficiently entrenched in the flysch so that exposure of the harder limestones has not caused a shift in their channels. Rather, they have incised the hard rocks, thereby fixing their courses transverse to the future mountain ranges of Luristān.

Several facts indicate that the system of *en échelon* axial basins is responsible for the development of transverse drainage, rather than the reverse. The consistent association of through-flowing streams and transverse culminations in the fold-belt, shows that the streams are structurally controlled, though hardly in the usual sense. Large axial

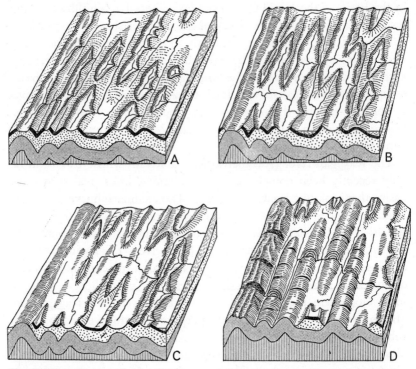

Fig. 66. Generalized evolution of transverse drainage associated with relief inversion in simple folds.

A. Anticlines being unroofed in initial phase of denudation. Major drainage lines follow structural routes. Anticlinal valleys enlarge by cliff recession controlled by spring-line sapping at the base of the upper limestone (*black*).

B. Expanding anticlinal valleys excavated in soft materials (*stippled*) merge, undercutting former consequent streams and producing compound subsequent valleys occupied by streams adjusted to lithology rather than tectonic structure. Soft materials are of sufficient depth so that adjacent subsequent basins coalesce before the centres of hard subjacent rocks are exposed.

C. Continued scarp retreat produces full relief inversion. Outcrops of non-resistant materials are continuous across the strike to the ridge on the left, and are drained by abstracted through-flowing subsequent streams that are transverse to the trend of the folds. Strips of hard rock begin to appear in the centres of those anticlinal basins, which are excavated through the full depth of soft materials. The syncline on the right is still intact and continues to function as a drainage conduit.

D. Continued uplift and denudation resurrect anticlinal mountains through erosional stripping of the mass of soft beds overlying the resistant subjacent formations (*toned*). Transverse subsequent streams superimposed upon the crests of hard-rock arches now produce transverse gorges through the anticlinal ranges. Large arch to left covered by erodable materials of insufficient depth to produce relief inversion prior to exposure of lower, resistant formation. Thus this range is not crossed by autogenic transverse drainage.

basins and embryonic transverse subsequent lowlands occur in areas not yet characterized by unified through-flowing drainage systems, thus the establishment of transverse streams is a gradual process of "capture" involving piracies between neighbouring subsequent stream systems. The varying orientations of the transverse reaches in successive anticlinal transections suggest an autogenic origin for each drainage anomaly.

The role of the Upper Cretaceous–Eocene flysch in the development of the transverse drainage is clear and consistent. Through-flowing transverse streams are found in every area in which the original depth of the flysch was of a greater magnitude than the amplitude of the folding, and in those areas only. Where the flysch was poorly developed, bringing the feature-forming limestones sufficiently close to one another to preclude large-scale relief inversion, all transverse reaches are demonstrably the result of local drainage antecedence, of superposition from orogenic sediments, or of headward extension; and no continuously anomalous reaches are present. This is the dominant condition south and east of the Bakhtīārī river—except in the basin of the Mālbūr river, where a flysch basin reappears and central transections of resurrected anticlines are once more conspicuous.

It is of extreme significance that transverse streams seemingly attracted to transections of resurrected anticlines are found in *every* region of the Zagros in which the original depth of the flysch accumulation exceeded local fold amplitudes. This unvarying relationship would appear to have implications beyond the Zagros region, for the combination of geological structure and lithology that has unfailingly produced transverse drainage involving successive anticlinal transections is common throughout the Alpine system in Europe and Asia. *En échelon* folding has affected immense masses of relatively easily erodible flysch sediments interbedded with more resistant materials in many older mountain systems as well. The development of more complex tectonic structures accompanying continued orogeny would tend to obscure the simple original relationship between structure and drainage that can be demonstrated in the Zagros. However, through-flowing streams, once fixed, will probably persist throughout continued deformation unless new patterns of highly erodible materials are bared deeper in the tectonic edifice. In this latter case adjustments similar to those sketched above should recur, with the transverse drainage lines continuing to be attracted to transverse structural culminations wherever they appear in conjunction with a critical thickness of erodible materials.

Hamadān
Shahr-i-Kurd
GAMĀS ĀB
QARA SŪ
Kirmānshāh
SAIDMARREH
KASHGĀN
KARKHEH
SEHZAR
BAKHTIARI
SHŪR
KĀRŪN
Dizfūl
DIZ
KARKHEH
Shustar
Ahvāz
MALBŪR
KHIRSĀN
MĀRŪN
Behbehān
HINDIJĀN
KHAIRABAD
ZUHREH
N
0 50 Miles
0 50 Km
● Reach developed in transverse subsequent valley, later superimposed upon adjacent resistant formations.
▿ Reach antecedent to structure.
o Reach superimposed from disharmoniously folded overburden.
x Reach extended headward across anticlinal axis.
? Origin of transverse reach undetermined due to lack of information on local geology.

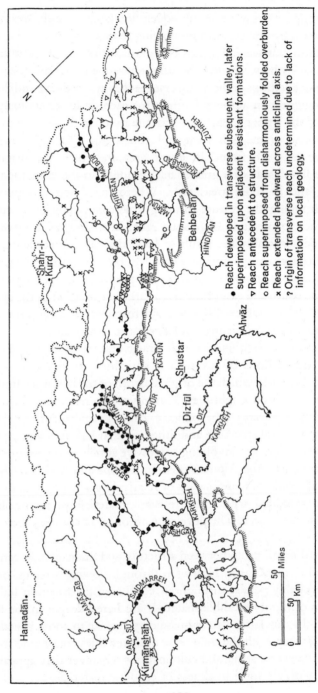

Fig. 67. Origin of anomalous transverse stream reaches in the central Zagros. Undifferentiated transverse reaches are channeled by structure or outcrops of erodable materials.

SUMMARY

Figure 67 summarizes the origin of transverse stream reaches and tangs in the central Zagros. The salient points from this figure are: first, drainage anomalies expressed almost identically in the landscape have originated simultaneously in a number of different ways; second, the through-flowing streams that cross the fold-belt most directly are of autogenic origin almost throughout, having developed in a simple logical manner not previously recognized in studies of drainage anomalies around the world; and third, despite the multitude and pattern of transverse defiles that so strongly suggest an allogenic origin for much of the region's drainage, neither regional stream antecedence nor superposition of drainage from an unconformable cover-mass have been significant in the genesis of the major transverse streams of the central Zagros.

CHAPTER 5

CLIMATE

INTRODUCTION

As with many other countries of the world, Iran is somewhat unfortunate in having recorded no long-term climatic observations. Climatic studies and observations are usually stimulated either by scientific interest or practical necessity; and whilst the weather exerts a decisive influence on nearly all phases of human activities, it is particularly in the fields of agriculture and aviation that a sound meteorological knowledge becomes essential, both for long-term planning as well as for day-to-day operations. Here it must be admitted, with regret, that until the World War II years, neither of the above incentives to meteorological studies received much attention in Iran. In the early years of the war, however, the country became a vital area, considered by the Allies the "Bridge of Victory" for the transport of essential wartime supplies to Russia. Roads had to be built under various climatic conditions, and traffic maintained in all kinds of weather. Soon a network of airways was established all over the country, and it was not long before Tehrān became the largest and most strategic air base of the Middle East. Then came the wartime food shortages and famines all over the Middle East, particularly in Iran where there occurred successive years of drought and crop failure. The country was made as self-supporting as possible. Consequently a great deal of attention was focused on its agricultural potentialities, the assessment of which required adequate knowledge of climatic conditions. A number of research projects were introduced and put into operation, and so a new movement began in the field of climatic studies.

In 1948 the Iranian government adopted its first Seven Year Economic Development Plan, and the help of foreign advisors was sought in making necessary surveys. The great importance of meteorological observations for agriculture and aviation was pointed out with due emphasis by various groups of consultants. The Plan Organization of Iran, a very effective body in financing the country's various economic projects, became interested in the subject of meteorology and sponsored a long-term project for its development.

Until that time the Iranian Ministry of Agriculture had been in charge of collecting climatic data from a number of stations in provincial centres. The stations of this ministry were increased in number, modernized in equipment, and to a certain extent staffed with better-trained observers. In addition a Department of Civil Aviation was created, and the existing airports classified according to their landing facilities and observational equipment.

The International Civil Aviation Organization, of which Iran has long been a member, offered technical help, and in 1951 three experienced Norwegian meteorologists were placed at the disposal of the Iranian government. A new era in the history of Iran's meteorological studies was thus opened and a sound start made under the supervision of U.N. advisors. The great necessity for co-ordinating activities was recognized in 1953, when a meteorological council, consisting of representatives of all interested government agencies, was formed under the authority of a decree by the council of ministers. The main object of this council was to make necessary preparations for the creation of the Iranian Meteorological Department, within the framework of the Ministry of Roads and Communication. The council received assistance from the World Meteorological Organization; and finally, in February 1956, the meteorological department was formed by virtue of a governmental decree, though it was not until March 1957 that it was firmly fixed by an act of parliament.

Once created, the department was able to implement a large number of development projects with the financial help of the Plan Organization and the technical assistance of the World Meteorological Organization. Between 1956 and 1964 the new department centralized within itself all the country's meteorological activities, and gathered together existing files and records. It then devoted its efforts to building up various meteorological networks, training technical staff, and processing the past data. By early 1965 the department operated some 400 stations, comprising:

4 Radar wind-finding stations,	44 Synoptic stations,
4 Radiosonde stations,	140 Climatological stations,
8 Pilot balloon stations,	200 Rain-gauge stations.

Their distribution throughout the country is shown in fig. 68.

It is on the basis of all existing records (especially those of the past fifteen years) available in the archives of the Iranian Meteorological Department that the following account has been compiled.

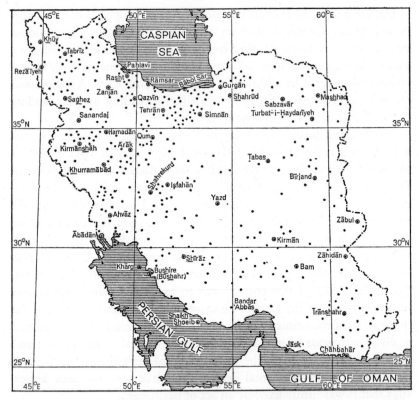

Fig. 68. Distribution of meteorological stations in Iran, May 1964. Only those stations included in the synoptic network have been named.

PRESSURE AND WINDS

Winter pressure conditions

During the cold winter months there develops over the interior of Asia a high-pressure belt, which results from the intensive cooling of a vast continent. Pressure is very high over Siberia (reaching 1,035 millibars), but it decreases outward in all directions. The winter high-pressure belt, however, is not a continuous one. Some outlying portions of this belt extend westward over the northern Caspian regions into Europe, and other tongues of high pressure exist on the Armenian and Anatolian plateaux. The interior of the Iranian plateau, too, is usually covered with a local centre of high pressure during the winter months.

In contrast with these centres of high pressure, there are a number of lows that also influence the climate of Iran. To the north there is a

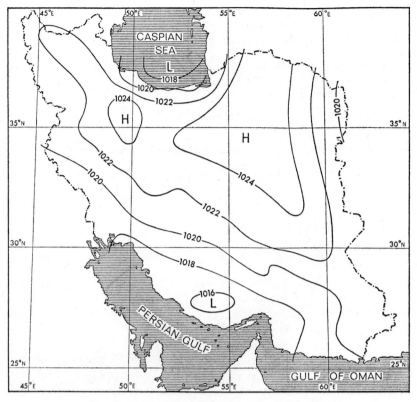

Fig. 69. Mean sea level pressure for January (in mb).

relatively low centre over the warm waters of the Caspian Sea. Farther west the effect of the Mediterranean Sea is to produce a zone of warmth surrounded by colder lands on all sides. Pressure over this large sea is therefore low, and it is in the eastern parts of this sea, namely in the neighbourhood of Cyprus, that a semi-permanent low centre of considerable importance exists. Other centres of barometric minima can be observed over the Persian Gulf and the Gulf of Oman.

Lying within this Middle Eastern pattern of pressure systems, Iran may be said to have a pressure field in winter that declines in intensity from north to south, as can be seen from fig. 69.

With the onset of spring in the northern hemisphere, the interior of Iran warms up rapidly, and by May the summer pressure pattern is fairly well established.

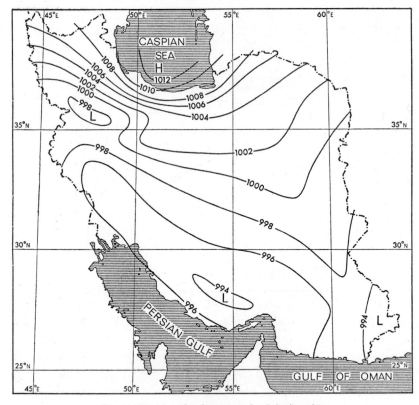

Fig. 70. Mean sea level pressure for July (in mb).

Summer pressure conditions

The general isobar pattern is almost the same in summer as in winter, except that the pressure centres and the gradient of isobars differ from one season to the other. Cooler air over the Caspian Sea causes relatively high pressure in this part of the country. In the south the excessive heating of the land produces one of the lowest thermal pressure centres in the world, within which the average pressure may amount to less than 994 mb. In winter the centre of this low is 20 mb higher: i.e. about 1,014 mb on average.

One interesting point about the pressure systems of Iran is that, contrary to conditions in certain other parts of the world, the pressure gradient increases in the summer. This is one of the main reasons for the strong winds that prevail in eastern parts of the country during the summertime. The mean difference of pressure between the south and the north of the country is 12 mb in winter and 18 mb in summer, with the higher pressure occurring in the north. Figure 70 shows the general distribution of pressure over Iran during the summer months.

As indicated by the winter pressure pattern over much of Iran, throughout the cold months the winds tend to blow consistently from the east or the north-east. This is because in the winter months there is a well-established and vigorous north-easterly stream of polar continental air over parts of the Iranian plateau. However, it should not be thought that the easterly or north-easterly winds of Central Asia are dominant at all times during the winter season. Frequently masses of relatively warm and moist (i.e. maritime) air from the Mediterranean break through over the Iranian plateau, not only raising the temperature conditions but also bringing rainfall and hence life to the country. The western half of Iran is more influenced by these western depressions; and in addition, masses of cold air reach it from the north-west, in the rear of eastward-moving depressions. Consequently the prevailing winds during the cold season in this part of the country are northerlies —sometimes from west of north, sometimes from east of north.

During the summer months the winds of Iran are dominated by the Indian monsoon system. However, in contrast with true monsoon areas, Iran experiences no reversal of wind direction from winter to summer, because higher pressure prevails in the north at all seasons, with a centre lying to the north-east in winter and to the north-west in summer. Summer wind directions over most of Iran are again more or less from the north or north-west, but topography and the nature of the terrain play a great part in modifying this general picture and in determining the actual directions of the local winds. Figure 71 shows winter and summer streamlines.

Local winds

In a country like Iran, where extensive flat deserts, highly complex mountain systems, closed basins, long valleys, coastal plains, lakes, and seas all lie in juxtaposition to one another, topography is a major modifying factor and surface winds are, almost in all cases, greatly influenced by local topographical features.

Over the mountainous regions winds are extremely variable and

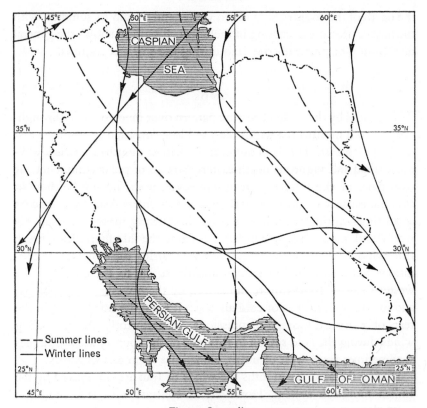

Fig. 71. Streamlines.

greatly influenced by topography. In the narrow mountain valleys, however, they tend merely to alternate in the two opposite directions that are determined by topography: thus "up and down" flows are a common feature of all such valleys. During the day, as would be expected, winds blow up valley, but as soon as the sun sets and the air on the higher levels is chilled, a down-valley flow of cold dense air sets in.

The air streams that cross the high ranges of Alburz and Zagros produce considerable "föhn" effects over the Caspian Sea littoral zone, as well as within the interior of the country and over the Mesopotamian lowlands. On the other hand, *bora* (i.e. katabatic) winds occasionally descend from the Alburz to bring cold waves over the flat deserts to the south. Similarly, down-slope winds of the bora type sometimes flow off the Zagros ranges into the coastal areas of the Persian Gulf.

The *sirocco* or *khamsin* of the Mediterranean have no real counterpart in Iran. However, along the northern shores of the Persian Gulf, and particularly in Khūzistān, a south-westerly warm wind that has its origin in Saudi Arabia blows occasionally during the cold months with gale force; but unlike the sirocco of the southern Mediterranean region, it brings a good deal of moisture because of its passage over the Persian Gulf.

In the mountainous areas the canalization of the air-stream in narrow mountain valleys and gorges causes unexpectedly strong winds in certain localities. This phenomenon is best exemplified in Manjīl (lat. 36° 37′ N.; long. 49° 31′ E.), where the Safīd Rūd valley provides a channel between the pressure system of the Caspian Sea and that of the interior.

Over the flat and barren lands of the interior of Iran, eddies and squalls are of common occurrence, especially in the hot afternoons when strongly heated air near the ground rises in funnel-shaped dust currents.

Land and sea breezes are common over the coastal areas, but because of the nature of the terrain their effect is closely restricted to the narrow littoral zones. Along the southern shores of the Caspian, where there is a general combination of moisture and high temperature in summer, the night winds blowing off-shore mingle with and are reinforced by cool and dry down-valley currents originating in the Alburz ranges behind the coast. The effect is to bring considerable relief to the inhabitants.

Along the Persian Gulf coast, on-shore winds are accompanied by great humidity, which, when combined with excessive temperature, produces considerable discomfort. The shores of the Persian Gulf have gained a bad reputation among the mariners, and have been called "hell's kitchen", and the like, by those who have suffered the nearly unbearable conditions found there.

Of all the local winds that blow over Iran during the summer months, two are very well known: the *shamāl* of the Persian Gulf coast and the Wind of 120 Days in Sīstān. Both these winds result directly from the prevalence of low pressure centred over West Pakistan, and both become strongly established currents during the dominance of this low pressure. The Shamāl is a north-westerly wind (*shamāl* means north) that blows down the valley of the Tigris and Euphrates; it affects the head and coastal areas of the Persian Gulf from February to October, though its greatest intensity and steadiness are during the hottest summer months. The Wind of 120 Days blows during May to September from the north-west with great regularity, steadiness, and sometimes violence. The wind normally begins towards the end of May. Actually the local inhabitants expect its commencement two months after the Iranian New Year, i.e. about sixty days after the spring equinox. The direction of this wind appears fairly constant, and although its speed varies, it does not often exceed 65 or 70 miles per hour.

TEMPERATURE

A fundamental climatic control in any part of the world is that exerted by latitude, for latitude determines the amount of heat received directly from the sun in the form of radiant energy. Iran is situated wholly within the extra-tropical warm temperate belt, since the southernmost portion of Iranian territory on the Gulf of Oman, slightly to the west of the port of Gwadar, in Pakistan, is located a short distance north of the Tropic of Cancer. Northward, Iran extends almost to the fortieth parallel.

Next to latitude, altitude is the most important control in the distribution of temperature. As already indicated, Iran is a plateau country of considerable elevation, in which the total area of land below 1,500 ft altitude constitutes a small portion of the total land surface: in fact, it is limited to very narrow coastal plains. Of the total surface area of Iran, no less than 103,000 square miles, or about one sixth, has an elevation exceeding 6,500 ft above sea-level.

In Iran, because of the special disposition of the mountain ranges, the influences of the seas tend to be limited to their immediate neighbourhood, and it is seldom that maritime areas play an important part in controlling temperature other than within narrow coastal strips.

There is one more fact that deserves special attention in this brief survey of general temperature control. From time to time, the country is exposed to the movement of air masses that originate in distant places and are therefore initially of totally different temperatures from those prevailing in Iran. Such air masses can exert a great influence on the pattern of temperature distribution within Iran, more especially during the winter season when the local effects due to insolation are relatively weak. "Imported" temperature is therefore in large measure responsible for the actual distribution of temperature over Iran. This is best observed when the country is invaded by cold continental air from the heart of Asia, but warm air can also flow in from outside in summer.

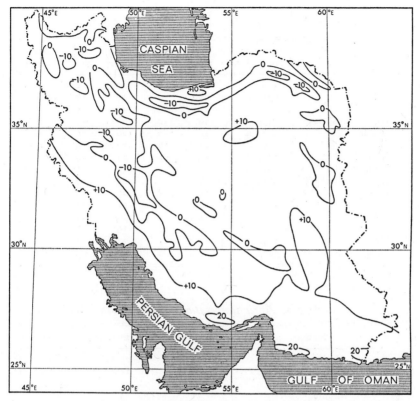

Fig. 72. Mean daily temperature for January (° C).

January temperature conditions

Figure 72 shows the average January temperatures within Iran. Except in the narrow coastal region of the Caspian Sea, January is everywhere the coldest month of the year in Iran. Mean monthly temperatures vary from 20° C in S.E. Iran to less than − 10° C in some of the higher stations in Āzarbāījān.

January is the month when most of the absolute minima are recorded at many stations, and table 1 below illustrates conditions prevailing in some representative localities.

April temperature conditions

Except along the southern shores of the Caspian Sea, where the annual minima are reached in February, the passing of January marks the beginning of a warming up of the land, a process that continues until

TABLE I. *January temperatures at selected stations*

Station	Elevation above sea-level	Av. max.*	Av. min.	Abs. max.†	Abs. min.	Mean monthly
Ābādān	3 m	19° C	7° C	27° C	−4° C	13° C
Arāk	1752 m	45	−5	17	−25	0
Bandar 'Abbās	6 m	23	14	30	5	19
Bushire [Būshahr]	14 m	19	10	28	−1	15
Iṣfahān	1590 m	10	−2	20	−16	4
Jāsk	4 m	24	16	29	9	20
Kirmān	1749 m	13	−1	24	−24	6
Kirmānshāh	1322 m	8	−4	19	−21	2
Mashhad [Meshed]	985 m	8	−2	24	−24	3
Pahlavī	−15 m	11	5	27	−9	8
Shīrāz	1530 m	12	0	22	−10	6
Tabrīz	1405 m	4	−5	16	−25	−1
Tehrān	1190 m	9	−1	19	−16	4
Yazd	1240 m	13	1	27	−14	7
Zābul	500 m	14	2	29	−4	8

*Av. = Average.   †Abs. = Absolute.

TABLE 2. *April temperatures at selected stations*

Station	Av. max.	Mean monthly	Av. min.
Abādān	32° C	25° C	18° C
Arāk	20	13	6
Bandar 'Abbās	29	26	23
Bushire	31	25	19
Iṣfahān	23	16	9
Jāsk	30	27	24
Kirmān	24	17	10
Kīrmānshāh	20	12	4
Mashhad	19	14	9
Pahlavī	16	13	10
Shīrāz	24	16	8
Tabrīz	17	11	5
Tehrān	22	16	10
Yazd	27	20	13
Zābul	28	22	16

July or even August. All isotherms therefore show a tendency towards a gradual upslope and northward movement. This can be easily seen from a comparison of fig. 73, which shows the daily temperature conditions in April, with fig. 72, which relates to January. It will be noted that in the south the 25° C isotherm makes a significant appearance during April.

The effect of rapid heating is more prominent in the interior, where

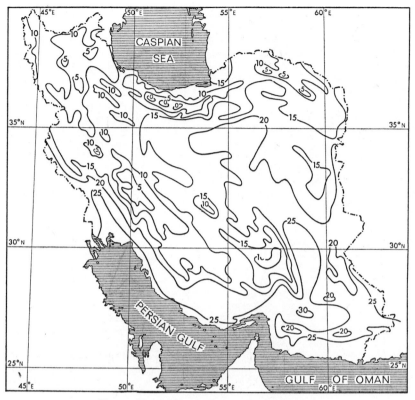

Fig. 73. Mean daily temperature for April (° C).

the 20° C isotherm now dominates. A similar change to warmer conditions is also observed along the Caspian shores, where most stations show an average mean daily temperature of about 15° C.

Over the highlands of the Alburz and the Zagros, the upslope and northward movement of the isotherms—a process that goes on from March to July or August—continues at a fast rate, with the result that the 0° C isotherm disappears from most of the mountainous sections and is to be found only over the higher Alburz.

Table 2 brings out a general picture of the thermal conditions during April.

July temperature conditions

The most critical months of the year, from the point of view of temperature studies, are the midsummer and midwinter months, during

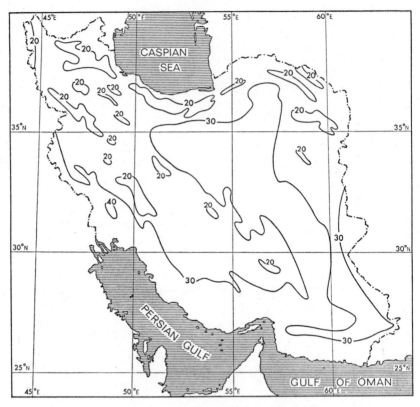

Fig. 74. Mean daily temperature for July (° C).

which extremes of temperatures usually occur. July and August are
the warmest months of the year in Iran.

Detailed study of the temperature records of Iranian stations for the
months of July and August brings out certain interesting facts regarding the distribution of temperature in Iran. It appears that the low and
flat deserts of the interior and their surrounding regions become
heated earlier in the year than the coastal areas, where the retarding influences of the sea play a decisive part in temperature conditions. Stations
below the 5,000 ft contour, with the exception of coastal stations,
record their highest monthly mean in July. But on the higher ground
of the Alburz and Zagros, as well as on the shores of the Caspian Sea,
the majority of stations record their maximum mean temperatures in
August.

The southern shores of the Caspian Sea are cooler in July than in

August, because of the retarding influence of the sea. During July the middle sections of the Caspian shores enjoy relatively lower temperatures, whereas in August the 25° C isotherm extends to the northern foothills of the Alburz, thus leaving the entire coastal areas within the same thermal averages as those of Tehrān to the south. However, in the capital the dry air makes conditions much more pleasant than in the humid coasts (fig. 74).

Table 3 illustrates the general thermal conditions at selected stations during July.

TABLE 3. *July temperatures at selected stations*

Station	Elevation above sea-level	Av. max.*	Av. min.	Abs. max.†	Abs. min.	Mean monthly
Ābādān	3 m	45° C	28° C	53° C	22° C	37° C
Arāk	1752 m	36	19	43	8	28
Bandar ʿAbbās	6 m	39	31	45	28	35
Bushire	14 m	39	28	50	23	34
Iṣfahān	1590 m	37	19	42	11	28
Jāsk	4 m	35	28	42	21	32
Kirmān	1749 m	35	18	41	9	27
Kirmānshāh	1322 m	37	16	44	7	27
Mashhad	985 m	34	18	43	11	26
Pahlavī	−15 m	30	22	35	15	26
Shīrāz	1530 m	37	20	41	14	29
Tabrīz	1405 m	32	17	40	7	25
Tehrān	1190 m	36	22	43	15	29
Yazd	1240 m	39	24	45	16	32
Zābul	500 m	38	23	45	22	31

* Av. = Average.   † Abs. = Absolute.

October temperature conditions

October is the typical autumnal month of the year, when more moderate temperatures make the climate of most parts of Iran distinctly agreeable. During October Tehrān, like many other cities, has a pleasant climate that attracts many visitors and tourists. Temperature conditions are in general similar to those of April, except in the southwest and along the Persian Gulf, where maritime influences produce a lag in the lowering of temperatures. Bandar ʿAbbās and the southeast of Iran are now the warmest parts of the country: averages of about 30° C are recorded in these parts of Iran even in October. The effect of quick cooling of the interior of Iran is seen in the trend of the 20° C isotherm, which comes to dominate an extensive area.

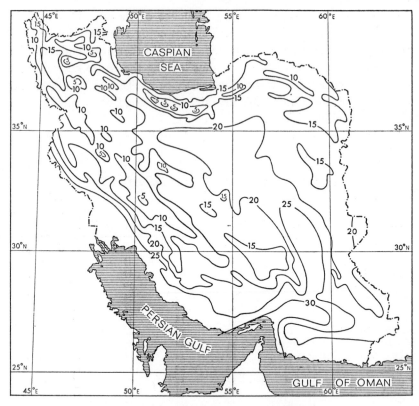

Fig. 75. Mean daily temperature for October (° C).

Table 4, as well as fig. 75, brings out the general thermal conditions that prevail during October.

TABLE 4. *October temperatures at selected stations*

Station	Mean monthly	Station	Mean monthly
Ābādān	27° C	Mashhad	14° C
Arāk	15	Pahlavī	18
Bandar ʿAbbās	30	Tabrīz	14
Bushire	26	Tehrān	18
Iṣfahān	16	Shīrāz	19
Jāsk	28	Yazd	19
Kirmān	17	Zābul	20
Kirmānshāh	16		

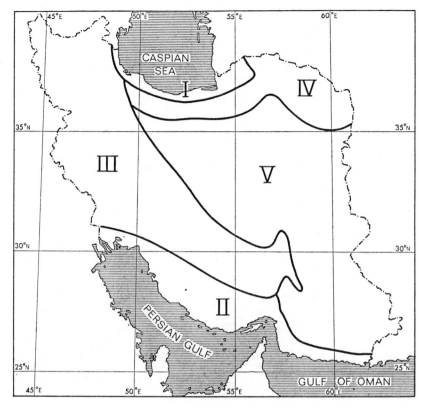

Fig. 76. Temperature provinces of Iran.

TEMPERATURE ZONES OR THERMAL PROVINCES OF IRAN

A study of the temperature data for Iranian stations has enabled the writer to recognize five distinct groupings, for which boundaries were worked out as here shown in fig. 76. The groups may each be called a "temperature type", and the approximate area dominated by each group may be referred to as a "temperature province" because of the similarities displayed by the individual stations within each group.

The five temperature provinces thus recognized are:

1. *The Caspian zone.* Characterized by a low annual range of temperatures, with relatively high values in winter and lower ones in summer. This is the only type in which the mean monthly minimum is reached in February; August is the month with the highest mean temperature, and both these characteristics are due to the retarding influences of the sea, as has already been initiated.

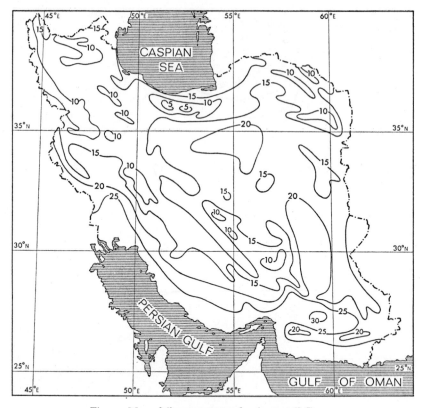

Fig. 77. Mean daily temperature for the year (° C).

2. *The Persian Gulf zone.* The Persian Gulf temperature zone stands out by reason of its high values and relatively small range, as compared with the curves for other types. January is the coldest month, but it is interesting to note that the mean for this month is higher than that for April in all the other types. July is the hottest month, but here again the mean for this month is 4° to 10° C above those of other types.

3. *The Zagros zone.* This is characterized by a very low January mean value, which almost approaches freezing point. August is the warmest month, but the average for the month is distinctly below those of the other types shown on the chart. The higher annual range in this zone, when compared with those of the maritime zones, (1), (2) above, is quite striking.

4. *The Alburz zone.* The trends here are not markedly different from the general Zagros trends, though this region experiences generally

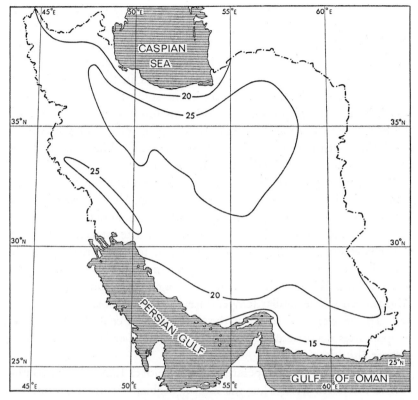

Fig. 78. Mean annual range of temperature (° C).

higher temperatures and also a relatively greater annual range. July is the warmest month of the year in this temperature zone.

5. *The Interior zone.* This is striking because of its great annual range —the widest of all the Iranian regimes—and also for its relatively high values.

It should be noted, however, that the mean monthly temperatures of the "Interior" zone, although high, are somewhat below those recorded along the Persian Gulf, which therefore represent the highest absolute temperatures occurring in Iran.

Mean annual temperature

Figure 77 illustrates the national average temperatures occurring, whilst fig. 78 illustrates the mean annual range of temperature occurring in the country.

The influence of latitude and elevation as highly significant major controls in the distribution of temperature throughout Iran can be clearly seen from this figure, which shows that isotherms decrease in value from south to north and from lower to higher elevations.

Maritime influences due to the Caspian Sea in the north and the Persian Gulf and the Gulf of Oman in the south are indicated by the way in which the disposition of isotherms follows the main trend of the coastline in both areas. Similarly, the main ranges of the Alburz and Zagros stand out quite distinctly on the map, while all other parts appear as islands of distinctly lower temperature.

The warmest parts of the country are shown to be the coastal areas fronting the Persian Gulf and the Gulf of Oman. Here, extremely high temperatures are recorded in summer, and the whole region appears as one of the most desolate in the entire country. The interior deserts are also characterized by higher average annual temperatures, and these conditions extend in a major belt from the neighbourhood of Tehrān in the north to Kirmān in the south, with a continuation eastward into Afghanistan where similar temperature conditions most probably prevail. To the west and north of the desert belt of central Iran, annual temperatures decrease under the influence of higher latitudes and also greater altitudes.

Generally speaking, temperatures decrease over Iran from the south-east to the north-west. Thus the Zagros highlands form a continuous zone of lower temperatures from the neighbourhood of Shīrāz as far as Āzarbāījān, with the coldest parts of Iran centred in the latter province. Āzarbāījān is well known for its very severe winters, when the entire plateau is invaded by cold air masses from Russia. Lowest annual temperatures are recorded at certain stations in these parts of the country, and these are much affected by spells of winter cold that can be of exceptional severity. Early in 1964, when a very cold, stagnant air mass covered most of the country for a few days, Bījār (lat. 35° 52′ N., long. 47° 36′ E.)—at an elevation of 6,360 ft above sea level—reported the lowest minimum temperature ($-36°$ C, $= -33°$ F) in the country. In the same period Darreh Takht (33° 22′ N., 49° 18′ E.), at 6,500 ft, had $-35°$ C. Bustānābād (37° 51′ N., 46° 50′ E.), at 5,650 ft, showed $-35°$ C; and Hamadān (34° 47′ N., 48° 30′ E.), at 6,160 ft had $-34°$ C.

In sharp contrast, the warming effects of the Caspian Sea on its southern shores are distinctly brought out in the annual temperature map. Temperatures are fairly uniform in this coastal belt: averages range from 15° to 17·5° C. Sub-zero temperatures are occasionally recorded, and the highest record available for this region is 44° C (111° F) in Gurgān. Farther east of Gurgān the outlying branches of the Alburz experience colder temperatures, especially in the north-eastern corners of the country which are in the direct path of the Asiatic cold waves. In Mashhad an absolute minimum of −35° C has been recorded; whilst −35° C is also reported from a high station of this part: Turuqbeh (lat. 36° 10′ N., long. 59° 31′ E.), which lies at an elevation of 7,600 ft.

In contrast to conditions within Āzarbāījān, very high temperatures can be observed in the summer months within the mountainous districts of Khurāsān. This is because the region is a territorial link between the hot deserts of the interior of Iran and the strongly heated wastes of southern Turkistān. Mashhad has recorded an absolute maximum of 43° C, to which there is nothing analogous in Āzarbāījān.

Annual range of temperature

Annual range of temperature, defined as the difference between the mean temperature of the warmest month and that of the coldest month, increases generally with an increase in latitude. This is because there are greater differences between winter and summer insolation as the distance from the equator becomes greater. The distance from large bodies of water is another factor that influences the annual range in temperature of any place on the earth's surface. Within Iran the effects of both these factors are clearly observable in the mean monthly temperatures, which vary considerably from season to season and place to place.

The lowest annual range is found along the coast of the Gulf of Oman, in south-eastern Iran. In Jāsk, for example, the difference between the coldest month (January) and the warmest month (July) is only 12° C, whilst Bushire [Būshahr], a port on the Persian Gulf, and some three degrees north of Jāsk, shows a mean annual range of 19° C. These two stations portray very well the general conditions prevailing along the southern seas of Iran, except in the low-lying and extensive plain of Khūzistān, where the annual range of temperature suddenly assumes a continental aspect and rises to 25° C. The Caspian littoral belt is another area with great maritime influences and consequently low annual ranges. Along this coast the annual range in temperature varies from 16° to 22° C.

Outside these maritime provinces, the annual range of temperature is considerable everywhere. Generally speaking, it varies from 22° to 25° C for stations in Āzarbāījān and the high Zagros, with possibly even greater figures for those areas surrounding the interior deserts. As will be seen from fig. 78, the isopleth of a 25° C annual range in temperature encloses the central deserts of Iran, with a north-westward extension towards Āzarbāījān. Another closed curve of similar value (25° C) occurs over the Khūzistān area.

Maximum and minimum temperatures

The study of mean and absolute extremes of temperature gives some idea of the average thermal conditions experienced by day and by night. In addition, of course, it furnishes information about the daily range of temperature. Highest values in the mean monthly maximum temperatures naturally come from the southern part of the country. Shustar, in the low-lying plain of Khūzistān, has a mean maximum temperature for July of 47·3° C, which is the highest for the country; whilst the lowest value in this respect comes from some stations in Āzarbāījān, which in the hottest month show a mean maximum temperature of between 21° and 25° C. As regards mean monthly minimum temperatures, the highest is recorded from the south-east—at stations on the coastlands of the Gulf of Oman (around 20° C); and the lowest comes from Bustānābād, in Āzarbāījān, with a mean monthly minimum temperature of − 10° C.

More interesting perhaps than the mean extreme values of temperature are the absolute extremes, i.e. the highest and the lowest on record during the period of observation, for they indicate the extreme temperature conditions to which an area can be subjected because of local conditions or the influence of external climatic factors. Summer heat is so strong that extreme maxima of more than 50° C are observed at several stations in the Khūzistān area in the south-west, as well as in the interior basins of the south-east. However, this latter area is influenced by the summer monsoon, and therefore attains its maximum temperature before July. In Tehrān, the daily temperature normally rises to above 40° C three to four times during the summer, and temperatures as high as 44° C have been recorded in the capital.

The highest temperature recorded in Iran during the period of observation is 53° C (127° F) registered at Gatvand (32° 17′ N., 48° 30′ E.) in the northern part of the Khūzistān lowland; and the lowest official record from existing data comes from Bījār in the northern Zagros, where the lowest temperature ever recorded in the country, − 36° C (− 33° F), was experienced in January 1964.

PRECIPITATION

Average annual precipitation

Discussion of annual precipitation in Iran is based on data for 125 stations within the period 1951–60. Of these stations, only forty-one had a complete record for the period; the others each had less than a ten-year run. Attempts have therefore been made, wherever possible, to extend by extrapolation the figures for stations whose data are incomplete. Unfortunately, the geographical distribution of recording stations does not permit a full basis for comparison, especially as between mountain and desert areas, and between mountains and the rest of the country. Moreover, closer examination of the location of cities within the highland zone would reveal that these tend to lie in rain-shadow areas, and therefore they report a generally reduced amount of rainfall compared with that experienced at higher levels or at sites more open to direct westerly influences. It is significant that many major towns within the upland regions—e.g. Iṣfahān, Shīrāz, and Kirmān—lie in basins of lower relief.

In preparing the rainfall maps (figs. 79–83) it was necessary to take into account a number of diverse factors: the general wind circulation, paths followed by atmospheric disturbances (especially the "depression tracks"), aspect in relation to rain-bearing winds, and of course topography.

Orography is clearly a major factor in the distribution of precipitation in Iran, and its influence, immediately clear on all rainfall maps, should be emphasized in all climatic studies of the country. Relief becomes an important factor in the climate of any region, especially where highlands or mountain ranges lie across the paths of prevailing moist winds. The parallel ridges of the Zagros range, which have a generally N.W.–S.E. trend, obstruct the prevailing westerlies of the winter season. Similarly the Alburz, trending east–west and lying to the south of the Caspian Sea, is at right angles to the dominant northerly winds.

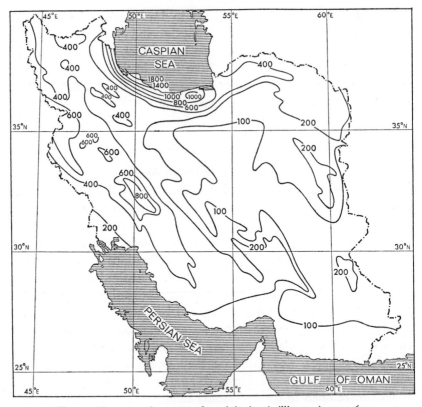

Fig. 79. Mean annual amount of precipitation (millimetres), 1951–60.

Over Iran as a whole it can be said that precipitation decreases from north to south and from west to east, except where relief of the land upsets the regularity in this arrangement. The mean annual precipitation for the entire country is 400 mm (15·7 in.). This value by itself is somewhat misleading, because only a small proportion of the land surface of Iran— namely, those parts of the Alburz and the Zagros foothills which have an elevation of 3,000 to 5,000 ft above sea-level—actually receive annual falls of this amount. Mean annual precipitation is much higher than this average on the high mountains and also along the Caspian Sea; and it is much lower in a major part of the interior as well as all along the southern sea.

The highest annual precipitation is recorded to the south-west of the Caspian Sea, at Pahlavī, which has an annual average rainfall of around 1,950 mm, or five times the average for the country. Mīrjāveh, a railway station on the Irano-Pakistani frontier, with an average annual rainfall of 48 mm only, is one of the driest recording stations of Iran, with less than one eighth of the country's average.

Circulation conditions and types of rainfall

During the entire winter season, from October/November to April/May, Iran is under the influence of the middle-latitude westerlies, and almost all the rain that occurs over the region during this period is caused by depressions moving over the area, after forming in the Mediterranean Sea on a branch of polar jet stream in the upper troposphere, which exists in this part of the world only during the wintertime.

These atmospheric depressions are basically of two different types:

1. One type is connected with shallow waves moving rapidly in the upper troposphere on a westerly air stream. These waves pass over the area along two principal tracks, a northerly one that brings the main rainfall of the country, and a southerly one travelling over the southern part of the plateau. Rainfall occurs from these streams on the western highlands of Iran; but on the lee of the mountain mass and in the interior of Iran there is little or no precipitation.

2. The second type of depression is related to the development of cold troughs in the upper atmosphere, which tend to create stationary or slow-moving depressions in the lower troposphere. These "lows", which absorb much moisture from the Persian Gulf and humid lowlands of Iraq, give rise to heavy rainfall over the western mountain ranges and also, to some extent, over the inner plateaus, owing to the persistence of damp air currents beyond the hill zone itself.

In spring the heating effect from the ground, which in these latitudes is sudden and rapid, creates a considerable amount of convectional rainfall, especially over the mountains. This is the reason why the northern mountainous parts of Iran receive their maximum rainfall during spring. In April and May, with the approaching summer season, the upper-air circulation over the region becomes dominated by the subtropical centre of high pressure—the subtropical jet stream is located to the north, in the high levels of the troposphere—and the rainfall season ends with the northward migration of this jet stream.

Except for the Caspian area rainfall is basically of cyclonic origin during practically all the rainy season; and in all cases when a cold upper trough is connected with the cyclones, the latter are considerably intensified by convection and instability. Such conditions are also associated with high intensities of rainfall.

The average fall of rain over the area is around 4 mm a day, while a maximum of 40–80 mm per day may occur once a year in the Zagros mountains. Such intensity is frequently observed along the Caspian coast, where daily falls of up to 100 mm (4 in.) are very occasionally reported at stations in the south-west of the Caspian region.

Seasonal distribution of precipitation

In the discussion that follows, seasons are considered according to the Iranian calendar: i.e. the year begins on the first day of spring (20 March), and each season covers three calendar months. In addition to seasonal maps of the actual distribution of precipitation, percentage isolines have also been prepared to illustrate the time of maximum rainfall at various groups of stations. These are based on the proportion of the annual precipitation occurring in each season of the year, and should prove helpful in explaining the actual distributions. Finally, it should be recalled that the terms "rainfall" and "precipitation" have been used interchangeably throughout this discussion, since of course all maps are based on figures that include both rain and snowfall.

Winter precipitation

In general, winter is the rainy season of Iran, and though there are stations that receive their maxima in spring or autumn, it is during the winter months that more than two thirds of the surface area of the country receive more than half of their annual precipitation (see fig. 80). The percentage value of winter precipitation decreases from south to north. Consequently, parts of southern Iran receive as much as 75 per cent, or even more, of their annual precipitation during the three winter months. The percentage lines on the map of winter precipitation bring out some interesting facts regarding stations in the high Zagros and the Alburz regions. It appears that the percentage value decreases as one goes farther north, and also as one reaches higher elevations: thus all the highlands of northern Khurāsān, together with the southern foothills of the Alburz, the southern half of Āzarbāījān, and the Zagros as far as the neighbourhood of Iṣfahān, all receive between 25 and 50 per cent of their annual precipitation in the winter months. The

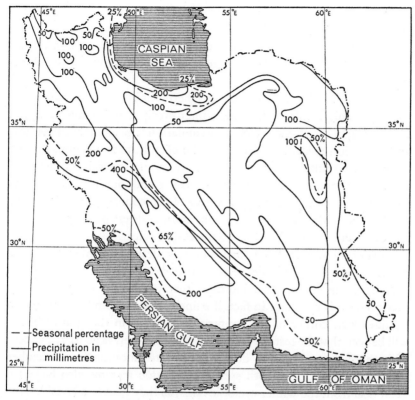

Fig. 80. Mean seasonal amount of precipitation and percentage of annual precipitation for winter.

percentage value for the winter rainfall is at its minimum along the southern shores of the Caspian Sea.

Turning now to fig. 80 itself, we note that the striking feature of the map is the great extent of territory that receives less than 200 mm of rainfall during the winter season. This territory covers almost the entire area of the country, with the exception of the Caspian littoral and the higher sections of the two mountain systems. It has already been stated that winter is the rainy season for Iran, and therefore one need only glance at the map to appreciate the degree of aridity that prevails in the country. Winter is the season during which Iran gets most of its annual precipitation; and yet half the land surface of the country lies within the 100 mm (4 in.) isohyet, and more than two thirds of the remainder between the 100- and the 200 mm lines (4–8 in.).

The wettest part of Iran during the winter months is the Caspian region, although it has already been indicated that this favoured zone actually receives less than 25 per cent of its annual precitation during this season. Within the Caspian region itself, precipitation decreases from west to east.

After the Caspian area and the northern flanks of the Alburz come the Zagros highlands, with a total winter precipitation of over 200 mm. In Āzarbāījān the average winter precipitation is below that of Zagros, and no station records a total winter fall of more than 200 mm. But the snow-clad mountains of Sahand and Savalan must receive a distinctly higher precipitation, and therefore they stand out on the map as "islands" of wetter territory. The rest of the country is relatively dry even in the midst of its rainy season, and the driest part is the central desert of Iran and Dasht-i-Lūt, to the east of Kirmān.

Most of the winter rain, which is more widespread than that of other seasons, has its origin in depressions that develop over or close to the Mediterranean basin. This indicates that over most of the country precipitation is cyclonic. In fact, if a line is drawn from Sarakhs, in the north-eastern corner of the country, to Ābādān in the south-west, it will be seen that the territory south of this line receives 60 to 75 per cent of its annual precipitation during the winter months (20 December to 20 March). Stations with spring or autumn maxima also benefit a great deal from the winter cyclonic rains, as they receive a considerable proportion of their annual fall during this season.

Spring precipitation

Spring is the period when Mediterranean depressions, which during winter have frequented the country, begin to retreat. The average number of depressions that reach Iran from the west during the winter months (January to March) is twenty-five, and the corresponding number for spring (April and May) is twelve, which indicates that, on the whole, cyclonic activity declines by at least 50 per cent during the spring months. Furthermore, depressions are weaker during the spring months, and therefore less able to penetrate far into the interior of the country. On the other hand, temperatures rise rapidly all over the country, which produces a great deal of atmospheric instability and convectional rain and thunder over the snow-clad highlands in the west and north. A combined result of these factors is that topography exercises a strong control, with precipitation decreasing considerably in the extensive lowlands of eastern and southern Iran. Here, in consequence, maximum rainfall usually occurs in winter.

The map of spring precipitation (fig. 81) indicates that all along the Persian Gulf coast the amount of spring precipitation is less than 10 per cent of the annual total, which means that summer conditions could already be held to prevail over large portions of the southern coastal areas. Beyond the 10 per cent line on the map lies the whole length of the central desert as well as the hilly parts of Kirmān, Fārs, and the western Zagros, where the aggregate spring rainfall varies from 10 to 25 per cent of the annual total for those regions.

With reference once more to fig. 81, it is of interest to note that the percentage of spring precipitation increases from south-east to north-west, but falls off to the north and the south in the coastal areas. Over the highlands of the eastern Zagros, as well as on the southern foothills of the Alburz and in northern Khurāsān, snow still lingers during the early spring months and there is also a considerable amount of convectional rain; as a result, stations located in these areas receive between 25 and 50 per cent of their annual precipitation during the spring months.

Spring is a transitional season during which the winter high-pressure centre over Asia begins to weaken, and as the season advances the easterly and north-easterly winds that prevail over the Caspian Sea throughout the winter months become steadily weaker. Consequently, rainfall along the Caspian shores of Iran falls to 10 per cent of its annual total—and a similar reduction prevails along the coastal areas of the Persian Gulf. In spite of this drastic fall in the percentage value, however, the Caspian littoral still remains the wettest part of Iran in the spring months.

Outside the Caspian area, Āzarbāījān enjoys a relatively wet period, especially in its western half, where a great deal of convectional rain is produced. Rains of this type occur over the higher Zagros, too, and most of this area is still under a thick blanket of snow in the early months of spring. Over the rest of the country dryness prevails, and only occasional showers break the climatic monotony and help the growth of the short-lived natural vegetation.

Convectional rains occur mostly in spring, when longer days and bright sunshine produce considerable heating of the earth surface. Convection is greater in the mountainous and hilly regions, where solar radiation is more intense than in the lower areas, and where there

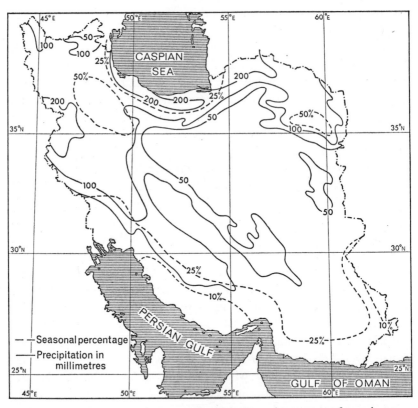

Fig. 81. Mean seasonal amount of precipitation and percentage of annual
precipitation for spring.

is great reflexion of heat over snow-covered surfaces of the ground.
The melting of snow also helps to increase the moisture content of the
air that is in contact with the ground. But in the upper layers of air
colder temperatures still prevail, so that when heating and expansion
cause the moist air near the surface to rise, condensation takes place at
comparatively low altitudes above the ground. Thunder showers of
typical convectional type are common over most of the higher grounds
of Iran during April and May. These are considered most important for
areas of unirrigated cultivation, for they occur during the growing
season, at a time when they are particularly needed by the plants.

It is perhaps useful to recall that while convectional rains are of short
duration, occurring mainly in the afternoons or early evenings, they
can be exceptionally violent and even disastrous on occasions. More-

240

over they sometimes give rise to hailstorms, which are even more dangerous to plants and sometimes to living creatures including man, especially
in the lower latitudes, where the size of an individual hailstone can be
much greater than it is farther north: a diameter of 4 in. has been known.

Summer precipitation

Summer is a dry season all over Iran except in the Caspian area.
With the onset of the summer heat, which in many places makes itself
felt as early as April, Iranians begin to change their living conditions.
During the winter months the south-facing rooms, which benefit
most from the warm rays of the sun, are made dwelling places. Iron
stoves or other heating devices are set up, and heavy clothing and
blankets used. But as soon as the warm season shows itself, a sudden
change takes place in domestic life. Those who can afford it change their
habitat to the more shaded and north-facing rooms, which offer more
protection from the scorching rays of the sun. All winter clothing and
blankets are packed away, not to be used for six to seven months.
Bādgīrs or "wind-catchers", like large open chimneys in appearance,
and so characteristic of Iranian architecture, are opened in all living
quarters. Dry and cool cellars, which in the more southern regions of
Iran are sometimes built very deep into the earth, are turned into
regular daytime dwellings. Bedding is transferred outdoors for use
throughout the summer, and during this season few would think of
spending a night indoors.

All through the long summer clear skies are generally the rule over
many places in the interior of the country, where there is no chance
even of a shower. Over the hills, however, an occasional shower of
very short duration may break the monotony. Many stations in the
Zagros, Āzarbāījān, and the northern Khurāsān highlands record such
occasional rainfalls, which for the whole season may amount to no
more than 15 mm. The possibility of summer showers outside the Caspian
region appears to be greatest in northern and western Āzarbāījān
where some stations receive as much as 6 per cent of their annual rainfall during the three summer months.

To the north of the Alburz, however, different conditions prevail:
indeed, as soon as one crosses this all-important mountain barrier, one
enters a totally different world. In contrast to the desolate scenery and
absolute dryness of the south, one finds on the northern slopes
luxurious forest, green fields, and above all frequent rainfall. The

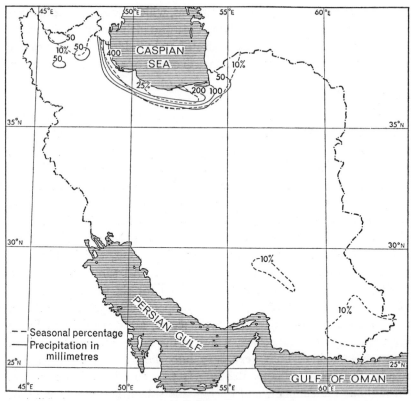

Fig. 82. Mean seasonal amount of precipitation and percentage of annual
precipitation for summer.

summer rains of the Caspian littoral are all orographic in nature,
caused mostly by the local winds of the sea and land breezes that bring
in moisture from the extensive water surfaces; these breezes produce
copious rain when they are forced to rise, e.g., by 5–10,000 ft over short
horizontal distances. Summer rains are more or less a daily occurrence
at many stations along the Caspian coastline and the northern foothills
of the Alburz. Some of these stations receive more than 25 per cent of
their annual rainfall during the summer months. In fact, the amount of
rain that some stations receive during the summer is generally high and
can be much higher than that recorded at the rainiest of stations over
the plateau interior during the whole year.

In summer the south-west corner of the Caspian is the wettest
section of the coastal area (see fig. 82). Pahlavī receives more than 200 mm,

in the three summer months alone; and this is higher than the average for more than half of the country.

The summer monsoon of India may on occasion affect south-eastern Iran. The disposition of the 10% isopleth brings out this effect very well; but being a short-term average, it conceals one other feature—a lack of regularity from one year to another. It is hardly true to say, therefore, that there is a regular monsoon effect in this part of Iran, and such effects as occur are confined to the extreme south-east.

Autumn precipitation

The Mediterranean depressions to which Iran owes most of its annual rainfall, especially in the interior, are least active during the summer months; but after the autumnal equinox, when the general pattern of the world's atmospheric pressure zones begins to shift, the depressions start to re-establish themselves over the Middle East. By mid-October some of these are sufficiently developed to reach the western portions of Iran and the Persian Gulf area. As time goes on their frequency becomes greater, and they are able to influence more and more of the western half of Iran during the autumn months. The Zagros and the Āzarbāijān highlands, as well as the Persian Gulf coasts, benefit more from the autumnal cyclonic activities than does the rest of the plateau country. Needless to say, in these areas orography plays a great part, since more plentiful precipitation occurs over the higher ground than on the lower slopes.

Another region that receives a considerable amount of precipitation during the autumn months is the Caspian littoral. In fact, it is at this season that the Caspian area receives its maximum seasonal rainfall. During the autumn months, cyclonic activity along the northern track, which by-passes the Anatolian plateau and follows the southern parts of the Black Sea, is far greater than the activity over the southern track, which eventually reaches Iran from the west via the Persian Gulf and Iraq.

Moreover, with the gradual formation of high atmospheric pressure over Central Asia the Caspian area draws in easterly and north-easterly winds that pick up considerable moisture during their passage over the Caspian Sea. Furthermore, land and sea breezes blow regularly now as in the other seasons; and it would seem to be the overlapping or combination of cyclonic influences from the west, together with the moisture-bearing winds from the north or north-east, as well as local

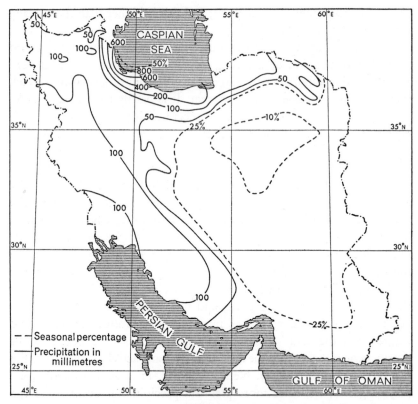

Fig. 83. Mean seasonal amount of precipitation and percentage of annual
precipitation for autumn.

winds, which produce the autumnal maxima at all stations along the
Caspian coastline.

During autumn, as in the other seasons of the year, the Caspian
littoral remains the wettest part of the country. The precipitation map
for autumn (fig. 83) brings this fact out clearly. It is interesting to note
that once again rainfall decreases from west to east. Other features on
the map bear out the facts already given for the rainfall of this region:
e.g. some stations along this coast receive as much as 50 per cent of their
annual rainfall during the three autumn months. However, this proportion decreases as one travels eastward along the coast, because the
eastern sections are farther away from the cyclonic influences. These
parts of the Caspian littoral are affected instead by the easterly winds,
which have not yet reached the sea—hence they have a land track for

part of the way, while farther west they travel over sea. They therefore bring rain to the western sections, but over the eastern parts they blow as dry interior winds that bring little more than intermittent clouds of dust. Consequently, stations like Gurgān not only record lower annual precipitation than the western stations, but they receive only 30 per cent of their total annual rainfall during the autumn.

Outside the Caspian littoral the autumn precipitation decreases both in actual amount and in its proportion of the annual total. Some stations along the western foothills of the Zagros, and also in the east of Āzarbāījān, appear to receive as much as 25 to 30 per cent of their annual precipitation during the autumn months. But over most of the Zagros and the northern highlands of Khurāsān, the amount and the percentage of rainfall are in close conformity: most stations in these sections of the country receive 10 to 25 per cent of their annual total during this season. As one goes south the percentage value increases, but the actual amount shows signs of decline due to the meagre annual precipitation along the Persian Gulf coastal areas. The driest part of the country during this season is in the east, where the few existing stations record as little as 10 per cent or less of their annual rainfall. This is perhaps because the atmospheric depressions in this season are not yet sufficiently developed to reach the eastern sections of the country from their regions of origin close to or over the Mediterranean. On the precipitation map for autumn this eastern area is left blank, and on the whole it can be regarded as receiving less than 50 mm of rain during the autumn months.

TABLE 5. *Monthly climatic data for selected stations*
(Temperature in °C. Rainfall in millimetres.)

No.	Station	Lat. N.	Long. E.	Height above sea-level (m)	Element	Jan.	Feb.	March	April	May	June	July	Aug.	Sept.	Oct.	Nov.	Dec.	Annual
1	Ābādān	30° 22'	48° 15'	3	Max. temp.	18·8	21·4	25·5	32·4	37·9	43·3	44·5	45·1	42·4	36·4	26·5	19·1	32·8
					Min.	7·2	8·7	11·9	17·5	22·2	26·2	27·7	26·8	23·0	17·8	12·5	8·3	17·5
					Rainfall	19·9	14·5	18·5	14·6	3·7	0·0	0·0	0·0	0·0	0·6	25·9	40·6	146·3
2	Āgh Darband	35° 58'	60° 50'	500	Max.	13·3	14·9	17·5	24·1	30·2	35·6	37·7	36·2	31·6	26·2	19·0	14·5	25·0
					Min.	0·0	0·2	2·1	7·2	11·3	14·8	17·9	18·1	13·1	7·6	2·8	0·2	7·9
					Rainfall	38·3	43·5	80·1	35·9	23·4	0·2	0·0	0·0	0·0	10·9	17·0	23·4	272·7
3	Ahvāz [Ahwaz]	31° 20'	48° 40'	20	Max.	17·7	20·7	25·3	32·3	38·9	44·5	46·1	45·9	42·1	36·0	26·0	19·2	32·9
					Min.	7·8	8·2	12·2	17·1	22·0	24·9	26·9	25·6	21·3	17·3	12·8	8·6	17·1
					Rainfall	33·5	25·2	16·9	17·3	3·5	0·0	0·0	0·0	0·1	1·8	26·7	33·5	158·5
4	Arāk	34° 06'	49° 42'	1753	Max.	4·5	7·9	12·8	19·6	26·5	32·6	35·8	34·4	29·6	22·7	12·6	6·5	20·5
					Min.	-5·1	-2·4	2·3	7·2	11·8	15·5	19·2	17·4	13·5	7·9	2·1	-2·8	7·2
					Rainfall	60·3	38·7	51·3	52·3	21·9	2·9	3·1	0·8	0·4	14·5	47·4	34·9	328·5
5	Ardabīl	38° 15'	48° 17'	1350	Max.	8·2	7·6	8·0	15·8	21·7	24·3	25·8	26·5	23·3	18·5	10·6	5·5	16·3
					Min.	-4·4	-4·9	-3·8	3·4	7·1	8·0	12·3	11·6	9·4	5·2	-0·7	-5·4	3·1
					Rainfall	16·5	39·6	58·7	52·7	42·1	15·4	5·3	5·6	10·1	33·2	45·0	25·8	350·0
6	Bābol Sar	36° 43'	52° 39'	-21	Max.	11·5	11·3	12·4	16·8	23·1	27·0	29·7	30·3	27·4	22·5	16·5	12·9	20·1
					Min.	4·1	4·2	6·3	10·4	15·5	19·5	22·1	22·1	19·4	14·5	8·7	4·9	12·6
					Rainfall	65·0	67·9	73·9	31·3	19·9	29·1	44·0	40·3	93·6	122·2	136·5	96·0	819·7
7	Bam	29° 04'	58° 24'	1062	Max.	16·6	19·9	24·4	31·6	33·6	37·4	37·7	37·1	34·5	29·9	21·5	16·9	28·4
					Min.	4·8	7·0	11·2	16·1	19·9	25·0	25·8	24·9	21·7	16·5	9·0	5·2	15·5
					Rainfall	23·5	3·2	15·4	10·6	10·5	0·0	2·9	0·0	0·0	0·1	6·1	3·6	75·9
8	Bandar 'Abbās	27° 11'	56° 17'	6	Max.	23·4	24·6	27·9	29·3	36·1	38·5	38·7	37·8	37·4	35·1	29·6	25·2	34·5
					Min.	14·0	15·0	18·5	22·5	26·5	28·9	31·0	31·0	29·2	25·6	19·7	14·2	23·0
					Rainfall	91·8	20·4	12·0	15·9	0·0	0·0	0·1	0·0	8·5	25·5	41·6		215·8
9	Biābānak	33° 19'	55° 02'	1200	Max.	14·4	15·8	19·3	27·6	32·8	38·6	39·3	40·5	36·0	29·5	18·3	14·2	27·2
					Min.	0·0	0·7	4·7	12·1	16·8	21·8	24·4	24·1	18·5	11·7	4·1	-0·7	11·5
					Rainfall	13·0	10·0	5·3	12·7	7·6	0·0	0·0	0·0	0·0	0·0	1·6	4·3	64·5

No.	Station	Lat.	Long.	Alt. (m)		Jan.	Feb.	Mar.	Apr.	May	June	July	Aug.	Sept.	Oct.	Nov.	Dec.	Year
10	Birjand	32° 52'	59° 12'	1465	Max.	11·4	13·9	18·9	24·5	29·6	35·2	36·6	35·6	33·0	26·9	18·8	13·3	25·1
					Min.	-0·9	0·2	5·0	9·4	12·2	16·7	19·5	17·2	12·8	6·4	1·6	-0·8	8·1
					Rainfall	45·0	19·3	39·6	40·4	12·8	0·8	0·3	0·0	0·2	0·1	9·0	16·4	183·9
11	Bushire	28° 59'	50° 50'	4	Max.	18·9	20·4	24·4	30·8	34·7	37·1	38·9	39·7	37·4	33·3	26·8	20·5	30·2
					Min.	9·7	10·4	13·7	18·1	22·3	24·9	27·6	27·3	24·1	19·2	14·9	11·5	18·6
					Rainfall	61·4	22·4	19·4	8·6	5·0	0·0	0·0	0·0	0·0	0·8	48·4	93·3	259·3
12	Dizfūl	32° 24'	48° 23'	143	Max.	19·0	20·5	24·1	31·2	37·7	43·9	46·2	45·6	42·7	36·6	26·8	19·6	32·8
					Min.	8·7	9·3	12·0	17·6	23·4	26·9	30·3	30·2	26·5	20·7	14·7	10·0	19·2
					Rainfall	65·0	45·9	48·6	30·3	4·0	0·0	1·0	0·0	0·0	5·0	80·0	75·6	355·4
13	Gurgān	36° 51'	54° 28'	120	Max.	13·4	14·3	13·9	19·1	25·9	30·3	32·3	33·0	29·8	24·3	17·2	13·4	22·2
					Min.	5·0	4·9	5·8	10·4	15·6	19·5	22·3	22·5	19·5	14·3	8·8	4·9	12·8
					Rainfall	61·6	50·4	87·2	72·7	41·0	43·8	40·1	29·2	26·7	77·9	71·6	48·1	649·8
14	Hamadān	34° 47'	48° 30'	1775	Max.	4·8	6·4	10·5	16·8	22·2	28·4	32·2	33·1	28·5	20·9	11·1	5·6	18·4
					Min.	-4·9	-3·7	0·1	5·4	8·2	12·0	15·1	14·5	10·9	6·1	-0·8	-3·5	5·0
					Rainfall	36·0	52·8	72·9	78·9	32·7	5·6	1·3	0·5	0·7	11·8	51·8	40·2	385·2
15	Iṣfahān	32° 37'	51° 40'	1590	Max.	10·0	13·4	17·2	23·2	28·3	34·6	35·6	36·1	32·7	25·9	16·8	10·5	23·9
					Min.	-2·2	-0·7	3·3	8·0	11·9	16·1	18·7	16·8	12·9	6·9	1·7	-1·5	7·6
					Rainfall	18·9	16·0	17·7	15·8	8·3	1·0	4·6	0·9	0·2	3·4	19·5	20·2	126·5
16	Kāzarūn	29° 37'	51° 40'	735	Max.	24·9	23·3	24·3	32·8	35·4	41·2	42·5	42·4	37·9	36·1	29·5	21·7	32·7
					Min.	2·6	2·4	3·3	10·1	15·5	20·0	22·9	22·6	18·9	12·9	7·1	3·7	11·8
					Rainfall	45·3	39·0	26·5	7·0	0·0	0·0	0·0	0·0	0·0	1·7	3·9	29·9	153·3
17	Khūy	38° 33'	44° 57'	1100	Max.	8·8	12·1	13·5	18·7	25·1	28·3	31·5	32·6	28·7	21·5	12·6	7·2	20·0
					Min.	-1·2	-0·6	2·2	6·6	11·8	14·3	16·9	17·7	13·7	7·9	3·5	-2·9	7·5
					Rainfall	18·7	10·6	18·0	15·1	48·9	16·7	6·8	0·7	1·7	8·5	26·6	5·2	177·5
18	Khurramābād	33° 29'	48° 22'	1171	Max.	11·7	13·3	16·7	22·4	29·3	36·3	39·9	39·8	36·0	29·1	18·7	13·0	25·5
					Min.	0·1	0·9	4·3	8·7	11·9	15·5	19·7	19·0	14·1	9·5	5·5	1·7	9·2
					Rainfall	66·5	73·2	88·1	82·8	28·4	0·9	0·5	0·0	0·4	10·4	76·7	75·6	504·0
19	Kirmān	30° 15'	56° 58'	1749	Max.	12·8	15·8	19·2	24·3	29·3	33·9	35·4	34·8	32·1	26·7	19·5	13·8	24·8
					Min.	-1·2	0·9	4·8	9·0	12·3	16·6	18·0	15·4	12·4	6·2	5·5	-0·8	7·9
					Rainfall	35·8	21·8	46·4	22·4	20·4	2·4	6·7	0·0	4·0	3·0	8·4	32·0	203·0
20	Kirmānshāh	34° 19'	47° 07'	1322	Max.	8·4	10·3	13·8	19·8	25·9	33·0	37·2	36·5	32·5	25·6	15·6	9·7	22·4
					Min.	-3·5	-3·1	0·4	0·5	7·6	10·9	16·0	15·0	10·0	5·4	1·3	-1·9	5·3
					Rainfall	37·8	46·3	67·8	68·0	30·0	2·9	0·0	0·1	1·3	12·3	55·3	50·9	372·7

TABLE 5 (cont.)

No.	Station	Lat. N.	Long. E.	Height above sea level (m)	Element	Jan.	Feb.	March	April	May	June	July	Aug.	Sept.	Oct.	Nov.	Dec.	Annual
21	Mashhad	36° 16′	59° 38′	985	Max.	7·5	9·3	12·1	19·4	25·8	30·8	33·7	32·5	28·5	22·0	13·0	8·7	20·3
					Min.	-2·9	-1·8	2·3	7·9	11·4	15·2	17·9	15·7	11·3	5·4	0·5	-2·2	6·7
					Rainfall	32·2	31·3	61·0	51·5	24·5	4·0	0·1	0·4	0·4	6·1	17·3	20·0	248·8
22	Mashīrān	38° 42′	47° 32′	600	Max.	9·8	9·7	12·4	19·2	24·6	28·2	30·4	30·4	25·9	21·2	13·1	9·4	19·5
					Min.	-2·9	-2·2	1·1	6·6	11·6	14·6	17·1	16·8	13·8	8·2	2·2	-1·9	7·1
					Rainfall	2·8	7·1	10·2	15·8	24·4	10·3	4·8	12·6	6·1	12·9	13·9	6·0	126·9
23	Pahlavi	37° 28′	49° 28′	-15	Max.	10·6	10·2	10·8	15·6	22·4	26·7	29·6	29·9	26·0	21·5	15·7	11·9	19·2
					Min.	4·5	3·9	5·3	9·8	15·2	19·0	21·3	21·3	18·8	14·6	8·7	5·5	12·3
					Rainfall	97·8	120·8	158·5	61·1	44·6	68·4	49·3	108·4	333·1	305·5	379·5	172·8	1899·8
24	Qasr-i-Shirin	34° 31′	45° 34′	500	Max.	15·5	16·4	20·4	26·7	32·3	40·9	41·7	41·2	38·1	33·1	24·2	17·1	29·0
					Min.	4·5	5·0	8·2	12·5	16·7	21·9	22·8	22·4	17·9	13·8	10·4	6·1	13·5
					Rainfall	80·4	71·5	67·1	36·7	26·4	0·6	0·0	0·0	0·0	0·6	42·6	87·8	414·0
25	Qazvin	36° 15′	50° 00′	1302	Max.	8·9	9·5	14·2	20·8	26·7	32·5	34·5	35·3	32·0	24·0	13·2	10·0	21·8
					Min.	-5·3	-5·1	-0·6	5·1	9·1	12·8	14·7	15·2	10·9	6·5	0·2	-2·5	5·1
					Rainfall	37·4	22·1	60·5	51·2	36·9	9·2	3·3	0·3	0·0	38·8	65·5	13·9	339·1
26	Qum	34° 38′	50° 53′	928	Max.	11·0	13·3	17·7	23·8	30·6	35·6	38·2	38·8	33·7	26·8	16·8	11·2	24·7
					Min.	0·2	2·7	5·6	11·3	16·1	19·4	22·2	20·4	16·7	11·2	5·2	1·0	11·0
					Rainfall	25·1	11·2	26·3	20·8	14·3	0·6	1·4	0·0	0·1	7·0	23·7	13·7	144·2
27	Rāmsar	36° 54′	50° 40′	-20	Max.	11·8	10·7	11·0	16·5	21·9	25·6	28·5	28·7	25·7	21·4	16·3	10·0	19·3
					Min.	5·0	4·3	5·8	9·5	14·5	18·3	20·3	31·2	19·2	14·5	8·9	6·1	12·3
					Rainfall	48·4	77·6	100·7	47·7	45·8	84·4	39·2	73·2	247·1	250·1	185·5	85·5	1285·6
28	Rasht	37° 15′	49° 36′	0	Max.	12·4	11·6	12·3	18·9	25·0	27·5	29·7	29·7	26·0	21·9	16·2	13·1	20·3
					Min.	2·8	1·6	4·0	8·4	12·8	15·9	17·9	18·6	16·4	12·3	6·1	3·1	10·0
					Rainfall	80·7	105·4	158·7	50·0	49·1	59·1	39·9	66·6	197·8	245·3	194·6	106·7	1355·4
29	Rezā'īyeh [Urumiyeh]	37° 32′	45° 05′	1332	Max.	4·0	6·2	10·4	17·5	23·5	28·2	32·0	32·2	28·2	21·6	11·8	5·2	18·4
					Min.	-4·2	-2·3	1·0	6·8	10·8	14·3	17·4	17·5	13·9	8·4	2·7	-2·1	7·0
					Rainfall	28·2	43·0	68·1	68·6	44·9	20·0	6·5	1·6	6·1	10·3	47·7	25·8	370·0
30	Sabzavār	36° 13′	57° 40′	940	Max.	9·8	13·2	16·8	24·4	29·3	34·8	37·6	36·5	32·6	25·9	16·0	10·0	23·9
					Min.	-1·9	-0·4	4·0	9·4	14·1	18·2	21·9	19·5	14·3	8·4	1·5	-1·5	9·0
					Rain.													

No.	Station	Lat.	Long.	Elev.													
31	Sangsūrākh	37° 38'	58° 45'	900	Max.	7·3	8·5	16·9	23·3	28·5	31·6	30·7	26·5	19·6	11·6	7·7	18·5
					Min.	-4·3	-3·6	4·4	8·3	12·9	15·7	13·6	9·9	4·3	-1·3	-4·3	4·5
					Rainfall	15·7	18·0	43·4	41·2	4·2	3·3	0·3	4·7	13·8	13·8	24·5	232·4
32	Saqqiz	36° 14'	46° 16'	1400	Max.	6·6	7·1	18·1	24·2	29·2	33·3	33·7	30·2	22·9	13·2	6·7	19·5
					Min.	-8·6	-7·8	2·9	5·6	8·1	11·6	10·7	5·5	1·1	-0·2	-4·6	1·8
					Rainfall	10·4	19·7	66·9	19·4	12·9	0·0	0·5	1·6	12·5	54·2	19·3	257·2
33	Shahr-i-Kurd	32° 19'	50° 51'	2066	Max.	4·4	6·7	18·4	22·2	31·0	33·3	32·9	29·6	23·2	14·0	8·0	20·4
					Min.	-9·3	-6·2	3·8	6·9	10·0	12·9	12·7	8·1	2·6	-1·5	-4·7	2·9
					Rainfall	52·5	35·2	25·2	11·0	0·4	7·3	0·2	0·0	1·8	21·4	31·0	227·7
34	Shāhrūd	36° 35'	55° 02'	1370	Max.	6·4	9·6	20·7	26·1	30·0	32·1	31·2	27·7	21·6	14·8	7·9	20·1
					Min.	-2·0	-1·0	8·6	12·8	16·9	19·6	18·8	14·7	8·7	3·1	-0·6	8·5
					Rainfall	12·9	14·6	24·6	18·4	4·8	2·8	0·3	4·7	5·9	9·9	10·1	134·7
35	Shīrāz	29° 36'	52° 32'	1490	Max.	12·4	14·6	24·1	29·8	34·9	36·9	36·0	33·5	27·6	19·8	13·5	25·1
					Min.	0·6	1·8	8·3	13·2	16·9	20·1	18·7	15·3	9·4	4·4	1·6	9·6
					Rainfall	76·9	47·3	63·4	12·7	0·0	1·2	0·0	0·0	tr	65·3	93·4	384·6
36	Ṭabas	33° 35'	56° 54'	1225	Max.	15·2	17·4	27·7	32·7	40·9	41·0	40·7	36·1	31·7	20·5	15·3	28·2
					Min.	1·4	3·4	14·0	17·6	22·9	24·8	23·1	19·4	12·5	4·8	0·9	12·7
					Rainfall	21·3	16·3	14·8	3·3	0·0	0·0	0·0	0·0	0·0	4·0	7·1	91·3
37	Tabrīz	38° 05'	46° 17'	1362	Max.	3·9	5·6	16·7	22·5	27·9	31·7	32·0	28·0	20·8	10·7	4·4	17·9
					Min.	-5·0	-4·0	5·8	9·4	13·6	17·0	17·3	13·1	7·3	1·4	-3·7	6·0
					Rainfall	15·1	32·2	47·1	42·5	23·2	11·1	1·2	8·7	14·0	29·4	1·59	285·6
38	Tehrān	35° 41'	51° 19'	1191	Max.	8·9	11·1	21·8	27·8	32·8	35·8	35·1	31·4	24·3	15·0	9·8	22·4
					Min.	-0·9	0·4	9·9	14·6	19·2	22·1	21·7	18·1	11·9	4·8	0·2	10·5
					Rainfall	31·4	29·5	34·8	13·9	3·4	1·1	2·3	1·9	8·2	37·7	24·4	223·5
39	Yazd	31° 54'	54° 24'	1240	Max.	12·7	15·7	26·5	31·6	37·0	38·8	38·1	34·1	27·2	17·6	12·4	26·0
					Min.	0·8	2·7	12·5	17·1	21·9	24·2	22·2	17·8	10·9	5·1	1·7	12·0
					Rainfall	15·4	3·2	9·5	3·9	0·9	1·3	0·0	0·0	1·0	15·9	8·4	67·5
40	Zāhidān	29° 28'	60° 53'	1370	Max.	14·1	18·2	27·3	32·4	35·4	36·8	35·3	33·0	27·3	21·2	16·8	26·4
					Min.	0·8	3·5	12·7	16·1	18·4	19·7	17·0	12·8	7·3	3·6	1·5	10·1
					Rainfall	36·1	16·8	14·6	7·5	0·1	6·3	0·0	0·0	0·8	7·5	15·2	116·6
41	Zanjān	36° 41'	48° 29'	1648	Max.	4·9	6·2	17·3	24·2	29·2	32·3	32·7	28·4	21·5	11·7	6·4	18·8
					Min.	-5·9	-5·4	4·5	7·4	11·5	14·4	14·7	10·4	4·9	0·1	-3·4	4·3
					Rainfall	11·5	18·5	55·3	30·7	32·9	1·7	1·4	4·4	16·2	31·5	18·5	293·4

CHAPTER 6

SOILS

Iran is covered to a large extent by the mountains which surround the saline, sandy, and rocky deserts of the central plateau, thus making the plateau a closed basin. Over 50 per cent of the total land surface is mountainous and highly broken in topography. There could be said to be four main physiographic areas in Iran, each with a distinctive character. These are:

1. The great Zagros and Alburz mountain ranges, which together form a great V-shape;

2. The area within the V, which begins as a high plateau with its own secondary ranges, and gradually levels towards the interior deserts;

3. The low-lying plain of Khūzistān, which is a continuation of the Mesopotamian plain; and

4. The Caspian coast, which lies below the sea-level and forms a separate climatic zone.

The major part of the country is arid or semi-arid; rainfall is restricted to the winter months, and is small in amount everywhere but on the northern flanks of the Alburz mountains, where it varies from 40 to 80 in. annually. On the plateau the average annual rainfall of over 8 in. in the north decreases to less than 5 in. in the south and south-east. At the head of the Persian Gulf the amount is somewhat greater. Snow is common in the high areas above 4,000 ft.

Vegetation varies according to climate. The climax-vegetation consists of oak and beech in the more humid sections of the north (of these trees a considerable number still remain), and a thin cover of grasses and/or scattered shrubs in the semi-arid and arid interior. Intermediates between the two extremes—such as tree and grass, grass and shrub, or tree–grass–shrub combinations—often occur within short distances of one another throughout the country. Because of destruction by man, the vegetation of many areas now bears little resemblance to the original cover.

From the point of view of soil-study, Iran can be divided into the following main geological units, from south to north:

1. The platform of Arabia. The north-east fringe lies in K̲h̲ūzistān, mostly covered by the deltas of the Kārūn and Kark̲h̲eh rivers.

2. The folded zone. The stratigraphic sequence in this zone starts in the Upper Palaeozoic and ends with the Miocene. The desolate character of the southern half of Iran is caused by the Mio-Pliocene sequence of the thick Fars Series (containing gypsum, anhydrite, salt, marls, silt, and sandstones, etc.) lying over Asmari limestone. Above the Fars series are the Bakhtiari series, mainly conglomerates.

3. Iranides. A structural complex consisting of three units:

(a) the radiolarite and ophiolite zones, consisting of red and green cherts, siliceous shales, and green eruptive ultrabasic rocks (serpentines);

(b) the Bīsitūn limestone zone, composed of thick massive Cretaceous limestone; and

(c) the Hamadān zone, of dark shales and sandstone, dark phyllites and chlorite schists, all of Mesozoic age.

4. The central plain. Characterized by gypsiferous and saline series of Eocene to Miocene age. The dissolution of gypsum beds has led to the formation of salt lakes (*kavīrs*).

5. The Alburz ranges. These are a thick stratigraphic sequence of Cambrian to Tertiary limestone, shales, sandstones, tuffs, etc. Gypsiferous and saline series are absent. The Turkoman and K̲h̲urāsān mountains to the east consist mainly of limestones and marls.

6. Caspian littoral. Composed of younger Tertiary sediments, alluvium, and some loess deposits.

In 1944 Dr Kovda prepared a general systematic map (on a scale of 1:6,000,000) of the soil cover of Iran; but the soil map presented here (fig. 84) is the first to be based on direct field observations for the country as a whole. Field-work was recorded on aerial photographs, photo indexes and field sheets at a scale of 1:250,000 and 1:500,000. These last were reduced to 1:1,000,000, eleven sheets of which were further reduced to 1:2,500,000 for publication purposes. Figure 84 is a further reduced summary and amalgamation from this. Reconnaissance, and detailed maps prepared for special projects have also been used.

The "soil association" appears to be the most adequate mapping unit for a 1:2,500,000 scale. An association is a selected group of soil units that are geographically related within the landscape; moreover, these units correspond to broad climatic and physiographic units, and they also have a common pattern of land use.

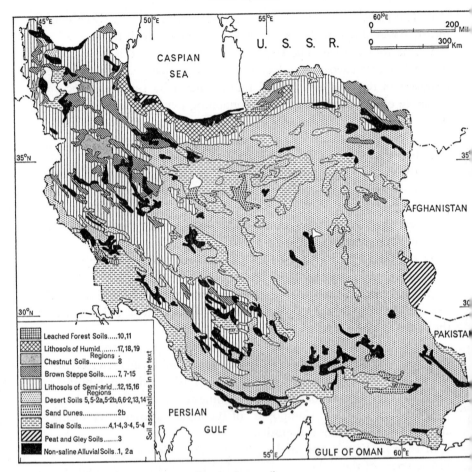

Fig. 84. Iran: soil types.

The mapping units in the legend are conveniently grouped into four physiographic units. This division is not exclusive, and units mentioned under one group may also occur to a minor extent under the others. Each association is given the names of its dominant soil groups. No attempt has been made to indicate soils below the level of major soil group, although phases of most of these were identified and recorded on the field map and a few are indicated on the soil map.

The soils "lithosols", "rendzinas", and "regosols" are included in the names of associations occupying dissected slopes and mountainous areas. This inclusion, while it may not always be justified in view of the small areas these soils cover, nevertheless serves to indicate the shallow development of most of the soils in these particular associations.

The legend of the map is given below:

I. *Soils of the plains and valleys*

		Approximate area mapped (in 1,000 hectares)
1	Fine-textured alluvial soils	4,750
2a	Coarse-textured alluvial and colluvial soils, and regosols	4,500
2b	Sand dunes (including coastal sands)	2,500
3	Low-humic gley, humic gley, and half-bog soils	750
4	Solonchak and solonetz soils (including gypsum soils)	6,000
1–4	Saline alluvial soils	5,000
3–4	Salt-marsh soils	7,000
	Total area of soils in plains and valleys	30,500

II. *Soils of the plateaus*

5	Grey and Red Desert soils	2,000
6	Sierozem soils	8,000
7	Brown soils	6,000
8	Chestnut soils	1,000
5–2a	Desert soils–regosols	8,000
5–2b	Desert soils–sand dunes	8,000
5–4	Desert soils–sierozem soils–solonchak soils	3,000
6–2	Sierozem soils–regosols (with sand dunes)	9,000
7–15	Brown soils–lithosols	2,000
	Total area of soils in plateaus	47,000

III. *Soils of the Caspian piedmont*

9	Red and brown Mediterranean soils	20
10	Red–yellow podzolic soils	30
11	Brown forest soils (including grey-brown podzolic soils)	300
	Total area of soils in Caspian piedmont	350

IV. *Soils of the dissected slopes and mountains*	Approximate area mapped (in 1,000 hectares)
12 Brown soils–rendzinas	400
13 Calcareous lithosols–desert and sierozem soils	35,000
14 Calcareous lithosols (from saliferous and gypsiferous marls)–desert and sierozem soils (including salt plugs)	12,000
15 Calcareous lithosols–brown soils and chestnut soils	24,000
16 Lithosols (from igneous rocks)–brown and sierozem soils	12,000
17 Lithosols–brown forest soils and rendzinas	2,500
18 Regosols (mainly from sandstones)–red-yellow podzolic soils	100
19 Lithosols (mainly from igneous rocks)–brown forest and podzolic soils	150
Total area of soils on mountains and dissected slopes	86,150
Total area of lakes	1,000
Total area of Iran	165,000

DESCRIPTION OF MAPPING UNITS

I. *Soils of the plains and valleys*

The soils of the plains and valleys are formed on transported material, brought by the usual agencies of water and wind.

Alluvial soils are composed of young, water-deposited sediments laid down on flat or gently sloping flood plains. They do not show a prominent "horizon differentiation" (i.e. with strongly differing layers) other than the formation of a surface organic horizon (A_1). The alluvial soils distinguished in this mapping unit are generally medium to heavy textured, and they are mostly calcareous.

Coarse-textured alluvial and colluvial soils and regosols are the colluvial soils of coalescing alluvial fans, called "diluvial" soils by Soviet soil scientists. They have been, and in most cases are still, in process of being built up by material carried by flood-waters from the mountains through relatively narrow valleys. Some profile development is observed in these soils. Lime accumulations are found as concretions or in pockets, as powder or as a deposit on gravel. Gravels and finer material are usually cemented by secondary lime; the degree of cementation varies with the region, rainfall, and with any other factors that affect the lime movement in the soil profile.

Sand dunes are common in most of the arid regions of Iran. They consist of deposits of loose sand, composed largely of quartz with fragments of many different minerals, occurring within or near the margins of deserts and coasts. These dunes may actually be in irregular active movement, or they may be fixed by vegetation growing upon them. The high wind velocities prevailing in some of the regions have been an important factor leading to the development of moving dunes in large areas.

Hydromorphic soils including Low Humic Gley, Humic Gley, and Half-Bog soils. The major hydromorphic soils found in Iran (and only in the north) are: low-humic and humic gley soils; pseudo-gley or grey hydromorphic soils, and a small area of half-bog soils near Pahlavī.

Low-Humic and Humic Gley soils, also called Wiesenboden or "Swamp meadow" soils, are dark-brown or black soils, rich in humus, grading into a greyish and rust-mottled colour. They are usually slightly acid or slightly alkaline. Gleization and calcification are the main processes by which these soils develop.

Grey Hydromorphic or Pseudo-Gley Soils. Actually degraded forest soils, these are the typical soils of the paddy lands in the Gīlān–Māzandarān area of the Caspian littoral. The soils have brown mottles, with black iron and manganese concretions, normally at a depth of 10 to 40 cm. The surface structure is usually fine-grained. The ground-water table is usually very deep, so there is no rising ground water from beneath the surface; but in winter and autumn there is a superficial or perched-water table, which is the reason for the hydromorphic nature of the soils.

Solonchaks and solonetz soils are the saline and alkaline soils of the arid, semi-arid and dry subhumid regions of Iran. They are poorly drained, and have been developed under consistently poor drainage conditions, particularly in cases where the sediment has come from gypsiferous and saliferous marls (as in mapping unit 4). Solonchak soils contain large quantities of soluble salts, mainly sulphates, but chlorides of calcium, magnesium, and sodium are known. The solonchaks are commonly light-coloured and poor in organic matter, and they have a lightly crusted friable granular structure. Solonetz soils are the result of the partial leaching and alkalinization of solonchak soils, which may happen following irrigation—especially irrigation without proper drainage and management. They often occur as spots scattered throughout Solonchak soils, and they have a surface layer of light-coloured leached material over a darker subsoil layer of tough, heavy material of columnar structure.

Saline alluvial soils (1–4) comprise areas of poorly drained alluvial soils, moderately to severely affected by soil salinity.

Salt-marsh soils are usually wet for all or most of the year. They occur in low-lying parts of the valleys that are seasonally flooded by rivers, and in great parts of the Da<u>sh</u>t-i-Kavīr. These soils combine the characteristics of salty soils, such as solonchaks, with those of the marshy soils. Salinity, alkalinity, and gleization are the main processes by which salt-marsh soils develop; and mottling, beneath as well as on the surface, is their most characteristic feature.

II. *Soils of the plateau*

A great part of Iran is a plateau about 3,000 ft or more above mean sea-level. Here arid or semi-arid climate is prevalent.

Grey and Red Desert soils. Desert soils are formed as a result of severe moisture deficiency. They commonly possess a thin surface crust, which consists of slightly cemented to strongly compacted materials—this last may sometimes be a distinguishing feature. Horizon differentiation is non-existent or barely visible. The organic content is low (0·1–0·2 per cent in the surface horizon), and the soils are calcareous throughout, usually having a shallow calcium carbonate horizon and an accumulation of soluble salts in the profile.

Sierozem soils. Light grey in colour, sierozem soils are humus-deficient (usually only about 0·5 per cent in the surface horizon) and extremely calcareous soils, with very little leaching. They carry sparse, open xerophytic plant cover with scanty soil life, and they occur primarily as the climax-formation of the desert steppe.

Common to all varieties of sierozem is a shallow humus horizon of 5 to 10 cm depth, contrasting only a little with the subsoil. At the surface there is a lighter-coloured, bright-grey A_1 horizon, which is either powdery or dusty; in many loamy soils, however, it may have a dense, partly leafy structure. This horizon results from the accumulation of wind-borne calcareous sediments which either remain loose or become puddled by rainwater. Under the A_1 horizon there usually is a darker, slightly brownish A_2 horizon richer in humus. This is followed by a light-grey A/Ca horizon, which passes gradually into a generally coarser C horizon. On highly calcareous parent material the Ca horizon often differs very little from the C horizon.

Brown soils. The brown steppe soils are probably the most widespread soils in Iran. They are brown to light-brown soils, slightly alkaline (pH 7–8), and thus usually containing calcareous horizons. These soils have very weakly developed greyish-brown granular surface

A_1 horizons, with an organic matter content of about 1 per cent or more. Usually eluviation is weak, although some brown soils show zones of accumulation of clay, in the form of clay-skins and clay-bridges between aggregates. Their subsurface horizons are brown or yellowish brown, granular or crumb in structure, and they grade at a depth of 15 to 30 cm into a pale brown or greyish, highly calcareous clay. The depth of the solum varies according to the slope of the area. Well-developed soil profiles with distinct texture, structure, colour, and reaction are rare and occur only on gentle slopes. The brown soils are developed in a semi-arid climate under grass vegetation, and suffer moisture deficiency during summer months.

Chestnut soils comprise dark-brown (chestnut-coloured) surface soil over a light-coloured material that overlies a calcareous horizon. The depth of the humus horizon varies from about 30–60 cm, and is usually 40–50 cm.

A typical chestnut soil profile consists of a lighter greyish-coloured loose A_1 horizon, occasionally showing slight leafy separation in the upper part, underlain by a chestnut-brown horizon (Munsell rating: 10 YR 4/3–3/3), which is normally spongy and rich in cavities. This changes gradually to a light brownish-grey transition A/Ca horizon, then to a whitish and more or less crusted Ca horizon, and finally into the loose parent material.

Chestnut soils are usually neutral at the surface, and unless they occur on highly calcareous parent materials, they effervesce only when taken from depths of about 30 to 40 cm. The humus content of the surface soil usually averages about 3 to 4 per cent.

Soil associations such as desert soils, sand dunes, etc., have been mapped, but they are not described separately here. These are complexes in which one predominant soil group and the other soils occurring together with it are indicated as an association.

III. *Soils of the Caspian piedmont*

The northern foothills of the Alburz mountains, as well as the slight to moderately sloping foothill areas bordering the southern coast of the Caspian Sea, are both characterized by a humid to subhumid, subtropical climate that is very different from that of the rest of Iran. (The Caspian piedmont includes the Caspian provinces of Gīlān, Māzandarān, and Gurgān.)

The abundance of vegetation, together with the intensity of chemical

weathering of Jurassic, Cretaceous, and Tertiary limestones, conglomerates, and sandstones, all of which compose the northern slopes
of the Alburz mountains, have given rise to the formation of *brown
forest*, *red-yellow podzolic*, and in some cases *grey-brown podzolic* soils.
In some transitional areas a few profiles of *red and brown Mediterranean*
soils have been mapped.

IV. *Soils of dissected slopes and mountains*

The soils of dissected slopes and mountains are in general stony,
shallow over bedrock, and without definite profile development. They
contain a high proportion of unweathered rock fragments, though there
may have been some incipient weathering and an accumulation of
organic matter. The absence of profile development may be due to
recent exposure of the parent material, or, more commonly, to the
forces of natural erosion which are vigorous enough to remove finer-
textured soil material as fast as it is formed. These soils may be called
lithosols. They are found in all climates, but are particularly associated
with arid and semi-arid areas.

Soil distributions occurring on mountains and in mountain valleys
occupy a large part of Iran and include a complex range of soil types.
These mapping units indicate areas generally unsuited for crop growth.
However, many of the mountain soils contain small areas of alluvial and
colluvial soils, or residual soils (mainly lithosols), that are suited for
cropland or improved pastures. The nomadic system of grazing in Iran
depends to a considerable extent on such areas of better soils. These
are small enclaves, comprising only a small percentage of the total soil
and it was impractical to show them on the map. Their existence is
recognized, however, and an attempt has been made to estimate the
proportion of each miscellaneous soil group composed of these soils.

It is clear that soils are the most valuable natural resource of Iran.
Out of 165 million hectares (408 million acres), 19 million hectares
(47 million acres) are under cultivation, including fallow and orchards;
ten million hectares (25 million acres) are pasture land; 19 million
hectares (47 million acres) are forest and woodland, while the remainder comprises wastelands, desert, and mountains (of which as
much as 33 million hectares (82 million acres) are unused but potentially productive). Of the 19 million hectares under cultivation, only
6·6 million hectares are under crops in any one year, and only 3 million
hectares are under irrigation. Of these, 700,000 hectares (1,730,000

acres) are vineyard and orchards, and 2·3 million hectares are under irrigated crops such as rice, cotton, sugar-beet, various oil seeds, and sometimes wheat.

The soil survey, land classification, and other soil research and investigations carried out in the last fifteen years by the government of Iran are being continued with the help of the F.A.O. and other agencies. Several problems in soil classification remain to be solved: notably among these are the soils of mountains and dissected slopes, the saline and alkaline soils, and the soils of irrigated areas. A beginning has been made in the preparation of maps of large areas of the country on a scale of 1:50,000.

All soil research has the following aims:

1. Each hectare of land must be used according to its capacity;

2. Any increase in the agricultural area of Iran should take place on the soils that have the greatest potentiality; and

3. All forms of land use, including the yields of every hectare under cultivation, should be improved.

To this end several irrigation, drainage, and reclamation projects have been started in the last decade. A great deal of investigation is being directed towards the improvement of yields through more efficient use of fertilizers, and by soil and water conservation.

NOTE ON CLAYS

A natural resource that affects everybody's life in Iran is mud. Until recently nearly all houses were of thick-walled mud construction and the roofs consisted of poplar tree-trunks overlain by a thick layer of mud; the well-compacted mud floors of these houses, insulated from the heat of the sun, were normally carpeted to some extent.

Even today, when they make bricks, they begin with the same raw material; and road-building on Iranian mud presents some special problems. When earthquakes strike, those heavy roofs so characteristic of many Iranian houses may crush their victims. So it may be said that the great majority of Iranians are born, live, and die in an environment of mud. It is all-surrounding, inescapable and often remarked on by the poets. It has not, however, been studied much by the scientists.

Instead of quoting Burton's somewhat laboured translation of a passage from Sa'di's *Gulistān*, Introduction 1, I shall give a spontaneous

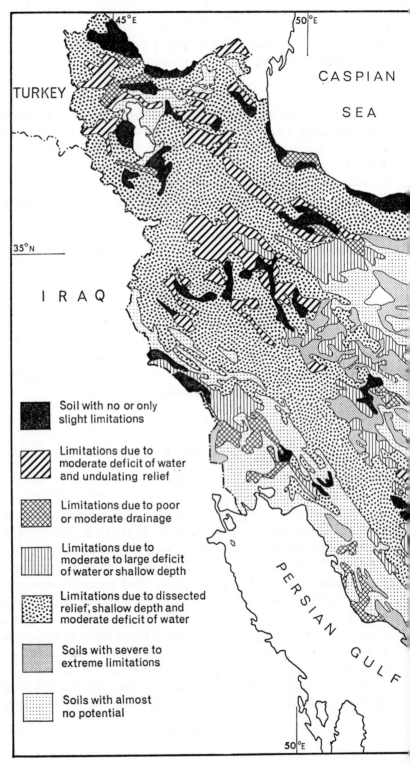

Fig. 85. Soil potentiality map of Iran.

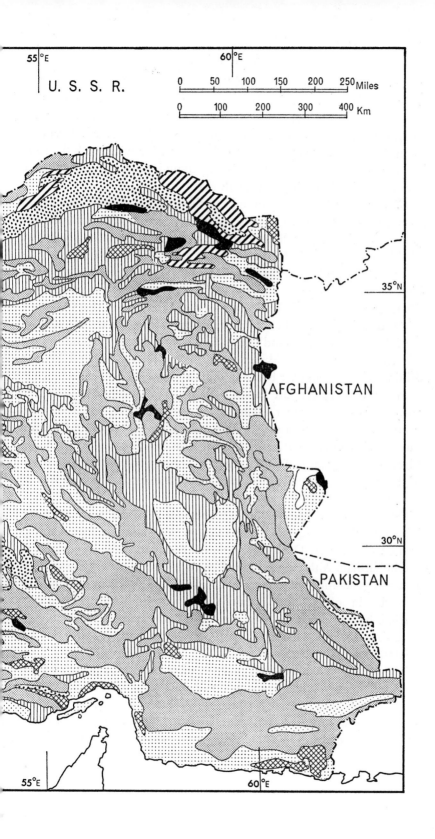

translation, made one day by P. W. Avery in a commercial office in Tehrān. "A sweet-scented clay one day in the bath came to me from the hand of my beloved. I said to it, 'Are you musk or ambergris? because I am drunk with your beautiful heart-ravishing smell.' It replied, 'I am just an ordinary piece of clay, but I sat for a while with the rose, and the perfection of my companion wrought its effect in me; and were it not so I should be just that earth that I am'."

Gil-i-Shīrāz (Shīrāz clay) bought in the bazaar at Tehrān was found to have a cation-exchange capacity of 24·8 milli-equivalents per 100 grammes (after all, Sa'dī came from Shīrāz); but a head-washing clay (*Gil-i-sar shūr*) bought in the bazaar at Kirmānshāh could rightly be described as a fuller's earth, since the cation exchange capacity was as high as 64·6 units per 100 grammes. This clay was said to come from Sāva, near Qum. J. V. Harrison has given an opinion that bentonite might one day be found in the volcanic tuffs and ashes associated with the calcareous series around Qum. With a little care in preparation the clay from the bazaar could be used in the refining of oils and fats, for drilling oil wells, and for bonding foundry moulds.

In the west of Iran pure kaolin is absent. The clay used at Lālīn, the pottery village near Bahār, Hamadān, is merely the calcareous alluvium from which the coarsest sand grains are allowed to settle out from a slurry. Clay from a *qanāt* near Lālīn has a similar chemical composition. Electronmicrographs show that the pottery clay contains a proportion of the clay mineral "palygorskite", a needle-shaped crystal, as well as the usual platy clay minerals.

Palygorskite has been found in many soils in Syria, in Israel, in the Diyala district of Iraq, and in the valley of Āb-i-Dilbī; in Iran it occurs in the foothills near Dar-i-Khazīneh, in the Kārūn delta in Khūzistān, and in Kirmān. Although palygorskite may be formed in saline swamps as a soil-generating clay mineral, I believe that much of this mineral occurring in soils on both sides of the Zagros mountains is essentially detrital, being derived by solution of the limestones and dolomites. I have found it in an Eocene limestone west of Kirmānshāh and in a dolomite near Khurramābād.

The minute crystals of palygorskite affect the permeability of soils, and exert strong shrinkage forces on drying. Water cannot easily drain through these soils; and roads, if they are not to be flooded or weakened by alternate wetting and drying underneath, should be built as raised causeways, or else should be very well waterproofed with crude petroleum below the road surface: a point not always realized by those involved.

It is difficult to make strong bricks with this calcareous alluvium since overheating melts the clay and underheating makes a weak brick. It seems certain that the Babylonian brickmakers at S̲h̲ūs̲h̲ achieved very accurate temperature control; but it is not known how they did this, for they made better bricks than have been made in recent times.

CHAPTER 7

HYDROGRAPHY

Since antiquity the distribution and intensity of human activity in Iran have always reflected the availability of water, either on the surface, or beneath it within the reach of primitive technology. Iran's most glorious days were inaugurated by achievements in water control that were incredible for their age, and her decline resulted as much from a misunderstanding of the implications of complete water control as from the more easily comprehended political and physical disasters brought by Arab rule and successive Mongol conquests. It is undeniable that contemporary Iran is among the leanest of countries by virtue of her climatic and hydrographic deficiencies. In honesty one must admit that her most legendary oases are verdant only by contrast with the fearful landscapes around them, and their sparseness of water is often disappointing to foreigners who are unacquainted with the desolation of their hinterland. In this desiccated country the congruence between procurable water and population density is maintained even where water is in excess of need. Since the collapse of the irrigation economy of ancient Khūzistān, the marshy coastal plain between the Alburz mountains and the Caspian Sea, though malarial, ill-famed, and isolated from the main currents of Iranian life, has continued to support the greatest concentrations of humanity between the Black Sea and the Indus valley.

GENERAL CONSIDERATIONS

Iran's most obvious hydrographic problems are compounded of the disadvantages of scanty and highly seasonal precipitation, and a surface configuration which tends to concentrate moisture on the periphery of the country, leaving its vast heart an area of irreconcilable sterility. South of the Alburz mountains there is no hope of rain during the summer months, when streams wither and the land is parched. Frontal precipitation occurs between October and May, its distribution and quantity being conspicuously related to elevation and exposure. Mountainous areas in the north and west may receive as much as 80 in. of precipitation, while many interior stations show a statistical average of less than 3 in. annually. Precipitation at all levels decreases in a south-easterly direction, but in most parts of Iran local orographic effects produce contrasts between relatively moist spots and rain-shadows. The country's physiography wrings enough moisture from eastward-travelling cyclonic depressions to support sizable populations in various regions, yet it provides dependable supplies of surface water only in relatively isolated areas around its margins. The pertinent relief elements are the vast and complex central plateau; and its encircling buttress of mountain chains, of variable height and breadth, whose exterior slopes lead downward everywhere to elevations little above sea-level. In the north and east this outward descent is abrupt; on the west it covers a distance of 100 miles or more. The significant streams of Iran trench these outer slopes, exporting the moisture collected seasonally on the highland rim of the central plateau. Only occasionally does a perennial stream snake out of the encircling ranges to bring a dependable supply of moisture onto the plateau itself, and all such streams wither and disappear in saline marshes and salt flats within sight of their highland catchments.

Only half of the outer slope, that of the Zagros mountains in the west and the Makran in the south, sends runoff to the sea. The northern slope is tributary to the Caspian basin and the sands of the Qara Qum, while the sparse contributions of the eastern highlands are lost in a series of salt flats and marshes that occupy the sump-like frontier zone between Iran and its eastern neighbours, Afghanistan and West Pakistan.

Nowhere in Iran is there an annual surplus of water, and significant seasonal surpluses occur in only the wishbone of high mountains that encloses the central plateau on the north and west. According to Carter (fig. 86), only the Alburz mountains, the high Zagros north of the thirtieth parallel, and the highlands of Khurāsān and Āzarbāījān show even a seasonal water surplus in excess of 8 in.[1] Additional small zones having a mean surplus of 4 to 8 in. extend the area of moisture available as runoff to small parts of the volcanic axis east of Iṣfahān, isolated high ranges in Fārs, and possibly the uplands in the vicinity of Bīrjand. Regions having a mean seasonal water surplus of less than 4 in. are not reliable sources of moisture, as shown by their want of perennial and even seasonal streams. In such areas (which constitute perhaps 80 per cent of the total of the country) the nature of human activity depends

[1] Douglas B. Carter, "Three Water Balance Maps of Southwest Asia", *Publications in Climatology*, Laboratory of Climatology, vol. XI, no. 1 (1958). Carter's figures are based upon calculations of the water balance using the Thornthwaite method, which considers evapotranspiration plus soil-moisture depletion and recharge.

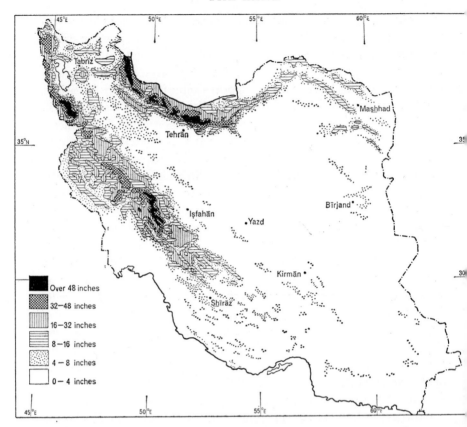

Fig. 86. Mean annual water surplus in Iran (adapted from Douglas B. Carter). All surpluses shown are seasonal, with summer a time of water-deficit throughout the country.

upon the availability of subsurface water that can be tapped by wells and *qanāts*. Runoff is episodic and occurs only because the precipitation, meagre as it is, momentarily exceeds the infiltration capacity of the surface. Such precipitation is of course capricious in terms of quantity, location, and distribution in time.

SEASONAL REGIME

The water surplus of 15 to 70 in. in the highland rim of Iran is seasonal, pertaining only to the winter months. During the summer even high-altitude stations indicate water deficits of 4 to 5 in.[1] A latitudinal effect

[1] Measured in terms of water needs to satisfy evapotranspiration and soil-moisture requirements. During the summer, deficits in the interior basins of the Iranian plateau probably range from 40 to 70 in.

is clear, the summer drought being increasingly noticeable as one moves southward through the ranges of the Zagros, which in the province of Fārs are as parched as the surrounding plains.

It follows that the regime of streams throughout the country is seasonal in the extreme, as well as being highly variable from year to year. The hydrological regime is, moreover, out of phase with the agricultural calendar. Peak flows arrive too late to benefit winter crops, and the period of minimum discharge occurs at the very time that summer crops are in greatest need of moisture.

Runoff is at a maximum in late winter when the biblical "latter rains" fall upon the highland snow-pack. At this time the discharges from large perennial streams moving westward out of the Zagros may increase tenfold over their late-summer minimum. Spring floods ordinarily inundate vast lowland areas, particularly near junctions of major streams. The Khūzistān plain suffers most in this respect, being a node for the drainage derived from 45,000 square miles of the Zagros mountains, carried down in five streams which converge on this lowland from the north-west, north, east, and south-east. South of Dizfūl and Shustar an area of perhaps 100 square miles, as well as far larger areas below Ahvāz [Ahwaz], are normally submerged by spring flood-waters, which have sometimes closed the Trans-Iranian Railway between Ahvāz and Khurramshahr for as much as 100 consecutive days. It is possible that the mere spectre of disastrous flooding has inhibited serious re-development of these potentially rich plains—the irrigated granary of Iran in Sassanian time. In Khūzistān alone, annual flood damage has averaged about £400,000 ($1,120,000), while the average loss in floods of thirty years expectancy has been estimated at some £2,000,000.[1]

During the spring and occasionally also in the winter, the principal streams of the Zagros and Alburz mountains become impassable barriers, washing away temporary bridges and filling slot-like gorges with waters too deep and too turbulent to be negotiated by any means. Even in open basins these torrents present formidable obstacles to man, especially to several hundred thousand transhumant nomads and their flocks, who must cross the streams frequently in their quest for grass. The migration routes of individual clans in various pastoral tribes are more or less circumscribed by custom, natural features, and conflict with adjacent groups, so that good fording places are not accessible to

---

[1] Development and Resources Corporation, *The Unified Development of the Natural Resources of the Khuzestan Region* (New York, 1959), p. 53. Figures converted from Iranian rials.

all, and in time of high water a normally dangerous crossing becomes a desperate struggle that is frequently attended by tragedy. During the period of spring snow-melt, many rivers in the Alburz and Zagros mountains can be forded only in the forenoon.

The perennial streams of the Zagros, Alburz, Āzarbāïjān, and Khurāsān are maintained throughout the rainless summer and early autumn by snow-melt and contributions from springs, which are especially copious in the limestone highlands of the west. Injections of clear spring water into the turbid greenish currents of the larger streams make the location and number of such sources quite evident. One of the great pleasures of the western highland, is in fact, the sweet water available at nearly all times. A significant number of streams, particularly in the Zagros, originate as flowing springs; among these is the Kūhrang, the traditional source of the Kūrān river. In the desolate eastern highlands, folded lavas store and transmit the sparse available moisture in the same manner as do the limestones of the more humid west, permitting a surprising degree of agricultural development in the bleak hinterlands of Qā'īn and Bīrjand.

Among the exterior ranges of the Zagros, much of the scenery itself has developed in response to the flow of springs. These mountains are, to an unusual degree, an area of great limestone and conglomerate "walls", some of them crenulate, others even-crested, produced by the unroofing, through denudation, of simple anticlinal folds. The massive limestones and conglomerates forming the great escarpments are underlain by relatively impermeable marls, with seepage of water at the interface between the cliff-making formations and their sub-stratum. Where the limestone–marl contact is exposed at the surface, scarps are almost monolithic, nearly vertical, and in rapid retreat because of sapping, as indicated by the accumulation of great detached blocks at their base. Where this contact is not exposed, the configuration of the scarps is the result of chemical weathering and frost action, producing more intricate cliffs and less spectacular scree.

STREAM DISCHARGES

A desert country, Iran possesses no truly great rivers. The discharges of Iranian streams are small, not only as a consequence of seasonal aridity, but also because individual drainage basins nowhere attain great size (fig. 87). This is a sign of the tectonic and physiographic youth of this part of the earth's crust. Few perennial streams exist other than in the mountain portions of Iran, where drainage systems are in their infancy. Drainage divides are unstable in the highlands, and stream captures, both complete and impending, are ubiquitous, particularly where head-waters encounter one another in synclinal valleys or subsequent lowlands. Contrary to expectation, the divide between interior and oceanic drainage does not coincide with the snowy "ridge-pole" of the Zagros. Instead, it is shifted towards the interior south of Hamadān, and follows a series of dry ranges of inferior elevation east of the line of great peaks. Thus streams running down to the Persian Gulf must first breach the very ranges upon which they are born—an initial manifestation of perplexing drainage anomalies which make the Zagros streams some of the world's most interesting in a geomorphological sense.

The position of this divide, along with the steeper gradients of the "exoreic" (i.e. outward flowing to the sea) streams, would seem to imply headward extension of the Persian Gulf drainage at the expense of "endoreic" (i.e. inward flowing) systems; but such may not have been the case. Both the Qum Rūd and the Zāyandeh Rūd, which empty onto the interior plateau, have captured significant headwaters from systems tributary to the Persian Gulf. Possibly this has been a temporary development related to local tectonic movements, only momentarily reversing a generally eastward movement of the endoreic–oceanic drainage divide. In time, greater streams with far-flung headwaters will emerge from the present competition, but stable hydrographic boundaries are not to be expected in this area in the current geological epoch.

The largest streams in Iran are the Kārūn, which moves south-westward out of the High Zagros; the Safīd Rūd, which breaches the western Alburz to reach the Caspian; and the Aras, which separates the Āzarbāījāni of Iran from their brothers in the Soviet Union. Only the Kārūn has been gauged long enough for its regime to be well known; this is the result of its navigability upstream as far as Ahvāz, where measurements have been made since 1894. The Kārūn has a maximum discharge in April of some 60,000 to 75,000 cu. ft per sec and a minimum discharge in October of about 7,000 cu. ft per sec. According to Pirnia, the natural flood discharge of the Safīd Rūd is twice that of the Kārūn, while its minimum flow declines to less than a tenth that of the more southerly stream.[1] The two catchments are of similar size

[1] H. Pirnia, "Experience in the Integrated Development of a River Basin", *Proceedings, U.N. Scientific Conference on the Conservation and Utilization of Resources*, vol. IV, *Water*

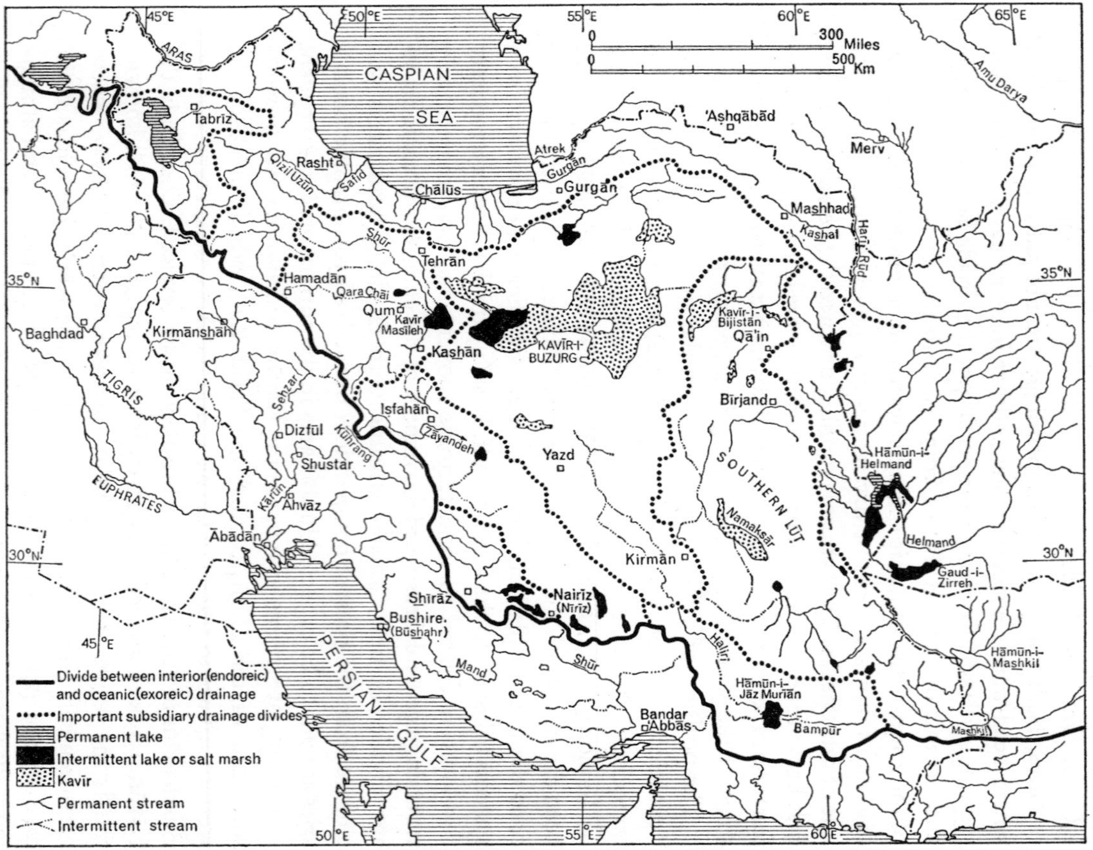

Fig. 87. The hydrography of Iran.

(about 21,000 square miles), but that of the Kārūn lies at a superior elevation and has a considerably greater snow-pack, which sustains the river throughout the dry season.

The largest individual catchment (23,000 square miles) is that of the Rūd-i-Mand, a wandering stream that collects the scant runoff of the dry Zagros of Lāristān. The discharge of the Mand, estimated generously, ranges from 71,500 to 360 cu. ft per sec.[1] The basins of the Kārūn (21,100 square miles), Safīd Rūd (20,900 square miles), and the Karkheh (16,600 square miles) follow in size, though they discharge more water, particularly during the dry period.

The westward-flowing streams of the central Zagros mountains, having relatively large catchments and being nourished by springs and snow-melt from extensive areas lying between 12,000 and 15,000 ft, maintain significant flows during the dry months. Measured at the mountain front, the minimum flows of the Karkheh, Diz, and Kārūn rivers have averaged 880, 1,765, and 3,000 cu. ft per sec respectively.[2] By contrast, the equally well-nourished but much shorter streams that course down the north slopes of the Alburz mountains cannot be relied upon for more than 200 cu. ft per sec during the dry season. The southern slopes of the Alburz are drained by several significant streams that disappear into the Kavīr Masīleh south of Tehrān. The Karaj river, now dammed, formerly discharged up to 4,400 cu. ft per sec in the spring, but dwindled to about 150 cu. ft per sec in the autumn months. The Kavīr Masīleh also receives runoff from the Zagros, carried down by the Qara Chai, Rūd-i-Shūr [Qara Sit], and Qum Rūd. The Qara Chai delivers as much as 11,000 cu. ft per sec in flood, declining to about 150 cu. ft per sec during October. The Qum Rūd probably has a comparable regime, with the Rud-i-Shūr being a lesser stream.

The Zagros sends but one other important stream eastward into the interior: the fabled Zāyandeh Rūd, which waters the oasis of Iṣfahān a short distance from the mountain front. The stream is eventually dissipated in the Gāvkhāneh salt marsh. The Zāyandeh Rūd rises in the highest part of the range and appears equal in discharge to some of the more important "exoreic" streams of the central Zagros, delivering at

Resources (New York, U.N. Dept. Economic Affairs, 1951), pp. 162–5. Figures converted from metric equivalents. The flow of the Safīd Rūd is now controlled by a high dam in the Alburz mountains.

[1] Pirnia, *Water Resources*, p. 164.

[2] Development and Resources Corporation, *Resources of the Khuzestan Region*, p. 40. Figures converted from metric equivalents.

least 60,000 cu. ft per sec in the spring; its flow declines to perhaps 1,000 cu. ft per sec in the autumn. Two additional streams of significance rise in the southern Zagros, but they never escape the highland. These are the Kur and Pulvar, which follow longitudinal valleys among the ranges, eventually becoming confluent on the Plain of Persepolis and terminating in the shallow Nairīz lake.

The interior basin of Lake Rezā'īyeh [Urumiyeh] receives several sizable streams from the east and south. The Zarīneh Rūd, entering from the south, discharges some 18,000 cu. ft per sec in the spring and maintains a flow of about 350 cu. ft per sec during the dry season. The highly saline Talkeh Rūd [Ajī Chāi], entering from the east, may have an even greater discharge, being nourished by snow-melt on the giant volcanic cones of Savalan and Sahand.

The highlands of Khurāsān in the north-east of Iran nourish three longitudinal streams of importance: the Gurgān and Atrak, which discharge westward to the Caspian, and the Kashaf, which flows south-eastward past Mashhad to join the Harī Rūd on the Afghan border. The watersheds of these streams are larger than those of the Alburz, being comparable to those of the central Zagros. Decreased precipitation and a smaller snow-pack in this area are somewhat compensated by reduced temperatures, so that the discharges of the streams of Khurāsān are inferior to those of the central Zagros, but well in excess of the streams of both the Alburz and southern Zagros.

About a quarter of the perimeter of Iran, extending south of the Kashaf basin and east of the Shūr, is essentially without permanent streams. This area contributes significant seasonal runoff to the marshes of the eastern frontier zone, and to the Gulf of Oman on the south. During the summer and autumn, even the better-known streams of the south and east are broad gravel channels containing only threads or pools of water. In their lower portions the streams of the Makrān (known as *kaurs*) consist largely of the seepage from gravel valley fillings. The Rūd-i-Halīl and Rūd-i-Bampūr, which flow towards each other in the Jāz Muriān Basin, rise at higher elevations and have more dependable flows. In fact, the water of their terminal basin is usually sweet, making it almost unique in interior Iran. The streams of the eastern highlands are short, and though nourished by springs they all but disappear late in the dry season.

In the province of Sīstān a number of such streams terminate in the Hāmūn-i-Helmand, a group of vast reed marshes and intermittent lakes fed primarily by the Helmand river, which flows westward some 700 miles from the mountain heart of Afghanistan. As a result of the demarcation of the Irano-Afghan frontier in 1903–5, only the delta distributaries of the Helmand presently lie within Iranian territory. Once an important source of irrigation water in the Sīstān basin, the flow of the Helmand has been largely wasted since the destruction of its control works by Tamerlane in the fourteenth century, an event which seems to have led to the depopulation of the region. Temporary barrages are erected at the head of the delta every autumn for diversion of irrigation water, the structures being carried away by the annual rise occurring in late December. Rising some 400 miles away in the outliers of the Hindu Kush, the Helmand usually delivers at least 60,000 cu. ft per sec in flood and 2,000 cu. ft per sec during the dry season. In times of flood, the waters of the resulting lakes (*hāmūn*) spill south-eastward through a well-defined channel to the Gaud-i-Zirreh, a salt flat some eighty miles distant in the south-western corner of Afghanistan.

HYDROGRAPHY AND COMMERCE

The streams of Iran are of little use for navigation. This is but another effect of the climatic regime and physiographic youth of the country. During periods of high water streams are not navigable owing to their strength, while the remainder of the year most are useless as a result of their weakness. Gathering in high mountains, the larger streams have steep and extremely irregular profiles. At some points their canyons are so constricted that a man can leap across hurtling waters that no ordinary boat or raft could survive. A stone's throw distant the stream may be a hundred yards across, divided in a plexus of gravelly channels only inches in depth.

Leaving the mountains altogether, streams dwindle quickly as a result of evaporation, seepage, and diversion for irrigation. Most disappear within sight of their highland sources, leaving their dry channels prolonged as gravel- or sand-filled depressions, the underflow of which now and then supports an exotic agricultural efflorescence.

Only the Kārūn is navigable for any significant distance, with shallow-draft steamers being able to work up to Ahvāz from the Shaṭṭ-al-ʿArab, a distance of 112 miles. Here ledges and rocks interrupt the channel, but even they can be passed by powerful craft during high water in April and May. Small native boats accomplish the passage at all seasons, though they must struggle against a strong current. Once past Ahvāz, light steamers and barges may proceed another seventy-three miles upstream—though not without difficulty—to the railhead at Dar-i-Khazīneh. Shoals, rapids, and narrows forbid further access to large craft, and even small native boats can make little use of the river above this point.

Not only are the streams of Iran generally unnavigable, but their valleys are of less than usual utility as routes of commerce and communication. Too often the mountain streams flow through impassable defiles in which waters too swift and too deep for wading are confined between perpendicular rock-walls hundreds or even thousands of feet in height. As we have seen, the streams of the Zagros mountains, in particular, are famed for their incredibly constricted *tangs*, some of which attain a depth of more than 8,000 ft. These canyons are refuges for mountain sheep and wild goats, but until the age of dynamite many remained inaccessible to man. As a consequence, a number of streams in the Zagros have different appellations above and below a single defile. Paths hacked out of sheer rock walls, together with the crumbling remnants of stone causeways perched high above mountain torrents, bear ubiquitous testimony to thousands of years of human efforts to overcome the isolation of these gorges. In the Zagros such defiles so disrupt riverine lines of communication that many of the historic commercial routes across the mountains have shunned the transverse valleys, and tortuously negotiated the Persian Ladder crest by crest. The migration routes of transhumant tribes are similarly affected, forcing certain groups to assault snow-clad ranges directly, in avoidance of the riverine "passes" provided by nature.

The unique gorges of the Zagros mountains are the physiographic expression of a disharmony between the drainage pattern and the tectonic structure of this region. Here we see one of the world's most impressive displays of anomalous transverse drainage, in which streams, large and small, cleave range after range of high mountains in apparent disregard for the geological structures that otherwise control the evolution of scenery in the region. The Zagros drainage anomaly is especially interesting as it cannot be explained by ordinary hypotheses of transverse drainage formation.[1]

---

[1] The origin of the Zagros streams and their significance for the general theory of transverse drainage are discussed elsewhere in this volume, in "The Origin of the Zagros Defiles", chapter 4, pp. 195–211.

HYDROGRAPHICALLY FAVOURED AREAS

The best-watered regions of Iran, outside of the highlands themselves, are the Caspian coastal plain and Khūzistān. The former, which receives the runoff of the northern slope of the Alburz mountains, is an area with upwards of 80 in. of precipitation annually. The coastal lowlands of Gīlān and Māzandarān may themselves experience rain at any season, so that the area is one of forest, jungle, and swamp, with rice the dominant crop on cleared land.

Khūzistān has a totally different aspect. Five great rivers funnel the runoff from 45,000 square miles of the High Zagros into this plain of 15,000 square miles, but its landscapes are hardly less sterile than those of the interior deserts. Throughout the long summer and autumn Khūzistān is essentially devoid of natural vegetation, and even in the spring cropland appears to be an intruder here. During the Sasanian period, however, this area was famed as one of the most bountiful regions of Asia: producing cereals, sugar cane, rice, and dates in abundance. The basis of this former prosperity was an elaborate system of barrages, tunnels, inverted siphons, lifting devices, and canals utilizing to the fullest degree the waters brought down from the Zagros in the Karkheh, Diz, and Kārūn rivers. What was not provided was artificial drainage of the irrigated land, an oversight that must have been a primary factor in the gradual decline of Khūzistān during 'Abbāsid times, when crews of slaves were conscripted to remove salt crusts from the fields. Rising water-tables under irrigated land probably also contributed to the 'Abbāsids' desperate and well-documented attempts to irrigate new lands of poorer quality. Waterlogging, induced alkalinization and salinization, increasing problems of security in the 'Abbāsid period, devastation by the Mongols, and the hazard of flood have all contributed to the depopulation of the Khūzistān region in the past millennium.[1]

On a smaller scale, a multitude of interior plains and open valleys in the mountain regions are amply supplied with water by through-flowing streams and rivulets fed by melting snows and generous springs. The most extensive and best-watered intermontane plains are found among the Zagros ranges, particularly in the basins of the Karkheh and Kārūn rivers. Some pockets in the Zagros are relatively verdant

[1] For an excellent discussion of the rise and fall of the Khūzistān region, see R. M. Adams, "Agriculture and Urban Life in Early Southwestern Iran", *Science*, vol. cxxxvi, no. 3511 (1962), pp. 109–22.

throughout the year, and there is little doubt that they offer the most comfortable living to be found in Iran. It is unfortunate, however, that the streams passing through these basins are often deeply entrenched, isolating separate sections of the plains from one another, and necessitating either diversion of irrigation water far upstream, or devices for lifting water directly to the fields. As a consequence, many plains otherwise suitable for cultivation are utilized only as pastures.

Some of the more important intermontane basins and valleys in the Zagros are those of Hamadān at the head of the endoreic Qara Sū; the plains of Kirmānshāh, Malāyer, and Nihāvand in the Karkheh headwaters; the Burūjird plain in the Diz watershed; the Malāmīr, Lurdagān, Simīrūn, and Shahr Kurd plains in the Kārūn catchment; and, farther south, the endoreic basins of Shīrāz and Nairīz. Scores of small oases of lesser fame but still greater verdure are scattered throughout the central Zagros and its foothills, as well as over the Alburz mountains and the highlands of Khurāsān and Āzarbāïjān.

ENDOREIC BASINS

The heart of Iran is a series of enclosed depressions of various shapes and sizes, each having near its centre a large salt flat or salt marsh. These sumps are seldom reached by surface flow. The exterior slopes of Iran on the north and east also drain into endoreic basins, so that only one fourth of the entire country sends runoff to the sea.

Three closed basins on the periphery of Iran contain large permanent bodies of water: the Caspian Sea, stretching away from the northern slopes of the Alburz range; Lake Rezā'īyeh in Āzarbāïjān, and the lakes (*hāmūn*) of Sīstān on the Afghan frontier. All of these saline lakes are shrunken remnants of formerly more extensive water bodies. Large parts of their shores are foetid mud flats and marshes, for each has been gradually reduced in size by the diversion of affluent waters for irrigation. This effect poses serious problems to Iran's important ports on the Caspian, all of which are impaired by progressive shallowing and rapid silting. Constant dredging is required to keep these harbours open, and large vessels must anchor a mile or more off-shore, trans-shipping into lighters and barges, which in turn discharge their cargoes at jetties many hundreds of yards in length. Gradual reduction in the elevation of the water surface in the Caspian, Lake Rezā'īyeh, and the lakes of Sīstān has caused their tributary streams to become incised well below the surface of the surrounding silts.

The great majority of the endoreic basins are unmitigated deserts, in which thin sheets of water collect only during wet seasons. These "lakes" may persist for several years, disappearing for a period, to return again after another humid cycle. Some are sufficiently well-established to be classified as semi-permanent marsh, with well-developed hydrophytic fauna and flora. During drier periods, evaporite efflorescences on the ephemeral beds of lakes lie exposed in sheets of startling whiteness dozens of miles in length and breadth, occasionally sending apophyses hither and yon between mountain ranges. Withering streams that approach the gleaming salt flats commonly disappear in marshes before reaching the terminal basin. Though saline and alkaline deposits crust the lake beds and their shorelines, sweet water may be present in the peripheral alluvial deposits, and its utilization by means of shallow wells and qanāts supports isolated concentrations of people around the perimeters of most of the desert basins of interior Iran.

Dry lakes and saline marshes are found in structural basins in the eastern Zagros; in the depression between the Zagros and the volcanic axis extending from Qum to Kirmān; to the east of the volcanic axis; in the Jāz Muriān basin, the Southern Lūt, Balūchistān, the eastern highlands north of Bīrjand, and, finally, at intervals along the frontier zone with Afghanistan and West Pakistan. Near the "shores" of these ephemeral water bodies are such oases as Iṣfahān, Shīrāz, Nairīz, Sīrjān, Qum, Kāshān, Ardistān, Nā'īn, Yazd, and Qā'īn.

The basins of Shīrāz and Nairīz in the southern Zagros contain large shallow lakes at present, which appear to be permanent. It has been pointed out that ancient accounts of the geography of this region do not indicate the presence of a lake in the Nairīz basin, suggesting that this vast body of water has appeared during historic time.[1] Curzon attributed the Nairīz lake to the decline in Iran's fortunes since the Mongol conquests, offering the hypothesis that large-scale diversion of water for irrigation during antiquity prevented runoff from reaching the terminal basin, which thus remained desiccated until the breakdown of the agricultural economy of the region.

Possibly the least tractable portion of Iran is the series of immense *kavīrs* occupying thousands of square miles south and east of Tehrān.

[1] George Curzon, *Persia and the Persian Question* (London, 1892), vol. II, pp. 111–12.

These areas, which resemble the beds of extinct lakes, are hazardous to travellers because of the peculiar character of their surface.[1]

The term *kavīr* implies a salt crust of variable thickness overlying deposits of silt that are laced with hidden channels of slimy mud. These mires, known as *shaṭṭs*, are fortuitously distributed, and both men and animals have been fatally trapped in them. The subsurface ooze appears to persist, despite the great aridity of these areas, as a result of the deliquescence of silts contaminated with hygroscopic salts, principally magnesium chloride. The kavīr surfaces become particularly treacherous when wetted by autumn rains. During the dry season the salt crust in many areas is an endless expanse of hard polygonal plates separated by jagged pressure ridges; some surfaces may become almost completely covered by sharp-edged fragments of the ruptured salt crust. The dangers of both laceration and engulfment in the slimy substratum have caused large parts of the kavīrs to be shunned by men and animals. Tracks through the kavīrs are rare and sharply defined: at least one is a causeway of imported rocks about eighteen miles long.

The Great Kavīr [Kavīr-i-Buzurg, Kavīr-i-Namak] lies between the Southern Lūṭ and the Alburz mountains, extending some 230 miles from west to east, with a breadth of forty to 150 miles. Two surface streams are known to reach the Great Kavīr at its eastern end; one of these is perennial, the other intermittent. Around the periphery of the Kavīr-i-Buzurg are smaller areas of similar character, the largest being the Bījistān Kavīr to the east, and on the west the Kavīr Masīleh, which lies directly south of Tehrān. The Kavīr Masīleh receives considerable runoff from both the Alburz and Zagros mountains, so that portions are ordinarily covered by standing water. The effect of the great kavīrs in the north and of the kavīrs, sands, and *yārdangs*[2] of the Dasht-i-Lūṭ, to the south is to give Iran an immense dead heart, which occupies some 200,000 square miles or nearly one third of the entire country.

[1] Curzon stated that Iranian tradition includes mention of great lakes in the desert basins south of the Alburz, one of them lapping at the outskirts of Rhagae [Ray], with the minaret of Sāva serving as a lighthouse on its shores. See *Persian Question*, vol. II, pp. 247–8. However, Hans Bobek's studies led him to conclude that the kavīrs are not former lake beds, but erosional surfaces of some complexity, which bevel subhorizontal sediments from which the saline materials are derived. H. Bobek, *Features and Formation of the Great Kavīr and Masīleh*, Arid Zone Research Centre, pub. 11 (U. of Tehrān, 1959), 63 pp. It seems that whatever the origin of the salines, these basins could at times have been inundated, at least in part, as folklore suggests.

[2] *Yardangs* are irregular sharp crested ridges, occasionally tens of feet in height, which alternate with smooth anastomosing grooves, both being a result of eolian erosion in silt deposits.

SUMMARY

On the whole, the hydrographic character of Iran does not serve the country well, since all of its influences are centrifugal. Plentiful surface water and procurable subsurface water make large areas habitable; but these are widely separated, most of them lying around the periphery of the country, isolated one from the other by high mountains, empty deserts, or treacherous kavīrs, across which communications are extremely difficult. Unnavigable rivers and impassable gorges further hinder contact between adjacent populations, fostering insularity and tribalism. Given such divisive physical circumstances it is somewhat surprising, and a tribute to the appetite and activity of the ancient despots, that this vast region could have been effectively subjugated and maintained under centralized authority at so early a date.

CHAPTER 8

VEGETATION

The extensive Iranian plateau constitutes a clearly defined physiographic and geologic unit; yet from the biogeographical and ecological points of view—that is, as a place to live for plants and animals, including man—the plateau displays marked variation. This is brought out very well by the regional changes in distribution and character of its natural vegetation cover, which in turn may be said to stem from four main factors:

First, *climatic situation*. Along its length of approximately 2,000 miles the Iranian plateau crosses—very much as a gigantic bridge—the full width of the great desert belt of the Old World; it does so at the point where this belt bends north-east to connect its Saharan–Arabian portion with its Central Asian section. With this geographical location, the Iranian plateau, while highly arid in its large and depressed central part, is exposed to a variety of climatic influences, some of which just touch its edges, while others penetrate or even submerge it for a restricted period. Of this latter kind is a temperate regime, with the westerlies and wandering depressions which in summer just impinge on the north-western fringe of the plateau in Armenia and Trans-caucasia, but which become more established during most of the winter half of the year. Also at this season the highly continental, anti-cyclonic regime of Central Asia and Siberia makes itself felt by sending its icy air masses against and over the plateau. The southern fringe of Iran, however, is exposed to the tropical or subtropical climatic con-ditions of the southern desert, which in the summer extend over all the lower parts of the plateau. Finally, the eastern and south-eastern edges show marked influences of the monsoon regime of the Indian sub-continent.

The second factor of diversification is the number of *phytogeographical regions*, which have contributed large groups of their characteristic plant species to the complex of Iranian vegetation. More than 10,000 plant species have been recorded in Iran, and whilst most of them belong to the Irano-Turanian group, which dominates the vegetation of the interior plains and uplands, many contributions from the Euro-

Siberian, the Nubo-Sindian, and Sudanian regions characterize the phytogeographic pattern along the Caspian, the Persian Gulf, and the Makrān shores, respectively. Less pronounced in numbers and distribution are the Mediterranean and Saharan–Arabian elements. Important again, however, is the recruitment from the Indo-Himalayan region in the north-eastern forests.

The third factor is the *pronounced and varied topography* of the plateau. Its more subtle features bring to bear the previously mentioned climatic influences, strengthening or weakening their effects according to location. The fact that over wide distances in the west and east the plateau is fringed by towering ranges, which include the highest elevations of the whole upland, brings about a striking contrast between the humid, forest-clad outward façades, which secure for themselves the greater proportion of rainfall, and the arid interior depressions, turned into poor steppes and deserts by the "Föhn effect" of descending dry air on the lee sides. Also, the interior ranges cannot compare with the coastal chains in respect to the precipitation available. Great altitudinal contrasts are to be found often at close distance, since ranges of more than 12,000 ft above sea-level are not at all infrequent, whereas the outer foothills or plains generally do not exceed a few hundred feet in altitude. Climatic–ecological diversity, with corresponding variation in vegetation type, is therefore a prominent feature of the Iranian highlands, at least on their strongly dissected margins, and more so in the western and eastern extremities than in the central parts. In the climatically more privileged regions, ecological diversity is further enhanced by the checkerboard, or ribbon-like, arrangement of highly diverse parent rocks and hence of corresponding soil formations.

The fourth factor to be considered is *the impact of human activity upon the vegetation*. Man has exercised a far-reaching influence on vegetation structure during his eight or more millenia as a cultivator and stock-breeder in Iran. During this long span of time he has implanted himself within the vegetal environment so intimately and thoroughly, and in so many ways, that only a few remnants of strictly natural vegetation may be found in the more remote corners of the country. Even in the dreariest deserts his interference is clearly evident.

Two of the most devastating human activities have been fuel-collecting and charcoal-making, vital though these may be in a country with low winter temperatures. Together with extensive cutting of timber for building, these activities have not only greatly reduced the

forest areas (which were restricted to begin with), but have also degraded the character of woodland. In addition, the steppes and even the
desert areas have also been deprived of their woody component; other
fundamental changes in the composition of the steppes have been
effected by continual animal grazing. This has led ultimately to the
disappearance of the perennial grasses and to their replacement by
non-palatable weeds or spiny shrubs. Finally, man's collection of edible
herbs, bulbs, and roots for food and medical purposes is by no means
negligible, and contributes to the same ultimate effects: that is, extreme
impoverishment.

Another very important form of interference with the natural plant
cover is, of course, cultivation. Irrigated cultivation has led to the
replacement of most of the natural oases by artificial ones, while
cultivation relying on rainfall has resulted in the destruction of large
forest and steppe areas. Because of the primitive methods of cultivation,
however, which include long periods of fallow, there is in fact no
clear-cut boundary between weed or fallow and natural steppe
vegetation.

All these modes of interference have given rise to many forms of
semi-natural vegetation, which may represent stages either in a process
of destruction or of regeneration. The latter, however, is rather exceptional and mostly incomplete. Thus, to establish the former character
and extension of the different types of natural vegetation is by no means
an easy task, nor has investigation reached anything like a satisfactory
state of knowledge. On the following pages a sketchy attempt has been
made to analyse the vegetal cover of the Iranian plateau and of some
adjacent areas into major units or types, on the basis of physiognomic,
ecological, and also floristic determinants and peculiarities. In fact,
each type comprises a whole series of habitats and corresponding
associations. But owing to the incompleteness of knowledge, and also
bearing in mind the rather general scope of this article, we shall confine
ourselves to some hints, rather than attempting to embrace the whole
array of such associations or classes of associations.

For a better understanding of their areal distribution we may arrange
all the relevant types of vegetation according to their dependence, first,
on atmospheric humidity (precipitation) or ground moisture; and
second, on temperature as expressed in elevation or exposure. Using the
first criterion we may arrange vegetation types into three main groups,
each of which displays a distinctly zonal location:

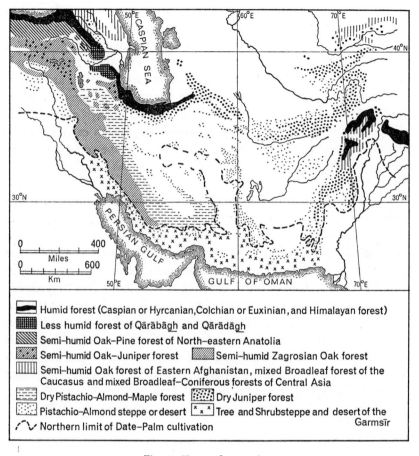

Fig. 88. Types of vegetation.

1. Humid forests.
2. Semi-humid and semi-arid forests.
3. Steppes and deserts with loose tree stands and brushwoods:
    (*a*) Interior plateau,
    (*b*) *garmsīr*.
To these must be added three azonal types:
4. Sand brushwoods.
5. Riparian forests.
6. Salt-marsh brushwoods and coastal forests.

The second criterion, that of temperature, allows us to subdivide the above vegetation types into altitudinal zones. It is noteworthy that the differences in climate, vegetation (natural and cultivated), and in general conditions are so striking that people have given to the altitudinal zones proper names familiar to every Iranian: e.g. *garmsīr* (or "warm land") for the southern, semi-tropical foothills and lowlands (including some of the lowest interior depressions), which are largely characterized by the cultivation of the date-palm. In contrast is the *sardsīr* (or "cold land"), i.e. the cool upland valleys and plateaus decidedly above the main zone of settled life, which carries no distinctive local or regional name. The highest or alpine zone, above any forests or cultivation, is called *sarhadd*, which means "land at the upper boundary".

In the western part of the Iranian plateau, which has always played a prominent part in Iranian history, there is only one area of a truly humid forest. It covers the lowlands along the southern shore of the Caspian Sea (including Tālish, Gīlān, Māzandarān, part of Gurgān), and also the northern slopes of the adjoining Alburz chain between the Aras canyon and the upper reaches of the river Atrak in Khurāsān. This "Hyrcanian forest", as it is called by most botanists, reminds one almost of a tropical forest by its vigorous growth, tall trees, and several-storeyed structure; its liana, its regenerative force, and also the number of species of trees and shrubs it contains (about fifty and sixty respectively). This broad-leaved, deciduous growth is a relic of the warm temperate forest that covered large parts of Europe and northern Asia in the late Tertiary; and there are also some Mediterranean and other ingredients. The lowland type of forest growth falls into several associations according to local conditions, which may include dry ground with deep dark-brown soils, riverain or swampy areas, and coastal dunes. Besides the normal linden, ash, elm, hornbeam, walnut, and maple (*Acer insigne*), along with evergreens such as *Buxus sempervivens*, *Ruscus hyrcanicus*, *Prunus laurocerasus* and *Ilex aquifolium*, there are also relic-species like the *Parrotia persica* (the "Persian teak wood"), *Pterocarya fraxinifolia*, *Zelkova crenata*, *Albizzia Julibrissin*, *Gleditschia caspica*, *Quercus castaneaefolia*, and others. There are also a great many shrubs. Artificial clearings are liable to become quickly infested by pomegranate, by *Paliurus spina christi* and other thorny shrubs, and the arable areas also by fern (*Pteris aquilina*).

The lowland forest also covers the foothills, as well as a transitional zone up to 3,000 ft above sea-level, in which some of its more cold-sensitive members perish. The montane forest falls into two zones. The lower open and fully exposed flanks are dominated by the Oriental or

European beech, while other associations gather on the more protected sun-facing slopes and in the ravines. From about 5,500 ft upward the beech is gradually replaced by a magnificent oak (*Quercus macranthera*), which dominates the upper zone and is accompanied by elm, ash, hornbeam, maple, wild pear and many shrubs, including the common juniper. This upper zone is slightly more xerophytic and forms the upper limit of the forest, which reaches 6,500 ft above sea-level in the Tālish hills, and 8,000 to 9,000 ft in the central and eastern Alburz.

The whole area of the Hyrcanian or Caspian forest receives annually about 30 to 80 in. of precipitation. While the maximum comes in the autumn, no season is without rain. Topographically the maximum probably falls in the beech zone, which is also the cloudiest one in a region that is notorious for its mist and cloudiness. Soils are mostly brown or reddish-brown forest soils with a more-or-less pronounced tendency to podzolization on non-calcareous rocks.

The Hyrcanian forest is much degraded, and largely destroyed in the lowland. Of the montane forest, up to one half may subsist though partly damaged. The rest has been changed into grassy pastures, enclosed fields, and worthless scrub, even of a xerophytic character, on the sun-facing parts. In some dry valleys, such as those of the Safīd Rūd and Chālūs, there exist natural stands of the wild cypress (*Cupressus horizontalis*) which in the Safīd Rūd valley are accompanied by the only place of extensive olive cultivation in Iran (Rūdbār).

The Hyrcanian forest extends north of the Aras (Qārābāgh) as a somewhat drier montane forest without beech, and then through Transcaucasia to join the "Colchian" or "Euxinian" Humid forest on the south-eastern shores of the Black Sea; this forest is also a Tertiary relic, but it is distinguished by an admixture of some spruces (*Abies nordmanniana*, *A. Bornmülleri*), rhododendron, and so on.

A semi-humid oak forest covers the outer slopes of the southern and south-western margins of the Iranian plateau, extending from the present Turkish frontier through Iranian and Iraqi Kurdistān and Lūristān into the province of Fārs. Using the name of the Zagros in a wide sense, we may call it the "Zagrosian forest". It is a somewhat dry, cold-resistant, and deciduous forest with broad-leaved, summer green, oaks as its dominant members. In appearance it differs widely from the Hyrcanian forest: its trees are low, round-topped, and so widely spaced that the ground cover receives enough light to take on the character of a grassy and herbaceous steppe. The whole forest displays an orchard-like appearance. Floristically it belongs to the Irano-Turanian complex, with a few Mediterranean ingredients. Its most characteristic members are *Quercus Brantii, Qu. libanii* and *Qu. Boissieri*, accompanied by elm, maple, celtis, walnut, Syrian pear, pistachio (*P. khinjuk, P. atlantica*), several almond trees, and a great many bushes. In the ravines there are special moisture-loving associations of poplar, willow, alder, elm, ash and plane tree, and also creepers.

No true foothill zone of this forest exists as it approaches its lower limit, at 2,300 to 2,600 ft above sea-level in the north (in the environs of Diyarbakr in Turkey), and at about 4,000 ft in the south. Its upper limit is at 7,500 ft or more (9,000 ft on Kūh-i-Manisht in the Pusht-i-Kūh ranges of Lūristān); whilst its boundary towards the interior plateau is confined to the more elevated crests of Zardeh Kūh (Lūristān) and Kūh-i-Dīnā (Fārs), but spreads far into the interior where the marginal ranges are low, as in Kurdistān. Here, and in the adjoining southern Āzarbāijān, in fact a link in the form of isolated patches seems to have existed across the interior plateau at one time before extensive degradation and destruction pushed the edge of the forest remnants far back towards the western ranges.

The annual amount of precipitation in the zone of the Zagrosian semi-humid forest seems to reach 20 to 30 in. (500–750 mm) or more, most of which occurs in winter and spring. With the exception of the calcareous lithosols found in some parts, brown and chestnut-brown forest soils predominate, together with blackish alluvial soils on some inter-montane plains.

The Zagrosian oak forest continues into eastern Anatolia with some changes in the floristic composition. More Mediterranean elements are to be found in the lower parts, whereas in the higher reaches an admixture of juniper (*J. oxycedrus, J. polycarpos*) makes its appearance. The lower limit of this forest towards the central depression of Āzarbāijān is at about 5,400 ft above sea-level.

On the intermediate plateau between the Caspian (Hyrcanian) forest on the one hand and the Zagrosian forest on the other, apparently nothing but various associations of open steppe are to be found nowadays, which gradually taper out towards the deserts of the central Iranian depressions. However, without paying further attention to the extensive stretches originally covered by, but later on cleared of, Zagrosian forest, we have now to consider the former existence of two "dry" forests in this area.

One of these is the Juniper-forest, which, as many remnants prove, once covered the southern slopes of the Alburz chain and both sides of the main ranges of K͟hurāsān. It is made up today of low trees of *Juniperus polycarpos* (=*J. macropoda*=*J. excelsa*) in thin stands, accompanied by a few or many shrubs, or even trees, such as pistachio (*P. atlantica*, *P. khinjuk*), almond, berberis, and cotoneaster; the hawthorn, crataegus sp., cerasus sp., maple, and various others. In ravines they form thickets together with walnut, wild fruit-trees, pomegranate, ash, poplar, willow, tamarisk, and so on. The ground cover of the forest is a complete steppe complex, either tragacanthic or herbaceous. While the upper limit of this dry forest approximates that of the Caspian montane forest, its lower limit is not easily established, but seems to lie at 3,600 to 5,400 ft above sea-level on the south side, and at 3,000 to 4,500 ft on the north side of the Alburz system and its eastward continuations (the Kopet Dāg͟h and K͟hurāsān). This forest belongs entirely to the cold-resistant type. A cold-sensitive lower zone may possibly be represented by the isolated patches of natural cypress forest in some valleys of the Alburz, mentioned above, as the requirements of humidity seem to be exactly the same for both types: annual precipitation 12 to 20 in. (300–500 mm). Because of the small amount of organic matter available, the soils are mostly of the chestnut and grey sierozem steppe types, if they are developed at all. This cold-resistant vegetation type continues both east and west of the area described here: into Armenia and Anatolia on the western side, and into Afghanistan and Central Asia on the east.

The second type of dry forest is the pistachio–almond–maple forest, which once seems to have covered the more elevated parts of the interior plateau next to the Zagrosian oak forest, either adjoining it or underlying it where the oak forest occurred as a capping on isolated ridges of the plateau. To the west of Tehrān, Arāk, and Iṣfahān, it has been almost completely removed, whereas in Fārs there still exist fairly extensive remnants to the north, south, and east of the Lake Nairīz. This forest also forms the markedly drier south-eastern continuation of the Zagros forest along the water-divide and onto the upland peaks and ranges south and east of Kirmān. The Kūh-i-Jamal Bārīz [Jabāl Bāriz], upward of 6,000 ft above sea-level, is covered by such a forest. Possibly it also extended to the Sarhad of Balūc͟histān (Kūh-i-Taftān) and to the Kūhistān (Qūhistān) of Qā'īn.

This forest is built up mainly of pistachio trees (*P. atlantica*) or shrubs of several species of almond, maple (*Acer cinerascens*), celtis, juniper (*J. polycarpos*), and a number of other shrubs. Natural stands are in no way thinner than those of the juniper forest. The ground cover is steppe-like.

The amount of precipitation required by this type of dry forest seems to be essentially the same as for the juniper type, that is, 12 to 20 in. annually. The soils, where they are not lithosols, are of the chestnut or sierozem type.

Very similar, though very much thinner, stands of pistachio trees, together with shrubs of several almond and other drought-resistant species (berberis, lonicera, lycium, pteropyrum, etc., but no maple or juniper), are to be found combined with steppe- and even true desert-formations at lower elevations throughout the interior plateau. These as a rule occur on rocky hill flanks only, avoiding the wide, gravel-covered *dasht* plains, where they were most probably destroyed by man, and the *kavir* and other alluvial soils, where they are absent for ecological reasons. Except for these topographic or edaphic restrictions, there do not seem to exist any climatic limitations upon this type of vegetation on the Iranian plateau (with the exception of the lowest parts of the Southern Lūt basin).

How to zone the vegetal ground cover on the plateau is an ever-vexing question: where should the boundary between steppe and desert be drawn? One answer is to identify this boundary with the limit of potential cultivation based on rainfall. This limit, though it is shifting through the years, runs somewhere between the isohyets of 10 and 12 in. of precipitation. Thus it broadly follows the limit which increasing aridity imposes on the two dry forests just described. Down to this boundary the steppe cover on the ground is very closely set and well developed except where destroyed. Within this cover two main groups of associations are to be distinguished.

1. Those of the tragacanthic type, or *astragaleta*, with the spiny bushes or brushwood of tragacanthic or other *astragalus* and *acantholimon* species, together with other dwarf brushes and many grassy and herbaceous ingredients including *artemisia*. These associations generally occupy the more elevated areas (from 6,000 ft upward), which may originally have been forested. They also extend to lower areas, following overpasturing. Far away from human abodes and thus protected from the insatiable need for fuel, these bushes may nearly reach the height of a man. In other associations they form spiny cushions which

often protect grasses that would otherwise have been eliminated long ago.

2. The *artemisieta* type of associations, where scrub composed of worm-wood (artemisia, mostly *Herba alba*) dominates together with other variable ingredients: dwarf bushes, grasses, and herbs. They generally cover areas of medium elevation, for the most part *dasht* plains and rolling country.

Cultivation, heavy pasturing, and other human uses have contributed to the degradation of both types, but especially of the latter, thus promoting the expansion of anti-pastural or post-segmental weeds like *Hulthemia persica*, *Peganum harmala*, *Sophora alopecuroides*, *Euphorbia sp.*, and others.

Outside the limit of potential cultivation based on rainfall, the steppe thins out naturally without greatly changing its composition. There is an intermediate zone where the patches of bare ground become considerable (desert-steppe). Finally the bare ground predominates, and the shrubby vegetation—except for the occasional stands of pistachios and almonds, and also the short-lived spring-time carpet of annuals—is more or less confined to some shallow rills or beds of occasional runoff, forming a sort of widely spaced network. This then is the true desert, and it is largely confined to the depressions below 3,000 ft in altitude. Annual precipitation is probably less than 4 in. and highly irregular. The largest area without any vegetation, because of sheer lack of precipitation, is the depression of the southern Lūṭ, which declines to about 800 ft above sea-level. The Great Kavīr of Khurāsān (about 21,000 square miles/55,000 sq. km) is another, even larger area that is completely barren, though not so much for climatic reasons but because of its high salinity. There are many other small kavīrs all over the central part of the interior plateau, and all equally devoid of vegetation.

The steppe with scattered pistachio and almond stands originally also covered the depressions of Āzarbāijān and adjoining Transcaucasia. It reappears in central Anatolia below the natural forest area. It also covers extensive areas on the northern foothills of the Kopet Dāgh and on the Zagros ranges below both the juniper and the oak forests. The vegetation on the foothills of northern Mesopotamia, as well as on the banks of the Kura river in Transcaucasia, belonged to basically similar steppe types. All of these are somewhat different floristically, yet remain within the Irano-Turanian domain.

Even more differentiated is the vegetation of the true *garmsīr*. Here, too, the predominant type is that of scattered trees and shrubs with a

steppe-like ground cover, which tapers out into more desert-like formations towards the east (Makrān) and, with growing distance from the
hills, towards the south-west (Khūzistān and southern Iraq). Floristically the vegetation of the garmsīr belongs to the Saharan-Arabian
and Nubo-Sindian groups. Most representatives of the former seem
to appear mainly in Khūzistān and in the upper reaches of the garmsīr,
where they mix with those of the pistachio–almond formation. The
kunār tree (*Ziziphus spina christi*), however, has a fairly wide distribution over the garmsīr. Prominent Nubo-Sindian trees are several species
of acacia, which are accompanied by shrubs like *Salvadora persica*,
Calotropis procera, *Stocksia brahuica*, *Prosopis spicigera*, *Euphorbia larica*,
Periploca aphylla, capparis, the dwarf palm *Nannorhops ritchiana wendland*,
and many other components.

Annual precipitation is about 8 to 12 in. in the west, and 5 to 10 in.
in the eastern parts, where sharply decreasing winter rains intermingle
with irregular monsoon summer storms. The upper limit of the
garmsīr is at about 1,200 ft above sea-level, on the road from Baghdad to
Kirmānshāh; at 3,000 ft south-west of Shīrāz, but at more than 4,500 ft
in Persian Balūchistān. It penetrates into the interior depressions at both
sides of the Sarhadd highland.

This zonal—that is, climatically controlled—vegetation structure
continues into the smaller eastern half of the Iranian uplands, which at
present are divided politically between Afghanistan and Pakistani
Balūchistān. Going east one encounters a symmetrical but reversed
arrangement of the main vegetation types. The floristic composition
of the Irano-Turanian group remains a feature on the interior plateau,
in the northern uplands and in the adjoining northern lowland, but it
changes basically on the eastern façade.

The large depression of Sīstān, 1,500 ft above sea-level, has a true
desert flora (Dasht-i-Marg, Rīgistān). It changes into a steppe of the
artemisieta type as one gains in height on approaching the northern and
eastern hill ranges. Still higher up it turns into the tragacanthic type.
From the foothills upward the pistachio–almond formation becomes
established (*P. cabulica* and, in the north, *P. vera*), together with several
almond species (e.g. *Amygdalus bucharica*), maple trees, trees of *Celtis
caucasica* and *Cercis griffithii*, and several shrubs. At altitudes above 5,500
to 6,500 ft the dry juniper forest is well preserved in extensive patches,
especially on the northern slopes of the Paropamisus and the Hindu
Kush (*Juniperus serafschanica*, with maple and other trees and shrubs);

from there it continues through Badakhshan right into the uplands of Central Asia, where it attains an upper limit of 9,000 ft above sea-level. It is also present on the south-eastern ranges, including the Sulaimān mountains. Here, however, while the juniper forest continues northward on the interior slope, on the outward (eastern) slopes, at about 32° 30′ N., a semi-humid forest of evergreen oak (*Quercus ballout*), together with many shrubs, becomes dominant and continues northward into Nūristān. Its lower limit is about 3,600 ft in the south, and 2,700 ft in the north. The juniper forest is topped by a zone of humid and semi-humid coniferous forests that stand between 5,500 and 10,000 ft, consisting of cedars (*Cedrus deodara*) and pine (*Pinus excelsa, P. gerardiana*) in the lower levels, and spruce and fir (*Abies webbiana, Picea smithiana*) in the higher reaches. Irano-Turanian and Indo-Himalayan elements intermingle in this forest zone, in the same way that the climatic regime integrates, as it were, features of the continental winter-rain type with those of the monsoon type. Precipitation probably exceeds 40 in. annually. Below this forest zone a kind of garmsīr vegetation is to be found, which approximates that found on the coasts of the Persian Gulf and Makrān.

A description of the vegetation structure of the Iranian upland is not complete without some discussion of the azonal vegetation types.

It is extraordinary to see how the moisture-holding capacity of sand, occurring in sheets and massive dune complexes on the southern or south-eastern edges of most of the interior depressions, enables extended thickets of bushes and low trees to exist under sheer desert conditions. This vegetation consists mainly of saxaul (Iranian "tāgh", *Haloxylon ammodendron* or *H. persicum*), calligonum ("iskambīl", *C. polygonoides* or *C. comosum*), and a few other species including stiff grass bunches (*Aristida pennata*). Unfortunately most of these species have now been completely destroyed since transport by trucks became available.

An all-pervading element are the riparian and wadi forests that follow running water or subterranean streams. Where they are most extensive, they merely form more or less distinct associations of moisture-loving trees and bushes, which are the much preferred hide-outs of wild beasts; but in the open areas, whether steppe or desert, such "natural oases" are features of great importance. Most of them have long been turned into cultivated oases, which, enlarged over the centuries, have developed into the most important population centres of the interior plateau. As regards their original vegetation, they fall into two large groups: those of the garmsīr, and those of the rest of the country. The latter group is very rich: willow and poplar, tamarisk, ash, elm, platan, maple, celtis australis, walnut, mulberry, plum, *Elaeagnus angustifolia*, *Zizyphus sativa*, and many others are represented, all interwoven with liana and vines. With a diminishing water supply and also with growing elevation, many members tend to fall away.

Equally, the garmsīr group is rich in species (some of which mix with the northern group in lower places) such as the tamarisk, poplar (*Populus euphratica*), myrtle, and oleander. More restricted to the true garmsīr are the *Calotropis procera* ("oshur"), *Razya stricta*, *Rubus sanctus*, and others; but the date-palm as a cultigen has largely replaced them. Also acacia or kunār trees (*Zizyphus jujuba* or *Z. spina christi*) gather to form closer stands in the wadis.

With growing salinity such riparian forests are bound to become infested by halophytes. Of the trees only tamarisk holds out, accompanied by saxaul and other halophytic bushes. Treeless salt-marsh is found along the shores of the kavīrs, or else where highly saline underground or surface runoff water is present periodically. Associations of *Halocnemum strobilaceum* together with several *salsola* and other halophytic species are characteristic of the plateau, while associations dominated by *suaeda*, with *salsola, anabasis, nitraria*, etc., are to be found in the hot garmsīr salt marshes.

Permanent or quasi-permanent lakes with low salinity are frequently fringed by reed swamps containing *Phragmites communis*, *Arundo donax*, cypress grass, juncus, carex, *Typha australis*, and *Saccharum spontaneum*. These offer a fine pasture for sedentary cattle-breeders around the Hāmūn lakes in Sīstān, at Lake Nairīz, and in the extensive swamps of the old Tigris delta.

Mangrove forests of *Avicennia officinalis* are known from the Persian Gulf coast, chiefly in the Strait of Hurmuz.

To conclude this sketchy description of the vegetation of Iran, it may be appropriate to raise the question: at what period in history or prehistory would the original vegetation of the Iranian highlands appear to have been at its best? In spite of the apparent conclusiveness arising from so much evidence of degradation and destruction caused by man and his animals, the answer cannot simply be that vegetation was at its most developed just before the beginnings of extensive cultivation and animal husbandry.

According to present knowledge, such activities may have begun about five to six millennia before our era. We know, however, that at this remote date the climate of Iran was not the same as it is today. The humid Caspian forest at that time did not yet cover the loess-clad foothills of the Alburz range in Gurgān; and Lake Marivan (Iranian Kurdistān), which is now situated within the oak-forest zone, was, according to the results of a recent pollen scrutiny, obviously surrounded by a kind of artemisia steppe up to the middle of the fourth millennium B.C. There is still other evidence for the existence of a prolonged dry phase just after the last cold (glacial) period, which later evolved towards the more humid conditions that linger on at the present day. The old familiar conception of a progressive desiccation of Iran must be dropped, in so far as a climatic mechanism is supposed to have been instrumental. However, regarded as a by-product of man's ever-expanding degradation and destruction of the vegetal cover, the idea may be considered valid. There is no doubt that general conditions have deteriorated in many ways in consequence of this erosion of the vegetation.

One is probably right in assuming that vegetal conditions in Iran were at their optimum during the third and second millennia B.C. There is also some evidence for believing that they were much better in the first millennium B.C., and probably for a good span of time afterwards, compared with conditions today. No doubt the many centuries of disorder and mismanagement have greatly contributed to progressive deterioration, which would seem to have accelerated in modern times, owing to the increased demands made on natural resources, together with the use of more powerful means of exploitation. It may, however, afford great satisfaction to know that climatic conditions have not substantially deteriorated; and thus it could be possible, with sound management and necessary investment, to reverse the course of deterioration.

CHAPTER 9

MAMMALS

By reason of its vast area and its position in the midst of widely differing zones—Indian lands, Arab lands, Turkistān, and the Caucasus—Iran is basically a meeting-place of foreign influences, pervaded by the highly original character of the country itself. All these factors presuppose an abundant fauna, which, even if it does not present the extraordinary multiplicity of forms apparent in the vegetation, is nevertheless of considerable interest both for its individuality and for its variety.

It is surprising that until recent years the country has never been seriously surveyed zoologically; existing records are sparse and much remains to be done. The only work of collation accomplished hitherto was an excellent book entitled *Eastern Persia*, a report by the Boundaries Commission, to which W. T. Blanford contributed the very lively and well-documented section on zoology. This work, which is already historic since it dates from 1876, was really the starting-point of Iranian zoology. The zoological exploration of the country is far from complete at the present day, but rapid progress is being made and certain principles have now been established which make it possible for the composition of the fauna to be understood.

About 129 species of mammals are found in Iran: 15 insectivora, 21 chiroptera, 28 carnivora, 1 pinniped, 12 ungulata, 4 lagomorpha, and 48 rodents. This is a considerable total; by comparison, Europe (without the Soviet Union), which is four times larger and much more varied ecologically, contains only about 133 species, very few more than are found in Iran.

Among carnivora, the tiger is still found in northern Iran, but has become very rare; it is of a magnificent breed with light-coloured fur. It is no longer encountered west of Rāmsar, although in the last century it was sometimes found as far distant as Mt Ararat and even Tiflis. Even now it still visits the forests of Māzandarān and Gurgān, and also the hill regions along the frontier of Turkistān, but its habitat has become increasingly contracted. The splendid forest of Māzandarān is being intensively developed and will soon be destroyed; hence it may be foreseen that within the next twenty years the tiger will vanish from Iran.[1]

The short-maned lion of Iran, which occurs frequently on the base-reliefs of Persepolis, has probably by now disappeared completely. Even in the last century travellers often referred to its incursions into the neighbourhood of Shīrāz, and it seems likely that it survived for some time longer in the region north-east of Dizfūl.

Wolves are still numerous, chiefly in Āzarbāījān, Kurdistān and the Alburz; they continue to flourish in spite of their being hunted mercilessly by the nomads. The wolf is a practical and cautious creature that knows how to exploit the nature of the terrain in which it lives. In summer it is not much in evidence, but it draws closer to the flocks in autumn; in the winter small packs of wolves invade the villages, even in broad daylight. Other carnivora include a few striped hyenas, various foxes, and ichneumon; cats, leopards (including the cheetah), and perhaps still some lynxes, such as the caracal. The Caspian Sea is the habitat of a seal (*Phoca caspica*) that changes its living-quarters according to the time of year; the existence of the Caspian seal was actually recorded by Herodotus, who observed that "the Araxes flows into swampy marshland where men are said to live who feed on raw fish and clothe themselves in seal-skins" (*Hist.* I, 202).

Mention should be made of some remarkable species among the ungulates. The Iranian onager lives on the edge of the central desert; it is not common but does not yet seem to be threatened with extinction, and herds of more than a thousand head were observed near the Afghan frontier in the last century. The Iranian fallow deer appears to have become very rare; in 1957 it was "rediscovered" north of Shustar, in the Kārūn valley, where it inhabits the thickets on the western slope of Zagros. The species generally is in urgent need of protection. The red deer and the roe deer are found on the higher levels of the Caspian forest. Gazelles (*Gazella subgutturosa* and *G. gazella bennetti*) are still fairly numerous, though they are hunted unceasingly. The wild goat (*Capra hircus aegagrus*) and particularly the red sheep (*Ovis orientalis*) fare better: the pursuit of them in the mountains is so arduous that these two species do not appear to be threatened. It is interesting to note that red sheep produce their young in the spring, about three weeks later than do domestic sheep.

[1] Vigorous measures have, however, been initiated recently by the Iranian government (1966) to ensure observance of a "close season" in respect of game generally.

There are a wide variety of lagomorpha and rodents. Pikas (*Ochotona rufescens*) inhabit the mountains of central and eastern Iran, as well as the eastern part of Alburz; they live in colonies which may be very numerous in certain years and then disappear completely in the years following. Six different types of jerboas are found in Iran; these are graceful little rodents that lead a solitary existence in desert regions. They store no food and sleep throughout the winter in shallow burrows, after blocking the entrances. The great majority of Iranian rodents, however, are the jirds and gerbils, and it is no exaggeration to say that these two groups make up 90 per cent of the whole order. They usually live in colonies, and certain species are largely responsible for the continued transmission of the plague from Kurdistān, where the disease is endemic. It would seem that some colonies of them have been infected for more than a hundred years, and probably even longer. Plague is pre-eminently a disease transmitted by rodents through their acting as hosts to infected fleas and other organisms. Usually at the time of an outbreak it is brought back to the villages by shepherds and may thus be the cause of a considerable number of deaths.

Other rodents are of small numerical importance. As regards chiroptera and insectivora, little is yet known; so far twenty-one species of bat have been discovered in Iran, but there probably exist many more. Insectivora do not include any species of outstanding interest; hedgehogs, however, are common.

CLASSIFICATION OF FAUNA

The mammals of Iran must in general be regarded as palearctic: certainly the red deer, roe deer, wild boar, fat dormouse, and common field mouse are palearctic; however, the links with other animals of this group are not very close, and genera such as *Meriones* and *Gerbillus*, which play an important part in Iranian fauna, are equally prevalent in the Sahara and must therefore be regarded as only marginally palearctic.

Two important characteristics are presented by the fauna of Iran: in the first place there is a high proportion of endemic species (18 per cent); and second, Iran has been penetrated by numerous species coming from outside, which have advanced to a greater or lesser depth within the country. The result is thus a composite fauna, in which autochthonous elements are combined with elements of a more general palearctic character, as well as with others of African or Indian origin.

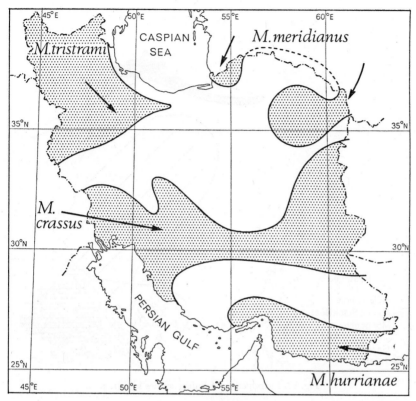

Fig. 89. Penetration by four species of the genus *Meriones* (Sand Rat) in Iran: *M. tristrami* coming from the north-west, *M. meridianus* from Turkistān, *M. hurrianae* from Pakistan and *M. crassus* from Iraq.

The endemic species, which are of special interest, may be divided into two groups corresponding to the two centres of presumed origin. The more important of these centres is situated in Khurāsān and extends into Balūchistān and West Afghanistan; fifteen species are found belonging to, or originating from, this region. They are: one hedgehog (*Hemiechinus megalotis*), one fox (*Vulpes cana*), two ungulates (*Equus hemionus onager, Ovis laristanica*), one lagomorph (*Ochotona rufescens*), and ten rodents (*Allactaga hotsoni, Jaculus blanfordi, Salpingotus thomasi, Myomimus personatus, Calomyscus bailwardi, Meriones persicus, Ellobius fuscocapillus,* and *Blanfordimys afghanus*). The members of these species are characteristic inhabitants of high-altitude semi-desert—quite different from the neighbouring and parallel group in Turkistān which characterizes the deserts of lower-lying plains.

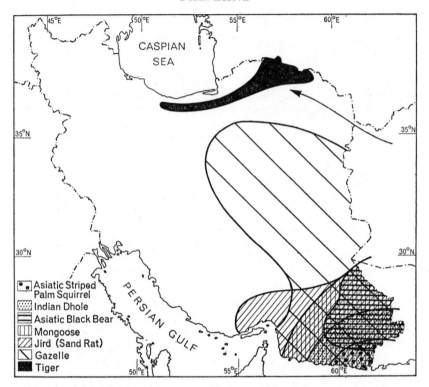

Fig. 90. Introduction of Indian species into Iran.

The second, less important, centre is situated in Kurdistān and provides the following eight species belonging to this region or based upon it: one ungulate (*Dama mesopotamica*) and seven rodents (*Sciurus anomalus, Allactaga williamsi, Mesocricetus brantsi, Meriones tristrami, Microtus irani, Ellobius lutescens*). The essential difference between the two centres is that Kurdistān has a much more severe winter than Khurāsān, and also that it is an enclosed region, in contrast to the open country of Khurāsān.

Numerous foreign elements have made their way into Iran by different routes (fig. 89); Indian fauna entered the country mainly from Balūchistān, and both the northern palm squirrel (*Funambulus pennanti*) and the Asiatic black bear (*Selenarctos thibetanus*) belong to this category; the tiger, on the other hand, certainly arrived by way of Afghanistan (see fig. 90).

Fauna from Turkistān were introduced from the north-east; certain

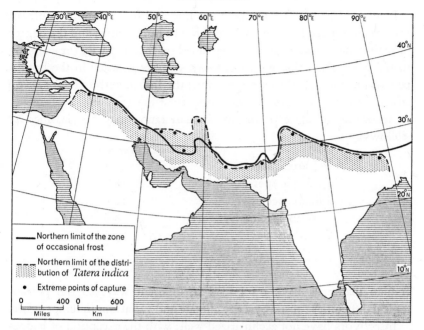

Fig. 91. Distribution of *Tatera indica* in relation to climate.

species, like the small corsac fox and the jerboa (*Alactagulus pumilio*), have remained close to the frontier, while others like *Rhombomys*, have advanced farther, so covering a large part of the country.

The introduction of African elements is more problematical, and the actual point at which they penetrated remains uncertain. It was probably in the region of Bandar 'Abbās, and the infiltration must have occurred during the Quaternary, when the mainland was still continuous across the present Strait of Hurmuz, which is now 40 miles wide. The African species did not penetrate very far into the country, settling mainly in Balūchistān. The Ethiopian hedgehog (*Paraechinus aethiopicus*) makes its home only in the island of Tumb [Tanb-i-Buzurg]; the Arabian fruit bat (*Rousettus arabicus*) has been found in Iran only in the island of Qishm; other African species, such as the sand fox (*Vulpes rüppelli*), settled on the mainland; and one type of bat (*Rhinopoma hardwickei*) in Balūchistān. An interesting animal is the sand cat (*Felis margarita*), which is found in the Sahara and in southern Saudi Arabia, while a species closely related to it (*Felis thinobius*) inhabits Turkistān; perhaps it will also be discovered in the kavīrs of eastern Iran.

Finally, contact was made between Iraq and India through southern Iran by two species originally belonging to hot regions, and the degree of their penetration northward depended on their capacity for adapting to the cold. The spiny mouse (*Acomys cahirinus*) settled in the hottest part of the country, the extreme south; the Indian gerbil (*Tatera indica*) advanced as far north as the occasional frost line (fig. 91).

According to place of origin, Iranian fauna may be classified as follows:

	Per cent
Palearctic species	55·1
Endemic species	18·1
Indian species	14·6
African species	8·6
Mixed species	3·4

ECOLOGY

Iranian mammals have responded in different ways to the physiological difficulties caused by a dry climate and variations in temperature.

Insectivora have not acclimatized well; with the exception of hedgehogs, they are limited in number and variety. Chiroptera have been more successful and there are many species, though overall they cannot be regarded as very numerous. They are difficult to find and must be sought in the *ganats*, which bring irrigation water down from the mountains to the fields and villages. Bats find in these canals both the humidity needed to protect them from the parching winds and a shelter from the cold in the winter.

Among ungulates, the wild boar has shown a remarkable capacity for acclimatization in such regions as Kurdistān, which is hot and dry in summer, but frozen, wind-swept, and covered with snow in winter; they are to be seen in large numbers and may be of considerable size and weight. The Iranian fallow deer, on the other hand, which in the Quaternary inhabited a large part of Asia Minor, is scarcely found today and exists only as a kind of residue among the thickets at the foot of the Zagros. The red deer and the roe deer have also found it difficult to survive in the higher zones of the Caspian forest.

It is among rodents that the most astonishing adjustments are to be observed. A remarkable example is the suslik (*Citellus fulvus*). This large rodent lives in great colonies and requires an assured water-supply; nevertheless it has succeeded in penetrating as far as the semi-desert zone when water is temporarily available in the spring. As soon as the summer heat has dried up the vegetation, it buries itself underground and spends the hot season estivating, a state which continues uninterruptedly throughout the autumn and is then converted into hibernation. The suslik stores no food and spends about 270 days of the year asleep. There remain 95 days for recovering from the long period of sleep, for producing offspring, and for acquiring enough fat to enable it to spend the next nine months underground. The young are born about 30 days after the end of the parents' hibernation. For them in particular the spring is a race against time, for they have only 65 days in which to reach adult stature and acquire the necessary reserves of fat. All vegetation dries up in a single week about the tenth of June, and any young which have not reached maturity by that time must die, since green plants are vital to them. Thus it is actually the life of the vegetation which chiefly determines the geographical distribution of this species: if the spring lasts for fewer than 95 days, *Cittelus fulvus* cannot survive. During their active period susliks eat without stopping, day and night. The area of Iran over which they are now distributed is not a continuous zone; whilst they occupy a considerable zone in Khurāsān, they also inhabit a small pocket north of Qazvīn and Hamadān. A slight increase in aridity with a corresponding shortening of the spring season in the region of the southern Alburz was probably enough to divide into two separate parts the tract of land occupied by them, which must formerly have been continuous.

The severity of winter conditions in Āzarbāījān and Kurdistān makes survival very difficult for the various species, which try to counter it in different ways. When the plateaus are frozen and swept by the winter winds, then moufflons, wild boars, foxes, and hares come down into the sheltered valleys; the rodents, on the other hand, remain where they are, reacting variously to these extremes of climate. Some, such as hamsters (*Mesocricetus brantsi*, *Cricetulus migratorius*) and jerboas (*Allactaga williamsi*, *Allactaga elater*), block the entrances to their burrows, which are not usually very deep, and go to sleep in them. Others do not hibernate, but in the autumn accumulate large stores of vegetable food, sometimes exceeding ten pounds in weight; they have burrows of some consequence and depth, perhaps containing several levels, which include a large chamber provided with thick litter. In this category are the various species of jird (*Meriones libycus*, *Meriones persicus, Meriones tristrami, Meriones vinogradovi*), though not all of them follow exactly the same ecology. *Meriones vinogradovi*, for example, appears to offer the best resistance to winter; its burrow is not so deep as some, and in the spring it is the first species to appear, to clean its winter-quarters, and to produce offspring. It is possible, however, that the shallowness of its burrow may be the very factor that prevents it from dwelling farther south, since burrows that are close to the surface offer less effective protection against the heat of summer.

The geographical distribution of a species may be checked by other causes. The black rat (*Rattus rattus*) and the Norway rat (*Rattus norvegicus*), for example, are both restricted to the coasts of the Caspian Sea and the Persian Gulf and are not found in the interior of the country; and it is observed that even though rats are continually arriving in Tehrān by train and lorry, their foothold in the city remains precarious. The reason is that these two species lose a large amount of body-moisture through evaporation and perspiration—almost twice as much as do the acclimatized species—and hence cannot survive without access to an unfailing water supply. The house mouse, on the other hand, resists dehydration very well and is found throughout the country.

One interesting species of rodent, *Ellobius lutescens*, has solved the problem of adopting a completely negative programme. It lives entirely underground, thus securing the best protection against hostile forces. After a summer of virtual inaction it withdraws into the deepest part of its burrow, where, from the time of the first autumn rains onward, it becomes very active and until the spring works ceaselessly on the excavation of new galleries. With the first signs of drought its industry slackens considerably and is soon at a standstill. The reproductive processes of this species must take place in midwinter, for no member of it has been found in a seminiferous condition between April and December.

DOMESTIC ANIMALS

Iranian saddle-horses are famous: the Türkmen of the Gurgān region ride quite large horses, while those of the Kurds are smaller, broader-backed and very hardy—merits which were noted by the Greeks of Xenophon. There are numerous donkeys, and it is claimed that the special breed called "bandari" results from a cross with onagers.

The cattle of the Caspian coast are of small stature; bulls (but not cows) have a hump like that of the zebu; on the plateau cattle are slightly larger and not humped. The Indian buffalo is quite common, especially in the Caspian provinces and in Āzarbāījān. Sheep are of the steatopygous breed; and goats belong to the same breed that is found throughout the whole of the Middle East. Less and less use is being made of dromedaries, but they are still to be seen in all parts of the country; camels remain mostly in the Gurgān province, and sometimes caravans of them are to be observed going up as far as Tehrān.

Dogs are of very mixed breed; the beautiful Iranian greyhound (*tāzī*) is sometimes seen; usually black and white in colour, it is swift and strong. The breed of greyhound known as "Afghan" of somewhat obscure origin, may also be encountered; on the plateau the sheep-dogs are of indefinite breed, but are purer-bred in Kurdistān and northern Āzarbāījān. They are large dogs of some ferocity, related to Himalayan dogs and perhaps to the stock from which European sheep-dogs, such as the Pyrenean and St Bernard, etc., are descended; the breed is quite uniform and occurs everywhere among the Kurds, even among those who have settled in the plain near the Syrian–Turkish frontier. The traveller arriving at a village is mobbed by these dogs and finds it difficult to get rid of them. Cats of the breed known as "Persian" seem to be unknown.

PROTECTION OF FAUNA

Unlike Syria, for example, Iran is not threatened with the imminent extinction of all her larger fauna. Nevertheless, certain species are already in the course of disappearing; the rarity of the Caspian tiger undoubtedly results from acts of man, namely hunting and the destruction of forests. The caracal and the cheetah are both extremely rare, but here it is probable that, as with the Iranian fallow deer and the recently disappeared lion, gradual changes in climate may be chiefly responsible for their diminution. Gazelles and onagers, by comparison, are still thriving, though these species have become rare over a wide belt surrounding the cities: living in the open they fall an easy prey to sportsmen in motor-cars. On the other hand, the moufflon and the wolf are flourishing, the best protection for both being the high ground of their habitat. The leopard must once have been common, for there are hills everywhere called *palang kūh* ("leopard mountain"); at the present day it is rare, except in the forests of the Caspian coast.

CONCLUSION

The richness and complexity of the fauna of Iran will be apparent from this brief survey. Although the country has not evolved a fauna as markedly original as that of India, which is in any case vastly greater in size, its generally high altitude has made it a kind of fortress, within which appreciable numbers of autochthonous species have been able to evolve and survive. Moreover, since the country is not completely enclosed, it has been penetrated in varying degrees by species coming from outside. The fact that the climate of Iran has changed very little since the end of the Tertiary is also of great importance. Glaciation occurred in Āzarbāījān and the Alburz, but only to a very limited extent; over the remainder of the country the prevailing climate appears to have been broadly similar to that of the present day. The Pontic strata of Marāgheh, near Tabrīz, have yielded traces of a fairly generalized fauna which is found in some degree everywhere at the same latitude in that period, and which includes the rhinoceros and orycterope. It appears that these remains correspond largely to the fauna of the present day, so that one type of fauna has continued to stock the country since the Tertiary epoch, though very little data is available on the subject. Consistency thus seems to be an important characteristic of Iranian fauna, and it can even be observed in the lack of variation among existing species, which differ very little from one region to another; moreover, there are very few subspecies. In this respect Iranian fauna is in complete contrast with the vegetation, which presents an extraordinary diversity. This unexpected antithesis between the consistency of mammals and the inconsistency of plants cannot at present be explained.

CHAPTER 10

ZOOGEOGRAPHIC ANALYSIS OF THE LIZARD FAUNA OF IRAN[1]

INTRODUCTION

An understanding of present distribution patterns of organisms in South-west Asia is essential to any meaningful generalizations concerning biogeography on a world-wide basis. The vast arid physiographically complex tract stretching across all of North Africa, South-west Asia, and north-western India today forms a barrier to the exchange of faunal elements of tropical and sub-tropical Africa with Europe, south-eastern Asia, and Central Asia. The extent to which communication between these faunas may have existed at various times in the past can be postulated only on the basis of our knowledge of palaeo-geography, past climatic conditions, and the distribution of living and fossil organisms.

The area covered by this paper is delimited by the political boundaries of Iran, which might be regarded as one of the most geographically complex areas of South-west Asia, and is centrally located with respect to the mingling of elements of the North African, southern Asian, Central Asian and European herpetofaunas (Anderson, 1963).

While many systematic problems remain on all levels, it is nonetheless possible to make a few generalizations regarding the zoogeography of South-west Asia, and Iran in particular. Thus far no zoogeographic analysis of the whole of South-west Asia has been attempted, and only the most cursory remarks on the zoogeography of the amphibians and reptiles of Iran have been published (Blanford, 1876; Wettstein, 1951; Anderson, 1964). In this report an effort is made to answer in the broadest sense the following questions: (1) What are the major distributional patterns? (2) What are the historical origins of these patterns?

[1] For critical reading of the manuscript in various stages of its development, I am indebted to my father, Howard T. Anderson, formerly Chief Geologist for the Iranian Oil Exploration and Producing Company, Alan E. Leviton, California Academy of Sciences, and George S. Myers, Stanford University. We have discussed the topics considered here over a period of several years, and whatever may be of value in this paper derives in large measure from these conversations.

(3) What factors determine present distributions? (4) To what extent can these generalizations be extended to the whole of South-west Asia?

The first attempt at a complete list of the herpetofauna of Iran was that of De Flippi (1865). Blanford (1876) added many species to this list as a result of his travels, and briefly discussed the zoogeography of Iran. In 1936, Werner attempted to bring the list up to date. His list was undocumented, and unfortunately contained many errors.

Material now in American museums, particularly in the California Academy of Sciences and the Field Museum of Natural History, forms a combined collection adequate as a basis for reviews of the faunistics of the South-west Asian herpetofauna. The present paper is a result of examination of this material.

Most previous work on the Iranian herpetofauna has consisted of brief reports on incidental material collected by travellers engaged in other types of work. I have drawn heavily on these reports, and in cases where identifications or localities were in doubt, I have attempted to examine either the specimens in question or other material from the particular region. In many cases such a check has not yet been possible. Also, an attempt has been made to locate every locality record in the literature, but again, this has frequently not been possible.

As a comment on the need for further investigations in Iran, it is worth remarking that only three individuals with a primary interest in reptiles and amphibians have collected in Iran: William T. Blanford in 1872; Alexander M. Nikolsky, around the turn of the century, who apparently visited the Gurgān region; and the present writer who collected in Iran during a nine-month period in 1958.

The zoogeography of any region can be viewed from three perspectives, all of which are closely interrelated.

(1) *Descriptive:* the distribution of organisms in relation to physiographic features of the region under study. This involves study of the morphology of the animals and taxonomic evaluation of available material and literature records. It is subjective in that it involves judgments based on the worker's knowledge of the groups involved, and includes all of the bias inherent in the taxonomic system employed. Obviously, it reflects the perceptiveness of the individual zoogeographer. The further he strays from familiar systematic ground, and the more he relies upon the judgment of previous workers for determination of material which he has not seen, the less reliable his zoogeographical description tends to become. The present paper is based upon

a comprehensive study of the systematics of the lizards of Iran which is in a final stage of preparation.

(2) *Ecological:* the distribution of organisms relative to environmental factors. This, too, is largely descriptive, containing many of the same pitfalls mentioned above, and usually it must be highly inferential, as available data are often diffuse and scanty, and knowledge of physiological responses to the physical factors of the environment is far from complete for any one species. Nevertheless, rough correlations are possible. These can at least prove stimulating to our speculations regarding the causes of present distribution patterns, and at times strongly indicate zoogeographical conclusions of considerable weight.

(3) *Historical:* this is often highly speculative, particularly in the absence of a fossil record. It involves a consideration of all discernible factors, in the dimension of time, which have produced present patterns of distribution. It is, therefore, an attempt to analyse observed distributional data in the light of available information regarding geomorphology, palaeogeography, palaeoclimatology, palaeoecology, and the evolutionary development of the organisms involved.

I have attempted to incorporate these three approaches in the following discussion, separating them as a matter of convenience. The third must follow as an effort at integration of the first two.

During the course of this study certain taxonomic changes have been necessary. The justification for these changes will be found in recent papers (Anderson and Leviton, 1966a, 1966b; Clark, Clark and Anderson, 1966; Anderson, 1966, 1968; Minton, Anderson and Anderson), and in the systematic treatment of the lizards now in preparation. All of the Iranian species recognized here are listed in table 6 (pp. 332–3).

Limitations of space prevent detailed discussion of the physical geography, palaeogeography, and vegetation of Iran essential to faunal analysis, and the reader is referred to the other contributions in this volume. I have drawn heavily upon the papers cited in the bibliography, and call particular attention to the following publications: Anderson (1963, 1966), Anderson and Leviton (1966b), Bobek (several papers), de Böckh, Lees and Richardson (1929), Butzer (several papers), Furon (1941), Hare (1961), James and Wynd (1965), Misonne (1959), Nairn (1961), Rechinger (1951), Schwarzback (1963), Shapely (1961), Stamp (1961), Walter and Lieth (1960), Wilson (1932), and Zeuner (1959).

While in Iran I was extended many courtesies by employees of the Iranian Oil Exploration and Producing Company. I particularly wish to acknowledge the friendship of William O. Williams, Dory Little, Jerry James, and Rufus Cook, who not only permitted me to accompany geological field parties under their direction, but were amiable companions in the field as well.

For several years I have had the pleasure of a lively correspondence with Mr Jeromie A. Anderson of Karachi, and with Dr Sherman A. Minton of the University of Indiana Medical Center. Both have first-hand experience with the amphibians and reptiles of West Pakistan, and our discussions have been most profitable.

DESCRIPTIVE ZOOGEOGRAPHY

Apart from those elements which it shares with other regions, South-west Asia has two major distributional components in its lizard fauna. One of these components occupies primarily the elevated regions that are generally termed the Iranian Plateau, in the broad sense of that term as defined further in this volume; and those species which occupy the Iranian Plateau may be termed the Iranian faunal element. The second major component, which may be designated as Saharo-Sindian, occupies the low desert areas from North Africa to north-western India.

Within these regions are species and associations of species with much more restricted distributional area. Only a few species of broad ecological tolerance extend throughout the greater part of either region. Also there is penetration of both areas by species characteristic of the other. Few species, however, are broadly distributed in both regions.

Entering South-west Asia on the north-west are elements with European affinities, primarily those having a Mediterranean distribution. Aralo-Caspian desert species penetrate the region on the north, and a few Oriental elements are found in the south-east.

The affinities of the lizard fauna of South-west Asia with the faunas of adjacent regions are principally at the generic level. An example of this is found in the genus *Lacerta*, the species (or subspecies) found within South-west Asia being distinct, and their distribution more or less limited to northern South-west Asia, but with near relatives in the Mediterranean countries of Europe. Where species are shared with other regions, these are usually the most widely ranging members of the genus. Examples are the agamid *Calotes versicolor*, which enters Balūchistān on the south-east and *Varanus bengalensis*, also in Balūchistān, representing the Oriental species of monitors.

Turning now to a more detailed consideration of the geography of Iranian lizards, attention will first be given to the distribution of species within the various physiographic regions of Iran.

The Central Plateau

(This term is here used to designate the internal drainage basin of the Iranian Plateau lying entirely within the confines of the Iranian borders, and rimmed by mountains.) Certain species range broadly over this entire region. These are:

Agama agilis[1]	*Teratoscincus scincus*
Agama microlepis	*Eremias guttulata*
Phrynocephalus maculatus	*Eremias velox*
Phrynocephalus scutellatus	*Eumeces schneideri*
Agamura persica	*Varanus griseus*

Collection has not been sufficient to permit detailed discussion of the distribution of these forms within the plateau region. *Agama microlepis* is known from the mountain slopes around the periphery of the plateau and from those ranges which cross the plateau. It probably does not stray far from large rock outcrops. *Phrynocephalus maculatus*, one of the most widely distributed members of the genus, probably occurs on sandy plains throughout the plateau; it is also one of the few lizard species to be expected in the salt depressions. *P. scutellatus* is distributed on gravel plains and slopes throughout the region. *Teratoscincus scincus* is also a sand-dwelling species, and probably occurs on the plateau wherever there are sandy soils and a sufficient beetle fauna. *Eremias guttulata* is one of the most widely distributed species of lizards in South-west Asia, the subspecies *E. g. watsonana* occurring throughout the region under consideration here. *Eremias velox* is widely distributed not only on the Iranian Plateau, but in the low deserts to the north as well; *E. v. persica* is the subspecies of the plateau. *Eumeces schneideri* has been collected in areas around the periphery of the plateau, and differs subspecifically from one area to another. It may not occur on the

---

[1] As used in this paper, the name *Agama agilis* Olivier covers the nominal species *A. sanguinolenta* (Pallas), *A. persica* Blanford (= *A. blanfordi* Anderson), and *A. isolepis* Boulenger. The systematic status of these forms is presently under study.

plateau proper. *Varanus griseus*, like *Eremias guttulata*, is one of a very few reptiles distributed throughout South-west Asia, in both the upland and lowland regions. *Varanus* is a genus of the Ethiopian, Oriental, and Australian tropics, *V. griseus* being the only species occurring in the intervening desert areas between the Ethiopian and Oriental Regions. The plateau form has been recognized by some as subspecifically distinct, *V. g. caspius*.

On the north and west of the plateau occur certain forms which are found also in contiguous regions. These species are:

Agama caucasica	*Lacerta saxicola*
Agama ruderata	*Ophisops elegans*
Phrynocephalus helioscopus	*Ablepharus bivittatus*
Bunopus crassicauda	*Mabuya aurata*

The plateau distribution of these species is largely confined to the inner slopes of the Zagros and Alburz Mountains bordering the plateau, and coincides with the Kurdish–Khurāsān rainfall pattern of spring and winter precipitation in excess of 200 mm.

Agama caucasica extends across the entire northern border of the plateau and into Afghanistan. It does not overlap with *A. microlepis* except in the mountains of the north-eastern corner of the plateau, where four species of large rock-inhabiting *Agama* have been recorded (but not all personally verified). *Agama ruderata* is a wide-ranging Saharo-Sindian species distributed primarily in the lowlands of western South-west Asia, but also ascending to elevations over 5,000 ft. The subspecies known from Afghanistan and Balūchistān, *A. r. baluchiana*, may not have its closest affinities with this species. *Phrynocephalus helioscopus* is essentially an Aralo-Caspian species, but perhaps more generally distributed on the plateau than indicated by the known localities. It differs ecologically from the two broadly distributed plateau species of the genus in its preference for clay soils and stony plains. *Bunopus crassicauda* presently is known only from the western part of the plateau, not extending into other areas. *Lacerta saxicola defilippii* does not occur on the plateau proper, but is the only species in the genus which crosses the passes in the Alburz Mountains and occupies the southern slopes of this range north of Tehrān. It is actually a Transcaucasian species with Mediterranean affinities. *Ophisops elegans elegans* is a lizard of lower and middle mountain slope elevations, and is found on the dry inner slopes of the northern, western and southern borders of the plateau. *Ablepharus bivittatus* has been recorded from the western part of the plateau, but the information on distribution and systematics of this genus in South-west Asia is so scanty as to render any discussion of it here meaningless. *Mabuya aurata*, a Saharo-Sindian species which also occurs in arid upland areas, may be more widely distributed on the plateau than is currently known, or at least it once may have been more widely distributed, since it is recorded also from the Transcaucasian and southern Türkmenistan regions.

Largely confined on the plateau to the south-eastern portion are several lizards, most of which occur also in the highlands of Balūchistān or in Sīstān. These are:

Agama nupta	*Acanthodactylus cantoris*
Uromastyx asmussi	*Acanthodactylus micropholis*
Cyrtodactylus agamuroides	*Eremias fasciata*
Cyrtodactylus kirmanensis	*Ablepharus grayanus*
Ophiomorus brevipes	

Agama nupta is primarily a species of the southern mountains of the Iranian Plateau, distributed on the plateau only on the inner slopes of the mountains along the southern border. It is reported from a few areas within the range of *Agama microlepis*. It may also overlap *A. caucasica* in the northern extremes of its range. All three species, along with *A. erythrogastra*, reportedly occur in extreme north-eastern Iran, an unexpected circumstance. *Uromastyx asmussi* is the only species in this Saharo-Sindian genus which penetrates the plateau. Apparently its ability to burrow in gravelly soils makes this possible. The distribution of the two species of *Cyrtodactylus* is very incompletely known, as they have been rarely collected. The two species of *Acanthodactylus*, sand-inhabiting Saharo-Sindian forms, do not really penetrate the plateau, reaching only as far as Bam. *Eremias fasciata* is found on plains in the eastern plateau region; whether or not the lizard identified with this species in southern Afghanistan is actually closely related remains to be demonstrated. *Ablepharus grayanus* also occurs in West Pakistan. The distribution of *Ophiomorus brevipes* has been fully discussed elsewhere (Anderson and Leviton, 1966b).

A few species, mostly Aralo-Caspian in distribution, are found in the north-east of the plateau. As far as known, these are:

Phrynocephalus mystaceus	*Cyrtodactylus fedtschenkoi*
Alsophylax spinicauda	*Eremias nigrocellata*
Crossobamon eversmanni	*Eremias arguta*
Cyrtodactylus caspius	

Alsophylax spinicauda is known only from Shāhrūd, which lies at the foot of the mountains on the north-central edge of the plateau. Whether or not this species is more widely distributed, perhaps in the mountains of Khurāsān, is not known. *Cyrtodactylus caspius* occurs in the northern mountains of Iran, being found in the plateau region on the arid inner slopes of these ranges. It is distributed in the Aralo-Caspian region along the eastern margin of the Caspian Sea. It occurs in Afghanistan, and perhaps will be found in the inner mountain ranges of the plateau in Iran. *Cyrtodactylus fedtschenkoi*, an Aralo-Caspian species, may not be on the plateau, although it has been taken in the mountains to the east. *Eremias nigrocellata* appears to be a form inhabiting the Kopet Dāgh, entering the plateau at Shāhrūd and perhaps elsewhere to the east. *Phrynocephalus mystaceus* and *Eremias arguta* are Aralo-Caspian species known only from the fringes of the plateau.

One of the least known areas of the Iranian Plateau, and yet one of the most interesting and most important faunistically, is the north–south chain of mountain masses separating the interior plateau basin from Afghanistan, including the drainages of both the Harī Rūd and the Sīstān basin. Many of the species recorded from this region are known from single records, or from a few localities all within this border district. Other species are shared with the Kopet Dāgh. Species of lizards known from this eastern region are:

Agama agilis	*Cyrtodactylus longipes*
Agama caucasica	*Stenodactylus lumsdeni*
Agama erythrogastra	*Teratoscincus bedriagai*
Agama microlepis	*Acanthodactylus cantoris*
Agama nupta?	*Acanthodactylus micropholis*
Phrynocephalus maculatus?	*Eremias arguta*
Phrynocephalus mystaceus	*Eremias fasciata*
Phrynocephalus ornatus	*Eremias grammica*
Phrynocephalus scutellatus	*Eremias guttulata*
Agamura persica?	*Eremias lineolata*
Cyrtodactylus agamuroides	*Eremias nigrocellata*
Cyrtodactylus caspius	*Eremias velox*
Cyrtodactylus fedtschenkoi	*Ablepharus grayanus*
Cyrtodactylus kirmanensis	*Varanus griseus*

Various factors account for the presence of this relatively large and varied fauna within a rather narrow strip of land. In this region several faunistically distinct areas are in contact. To the north and east, in the drainage of the Harī Rūd, various Aralo-Caspian species obviously ascend the eastern flanks of this region. Among these are *Phrynocephalus mystaceus, Eremias arguta, E. grammica,* and *E. lineolata.* These elements are largely confined to the northern half of this mountainous border zone. On the eastern slopes of the central section, certain species enter from the Helmand Basin. Most of these are Iranian faunal elements whose distribution is largely confined to the eastern half of the Iranian Plateau, that occupied by Afghanistan and upland West Pakistan. Included in this group are *Phrynocephalus ornatus, Stenodactylus lumsdeni, Teratoscincus bedriagai, Teratoscincus microlepis,* and *Eremias fasciata.* Entering through upland Balūchistān, and penetrating only the southern portion of this elevated border, are lowland Saharo-Sindian species such as *Acanthodactylus cantoris, A. micropholis,* and *Ablepharus grayanus.* Most of the species on the western flanks are wide-ranging plateau species, Iranian elements which cross the passes into Afghanistan and highland West Pakistan. Included here are *Agama agilis, Phrynocephalus maculatus, P. scutellatus, Agamura persica, Teratoscincus scincus, Eremias guttulata, E. velox,* and *Varanus griseus.* Other important Iranian elements are the mountain species, *Agama caucasica, Cyrtodactylus caspius, C. fedtschenkoi,* and *Eremias nigrocellata,* which penetrate the elevated plains and passes from the northern ranges, *Agama nupta* which enters from the south, and *Agama microlepis,* which is distributed through the elevated regions of the plateau and occupies the central area.

Of particular interest are the species apparently endemic to this region. *Agama erythrogastra* is known only from the northern part of this area, while *Cyrtodactylus agamuroides* and *Cyrtodactylus kirmanensis* have been found only in this region and similar arid mountain slope and valley situations in the southern extent of the plateau and adjacent Makrān. *Cyrtodactylus longipes* is known only from these mountains.

The road from Mashhad to Zāhidān runs the length of this border region. The terrain crossed by this road is one of plains and mountain masses, the road running through the mountains in some places, along the eastern front in others, thus traversing a considerable variety of habitats. Many of the collecting localities recorded for this region have not been precisely located on any map available to me, and I am unable to find information regarding the terrain of most localities. The best general account of this road is that given by Lay.

The majority of specimens collected in this region are deposited in the collections of the Zoological Institute at Leningrad, and were obtained by the ornithologist Zarudny at the end of the nineteenth century. The diversity of this fauna makes a detailed study of the region particularly desirable.

The Rezā'īyeh [Urumīyeh] basin

The following lizards are known to occur in the area that drains into Lake Rezā'īyeh:

Agama caucasica	*Lacerta brandti*
Agama ruderata	*Lacerta strigata*
Phrynocephalus helioscopus	*Lacerta trilineata*
Apathya cappadocica	*Ophisops elegans*
Eremias pleskei	*Ablepharus bivittatus*
Eremias velox	*Eumeces schneideri*
Mabuya aurata	

Doubtless other species, as yet unrecorded, occur on the inner slopes of the surrounding mountains; *Ophisaurus apodus*, *Cyrtodactylus caspius*, *Cyrtodactylus kotschyi*, and *Lacerta saxicola* are to be expected.

The faunal affinities of this region are with the eastern Mediterranean and Transcaucasia in the genus *Lacerta*, with Transcaucasia and Anatolia in the mountain fauna, and with the Iranian Plateau fauna in most other species. At the specific and subspecific level, however, this fauna where adequately studied, is distinctive. The subspecies *Phrynocephalus helioscopus horvathi* has been recognized by some workers, *Apathya cappadocica urmiana*, *Eremias pleskei*, *Lacerta brandti*, and *L. trilineata media* are also endemic to this basin and the contiguous areas of Transcaucasia and eastern Turkey. *Eremias velox strauchi*, a form occupying arid mountain habitats, ranges somewhat more widely, from the Armenian plateau into the Tālish Mountains, the Alburz, and the Kopet Dāgh.

The Sīstān basin

The inclusion of this portion of the Helmand drainage within the borders of Iran adds a number of interesting species to the lizard fauna of the country. The affinities of this basin are with the Iranian faunal element primarily, but exchange between the plateau and the lower eastern deserts has obviously occurred. There has also been contact with certain Aralo-Caspian species. Known from the Iranian part of the Sīstān basin are:

Agama agilis
Agama nupta
Phrynocephalus luteoguttatus?
Phrynocephalus maculatus
Phrynocephalus ornatus
Phrynocephalus scutellatus
Agamura persica
Crossobamon eversmanni
Cyrtodactylus agamuroides
Cyrtodactylus caspius
Cyrtodactylus scaber

Cyrtodactylus zarudnyi
Teratoscincus bedriagai
Teratoscincus microlepis
Teratoscincus scincus
Eremias fasciata
Eremias guttulata
Eremias velox
Eumeces schneideri
Ophiomorus tridactylus
Varanus griseus

The majority of species belong to two basic categories: widely distributed Iranian Plateau forms, primarily occupying the uplands, and an endemic, sand-adapted Helmand fauna, having plateau affinities. *Agama agilis*, *A. nupta*, *Phrynocephalus maculatus*, *P. scutellatus*, *Agamura persica*, *Cyrtodactylus caspius*, *Teratoscincus scincus*, *Eremias guttulata*, *E. velox*, *Eumeces schneideri*, and *Varanus griseus* belong to the former category, while *Phrynocephalus luteoguttatus*, *Phrynocephalus ornatus*, *Cyrtodactylus zarudnyi*, *Teratoscincus bedriagai*, *T. microlepis*, *Eremias fasciata*, and *Ophiomorus tridactylus* represent the latter. *Crossobamon eversmanni* is an Aralo-Caspian gecko; *Cyrtodactylus agamuroides* is an apparently narrowly distributed upland Iranian form, and *Cyrtodactylus scaber* is a Saharo-Sindian element.

The Caspian region

The following lizard species have been recorded from within Iranian limits in the region of the Caspian Sea:

Agama agilis
Agama caucasica
Anguis fragilis
Ophisaurus apodus

Eremias velox
Lacerta chlorogaster
Lacerta saxicola
Lacerta strigata

From this list it is readily apparent that this small lizard fauna finds its relationships almost exclusively with Mediterranean Europe and Transcaucasia, though a few Aralo-Caspian elements are to be found along the western shore of the Caspian north of the Aras river. To the east contact is made with the Aralo-Caspian fauna in the vicinity of Gurgān and Pahlavī Diẕh. Of the two Iranian elements represented, *Agama caucasica* is a species of rocky and mountainous terrain, whose range apparently extends through the passes to reach the northern slopes of the Alburz. *Eremias velox persica* may also have crossed these passes at some time, or the animals identified as this subspecies may actually be *E. v. velox*, the form found on the Türkmen Steppes. A single endemic species, *Lacerta chlorogaster*, is found along the geologically recently exposed southern Caspian coast. It is also reported from the valley of the Atrak in the Kopet Dāgh, from whence it undoubtedly moved westward as the Caspian Sea receded. *Lacerta saxicola defilippii* is a montane lizard found on both the northern and southern slopes of the Alburz. Its affinities are to the north-west.

The Khūzistān Plain and the Persian Gulf Coast

Geographically an extension of the Mesopotamian Plain, this region has a close faunal relation to lowland Iraq and northern Arabia. The Tigris has apparently served as a barrier to the distribution of some forms, however. The fauna is not uniformly distributed, certain species being reported only from the more humid gulf coastal plain. The Iranian part of the Mesopotamian lowlands has been neglected by zoological collectors, and the composition of this fauna has not been elaborated. The following lizards are known:

Agama agilis	*Acanthodactylus fraseri*
Agama nupta	*Eremias brevirostris*
Agama ruderata	*Eremias guttulata*
Uromastyx loricatus	*Ophisops elegans*
Bunopus tuberculatus	*Ablepharus pannonicus*
Ceramodactylus affinis	*Chalcides ocellatus*
Cyrtodactylus scaber	*Eumeces schneideri*
Hemidactylus flaviviridis	*Mabuya aurata*
Hemidactylus turcicus	*Ophiomorus blanfordi?*
Pristurus rupestris	*Scincus conirostris*
Acanthodactylus cantoris	*Varanus griseus*

With few exceptions these species may be termed Saharo-Sindian elements. *Agama agilis, Eremias guttulata, Eumeces schneideri, Mabuya aurata*, and *Varanus griseus* are species which are distributed widely in South-west Asia over the lowland deserts as well as across the plateau. *Ophisops elegans blanfordi* may or may not be distinct from the upland form, *O. e. elegans. Agama nupta* and *A. ruderata* are not widely distributed in this region, being species of the foothills and mountains. *Hemidactylus flaviviridis* is known only from Gulf ports, and its distribution is undoubtedly due to human agency. This may also be true of certain other species, such as *H. turcicus, Pristurus rupestris*, and *Chalcides ocellatus*, animals which may travel in thatch or in sand ballast used in the extensive trade by dhow. The record for *Ophimorus blanfordi* is simply "Fārs Province", and so presumably from the coastal dunes in the general area of Bushire. It, too, could have been introduced in sand ballast, but its presence in this region definitely requires confirmation.

Iranian Balūchistān and the Makrān coast

Species recorded from this region within Iranian limits are:

Agama agilis	*Teratoscincus scincus*
Agama nupta	*Acanthodactylus cantoris*
Calotes versicolor	*Acanthodactylus micropholis*
Phrynocephalus maculatus	*Eremias fasciata*
Phrynocephalus scutellatus	*Eremias guttulata*
Uromastyx asmussi	*Eremias velox*
Agamura persica	*Ophisops elegans*
Bunopus tuberculatus	*Ablepharus grayanus*
Ceramodactylus doriae	*Chalcides ocellatus*
Cyrtodactylus agamuroides	*Eumeces schneideri*
Cyrtodactylus brevipes	*Ophiomorus blanfordi*
Cyrtodactylus scaber	*Ophiomorus brevipes*
Hemidactylus flaviviridis	*Ophiomorus streeti*
Hemidactylus persicus	*Varanus bengalensis*
Hemidactylus turcicus	*Varanus griseus*
Tropiocolotes persicus	

This somewhat large lizard fauna is made up of two main elements: an Iranian faunal element, composed of widely ranging plateau forms, most of which are here confined primarily to the rugged, folded terrain of Balūchistān, and a Saharo-Sindian faunal element, more or less confined to the coastal plain, in so far as details of distribution are known. This latter group of species can be further subdivided into those forms which apparently range no farther west than Bandar-i-Lingeh, such as *Uromastyx asmussi*, *Acanthodactylus cantoris blanfordi*, *A. micropholis*, and *Ophiomorus blanfordi* (a questionable record of this species does exist for Fārs Province, however). There are also certain species which occur in Balūchistān east of the Iranian border, for which no definite Persian records yet exist. Among these are *Agama melanura*, *Agama megalonyx*, *Agama rubrigularis*, and *Stenodactylus orientalis*. Certain other elements of the Sind fauna stop short of the Iranian border, e.g. *Uromastyx hardwicki*, *Hemidactylus brooki*, *Teratolepis fasciata*, *Mabuya macularia*, and *Ophiomorus raithmai*. It may be that the western limits of certain of these species more or less coincide with the western termination of the Balūchistān precipitation type of winter and summer rains under the influence of the monsoon.

It is only in Balūchistān and the Makrān that any Oriental elements enter Iran. *Calotes versicolor* and *Varanus bengalensis*, both wide-ranging lizards with great ecological tolerance, are known from this region.

Cyrtodactylus brevipes and *Ophiomorus streeti* are endemic species from inland Balūchistān. The extent of their distribution is not known.

An area of particular interest in this region is the extensive internal basin known as the Jāz Muriān Depression. A low basin of internal drainage, rimmed by mountains, and having extensive aeolian sand deposits on its floor, its fauna is incompletely known. Most collecting in this basin has been in the neighbourhood of Īrānshahr, near the Bampūr river in the higher eastern portion of the depression. The two endemic species, *Cyrtodactylus brevipes* and *Ophiomorus streeti*, are known only from this vicinity. *Agama agilis*, *A. nupta*, *Phrynocephalus maculatus*, *P. scutellatus*, *Uromastyx asmussi*, *Bunopus tuberculatus*, *Teratoscincus scincus*, *Acanthodactylus cantoris blanfordi*, *A. micropholis*, *Ablepharus grayanus*, *Eumeces schneideri zarudnyi*, *Ophiomorus brevipes*, *Varanus bengalensis*, and *V. griseus* are also known from the depression and the surrounding slopes.

Of particular interest in comparing the fauna of the Makrān coast with that of the western coast of the Persian Gulf is that fact that while the climatic change in the lowland region stretching from North Africa to Sind occurs east of the Iranian border, there is an additional faunal change between Bushire and Bandar-i-Lingeh. Many of the species shared by the two regions are plateau forms, not requiring a continuous coastal distribution. Of the strictly Saharo-Sindian elements, the only shared species are *Cyrtodactylus scaber*, a form which ranges into the foothills, *Bunopus tuberculatus*, in which there is some evidence of geographically correlated variation, *Acanthodactylus cantoris*, subspecifically distinct in the two areas, and *Chalcides ocellatus*, a widely distributed species known within Persian limits only from two ports, Bushire and Jāsk. The possibility of human agency as a factor in the Persian Gulf distributon of this last species cannot be discounted.

Of additional interest is the distribution of *Eremias brevirostris*, known from West Pakistan and from the western Persian Gulf, but never recorded from the Makrān coast. It is known from Qishm Island and Jazīreh-ye Tanb-i-Buzurg, islands off the Makrān coast. This suggests that these islands may have been connected with the mainland at a time when distribution of Saharo-Sindian forms was continuous along this coast. Present distribution of the Saharo-Sindian fauna along the gulf indicates that coastal environments are interrupted between Bushire and Bandar-i-Lingeh, a question which could be settled easily through observation.

The Türkmen Steppe

The contact of the fauna of the plateau with the Aralo-Caspian elements has been briefly considered in the discussion of the eastern border of the plateau. Small portions of these low plains are enclosed by Iranian borders in the north-eastern corner of the country, and in a narrow wedge east of the Caspian Sea, between the shore and the mountains. Species found in this drainage are:

Agama agilis	*Eremias arguta*
Agama caucasica	*Eremias grammica*
Agama erythrogastra	*Eremias guttulata*
Agama nupta	*Eremias intermedia*
Phrynocephalus helioscopus	*Eremias lineolata*
Phrynocephalus interscapularis?	*Eremias nigrocellata*
Phrynocephalus mystaceus	*Eremias velox*
Ophisaurus apodus	*Lacerta chlorogaster*
Crossobamon eversmanni	*Eumeces schneideri*
Cyrtodactylus caspius	*Eumeces taeniolatus*
Cyrtodactylus fedtschenkoi	*Mabuya aurata*
Teratoscincus scincus	*Varanus griseus*

Even here on the fringes of the Türkmen Steppe, only 43·5 per cent of the lizard fauna are forms which can be considered truly Aralo-Caspian, the remainder being species from the Iranian Plateau, and species confined primarily to mountain slopes, e.g. *Agama caucasica*, *A. erythrogastra*, *A. nupta*, *Ophisaurus apodus*, *Cyrtodactylus caspius*, and *Eremias nigrocellata*. The only forms which may be said to have a primarily Aralo-Caspian distribution are *Phrynocephalus interscapularis*, *P. mystaceus*, *Crossobamon eversmanni*, *Cyrtodactylus fedtschenkoi*, *Eremias arguta*, *Eremias grammica*, *Eremias intermedia*, *Eremias lineolata*, and *E. velox velox*.

The three subspecies of *E. velox* have been reported together both in the Gurgān region and in the north-eastern corner of Iran. Intermediates are said to occur in the former but not the latter region. On the basis of material that I have examined I have been unable to verify this, or even to distinguish clearly between the three forms by means of the characters usually employed.

Comparison of this Türkmen Steppe fauna with that of the Iranian Plateau indicates that the great majority of species presently capable of negotiating the passes separating the two regions are those of the plateau.

The Mughān Steppe

This region, drained by the Aras River, falls within Iranian limits only in the northernmost part of Persian Āzarbāījān. Virtually no collecting has been done in the Iranian part of this region, but the fauna of the Mughān Steppe in U.S.S.R. has been listed by Sobolevsky (1929) in his analysis of the herpetofauna of the Tālish Mountains and Lankorān lowland. He includes the following species from the Mughān Steppe:

Ophisaurus apodus	*Lacerta strigata*
Cyrtodactylus caspius	*Ophisops elegans*
Eremias arguta	*Eumeces schneideri?*
Eremias velox	

Ophisaurus apodus and *Lacerta strigata* are species with Mediterranean affinities. *Eremias arguta* is a widely distributed Aralo-Caspian form which occurs also in Rumania, southern Russia, the Crimea, and Transcaucasia. *E. velox strauchi* and *Cyrtodactylus caspius* are lizards which occupy the intermediate upland areas between Iran and the U.S.S.R., while *Ophisops elegans* and *Eumeces schneideri* are primarily plateau forms.

Thus far the fauna has been discussed relative to the principal drainage areas of Iran, and species occupying the mountain slopes of these drainages have been included. The mountains themselves should now be discussed briefly, although our knowledge of the montane lizard fauna is very fragmentary.

The Zagros Mountains

This long mountain chain forms both a barrier between the plateau and the Mesopotamian lowlands and a corridor for the southward distribution of northern faunal elements. Unfortunately, zoological information for this range is very sketchy, though the southern extent of these northern species is known. The species known from the Zagros area itself are:

Agama agilis	*Lacerta strigata*
Agama nupta	*Ophisops elegans*
Agama ruderata	*Ablepharus bivittatus*
Ophisaurus apodus	*Ablepharus pannonicus*
Cyrtodactylus heterocercus	*Eumeces schneideri*
Cyrtodactylus scaber	*Mabuya aurata*
Eremias guttulata	*Ophiomorus persicus*
Lacerta princeps	*Varanus griseus*

Three species, *Cyrtodactylus heterocercus*, *Lacerta princeps* and *Ophiomorus persicus*, are endemic to the Zagros. The extent of their distribution is undetermined. The known fauna, is essentially that of the lower passes and consists mostly of wide-ranging South-west Asian species. These are *Agama agilis*, *A. ruderata*, *Cyrtodactylus scaber*, *Eremias guttulata*, *Ophisops elegans*, *Ablepharus pannonicus*, *Eumeces schneideri*, *Mabuya aurata*, and *Varanus griseus*, all species distributed through both lowland and arid mountain areas over much of South-west Asia. *Ophisaurus apodus* and *Lacerta strigata* are species entering from the north-west, and having Mediterranean affinities. *Agama nupta* is a species of the outer flanks of the mountains rimming the western and southern borders of the Iranian Plateau.

The western foothills of the Zagros Mountains

This area, too, has been little studied. Our limited knowledge of the fauna and general ecology of the foothills suggests that this belt should be considered separately from both the Zagros mountains proper and the Mesopotamian lowlands, although it shares species with each. The known species are:

Agama agilis	*Phyllodactylus elisae*
Agama nupta	*Ptyodactylus hasselquisti*
Uromastyx loricatus	*Eremias guttulata*
Cyrtodactylus scaber	*Ophisops elegans*
Eublepharus angramainyu	*Ablepharus pannonicus*
Hemidactylus persicus	*Eumeces schneideri*
Hemidactylus turcicus	*Mabuya aurata*
Tropiocolotos persicus	*Scincus conirostris*
Varanus griseus	

The three endemic taxa of this list are of particular interest. *Eublepharus angramainyu* and *Tropiocolotos persicus helenae* both have their nearest relatives in West Pakistan and Afghanistan; *Phyllodactylus elisae* is probably most closely akin to the New World species of *Phyllodactylus* than to other Old World forms presently included in the genus, according to James Dixon (personal communication).

Hemidactylus persicus is a species which has been recognized only from this region, Arabia, and areas to the east, in Balūchistān and Sind.

The remaining forms are the generally distributed South-west Asian species, *Agama agilis, Eremias guttulata, Ophisops elegans, Ablepharus pannonicus, Eumeces schneideri, Mabuya aurata,* and *Varanus griseus,* and Saharo-Sindian elements, *Uromastyx loricatus, Cyrtodactylus scaber, Ptyodactylus hasselquisti,* and *Scincus conirostris. Agama nupta* is restricted to rocky outcrops through the southern and western upland regions from Iraq to Sind.

Scincus conirostris and *Uromastyx loricatus,* both narrowly distributed species, are hardly characteristic of the foothill belt, the former being found only in aeolian dunes caught in the fringes of the hills, the latter in the lower alluvial fans and valleys.

Conspicuously absent from this region are the strictly Iranian elements; that is, those characteristic of the Central Plateau. In this respect the region differs sharply from the folds of Balūchistān where such species are an important element of the lizard fauna.

The Alburz Mountains

The fauna of this range consists of two fairly well-defined segments: that of the dry southern slopes (these species having been included in the discussion of the plateau), and that of the much wetter, forested northern slopes (included in the section on the Caspian coast). A few species cross the passes; a few range along the lower crests. The known species of the Alburz are:

Agama agilis	*Cyrtodactylus caspius*
Agama caucasica	*Eremias nigrocellata*
Agama ruderata	*Eremias velox*
Phrynocephalus helioscopus	*Lacerta saxicola*
Phrynocephalus scutellatus	*Lacerta strigata*
Anguis fragilis	*Ophisops elegans*
Ophisaurus apodus	*Eumeces schneideri*
Mabuya aurata	

Of all these species, only *Lacerta saxicola defilippii,* a montane species with Caucasian affinities, is known to occupy the mountain crests, occurring on both flanks of the range above tree line. Other species which at least cross the passes and occupy the mountain valley are *Agama caucasica*, *Ophisaurus apodus*, *Eremias velox persica*, *Lacerta strigata*, and *Mabuya aurata*. *Cyrtodactylus caspius* and *Eremias nigrocellata* are only known in the Alburz from the more arid eastern end of the range where it merges with the folds of the Kopet Dāgh. *Agama ruderata*, *Phrynocephalus helioscopus*, *P. scutellatus*, and *Ophisops elegans* are species of the southern foothills, *Agama agilis* and *Eumeces schneideri* probably ranging somewhat further up the southern flank, perhaps into the lower mountain valleys. *Anguis fragilis*, and perhaps other lowland Caspian species such as *Lacerta chlorogaster*, occur on the northern slopes.

The Kopet Dāgh

The more arid mountain folds stretching along the Iran–U.S.S.R. border east of the Alburz have not been studied in any detail, one reason being that routes crossing the border run to the west and east of these mountains. The relatively low Atrek valley divides the two main folds of the ranges, and has itself been little travelled by zoological collectors. Our scanty knowledge of the fauna suggests that transects of these ranges would yield interesting results. The known species within Iranian limits are:

Agama caucasica	*Eremias velox*
Phrynocephalus helioscopus	*Lacerta chlorogaster*
Anguis fragilis	*Lacerta strigata*
Ophisaurus apodus	*Ablepharus bivittatus*
Alsophylax spinicauda	*Ablepharus pannonicus*
Cyrtodactylus caspius	*Ablepharus persicus?*
Eremias nigrocellata	

I include in this list records from Shāhrūd, on the southern flank where these mountains contact the plateau. The two endemic species *Alsophylax spinicauda* and *Ablepharus persicus* are reported from this locality. Both are of uncertain taxonomic status, particularly *A. persicus* (Werner's record of this species from Fārs can be ignored). There is a record of *Eublepharis macularius* from the Kopet Dāgh within Russian limits. In light of recent comments on the distribution and status of this species (Anderson and Leviton, 1966*a*) these specimens should be re-examined.

Phrynocephalus helioscopus, *Ophisaurus apodus*, *Cyrtodactylys caspius*, and *Lacerta chlorogaster* are known in the Kopet Dāgh from the Atrak valley.

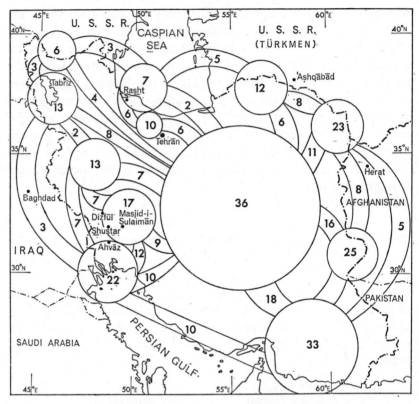

Fig. 92. Correlation of Iranian lizard fauna at the species level with physiographic regions. Figures within circles represent numbers of species recorded for the regions; figures in connecting arcs represent numbers of species in common to two regions.

Islands of the Persian Gulf

Almost nothing is known of the fauna of these islands, most of which lie close to the Iranian coast. A close study of these islands may provide an answer to some questions about earlier distributions along the gulf coasts. The few lizards known from these islands are listed here, with the island from which they were taken in parentheses:

Bunopus tuberculatus (Jazīreh-ye Tanb-i-Buzurg), Cyrtodactylus scaber (Bahrain Island), Pristurus rupestris (Jazīreh-ye Khārg; Bahrain Island), Acanthodactylus micropholis (Qishm Island), Eremias brevirostris (Qishm Island; Jazīreh-ye Tanb-i-Buzurg), E. guttulata (Jazīreh-ye Hingām, Scincus conirostris (Bahrain Island).

The distribution of turtles can be briefly considered here. Emys *orbicularis* is a Mediterranean species which occurs in Iran only along the Caspian coast. It ranges as far north as central Europe, and appears in the littoral fauna of north-west Africa, from Morocco to Tunisia. *Clemmys caspica* is a nearly circum-Mediterranean form, occurring in northern and western Iran, its distribution being limited to the areas where permanent streams, or at least regular and sufficient annual precipitation, occur. Thus it appears to range no further east than the extreme western portion of the plateau, or that area in which annual precipitation is in excess of 300 mm. No lizard species has a parallel distribution.

Trionyx euphraticus is a species endemic to the Mesopotamian drainage. It is the only representative of the genus (and its family) in South-west Asia, doubtless a relict of a moister period when this genus was more continuously distributed. An investigation of its affinities within the genus would prove interesting. The genus is known from the Upper Cretaceous of North America, Europe and Asia, from Africa since the Miocene, and from the East Indies since the Pleistocene (Romer, 1956).

The Mediterranean distribution of *Testudo graeca* parallels that of *Clemmys caspica*, *Testudo graeca graeca* ranging from southern Spain through North Africa, *Testudo graeca ibera* occupying the area from the Balkans east through Iran, the hiatus in the distribution of the species in southern Europe being occupied by the related *Testudo hermanni*. The form occupying the plateau region of Iran has been recognized as a distinct subspecies (or species), *T. graeca zarudnyi*, by most workers, although the distinction between the populations of *T. graeca* is not by any means great. Loveridge and Williams (1957) suggest that a continuous population of *T. graeca* formerly extended across southern Europe, the invasion of Africa taking place via Spain, with the present Iberian population constituting a relict of this former distributon.

Testudo horsfieldi, while its affinities are with the *graeca* group (Testudo *sensu stricto* of Loveridge and Williams), is quite distinct, and is an Iranian Plateau species extending into the Transcaspian region. This is the only turtle occupying the large area of South-west Asia between the range of *T. graeca* and the Indus valley, where turtles suddenly become an important faunal element.

The single amphisbaenian within Iranian limits, *Diplometopon zarudnyi*, is restricted to northern Arabia and the Mesopotamian lowlands in aeolian sand deposits. The only known member of the genus, it is the north-eastern representative of the trogonophine amphisbaenians, discontinuously distributed in the deserts of North Africa and Arabia.

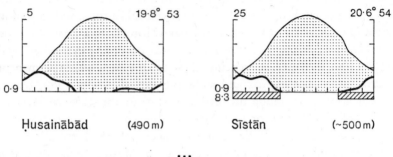

III₃ₐ

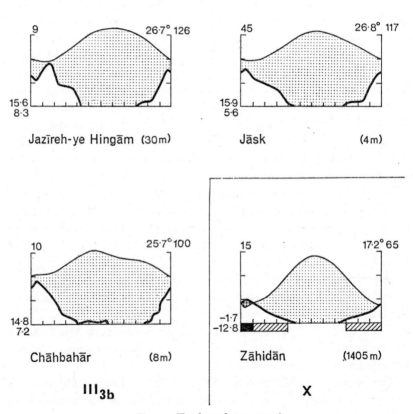

Fig. 93. (For legend see p. 329.)

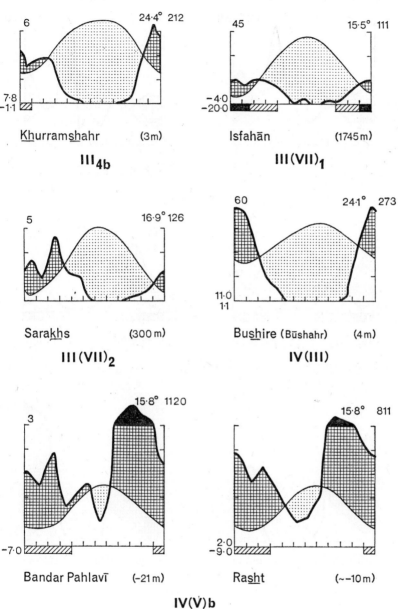

Khurram**sh**ahr (3 m)

III₄b

Isfahān (1745 m)

III(VII)₁

Sara**kh**s (300 m)

III(VII)₂

Bu**sh**ire (Būshahr) (4 m)

IV(III)

Bandar Pahlavī (−21 m)

Ra**sh**t (~ −10 m)

IV(V̇)b

Fig. 93 (*cont.*)

327

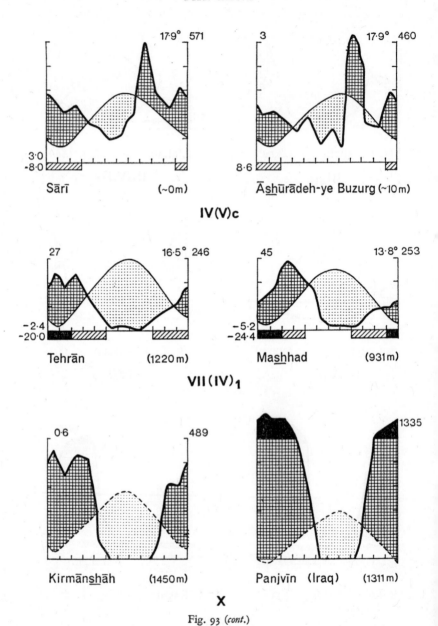

IV(V)c

VII(IV)₁

X

Fig. 93 (cont.)

Fig. 93. Climatic types in Iran (from Walter and Lieth, 1960; redrawn).

I   equatorial, humid
II tropical, summer rains
III subtropical, hot and arid
IV Mediterranean, winter rains
V   warm-temperate, humid

VI   humid, with cold season
VII arid, with cold season
VIII boreal
IX   arctic
X   mountain areas in the other regions

Explanation of graphs:

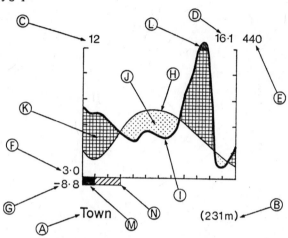

A. Station.
B. Altitude.
C. Number of years observation (first figure for temperature, second for precipitation)
D. Mean annual temperature in degrees Centigrade.
E. Mean annual sum-total of precipitation in mm.
F. Mean daily minimum of coldest month.
G. Absolute minimum.
H. Monthly means of temperature (thin line).
I. Monthly means of precipitation (thick line). Both *h* and *i* stand in a fixed proportion to one another, 10° C corresponding to 20 mm precipitation.
J. Dotted area—arid period prevailing when precipitation falls below temperature curve.
K. Cross-hatched area—humid period prevailing when precipitation is above temperature curve.
L. Precipitation above 100 mm is printed in the scale of 1 : 10 and marked in black.
M. Black block—frost, where mean minimum of month falls below 0° C.
N. Hatched block—where absolute minimum falls below 0° C.

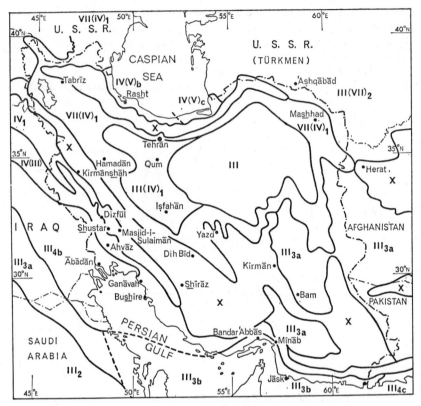

Fig. 94. Distribution of climatic types in Iran. After Walter and Lieth, 1960 (redrawn).

ECOLOGICAL ZOOGEOGRAPHY

So little is known about the Iranian lizards in nature, and information about the physical environment so lacking in detail, that only a few very general remarks can be made relative to the immediate factors determining present distributions.

One of the greatest difficulties in attempting to make ecological correlations is the fact that so little of the available climatic data is directly applicable to a consideration of the actual environmental conditions faced by small organisms. Lizards are subject to the temperatures and temperature fluctuations two in. or less above the ground, not those one metre above the ground in a sheltered meteorological screen, which is the standard basis for climatological measurement. The relative humidity affecting their lives is that to be found in burrows, under rocks, and in other areas of retreat. They may depend almost totally for water on dew, an element rarely measured in South-west Asia. By examining the gross correlations of distribution with climatic type (table 6), however, certain clues as to the direction ecological studies should take may appear, for we should expect that differences in climate over a broad area will be reflected to a considerable extent by the many microhabitats of the region.

Environmental factors influencing lizard distribution in South-west Asia

Temperature

It is now well known that lizards are able to maintain their body temperatures within a fairly narrow range. Although some physiological mechanisms, such as vasodilation and vasoconstriction, and changes in albedo (colouring) are involved, these are generally accessory to the primary, behavioural means of temperature regulation. Thus the animal's body temperature at any given time is a product of its relation to ambient temperature, and reflected radiation from substrata. For this reason, the mean air temperature, either on a daily or a seasonal basis, is less meaningful than the extremes from which the animal is unable to escape. So too, the number of hours and days during which the combination of climatic events enable the lizard to maintain a suitable activity temperature must be considered.

Temperature may be most critical to developmental stages, as the lizard must be able to place its eggs where they will be protected from lethal extremes as well as exposed to temperatures sufficiently high for development to proceed. Such species must be developmentally labile to the extent that they are able to endure the inevitable fluctuations and inconsistencies in temperature and moisture characteristic of arid regions.

The behavioural means by which temperature is regulated differs considerably from group to group. Most lizards (at least diurnal species) bask, utilizing direct insolation to raise the body temperature to the activity range. Normal activity temperatures for agamid lizards in the foothills of Khūzistān were found to lie between $38°$ and $43°$ C, the larger *Uromastyx* foraging with anal temperature as high as $44°$ C. A change in albedo correlated with body temperature was observed in these lizards, basking individuals being the darkest in appearance, those near or past the voluntary maximum being extremely light in

TABLE 6.

Correlation of Iranian turtles, lizards, and amphisbaenians with the climatic types of Walter and Lieth (see figs. 93 and 94). N.B.: X refers to mountain areas within the other climatic regions, and thus does not refer to a climatic type comparable in all regions.

+ = known presence within climatic type.
? = questionable presence within climatic type.
AC = Aralo-Caspian faunal element.
I = Iranian faunal element.

M = Mediterranean faunal element.
SS = Saharo-Sindian faunal element.
O = Oriental faunal element.

	Faunal class	III	III_{3a}	III_{3b}	III_{4b}	$III(IV)_1$	$III(VII)_2$	IV_1	$IV(III)$	$IV(V)_b$	$IV(V)_c$	$VII(IV)_1$	X
Clemmys caspica	M	.	.	.	+	+	.	+	+	+	+	+	.
Emys orbicularis	M	.	.	.	.	.	.	.	.	+	+	.	.
Testudo graeca ibera	M	.	.	.	.	+	.	+	+	+	.	+	+
Testudo graeca zarudnyi	I	+	+	.	.	+	.	.	.	.	.	+	+
Testudo horsfieldi	I	+	+	.	.	.	.	.	.	.	.	.	.
Trionyx euphraticus	SS	.	.	.	+	.	.	.	+	.	.	.	.
Agama agilis	I/SS	+	+	.	+	+	+	.	+	+	+	+	+
Agama caucasica	I	.	.	.	.	+	.	.	.	.	+	+	+
Agama erythrogastra	I	.	.	.	.	.	.	.	.	.	.	+	.
Agama kirmanensis	I	.	.	.	.	+	.	.	.	.	.	.	.
Agama megalonyx	I	.	?	.	.	.	.	.	.	.	.	.	.
Agama melanura	I	.	?	.	.	.	.	.	.	.	.	.	?
Agama microlepis	I	+	+	.	.	+	.	.	.	.	.	+	+
Agama microtympanum	?	.	.	.	.	.	.	.	.	.	.	.	.
Agama nupta	I	.	+	.	+	+	?	+	+	.	.	+	+
Agama rubrigularis	I	.	.	.	.	.	.	.	.	.	.	.	.
Agama ruderata	I/SS	.	.	.	.	+	.	.	+	.	.	+	+
Calotes versicolor	O	.	+	.	.	.	.	.	.	.	.	.	.
Phrynocephalus helioscopus	AC/I	.	.	.	.	+	+	.	.	.	.	+	.
Phrynocephalus interscapularis	AC	.	.	.	.	.	+	.	.	.	.	.	.
Phrynocephalus luteoguttatus	I	.	+	.	.	.	.	.	.	.	.	.	.
Phrynocephalus maculatus	I	+	+	.	.	.	.	.	.	.	.	+	.
Phrynocephalus mystaceus	AC	.	.	.	.	.	.	+	.	.	.	.	.
Phrynocephalus ornatus	I	.	+	.	.	.	.	.	.	.	.	.	.
Phrynocephalus scutellatus	I	+	+	.	+	+	.	.	.	.	.	+	+
Uromastyx asmussi	SS	+	+	.	.	.	.	.	.	.	.	+	+
Uromastyx loricatus	SS	.	.	.	?	.	.	+	+	.	.	.	.
Uromastyx microlepis	SS	.	.	.	+	.	.	+	.	.	.	.	.
Anguis fragilis colchicus	M	.	.	.	.	.	.	.	.	+	+	+	?
Ophisaurus apodus	M	.	.	.	.	.	.	+	.	+	+	+	+
Agamura persica	I	.	+	.	.	+	.	.	.	.	.	+	?
Alsophylax spinicauda	I	.	.	.	.	.	.	.	.	.	.	?	?
Bunopus crassicauda	I	.	.	.	.	+	.	.	.	.	.	.	.
Bunopus tuberculatus	SS	+	+	+	.	.	.	.	+	.	.	.	+
Ceramodactylus affinis	SS	.	.	.	.	.	.	.	+	.	.	.	.
Ceramodactylus doriae	SS	.	+	+	+	.	.	.	.	.	.	.	.
Crossobamon eversmanni	AC	.	+	.	.	.	+	.	.	.	.	.	.
Cyrtodactylus agamuroides	I	.	+	.	+	.	.	.	.	.	.	.	+
Cyrtodactylus brevipes	I	.	?	.	.	.	.	.	.	.	.	.	?
Cyrtodactylus caspius	I	+	+	.	.	.	.	+	.	.	+	+	+
Cyrtodactylus fedtschenkoi	I	.	?	.	.	.	.	+	.	.	.	+	.
Cyrtodactylus gastropholis	?	.	.	.	.	.	.	.	?	.	.	.	?
Cyrtodactylus heterocercus	I	.	.	.	.	.	.	.	.	.	.	+	?
Cyrtodactylus kirmanensis	I	.	+	.	.	.	.	.	.	.	.	.	?
Cyrtodactylus kotschyi	M	.	.	.	.	.	.	.	.	.	.	?	?
Cyrtodactylus longipes	I	.	+	.	.	.	.	.	.	.	.	.	.
Cyrtodactylus russowi	AC	.	.	.	.	.	?	.	.	.	.	.	.
Cyrtodactylus scaber	SS	.	+	+	+	.	.	+	+	.	.	.	.
Cyrtodactylus zarudnyi	I	.	+	.	.	.	.	.	.	.	.	.	.
Eublepharis angramainyu	I	.	.	.	.	.	.	.	+	.	.	.	.
Hemidactylus flaviviridis	O	.	.	+	+	.	.	.	+	.	.	.	.

TABLE 6 (*cont.*)

	Faunal class	III	III_{3a}	III_{3b}	III_{4b}	$III (IV)_1$	$III (VII)_2$	IV_1	$IV (III)$	$IV (V)_b$	$IV (V)_c$	$VII (IV)_1$	X
Hemidactylus persicus	SS	.	.	.	.	.	.	+	+	.	.	.	+
Hemidactylus turcicus	SS	.	.	.	.	.	.	.	+	.	.	.	?
Phyllodactylus elisae	?	.	.	.	.	.	.	+	+	.	.	.	+
Pristurus rupestris	SS	.	.	.	+	.	.	.	+	.	.	.	.
Ptyodactylus hasselquisti	SS	.	.	.	.	.	.	.	.	.	.	.	+
Stenodactylus lumsdeni	I?	.	+	.	.	.	.	.	.	.	.	.	.
Teratoscincus bedriagai	I	.	+	.	.	.	.	.	.	.	.	.	.
Teratoscincus microlepis	I	.	+	.	.	.	.	.	.	.	.	.	.
Teratoscincus scincus	I	.	+	.	.	+	+	.	.	.	.	+	?
Tropiocolotes persicus helenae	SS?	.	.	.	.	.	.	+	.	.	.	.	.
Tropiocolotes persicus persicus	SS?	.	+	.	.	.	.	.	.	.	.	.	.
Acanthodactylus cantoris blanfordi	SS	.	+	+	+	.	.	.	.	.	.	.	.
Acanthodactylus cantoris schmidti	SS	.	.	.	.	.	.	.	+	.	.	.	.
Acanthodactylus fraseri	SS	.	.	.	+	.	.	.	+	.	.	.	.
Acanthodactylus micropholis	SS	.	+	+	.	.	.	.	.	.	.	.	?
Apathya cappadocica	I	.	.	.	.	.	.	.	.	.	.	+	.
Eremias arguta	AC	.	.	.	.	.	+	.	.	.	.	+	.
Eremias brevirostris	SS	.	.	+	.	.	.	+	+	.	.	.	.
Eremias fasciata	I	.	+	.	.	.	.	.	.	.	.	+	+
Eremias grammica	AC	.	+	.	.	.	+	.	.	.	.	.	.
Eremias guttulata watsonana	I	.	+	+	+	+	+	+	+	.	.	+	+
Eremias intermedia	AC	.	.	.	.	.	+	.	.	.	.	.	.
Eremias lineolata	AC	.	.	.	.	.	+	.	.	.	.	.	.
Eremias nigrocellata	AC	+	.	.	.	.	.	.	.	.	.	+	+
Eremias pleskei	I	.	?	.	.	.	.	.	.	.	.	+	.
Eremias scripta	AC	.	?	.	.	.	+	.	.	.	.	.	.
Eremias velox persica	I	+	+	.	.	+	?	.	.	?	.	+	+
Eremias velox strauchi	I	.	.	.	.	.	.	.	.	?	.	+	+
Eremias velox velox	AC	.	.	.	.	.	+	.	.	.	+	.	.
Lacerta brandti	I	.	.	.	.	.	.	.	.	.	.	+	?
Lacerta chlorogaster	?	.	.	.	.	.	?	.	.	+	+	.	+
Lacerta princeps	I	.	.	.	.	.	.	.	.	.	.	.	+
Lacerta saxicola defilipii	I	.	.	.	.	.	.	.	.	+	.	.	+
Lacerta strigata	I/M	.	.	.	.	.	.	.	.	+	.	+	+
Lacerta trilineata media	I	.	.	.	.	.	.	.	.	.	.	+	.
Ophisops elegans blanfordi	SS	.	.	.	.	.	.	+	+	.	.	.	.
Ophisops elegans elegans	I	.	.	.	.	+	.	.	.	.	.	+	+
Ablepharus bivittatus	I	.	.	.	.	.	.	.	.	.	.	+	.
Ablepharus grayanus	I?	.	+	.	.	.	.	.	.	.	.	+	+
Ablepharus pannonicus	I	.	.	.	.	.	+	+	+	.	.	+	?
Ablepharus persicus	I	.	.	.	.	.	.	.	.	.	.	?	?
Chalcides ocellatus	SS	.	.	+	.	.	.	.	+	.	.	.	.
Eumeces schneideri	SS/I	.	+	.	.	.	+	+	+	.	.	+	+
Eumeces taeniolatus	I	.	.	.	.	.	+	.	.	.	.	.	.
Mabuya aurata	SS/I	.	.	.	.	+	+	+	+	.	.	+	?
Ophiomorus blanfordi	SS	.	.	+	?	.	.	.	.	.	.	.	.
Ophiomorus brevipes	I	.	+	+	.	.	.	.	.	.	.	.	.
Ophiomorus persicus	I	.	.	.	.	.	.	.	.	.	.	.	+
Ophiomorus streeti	I	.	+	.	.	.	.	.	.	.	.	.	.
Ophiomorus tridactylus	I	.	+	.	.	.	.	.	.	.	.	.	.
Scincus conirostris	SS	.	.	.	+	+	+	.	.	.	.	.	.
Varanus bengalensis	O	.	.	.	+	.	.	.	.	.	.	.	.
Varanus griseus	SS/I	.	+	.	?	+	+	+	+	.	.	+	+
Diplometopon zarudnyi	SS	.	+	+	+	.	.	.	.	+	.	.	.

colour. Similar activity temperatures were recorded for lacertids and for *Varanus griseus* (Anderson, 1963).

Probably most species exhibit a seasonal shift in the daily hours of activity. In Khūzistān the lizards first become active in early spring for a few hours from mid-day when temperatures are highest. As the season wears on they begin activity progressively earlier in the day and remain active longer. Eventually they seek cover during the hottest hours, and by mid-summer they are active only during the early morning and late afternoon, a reversal of this shift occurring in autumn.

Some species, such as the sand-dwelling *Ophiomorus* and *Scincus conirostris*, are able to maintain fairly constant body temperature through their burrowing habits in aeolian sand dunes. By moving on to the sand surface, or near the surface, during the warm hours they come quickly to activity temperature, while both high and low extremes are readily avoided by burrowing a few inches below the surface.

The small lacertids are able to extend their activity periods into the hottest hours of the day by utilizing the small areas of shade provided by rock or bush, making brief forays into the sunlight to catch insects.

The agamids position themselves relative to the incident sunlight so that the maximum surface area is exposed during basking, the minimum during the hottest period. The small agamids ascend low bushes at mid-day and thus escape some of the heat re-radiated from the ground. A darkly pigmented peritoneum is characteristic of diurnal species in South-west Asia, and is presumably related to the thermal environment affecting these animals.

One of the striking aspects of the lizard fauna of this desert region is the diversity of gecko species. These creatures are able to circumvent the problem of high daytime temperatures through exploitation of nocturnal activity. During the hottest season, when diurnal lizards are restricted to brief activity periods, nocturnal air temperatures remain high, due to the re-radiation from the heated ground surface. The activity of many insects and other arthropods is also largely confined to the night hours during this period. A few geckoes apparently have become secondarily diurnal, or partially so. Such behaviour is indicated for *Pristurus*, *Agamura*, and some *Cyrtodactylus* (*C. agamuroides*, *C. gastropholis*), all of which have darkly pigmented peritoneum. The habits of these lizards have not been studied, however, and only a few observations have been recorded.

Only the most cursory temperature observations have been recorded for lizards in South-west Asia (Anderson, 1963), but considerable study of thermal problems in regard to lizards of the deserts of the south-western United States has been undertaken in recent years (see particularly Cowles and Bogert, 1944; Mayhew, 1963, 1964, 1965 *b*).

Mountain ranges may serve as barriers to animal distribution for several reasons, but certainly one of the most important is their imposition of a vertical temperature gradient. For instance, if continental temperature zones move southward in response to general lowering of temperatures, lizards living on the low Aralo-Caspian steppes find an increasing temperature barrier to their ascent of the passes through the east–west ranges separating the low steppes from the Iranian Plateau. Conversely, north–south ranges, such as the Zagros, may provide corridors for the southward penetration of upland northern elements. With general increase of continental temperatures, and increased aridity, some plateau species may find refuge in the higher elevations of the mountain masses present on the Iranian Plateau, while in response to climatic cooling and increased precipitation, species isolated in such mountain areas may descend to the plateau to become more widely distributed.

Precipitation and humidity

Reptiles as a group have various physiological adaptations which enable them to exploit arid environments. The more obvious of these are well known, namely, a relatively impermeable integument, excretion of uric acid, and high degree of resorption of water in the kidneys. Many other aspects of their osmoregulatory physiology remain relatively unstudied.

Certainly the amount of available water must be a limiting factor for many species in arid regions, more so perhaps than extremes in temperature. Undoubtedly behavioural adaptations play an important role in conservation of water in desert species. Many lizards spend the hours when evaporative rates are highest in burrows, where the relative humidity must be considerably higher than that of the general environment.

It has often been noted that while many desert lizards in captivity will not drink water standing in a vessel, they will, however, lap water sprayed in droplets on rocks, leaves or other objects (including other individuals) in their cages. This suggests that atmospheric water condensing as dew may be important to the survival of such species.

TABLE 7. *Elevational distribution of lizards in Iran*

Elevation in thousands of feet

0 1 2 3 4 5 6 7 8 9 10

Agama agilis.
Agama caucasica
Agama erythrogastra
Agama kirmanensis
Agama megalonyx
Agama melanura
Agama microlepis
Agama microtympanum
Agama nupta
Agama rubrigularis
Agama ruderata
Calotes versicolor
Phrynocephalus helioscopus
Phrynocephalus interscapularis
Phrynocephalus luteoguttatus
Phrynocephalus maculatus
Phrynocephalus mystaceus
Phrynocephalus ornatus
Phrynocephalus scutellatus
Uromastyx asmussi
Uromastyx loricatus
Uromastyx microlepis
Anguis fragilis
Ophisaurus apodus
Agamura persica
Alsophylax spinicauda
Bunopus crassicauda
Bunopus tuberculatus
Ceramodactylus affinis
Ceramodactylus doriae
Crossobamon eversmanni
Cyrtodactylus agamuroides
Cyrtodactylus brevipes
Cyrtodactylus caspius
Cyrtodactylus fedtschenkoi
Cyrtodactylus gastropholis
Cyrtodactylus heterocercus
Cyrtodactylus kirmanensis
Cyrtodactylus kotschyi
Cyrtodactylus longipes
Cyrtodactylus russowi
Cyrtodactylus scaber
Cyrtodactylus zarudnyi
Eublepharis angramainyu
Hemidactylus flaviviridis
Hemidactylus persicus
Hemidactylus turcicus
Phyllodactylus elisae
Pristurus rupestris

TABLE 7 (*cont.*)

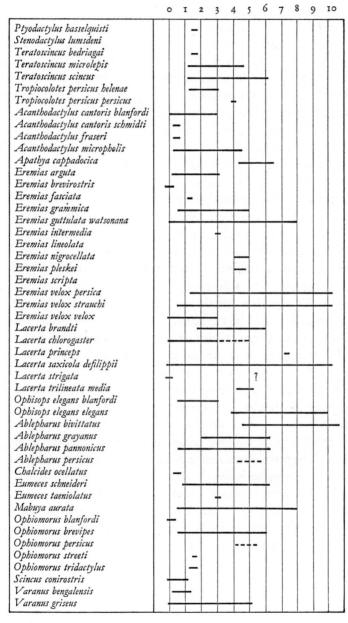

Elevation in thousands of feet

	0	1	2	3	4	5	6	7	8	9	10
Ptyodactylus hasselquisti											
Stenodactylus lumsdeni											
Teratoscincus bedriagai											
Teratoscincus microlepis											
Teratoscincus scincus											
Tropiocolotes persicus helenae											
Tropiocolotes persicus persicus											
Acanthodactylus cantoris blanfordi											
Acanthodactylus cantoris schmidti											
Acanthodactylus fraseri											
Acanthodactylus micropholis											
Apathya cappadocica											
Eremias arguta											
Eremias brevirostris											
Eremias fasciata											
Eremias grammica											
Eremias guttulata watsonana											
Eremias intermedia											
Eremias lineolata											
Eremias nigrocellata											
Eremias pleskei											
Eremias scripta											
Eremias velox persica											
Eremias velox strauchi											
Eremias velox velox											
Lacerta brandti											
Lacerta chlorogaster											
Lacerta princeps											
Lacerta saxicola defilippii											
Lacerta strigata							?					
Lacerta trilineata media											
Ophisops elegans blanfordi											
Ophisops elegans elegans											
Ablepharus bivittatus											
Ablepharus grayanus											
Ablepharus pannonicus											
Ablepharus persicus											
Chalcides ocellatus											
Eumeces schneideri											
Eumeces taeniolatus											
Mabuya aurata											
Ophiomorus blanfordi											
Ophiomorus brevipes											
Ophiomorus persicus											
Ophiomorus streeti											
Ophiomorus tridactylus											
Scincus conirostris											
Varanus bengalensis											
Varanus griseus											

Unfortunately as we have noted, there is very little precise information regarding dew in South-west Asia, although it is well known to desert travellers that heavy dew frequently forms during late night and early morning hours, even in extremely arid areas.

The possibility exists, of course, that some lizards make use of metabolic water, as do kangaroo rats. Metabolic water may be indirectly utilized: the water which is an end-product of carbohydrate metabolism, when exhaled in the confines of a burrow, will rapidly and significantly increase the relative humidity of the atmosphere, greatly reducing the evaporative loss of water through the integument (personal communication by Tyson Roberts). Since this water is the result of carbohydrate metabolism, there may be a net gain in metabolically available water, since condensation on the burrow walls and objects in the burrow may occur as the temperature drops at night, and this can be lapped by the animal, or possibly actively absorbed through the integument. The question remains to be investigated as to whether or not the acquisition of free water through this means exceeds water loss through evaporation (since obviously there must be a net loss to the environment of *total* water: free water plus metabolically derived water). Suggestive in this regard is the fact that certain desert reptiles readily absorb water through the skin. Unless active uptake of water occurs, it would be expected that evaporation through the skin ought equally to occur, which is a peculiar adaptation for animals living in areas where little or no standing water is encountered: it is observed, for example, that the skin of a living *Varanus bengalensis* is observed to soak up water spectacularly, that of *V. griseus* showing only slightly less tendency to do so.

A salty incrustation accumulating between the eye and nostril of captive specimens of *Varanus griseus* in Iran was observed during my stay there. The possible existence of a salt-excreting gland, such as that known in the 'marine iguana', *Amblyrhynchus cristatus*, and in certain marine birds, warrants investigation.

Schmidt-Nielsen (1959) has demonstrated the role played by the blood in the water balance and metabolism of the camel. Studies along this line might well prove enlightening in other groups of desert animals as well.

Distribution of the turtle *Clemmys caspica* is definitely correlated with the occurrence of permanent water, or seasonal water which is regular and dependable from year to year.

In the case of some lizards distributed only along the coasts of the Persian Gulf in Iran, humidity may be the limiting factor. Certain species, notably geckoes, transported through human agency have become established only in coastal areas of human habitation in the areas of introduction. Humidity may play a role in these cases, although the inability of these introductions to compete successfully with existing faunal counterparts is undoubtedly the result of various factors.

Surface character

While the nature of the substrate is obviously an important factor in determining plant distribution, it has seldom been emphasized in studies of terrestrial reptile distribution. There is however considerable correlation of substrate type and local distribution of lizards in Southwest Asia, and this has distinct general significance.

Certain Iranian lizard species are adapted for life in or on aeolian sand dunes, or at least on sandy soils, and are more or less restricted to such zones. Among these are the species of *Acanthodactylus*, *Scincus*, *Teratoscincus*, *Crossobamon eversmanni*, *Phrynocephalus maculatus*, *Eremias grammica*, *E. scripta*, and several species of *Ophiomorus*. The amphisbaenian *Diplometopon zarudnyi* is also a sand-dweller. *Ophiomorus* and *Diplometopon* live beneath the surface of the sand, and their limbs have been greatly reduced, an adaptation facilitating the types of subsurface locomotion which these animals employ. The other species named above have the digits equipped with comb-like fringes of scales, an adaptation which has arisen independently in many groups in various sandy deserts throughout the world. *Scincus*, and to a lesser extent, species of *Phrynocephalus*, are adapted both for burrowing and for sand-running.

The large species of *Agama* appear to be restricted to areas such as limestone outcrops and rocky cliff faces where both basking surfaces and deep crevices for retreat are provided. Species in this group include *Agama caucasica*, *A. erythrogastra*, *A. melanura*, *A. microlepis*, and *A. nupta*. Such terrain is characteristic of the Iranian Plateau and the mountains and upland regions of its borders. The smaller species of *Agama* occur on plains, valleys and alluvial fans, on sandy, loam, clay, and gravel soils. Species specificity in regard to these different soil types has not been well established. These lizards are usually found in the vicinity of small rock piles such as those erected by local inhabitants to mark the boundaries of grain fields. Such rock piles provide vantage points and basking areas upon which the lizards are able to orient themselves relative to sunlight for temperature control. They retreat into these piles for shelter. They also ascend low shrubs, and presence or absence of low bushes may be a factor in distribution of some species. Such areas frequently interdigitate with the outcrops and boulder slides occupied by the larger species, but the occupancy of the two environments is usually sharply defined.

Species of *Phrynocephalus* and *Eremias* show distinct preferences for particular soil types. *Phrynocephalus helioscopus*, *P. ornatus*, *P. scuttulatus*, *Eremias fasciata*, and *E. guttulata* preferring open clay and gravel plains, while *Phrynocephalus interscapularis*, *P. maculatus*, *P. mystaceus*, *Eremias intermedia*, and *E. lineolata* are usually found on sandy plains and steppes. *E. pleskei* and *E. velox strauchi* apparently prefer dry mountain slopes. Local distribution of many lacertid species may be determined by the availability of cracks and holes in clay and gravel soils, or burrows in plant-stabilized sandy soil. These crevices provide a retreat from predators and from temperature extremes.

Among the geckoes, *Teratoscincus* and *Crossobamon* have been mentioned as sand-dwelling species. The various species of *Stenodactylus*, *Ceramodactylus*, and *Bunopus* also occur on sand, but to what extent they occupy substrates is not known. *Agamura*, *Pristurus*, *Tropiocolotes*, and *Cyrtodactylus* usually are collected on non-sandy substrate. The various species of *Cyrtodactylus* are found on rocky slopes and cliff faces, in crevices and caverns, and in and about places of human habitation (particularly true of *Cyrtodactylus scaber*). *Phyllodactylus elisae* is found in caverns in gypsum deposits and limestone, and occasionally as a house gecko. *Hemidactylus* and *Ptyodactylus* are similarly adapted to life on vertical surfaces. The discontinuous distribution of geckoes of the genus *Eublepharis* should be investigated from an ecological standpoint. In Khūzistān *E. angramainyu* was found only in the foothill areas where extensive gypsum deposits exist. It may be that these large geckoes are dependent upon the cavernous areas in the gypsum where water persists throughout the year and a high relative humidity may be maintained.

Man-made edifices (usually constructed from mud-brick) provide additional habitat situations not only for the geckoes mentioned above, but for the large, rock-dwelling species of *Agama* as well. These lizards are often quite numerous on walls, houses, and monuments. There is usually an abundance of insect prey in such situations, attracted by the human inhabitants and their domestic animals and cultivated plants.

The Iranian species of *Uromastyx* are confined in their local distribution to well-drained alluvial soils wherein they are able to excavate their burrows. *Uromastyx asmussi* reportedly favours gravelly alluvium, whereas *Uromastyx loricatus* prefers silty-clay soils.

The most widely ranging forms in South-west Asia are those occupying the greatest range of substrates, such as *Varanus griseus, Eremias velox, Agama agilis, Mabuya aurata, Eumeces schneideri,* or those inhabiting the most continuously distributed substrates, such as *Eremias guttulata.*

Evolution of the various lizard groups in South-west Asia may be significantly correlated with this specific affinity for substrate-type, and the discontinuous distribution of these substrates. Many populations or subpopulations may be rather effectively isolated genetically from one another over protracted periods of time. This has been discussed in the case of the obligate dune-dwelling species of *Ophiomorus* in a previous paper (Anderson and Leviton, 1966b). Even species physically and physiologically capable of crossing fairly narrow stretches of intervening unsuitable substrate may rarely do so.

As a casual observation, I have noticed that the greatest number of individual lizards occupying the fringe areas of a population are often juveniles. It is these animals, unable to wrest already established territories from adults, that are most easily picked off by predators. It is among these juveniles also that one expects the greatest phenotypic variation, and from this peripheral group the occasional colonizers of unoccupied habitat separated by unfavourable terrain must usually be drawn. It is thus possible to visualize these patches of discontinuously distributed substrate types as analogous to islands, and the effects of "waif disperal" and "genetic drift" readily imaginable.

Dependence on substrate may also serve as a limiting factor on one or more fronts as populations migrate in response to climatic change. Species inhabiting low sandy plains, possibly physiologically able to negotiate the temperature and/or moisture gradient imposed by a bordering mountain range, may yet fail to cross the passes when confronted by the rocky cliffs, slides, and aluvial fans along the mountain front.

Food

Food availability as a limiting factor is, of course, a reflexion of the physical factor of the environment which restricts the distribution of the food organism.

It is interesting to note that the great majority of lizard species examined in this regard exhibit a fairly wide latitude in dietary items. Most of these lizards apparently eat any small arthropod with which they come in contact and are able to capture and overcome. Vegetable matter also appears in the stomach contents of several carnivorous species, sometimes in such quantity that its ingestion incidental to capture of insects can be ruled out. Similar observations have been recorded for lizards in desert regions of North America (Banta, 1961). This non-specificity or limited specificity as to diet is obviously an important adaptation in arid regions where population densities of prey species are usually low, and the appearance of any one species of insect tends to be seasonal. Even the vegetarian *Uromastyx* are reported to take animal food in captivity, and may occasionally do so in nature as well.

Present data are insufficient to demonstrate dietary specificity in any Iranian lizard species, but it has certainly not been ruled out for some. Ants undoubtedly predominate in the stomach contents of the smaller species of *Phrynocephalus*, and in *P. ornatus* and *P. luteoguttatus* no other food material was found. This may, of course, only indicate the seasonal availability of these insects. Only beetles were found in the digestive tract of the few specimens of *Teratoscincus scincus* and *T. bedriagai* which I examined. In captivity, specimens of *Teratoscincus scincus* regurgitated mealworm larvae (*Tenebrio molitor*) and crickets, feeding successfully only on adult beetles. *Anguis fragilis* reportedly shows a preference for slugs and snails, its dentition being particularly adapted to these dietary items. It also feeds on earthworms and soft-bodied insect larvae.

The possible importance of desert locusts in the food chains of predatory animals in South-west Asia has been alluded to previously (Anderson, 1963). In the foothill belt of Khūzistān a large number of insect species and individuals appear coincident with the spring growth and bloom of annual herbaceous plants and the appearance of cultivated grain crops. The number of insects rapidly diminishes as the ephemeral vegetation dies and the crops are harvested. It is during this period that large numbers of desert locusts arrive (or so it was observed in 1958) to assist the goats in eliminating the last vestiges of vegetation from the hillsides and stream courses. These grasshoppers remain in gradually diminishing numbers, presumably making use of stored fat deposits. In the autumn as the locust population has nearly expired, there is a brief resurgence of plant growth and an attendant increase in the local insect fauna. Observation indicated that the population density of reptiles, particularly *Agama nupta*. *A. agilis*, and *Eremias guttulata watsonana* remained high throughout this period. The number of avian and mammalian predators was remarkable for such an arid region, so barren of vegetation. Large numbers of foxes (*Vulpes vulpes*), occasionally observed feeding on reptiles killed on the roads, could be seen each evening throughout the summer; wolves (*Canis lupus*), jackals (*C. aureus*), and mongooses (*Herpestes* sp.) were not uncommon, a hyena (*Hyaena hyaena*) being seen on one occasion. A large *Buteo* hawk, small owls, shrikes, and falcons were frequently observed. It seems likely that rodent populations undergo considerable cyclic fluctuation in this region, yet the reptile and predaceous mammal and bird populations remain high. One hypothesis, which suggests itself on the basis of these casual observations, is that energy is brought into the area in the form of the considerable influx of desert locusts, which sustain the commonest lizard species. These in turn provide sustenance for the secondary predators until rodent populations again increase.

Kraus (1958) briefly summarized the life-history of the desert locust and its relation to meteorological conditions. All of Iran (and indeed most of South-west Asia and all of North Africa) lies within the total invasion zone of the desert locust, and southern Iran is in the area in which breeding or swarms are to be expected in at least 50 per cent of the years. The locusts only multiply under conditions which are of rare occurrence at any one point in the great arid tract of South-west Asia and North Africa; but where successful breeding occurs, great numbers are produced, and it is their dispersal to all parts of the desert which assures their success in the next generation. They thrive best under conditions which fluctuate between great dryness and markedly seasonal or periodic rainfall. Green food is essential only in the hopper stages, the adults being able to withstand extreme dryness and heat without food for long periods. Relatively high humidity or succulent green food is necessary, however, for the locusts to attain sexual maturity.

This explanation of the life-cycle of the locust as a highly important link in the food chain is purely speculative, and based on inadequate observations. It is worthy of further investigation, however, since were it to prove correct there would be dire implications of a wider economic nature. If locusts are so reduced in numbers to the point where they no longer provide an alternative food supply for creatures that normally prey on rodents, the unchecked numbers of rodents following diminution of predators in agricultural areas may turn out to be an even greater and more general problem than the prevention of locust swarms.

Vegetation

The distribution of lizards in relation to the flora is neither a result of dependence upon common physical factors of the environment, substrate, precipitation, etc., nor a consequence of certain physical requirements provided for the lizards by the vegetation. Certain types of shrubs, for instance, stabilize dune sands and provide suitable sites for burrow excavation among their roots. These burrows may be constructed by rodents, and thus the lizards are also dependent upon the presence of these animals as well as on the plants. In the arid areas of sparse vegetation many lizards may depend for sustenance upon the insect species attracted to the vegetation, and consequently their local distribution depends upon the frequently narrowly restricted occurrence of certain plants.

The small species of *Agama* climb into the branches of low steppe and desert vegetation such as wormwood (*Artemisia*) and camel thorn (*Alhagi camelorum*) to orient themselves relative to the sun's rays and to escape the hot soil surface for temperature control. Such vantage points also enable them to survey their territories. Vegetation may play a similar role among forest species in the mountains and along the Caspian coast, the patches of alternate light and shadow enabling efficient behavioural temperature control. A few species adapted to climbing tree trunks may extend their territories vertically as well as horizontally, and the ability to move quickly around the circumference of a tree trunk offers considerable protection from the larger predators.

While the relationship of South-west Asian lizards to vegetation has been little studied, whatever dependence does exist is probably in relation to vegetation type rather than to particular species of plants.

Certainly the role of vegetation in the creation and maintenance of soil and moisture conditions and other factors of the microclimate is obvious.

Light

Light as a limiting factor in reptilian distribution has been little considered. Very few studies on the quality and quantity of light affecting the biology of reptiles exist, although it is known that reproductive cycles in some but not all lizards in temperate areas are related to photo-period (Mayhew, 1961, 1964 1965 a). Doubtless other physiological cycles are similarly related to light.

It is possible that when continental or regional warming occurs, northward migrating species (particularly tropical elements) may find that light and photoperiodic factors rather than thermal factors become limiting.

Regional differences in qualitative and quantitative light distribution, particularly in relation to microhabitat situations, have not been studied in South-west Asia, but should be considered. Certainly cloud-cover and humidity, factors relating to this question, differ regionally as well as seasonally.

Wind

Air movement is obviously important in ecology, primarily as it affects the other physical factors of the environment. Thermal convection, rainfall distribution, and humidity are interrelated with differences in atmospheric pressure and air movement.

Analysis of the morphological adaptations for sand-dwelling in species of the skink genus *Ophiomorus* suggests that their evolution is correlated with the migration of aeolian sand dunes in a N.W.–S.E. direction due to the strong winds blowing from the north-west along the eastern borders of Iran. In this group there has been increasing specialization in certain morphological features from northwest to south-east (Anderson and Leviton, 1966 b). Similar analysis of other groups may prove enlightening in regard to the distributional history of the organisms, as well as providing clues to the development and sequence of certain landforms. It is noteworthy in this regard that while *Ophiomorus*, an Iranian element, has moved south and east down off the plateau into coastal environments, the sand-dwelling Saharo-Sindian elements *Scincus* and *Acanthodactylus* have not penetrated the plateau. In fact, the genus *Scincus* apparently does not occur in South-west Asia east of the Persian Gulf coast in the Bushire region, in spite of the supposed record of *Scincus mitranus* from the Hab river region of West Pakistan. This Arabian species has never been collected in the West Pakistan subsequent to the original record (Murray, 1884a), and J. A. Anderson, who has collected extensively in this region, believes the record to be in error (personal communication), an opinion in which I fully concur.

HISTORICAL ZOOGEOGRAPHY

Analysis of the Fauna

Endemism

To be at all meaningful from the standpoint of zoogeographic analysis, the term 'endemic' must be used with reference to a geographically defined region of rather narrowly limited extent. Hence, in a state like Iran, which takes in the entirety of certain geographic regions while including small portions of others within its boundaries, it is meaningless to refer to a species as 'endemic to Iran'. Rather we must consider forms restricted to the Central Plateau, the Helmand Basin, the western foothills of the Zagros, etc. Some of these 'endemics' will consequently also be found beyond the borders of Iran.

The significance of endemic species (or subspecies) from the standpoint of historical zoogeography is threefold: (1) a narrowly restricted form may be "relictual", occupying the remaining habitable area of a once much broader distribution. Frequently its nearest relatives are to be found at some considerable distance. In continental situations this may be taken as an indication that the environment in which the animal is found was once of greater extent. The fact that adaptation to environmental change may have occurred *in situ* must not be overlooked. Nonetheless, such a situation suggests that a previously widespread environment has become discontinuously distributed, perhaps with subsequent modification even in the areas of least drastic change. *Phyllodactylus elisae* and *Trionyx euphraticus* are endemics of the above type. (2) An endemic population may be in the process of expanding its range, often at the expense of closely related neighbouring species, in response to the spread of its environmental type with climatic change. It is usually assumed that spatial isolation is necessary for the differentiation of animal populations. Endemics which are in progress of expanding their range are difficult to recognize at any one moment in time. The range of a species may be advancing on one front and retreating on another; indeed, this must be the case almost invariably, due to the climatic fluctuations that occur even within a general trend toward increased aridity, or toward increased precipitation. Certain speculations of a general nature can often be made, however. For instance, where aeolian sand dune formation has progressively increased, and dune areas are expanding and covering alluvium, we can draw the obvious conclusions that sand-dwelling populations are spreading and encroaching upon the areas inhabited by species better adapted to clay or gravel soils. Usually the changes which affect animal distribution are far more subtle, however, and our insufficient knowledge of the ecology of the species in question makes meaningful speculation impossible. With regard to lizard species, recognition of expanding populations is almost always inferential, since we have little information regarding changes in extent of distribution over even brief periods. The expansion of economically important animals is much better documented. (3) A population (most often recognized at the subspecific level) may have differentiated fairly recently out of a larger population through isolation, and may have remained relatively static in its distribution since its isolation from the parent population. With climatic change, and/or changing landform, this population will expand or contract, hence it is the incipient form of the other two categories of endemic species.

The Central Plateau

As mentioned previously, the Central Plateau region can be subdivided geographically. It consists of several drainage basins of individual character, such as the Dasht-i-Kavīr and the Dasht-i-Lūt. Unfortunately, our knowledge of the fauna is far too limited to enable a detailed zoogeographical analysis of the plateau region. The distribution patterns within the plateau reflect more our ignorance than our knowledge. The following species are thus far known only from the Central Plateau: *Agama kirmanensis*, *A. microlepis*, *Bunopus crassicauda*, *Cyrtodactylus kirmanensis*.

Thus four species, or 11 per cent of the fauna of the Central Plateau, are endemic, and there are taxonomic problems associated with each of these nominal species. All belong to genera well represented not merely on the Central Plateau but in the highest parts of Iran generally. It is hence not unreasonable to surmise that they are autochthonous forms which have differentiated in response to the vicissitudes of local isolation and environmental change on the plateau.

Sīstān basin

Three species endemic to this basin occur within the borders of Iran. They compose 12 per cent of the fauna of this region. They are: *Cyrtodactylus zarudnyi*, *Teratoscincus bedriagai*, and *T. microlepis*.

The remarks in regard to the endemics of the Central Plateau apply equally to these species.

Balūchistān and Makrān coast

In this region three Iranian species, *Cyrtodactylus brevipes*, *Tropiocolotes persicus*, and *Ophiomorus streeti*, or 9 per cent of the lizard fauna, are endemic. As discussed in a previous paper (Anderson and Leviton, 1966*b*), the genus *Ophiomorus* appears to have had its centre of origin on the Central Plateau, isolation through aeolian distribution of sand dunes having resulted in differentiation of several sand-dwelling species.

The problems regarding the affinities of forms here assigned to the genus *Tropiocolotes* will be discussed in forthcoming systematic studies of the lizards of South-west Asia (e.g. Minton, Anderson and Anderson). In so far as can be determined from material in collections, this group of small geckoes is discontinuously distributed through North Africa and South-west Asia, and the recognized populations may represent the fragmentation of a more continuous distribution. It is perhaps significant that none of these lizards (variously assigned to *Tropiocolotes, Alsophylax, Microgecko*) is yet known from the interior Iranian Plateau, but occurs rather along its western, southern, and northern margins. *Alsophylax pipiens* occurs at Kabul, Afghanistan, however, and *Tropiocolotes depressus* is found at 6,500 ft in northern West Pakistan. It may be that this group of small geckoes (if they are a natural group) is more continuously distributed than has yet been recognized. Unfortunately, to date nothing has been published on the ecology of these forms.

Cyrtodactylus brevipes is a member of a species-group distributed primarily on the Iranian Plateau.

South-eastern Iran

If we view the south-eastern portion of Iran from a somewhat different perspective, and include a portion of the eastern Central Plateau, including the Dasht-i-Lūt, a portion of Balūchistān, including the Jāz Muriān depression, and Sīstān as well, we find a number of lizards endemic to a region which approximately corresponds to the climatic type III$_{3a}$ of Walter and Lieth (see figs. 93 and 94). These are: *Cyrtodactylus agamuroides, C. brevipes, C. kirmanensis?, C. longipes, C. ʒarudnyi, Tropiocolotes persicus persicus, Stenodactylus lumsdeni, Teratoscincus bedriagai, T. microlepis, Eremias fasciata, Ophiomorus brevipes, O. streeti.*

This is perhaps too large an area to be really meaningful; if one extends it to the east into West Pakistan and Southern Afghanistan, such species as *Phrynocephalus ornatus* and *Agamura femoralis* should be included. It is interesting, however, that all of the forms restricted to this region have their affinities with Iranian Plateau species, and not with Saharo-Sindian elements. All are adapted to live in a region with very low mean annual precipitation (under fifty-five mm) all falling during the winter months, and high daily and mean annual temperatures. Such conditions may have been more widely spread on the Central Plateau both in the recent past and at times during the Tertiary period.

Rezā'īyeh basin

Two lacertid lizards, *Apathya cappadocica urmiana* and *Eremias pleskei*, or 15 per cent of the known fauna of the Rezā'īyeh area are endemic.

If the area considered is enlarged to include adjacent areas of eastern Turkey and the southern Transcaucasian provinces of the U.S.S.R., the species *Apathya cappadocica (sensu lato)*, *Lacerta brandti*, and *L. trilineata media*, as well as *Eremias pleskei*, may be considered "Armenian" endemics. The two forms of *Lacerta* are Mediterranean in their affinities. Representatives of this European genus probably entered Iran during the Pleistocene in a period of decreased evaporation, and may never have penetrated far into the Central Plateau. *Eremias pleskei* was regarded by Nikolsky as closely akin to *Eremias fasciata*, which is a species of the most arid region of the Central Plateau and adjacent Afghanistan and Balūchistān. It remains to be determined whether its nearest relatives are Iranian or Aralo-Caspian elements. *Apathya*, a monotypic genus, has been regarded both as a subgenus of Lacerta and as congeneric with *Latastia* by different workers. If its affinities are with the latter, its nearest relatives are now to be found in north-eastern Africa and in Arabia; if the former, it is of European or Mediterranean derivation. My limited acquaintance with these groups does not warrant the expression of an opinion in regard to its systematic position. In either case, however, *Apathya* would appear to be a relictual endemic.

No endemic lizards are recognized from the Mughān Steppe, the Caspian coast, or the Alburz mountains. *Lacerta chlorogaster*, however, occurs only on the Caspian coast and the valley of the Atrak river in the Kopet Dāgh. Since the southern coast of the Caspian Sea has only been exposed since the close of the Pleistocene as a result of continuing recession of the sea since the Chvalyn Transgression, the small lizard fauna of this region has only recently become established. The present distribution of *Lacerta chlorogaster* suggests that it may have entered Iran during the Tertiary or early Pleistocene, having been restricted to the lower elevations of the Kopet Dāgh during the Chvalyn Transgression; and it would seem at present to be extending its range with the return of favourable conditions to a more extensive area. It is quite distinct morphologically from all other Iranian species in the genus.

With the depression of snowline during the last glaciation, the Alburz Range must have been one of the areas of Iran most affected by the climatic changes of the Pleistocene. On the south slope the lizard fauna would hence have retreated to lower elevations and on to the Central Plateau. On the north flank any lizards which remained (and perhaps none did) would have been confined to a narrow belt above the more extensive Caspian Sea, and this belt would probably have had ecologically continuous connexions to the west and east. This sort of situation could not have provided the isolation conducive to the production of an endemic fauna.

Kopet Dāgh

Only two species, 17 per cent of the known fauna, may be construed as endemics to the Kopet Dāgh. This area has been very inadequately investigated, however. The two lizards, *Alsophylax spinicauda* and *Ablepharus persicus*, are of doubtful taxonomic status. Both are known with certainty only from the vicinity of Shāhrūd at the edge of the Central Plateau.

Türkmen Steppe

A single Iranian species, *Agama erythrogastra*, is endemic to the Türkmen Steppe drainage area. However, it occurs only at relatively high elevations of this drainage (3,000–5,000 ft) in the region included in climatic type VII (IV)$_1$ (Walter and Lieth, 1960), while most of the Türkmen Steppe proper has a climatic type designated III (VII)$_2$ (see figs. 93 and 94). This lizard is one of several species of large, rock-dwelling *Agama* autochthonous to the Iranian Plateau.

Zagros Mountains

Three species of lizards, *Cyrtodactylus heterocercus*, *Lacerta princeps*, *Ophiomorus persicus*, 25 per cent of the known fauna within Iranian borders, are endemic to the Zagros mountains. *Cyrtodactylus heterocercus* is a member of the South-west Asian group of the genus. According to Mertens (1952) it may be most closely allied to *C. kotschyi*, species at present having a Mediterranean distribution. This relationship is by no means certain, however. In Iran *C. heterocercus* is known only from Hamadān, the type locality. A related subspecies, *C. h. mardinensis*, is known from south-eastern Turkey, where it occurs at elevations of about 3,000 ft.

Lacerta princeps, known from the Zagros as far south as the vicinity of S̲h̲īrāz in Iran, but also reported from Iraq and south-eastern Turkey, is the only member of the genus to penetrate Iran to any extent. It is apparently restricted to the high forested areas of the Zagros, and whether or not it is continuously distributed between the recorded localities is an open question. Like *Lacerta chlorogaster*, it is a quite distinct species, and probably represents a penetration of Iran during a moister climatic regime in the Pleistocene or earlier.

Ophiomorus persicus is the least specialized member of this genus which appears to have diversified in the elevated regions of South-west Asia, the Iranian Plateau in the broadest sense. The diversification of the three western species, all of which live under rocks (the other two species occurring in Turkey, Greece, Israel and Jordan) may date from the increasing orogeny of the Tertiary, and *O. persicus* may have evolved *in situ*.

The Western Foothills of the Zagros

Of particular interest are the two species (12 per cent of Iranian lizards) endemic to the foothill belt. *Eublepharus angramainyu*, a recently described species (Anderson and Leviton, 1966a), long considered conspecific with *E. macularius*, is found in this region of Iran and Iraq. Its nearest relatives are found in West Pakistan, southern Afghanistan, and the Salt Range of the Punjab. *E. macularius* has also been reported from the Kopet Dāg̲h̲ in the U.S.S.R., and this may prove to be yet another distinct population of the genus. There are no records of the genus as yet from the interior of the Iranian Plateau proper, the known populations occurring at localities on the periphery of the plateau. This negative evidence, and the markedly discontinuous distribution of the genus as at present constituted in Asia, suggests that these large geckoes are the remnants of an older, more continuous distribution, perhaps of considerable antiquity. Indeed, the distribution of the eublepharid geckoes as a whole (if they are a natural group) supports this hypothesis. Notably, all occur on the margins of areas with a long continental history. The relatively large size of most species and their nocturnal, ground-dwelling habit set them apart ecologically both from the active diurnal lizards and the smaller, agile geckoes of the regions they inhabit.

Interestingly enough, the second foothill endemic, *Tropiocolotes persicus* also has its nearest allies in West Pakistan (Balūchistān, Sind, and Rajasthān) and in extreme south-eastern Iran. As mentioned above, the group of small geckoes variously assigned to the genera *Tropiocolotes, Alsophylax,* and *Microgecko* are discontinuously distributed along the margins of the Iranian Plateau.

A third narrowly distributed species, *Phyllodactylus elisae,* also a relictual species, should perhaps be considered here, although it is also found on the Mesopotamian Plain (in the upper extent). According to Dixon (personal communication) this species is not closely related to *P. europaeus,* which is a relictual species of the Mediterranean primarily confined to islands. These two species are the only palearctic members of the genus, and *P. elisae* is more closely related to the American species than to those of Africa, Madagascar, or Australia.

Khūzistān Plain

Two species (9 per cent), *Ceramodactylus affinis* and *Acanthodactylus fraseri* are the only Iranian lizards which are known as endemics from the Khūzistān Plain (here including the western portion of the Iranian coastal plain of the Persian Gulf). Both are Saharo-Sindian derivatives. Two other Saharo-Sindian derivatives of limited distribution should also be included as endemic members of this faunal assemblage, although one (*Uromastyx loricatus*) also occurs in the foothills (only in alluvium-filled valleys) and the other (*Uromastyx microlepis*) is found along the Arabian coast of the Persian Gulf. *Acanthodactylus fraseri* is probably most closely related to other North Arabian Desert species in Syria, Jordan, Iraq, and Arabia, while *Ceramodactylus affinis* is scarcely differentiated from the more widely distributed *C. doriae. Uromastyx loricatus* has its nearest relative in *U. asmussi* of the eastern gulf region, and *U. microlepis* is a close ally of *U. aegyptius*. It is likely that the Khūzistān Plain became separated to a certain extent (at least ecologically) from the Mesopotamian Plain and northern Arabia at some period (or periods) of changing position and/or extent of the Persian Gulf, just as it appears to be separated at present from the coastal region east of Bandar-i-Lingeh. The valley of the Tigris, with its marshes in the lower reaches, may form a barrier of consequence to some forms at the present time. Caution is, however, necessary in assuming too readily any major change in the extent of the Persian Gulf within relatively recent times.

The Iranian faunal element

Some forty-three Iranian lizards, 46 per cent of the total Iranian lizard fauna, have a distribution largely confined to the Iranian Plateau in the broad sense. These species have been termed in this study the "Iranian" element. Other students of biogeography in South-west Asia have used the term "Irano-Turanian" for the Iranian Plateau species, and have included the Aralo-Caspian species as well. Still others have used "Eremian" to refer even more broadly to the fauna of the entire palearctic desert region. Neither of these two terms, however, has significant application to the lizard fauna.

Only three species, *Phrynocephalus helioscopus*, *Teratoscincus scincus*, and *Eremias velox* could legitimately be termed Irano-Turanian, and all seem to be subspecifically distinct in the two regions.

Eremias guttulata and *Varanus griseus* are the only species which could be termed Eremian, and here, too, there are populational differences.

Iranian elements constitute 55·5 per cent of the lizard fauna of the Central Plateau, 64 per cent of the Sīstān Basin fauna, 38·5 per cent of the Rezā'īyeh Basin fauna, 16·6 per cent of the Mughān Steppe fauna, 14·3 per cent of the Caspian coast fauna, 4·5 per cent of the Khūzistān Plain fauna, 42·4 per cent of the Balūchistān and Makrān fauna, 21·7 per cent of the Türkmen Steppe fauna, 38·5 per cent of the Zagros Mountains fauna, 17·6 per cent of the fauna of the western foothills of the Zagros, 20 per cent of the Alburz Mountains fauna, and 25 per cent of the fauna of the Kopet Dāgh.

With regard to the relationship of the Aralo-Caspian fauna to the Iranian element correlation at the generic level is particularly noteworthy. Only *Crossobamon* is not represented in the Iranian element.

A number of South-west Asian genera seem to be predominantly distributed on the Iranian Plateau: *Agama*, *Phrynocephalus*, *Agamura*, South-west Asian species of *Cyrtodactylus*, *Teratoscincus*, *Eremias*, *Ophiomorus*. It is not too unreasonable a speculation to propose the Iranian Plateau as the centre of dispersal for these groups. It is quite possible that other groups, now distributed in the Saharo-Sindian region, also had their origins on the Iranian Plateau.

On the basis of the foregoing discussion, speculation is possible regarding the Central Plateau and similar inland basins as a source of faunal origins. Surrounded by high mountains, such basins are protected from faunal invasion to a considerable extent, the only species capable of entering such regions being those with the greatest range of ecological tolerance.

Inland basins of this type in subtropical latitudes are also protected from the drastic climatic changes that affect less sheltered regions. Thus, in a region like the Central Plateau climatic change is less likely to lead to extinction or migration of an entire lizard fauna than to create local environmental situations in which isolation results in speciation.

With general lowering of temperatures, species distributed to the north of such basins are unable to move south across the elevational and temperature gradient of the mountains bordering the elevated basin on the north. Similarly, the plateau species find a barrier to their southward migration; this is of less significance for plateau species, however, since those whose ecological tolerance enables them to negotiate the southern passes are able to move to lower elevations south of the plateau. Further, the lowering of temperature is likely to be less severe in the basins than on the mountains.

As temperatures rise and aridity increases, plateau-forms again move off the interior plateau to lower elevations, but this time to the north. They also could be expected to move into the higher elevations of the internal mountain ranges, populations thus becoming discontinuously distributed. The rock-dwelling species of *Agama* may be representative of the results of just such climatic fluctuation, with certain forms distributed to the north, e.g. *A. caucasica* and *A. erythrogastra*, while *A. nupta* and *A. melanura* border the plateau on the south. The internal mountains are held by *A. microlepis*.

Species distributed immediately to the north of the Central Plateau, particularly along the outer mountain flanks, may move to higher elevations with rising temperatures, and ultimately on to the plateau, but the net faunal movement will be to the north, off the plateau, due to the greater number of reptilian forms in the warmer regions. As for the forms to the south of the plateau, again a tendency to move north and to higher elevations, hence on to the plateau, would be expected. However, such species, adapted to a maritime environment, would face the problem of moving into the more rigorous conditions of a continental climate.

In the case of the lizard faunas, movement either off or on to the plateau must (at least for many species) presuppose the existence of suitable local environments through the passes. For example, temperature conditions may prove less of a barrier to lizards native to the sandy Aralo-Caspian steppes than the terrain itself—rocky, precipitous scarps. It would appear more likely that species on the Central Plateau, with its diversified conditions of terrain, would at certain times find suitable passes to the lower elevations than the reverse.

In summary then, the plateau is expected to be a centre of evolution, the fauna being pre-adapted to move off the plateau as the climate fluctuates, to the south with general lowering of temperatures, to the north with elevation of temperature. At the same time, the plateau remains relatively sheltered, both from faunal invasion and from the extremes of climatic change. If remnants of an older plateau fauna are to be found, they must be sought on the periphery of the plateau, in the surrounding mountains (remnants of a cooler, moister period) and in the peripheral surrounding lowlands. In the isolated higher elevations of the interior mountain ranges, and in the low, hot interior basins one would expect to find isolated populations undergoing speciation.

In this regard, it is interesting that the known endemic species have been found in the regions peripheral to the Central Plateau. This picture of endemism is however undoubtedly biased by the fact that far less time has been spent by collectors in the interior mountains and basins of the plateau than in the more habitable areas on the plateau margins. The Iranian faunal element is visualized here as largely autochthonous to the Iranian Plateau.

The Aralo-Caspian faunal element

In so far as the lizards are concerned, the Aralo-Caspian faunal element seems to be derived, at least at the generic level, from the Iranian element. At the species level the lizard fauna of the Aralo-Caspian desert is at present quite distinct from that of the Iranian Plateau, with the genera of this area being nearly all represented by an even greater number and variety of forms on the Iranian Plateau. But as well, there are in this Aralo-Caspian fauna Eurosiberian elements, such as *Lacerta vivipara* and *L. agilis*, which do not enter Iran.

This element actually enters Iran only in the areas of physical extension of the Türkmen Steppe within the Iranian political boundaries. Only 8·3 per cent of the Central Plateau fauna is composed of Aralo-Caspian elements, while even in the low-lying Sīstān Basin they represent only an estimated 8 per cent of the lizard fauna. In the poorly known Kopet Dāgh 16·7 per cent of the lizard species are Aralo-Caspian forms. Even in the Iranian areas of the Türkmen steppe the Aralo-Caspian lizards constitute but 43·5 per cent of the total assemblage.

The Mediterranean faunal element

As pointed out by Heptner (1945) the Mediterranean element is probably a meaningless category in terms of faunal origin. This appears to be true for the lizards at least, since the Mediterranean area provides a mild climatic haven for the vestiges of a once more widely spread European fauna. Nonetheless, from the standpoint of present distributions, there does exist an assemblage of lizard species now confined to the Mediterranean region, and it is through this area that certain members of the allochthonous Iranian fauna entered.

Mediterranean lizards do not occur on the Central Plateau at present, but approximately 31 per cent of the species of the Rezā'īyeh Basin are either Mediterranean elements or biregional elements with their nearest relatives in the Mediterranean region. This is true of 50 per cent of the Mughān Steppe fauna and Caspian coast fauna, while about 25 per cent of the known Zagros mountains species have Mediterranean affinities. In the Alburz mountains 44·4 per cent and in the Kopet Dāgh 30·8 per cent of the lizards find their closest allies in the Mediterranean area. These percentages are somewhat misleading, as they represent not species classified here as Mediterranean elements, but for the most part species having their relationships with such elements. Some are biregional, while others are strictly Iranian in their present distribution.

The Oriental faunal element

This is a broader category than the others employed in this discussion, and would perhaps be inappropriate to regional considerations in other Asian areas. However, only three species, *Calotes versicolor*, *Hemidactylus flaviviridis*, and *Varanus bengalensis*, having their principal distribution in the Oriental region, enter Iran. *Hemidactylus flaviviridis* is found along the Persian Gulf and its occurrence here is due to human agency as it is in other coastal port areas in Asia and Africa. *Calotes versicolor* and *Varanus bengalensis* are the most widely distributed members of their respective genera and among the most widely ranging species in the Oriental region. They enter Iran through Balūchistān and are present only in the extreme south-east of the country.

The Saharo-Sindian faunal element

The Saharo-Sindian element is secondary in importance only to the Iranian element in consideration of the lizard fauna of Iran. Besides the species categorized here as Saharo-Sindian, a number of forms are regarded as bi-regional: *Agama agilis, Agama ruderata, Eremias guttulata, Eumeces schneideri, Mabuya aurata,* and *Varanus griseus* occurring widely on the Iranian Plateau as well as in the Saharo-Sindian regions. Regional population differences exist in these species, but have been inadequately studied.

While certain species, such as *Ceramodactylus doriae, Cyrtodactylus scaber, Hemidactylus turcicus, Acanthodactylus cantoris (sensu lato), Eremias brevirostris* occur both to the east and west of Iran as well as along the Iranian coast of the Persian Gulf, others are found only to the west or to the east. *Uromastyx loricatus, U. microlepis, Ceramodactylus affinis, Acanthodactylus cantoris schmidti, A. fraseri,* and *Scincus conirostris* apparently are encountered not much further east than Bushire, while *Uromastyx asmussi, Acanthodacylus cantoris blanfordi, A. micropholis,* and *Ophiomorus blanfordi* find their western limit at Bandar-i-Lingeh.

In so far as it has been investigated, the Persian Gulf coast of Arabia has its affinities with the western Saharo-Sindian region rather than with Balūchistān and Sind. There large numbers of Saharo-Sindian species found in North Africa and the North Arabian Desert which do not extend as far east as Iran, while several North-west Indian and West Pakistan lizards stop short of the eastern border of Iran. In short, the Saharo-Sindian element is relatively homogeneous at the generic level, but at the species level can be partitioned at least into eastern and western components, even within the borders of Iran. This is due in large part to two factors: the changes in position and extent of the Persian Gulf relative to the associated landforms, and the influence of the monsoon in the area east of Iran, adding some summer precipitation to the pattern of winter rains experienced by the western part of the Saharo-Sindian desert.

Except for those forms having a biregional distribution, the influence of the Saharo-Sindian element is little felt in the interior of Iran, even in the low Sīstān Basin. On the K͟hūzistān Plain, however, 82 per cent of the lizard species are either Saharo-Sindian or biregional elements, while in Balūc͟histān and Makrān these elements make up approximately 45 per cent of the fauna. In the western foothills of the Zagros mountains 70·6 per cent of the species are Saharo-Sindian or biregional.

In his discussion of the desert and steppe fauna of the Palearctic region, Hepter (1945), on the basis of his studies of the mammalian fauna, felt that five independent centres of origin could be distinguished: Sahara; South-west Asia (Iran and Afghanistan); Tūrān; Kaza͟khstān; and Mongolia. He, too, regarded the nature of the terrain as important, and felt that each of the centres had developed a fauna characteristic of the prevalent soil type, for example, 'plain deserts with compact soil' in Mongolia and Kaza͟khstān, sand deserts in Tūrān, 'upland deserts' in Iran and Afghanistan.

Faunal connexions with Europe

In the absence of a fossil record of any extent, past faunal connexions are largely conjectural. Present distributions indicate that there has been a faunal exchange between Iran and Europe through the Mediterranean area. Of particular note with regard to the lizards is the fact that, with the exception of *Anguis fragilis*, no Eurosiberian elements exist in Iran. This is in considerable contrast to certain other groups such as the mammals, where such forms as *Erinaceus europaeus* (hedgehog), *Talpa europaea* (mole), *Canis lupus* (wolf), *Vulpes vulpes* (fox), *Ursus arctis* (bear), *Martes foina* (marten), *Meles meles* (badger), *Lutra lutra* (otter), *Felis lynx* (lynx), *Sus scrofa* (pig), *Lepus europaeus* (hare), and *Castor fiber* (beaver) are known from Iran (several of these are subspecifically distinct in South-west Asia, however). Among the amphibia such forms as *Bufo viridis* (toad), *Hyla arborea* (tree frog), *Rana ridibunda* (frog) and *Triturus cristatus* (crested newt) are important faunal elements. *Coronella austriaca*, *Elaphe dione*, *Natrix natrix* and *Agkistrodon halys* among the snakes represent this faunal element.

There is also no indication of faunal exchange with Europe through Iran in the lizard fauna of South-east Asia, with the possible exception of the genera *Ophisops* and *Ophisaurus*. The genus *Agama* is recorded from the Eocene of Europe, however, and *Varanus* is known from the Miocene to the Pleistocene. Thus there appears to have been at least periodic faunal connexion of Europe with South-west Asia during the Tertiary either through Turkey or via Transcaucasia.

It is perhaps worth remarking that with the exception of *Tarentola* and *Chamaeleon*, which occur in Europe along the margin of the Mediterranean Sea, all of the lizard genera found in Europe are represented in Iran.

Faunal connexions with Central Asia

Iran has been connected with Central Asia continuously since the Oligocene, and at least intermittently during prior periods. The ecological relationships between the two areas have certainly differed from their present state, probably throughout much of the past. During much of the Tertiary, the climate was probably warmer than at present in Central Asia and likely more uniform between the two areas. The present contrast is a result of climatic events during the Pleistocene and later, and the Tertiary orogeny which resulted in the present elevation of the Kopet Dāgh, Hindu Kush, and Himalayas. At times the faunal exchange was undoubtedly greater than at present, but with the uplifting of the Iranian Plateau, the net faunal movement has been increasingly from the plateau to Central Asia (or is so postulated for the reasons stated above in the discussion of the Iranian faunal element).

Faunal connexions with the Oriental region

The lizards common to Iran and to Indian and other southern Asian areas, even at the generic level, occur primarily in the north-western desert of the Oriental region. The following genera occur both on the Iranian Plateau and in the Asian tropics: *Cyrtodactylus*, *Hemidactylus*, *Mabuya*, *Eumeces*, *Ophisops*, *Ophisaurus*, and *Varanus*. Of these, the South-west Asian species of *Cyrtodactylus* belong to a distinct species group which appears to have no tropical representatives. This genus is in serious need of careful revision. *Hemidactylus*, *Mabuya*, and *Eumeces* are pan-tropical genera having a few representatives in various subtropical areas of the world, while *Ophisops* and *Ophisaurus* have discontinuous distributions through eastern Europe and South-west Asia, each having two species entering the tropics. *Varanus* is now a genus of the Old World tropics, having a single species, *V. griseus*, in the intervening desert areas of South-west Asia. In the Tertiary, however, it was present in Europe, and its near relatives date back to the Cretaceous of North America. It has clearly retreated to its present range as a result of climatic change.

The distribution of the genus *Ophisaurus* is particularly interesting, for it has a living species in the southern and eastern United States (south to Veracruz, Mexico), and is known from the Oligocene to Miocene of Europe. Hence its present discontinuous distribution is the remnant of a Tertiary Holarctic distribution.

Faunal connexions with Africa

S. Bodenheimer (1938) listed several species of North African animals, including mammals, birds, beetles, butterflies, orthopterans and hemipterans which he considered the remnants of an Irano-Turanian fauna. No reptiles are included in this list however, and as regards the lizard fauna any present relationship of Iran with the North African desert is not between the Iranian Plateau and North Africa, but involves only the Khūzistān Plain and the low coastal areas of the Persian Gulf. There are a few widely distributed biregional species common to North Africa and the Iranian Plateau, but as these are more or less continuously distributed, they can scarcely be regarded as representing a relictual Iranian element in North Africa.

From his consideration of the several animal groups studied Bodenheimer draws the following conclusions:

A small, but significant relict fauna is discontinuously distributed over North Africa in such enclaves as the Hoggar and Sinai mountains. Its affinities are with the present fauna of the steppes and high plateaus of South-west and Central Asia, i.e. Irano-Turanian. Considerable remnants of this fauna are met also in all the Mediterranean islands from Cypress to Sardinia and in the steppes of Spain. It appears to represent a once continuously distributed steppe fauna.

While the present composition of the known lizard fauna contributes nothing to this hypothesis, on the other hand it offers nothing contradictory. As is apparent by comparing distribution patterns of different animal groups, different ecological factors determine distribution from group to group; hence historical events have affected lizards in a way different from that affecting mammals, birds, insects, or even other reptilian groups. We see evidences that these varying responses to historico-ecological events exist among lower taxonomic categories as well.

It is to be expected that studies of the systematic relationships between species of Saharo-Sindian lizards and Iranian species will provide evidence in regard to Bodenheimer's speculations.

The present geographic contact of South-west Asia with Africa is through Sinai. In an earlier paper Bodenheimer (1937*a*) analysed 756 species of animals known from Sinai. Of these, he regarded 13·9 per cent as Irano-Turanian faunal elements. He regarded only one snake, *Eirenis coronella*, and no lizard as Irano-Turanian. This snake occurs primarily in the higher elevations of the Sinai Massif, which Bodenheimer regards as an Irano-Turanian enclave. The Saharo-Sindian element is dominant in the northern part of the peninsula, the Tih-territory, and in the dunes and southern lowlands. This is certainly true of the lizards as well as the other groups he examined. Mediterranean elements occur on the northern dunes, in parts of north-eastern Sinai, and in the higher elevations of the Sinai Massif, being penetrants in the north, relics in the south. This applies to the lizards, also, and Bodenheimer lists the following species from the Sinai Massif: *Agama stellio*, *Chamaeleon chamaeleon*, *Abelpharus kitaibeli*, *Chalcides ocellata*, and *Ophisops elegans*.

Bodenheimer's interpretation is that one wave of relatively recent faunal elements replaced another in Sinai, the once dominant Paleotropical fauna of the savannah being replaced by a steppe Irano-Turanian fauna contemporaneously with a period of strong Mediterranean penetration or partial dominance, until the Saharo-Sindian fauna became the most prominent element. Relics of these older faunas remain in the south and in the higher elevations.

A consideration of the fauna of Palestine (Israel and western Jordan) is interesting from the standpoint of past faunal relationships between Africa and South-west Asia. This region is one of varied environmental situations and is subject to the maritime climatic influence of the Mediterranean Sea. There probably has been at least intermittent contact between Africa and Eurasian regions through this area even during periods of greater extent of the Tethys Sea. For these reasons certain parts of Palestine might be expected to serve as refuge areas for remnants of older faunas.

Bodenheimer (1937*b*) has analysed the entire known fauna of Palestine, while Haas (1952) has considered the origins of the herpetofauna. As in Sinai, there were no tropical species of lizards still extant in Palestine. From what we have seen so far, it would appear that lizards survive less well as relicts in South-west Asia than do some other animal groups. For this reason lists of lizards at the species level of differentiation may be less useful than other groups in revealing historical faunal affinities. But once their systematic relationships are adequately known, however, they may nevertheless provide important clues. The presence of the Mediterranean species of chamaeleon, *Chamaeleon chamaeleon*, in Israel–Jordan is particularly interesting, for this is the single represenative in the Palearctic region of this now tropical family. Unlike *Varanus griseus*, it is not widely distributed but is confined to the Mediterranean margins.

The distribution of *Ptyodactylus hasselguisti* should be carefully studied in relation to past faunal history. Said to occupy a wide latitude of environmental situations, and apparently common in the countries of the eastern Mediterranean, it nonetheless has been recorded only once from Iran, in the western Zagros. It is not certain whether or not this distribution in South-west Asia is continuous. It would be interesting to know whether its presence in the arid region of the Palearctic is relictual, or represents a recent incursion. Remains of another species (of similar size, but larger teeth) occur in the Acheulean of the Judaean Desert (Haas, 1952).

Among other reptilian groups of tropical affinity, the disjunct distribution of the genus *Trionyx* has already been mentioned. *Crocodilus* existed up to the turn of the century in the Kabara swamps south of Haifa (Haas, 1952), and has survived in isolated areas of North Africa as well. As Haas points out, such aquatic animals are less subject to changing conditions of humidity than are the terrestrial groups. Two snakes are similarly noteworthy. *Micrelaps muelleri*, a nocturnal opisthoglyphous colubrid, is found at relatively high elevations with 550 mm of annual rainfall. Its only congener is in Somalia. *Atractaspis*, a tropical African genus of viperids, has a single South-west Asian member, *Atractaspis engaddensis*, known only from the En Geddi oasis in Jordan. Another species is known from southern Arabia.

Bodenheimer considers 5 per cent of the 2,852 species of the fauna of Israel–Jordan as tropical. He concludes that the effect of the glacio-pluvial period was minimal on the fauna, while the most important recent event has been a "neo-Sudanian" faunal eruption on a broad front of the Saharo-Sindian region, and a subsequent penetration of this element into the southern Mediterranean area.

Faunal connexions with Arabia

The Arabian Peninsula has a large lizard fauna, many species of which are endemic. Unfortunately, this fauna is very incompletely known, and details of distribution within Arabia poorly worked out. Further collecting, particularly in the higher elevations along the coasts, will undoubtedly increase the list of species known, and will certainly increase the value of our zoogeographic speculations. In view of its long stability as a continental area and its previous connexion with Africa along its southern Red Sea coast, a study of its faunal relations with other regions should prove most enlightening.

At present, the faunal connexion of Iran with the Arabian Peninsula is through the Mesopotamian Plain at the head of the Persian Gulf. Even this contact is limited by the presence of the Tigris river. The only area of Iran having a close affinity with Arabia is the Khūzistān Plain and the associated western coastal plain of the Persian Gulf. The species shared by Iran and Arabia are either Saharo-Sindian elements, or wide-ranging biregional forms, such as *Eremias guttualata* and *Varanus griseus*.

According to Misonne (1959), the distribution of a few mammalian species indicates faunal contact of the two areas across the Strait of Hurmuz, at least three species having entered Iran by this route.

The lizard fauna provides no evidence of extensive faunal contact in the vicinity of the Strait of Hurmuz or to the east. This is somewhat surprising, in that the present position of the Persian Gulf is thought to be relatively recent, and even since its formation eustatic lowering of sea level during the Pleistocene must have established dry land contact between Iran and Arabia. Nonetheless, evidence for extensive ecological continuity across this contact is lacking. As stated previously, a faunal break for Saharo-Sindian elements is indicated on the Iranian coast of the Persian Gulf between Bushire and Bandar-i-Lingeh, and the lizard fauna of the Arabian coast is related to the Iranian fauna west of this break.

Three lizard species may have some bearing on the question of an eastern faunal contact, however; *Phrynocephalus maculatus*, an Iranian element not crossing the Zagros mountains and the western foothill belt, and not recorded from the Khūzistān Plain, is represented by a subspecies in Arabia. This species and the closely related *P. arabicus* are the only representatives of this Iranian Plateau genus in Arabia or westward. *P. maculatus* is a widely distributed sand-living form, which ranges down from the Iranian Plateau into Balūchistān on the Iranian side of the Persian Gulf.

Less certain is the distribution of *Eumeces taeniolatus*, an Iranian element distributed primarily in the eastern part of the Iranian Plateau. It has twice been recorded from Arabia, once from El Kubar in south-western Arabia (Taylor, 1935) and by Haas (1957) from twenty-three miles north of Hail, Saudi Arabia. Haas also cites a British Museum specimen from Muscat. This species does occur in the Saharo-Sindian region in lowland West Pakistan (Minton, 1962). Not having seen the Arabian material, I cannot verify that the various records refer to the same species.

Thirdly, the swimming skink, *Scincus mitranus*, an Arabian form, was reported from the Hab river region of West Pakistan by Murray (1884 a), who recorded seven specimens (as *S. arenaria* Murray). As remarked earlier this species has never been taken again outside of Arabia, and its occurrence in West Pakistan is open to serious doubt. Indeed, this single record is the only report of this genus on the northern side of the Persian Gulf coast of Bushire.

Faunal affinities between the African and Asian tropics

There are no lizard species, apart from those distributed through human intervention, common to both the African and Asian tropics. A number of genera are found in both regions, however. These include the following: *Cnemaspis, Phyllodactylus, Hemidactylus, Phelsuma, Agama, Chamaeleon, Mabuya, Lygosoma, Leiolopisma, Ablepharus, Riopa, Eumeces,* and *Varanus*.

In several of these genera serious systematic problems remain, and careful study may reduce the degree of apparent correspondence at the generic level between the African and Asian tropics. Of the above genera, *Hemidactylus, Agama, Mabuya, Abelpharus, Eumeces,* and *Varanus* are now represented in South-west Asia in the region between the African and Asian tropics. *Agama* has a single, specialized species, *A. minor*, entering the Indian tropics, and the several closely related African tropical species probably represent a single radiation of savannah and forest forms. The genus appears to have had its major evolutionary centre on the Iranian Plateau. It is interesting that the Agamidae are represented in tropical Africa by this single, little-diversified genus.

With the exception of *Chamaeleon*, which has a single Mediterranean species, none of the genera show a discontinuous distribution in Asia between the two tropical areas, thus there are no relict populations of tropical genera existing on the Iranian Plateau. Most of the tropical genera which do occur in South-west Asia are represented by one or more widely distributed desert-adapted species, such as *Eumeces schneideri*, *Mabuya aurata* (and the related *M. vittata* and *M. dissimilis* to the west and east respectively) and *Varanus griseus*. *Mabuya* and *Eumeces* occur in the New World tropics, the latter having a few Neoarctic species as well. *Varanus* is known from the Tertiary of Europe, and closely related fossil genera are recorded from the Cretaceous of North America.

The relationships of the genus *Phyllodactylus* as presently constituted are being studied by James Dixon. The South-west Asian relict *Phyllodactylus elisae* appears to be related to the New World species rather than to *P. europaeus* or to the African, Malagasy, and Australian species of the nominal genus (Dixon, personal communication).

Cnemaspis is about equally represented in Africa and Asia. *Phelsuma* has a single Asian species, *P. andamanense*, found on the Andaman Islands. The other species live on Madagascar, the Comoro, Seychelles, and Mascarens Islands, but not in Africa. *Chamaeleon* is a primarily Malagasy and Africa genus, although *C. chamaeleon* is found on the eastern shores of the Mediterranean. A single species, *C. zeylanicus*, is known from Ceylon. *Riopa* has a dozen African species and an equal number of Asian members.

It is particularly interesting that most of the lizard genera residing in both the African and Asian tropics (some of them in the New World and Australia as well), but not represented in the intervening areas, nor known from the fossil record, are skinks and geckoes. The majority of these genera have island species (indeed, are often the most important elements of island lizard faunas). They represent the most successful trans-oceanic travellers among the lizards, and are the least dependent upon continuous ecological connexions for their distribution.

The explanation of faunal similarities between Africa and Asia (also Australia and the New World) through the development of land bridges and continental drift is an old story. Others would reject the theory of drift, and derive these faunal similarities solely through past continuous distribution of tropical and subtropical climatic conditions in the Holarctic Realm. Present distributions of lizards in South-west Asia contribute little to any of these hypotheses. The majority of pantropical lizard genera are represented at present in the arid regions between the tropics; hence there is faunal contact at the generic level even today. Those not represented in South-west Asia are genera which perhaps require no faunal contact for their distribution.

As we deduce from the fossil evidence and differences in present distribution, evolution proceeds neither at the same rate nor contemporaneously in all animal groups. Some modern lizard genera are also known as fossils, and reach back almost unaltered to the early Tertiary. For this reason, analogies cannot be drawn with the history of mammalian distribution.

SUMMARY

Iran comprises the most geographically complex area of South-west Asia, and is centrally located with respect to the mingling of elements of the North African, southern Asian, Central Asian, and European herpetofaunas. There are found in Iran five species of turtles in four genera and ninety-three species of lizards in thirty-two genera. A single amphisbaenian occurs within the country.

Apart from those faunal elements which it shares with other regions, South-west Asia has two major distributional components to its lizard fauna. The Iranian faunal element is viewed here as autochthonous to the Iranian Plateau, and occupies primarily the elevated regions extending from the Anatolian highlands, across the southern border of the U.S.S.R. through Afghanistan, and extending south, bordered on the west by the Zagros mountains, to the narrow coastal plain of the Persian Gulf, and east through upland Balūchistān. The Saharo-Sindian faunal element occupies the low desert areas from North Africa to north-western India. It is seen here as allochthonous to Iran, its origins probably lying in the low elevations to the south. Origins and subdivisions of this element await study of conditions in South-west Asia as a whole, and are not elaborated here. Although there is penetration of both areas by species characteristic of the other, few species are broadly distributed in both regions.

Entering South-west Asia, on the north-west are elements with European affinities, primarily those having a Mediterranean distribution. Aralo-Caspian desert species penetrate the region from the north, and a few Oriental species are found in the south-east.

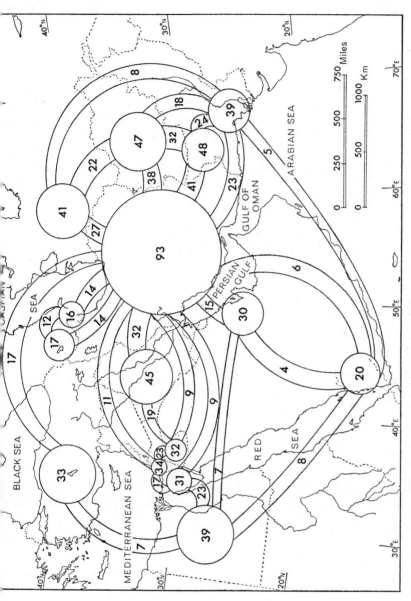

Fig. 95. Correlation of the Iranian lizard fauna at the species level with the faunas of countries elsewhere in South-west Asia. Figures within circles represent numbers of species known for the countries; figures in connecting arcs represent numbers of species common to two countries.

The affinities of the lizard fauna of South-west Asia with the faunas of adjacent regions are primarily at the generic level. In this paper the lizard fauna of thirteen physiographic areas of Iran is examined in detail.

TABLE 8. *Summary of distribution of faunal elements in Iran*

Figures represent percent of total fauna for each physiographic region represented by each faunal element. Numbers in parentheses represent total species in fauna.

	Iranian	Saharo-Sindian	Aralo-Caspian	Mediter-ranean	Oriental	Biregional or doubtful
Central Plateau (36)	55·5	8·3	8·3	0	0	27·7
Sīstān Basin (25)	64·0	8·0	8·0	0	0	20·0
Rezā'īyeh Basin (13)	38·5	0	0	7·7	0	53·8
Mughān Steppe (6)	16·6	0	16·6	16·6	0	50·0
Caspian Coast (7)	14·3	0	0	28·6	0	57·1
Khūzistān Plain (22)	4·5	50·0	0	0	4·5	40·9
Balūchistān and Makrān Coast (33)	42·4	30·3	0	0	9·1	18·2
Türkmen Steppe (23)	21·7	0	43·5	4·3	0	30·5
Zagros Mountains (13)	38·5	7·7	0	15·4	0	38·5
Western Zagros Foothills (17)	17·6	41·2	0	0	0	41·2
Alburz Mountains (10)	20·0	0	0	20·0	0	60·0
Kopet Dāgh (12)	25·0	0	16·7	16·7	0	41·7

The Central Plateau, which has apparently existed as a terrestrial environment continuously since the Oligocene or Miocene. Encircled by developing mountain chains, the plateau has been less subject to climatic change throughout the Quaternary and much of the Tertiary than less protected continental areas. It is postulated here that such enclosed basins, containing a diversity of habitats, may be centres of origin and dispersal for many of the Asian faunal elements.

The lizard fauna of the Central Plateau is composed primarily of species belonging to the Iranian faunal element and wide-ranging biregional species (see table 8). Five patterns of distribution within the plateau are discussed.

The Sīstān Basin. The lizard fauna of this basin is derived from the Iranian faunal element and has its greatest affinities with the Central Plateau (see fig. 92).

The Rezā'īyeh [Urumīyeh] Basin. The faunal affinities are Mediterranean and Transcaucasian in the genus *Lacerta*, Transcaucasian and Anatolian in the fauna of the mountains bordering the basin, the remainder of the species being plateau-derived. Endemics account for 15 per cent of the species. The majority of the species are biregional, or belong to the Iranian faunal element (table 8).

The Caspian Coast. The emergence of this low-lying coastal zone is a post-Pleistocene phenomenon. Consequently, its small lizard fauna contains no endemic species, and has faunal relationships with Mediterranean Europe and Transcaucasia.

The Khūzistān Plain and Persian Gulf Coast. The majority of lizard species in this fauna belong to the Saharo-Sindian element, and the fauna has its greatest relationships with Mesopotamian Iraq and gulf coastal Arabia. There is a distinct break in the continuity of Saharo-Sindian species composition between Bushire and Bandar-i-Lingeh on the Persian Gulf coast. In so far as Iran is concerned, western component of this element occurs in Khūzistān, and an eastern component in Balūchistān.

Iranian Balūchistān and Makrān Coast. Almost half of the lizard species of Iranian Balūchistān belong to the Iranian faunal element, Saharo-Sindian species forming the bulk of the remainder (table 8). It is in this region that a few representatives of the Oriental element enter Iran. Three species, 9 per cent of the total fauna, are endemic to this region. If south-eastern Iran is considered more broadly, however, including part of the Central Plateau and the Sīstān Basin, we find twelve species endemic to a region approximately corresponding to climatic type III_{3a} of Walter and Lieth (see figs. 93 and 94).

Türkmen Steppe. In extreme north-eastern Iran the lizard fauna of the Tūrān lowlands of Central Asia extends into Iran. This Aralo-Caspian element is closely related to the Iranian element at the generic level, and the two elements have been considered a single faunal association, the Irano-Turanian, by most previous authors. The Central Plateau and the Tūrān lowland have had at least intermittent contact since the Eocene. It is proposed in this paper that the net faunal movement has been from the Iranian Plateau into the Tūrān lowland.

Mughān Steppe. This fauna, having species of the Mediterranean, Aralo-Caspian, and Iranian elements, has without doubt assembled since the recent regression of the Caspian Sea.

Zagros Mountains. Because of their N.W.–S.E. strike, these mountains form a distribution corridor enabling a few northern species to penetrate southward. The lizard fauna is poorly known, but does contain relictual endemics. Wide-ranging, biregional species cross the passes, and species with Mediterranean affinities are present.

Western Foothills of the Zagros Mountains. The great majority of lizards belong to the Saharo-Sindian faunal element and biregional species, although the influence of the Iranian element is also felt. In contrast with upland Balūchistān, however, the fauna of the Central Plateau is conspicuously absent, due to the intervening Zagros ranges. Relictual endemic species also occur in this area, which lies at the extreme south-western margin of the Iranian Plateau (*sensu lato*).

Alburz Mountains. Since the post-Pleistocene recession of snowline to higher elevations, the lizard fauna of the Central Plateau has invaded the dry southern slopes, while forest species with Mediterranean affinities have entered the lush vegetation on the northern flanks of the range.

Kopet Dāgh. The lizard fauna of this elevated region is little known. Some lizard species may have found a Pleistocene refuge in these drier mountains of intermediate elevation, re-invading the Caspian lowlands as the Caspian Sea receded. Iranian elements enter the ranges from the south, while Aralo-Caspian species have entered via the valley of the Atrak river.

Present distributions indicate that there has been a faunal exchange between Iran and Europe through the Mediterranean area. Strictly Eurosiberian species are notably lacking in the Iranian lizard fauna, in contrast to certain other animal groups. It is here suggested that with the uplifting of the Iranian Plateau, the net faunal movement has been from the plateau towards Central Asia. The lizards common to Iran and to India and other southern Asian areas, even at the generic level, occur primarily in the north-western desert of the Oriental region, and communication is through Balūchistān. In the lizard fauna, relationships with Africa are largely in the Saharo-Sindian element and wide-ranging biregional species. At present, the faunal connexion of Iran with the Arabian Peninsula is through the Mesopotamian Plain at the head of the Persian Gulf. Despite evidence of land connexion across the gulf during the Pleistocene, the present distribution of lizards does not indicate extensive faunal exchange between the two areas via this route.

Little ecological information is available for Iranian lizards, other than that contributed in an earlier paper (Anderson, 1963). The physical factors of the environment are briefly considered with regard to their possible effects on lizard distribution. Since there is little climatic data for South-west Asia directly applicable to microhabitats of lizards, only the broadest speculations and correlations (see table 6) can be made in regard to temperature, rainfall, humidity, light, and air movement. Examination of known distributions and gross morphological adaptation, as well as personal observation, reveals that a large number of South-west Asian lizards are rather narrowly restricted to specific types of environment, and it is suggested that this factor plays an important role in determining distribution.

CHAPTER 11

ORNITHOLOGY

Iran from the ornithological viewpoint is situated within the Palearctic region, one of the major zoogeographical areas of the world which includes the whole of Europe, Africa north of the Sahara and Asia north of the Himalayas. Broadly speaking, therefore, the avifauna of Iran is similar to that of Europe and a large number of the species found in the latter area also occur in Iran. In addition a number of birds from Siberia reach Iran, as do a few representatives of the Ethiopian and Oriental regions in the south-west and south-east respectively.

Within Iran there are found approximately 450 species of birds which can be broadly divided into the four main categories of (*a*) residents, (*b*) summer visitors, (*c*) winter visitors and (*d*) passage migrants. The exact status of some of these birds is still not entirely clear since, with the exception of the Caspian area, Iran has not been closely studied by modern ornithologists.

Before considering the avifauna of Iran in detail, it is of interest to trace the history of its general ornithology and consider what literature is available on the subject. Unfortunately, particularly in the case of the older authors, it is often extremely difficult to come by copies of their books and papers outside the great Natural History libraries in the various capitals and universities of the world. In addition, much of the small amount of published material is in German, Russian or French. There is little or no material available in Persian.

W. T. Blanford's *Eastern Persia Volume II* published in 1876, described 384 species of birds, drawing not only on the author's own observations and experience, but making use of all material previously published. This was the first, and to date the last, attempt in English to describe the birds of Iran as a whole.

From 1884 to 1904, the great Russian ornithologist N. Zarudny was active in Iran. During these twenty years he travelled all over the country from east to west and north to south, producing as a result of his journeying some fifty-one papers, and making large collections wherever he went. Most of these papers were written in German or Russian and ranged from a one-page account of a new species (e.g.

"Vorläufige Bemerkungen über drei ornithologische Neuheiten aus Persien—*Certhia familiaris persica* subsp. nov.; *Troglodytes parvulus subpallidus* subsp. nov; *T. parvulus hyrcanus* subsp. nov." published in *Ornithologische Monatsbericht*, 1905, page 106) to whole books describing his journeys and ornithological findings in detail (e.g. *Marschroute der Reise in Öst-Persien im Jahre 1896* published in Russian by the Imperial Academy of Science in St Petersburg). A number of these papers were written in collaboration with Baron H. Loudon. The collections which he made are mostly held in the U.S.S.R. and largely unavailable for detailed study. In 1911 Zarudny produced a paper in tabular form which was published in April of that year in the German *Journal für Ornithologie*. This paper, which listed 716 species and subspecies of birds for Iran, was a summary of all the then available knowledge; and described the status of each bird—resident, breeding, winter visitor, passage migrant, vagrant, etc.—for the thirteen areas into which, for the purpose of his tables, he divided Iran. This was the second, and to date the last, attempt to describe the status and distribution of the birds of Iran. After 1911 Zarudny, in collaboration with M. Härms, produced three further papers on Iran making, in all, a total of some fifty-five publications on the birds of the country.

Up to the end of the First World War, the only other prominent ornithologist to study Iran was the Englishman H. Witherby, who published three papers in *Ibis* on the birds of the province of Fārs, Western Iran and the Caspian.

Between the war years C. B. Ticehurst published two lengthy papers on the birds of Mesopotamia and the Persian Gulf, C. E. Capito described the birds of North-west Fārs, where he was then resident, Buxton wrote some notes on the Rasht/Pahlavī area and Professor Stresemann discussed the birds of the Elburz. Apart from these authors, only K. Paludan, a Dane, published any other material at all during this period. 1940 saw the production of the important work in Russian by J. A. Issakov and K. A. Vorobiev entitled *Wintering Birds and Migration on the South Coast of the Caspian* but it was not until after the Second World War that interest in Iranian ornithology revived and a certain amount of material, mostly in German or English, was produced. Unfortunately, apart from B. Löppenthin's 1950 paper on the "Sea Birds of the Persian Gulf", the great majority of these papers were concerned with the Caspian area of northern Iran. Prominent among the authors who wrote about this region were Professor Schuz, R.

Passburg and X. de Misonne; and their writings provide an accurate and up-to-date picture of the distribution of the birds of the two provinces of Māzandarān and Gīlān.

For the amateur ornithologist who may be visiting Iran or who is stationed there for a period of years, there is vast scope for further study since, ornithologically speaking, huge areas of the country are virtually unexplored and, with the exception of the Caspian, very little has been published recently about the avifauna of the area. For such a person a small number of basic reference books are essential and these include Collin's *Birds of Europe*, Meinertzhagen's *Birds of Arabia* and volumes I and II of Vaurie's *Birds of the Palaearctic Fauna*. Such a library will enable the amateur satisfactorily to identify most of the birds he sees. A further difficulty which will face him, however, is one of distance and communications. Iran is a large country in which travel is arduous on rough roads. Moreover, except in the larger cities such as Tehrān, Tabrīz, Shīrāz, etc., accommodation may be difficult, and in places it may be necessary to camp. These drawbacks, however, do not apply to the Caspian area which is easy of access from Tehrān, and is served by reasonably good roads. It also has a wealth of bird-life and in consequence has been studied in greater detail than any other part of the country.

Virtually all aspects of ornithology in Iran still require further study. One of the major gaps is an up-to-date account of the status and distribution of the birds of the area as a whole, since Zarudny's 1911 tabular paper is not only now out of date, but also suffers from the disadvantage that the distribution of each bird as listed for the thirteen geographical areas is not supported by detailed evidence except in his previously published papers which are virtually unobtainable. For instance, the rare Desert Jay (*Podoces pleskei*) is listed by him as resident in Sīstān, the Kirmān area and the whole of Balūchistān, but no precise details are available of exactly where it is to be found within the huge areas mentioned nor does he provide any ecological or other data.

Apart from this basic gap in current ornithological knowledge, modern regional studies of virtually the whole country—with the exception of Māzandarān, Gīlān and the immediate area of Tehrān—are sadly lacking. A limited amount of work has been done on migration in the Caspian provinces but elsewhere in Iran this subject, too, has received hardly any attention whatsoever. Little work has been done on taxonomy and there is no published material on ecology, population or breeding biology. It will be apparent, therefore, that the gaps in our ornithological knowledge of Iran are very large and that there is more than ample scope for both the amateur and the professional in the field of general and specialized studies.

Apart from the professional ornithologist, who can undertake an organized field expedition to any part of Iran, the amateur bird-watcher who is posted to that country is most likely to find himself in Tehrān. There he will be reasonably well situated to indulge in week-end ornithology and will have the opportunity of visiting many areas rich in bird-life. To the west of Tehrān and south of Karaj lie the Aḥmadā-bād marshes; in winter the haunt of many species of duck, in spring and autumn traversed by thousands of migrants and in summer a hard-baked mud plain with nesting larks and Sandgrouse. Immediately to the north of Tehrān rise the Alburz mountains with Mt Damāvand's snow-capped peak towering over all. In the high valleys of the foothills, such as the Lār, where the only inhabitants are an occasional shepherd, the bird-watcher will come across the Wall Creeper, the Alpine Accentor, the Twite and the Red-fronted Finch, and in winter the Snow Finch and the Caspian Snowcock. As one drives from Tehrān over the Alburz mountains to the Caspian, the road passes through a tunnel at a height of some 10,000 ft. In summer the whole of this area is full of Horned Larks, Choughs and Wheatears of several kinds un-known in Europe, with the occasional Vulture and Lammergeier circling overhead. Descending the northern slopes of the Alburz towards Chālūs, one passes through heavy bush and forest country, full of Pheasants, small Warblers, Woodpeckers, Jays and other birds differing only sub-specifically from their relatives in western Europe. Driving west along the shore of the Caspian Sea, one can expect to see a variety of birds—Cormorants nesting in trees in company with Grey Herons and little Egrets, Terns fishing just off the beach, Ringed Plover running to and fro on the shingle, the huge White-tailed Sea Eagle and the smaller Osprey at their eyries, the woodland clearings full of Tits, Redstarts and Flycatchers. At Pahlavī the landscape changes and all around is the vast swamp of the Murd-Āb, traversable only in flat-bottomed boats. In summer the whole area is a waving mass of tall reeds filled with breeding marsh birds such as the Crakes, probably the Purple Heron, small Warblers, Terns and enormous numbers of other species. In autumn the area is used as a staging area by tens of thousands of migrants which pour in from the north. At the height of the migration period it is comparatively normal to see over one hundred different species in a single day's bird-watching.

In winter the whole area is one enormous wild-fowl paradise for duck and geese which, although heavily shot and netted, is so vast that the birds are not driven away. One authority has estimated that the total annual bag by shooting and netting along the whole Caspian coast may be something in the order of 1,200,000 birds per year, largely Mallard and Teal. Of these it is reckoned that 100,000 are shot, 50,000 are taken in decoy ponds and the remainder by net, gong and flare. On the Murd-Āb alone, some 250 boat teams operate in winter using the last three methods, and are reckoned to take some 875,000 duck per year; indeed this form of crop provides many of the peasants in the area with their livelihood in the winter months.

Returning from Pahlavī over the road through Rasht, the country-side is more open and rocky with occasional stretches of woodland interspersed with strips of cultivation. Here one hears the ringing call of the Rock Nuthatch and sees coveys of Rock Partridge and, in the more desert areas, the self-effacing Persian See-See, a form of desert partridge.

Even a trip of this nature, however, is a considerable undertaking in Iran. The round journey Tehrān–Chālūs–Pahlavī–Rasht–Tehrān by car, which is the only method, may well, even under normal circumstances take all of eighteen hours' motoring. If therefore one wishes to devote any reasonable amount of time to bird-watching, it becomes nearly impossible to do such a trip in a single week-end.

One long week-end trip which can however be undertaken is to drive north-east from Tehrān over the Alburz through Fīrūzkūh and Pul-i-Safīd, where in autumn small boys sell snared pheasants at the road-side for five shillings each, to Bābol Sar on the Caspian. Here there are no open marshes, but high sand dunes along the Caspian shore, with cultivated fields behind full of Larks and Warblers. In winter this area and further east along the coast to Bandar Shāh is the haunt of tens of thousands of geese—not the grey geese of Pahlavī, but the Lesser White-fronted Goose which is far rarer in Europe, and occasionally the Red-breasted Goose. This latter species, seems unfortunately, to be getting rarer and rarer in Iran. Of recent years it has only been recorded in one's and two's from the South-east Caspian area where previously it was reported in thousands.

South and east of Tehrān bird-watching opportunities are more limited and one has to drive for many hours through the desert to reach any really promising areas. This precludes anything but really long week-end trips of at least three to four days' duration. On the other hand, day trips into the desert and rocky areas south of Tehrān are often rewarding, as one can expect to see several kinds of Wheatear, the Rollers in rows on telephone wires, the Desert Warbler, the Desert Lark, Sandgrouse, and other birds of the area. If one is lucky enough to find some cultivation where there is running water and a little greenery and cover, the variety of bird life is quite extraordinary with Fan-tailed Warblers, Golden Orioles and Shrikes present in considerable numbers.

This perhaps gives some idea of the opportunities available for anyone who is living in Tehrān. Similar opportunities exist, of course, around Tabrīz, Mashhad, Iṣfahān, Shīrāz or the Khurramshahr/Ābādān area, where, dependent on the surrounding habitat, much of interest can be seen. In all areas, however, it will be necessary to make fairly long and exhausting trips and to be prepared to camp out in the open country.

The birds which are to be seen in Iran are, in the main, very similar to those in Europe and for anyone used to the latter little difficulty in identification will be encountered. The few totally non-European birds are readily identifiable with the aid of the text-books mentioned above.

In the succeeding paragraphs an attempt is made to describe in broad outline the various groups of birds in Iran, commenting in particular on those members of each family which do not occur in Europe. Some idea will be given of their status and habitat.

Of the truly pelagic birds, there are representatives in Iran of only three families, the Skuas, Petrels and Shearwaters. Both types of Skua which have been reported from the Caspian in winter and the Petrel from the Persian Gulf can only be regarded as rare vagrants, while the Persian Shearwater, which occurs in the latter area in some numbers, is not likely to be seen by the casual observer unless he is travelling by ship. The Gulls and Terns, however, are well represented and many of the latter are to be found inland both on migration and nesting. In addition to the Common, Herring, Black-headed, and Lesser Black-backed Gulls (all of which frequent the Caspian), the Great Black-headed, Slender-billed, Sooty and Hemprich's Gulls occur in Iran, largely as winter visitors. No less than twelve different sorts of Tern

are to be found including all of those common to Europe as well as the
Bridled, White-cheeked, Swift and Crested Terns, the latter mostly
occurring in the Persian Gulf area. Many of these Terns migrate through
Iran, and a Sandwich Tern, ringed in Russia, was picked up near
Tehrān in the autumn of 1957.

Two other seabirds which are to be found in the Persian Gulf are the
Red-billed Tropic bird, nesting on the islands there, and the Masked
Booty, whose status is not exactly clear, but which may breed on the
islands off the Makrān coast. Both birds are unknown in Europe.

The Grebe family is represented by five members, two of which, the
Little and Great Crested, are resident. The Horned and Red-necked
Grebes are both uncommon winter visitors, while the Black-necked
Grebe is a rare breeding species, but a fairly common visitor in winter.

Both the White and the Dalmatian Pelican occur in Iran, and can be
seen on the Caspian in large winter herds and in the south all the way
down the length of the Shaṭṭ-al-ʿArab as far south as Fao. Both species
appear to be resident in the marshes of Sīstān but this area has been
little explored in recent years.

Apart from the Shag and the Common Cormorant, both the Pygmy
and the Socotra Cormorant occur in Iran, the latter only in the Persian
Gulf. The former is resident in Sīstān and is a winter visitor and passage
migrant to the Caspian area. In addition that snake-like fishing bird
the Darter, although not yet reported from Iran, is common in the
Amara marshes on the Iraqi side of the Iran–Iraq frontier in the south-
west and is likely, sooner or later, to be seen on the Iranian side of the
frontier.

Herons abound in Iran where, on the Caspian, the Grey Heron can
be found breeding in a colony of tree-nesting Cormorants. The Purple
Heron also nests in certain parts of the country, as do the Night Heron
and the Great White Heron, although the last is largely a winter visitor.
Along the shores of the Persian Gulf the Reef Heron is common in both
the blue and the white phases, with the former colour predominating.
The commonest heron of all in North Iran, however, is the Little
Egret, and the lush meadows of the Caspian are often alive with these
stately white birds feeding among the grazing cattle. In autumn, their
numbers are increased by thousands of migrants arriving from the
north; and sometimes in late September whole areas of the Murd-Āb
appear to be one white sheet of birds.

One of the commonest nesting birds in North Iran is the White

Stork whose huge nests adorn many a mosque tower. Its near relative, the Black Stork, is now, however, very scarce and little is known of its exact status throughout the country. In southern Balūchistān a third member of this family, the White-headed Stork from India has been recorded but it is probably only a rare vagrant to the area.

The Hermit Ibis and the Sacred Ibis, both of which have been reported from the west of the country, are not likely to be seen by the average ornithologist, but the Glossy Ibis is present in the Murd-Āb marshes and may well breed there. The local sportsmen are unfortunately inclined to shoot them, since their fat, boiled down, is said to be a certain specific against rheumatism, as is that of the Coot. Another bird which also tends to be pursued by the locals is the Flamingo, whose flesh is credited with aphrodisiacal properties. The Flamingo certainly nests in the north-west and Sīstān but no longer does so on the Caspian where it is, however, present during mild winters in considerable numbers.

Iran is a paradise for wild-fowl, and nearly all the European species occur in the country, mostly as winter visitors. The two great areas of concentration are the Caspian provinces and Sīstān but little is known of the latter area. Although vast numbers are taken by professional duck catchers each year in the two provinces of Māzandarān and Gīlān, uncounted millions still frequent the area and it is an unforgettable sight to go out at dawn into the heart of the Murd-Āb to watch the morning flight and later to see huge rafts of Mallard, Teal, Garganey and Shoveler dibbling in the shallow water. To give some idea of possible numbers one such raft of many which were seen by a qualified observer was estimated to be some 1,100 yd long by 60 yd wide and was made up almost entirely of Mallard, packed so close together that the water between individual birds was no longer visible. Both Swans and Geese winter along the Caspian, the former in comparatively small numbers. In the south-west Caspian the geese are predominantly Greylag, but in the south-east it is the rarer Lesser White-front which is present in thousands, making the clear winter sky resound with its wild call. In previous years this area was the main wintering haunt of the little Red-breasted Goose from Siberia, but recently its habits appear to have changed and it is now seldom to be seen in the area.

Apart from all the normal Duck which are to be found throughout Europe, four species of particular interest, all of which breed in the area, occur in Iran. They are the Ruddy Shelduck, the Marbled Teal, the

White-eyed Pochard and the Stiff-tailed Duck. Of these the Ruddy Shelduck and the Marbled Teal are fairly widely distributed but the other two have only a very limited range and are hard to find. Indeed the Stiff-tailed Duck, a winter visitor except for Sīstān where it is said to be resident, appears to be becoming very rare indeed. Further information on its status throughout the country is urgently needed.

The birds of prey are well represented and are widely distributed throughout the whole area. Seven species of eagle occur in Iran, and some of them such as the Golden and Bonelli's Eagles are used in combination with greyhounds for hawking gazelles in the deserts of the south. The White-tailed Sea Eagle and the Osprey are common along the Caspian coast, but there is some recent disturbing evidence to suggest that there has been a sharp decline in numbers of occupied eyries. This decline, if correct, is almost certainly not due to shooting but can more likely be attributed to an increase in the indiscriminate use of pesticides. The third sort of fishing eagle which occurs in Iran is the rare Pallas' Fishing Eagle, which is only a winter visitor to Sīstān and the extreme south of the country. Vultures are widely distributed throughout the mountains, and that ubiquitous scavenger the Egyptian Vulture can usually be seen on rubbish dumps in cities and villages throughout the country. The Bearded Vulture or Lammergeier, however, is very much a bird of the cliff faces, not usually soaring high overhead like others of his tribe but swooping on out-stretched wings along the barren rock faces.

Of the true falcons the Lanner and the Peregrine are in most demand for falconry, a sport still practised to a very large extent in southern Iran particularly amongst the nomadic tribes. The Hobby and the Merlin and the two kinds of Kestrel are found wherever the habitat is suitable, the Lesser Kestrel nesting colonially in holes in the cliff faces, in ruins such as, for example, those of Persepolis, or high up in the great tower at Gunbad-i-Qābūs. In south Balūchistān the rare Red-headed Falcon is reported to breed but recent confirmation of this is still required, as is modern evidence of the nesting in the same area of the White-eyed Buzzard.

All along the Caspian in the northern foothills of the Alburz the Pheasant is plentiful and is much shot by local sportsmen and hunters from Tehrān. On account of the thick thornbrakes and heavy cover its habits are rather different from those of its cousins in Europe. In Iran it rarely, if ever, flies and then only as a last desperate escape measure. It relies entirely on its legs and, in the thick ground cover, can outrun the fastest dog. As a result the birds are mostly taken in snares and nooses or, when shot, are fired at on the ground as they rush across a glade or clearing. At night they roost on the ground or in a small bush, never high up in trees as they do in England. The Quail is widely distributed wherever there is land under cultivation but is not regarded by the Iranians as a gamebird and is not hunted, all the attention of local sportsmen being devoted to the partridge. In the north-west the English partridge is found, but the common bird throughout Iran is the Rock Partridge, another determined runner and outstandingly difficult of approach. In the more open areas are to be found the Persian See-See, a form of near-desert partridge, the Francolin or Black Partridge, surely one of the most beautifully coloured birds in the world and, in the extreme south in Balūchistān and along the Persian Gulf, the Grey Partridge. One method used by local hunters to approach these birds is unique to Iran and is known as the scarecrow method. It is used primarily to shoot the Rock Partridge and can only be applied in certain parts of the country where the hunter can locate his coveys feeding on open stubble. He does this by observation from rocky outcrops surrounding the fields and then approaches the birds upwind, holding in his left hand a wooden frame, covered in brown cloth, big enough to hide his whole body. In his right hand he has his gun fully cocked and moves slowly over the field at an angle to the birds, taking short careful steps. As he comes within range he slips the barrel of his gun through a ready-made flap in the screen and takes a pot-shot at the covey on the ground. This is a deadly method in the hands of a skilled hunter since, for some unexplained reason, these otherwise very wild birds are usually fooled by this approach. Luckily for them there are not very many practitioners of this art and bags made by this method are probably not excessive.

Another gamebird which must be mentioned is the Snowcock, the king of the high mountains. This magnificent bird, whose distribution is limited to the high mountains of Central Asia, the Himalayas and the Caucasus, is found in Iran only in the Alburz and the mountains of the north-west. It is shy and elusive and not often seen, although sometimes in hard and snowy winters it comes down to the lower levels and can be found fairly near Tehrān. In hard weather it burrows deep into the snow and this is often its undoing, since local hunters follow its tracks and dig it out of its snow house. Not many are taken by this method, though, since it is arduous in the extreme and demands extraordinary skill and endurance on the part of the hunter.

The only other game-birds which are found in Iran are the Sandgrouse and the Bustard, the former a large partridge-like bird living in the wilder, less cultivated parts of the country. In northern Iran the Blackbellied Sandgrouse is the commonest member of its family and the one most likely to be encountered. These birds usually move to water once a day, most often at dawn, and it is then that comparatively large bags can be made. In the southern parts of the country other types of Sandgrouse are found but these tend to be more birds of the real desert. Over recent years a regrettable habit has grown up amongst Iranians of shooting these birds from a moving Land Rover, and fairly considerable bags can be made in this way. This is by no means so unsporting as might be thought, however, since it is a matter of no little difficulty to bring down a bird on the wing when shooting from a moving vehicle bucking over the rough desert.

Three kinds of Bustard are found—the Great, the Little and the Houbara. The first two species are largely confined to the huge open plains of the north-east and the north-west, while the Houbara inhabits the southern part of the country and is still hawked by horsemen with eagles on their fists. In autumn a certain amount of local migration takes place and it is by no means unusual to find small groups of Great Bustard in the open cultivated plains around Tehrān. It is astonishing to see how a bird of this size can virtually disappear in a stubble field. One can watch them land, the white signal patches on their wings flashing bravely in the sun, and then suddenly lose sight of them in a field of stubble only a few inches high. Although the landing place is carefully marked, there is no sign of the huge birds by the time the area is reached—they have long since run off to the nearest cover.

Snipe and Woodcock are particularly abundant in Iran. The former, mostly the Common and the Jack, are found in winter and on passage wherever suitable habitat prevails, while occasionally the Great, the Solitary and the Pintail Snipe are to be seen. Woodcock abound on the northern slopes of the Alburz in winter and are much sought after by local hunters. One of their principal migration routes is over the Caspian and, given a suitable combination of wind and weather, the sand dunes on the seashore are at times littered with exhausted birds which allow approach within a few feet.

The Cranes are largely passage migrants through Iran, but apparently in no great numbers. Some may winter in Sīstān, but elsewhere they are only transient visitors although old records, unsubstantiated in recent times, show the Siberian Crane wintering on the Caspian.

The Rail family is well represented by the Land and Water Rail and the Little Baillon's and Spotted Crake, but so inconspicuous are the latter trio that their presence tends to pass unnoticed. The most outstanding member of the family is the Purple Gallinule which occurs in most of the marshes of Gīlān and Māzandarān and, comparatively speaking, is unafraid of man. This charming bird, handsome in its purple-shot plumage and scarlet face knob, can be seen in almost any marshy area picking its way delicately over the floating leaves.

In addition to nearly all Plovers such as the Green, Golden, etc., which are to be found throughout Europe, there are a number of interesting species which are likely to be unfamiliar to the European observer. These include the White-tailed Plover, the Sociable Plover, the Red-wattled Plover, the Spur-winged Plover (this last recently rediscovered as a breeding species in Greece), the Large, Sand, Mongolian Plover, and the Caspian Plover, the latter not to be found anywhere near the Caspian. In addition, although not strictly belonging to the same family, the hole-nesting Crab Plover is found on the shores of the Persian Gulf.

As a country, Iran is immensely rich in waders, although the great majority occur only on passage through the area. One of the best places to see this passage is at Pahlavī in the autumn, where the seashore and the marsh edges are alive with waders of different species. In addition to the normal species associated with Europe, such as the Curlews, Shanks, Sandpipers, Godwits, Stints, etc., both the Slender-billed and Australian Curlews have been recorded, while the Avocet and the Blackwinged Stilt are common breeding species. The latter nests on the Aḥmadābād marshes to the west of Tehrān and, for the ornithologist, there is nothing more exciting than the frantic crying of these birds as they circle the area of their nest with their long pale legs protruding far behind their tails.

Another interesting group of birds with which the average European ornithologist is unlikely to be well acquainted is the Courser/Pratincole species. The Cream-coloured Courser is largely a bird of the desert edges and, except in movement, is virtually invisible. When it runs, however, its long legs and eyestripe are clearly to be seen, but to get it to fly is a matter of difficulty. The Pratincoles, too, are birds of the near desert but in northern Iran they are birds of passage that sometimes linger in suitable habitat, particularly in spring, for a matter of weeks. As they swoop and sweep over the flat marshes, their swept-back swallow-like wings slice through the clear air with indescribable beauty.

Another lovely visitor to the pools of the Aḥmadābad marshes is the Red-necked Phalarope. These are purely birds of passage, nesting as they do in the far north, but every spring and autumn the marshes are full of them for a few days. They are in every stage of plumage; in spring some just acquiring the glossy red breeding plumage with others still in winter grey: in autumn birds losing their breeding colours and some already in their drab winter dress. At both seasons of the year they are unbelievably tame and take no notice of human beings. A brackish pool, only some five or six yd across may contain upwards of fifty to sixty birds in every stage of plumage change—all milling round in feeding circles utterly unconcerned about the observer standing a few yards away. The rarer Phalarope, the Grey, has also been recorded on passage through the area and may, indeed, winter in small numbers on the shores of the Persian Gulf, but modern evidence of this is lacking, largely due to the fact that no competent ornithologist has adequately studied the birds of the Gulf in winter.

The pigeon family is well represented in Iran. The European Wood Pigeon occurs in the Caspian but is by no means so common as his cousin in England. Outside the Caspian area the most common Pigeon is the Rock Dove which breeds in hundreds in qanāts all over the country. Except in the most isolated areas few of these birds are of pure breed, since they have interbred with the tame pigeons which infest every Iranian town and village. In the south the Palm Dove is common wherever the habitat is suitable, while in the high mountains of the north-east it is possible to see the rare Eversmann's Pigeon, but this is not a common species and is unlikely to be seen by anyone who does not expressly set out to find it.

The European Cuckoo is common both as a breeding species and on passage but, strangely enough, it does not seem to call as much as it does in Europe. Three other Cuckoos largely unknown in Europe also occur in the area—the Great Spotted Cuckoo nesting in the south-west, the Pied Crested Cuckoo found only in Baluchistan and the Himalayan Cuckoo breeding in Khurāsān and the north-east.

Iran is rich in Owls, and for anyone who drives around the country-side the Little Owl is one of the commonest birds. In some parts of the country each and every well has its unblinking Little Owl perched on the parapet. Like their counterparts in Europe, the other kinds of Owl are more difficult of observation, but in most areas one can hear at night the monotonous call of the Scops or the deep pulsing hoot of the Eagle Owl, the latter mostly in the rocky desert areas of the central plateau. In the Zagros mountains of the south-west the rare Brown Fish Owl is resident, but the casual traveller through the area is unlikely to record it.

The European, Egyptian and Indian Nightjars all occur in Iran but, secretive as they are, they are invisible to an average observer unless he stumbles across them on passage. Only the Egyptian Nightjar is widespread through the country, the European being largely a passage migrant and the Indian Nightjar little more than a rare vagrant to the south-east.

Everywhere in summer in Iran one sees Swifts circling high in the sky; these are mostly the Alpine Swift of Europe since the Common Swift is principally a bird of passage. In the south and east two other species occur, the Pallid and the White-rumped Swifts but these need careful observation to be sure of their identification.

In northern Iran the flashing blue of the European Kingfisher is a common sight on the streams of the Alburz, but in the south its place is taken by the gaudy White-breasted and Pied Kingfishers, the latter a perfect symphony in black and white as it hovers above the slow moving streams of the south-west.

Perhaps the most colourful of all the birds in Iran and possibly also the most typical are the Bee-eaters, the gay summer visitors whose excited calling in the blue skies greets the traveller wherever he goes. The two most common species are the European and the Blue-cheeked or Persian Bee-eaters, both of which nest in Iran. Nearly every village in the north seems to have a colony near it, and the day-long calling of the hawking birds high in the summer sky is indelibly associated with the hot months of summer. During spring and autumn vast flocks pass through on migration and the telegraph wires alongside the straight desert roads seem to sag under the twittering thousands of birds, first the Blue-cheeked and then the Common Bee-eaters. In the extreme south and east their place is taken by the smaller green form, the Indian Bee-eater which seems, on the whole, to be less gregarious than its cousins elsewhere.

The other species eternally associated with telegraph wires in Iran

is the Roller, widespread over the whole plateau country. Almost anywhere in the flat plains of central Iran every stretch of wire along the
road appears to have its Roller, a single bird sitting motionless in the
shimmering light occasionally launching itself into space to snap up a
passing insect. In the south and east its near cousin the Indian Roller
also occurs but the two species appear to live happily side-by-side with
no inter-specific competition.

In contrast to the Rollers of the open plains area, the Woodpeckers
are essentially birds of the copse and forest. By far the commonest
species is the Syrian Woodpecker, which is found in almost any large
garden or piece of woodland in northern Iran. Among the forests of
the Caspian both the Green and the giant Black Woodpeckers are to be
found but neither could be described as common; while in the eastern
areas the rare White-backed, White-winged and Slaty-bellied Green
Woodpeckers have been recorded.

Before turning to the last major group of birds—the Passerines—
it is worth making mention of one brilliant member of a family which
will be quite unknown to European ornithologists but familiar enough
to those who have watched birds in Africa or the Far East. This is the
Sunbird, an Old World cousin, though anatomically unrelated, of the
Humming Birds of the New World. This family represented in Iran
only by the Purple Sunbird, is widespread throughout Africa and the
Far East; but in the area under consideration it occurs only in Balūchistān and along the shore of the Persian Gulf. Even there it is somewhat local in its distribution. Detailed study of its ecology still remains
to be undertaken, but once an observer has seen its jewel-like beauty,
the memory is likely to stay with him for ever and will probably, so far
as Iran is concerned, be one of the ornithological highlights of his time
in the country.

The last group of Iranian birds to be considered is the huge Order of
the Passeriformes largely, but not exclusively, summer visitors to the
area. Included in this Order are all the songbirds such as the Larks,
Thrushes, Warblers, the Crow family, the Wagtails, Shrikes and
Bunting. It is mostly birds from this Order which will strike the eye of
the amateur observer in Iran since members of the different families
contained in it can be seen in all parts of the country from the high
Alburz to the desert plateau.

The first, and one of the most widely spread families in Iran is the
Lark group. Including not only those Larks, such as the Sky, Wood

and Short-toed Larks commonly found in Europe, the family is represented throughout the whole of the country. In the high Alburz the alpine meadows are alive in summer with nesting Horned Larks while cultivated fields ring with the Calandra's brazen song. In the extremes of the desert areas the long-legged Bifasciated Lark, looking for all the world more like an elongated, rather faded, partridge, can be seen creeping over the rocky sands. Many of the Larks which live in desert or in semi-desert areas tend to assume a coloration in keeping with the hue of the local soil; and in a species so widespread as the Crested Lark astonishing colour variations occur over comparatively short distances.

Of the Swallow family the ordinary European Swallow, the House and the Sand Martins are all common in the area, while in the mountains the ubiquitous Crag Martin is dominant. In the south and south-east the Red-rumped Swallow largely replaces its European cousin and may possibly overwinter in the area.

A very typical bird of northern Iran is the Golden Oriole. The vivid gleaming yellow of the male can be seen flitting through the trees in Persian gardens, while its liquid whistling call is one of the most lovely sounds to be heard in spring. There is one particular garden a few miles north of Tehrān which is full, every year, with these lovely birds. A little stream runs through, lined on each side by stately poplars, with occasional clearings covered in short lush green grass. These clearings are much beloved by both Hoopoes and Orioles and it is rare not to see half a dozen or more of these birds perched in the surrounding trees or strutting on the close-cropped sward.

The Crow family is represented by all the species commonly found in Europe, except the Carrion Crow, but the latter's cousin, the Hoodie, abounds all over the country, one particular form in the south-west having far more white on it than its European cousin. By far the most exciting member of the Crow family, however, is the Desert Jay. This bird, of which little is known in Iran, is to be found in the sandy wastes of Sīstān, Kirmān and Balūchistān but definite details of its range and distribution in the area are largely lacking.

All the Tits which occur in Europe are found in Iran; and the Great Tit is one of the commonest birds to be seen in Tehrān inhabiting virtually every moderately sized garden in the area. Outside Tehrān, all through the foothills of the Alburz, the ringing metallic cry of the Rock Nuthatch echoes through the hills. Every little valley in the hills holds a pair or more, and it is not difficult to find their rounded mud-nests stuck to the side of a sheer rock. These nests are almost certainly used year after year, the sun-baked mud standing up astonishingly well to the ravages of winter. Two other birds associated with the foot-hills of the Alburz are the Dippers, a pair of which is present on nearly every stream in the area, and the rare Wall Creeper which is sparsely distributed in certain favoured localities.

In the south-west and along the Gulf and as far north as Sīstān a common garden bird is the exotic White-eared Bulbul. This species, so very alien to any observer used to the birds of Europe, is friendly and confiding and seems to prefer trees and bushes near human habitation of some sort.

In Iran the Thrush family is of great interest to ornithologists. Over the northern part of the country the Blackbird is resident and, in winter, is joined by its cousin from Russia, the Black-throated Thrush which arrives from the north often in company with Fieldfares and Redwings. In the mountain valleys the Ring-Ousel, a handsome bird, is far exceeded in glorious colours by the Rock Thrush and that wonderful symphony in blue, the Blue Rock Thrush. These two latter species are resident and can be found in the bare hill-sides usually occupying some conspicuous vantage point.

The next group in the family of Thrushes is the Wheatears, which are particularly well represented in Iran. The name Wheatear is often confusing to people interested in birds, since members of the family are not usually connected with corn cultivation nor are they possessed of ear-tufts. The probable origin of the name, according to the Shorter Oxford English Dictionary, is from the word "whiteeres" formed from the adjective "whit"=white and "eeres" or "ers"= arse in allusion to the bird's white rump. The word itself dates from the end of the sixteenth century. Indeed, in most but not all members of this family, this white rump is a very distinctive feature and a great help to rapid identification. In addition to the ordinary species found in Europe, the Arabian or Finch's, the Red-tailed, the White-rumped Black, the Hooded and the Mourning Wheatears all occur in Iran. Their specific identification is often a matter of some difficulty to the amateur since not only is it difficult quickly to analyse accurately the various colour patterns, but a number of species have different colour phases. For identifying any particular species in the hand the black and white drawings of the various tail patterns in Meinertzhagen's *Birds of Arabia* are most helpful.

Still in the Thrush family are the Redstarts. Both the Common and the Black are abundant throughout Iran while two rare species, both "pièces de résistance" for any European ornithologist, also occur in the mountains of the North and East. These are the Alburz Redstart, probably resident in the area, and Eversmann's Redstart, largely a winter visitor and passage migrant to the north and east.

In Iran the European Robin is a not very common winter visitor and passage migrant, but the White-fronted or Iranian Robin is resident in many rocky scrub-covered areas of Iran. It is, however, secretive and hard to find.

Both the Nightingale and its very close cousin the Thrush Nightingale breed in Iran and sometimes on a warm evening in a large Persian garden up to half a dozen or more can be heard competing with one another in a song-battle.

Another very large family is the Warblers, members of which are to be found all over the country, whether in the high mountains, the marshes or the deserts of the central plateau. All the species found in Europe either pass through or nest in Iran—indeed two of the most typical birds in the gardens and thickets of northern Iran in the summer months are the Olivaceous and the Fan-tailed Warbler, the former slipping inconspicuously through the bushes, the latter attracting attention with its up-cocked, white-spotted chestnut tail.

Of the typical larger Warblers, the three genera *Sylvia*, *Hippolais* and *Locustella* are all well represented. The most unusual members of this group, for European observers, are the Desert Warbler, a bird of the arid scrub of the central and southern regions of Iran, the Olivaceous Warbler mentioned above, Upcher's Warbler, largely in the south and east of Iran, and the Moustached Warbler, noted for its skulking and unobtrusive habits.

The Reed Warblers are common throughout the area anywhere where suitable habitat is available—in particular the Great Reed Warbler whose deafening song echoes through the reedbeds in the summer months. In this group is also included Cetti's Warbler, preferring apparently a drier habitat than its near relatives and, owing to its exceptionally skulking habits, very difficult to observe.

The Leaf Warblers, so called on account of their fairly uniform grey–green–yellow colouring, are poorly represented by some five or six species, most of which are largely passage migrants, although the Chiffchaff appears to winter in the south and east.

The only Wren-Warbler is the Graceful Warbler, a small long-tailed bird of the more arid southern and eastern parts of the country and not a species which the casual observer is likely to come across unless he goes out deliberately in search of it.

The Fan-tailed Warbler mentioned above is the only Grass Warbler which occurs. It is widely distributed throughout the area and its tail-cocking habits and tendency to move in small flocks make it very conspicuous.

That enchanting bird of the European forests, the Goldcrest, must now, according to modern systematists, take its place in the Warbler family in the Kinglet group. In Iran it occurs only in the Caspian forests where Zarudny states that it breeds but in no great numbers. It is certainly not common but can be seen in winter around Tehrān.

The last member of this large family which is worth mentioning is the Grey-backed Warbler which, despite its name, is regarded by modern experts as being far closer to the Thrushes. It is widely distributed as a nesting species and passage migrant throughout Iran, but is by no means common. With its, for a Warbler, largish size, graduated tail and strong feet, it seems more babbler than warbler-like and will be quite unfamiliar to the average European observer.

The Babbler is another bird which, though easy to identify, will be strange to people accustomed only to the birds of Europe. Hutton's Babbler is resident in the south and east of Iran and is a largish rather nondescript brown bird with a long tail and slightly curved beak. It lives in the scrub on the desert edges and around villages and is remarkable for its jumping gait and the fact that it often goes round in troops numbering four to as many as a dozen birds all hopping after each other through the bushes.

The Flycatchers of Iran are similar to those of Europe and in summer are to be ranked among the common birds of the garden and forest edge. The Pied Flycatcher is largely a bird of passage but the Spotted breeds in the area, as does the Red-breasted. The latter also migrates through Iran, since there is a case on record of a young bird of the year ringed at Ottenby in Sweden in the autumn and picked up a few months later in the province of Māzandarān.

The Sparrow family has a number of interesting representatives in Iran which are unknown in Europe. These include the Desert and Yellow-throated Rock Sparrows, the very rare and local Dead Sea Sparrow and the Saksaul and Desert Sparrow. The House and

Tree Sparrows are probably the commonest birds in Iran and are to be found wherever there is human habitation.

One of the most fascinating sights to be seen on the Caspian coast is the spring and autumn passage of the Yellow Wagtails. At certain times of the year the pastures there are, quite literally, yellow with birds, the flocks lingering for a day or two, depending on the weather, and then moving on. The Yellow Wagtail has many races distributed from Europe in the west to the eastern regions of the U.S.S.R.; and many of the various subspecies—and apparently intermediates between the races—pass through Iran, only a few, particularly of the Black-headed race, staying on to breed.

The Waxwing, so well-known to West European observers as a winter invader in occasional years, is only a vagrant to Iran; but an unusual bird (in that it is classified by the systematists as an aberrant species although near the Waxwings) is found along the Persian Gulf and in the south-west. This is the Grey Hypocolius, a slightly smaller bird than the Waxwing and one prone, like the latter, to make irregular migrations from its main centres in south-west Asia.

Two other genera, both rare and represented by a single species in Iran, are the King-Crow, found nesting only in south Balūchistān; and the Common Mynah—a relative of the well-known talking species so beloved as a cage-bird in the Far East and in Europe—which is resident in small numbers along the Persian Gulf. One wonders whether this resident population does not indeed stem originally from escaped cagebirds?

The last family to be considered is that of the Finches and Buntings. In addition to the normal species found in Europe which in Iran are largely, but not entirely, summer visitors and migrants, there are a number of attractive birds which will excite the interest of the ornithologist. These include the Red-fronted Finch, resident in the Alburz, the Desert Finch, the Trumpeter Bull-Finch, the Crimson-winged Bull-Finch and the White-winged Grosbeak, said to be also resident in the Alburz.

The Buntings, too, are largely summer visitors and passage migrants, some of them such as the White-capped, the Yellow-breasted and the House Buntings being very rare indeed. One of the commonest is the Black-headed, which was shown by Dr Paludan to hybridize with its Red-headed cousin in the area of Zarangul in North Khurāsān. Around Tehrān the foothills of the Alburz are alive in summer with Ortolan and Rock Buntings, both of them breeding in considerable numbers.

The above very brief survey of the birds of Iran will, it is hoped, give some idea of the variety of the avifauna to be found in the country and shows, to a limited degree, how it differs from that of Europe. There is little doubt that, for the amateur observer, Tehrān is the best place to be stationed since, within its immediate surrounds, an extremely representative selection of birds can be seen and, with occasional trips to the Caspian and into the desert, the numbers of species observed can be sharply increased. One of the main advantages of living in this area is that so many birds pass through on passage and, bearing climatic conditions in mind, it is possible to see huge falls of waders, ducks and small passerines as they traverse the area. The same, however, applies to a greater or lesser degree to the other principal cities of the country and there is no doubt that, for any amateur observer, there is vast scope and interest wherever he may live. For the professional the field is wide open, as there is a serious lack of definitive material on almost all aspects of ornithology in Iran, both in the general sense such as studies on migration, regional distribution, etc., and in the particular, of studies of individual species, their ecology, or breeding.

PART 2

THE PEOPLE

CHAPTER 12

EARLY MAN IN IRAN

Fossilized remains of early forms of man are rare in all parts of the world, and in this respect the Middle East is no exception. Claims have been made for Africa as the place of origin of humanity; other claims favour an Asian origin. As for the Middle East, "Here was the nursery of modern man (*Homo sapiens*) in an area equidistant from our two hypothetical cradles, one in Central Asia, the other in East-South Africa".[1] Field suggests that whilst the first man evolved in an area other than the Middle East—and the weight of the fossil evidence is now very much in favour of an African origin—the Middle East became the area where, in comparatively recent times, his modern form evolved.

Moreover it is virtually certain that the early forms of man, presumably of the *Pithecanthropus* variety, spread quickly and extensively through the tropical and subtropical areas of the Old World from one of the two proposed areas of origin (Africa or Asia)—and in either case, of necessity, via the Middle East. Early human migrations of great importance must therefore have occurred in this area, but as yet there is no fossil evidence from the Middle East as a whole, let alone Iran, for anything but the most limited traces of very early human occupations.

It has been claimed that "Stone Age Man" lived in and migrated across south-west Asia for perhaps 100,000 years, during which time rapid cultural advances occurred.[2] Field further asserts that this was the "Nursery of Man" where *Homo sapiens* developed, from which he subsequently migrated in every direction, and into which later immigration occurred. This may well be an oversimplification, since part of the sequence of development may have taken place in other Old World areas, possibly contemporaneously with the south-west Asian events. It is also possible that the evolution of modern man occurred elsewhere, and that these evolved *sapiens* forms later spread from eastern Asia or Africa, or both, into south-west Asia.

Since there is little fossil evidence for these processes in all South-

---

[1] H. Field, *Ancient and Modern Man in South Western Asia*, p. 165.
[2] *Ibid.* p. 163.

west Asia, it is evident that there must be extremely little available from Iran itself, or even from Iran together with contiguous parts of Iraq, Turkey, the U.S.S.R., and Afghanistan. But even this limited evidence is sufficient to prove that Palaeolithic man lived in many parts of Iran, ranging from Lake Rezā'īyeh [Urumiyeh] in the north-west to Shīrāz in the south-west, to the south-eastern littoral of the Caspian and eastward into southern Khurāsān.

A great deal of Lower Palaeolithic material has been found in south-west Asia, including Israel, Lebanon, Jordan, Syria, Saudi Arabia, and the Caucasus. None has yet been discovered in Iran itself, which is perhaps surprising in view of the extensive area known to have been occupied by Lower Palaeolithic man in Africa, Europe, and eastward into Asia.

The Middle Palaeolithic period is frequently identified with Neanderthal man and the Mousterian culture; and in South-west Asia, Neanderthaloid remains are known from Israel, Iraq, Turkey, and Iran. In terms of glacial chronology, Neanderthal man first appeared in both Europe and the Middle East towards the very end of the third or "Riss–Würm" interglacial period. Before this time Neanderthaloids are unknown, and so one may justifiably assert that during the third interglacial period a dramatic change occurred in the constitution of the population of the European and South-west Asian area.

Comparatively few fossil bones of third interglacial age and older are known in Europe. Among the finds are Heidelberg (first interglacial period); Swanscombe (second interglacial); Steinheim (third interglacial), and Ehringsdorf, Fontéchevade, Montmaurin, and Krapina (all third interglacial). Among other attributes this group of men, or possibly this number of racial groups, had brains that were modern in both sizes and shape, and at least some individuals had small faces in relation to total head size. This population, if in fact it is singular, has been termed "Archaic European".[1]

As regards the Middle East, very few remains have been discovered that are as old as those of the "Archaic Europeans", though certain finds probably fall into this category, such as those at Mughāret el Zuttiyeh, near the Lake of Galilee, and also some of the remains on Mt Carmel. As with some of their European contemporaries, these manifest affinities with modern European forms of man as well as with the long-extinct Neanderthaloids.

[1] C. S. Coon, *Seven Caves*, p. 301.

It is interesting to consider the relationships of the Neanderthaloids both with the "Archaic Europeans" and also with the subsequent peoples in this area of Europe and South-west Asia. Did the Neanderthaloids usurp their forerunners, and if so what was the fate of the earlier forms of men?

There are a number of theories suggesting the relationship between the Neanderthaloids and the men who lived before and after them, and these have been adequately summarized by Coon.[1] First, it has been put forward that the Neanderthaloids were descended from their European forerunners, and were later the ancestors of those men who followed them. This is a simple unilineal evolutionary scheme; and although the first part of the theory may be soundly based it is very difficult, if not impossible, to believe that so highly specialized a group as the Neanderthaloids ultimately became could have evolved into modern European forms of man.

Second, it has been claimed that from the original "Archaic European" population Neanderthaloids evolved in one direction whilst modern European man evolved in another. Their progressive specialization, both anatomical and physiological, in order to cope with the particular environment that existed towards the end of the Riss–Würm interglacial and during the Würm glacial period, eventually led to the extinction of the Neanderthaloids; for as environmental conditions changed, so alternative constitutional adaptations became more successful. These new forms were to appear as men of modern type.[2]

A third possibility is that the Neanderthaloids invaded Europe and South-west Asia from the Far East.[3] It is evident that the skeletons of early cave dwellers at Chou kou tien were in some respects like those of the later Neanderthaloids. For instance, the limb bones of the Chou kou tien skeletons had thick walls and thin channels, as in the Neanderthaloids, and features such as these are unlike those of the Europeans who either preceded or followed the Neanderthal form of man.

With the currently available evidence it is still impossible to indicate the origins of the Neanderthaloids who lived in Europe and South-west Asia. It is clear that the Neanderthaloids, both the eastern variety in Iran and in other parts of South-west Asia, and the western variety (of Europe in particular), were largely derived from the preceding

[1] *Ibid.* pp. 301 ff.
[2] W. E. le Gros Clark, *The Fossil Evidence for Human Evolution*, pp. 62–3.
[3] J. E. Welker, "Neanderthal Man and *Homo sapiens*", *Am. Anthrop.* (1954), pp. 1003–25.

Caucasoids of the last interglacial; but "it is not certain whether the distinctive Neanderthal traits, both cranial and post-cranial, arose through mutation and selection alone, or were introduced into Europe and western Asia by mixture with a non-Caucasoid population".[1] Their subsequent fate is clearer, for they were probably absorbed into the populations of southern Europe, the Middle East, and possibly North Africa at some time during the middle of the Würm glacial period. The Middle East Neanderthal type seems to have overflowed into Africa, for there is marked similarity among the men of Shanidar, Amud, Haua Fteah, and even Djebel Mirud in Morocco. The Neanderthaloids seem to have favoured the comparatively mild areas of western and southern Europe, and few of their remains are found in colder regions. However, some of them lived on the western slopes of the Zagros mountains in Iraq and Iran, as well as in areas to the north of the Alburz and Hindu Kush mountains in Iran, Soviet Central Asia, and Afghanistan.

In 1949 C. S. Coon excavated the cave of Bīsitūn, located some thirty miles east of Kirmānshāh, and in it he discovered one ulna fragment and one human incisor tooth, in association with a highly developed Mousterian industry. The implements would seem to be Middle Palaeolithic flakes; thus Bīsitūn was evidently occupied during the Würm glaciation and probably during Würm I. No absolute dating is available since the application of the carbon-14 method was impracticable there.

During the period of occupation, the men of Bīsitūn became increasingly skilful craftsmen. This Middle Palaeolithic flake industry is broadly comparable with such industries in Syria, northern Iraq, and Israel, except that implements in Bīsitūn are more limited in number and variety. Moreover, there is in Bīsitūn a much higher proportion of blades than in the other areas, suggesting either that the industry here was later and so more highly evolved, or else that Bīsitūn was an isolated settlement where the people independently invented and modified their own variants of a widespread tool assemblage, whilst other techniques with similar tools were being invented and perfected elsewhere. The blade-users of Europe were making comparatively far more advanced tools during the Würm I–II interstadial period. An isolated site in Iran, "Bisitun appeared to have been off the main line of history".[2]

Tamtameh is a cave at 5,000 ft located some thirteen miles north-west of

[1] C. S. Coon, *The Origin of Races*, p. 576.   [2] Coon, *Seven Caves*, p. 125.

Lake Rezā'īyeh, and in it a small number of flint fragments were discovered. These unworked pieces of flint had been struck off their cores, as at Bīsitūn, suggesting that people with the same culture lived at both sites, although the Tamtameh group might have been less proficient tool-manufacturers. In this cave a fragment of a human femur was also found.[1]

Again, Palaeolithic implements of the same general kind as at Bīsitūn (in this case patinated Mousterian implements) were found near Khurnik, a village on the Zābul–Mashhad road and in the so-called "Sarakhs corridor".[2] Had any considerable Palaeolithic migrations and other population movements occurred along the corridor during this period, it is very likely that there would have been archaeological remains in the area to mark such events. Yet the Khurnik industry, whilst basically resembling that of Bīsitūn, demonstrates mastery of even more sophisticated techniques; however, there is no evidence of a large-scale production of blades or of any production of burins. At Khurnik, as at some other contemporaneous sites in Iran, Neanderthal man or possibly some other Middle Palaeolithic form of man continued to survive for a considerable period, during which his tool-making techniques were very much perfected but without innovation or radical departures in style that might have come from contact with new ideas. In sum, this is quite unlike the tool equipment one would expect to find in a much-travelled corridor.

In 1933 W. E. Browne collected unstratified Middle Palaeolithic implements some twenty-seven miles from Lake Nairīz, south-east of Shīrāz at approximately 8,000 ft above sea-level. Nairīz, now salt lake, may have been a freshwater lake in Middle Palaeolithic times.

At most of the sites so far considered, there is much evidence of a Middle Palaeolithic flint industry and very much less skeletal material. What there is consists of the strongly bowed fragment of ulna and the incisor tooth from Bīsitūn and the piece of femur shaft from Tamtameh. "I am not certain that these three specimens belonged to Neanderthals, although the ulna fragment looks as if it did; all I know is that some kind of man lived in or near the Zagros Mountains during Würm I or the Würm I–II Interstadial."[3] The contemporaries of this man favoured southern and south-western Europe, which possibly constituted

[1] Coon, "Cave Exploration in Iran, 1949", *Univ. Museum Memoirs*, Univ. of Pennsylvania, Philadelphia (1951), pp. 1–124.
[2] Coon, *Seven Caves*, p. 127. [3] Coon, *The Origin of Races*, p. 562.

one of the Neanderthaloids' main living areas; but some men of this type lived in regions to the east of this primary area, extending into Soviet Central Asia if not beyond. The probable Neanderthaloid men of the Iranian sites "lived on the frontiers of the Palaeolithic world past the time when, in certain other places, men of our own race had begun making a large variety of tools, using blades instead of flakes . . ."[1] During the Würm glaciation, Bīsitūn was "a rustic refuge inhabited by already outmoded types of humanity".[2]

Flints of the general Bīsitūn variety were found by Garrod in 1928, some 120 miles north-west of Bīsitūn in the cave of Hazār Mard in Iraqi Kurdistān. Again, teeth of the Neanderthaloid type have been discovered in Turkey in a Mousterian deposit, in a cave near Adalia on the southern coast of Anatolia.[3] Bostanci found three such teeth in a lake-shore cave at the foot of the Musā Dāgh, some 700 miles to the east-north-east.[4] These widely separated sites indicate the presence of Neanderthal man and his Mousterian culture in Turkey, which was thus part of the eastern area of his distribution.

To date, however, the principal eastern site at which the Neander-thaloid–Mousterian complex has been revealed is Shanīdār, where Solecki found seven Neanderthal skeletons between 1953 and 1960. Shanīdār is a large cave in the western Zagros of northern Iraq which has been intermittently occupied from Würm I times onward. In the cave's Mousterian deposits, Solecki found a baby's skeleton in 1953, three adult skeletons in 1957, and three more in 1960. Absolute dates are available for this cave, by the use of the carbon-14 method. The skeletons found in 1957 are termed Shanīdār 1, 2, and 3. Shanīdār 1 has a C14 age of 46,000 ± 1,500 years; Shanīdār 3 is probably a few hundred years older, while Shanidar 2 and the baby are probably about 60,000 years old. The 1960 skeletons are probably 60,000 years old or older.[5]

The remains are undoubtedly those of Neanderthaloids; and as has been pointed out, both Shanīdār 1 and 3 lived late in Würm I within "what has always been a marginal refuge area", and certainly too late

[1] Coon, *Seven Caves*, p. 126.
[2] *Ibid.*
[3] M. S. Senyürek, "A Short Preliminary Report on the Two Fossil Teeth from the Cave of Karain", *Belleten* (1949), pp. 833–6.
[4] Senyürek and E. Bostanci, "The Excavation of a Cave near the Village of Magracik in the Vilayet of the Hatay", *Anatolia* (1956), pp. 81–3.
[5] R. Solecki, "Three Adult Neanderthal Skeletons from Shanidar Cave, Northern Iraq", *Smithsonian Report Publication* (1959–60), pp. 603–35.

to have been possible ancestral forms for modern man.[1] Moreover some of the finds, especially S̲h̲anīdār 1, are classic Neanderthaloids and therefore improbable ancestors for *Homo sapiens*.

The skeleton of a young Neanderthaler was found in 1938 in Mousterian deposits in the cave of Teshik Tash, located in a gorge in the Baisun-Tau mountains of south-west Uzbekistan, approximately eighty miles south of Samaqand and sixty miles north of the Afghan frontier. The skeleton probably dates from the Würm I–II interstadial period, when the climate was very much like today's and there was a modern fauna and a fully developed Mousterian industry. Such a dating, if correct, indicates that this skeleton is contemporaneous with the Upper Palaeolithic blade culture found in the Afghanistan cave of Kara Kamar near Haibak.

The Teshik Tash skull distinctly resembles that of a western Neanderthaler, though it is morphologically more "modern" than those of most, if not all, the western Neanderthalers, particularly because it has a higher cranial vault. This is the type of skull one would expect to find in a Neanderthal population less specialized than that of western Europe, either because the specialization never occurred, or else because the specialized features were lost in the evolutionary process, perhaps by admixture with features of a more modern type of human being. The post-cranial skeleton is even more developed than the skull itself. Altogether the find is of considerable significance, since "it bears witness to the fact that the Neanderthaler lived (in Würm I–II times) in the interior of the Asian continent in an environment that differed little from that of today".[2] On the other hand, "The finds from Teshik Tash and S̲h̲anīdār do not support, nor do they completely disprove, the theory of mixture with Sinanthropus-descended Mongoloids across the mountain spine of North Central Asia".[3]

In Europe the climate of the Würm I–II or "Göttenweig" interstadial period (c. 40,000–29,000 B.C.) was rather like that of the present-day. During this period important racial and cultural changes occurred, for the Neanderthaloids were replaced by Upper Palaeolithic people who essentially resembled modern Europeans; and the Mousterian flake culture was succeeded by a blade culture, which was to assume many forms and to last until the close of the Pleistocene era around 8,000 B.C. Similar but not identical Upper Palaeolithic blade cultures

---

[1] Coon, *The Origin of Races*, p. 565.   [2] M. Nesturkh, *The Origin of Man*, p. 256.
[3] Coon, *The Origin of Races*, p. 576.

occurred in Siberia, parts of Afghanistan, the Iraqi–Iranian Zagros, Turkey, Syria, Lebanon, and Israel. Upper Palaeolithic man had a specialized tool kit of flakes and especially burins, which in no way resembled the Neanderthal kit of his predecessors, and was very much superior to it.

The question of the geographical and hence biological origin of the newcomers again poses itself. They could not have been direct descendants of the Neanderthaloids, either in Europe or elsewhere. One is therefore seemingly presented with two alternative explanations. Either the newcomers could have been descendants of the "Archaic Europeans", e.g. of Fontéchevade and Krapina, who had lived on somewhere during the Neanderthal interlude and then returned to areas formerly occupied by their ancestors; or the newcomers may have moved into Europe and western Asia from some other geographical area where they had separately evolved their distinctive physical features and their blade-making culture. It is theoretically feasible to accept either explanation. Which ever is favoured, the Middle Eastern sites may well yield valuable data with regard to the flake-blade evolutionary sequence from the Middle to the Upper Palaeolithic, possibly accompanied by skeletal material showing both modern European and other features—Neanderthaloid and/or "Archaic European".

Upper Palaeolithic man and his cultures were very widely distributed throughout South-west Asia. During a period dated approximately 15,000 to 25,000 years ago, this "Aurignacian" man wandered extensively along the Mediterranean coastal areas, the Fertile Crescent, the shores of the Caspian, and in other places. It has been claimed that the origins of Upper Palaeolithic culture have been determined in a general way; and Coon ascribes to both the culture and its associated racial types an Asian origin, with a subsequent introduction to Europe. "The only part of the Old World in which a blade culture is known to have arisen from a flake culture in Würm I is the Near East—Palestine, Syria, Lebanon and possibly Western Iran."[1]

There is a detailed review of the literature on this subject available,[2] as well as a consideration of the Iranian material.[3]

The geographical distribution of the Upper Palaeolithic sites is

[1] Coon, The Origin of Races, p. 578.
[2] F. C. Howell, "Upper Pleistocene Stratigraphy and Early Man in the Levant", Proc. Am. Phil. Soc. (1959), pp. 1–65.
[3] R. J. Braidwood, B. Howe and C. A. Reed, "The Iranian Prehistoric Project", Science (1961), pp. 2008–10.

similar to that of the Neanderthaloid sites of the Middle Palaeolithic, since areas of extreme environmental difficulty in Würm I would have been equally difficult in Würm II, III, and later.

In general there is very little Upper Palaeolithic skeletal material from western Asia, but some of the important finds in the area are in Iran. The first bones of these men of modern, non-Neanderthal type were found by Coon in Hotu cave, where three skeletons, one male and two female, were excavated. These are indistinguishable from their European contemporaries in the Dordogne, Grimaldi, and other sites. The Hotu finds may be variously described as Upper Palaeolithic, Mouillian, or Capsian. According to the C^{14} dating from the earth found under skulls 2 and 3, all the finds are 9,335 years old. That is, this cave together with the nearby Belt cave were dry enough to be inhabited around 10,000 years ago, in the closing stages of the last glacial period in Europe. The Pleistocene deposit shows a sequence of four gravels and three intervening sands above a succession of three complexes of red gravels and sands, all underlain by black humus. The fauna shows an alternation of wet and dry forms. Flints included an assemblage of cores, flakes, flake blades, and blades, some of Aurignacian type; whilst the skeletons were found in the lowest gravel bed. The man was placed in the general Cromagnon category; the females seem to represent an adapted form from the Upper Palaeolithic period, with no trace of the Neanderthaloid characters shown, for instance, by the two Mesolithic skeletons from Belt cave.

In terms of European chronology the lowest level in Hotu is, or could be called, very late Upper Palaeolithic; but it is technologically Mesolithic, especially since it is characterized by the presence of the bow and the dog. This Mesolithic, however, is earlier than that in northwest Europe. Both the implements and the animal bones from the lowest deposits of Hotu could have come from the Seal Mesolithic of Belt cave, which has the same C^{14} date. Moreover, the people who lived in Hotu from its first occupation, through the so-called "Red 1" period, were very probably similar to the Belt cave seal-hunters; and their tool-making tradition was like that of the so-called "vole-eaters" who followed them after a considerable time interval.

The gazelle-hunters of Belt cave could also have shared this tool-making tradition. Moreover, of course, the Belt Mesolithic can be compared in detail with that from Shanīdār; and the two assemblages, in addition to being very similar, are also of approximately the same date.

C¹⁴ dates for vole-eaters

3 skeletons	9,190 ± 590 B.P.*	7,240 B.C.
2 other samples	9,220 ± 570 B.P.	7,270 B.C.

C¹⁴ for seal-hunters

11,860 ± 840 B.P.   9,910 B.C.[1]

* B.P. = Before Present.

The Belt cave, otherwise known as Ghār-i-Kamarband, is located five miles west of Behshahr and about 120 ft above the level of the Caspian. The Mesolithic material here lay beneath Neolithic strata and it dates from approximately 10,000–5,600 B.C.

C¹⁴ dates for Gazelle Mesolithic

2 samples   8,570 ± 380 B.P.   6,620 B.C.

C¹⁴ for seal Mesolithic

2 samples   11,480 ± 550 B.P.   9,530 B.C.

The flints are primarily blades, including scrapers and many beautifully retouched geometric specimens. The human skeletal material from the Gazelle Mesolithic is basically modern in type, but it also reveals some Neanderthaloid traits as, for example, in the region of the mouth of a twelve-year-old girl whose skeleton was found there.

The Ghār-i-Kamarband material tells us little of the fate of Neanderthal man, or of the origins of the Upper Palaeolithic blade-making peoples who lived farther west. Yet it gives much information concerning the Mesolithic and Neolithic peoples and cultures of this area.

It appears that early in post-glacial times the shores of the Caspian constituted an important passageway of east–west movement of peoples. This is geographically understandable; the archaeological material is confirmatory.

Some of the sites already mentioned—for instance, Bīsitūn—contain no Upper Palaeolithic material. In others the Upper Palaeolithic stratigraphy is unsatisfactory. However, in northern Afghanistan at Kara Kamar there is a properly stratified Upper Palaeolithic flint-blade industry in which the blades are broadly comparable with those of the Upper Palaeolithic of Syria, Palestine, and Iraq, though the Kara Kamar assemblage contains a much smaller number of specialized tools, many more crudely worked pieces, and no burins. The key tool

---

[1] E. K. Ralph, "Univ. of Pennsylvania Radiocarbon Dates I", *Science* (1955), pp. 149–51.

here is the fluted steep scraper, and specimens found at Kara Kamar are indistinguishable from those found in Iraq, Palestine, and Syria. In fact it is difficult to believe that there was no cultural connexion between northern Afghanistan and the eastern shores of the Mediterranean during Upper Pleistocene and Upper Palaeolithic times.

The carbon-14 age for Kara Kamar is more than 34,000 years, which makes the culture contemporaneous with most of the western European blade industries, though it doesn't tell us which of the two is older, nor what was the precise relationship, if any, between European settlements and the Kara Kamar and Levant series. There is a considerable geographical gap between Kara Kamar and the Aurignacian material of Shanīdār, in which very little Upper Palaeolithic material is known. The sites of Hazār Mard and Zārzī, south of Shanīdār, do contain implements which resemble those of Belt, Hotu, and Kara Kamar; and Upper Palaeolithic (Aurignacian) skeletal remains are known from Devis Khreli in Georgia, but the geographical discontinuity previously mentioned is still a very real one. Interestingly enough, it has been suggested that the search for caves and shelters in which Palaeolithic man might have lived should be concentrated within the Shīrāz–Mashhad–Zāhidān triangle, and particularly within the Bam–Kūh-i-Taftān area.[1]

In 1950 the Peabody Museum–Harvard Expedition conducted a reconnaisance survey in Khūzistān and Luristān during which flint implements were found at Minūchihrābād, south-west of Dizfūl; at Papīleh, south-east of Dizfūl; Sārib-Darreh, seven miles south-west of Khurramābād; and in two rock shelters overlooking Khurramābād. In one of the latter, the Kunjī rock shelter, 300 ft above the valley floor, Upper Palaeolithic implements were found.

Yet in Kara Kamar, which is 1,500 miles east of the nearest known site of the same general class (i.e. Shanīdār), there are carinated steep scrapers and nosed scrapers characteristic of the Aurignacian phase of the Upper Palaeolithic cultures of Palestine and Europe. The people of Kara Kamar, of whom there are no skeletal remains, either had a poor tool assemblage or else they did not leave a comprehensive sample of their tools in the cave.

The Kara Kamar tool sequence is difficult to date precisely, since it comprises, respectively, crude flakes, Upper Palaeolithic blades, then more crude flakes, and lastly Mesolithic blades. All the material from

---

[1] H. Field, *Ancient and Modern Man in South Western Asia*, pp. 127, 230.

this site, apart from the Mesolithic, is over 34,000 years old (see p. 405 above); and this C¹⁴ figure is based on five samples from the blade and steep-scraper culture, which is very similar to the Aurignacian material, including steep scrapers, found at Shanīdār. The steep-scraper material at Mt Carmel has no C¹⁴ date since the technique was unknown at the time of excavation. The Kara Kamar blade culture is probably from early in Würm II. Although much excavation has been undertaken in contiguous Soviet areas to the north, nothing comparable with the Kara Kamar material has yet been found there.

It may be that the Kara Kamar people, too, were an isolated eastern group of a predominantly more westerly distributed Upper Palaeolithic population. This is perfectly feasible, for there is evidence of considerable population movement in the whole of south-west Asia during the Palaeolithic period. At the height of the Würm I glaciation, for example, Shanīdār was probably deserted, to be re-occupied by Upper Palaeolithic people no more than *c.* 35,000 years ago during the Würm I–II interstadial period. Similarly, in Afghanistan a group may have wandered into the Kara Kamar area from elsewhere, and might have been subsequently isolated there once its mobility was limited by environmental changes.

The Mesolithic material from Kara Kamar is meagre, comprising but fifty-eight definitely used tools. The assemblage closely resembles that from the Seal Mesolithic of Belt cave at the closing stages of the Würm glacial period. The C¹⁴ dating method gives values of 10,580 ± 720 B.P., or 8,630 B.C., for the Kara Kamar Mesolithic, which are similar to the values for the Hotu Mesolithic sequence and thus somewhere between the time of the seal-hunters and that of the two female skeletons. The Shanīdār Mesolithic is 12,000 ± 400 B.P., or 10,450 ± 400 B.C. The Kara Kamar Mesolithic therefore appears to have been an early phase of the general culture. The findings from Kara Kamar, Belt, Hotu, and Shanīdār show that this early Mesolithic was distributed from the north-west Zagros mountains to the Caspian shores, and from there to the northern slopes of the Hindu Kush mountains.

Thus towards the end of the last glacial period, people living on the fringes of the northern Eurasian area in Iraq–Iran–Afghanistan and contiguous areas had already become Mesolithic hunters, and by that time some areas like the Caspian shores of Iran might have become important avenues for human movement and migration. With the post-glacial climatic amelioration, this Mesolithic way of life was to spread into more northerly parts of Eurasia, where it was to persist until the coming of the Neolithic farmers from about 3,000 B.C. onward. The Neolithic culture, like the Mesolithic culture before it, was established earlier in restricted localities of the south than in areas to the north, because southern climatic conditions could more quickly support the Neolithic way of life. It has been claimed that the place of origin of the Neolithic is probably "a few miles at most from Belt and Hotu".[1] Certainly the Neolithic C[14] ages from these caves are among the most ancient yet known. The Neolithic dates in this region are much earlier than those of Europe, and according to Coon the Caspian area could well be the place from which the European Neolithic, was derived. With much more certainty one might claim Iran and contiguous areas of South-west Asia generally as the area of origin, since Neolithic men were widespread in the whole region, from the shores of the Mediterranean to the Caspian and beyond.

The highest rubbles at Hotu seem to be unique, for they include very coarse flint implements and the bones either of domesticated animals or of animals in the process of being domesticated. This culture is termed the "Sub-Neolithic", and it dates from between the truly Mesolithic and the Neolithic industries of the Belt cave. Also from the Hotu cave the skeleton of a Neolithic male and those of two infants were excavated. One of the Hotu dates, 6,135 ± 1,500 B.C., is among the oldest Neolithic dates known. Other Neolithic dates are known from the Belt cave:[2]

Ceramic Neolithic. 3 samples. 7,280 ± 260 B.P. 5,330 B.C.

Pre-Ceramic Neolithic. 2 samples. 7,790 ± 330 B.P. 5,840 B.C.

For Hotu cave there are comparable figures:[3]

Software Neolithic. 6,385 ± 425 B.P. 4435 B.C.

Sub-Neolithic. 8,070 ± 500 B.P. 6120 B.C.

From these early beginnings the Neolithic record is continuous. For instance, "the Neolithic specimens began with the soft ware of the Upper Neolithic of Belt Cave and continued into a transition to painted pottery similar to Sialk II".[4] Continuity from both these early men and their cultures to their descendants is well known and authenticated, especially in Iran and also in South-west Asia generally.

It should perhaps be noted that in Hotu the Painted Pottery level is given a C[14] date of 4,830 ± 480 B.P. Subsequently twelve Iron Age

---

[1] Coon, *Seven Caves*, p. 299.   [2] *Ibid.* p. 266.   [3] *Ibid.* p. 197.
[4] H. Field, *Ancient and Modern Man*, p. 126.

samples were dated from 2,685 ± 210 B.P. to 2,950 ± 230 B.P. The 2,000 years separating the Painted Pottery from the Early Iron Age, elsewhere occupied by the Bronze Age, are not at all documented in the Caspian caves, which have otherwise told us so much of the evolution of man and his culture in Iran.

Now we reach the threshold of history, and in place of the meagre finds of human bones and artifacts which must suffice for the prehistoric period, there is a wealth of data which continues the tale of the evolution of man and his culture.

CHAPTER 13

GEOGRAPHY OF SETTLEMENT

A. GENERAL CONDITIONS OF SETTLEMENT

*The habitats of nomadic and settled peoples; natural environment
and present-day distribution*

The life of Iran is dominated above all by the disparity between the
nomadic peoples and those who are settled—between the shifting
habitat of the former and the permanent homes of the latter. The
ecological conditions responsible for this division are, broadly speaking,
well-known,[1] and a reasonably accurate delimitation has been possible,
especially of those regions where the rainfall permits regular cultivation
and permanent settlement.[2] These areas include the mountain chains
of the Caspian and of Khurāsān (south of the river Atrak); a large
part of Āzarbāījān (with the exception of the basins of the river
Aras and Lake Rezā'īyeh); and virtually the whole of the Zagros
mountains north-west of Shīrāz. Fārs is made up partly of cultivable
mountain slopes and partly of basins too arid for agriculture. Scattered
areas of rain-cultivation also exist in the south-eastern parts of the
Zagros, in the mountains of central Iran north of Yazd and Kirmān,
and in Kūhistān, over to the east of the country and north of Bīrjand.

Much less is known, however, of the distribution and the itineraries
of the great nomadic groups. One still has to rely above all on the data
gathered together in Field's massive compilation—a useful work even
though its geographical information is far from complete.[3] Nevertheless, a study of the facts relating to the two ways of life does lead one to
some remarkable conclusions. Though, understandably, there are but
few nomads in the humid, cultivable areas in the north of the country
and in the mountains of Āzarbāījān, and though their importance pre-
dictably increases when one comes to the arid regions of Balūchistān,
they are nevertheless few in number in the great deserts of east-central
Iran; while the huge nomadic confederations of the Qashghai, the

---

[1] H. Bobek, "Die Natürlichen Wälder...", *Bonner Geogr. Abhandl.* (1951); "Beiträge
zur Klima-ökologischen Gliederung...", *Erdkunde* (1952), pp. 65–84; and "Die Klima-
ökologische...", *Proc. 17th Int. Geogr. Congr.* (1952), pp. 244–8.

[2] Bobek, "Die Verbreitung des Regenfeldbaues...", *Festschrift J. Sölch* (1951), pp. 9–30.

[3] H. Field, *Contributions to the Anthropology of Iran*.

Bakhtīārī, and the Khamseh dominate the Zagros mountains, where climate might have been expected to favour cultivation and a settled way of life. Moreover, the remaining areas of the Zagros are inhabited principally by semi-nomads, Kurds or Lurs, who, while possessing permanent homes, occasionally undertake lengthy migrations along the mountain valleys, venturing well beyond the summer pasturage above their own villages.

The distribution thus appears to be to a large degree anomalous and contrary to the exigencies of the natural environment. The fundamental problem is to determine as far as possible what human and historical factors have combined to bring about such a state of affairs.

Historical factors contributing to the reduction of settled areas

(a) Ancient times

In prehistoric times and in the first recorded periods of man's occupation in Iran, i.e. the Neolithic and Bronze ages, the settled areas appear to have been much more extensive than they are now. Stein has noted that Luristān, which has for centuries been given over to the migrations of the semi-nomadic Lurs, was permanently settled during the two thousand years immediately prior to the Christian era;[1] yet since that time there seems to have been no perceptible variation in the boundaries of cultivable or irrigable land.[2] Bobek, who has examined the data of prehistoric settlement in the light of regional differences in climate and vegetation, has arrived at similar conclusions and confirmed that in many parts of the country, even including some semi-desert areas, settlement was once far more extensive than it is today.[3]

There is indeed abundant evidence pointing to a decline in the settled way of life—a decline continuing in comparatively recent periods as well as in the distant past. Frequently one comes across traces of former cultivation, now discontinued.[4] The prevalence of certain weeds, such as *Phlomis persica*, over large areas of the Zagros mountains between 1,500 and 2,000 m above sea-level strongly suggests that cultivation was once practised there.[5] A study of the technicalities of the black tent (certain forms of which, especially those in Balūchistān, seem to have derived directly from the arched huts of semi-nomadic peasants)

---

[1] A. Stein, *Old Routes of Western Iran*, p. x.   [2] Ibid. p. 221.
[3] H. Bobek, "Klima und Landschaft Irans . . .", *Geogr. Jahresb.* (1953–4), pp. 28–37.
[4] See E. Herzfeld, "Eine Reise durch Luristan, Arabistan, und Fars", *Peter. Mitt.*, p. 60; and C. G. Feilberg, *Les Papis*, p. 85.   [5] H. Pabot, *Rapport au Khuzistan* . . .

leads one to conclude that full and warlike nomadism developed out of a period of limited semi-nomadism.[1] Everywhere there is evidence of such changes.

It is much more difficult to date these transformations. Apart from anything else, they probably took place more than once. Bobek is inclined to think that the principal episode was the *Verreiterung*: the development of warlike nomadism that is known to have taken place mainly in the second half of the second millennium B.C.[2] And indeed the sparse information we have regarding the location of nomads and settled folk in the Achaemenid period tends to suggest that the nomads were restricted to a much smaller area than they occupy today. The account left to us by Herodotus shows that true nomads were relatively few in number. In the army of Xerxes they made up merely one tenth of the cavalry;[3] and their principal tribe, the Sargatians (the only tribe of any real significance in the army), came predominantly from the desert of south-east Iran—which should have been their true home; for all that elements of the same tribe are known to have existed in the Zagros mountains. The other tribes, the Mardeans, Dropitians, and Dahans, were backward peoples, referred to disparagingly as barbarians, rogues, and wretches.[4] The Mardeans are described as impure, hairy creatures of disgusting habits; they lived exclusively on the flesh of their herds and of animals they slew in the chase, and they sheltered in the depths of caverns.[5] These remnant peoples lived in widely scattered areas, particularly around the Caspian Sea, and appear to have been on the fringes of Iranian society, rather like the "tribes" of present-day India. This marginal character and the fact that the same essentially pejorative epithets could be applied to several quite unrelated groups are sufficient explanation of a ubiquity which certain writers have erroneously ascribed to complicated movements of population.[6]

Herodotus gives us a picture of a society composed overwhelmingly of settled people. In addition to the nomads, he speaks of tribes "which till the soil": Panthialeans, Derousians, Germanians, who each had certain peculiarities, though they were all basically similar to other Persians. The semi-nomadic tribes of the Zagros mountains were

---

[1] K. Ferdinand, "The Baluchistan Barrel-vaulted Tent," *Folk* (1959), pp. 27–50; and "Supplementary Material", *Folk* (1960), pp. 33–51.

[2] Bobek, *Geogr. Jahresb.* (1953–4), pp. 36 ff.   [3] Herodotus, *History*, VII, 84–7.

[4] Herodotus, I, 125; and see A. W. Lawrence's notes to Rawlinson's translation, reproduced in Field, *Anthropology*, vol. I, pp. 38–9.   [5] Quintus Curtius Rufus, *Works*, V, 6.

[6] Recently reiterated in the case of the Mardeans, in L. Dillemann, *Haute Mésopotamie Orientale* . . ., pp. 95–9.

integrated within the framework of the Achaemenid state. And though the pastoral peoples of more out-of-the-way areas must have been but lightly curbed (e.g. the Ouxians, a mountain people, exacted a toll even from the "Great King" himself),[1] the road from Persepolis to Ecbatana nevertheless ran through the very heart of the mountains, following the longitudinal valleys which afforded the most direct route. The situation today is very different: the main road from Shīrāz to Hamadān runs along the northern flank of the mountains.[2]

The way of life in the Zagros mountains seems to have been formed essentially by the gradual arrival, during the second and first millennia, of semi-nomadic Iranian tribes, pastoral folk who had more in common with the *Fahrer* (= wanderer) than the *Reiter* (= horsed warrior). Wagons being unsuitable for use in mountain valleys, oxen were the basic means of transport (they are still used in Luristān);[3] and they remained so in the mountainous regions of Iran until the seventeenth century, when it was the custom for them to be shod.[4] In the thirteenth century, Marco Polo commented admiringly on the virtues of the great white oxen of the country between Kirmān and Hurmuz.[5] Such journeying was very different from that of the true nomads, with their horses and camels. In the course of these complex migrations of peoples (which doubtless resulted in the ethnogenesis of the Kurds and the Lurs), there came into being the widespread semi-nomadism of the mountain valleys, which has so close a connexion with the present-day way of life.[6] Less sedentary than the shortlived pastoral village life of the Neolithic and Bronze ages, it was nevertheless in no way comparable with the wide-ranging nomadism of today's powerful confederations. The *Verreiterung*, whose influence was doubtless felt throughout the great Iranian desert and perhaps also in the arid south-eastern part of the Zagros, had in general little effect in mountainous regions.

(b) The rise of Bedouinism in the Middle Ages, and its consequences

In the Middle Ages there were massive invasions of nomads. Arabs came first, though their numbers were appreciable only in the coastal strip running along the Persian Gulf, and in *garmsīr* (= warm) regions

---

[1] Arrian, *Anabasis*, III, XVII, 2–5.
[2] As has been truly remarked by A. Gabriel, *Die Erforschung Persiens*, p. 9.
[3] Feilberg, *Les Papis*, p. 59.
[4] Chardin, *Voyages en Perse*, ed. Lecointe. Nouvelle Bibliothèque des voyages (Paris, 1830), vol. VI, p. 186.
[5] Ed. Hambis (Paris, 1955), p. 41.   [6] Feilberg, *Les Papis*.

where their dromedaries could travel with ease. Above all there were Turks and Mongols, who came down from the cold steppes and swept over almost the whole of the Iranian plateau. And it was these invasions that were principally responsible, both directly and indirectly, for reducing the number of agricultural settlements.

The medieval Arab geographers help us to follow these transformations.[1] The earliest of them, Iṣṭakhrī and Ibn Ḥauqal, writing in the tenth century, still name the Kurds as the principal nomads; and they also remark on the relative inferiority of their horses.[2] We are a long way from the Reiter. Iṣṭakhrī, who, with some exaggeration, says that the Kurds have half a million black tents and are scattered all over Persia, shows them seeking pasturage both summer and winter, after the manner of the Bedouin; but he adds that the tribes close to the limits of *sardsīr* (= cold lands) and garmsīr do not migrate.[3] Ibn Ḥauqal makes the same observation with regard to all the people of the garmsīr: these folk do not wander far, but seek summer pastures within the limits of the territory they occupy. In the Fārs, nomads occupy only four clearly defined districts, each one centred upon a permanent habitat. These people were in fact only semi-nomads, and in one of the "nomadic" areas (that of Bāzandjān, north-west of Shīrāz) the herds of the distant governor of Iṣfahān mingled with those of the local inhabitants.[4] Farther to the east, the country south-east of Jīruft (stretching from Hurmuz in the west to Makrān in the east) was occupied by the Qufṣ, who were brigands rather than nomads; we are told that they travelled more often on foot than on horseback.[5] No significant numbers of nomads are mentioned as being present elsewhere. The mountains of Āzarbāijān were occupied by the Kurds, who carried out regular migrations along the flanks of the ranges—in the Savalan, for example, where the first Arab invaders undertook not to interfere with their movements.[6] If we are to believe all that Iṣṭakhrī has to say about the Kurds (though he seems to exaggerate somewhat), it would appear that they had already begun to practise long-range nomadism, doubtless as a result of the Arabs' invasion of the Zagros area. But even at this

---

[1] The information they give is conveniently gathered together in Schwarz's monumental work, *Iran im Mittelalter*.

[2] Iṣṭakhri 115, 7; in Schwarz, vol. III, p. 155.

[3] Iṣṭakhri, 115, 6; Ibn Ḥauqal, 186, 17: for all of this see Schwarz, III, pp. 155–7.

[4] After Ibn Khurdādbeh: see Schwarz, III, pp. 135–9.

[5] Iṣṭakhri, 164, 4; Ibn Ḥauqal, 221, 1: see Schwarz, III, pp. 260–7, and V. Minorsky, *Hudūd al-'Ālam*, p. 374 on "*Kūfich, Qufs*".

[6] Belādsori, 326, 4; Yāqūt, I, 160, 21: see Schwarz, VIII, pp. 1246 ff.

date a tendency towards a more settled way of life can be observed. Qundurīja, near Usnūh, was founded by the Kurds.[1]

Later authors leave us with a rather different picture, in which true nomads, the Türkmen, make their appearance and, with the passing of time, seize upon vast areas of land. The Mughān-steppes, to the south of the river Aras, are a particularly good example. Ibn al-Faqīh, Iṣṭakhrī, and Ibn Ḥauqal all know Mughān as a small town; in the same period Muqaddasī gives a flattering description of it; while to Yāqūt, the Mughān is a region, inhabited principally by Türkmen and remarkable above all for its numerous pastures, though towns still exist there. For Qazvīnī, it was no more than a winter home for the Tartars (Mongols), who had over-run the Türkmen.[2]

That is an example of direct Bedouinization. But the indirect results were of no less importance. One of the principal changes that came about, apparently as a result of the Saljuq invasion, was the Bedouinization of Balūchistān. The Balūchīs were probably of northern origin; linguistic arguments have recently been adduced in support of the theory that they came from the regions to the north of the Great Kavīr.[3] From there they were driven by the earliest Turkish invasion into Kirmān, where they were reported by the Arab geographers of the eleventh and twelfth centuries. The Saljuq conquest of Kirmān and then the Mongol invasion pushed them farther to the east, into the Sīstān and the Makrān, where they submerged the Dravidian-speaking peoples who had inhabited those regions from time immemorial.

At all events, a crucial period seems to have followed on the ravages and devastation caused by the Mongol invasion. In many regions the peasants were obliged to leave their homes and adopt a nomadic way of life. Marco Polo, whose travels date from this period, has left us valuable evidence of villages being abandoned in the mountains to the south of Kirmān—an area frequented even today only by wandering shepherds.[4] A highly significant text describes the "flight to the mountains" undertaken in Luristān by settled people who turned to nomadism and adopted a way of life similar to that of the invaders.[5] It is not surprising

---

[1] Schwarz, VIII, p. 1249.

[2] Ibn al Faqīh, 285, 17; Iṣṭakhri, 182, 1; Ibn Ḥauqal, 239, 13; Muqaddasi, 259, 10; Yāqūt, 5,226; Qazvīnī, 2,379, 8: all in Schwarz, VIII, pp. 1086–94.

[3] R. W. Frye, "Remarks on Baluchi History", *Central Asiatic J.* (1961), pp. 44–50.

[4] Ed. Hambis, *Travels*, p. 40.

[5] Here is the text, which deserves to be quoted in full: "Section on the Atabegs of the Great Lur . . . One of the reasons for the prosperity of the country was the fact that the Atabeg Shams al-Dīn adopted the yailāq and qishlāq system after the fashion of the

that the Turkish words for winter quarters and summer quarters, *qishlāq* and *yailāq*, should have passed, with no change of meaning, into the Iranian language.

The full consequences of this Bedouinization did not, however, make themselves felt immediately; this was a process that continued intermittently until very recent times, as a result of the movements, depredations, and conflicts of the various nomadic groups. Even in the early years of the twentieth century the oases of Nih and Dih Salm, in the Lūt desert, were laid waste by marauding Balūchīs.[1] The policy of large-scale tribal displacement carried out by certain rulers—Nādir Shāh and the early Qājār monarchs in particular—also tended to prolong the period of instability.

Small groups of settled people remained as islands amid the rising tide of nomadism: sadly depleted, turned in upon themselves, and hanging on to areas that were particularly suitable for their way of life. Thus nomads occupied the southern and western parts of the great Damāvand massif, where there are many traditions and much evidence to show that cultivation was carried on in ancient times. This area became a favourite yailāq of the Tartars, who wintered on the southern slopes of the Alburz mountains; and it was here that Clavijo, the Spanish ambassador to the court of Tīmūr, in 1404 visited that prince's son-in-law, whom he found leading a horde of nomads estimated at three thousand tents. In the middle of the nineteenth century these same grassy slopes were a favourite summer retreat of the Qājār monarchs. All the while, however, in a small region upon the northern and eastern slopes of the volcanic cone a few settled village dwellers were tenaciously existing on terraces cut out of the tuff above the precipitous Harāz gorge; this district, Lārījān, thus commanded one of the essential routes between the Iranian plateau and the Caspian, and was the base for a small principality which remained virtually independent of Tehrān until the middle of the nineteenth century.[2]

Mongols. He wintered at Idaj and Susa and in summer came to Kūh-i Zardak, which is the source of the Zanda [Zāyandeh] Rūd. Thus, the animals did not need barley, and the peasants were not exposed to the violence of whosoever first came upon them", *Muntahab al-tavārīh-i Mu'īnī*, ed. J. Aubin (Tehrān, 1957), p. 44. The work was composed in A.D. 1414–15, and the events here recounted took place in the period 1260–70. I am grateful to Jean Aubin for this text.

[1] G. Stratil-Sauer, "Route durch die Wüste Lut . . .", *Abhandlungen der geogr. Gesellsch.* (1956), p. 20.

[2] All the references to the Bedouinization of Damāvand and the resistance of Lārījān are gathered in X. de Planhol, *Recherches sur la Géographie Humaine de l'Iran Septentrional*, ch. 2, sec. A.

Only one region of major significance escaped these upheavals: the damp, wooded areas near the Caspian offered an almost insurmountable biogeographical barrier to the advance of the nomads, and the only ones to penetrate were wretched detribalized groups or individuals frequently reduced to an artisan condition similar to that of the Tziganes.[1] Situated between drier and forest-like areas—in the west were the Mughān steppes, which served as winter pasture for the nomads who summered in the uplands of Āzarbāījān; in the east was Gurgān and the turbulent frontier with the Türkmen of the Atrak—Māzandarān and Gīlān formed a fever-ridden "jungle" which remained but sparsely peopled until the fostering of colonies by Shāh 'Abbās and Muḥammad Shāh Qājār. But the continuity of human occupation there was never interrupted, and the seeds of today's vast demographic accumulations were thus preserved.

Towards the settling of the nomads

With this exception, the settled areas emerged considerably reduced from this period of unrest. But their recovery, though slow, had an early beginning. From the thirteenth century the Jurmā'ī, qualified as Mongols, are reported to be in the process of settling in the garmsīr of Lār (Kurbāl).[2] This tendency towards *spontaneous settlement* on the part of the nomads continued without a break, reinforcing a sedentary population whose territorial expansion nevertheless remained extremely slow. The apparent contradiction in this has recently been resolved in a decisive way by Barth's excellent studies of the Bāṣirī. The explanation lies basically in the fact that the nomads, who lived a relatively healthy life and were spared the worst ravages of epidemics, developed large population surpluses; and these groups found themselves obliged to settle after all available pasture land had reached saturation-point. Conversely, the ill-health which prevailed among settled peoples right up to the beginning of the twentieth century seems to have excluded any possibility of numerical increase, and thus they could easily absorb those surplus nomads who were being continuously expelled from their own, nomadic communities.[3]

Though the advances in peasants life prior to the last fifty years were

---

[1] See, for example, G. Melgunof, *Das südliche Ufer des Kaspischen Meeres* . . ., p. 212; and De Planhol, *Recherches*, p. 56.

[2] J. Aubin, "Références pour Lar médiévale", *J. Asiatique* (1955), pp. 491–505.

[3] F. Barth, *Nomads of South Persia*, chs. 7, 10.

slight, they were nonetheless sufficient to cause relations between nomads and settled people to be reorganized on a new footing. The sharing of pasture land among nomad groups living at maximum density amid increasing numbers of fixed settlements called for the most detailed regulation—indeed a calendar had to be worked out to control migratory movements and the pastoral groups' successive tenure of grazing land along the trail. A considerable degree of co-operation was also rendered necessary among the nomads if they were to resist the country's growing central political authority, concerned always to extend its power and protect the peasants, who were a profitable source of taxation. The progress of sedentary life thus brought about those great nomadic confederations which became the characteristic feature of the Zagros.[1] The Qashghai make their appearance in 1415, in summer quarters to the south-west of Iṣfahān;[2] but the main development of the confederation did not begin until the seventeenth century. The organization of the Bakhtiārī must also have taken place about the seventeenth century, while the confederation of the Khamseh—which was created by the Qavām family, merchants of Shīrāz, in order to protect caravans and balance the power of the Qashghai—dates only from the middle of the nineteenth century. These huge groupings remained essentially pastoral in character; but at the same time, as a result of the periodic expulsion of their surplus members, other settlements were founded upon the nomads' territory: meagre hamlets which remained strictly subordinate to the tribal leaders.

A new phase opened in the twentieth century. Population growth in settled communities inevitably restricted the areas that wandering tribes could claim; and the sharing of pasturage required stricter organization than before. As the seasons passed, successive groups of nomads, in accordance with time-tables stipulating the altitude at which they should travel, would occupy an area of pasture land, with one group arriving hard upon the departure of another.[3] Conflicts with settled communities became more frequent. With the eventual strengthening of the central authority, the Pahlavī dynasty (1920) sought to ensure their control of the nomads by means of *imposed settlement*. The first attempt at this was made by Reẓā Shāh, but little is known of this venture. Travellers who were able to visit the Zagros in the thirties,[4] however,

---

[1] Aubin, *J. Asiatique* (1955).
[2] Barth, "The Land Use Pattern of Migratory Tribes of South Persia", *N. Geogr. Tids.* (1959–60), pp. 1–11.   [3] Barth, *op. cit.*
[4] Stein, *Old Routes*; and K. Lindberg, *Voyage dans le Sud de l'Iran* (the journey dates from 1940).

have left us moving accounts of tents being destroyed by the authorities and replaced with dead-straight rows of mud huts. Some of the more artful nomads hid their tents in ravines and were soon forsaking their homes, at least during the summer months.[1] The utter lack of consideration for the wishes of the people who were placed in settlements in the sardsīr or garmsīr; the hardships which the forced settlers had to undergo in winter, often at altitudes approaching 1,800 m;[2] the high death rate among their cattle (Barth has shown that in cases of brutal settlement, whether in sardsīr or in garmsīr, the rate sometimes reached 70 to 80 per cent)—all these factors led to the complete failure of this first attempt to control the nomads. Following the abdication of Rezā Shāh and the consequent weakening of the central authority, the confederations reformed and went back to their old wanderings. A second phase of forced settlement began in 1957, though its spirit and its methods seemed little different from before. This time there seems to be no doubt about the final outcome, even if the price will be a heavy one.[3] It will take a long time for the enterprise to be brought to completion.

B. TYPES OF RURAL HABITAT

In the light of the general data outlined above, any classification of the types of human settlement in Iran must be made on a scrupulously genetic basis; and care should be taken to distinguish among the various forms arising at different periods, the marks of which are usually clearly recognizable in the landscape.

Ancient village settlements

A first grouping would thus include those long-established settlements which withstood Bedouinization both in the Middle Ages and in modern times. We are far from being able to present a detailed geographical picture of such settlements: this remains one of the major fields for research in Iran, for the need to distinguish among the various types of settled areas dominates any analysis of land utilization.[4] Nevertheless, a rough outline of the distribution may be given.

A certain number of large oases—Iṣfahān, Yazd, and Kirmān, for

---

[1] Stein, p. 303.   [2] Stein, p. 276; in the plain of Alishtar.
[3] C. Stauffer, "The Economics of Nomadism", *Middle East Journal* (1965), pp. 283–302.
[4] X. de Planhol, "Traits généraux de l'utilisation du sol dans l'Iran aride", *Actes Symp. Heraklion* (1962).

example, as well as others on the edge of the great desert—survived the Turk and Mongol invasions; they were saved by their size, which prevented their complete destruction and facilitated defence by means of roads bordered by thick hedges. Besides containing towns (which remained largely rural in function, though they surrounded themselves with fortifications), these oases also comprised numerous large, closely packed villages, which flanked water-courses or clustered about the outlets of qanāts. Unfortunately, research has not yet determined their internal organization or their relationship with the soil.

But the settled way of life endured above all in the mountainous regions of the north, particularly in the Alburz,[1] and in the massifs of Āzarbāījān, such as the Sahand;[2] in these latter areas the Turkish language gained ascendency without violence, which permitted a true continuity of rural life.[3] In other regions, too, such as Khurāsān[4] and Balūchistān,[5] and even in those areas which seem to have been most seriously devastated, ancient villages are still to be found, characterized by terrace cultivation and intensive agricultural techniques.

A number of detailed descriptions of these mountain villages have been given recently.[6] Even in a region where rainfall would be sufficient for cultivation, the position of the village is invariably characterized by the presence of an irrigable area, however small; and the resource of water (e.g. a spring) served as a focal point for the community. Considerations of defence and security do not seem generally to have influenced the siting of a village. As a rule, it is situated on the first rocky slopes rising above a valley floor, and these slopes are terraced and roughly divided into meadows by means of low dry-stone walls or willow hedges. In the volcanic region of Damāvand, as we have seen, some villages are sited upon ledges in the tuff above the deep gorge of Harāz. The central portion of the village land is laid out in irregular fields of lucerne and cereals; these are irrigated, intensively worked, terraced, kept free of stones, and regularly manured. Farther out the

---

[1] De Planhol, "Observations sur la geogr. humaine", *Bull. Assoc. Géogr. Fr.* (1959), pp. 57–64; and *Recherches.*
[2] De Planhol, "La vie de montagne dans le Sahene", *Bull. Assoc. Géogr. Fr.* (1958), pp. 57–64.
[3] De Planhol, "Caracteres généraux de la vie montagnarde . . .", *Annales Géogr.* (1962), pp. 113–30.
[4] Village described by C. S. Coon, *Caravan, the Story of the Middle East*, pp. 179–82.
[5] F. Balsan, *La colline mystérieuse*, p. 143, and pl. XII, 1, p. 129.
[6] De Planhol, "Pressione demografica e vita di montagnea . . .", *Boll. Soc. Geogr. Ital.* (1960), pp. 1–7; "Un village de montagne de l'Azerbaidjan . . .", *Rev. Géogr. Lyon* (1960), pp. 395–418, ch. *Recherches*; *Aspects of Mountain Life* (1966).

fields become rectangular in shape and are much larger; they depend for moisture exclusively on the rainfall, are allowed to lie fallow, and are manured only when the cattle are turned onto the stubble. In this same area and at the same altitude the winter pasture (qishlāq) is to be found—in a sheltered valley which is not far from the village. Frequently the qishlāq is dotted with rudimentary shelters or rough stone stables in which the smaller livestock may be housed during the early months of the bad season before their final removal to the stables in the village. The summer grazing (yailāq) lies slightly farther out still, occasionally accompanied by yet more cultivable fields. Here are to be found dry-stone shelters roofed with loose-fitting planks, which are removed during the winter; in areas where wood is not available, black awnings (imitated from the nomads) are stretched over fixed and permanent bases during the fine season.

In the middle of this neatly arranged area, the village itself invariably seems a huddled and haphazard agglomeration, though the terrain some-times encourages the development of well-defined quarters of quite individual character: as, for example, when the village is built on a number of mounds separated one from the other.[1] The aspect of the mountain village is generally more open than that of an oasis village. The dwellings are square mud buildings. When a wooden framework (willow or poplar) is practicable, the houses have flat roofs, while in the more desert regions they are topped by wooden domes. Usually they have no windows. But the need to shelter the animals during the winter has frequently led to the construction of more complex buildings, with courtyards, a variety of outbuildings, barns, and stables for the cattle (see fig. 96). When natural conditions are favourable, a good deal of troglodytism is encountered: an ancient Iranian expedient against the winter cold in treeless areas. Stabling in particular is apt to be under-ground, beneath the dwelling-house. In regions where the rock is soft—in Sahand, for example, with its volcanic tuff, and in those areas where limestone is found—the villages are veritable beehives, and the ground beneath each is honeycombed. In Sahand the recent growth in population and the increased quantity of livestock, together with the impossibility of extending the stabling beneath the dwellings, for fear of collapse, have led to the practice of stabling the smaller livestock in caves just outside the village. Thus a type of village with separate stabling has come into being.[2] In other places this arrangement may

---

[1] Lighvān in the Sahand: De Planhol, *Rev. Géogr. Lyon* (1960).   [2] *Ibid.*

well be much older: for example, the existence of a crumbling rock-face near a village probably caused the stabling to be concentrated there from the very earliest times.[1] Separate stabling close to the open countryside has been encouraged by the additional fact that the small livestock are frequently put out to graze, weather permitting, during the winter. The larger animals, on the other hand, are never housed far from the dwelling occupied by their owner.

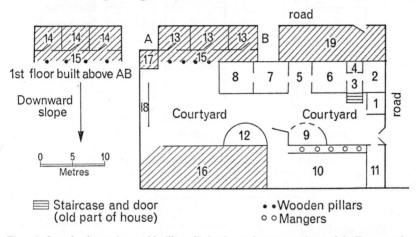

Fig. 96. Complex house in an old village (Rā'ineh, on the eastern slope of the Damāvand). This is in fact a double house. The hatched area was constructed within the last thirty years, and is occupied by the brother of the man who owns the older part of the building. The newer part is similar to the old, but its summer quarters are, according to the modern practice, placed on the floor above and not merely juxtaposed with the winter quarters. Note the absence of shelter for the smaller livestock, which are moved down the mountain during the winter.

Old part of house: 1. Kitchen. 2. Winter habitation. 3. Winter hall. 4. Small storeroom. 5. Summer hall. 6. Summer reception-room. 7. Summer habitation. 8. Storeroom. 9. Bread oven. 10. Cattle shed. 11. Dungheap. 12. Lavatories.

Newer part: 13. Winter rooms. 14. Summer rooms. 15. Verandah. 16. Cattle shed. 17. Kitchen. 18. Young trees. 19. Barn shared by the two brothers (of more recent construction).

Thus dwelling-houses are often superimposed upon the underground accommodation for the cattle (see fig. 97). Proper two-storey houses, with stabling on the ground floor and habitation above, would seem, in the light of present knowledge, to be very rare if not completely unknown in the old village settlements of the plateaus. Single-storey houses are essentially the rule here. And the two-storey ones now being erected, as a result of a certain rise in the standard of living, are "false",

---

[1] For example at Nīak, in the high valley of Harāz: De Planhol, *Recherches*, p. 26, pl. vi *b*.

in the sense that the ground floor is devoted to living space and never to stabling. This two-storey elevation reflects the inhabitants' desire to distinguish between the winter living-quarters on the ground floor,

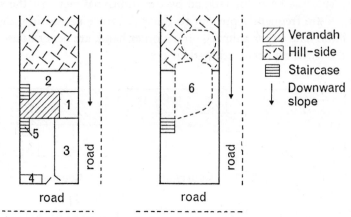

Upper drawing: 1. Kitchen. 2. Bedroom. 3. Barn and storeroom. 4. Lavatory. 5. Entrance to underground stable. 6. Stable.

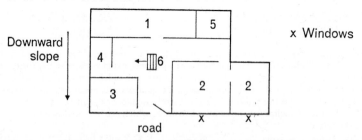

Lower drawing: 1. Kitchen. 2. Bedrooms (modern construction, higher, with windows). 3. Old room, now a barn. 4. Lavatory. 5. Storeroom and granary. 6. Entrance to underground stable.

Two-storey house, simple type. 1. Stable. 2. Habitation. 3. Verandah with wooden pillars. Height of stable: 1·5 m. Construction of logs and rough-cast. Roof in four sections.

Fig. 97. Semi-troglodytic dwellings with superposition (village of Līgvān, northern slope of Sahand; 2,200 m above sea level). (After de Planhol, "Un village de montagne de l'Azerbaidjan iranien", *Revue de Géogr. Lyon,* 1960.)

and the summer quarters above. In the past, the winter and summer rooms were on the same level, differentiated merely by the degree to which they were closed in from the air outside; nowadays the distinction tends to be vertical rather than horizontal (see fig. 97 above).

Rural habitat in the areas of heavy rainfall along the shores of the Caspian

A settled way of life is traditional also in the humid regions along the Caspian: in Gīlān, Māzandarān, and the western part of Gurgān. But the generally recent dates of land clearance, together with the influences of an environment very different from that of the Iranian plateau, have given this region a number of its own characteristics.

One of these is the way in which the buildings are grouped. The loosely knit village—rather like a nebula—is that most commonly found; it is made up of a number of hamlets, disconnected, yet closer to one another than to any neighbouring villages. Qāsimābād, for example (in the district of Rānikūh, eastern Gīlān), stretches for several kilometres along a stony ridge crossed by torrents and rising above a recently warped plain; the village lies among orchards, and so appears as a narrow belt of woodland winding across the flat, bare rice plantations.[1] Other and rather more compact villages are situated upon artificial mounds, though the plan of these villages is not invariably haphazard. Frequently there is a sort of rudimentary village green among the houses and gardens; here are gathered the cattle, which are led to their pasturage in the "jungle" only by way of carefully marked paths running across the rice plantations. At night the cattle are often allowed to roam about this central "green" area—from which, in any case, they would find difficulty in escaping. (Personal observation confirms that this is the practice in the village of Kalār Chan, to the west of Chālūs.)

The "nebula" villages, of an extremely scattered nature, are by no means uncommon, especially close to the shore. The reasons for their development are clearly discernible. They result from land having been brought into cultivation piece by piece, the whole process extending over a very lengthy period. In the beginning the settlements were small, their development being limited by the difficulties of soil clearance; but the original hamlets gradually fused together as the population increased. Because of the varying dates at which the land was brought into cultivation, there are often great differences in ownership and methods of cultivation even within a single village. At Qāsimābād, for example, the oldest hamlets belong in their entirety to big landlords; while in the more recent hamlets, especially those which have been developed since the middle of the last century by refugees from the Caucasus, the houses and gardens are individually owned.

---

[1] C. Collin-Delavaud, *Trois types de terroirs dans les provinces caspiennes d'Iran*, p. 107.

Moreover, the houses themselves are very different from those of the ancient villages on the plateaus. The materials are drawn from the richly wooded surroundings, and the style is adapted to the heavy rainfall of the region. Roofs are steeply sloping and are covered with rice straw or shingles; in the towns (e.g. Rasht) the roofs are less steep and made of round tiles. Sometimes the houses are of timber and plaster, but wood is always the basic material employed, and the fine framework is clearly visible. Almost always the houses have two storeys —an arrangement that seems to have derived from the use of piling, which is common on account of the wetness of the terrain. Today in the Caspian region there are examples of houses that illustrate each stage of the transition: the simple one-storey habitation standing upon the ground; the same dwelling raised upon stout beams in order to allow the rainwater to drain away beneath; the house built upon true piling; and finally the two-storey building with a walled ground floor. The upper floor is surrounded by a broad, open gallery, where the occupants can take the air during summer.

But the Caspian house is characterized above all by its separate out-buildings and open courtyard. When the ground floor of the house is given over to stabling, there is frequently an adjacent cage-like structure set on piles and consisting merely of a wooden floor, thatched roof, and a series of mats fixed to the uprights to serve as walls. This outbuilding is approached by means of a ladder,[1] and the owners make use of it in summer, when the main dwelling-house is rendered uninhabitable by vermin and mosquitoes. Fumigation is sometimes practised be-neath the flooring in an effort to keep the mosquitoes away. The barn, in which unthreshed rice is stored, is also frequently detached from the main dwelling, and it, too, generally stands on piles and has a deep roof. There may also be a separate building for the rearing of silk-worms, and a henhouse raised on piles out of reach of the smaller predatory animals.

Only in the mountain forests of the Caspian and in the narrow plains among the slopes of the Alburz do the villages tend to be more closely knit. Individual houses are also more compact in these regions, built in a style midway between that of dwellings on the coastal strip and of

---

[1] This summer house is often called the *tālār*, though the terminology varies from place to place. In Gīlān the word *tālār* is often used for the open gallery running along the first floor of the building (Chodzko, quoted from Rabino, "*Les provinces caspiennes de la Perse*", p. 25); while in Māzandarān *talak* signifies the whole of the rural house and its out-buildings (A. K. S. Lambton, *Landlord and Peasant in Persia*, p. 440).

dwellings on the plateau; yet the frequent use of rough, unplaned logs makes their appearance typically Caspian.[1] Genuine two-storey houses exist in these areas, though the superposition is no more than partial whenever one room has to be particularly lofty to accommodate the loom used in the manufacture of carpets (see fig. 98).

Rural habitat of the open plains.
Fortified villages of the qal'eh *(=fortress) type*

The open, loosely knit village reflects the comparative security of the mountainous or nomad-free regions. In the open plains and plateaus, which are on the other hand much frequented by nomads, the villages are strongly fortified. They are rectangular in layout, with high walls, corner towers, and a single large gateway dominated by a watchtower. The internal arrangement sometimes turns on a central street running from the gateway and flanked by houses, each having its own little courtyard for the use of the family and the sheltering of the cattle. Usually, however, the houses are all joined together and strung out against the inner face of the defensive wall, this being the typical "habitable wall"—a sort of long-drawn-out honeycomb—of the *qal'eh*. The whole of the central part of the village is a communal park for the cattle.

Architecturally this arrangement is extremely ancient, going back to the communal wall-dwellings (huge, multicellular blocks) noted by Herzfeld in Neolithic Persepolis and by Tolstov in Khorezm in the second half of the first millennium B.C.[2] The fortified rectangular village (in the true sense of the word) derives from this form. It appears in Fergana, following the conquest by the Kuchans, in the fifth and sixth centuries, but it was already common throughout this part of Asia at the time of Alexander, and was present, under Iranian influence, in Qara Qum during the Achaemenid period. A. Z. Rosenfeld has made an extensive study of the fortified village in Iran, and has noted its limited defensive properties: its walls of insufficient thickness; a frequently unfavourable strategic situation on low-lying ground dominated by nearby hills; its inability to withstand a siege, owing to lack of water; and the location of irrigation ditches, often well outside the defensive wall.

---

[1] For example at Rūdbārak in the Kalār Dasht: De Planhol, *Recherches*, p. 53 and pl. xi b.
[2] E. Herzfeld, *Iran in the Ancient East*, p. 11; S. P. Tolstov, *Villages with "Habitable Walls"* (in Russian), pp. 4–5; I quote from A. Z. Rosenfeld, "The Qala, the Iranian Fortified Village" (in Russian), *Sovietskaya Etnografiya* (1951), pp. 22–38.

These features, together with the age of the fortified village and its appearance in all parts of the Iranian world, have led Rosenfeld to conclude that it is not so much the product of especially difficult circumstances as a perfectly normal expression of Iranian culture, for this is a society that originated essentially from "clan-communities".[1]

But even if these villages express primarily an architectural (and social) theme, which is encountered in isolated houses as well as in whole villages, their actual diffusion is strongly linked with the degree of security enjoyed in the locality. The villages are found in a great variety of regions: in Fārs, around Iṣfahān and Tehrān, in Khūzistān, in the north-west, and in Sīstān. They are particularly numerous in Khurāsān; and it has been observed that this type of habitation occurs above all in the plains and in areas open to invasion.[2] It is also found with some frequency in hamlets or villages that are physically isolated from, but owe their origin to, a larger agglomeration, which itself, by reason of its size and large population, does not need such protection against roving brigands or robbers. Though the walled village could hardly withstand a proper siege, there can be no doubt about its value in countering the attacks of wandering marauders. So that to attribute only a social significance to this type of habitation and to see it as a specifically Iranian phenomenon might well seem a false assessment of the problem. Rather, the qal'eh village is the product of a pastoral civilization that was fraught with insecurity; it reflects the settled people's need to defend themselves, and their cattle, against the repeated incursions of the nomads. The spread of this type of village, in about the middle of the first millennium B.C., coincided with the Verreiterung of the Iranian steppes.[3]

Recent progress towards a more peaceful way of life would seem to imply the end, sooner or later, of this village; and in fact many qal'eh are to be found in varying stages of dilapidation.[4] In those which remain intact—and these are numerous, for they continued to be built right up to the beginning of the twentieth century—population increases have led to the erection of new dwelling-houses, which now encroach upon the communal space on the centre of the village, and the removal of cattle enclosures to new positions outside the defensive wall.

[1] Rosenfeld, *op. cit.*
[2] A. K. S. Lambton, *Landlord and Peasant in Persia*, pp. 8–9.
[3] De Planhol, "Les villages fortifiés en Iran et en Asie Centrale", *Ann. Géogr.* (1958), pp. 256–8.
[4] De Planhol, *Recherches*, ch. 1.

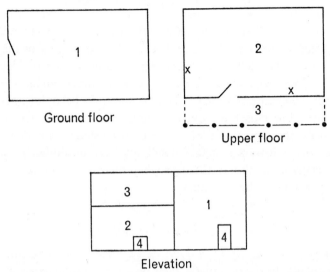

Ground floor

Upper floor

Elevation

House with partial superposition. 1. Habitation (the height of the ceiling is determined by that of the loom used in carpet-making). 2. Stabling. 3. Barn. 4. Doors. Access to the barn is by way of a ladder. Construction of logs, puddled clay, rough-cast.

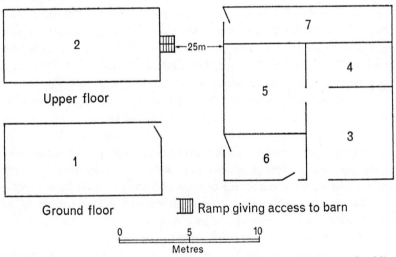

Upper floor

Ground floor   ▥ Ramp giving access to barn

0   5   10
Metres

Complex upper-class house. (Note the separate building containing the barn and stabling; the partial superposition of the dwelling-house; the separation of winter and summer quarters.)

1. Stabling. 2. Barn. 3. High room used for carpet-weaving. 4. Winter quarters. 5. Summer quarters. 6. Storeroom. 7. Charcoal store (with lattice-work). Granary placed above 4–5–6.

Fig. 98. Types of rural habitation at Rūdbārak (Plain of the Kalār Da<u>sh</u>t, northern slopes of the Ālam Kūh massif; alt. 1,350 m; Caspian mountain-forest region).

These new enclosures are protected by walls far less formidable than the "habitable wall" of the village, and this fact in itself gives evidence of the greater security of life today.[1] Though now a thing of the past, the qal'eh has nevertheless had a considerable influence on the development of Iranian villages in general. A great many villages in the Bedouin-frequented plains seem, at first sight, to be quite open and loosely knit; but closer examination reveals a distinctly rectangular ground-plan, showing that they began their existence as qal'eh. Long after the corner towers and wall-dwellings have crumbled away, the villages retain something of the days when their high walls were essential for the safety of the inhabitants.

Rural habitat with nomad traditions

The villages occupied by recently settled nomads differ from those of earlier peasants. In the first place, their position is rarely determined by the availability of water for irrigation; generally it depends on the proximity of land that may be cultivated solely with the aid of rainfall, or on the ready availability of rich pasture land. Thus the villages are generally to be found in fertile plains, and sometimes right in the middle of such plains, rather than in mountain valleys or on piedmonts which might be irrigated by means of qanāts. For example, the Türkmen settled at Qumishān, in Gurgān, established themselves in 1951 on a clayey steppe which had formerly been a summer pasturage.[2]

The structure of this kind of village usually includes a geometrically, or at least a regularly, planned centre. But at the same time the settlement is looser and more open in appearance than those of older foundation, which have grown without expanding, due to the custom of putting up new buildings within the limits drawn by those already existing. Moreover, the absence of trees and the generally bare appearance always characterize the recently developed village. Some of its dwellings long remain movable nomadic shelters: for example, the felt yurts of the Türkmen (ūbeh); black tents in the Zagros; or osier, cradle-vaulted huts in Balūchistān. But in time permanent dwellings are constructed, similar to those found in villages of a settled tradition. Thus the Türkmen of Qumishān, in the midst of their bare steppe, put up

[1] Qal'eh Nau, near Varāmīn: De Planhol, *ibid*. For the recent evolution of this type of village, see also Tuzzi, "Villaggi Fortificati in Iran", *Revista Geografica Italiana* (1964), pp. 20–34.

[2] C. Collins Delavaud, *Trois types de terroirs*, p. 111.

two-storey houses of timber and plaster, complete with open wooden galleries. They were copying the design from the peoples of Māzandarān, who are their nearest neighbours;[1] but genuine two-storey houses, with stabling on the ground floor beneath the living accommodation, are by no means unusual among communities of recently settled nomads.

Though the morphology of the village enables us to identify without difficulty a community of recently settled nomads, it is not always easy to distinguish between the establishments belonging to semi-nomads of true nomadic tradition (whose settlement took place in the comparatively distant past), and those of semi-nomads who originated as sedentary shepherds and were forced by the insecurity of their environment drastically to extend their pastoral migrations. In the latter case, however, the villages' physical appearance and regional organization may prove reliable criteria. Thus the oasis of Nīkshahr, in Balūchistān, is in reality made up of a score of little hamlets of hemispherical or conical huts scattered about mostly on the extremities of the palm groves at the edge of the cereal plantations. True houses, i.e. flat-roofed rectangular constructions of unfired brick, are few in number. Nine of these hamlets each contain a mosque: that is to say, they have at least the minimum requirement for a village community. But there is no regional centre, no market which might serve as a focal-point for the oasis as a whole.[2] The social organization is essentially the same as in other sedentary communities, being related to ownership of land, even though this land is under the nominal authority of a *sardār* (= headman).[3] Nevertheless, one has the impression of a close affiliation with and recent family descent from the nomads of the region. This kind of oasis settlement—scattered, rudimentary, frequently inhabited by pastoral folk—predominates throughout Balūchistān.

In Bashkird, immediately to the west, the vast majority of the dwellings are likewise hemispherical huts, or *lahar*, grouped by dozens into semi-nomadic hamlets, a number of hamlets together making up a *shahr*. Here, however, a far more ancient tradition is at once apparent from the groups of semi-troglodytic date-stores which serve as fixed centres for the communities. (These storehouses are known as *kat*, a word which was already in existence, and with the same signification,

---

[1] *Ibid.*

[2] G. B. Castiglioni, *Appunti geografici sul Balucistan Iraniano*, pp. 40–6.

[3] But also with a vestigial military connotation, and distinct from the term now normally used in cultivated areas (*kaīkhudā*).

in the Achaemenid period.[1]) It is thus extremely probable that the semi-nomadism of Ba_sh_kird dates from long before the medieval Bedouiniza-tion. Moreover, a number of other factors tend to confirm this con-clusion. There are signs of an unbroken cultural tradition going back into the distant past (e.g. during migration these nomads use a certain breed of donkey well known in ancient times),[2] while the terracing of land for cultivation points to a long tradition of settled life. The same is doubtless true of the Papi of Luristān; these ancient semi-nomadic people, who make use of oxen for transport, were obliged to extend their migrations during the period of medieval Bedouinization.[3] One of the major results of their contact with true nomadism was their adoption of the black tent in their summer encampments, far from the flat-roofed villages they occupy during the winter. (In recent times, following Rezā _Sh_āh's prohibition of the black tent, they have made their huts of branches, which is probably a return to the most ancient tradition of all.) The winter villages often resemble the hamlets of recent nomads, but thickly wooded gardens indicate the nuclei of a much earlier settlement.[4] At all events, the relative length of the migrations has led more and more peasants (*ra'īyat*) to settle down, either in the winter villages or in new ones that have grown up in sheltered valleys near the summer encampments. From these latter they now content them-selves with brief summer journeys, which are mere changes of air rather than true migrations. The landowners (*_kh_ān*), on the other hand, make the same long migrations as they did formerly, in order to inspect their lands and crops in different areas.

Agrarian patterns and the rural scene

As we have seen, the population density in the villages of Iran is very high—even in the Caspian regions, where settlements tend to be slightly less closely knit than elsewhere. To what extent has this concentration led to the use of communal methods in the control and exploitation of land? Research in this field is still in its infancy. Aerial photography, however, has shown the existence of a zone characterized by strip-cultivation arranged in large fields (*gewannflur*)—though most of Iran is dominated by broad, irregular fields (which do occasionally achieve a

[1] I. Gershevitch, "Travels in Bashkardia", *Royal Central Asian J.* (1959), p. 219.
[2] After Strabo (*Works* xv, 2, 15) quoted by Gershevitch, p. 215.
[3] Feilberg, *Les Papis*.
[4] See for example, *Les Papis*, "Le paysage rural à Kouppa", fig. 20, p. 45.

certain regularity in irrigated districts).[1] The zone runs almost un-interruptedly from eastern Āzarbāījān by way of Qazvīn to a point between Kirmānshāh and Arāk, and by way of Iṣfahān to the basins of Fārs; while isolated areas of strip-cultivation are also to be found in Khurāsān and Khūzistān. This feature, which goes with a strict communal organization and thus overall control of the land, is designed to further the almost exclusive production of cereals. It is not found in densely populated oasis areas where a greater variety of crops is cultivated, nor in tribal areas that have only recently come under cultiva-tion. The oasis zones are typified by large numbers of small landowners, while the tribal zones are given over to broad irregular fields and open-field cereal cultivation on a much less rigid framework. It could be that these areas of strip-cultivation, as distinct from the irrigated oasis districts, are evidence of a survival in the plains of the old agricultural methods once practised by settled communities. But even in tribal areas the utilization of land is fast becoming more organized. In the Kalār Dasht, a mountain plain on the Caspian slopes of the Alburz, an open-field cultivation of cereals is now being operated on a strict, two-field rotational basis; there are even intervillage agreements to determine the order of rotation.[2] And the population of this region has only been properly installed since the settling of the Kurdish tribes by Muḥammad Qājār at the end of the eighteenth century. The total area of land culti-vated in Iran on a collective and rotational system must greatly exceed that under strip-cultivation.

In all areas of Iran today the rural scene shows evidence of powerful collective organization, and almost everywhere there are communal measures for the herding of the cattle. Except for the rice- and fruit-growing areas of the Caspian, the irrigated oasis districts, and the mountain valleys, the open fields are almost entirely without hedges or fencing. And even in the mountain valleys, the terraced and irrigated areas permanently devoted to cereal production are sometimes thrown open in their entirety, during the two-month interval between harvest and sowing, to the wanderings of the cattle; the harvest having been gathered simultaneously in all sections of the area, the cattle are at complete liberty to roam where they will.[3] There are, however, a few areas given over to specialized crops or late harvestings—fields of millet, for example (this crop is grown in the summer and harvested

---

[1] Bobek, 1960. [2] De Planhol, *Recherches*, ch. 3.
[3] This is the case at Raineh, at the foot of the Damāvand: De Planhol, *ibid.* p. 24.

later than the winter-sown cereals), form tightly enclosed patches in the midst of the open field in the Bīrūn Ba<u>sh</u>m, a country of the middle <u>Ch</u>ālūs Rūd, below the Kalār Da<u>sh</u>t.[1] Even in the Caspian regions, where abundant rainfall encourages little hedges to sprout up among the different parcels of land, these serve no enclosing purpose and have no significance at all with regard to the exploitation of the land. The widespread existence of common pasture land, and of communal arrangements whereby specially detailed individuals guard both cattle and smaller livestock, are two particularly tangible proofs of the strong sense of community existing among the villages of Iran.

C. URBAN HABITAT

Centres of urban life

Iran, with her ancient tradition of settled life, has undergone a variety of demographic upheavals which have left their mark upon the different types of rural communities. Her town life is no less remarkable for its antiquity, proliferation, and its instability. Through the years, as the settled way of life has contracted, many towns have simply disappeared; occasionally there are ruins to mark their position, but in some cases no trace at all remains. The instability has been particularly marked in the life of the capital cities: these have risen and fallen with changes in power, and in accordance with their geographical value in dealing with the problems of centralization in the Iranian plateau. The critical areas of this plateau, however, are in the centre and south-east of the country, and these are desert zones decidedly unfavourable to urban life.

A map of the urban network as it is today (fig. 107, p. 474) shows the fundamentally asymmetrical disposition of the towns within Iran, and their relationship both with natural conditions and with the density of the rural population. Cities and towns are numerous in all those regions where rainfall is sufficient for agricultural purposes; thus they are few in the centre, the east, and the south-east of Iran. Nevertheless, a line of oases penetrates the desert regions by way of Yazd and Kirmān, and a careful study of the map reveals a number of other such lines. A particularly important one runs along the junction between the central plateau and the chains of the Zagros, by way of Hamadān, Iṣfahān, Yazd, and Kirmān. In the north a similar line follows the foothills of the Alburz,

[1] De Planhol, *ibid.* p. 43 and pl. VIII.

taking in Zanjān, Qazvīn, Tehrān, Simnān, Dāmghān, and so on, and linking the urban centres of Āzarbāïjān with those of Khurāsān. Another important urban group comprises the towns and ports of the south-western foothills of the Zagros. These centres of urban life have had an extremely chequered history, since they have always been influenced by political and economic factors; for instance, their position has often been modified by the extension of the area under Iranian political domination.

With its central position, the north-eastern edge of the Zagros mountains would appear to be the most favourable area for a capital of Iran. The very names of the cities are proof of a centralizing function: Hamadān, for example, was originally *Ecbatane*, from the old Persian *Hamagtana* (= place of meeting); and Iṣfahān was once called *Aspadana*, probably from *çpādhānā* (= the armies, meeting-place of the army) rather than from *açpādhānā* (= cavalry station).[1] But a permanent capital has never managed to establish itself in this region. Yazd and Kirmān have always been too remote from the humid and more prosperous areas of the country, and Kirmān achieved its greatest eminence only as the seat of a local Türkmen dynasty during the Saljuq period, in the eleventh and twelfth centuries. In Ecbatana, protected by the mountains, the political unity of the Medes asserted itself in the eighth century B.C. against the power of the Assyrians, but this city yielded pride of place to cities farther south when the Achaemenid empire expanded to include the rich plains of Mesopotamia and Asia Minor. Susa, the cradle of the Achaemenids, then became the lowland winter capital, with Ecbatana reduced to the status of summer residence.[2] Persepolis and Pasargadae were too deeply embedded in the mountains to come into the reckoning. And the two periods during which the capital was fixed at Iṣfahān—under the Saljuqs in the eleventh and twelfth centuries, and under the Safavid dynasty from 1598 to 1722— cannot be regarded as more than episodes.[3] Centrifugal tendencies always won in the end.

The most tenuous seats of national government have always been those towards the south and south-west. Shīrāz, whose development, if not foundation, dates from the Islamic period, has never been anything more than the regional capital of Fārs; it was due purely to ephemeral circumstances that it became the main seat of the Zand

---

[1] L. Lockhart, *Persian Cities*, p. 18.   [2] Lockhart, p. 95.
[3] Lockhart, p. 42.

dynasty during the second half of the eighteenth century. On the other hand, the rebirth and swift development of the towns in Khūzistān (Ahvāz and Ābādān, for example) have been a result of twentieth-century economic circumstances. The opening up of the oilfields has given their expansion a solid regional basis, while the national overseas trade has centred on the Persian Gulf following the construction of the Trans-Iranian Railway.

In fact it is the northern fringe of the country, or at least the inward-looking flanks of the northern mountains, that have always held the greatest attraction as a seat of political power. The establishment of the Qājār capital in Tehrān at the end of the eighteenth century was merely the last manifestation of what may well be a permanent tendency in the life of Iran. There are manifold reasons for this phenomenon. Moreover, the Turkish and Mongol origins of the earliest dynasties certainly played a major part in causing the capitals to be situated in the north, and especially along the main invasion route following the Alburz into Āzarbāījān. The princes of these basically nomadic states were anxious both to be near their tribes and to avoid the excessive heat of the climate farther to the south. This helps to explain the evolution of Tabrīz, which, despite all vicissitudes, was the capital successively of the Mongols, the Qarā Qoyūnlū, the Aq Qoyūnlū, and finally the Safavids, all of whom stemmed originally from the Türkmen tribes of the north-west from the thirteenth to the sixteenth centuries. Tabrīz was abandoned only for short periods, and always for other cities in the same region: Marāgheh, whose fertile pasture land had attracted Hülagü; Ardabīl, the cradle of the Safavids; and Sultānīyeh.

But there were other factors, too, which contributed to this preponderance of northern towns. For instance, strategic considerations played their part in the removal of the Safavid capital to Qazvīn during the great sixteenth-century wars against the Ottomans;[1] and in Nādir Shāh's decision to make Mashhad the centre of an empire whose ambitions lay far away to the east, towards Afghanistan and India. Many of these northern towns grew up as frontier towns during the "marches"; Ardabīl and Qazvīn, for example, were for a long time Islamic bases, against the Dailamites, or the "Assassins", holding the nearby mountains. In the Caspian lowlands the town network did not properly develop until the modern period; in all probability the foundation of Rasht does not go back beyond the end of the thirteenth century.[2]

[1] Lockhart, p. 69.   [2] Lockhart, p. 73.

For a long time, too, economic factors have worked in favour of the northern towns. Today, as in the Middle Ages, the bulk of cross-country traffic passes by way of the route following the foothills of the Alburz, to the north of the desert; and until the beginning of the twentieth century, Tabrīz was the country's greatest emporium, the centre of caravan routes to Turkey, and the starting-point of Iran's first railway, which ran towards Russia. Later on we shall examine the part played by these different elements in the selection of Tehrān as capital.

Structure and evolution of urban life

At the present time the towns of Iran are in the process of transformation. They have not escaped the great movement of westernized urbanization which is affecting towns in all Middle Eastern countries. Buildings of very different periods, for instance, can often be found in close juxtaposition to one another. What is remarkable in Iran, considering how long ago the land was settled, is that it is possible to distinguish elements even prior to those of the Islamic period.

(a) Ancient elements

The sites of towns are among the most important of the truly autochthonous features of Iran. Throughout almost the whole of the country the locations of early villages were determined by the availability of water. Even though some towns, such as Iṣfahān and Ahvāz, may be situated on rivers, most are supplied by qanāt. The most favourable site of all for town growth is thus a gentle slope some short distance from the foot of the hills that feed the qanāt; and *jūb*, a small open canal, is an essential feature of the traditional Iranian street. Nothing could be further from the Iranian conception of a town than the lofty, fortified site chosen by the Greeks even for the most modest acropolis, such as Rhagae, or Ray, refounded by Seleukos Nikator under the name of Europos, in the plain near Tehrān.[1]

The types of houses most commonly found in the towns are to a large extent strongly characteristic and special to Iran, reflecting ancient efforts to adapt dwellings to prevailing geographical conditions. By the Islamic period at least the alternation of severe winters and torrid summers had already led to the widespread adoption of at least a partial troglodytism: the *zīr-i-zamīn*, a sort of semi-basement, did much to

[1] Bobek, "Teheran", *Geogr. Forsch.* (1958), p. 15.

temper these extreme variations of heat and cold.[1] The most common house-plan today—with the main habitation at the end of a courtyard, into which it opens by way of a wooden-pillared gallery that is occasionally enclosed by two slightly protruding wings on either side—appears to derive directly from the simple cell of the ancient wall-dwelling. At all events, this type of structure originates from an epoch considerably antedating the Islamic period, and makes no concession at all to the Islamic need for the interior to be divided into two parts. In general, this separation of *anderūn* and *bīrūn* (outer and inner apartments) has been satisfactorily achieved only by the erection of separate buildings.

The same can be said of the more luxurious houses, whose style is certainly also of great antiquity, and their geometrically planted gardens and pools of running water earned the admiration of the Greeks.[2] The cross-shaped garden, with one arm longer than the other and a pool placed at the point of intersection, seems to have existed on the Iranian plateau from the very earliest days of agriculture;[3] and in the Sasanid period (A.D. 226–642) the same layout was adopted for the hunting park, except that there was a pavilion at the intersection instead of a pool. This arrangement is strictly dependent on the availability of flowing water and the presence, on a slope, of qanāt-fed canals.

It is rather more difficult to determine to what extent the plans and construction of towns as a whole are pre-Islamic. The oldest Iranian towns were doubtless of oriental type, loosely knit about a nucleus, rather than of the square, geometrical Greek pattern. But it is impossible to judge the accuracy of the only actual description that has come down to us: that in which Herodotus depicts Ecbatana as a circular town ringed by no fewer than seven concentric walls (*History*, I, 98). Such a description has a decidedly mythical ring about it; and it must be remembered that Herodotus himself had never visited the town. However, the existence of the bāzār as an autonomous quarter within the town must go back to very ancient times; the word *bāzār* itself derives from the Pahlavī *vajar* (=market).[4]

---

[1] Known in most regions, under widely differing local names: *shabādān* at Shustar, and *sardāb* at Dizfūl, for example (Lockhart, pp. 150, 155).

[2] Quintus Curtius Rufus, VIII, 2.

[3] D. N. Wilber, *Persian Gardens and Garden Pavilions*, p. 19.

[4] Lockhart, p. 158.

(b) Islamic town structure

However much they may have retained or assimilated more ancient structures, the towns, and cities, at least as they stood about the year 1925, owed their appearance above all to the influence of Islamic civilization. Indeed, they contained all the essential features of Muslim towns, notably the strict, hierarchical division into quite separate quarters: the princely quarter, with its palace and citadel (*ārg*); the bāzār, and the residential districts.[1] Then there was the segregation of religious minorities. In some towns there were clearly defined Jewish quarters (*maḥalleh*): at Shīrāz, for example, and at Iṣfahān, where the Jewish area, *Yahūdiyeh*, had long been distinct from the Muslim town. There were Armenian quarters, like the one that had been grouped round its church in the old town of Shīrāz since the sixteenth century;[2] and finally there was the new quarter of *Julfā*, established at Iṣfahān beyond Zāyandeh Rūd and separated from the old Muslim town by the new royal town of Shāh ʿAbbās. Yet another Muslim feature was the inorganic structure and the confused maze of streets, many of them culs-de-sac or alleys (= *bunbast* or *kūcheh*).[3]

Yet it must not be thought that there were no attempts at controlled, organic urbanization before the present period. Monarchs and governors left marks on certain towns which are still to be seen. In Mashhad Shāh ʿAbbās built a magnificent avenue running north-west and south-east of the mausoleum of Imām Riżā. The north-western part, the *Khīābān-i-Bālā* (= the upper avenue, nowadays called *Khīābān Nādirī*), is very attractive, being divided into two carriageways by a central canal shaded by plane trees and elms; this has been described, somewhat grandiloquently, as the *Unter den Linden* of Mashhad.[4] In Shīrāz the improvements carried out by Imām Qulī Khān at the beginning of the seventeenth century (e.g. the construction of a broad avenue carrying the Iṣfahān road) were followed in the late eighteenth century by Karīm Khān Zand's reorganization of the entire north-western part of the town about a broad avenue and a large square surrounding the ārg.[5] These, however, were relatively trifling changes. The only major enterprise in these years was Shāh ʿAbbās's creation of a truly

---

[1] In this connexion see De Planhol, *Le Monde Islamique*, pp. 12–26.
[2] J. I. Clarke, "The Iranian City of Shiraz", pp. 14, 23, and 50.
[3] Clarke, pp. 14, 50.
[4] Sykes, quoted by Scharlau, "Moderne Umgestaltungen im Grundriss iranischer Städte", *Erdkunde* (1961), p. 191.   [5] Clarke, p. 15.

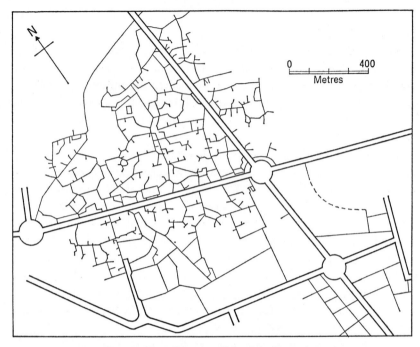

Fig. 99. Plan of Gurgān. (After Scharlau, 1961.)

royal town at Iṣfahān—with a great square, an harmonious expanse
of gardens, and the great avenue of Chahār Bāgh, which goes as far
as Zāyandeh Rūd and even beyond the river. With these exceptions
(together with Nāṣir al-Dīn Shāh's work at Tehrān in the nineteenth
century, of which more will be said on pp. 445–61), town morphology in general remained in the habitual Islamic state of disorganization
right up to the Pahlavī period. This lack of order was particularly
marked in the residential areas, for any reorganization had been strictly
limited to the official, royal, and religious quarters of towns. In Shīrāz
some of the structures of the Zand period had already been partially
obliterated by the time of the Qājār monarchs.[1]

(c) Contemporary changes

In 1925, when Rezā Shāh came to the throne, a new era began.
Under the great reformer a programme for bringing the country up-
to-date was carried on, and introduction of methodical urbanization
was one of its major features.

[1] Clarke, p. 15.

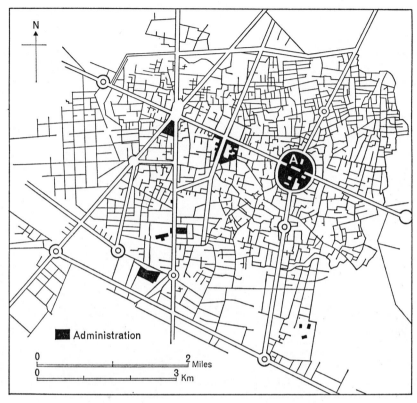

N

Administration

0 ⸻⸻⸻ 2 Miles
0 ⸻⸻⸻ 3 Km

Fig. 100. Plan of Ma<u>shh</u>ad. *A*, Holy Circle. (After Scharlau, 1961.)

Town-plans were completely redrawn. The guiding principle was the construction of broad, straight highways, which would permit the circulation of modern traffic, right through the maze of ancient streets and with complete disregard for the existing structure. The course and position of these new thoroughfares were extremely varied. Often, especially in the smaller towns, they were continuations within the built-up area of external roads leading to the town. (This was the case at Gurgān; see fig. 99). It was natural that the new streets should fit in with improvements that had already been made: this happened at Ma<u>shh</u>ad,[1] where the new thoroughfares in the old town were exactly at right angles to <u>Sh</u>āh 'Abbās's broad avenue (fig. 100); and at <u>Sh</u>īrāz, where modern plans were based upon the work of Karīm <u>Kh</u>ān Zand (fig. 101).[2] Other roads were constructed along the line of the ancient

[1] See Scharlau, *Erdkunde*, 1961.　　　　[2] Clarke, pls. III, IV, fig. 5.

439

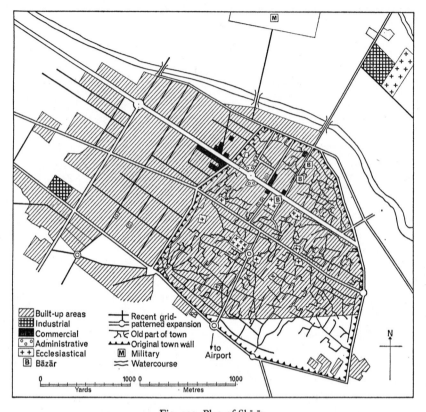

Fig. 101. Plan of S̲h̲īrāz.

walls, thus forming a system of ring-roads (S̲h̲īrāz, Tabrīz, and the
north-eastern quarter of Iṣfahān). But sometimes the plan was completely artificial, superimposed on a background with which it had
nothing whatever in common. This was the case at Hamadān, where
the roads radiate out from a great central square to boulevards which
describe a rough circle about the city (see fig. 102).

A similar geometrical layout exists in the more modern parts of the
Iranian town as well, the main thoroughfares generally being continuations of those cut through the old quarters. In the new quarters,
however, the smaller streets are laid out within the framework of the
great arteries, whilst the old quarters are ruthlessly pierced by the
new main roads. The relative importance of the old and new quarters
obviously varies from town to town. At Mas̲h̲had, for example, which
as a centre of pilgrimage has always retained its prosperity, the new

440

Fig. 102. Plan of Hamadān.

quarters are relatively less important than at Shīrāz, which had seriously declined during the Qājār period. In Iṣfahān, which has never re-captured the splendour it had at the time of the Safavids, the new quarters are very small, and the contemporary building has been virtually confined to the avenues of the royal town, which was

441

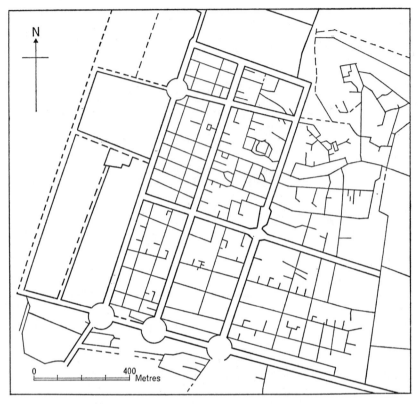

Fig. 103. Plan of Bujnūrd. (After Scharlau, 1961.)

originally planned as a resort of pleasure, but has now been invaded by offices and various other kinds of buildings. Lastly, there are a number of smaller towns, founded during the Pahlavī period, which have a completely geometrical layout in keeping with modern ideas. (The ground-plan of Bujnūrd in Khurāsān, for example, resembles a rectangular checkerboard; see fig. 103.) One must also refer here to the exceptional instance of Ābādān, which is an "artificial" town with strictly defined "quarters" and a systematic ground-plan. It could be said to be a real "colonial" impress brought about by the oil industry in a country where, by comparison, it appears foreign and outlandish.

These changes in the layout of towns have been accompanied by the construction of new communal and professional buildings. Religious segregation has considerably declined, though it has not yet disappeared completely. More than a quarter of the Jewish community in Shīrāz have already moved out of the traditional *mahalleh* into districts, as have practically all the Armenians.[1] At Kirmān the old Zoroastrian quarter, partly abandoned as the result of heavy migration to Tehrān, has acquired a recent population of Muslims.[2]

Commercial segregation is also in eclipse. The old bāzārs continue to exist, but the strict grouping of the past is now much relaxed, especially where modern thoroughfares have cut through bāzārs and encouraged them to spill over into other districts.[3] New business areas have developed (no longer grouped by trades or professions) along the new arteries, especially in town centres. In Khīābān Luṭf 'Alī Khān-i-Zand at Shīrāz, for example, the presence of numerous pavement-traders emphasizes the commercial nature of the central areas.[4] The broad avenues of the royal town at Iṣfahān have been invaded by commerce; even the new residential districts have here seen the development of small establishments housing the more essential crafts and trades.

The new quarters, as well as the modern streets that have been driven through ancient parts of the Iranian town, are characterized also by the presence of new types of buildings, constructed of different materials from those used previously. The unfired bricks of the older quarters have given way to fired bricks and sometimes polychrome surfaces. Within the Iranian plateau region, the roofs of houses are usually terraces—but they are terraces of brick and steel, very different from the old flat roofs of beaten earth, which had to be rolled with great cylindrical stones after each rain. Flat roofs of metal have come into use for more modest houses. Though houses of the plateau are still comparatively low, nowadays they frequently have two or three storeys, whereas in the past the great majority had one storey only. The old kind of house, with the main building fronting upon a closed courtyard, has almost totally disappeared, and ground-plans are coming more and more to resemble those of European apartment blocks. The frequent survival of the *zīr-i-zamīn* alone shows the vitality of certain traditional elements. In the early years of the Pahlavī period, new building underwent a great variety of influences. The predominance of Russian colonial style—broad, two-storeyed buildings with square windows—has been noted among the earliest "Western" buildings at Mashhad. Then followed a period of Western European construction overlain with an amazing proliferation of Persian adornment and decoration.[5] Following

---

[1] Clarke, p. 50.   [2] English, *City and Village*, pp. 48–9.
[3] Clarke, p. 28.   [4] Clarke, p. 34.   [5] G. Stratil-Sauer, *Meschhed*, pp. 12 ff.

such excesses, there has been a general progression towards an agreeably sober and square style of building, quite in keeping with present-day materials and the breadth and regularity of the streets.

The attractive appearance of these new quarters, with their avenues and modern buildings, readily explains the recent development of internal social distinctions and a class segregation that was previously extremely rare. Though statistics are not yet available, it is clear that the density of population, based on the number of people per room, is considerably lower in the new sections than in the old; while the comfort and amenities of the modern buildings are immeasurably superior. Almost all well-to-do families have by now migrated to these newer districts, so that the older quarters have become more and more exclusively occupied by the poorer classes. Luxury shops, cinemas, and other entertainment tend to be concentrated in the newer quarters; while public baths are situated above all in the older districts, testifying to the lack of bathrooms in private homes.[1]

We have no reliable information on the migrations and population movements which may have accompanied these changes. Nevertheless, it does seem probable that immigrants from the countryside into the towns have congregated in the older sections, replacing wealthier citizens who have moved out. Thus the older districts have sunk into an even deeper degradation. One feature of Iranian cities, however, is the almost complete absence of shanty-districts. The relative weakness of the country's urge towards urbanization may well be one reason for this situation,[2] though the absence of shanty-towns around Tehrān, whose growth has been extremely rapid, leads one to suspect that other causes may have operated. The lack of shanty-towns may be attributed in part to the Iranians' long tradition of settled life and their attachment (much stronger than any to be found among Turks or Arabs) to stable, permanent homes. Even when the conditions requisite for the creation of a shanty town are fulfilled (land to which no legal right is held, and the illicit construction of *muftābād*, or shanties), the buildings are still of bricks. In many cases, the expansion of towns seems to have come about as a result of internal population growth rather than of immigration. Of the 170,659 inhabitants of Shīrāz recorded in the census of 1956, 150,901 (or 88·4 per cent) had been born in the district of Shīrāz, which had at the time no more than 410,458 inhabitants.[3]

The weakness of urbanization is understandable when one considers

---

[1] Clarke, pp. 21–3.   [2] Clarke, p. 23.   [3] Clarke, p. 45.

the low degree of economic activity, as revealed by a study of the country's professional structure. In Shīrāz in 1956, the working population over the age of ten years amounted to no more than 43 per cent of that age-group (this low figure was due largely to the inactivity of women, of whom no more than 7 per cent were working, compared with 76 per cent of the males); and barely a third of this whole group were artisans or engaged in construction work. It is difficult to establish to what extent these statistics—the first to be published for a city in Iran—would hold good for the other provincial capitals. They seem representative enough, provided one excepts those few cities in which large-scale modern industries have developed. At Firmān, which is a small carpet-manufacturing town, the figure of 8 per cent of male unemployment given by the census of 1956 appeared to one observer to be somewhat low.[1] The overall impression is that the amazing physical changes in Iranian towns have not been accompanied by a corresponding economic and social evolution.

Tehrān

The capital of Iran presents all the general features outlined above; but in some respects—size and, above all, rate of growth—it is quite exceptional. The population advanced from a presumed 120,000 in 1860, to 210,000 in 1922, 540,000 in 1939, to an overall 1,600,000 in 1956, and an estimated 2,000,000 in 1960–1 (account being taken of the great spread in area). The fact that this remarkable growth has taken place virtually within the Pahlavī period explains why, of all Iranian towns, Tehrān has the least "oriental" aspect.[2] But the development of this vast agglomeration has brought with it a striking degree of social segregation and a train of related problems.

(a) Location: conditions and stages of growth

There are good reasons for the relatively late growth of Tehrān, and numerous factors may have played a part in eventually deciding the site on which the capital should stand. It may have been conveniently close to the territory covered by the original tribe of the new ruler; strategic interests may have been involved, with the menace of Russia already apparent after the seventeenth century A.D. in the north-west and the ever-present danger of the Atrak Türkmen to the north-east. Then,

---

[1] English, pp. 48–9.   [2] Scharlau, *Erdkunde*, p. 190.

too, by the eighteenth century the tradition in favour of a northern capital was already deeply embedded in Iranian political thinking. But more than anything else, it was probably his interest in the Caspian provinces (an interest which dates back to the time of the Safavids) which led Muḥammad Shāh Qājār to site his capital at the foot of the Alburz mountains in 1786. At all events, it was because of the general conditions of life, together with exigencies of communications, that Tehrān was founded on the east–west road at the foot of the mountains, just at the point where this road divides into two and continues on either side of the foothills.[1] From this central position the town is able to command the valleys leading to the Caspian, while roads leading to Qum, to the oases of central Iran, and to the basins of Fārs lie conveniently west of the great *kavīrs*.

The simple, partly troglodytic village that had long existed on the site gained somewhat in importance when the city of Ray (ten km away to the south), which had hitherto served as urban centre for the district, was destroyed during the Mongol invasion.[2] But Tehrān's position, for all its undeniable strategic value, seems oddly remote for a capital city. It was inevitable that centrifugal forces should predominate in other provinces, especially in those to the south of the central desert, so long as there was no vigorous political centralization to ensure the supremacy of the new metropolis; for Tehrān's economic importance as a communications centre was not in itself sufficient to raise it above other cities that were equally well endowed in this respect. The unification of Iran remained very incomplete under the Qājārs, and the central authority was often challenged, so that it was only with the power and energy of Rezā Shāh that the political conditions necessary for the dramatic rise of a metropolis were created. Viewed in this light, Tehrān appears as the personal creation of this reformer.

He left his mark clearly on the plan of the city, too. Tehrān had been much enlarged, and embellished with a palace after 1786–9. Its exaltation

---

[1] For a good study of the elements of the situation in Tehrān, see Bobek, "Teheran", *Geogr. Forsch.* (1958), pp. 14–15.

[2] For the historic evolution of Tehrān, see Minorsky, article on Teheran, in *Encyclopédie de l'Islam*, vol. IV, pp. 750–6. Recent studies of contemporary evolution: F. C. Clapp, "Tehran and the Elburz", *Geogr. Rev.* (1930), pp. 69–85; Bobek, *Geogr. Forsch.* (1958), pp. 5–24; and De Planhol, *Recherches*, ch. 4 ("De la ville islamique à la métropole iranienne—Quelques aspects du développement contemporain de Téhéran"). These last observations, which date substantially from 1958, have supplied me with raw material for the following account. I am grateful to M. P. Vieille for having helped me to unearth them. Finally, Ahrens, *Die Entwicklung...* is a fine study for those interested in urbanism.

to a capital by Āg̱h̲ā Muḥammad Qājār Nāsir ed-Din Shāh (1848–96) had furthered its enlargement and begun modernization on European lines; in his time its original walls, dating from 1553 were still standing. Under the Qājārs the town gained a number of large, modern thoroughfares; but its main feature, within the octagonal circumvallation, was the confused intermingling of residential suburbs, palaces, and gardens in the north, and of brickworks and potteries in the south. Much more important changes were carried out by Reżā Shāh. In the early thirties, he riddled the whole of the old town with a geometrically planned network of broad avenues. Some of these followed earlier alinements, notably the course of the ancient fortifications; but the majority of them were pushed through with a supreme disregard for pre-existing buildings. The penetration of the older quarters was carried much further in Tehrān than in any other town in Iran, and it is this network of streets, extended in all directions because of the growth of the city, that provides the present-day framework of the capital and determines its essential character. One has to leave the broad avenues and plunge into the maze of narrow *kūcheh* in order to recapture something of the town's earlier, closed-in atmosphere.[1] More recent operations have been limited to the construction of relatively wide and similarly geometrical secondary thoroughfares.

So the ground was laid for the development of a great metropolis, though the expansion was accompanied by chaotic methods of building and fierce speculation in land. Building was dominated by an almost indiscriminate private enterprise, scarcely held in check by the existence of building permits whose issue depended, at least in theory, on the preliminary depositing of plans. Much of the building is still carried out by contractors, who purchase building sites and erect houses for sale. Plots of land are sometimes too large for a single house, even with a garden, and this may explain the frequency with which one sees pairs or groups of identical houses of exactly the same age. With building carried on in this way, it has been impossible to meet the enormous demands for housing created by the inordinate growth of the population. Tehrān, indeed, suffers from an acute housing shortage. Rents are extremely high, and annual profit from investment in this field would appear to average out at almost 20 per cent. Land speculation is the principal financial activity in the capital. It has been calculated that

---

[1] For a sensitive evocation of the atmosphere of the old town, see E. Pākravān, *Vieux Téhéran*.

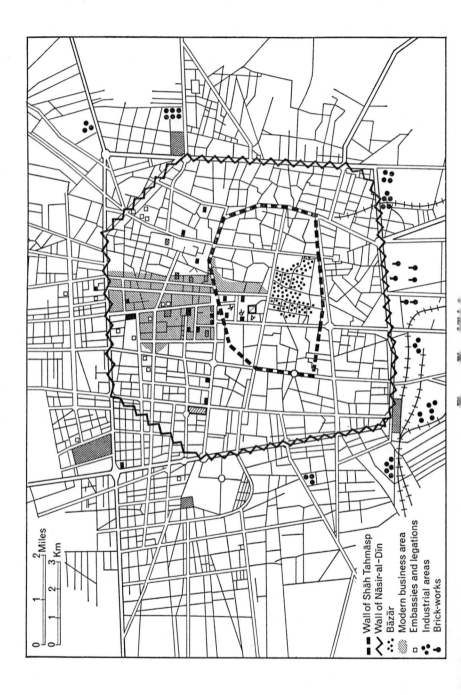

Wall of Shāh Tahmāsp
Wall of Nāsir-al-Dīn
Bāzār
Modern business area
Embassies and legations
Industrial areas
Brick-works

0 1 2 Miles
0 1 2 3 Km

in 1960 there remained sufficient building land to allow for an increase in population of up to six million inhabitants, and for another fifteen years of construction at the present rate.[1] Building by the authorities is slowly creeping in, especially in the eastern part of the city, where public money financed the construction of the Chahār Ṣad Dastgāh ("The Four-hundred House Plan") in 1946–9, and Kūh-i-Narmak in 1956–7 on the Māzandarān road; while Tehrān-Nau, for the poorer classes, was built with public money in the same area in 1950.[2] The first "new town" development was Tehrān-Pārs, privately financed by capital belonging to Zoroastrians. Starting in 1958 a complex unit containing a full range of accommodation, from simple to luxurious, was built in the middle of the desert to the east of the city. By commencing building operations at various, widely separated points, it was possible to combat speculation by ensuring that land should increase in value uniformly throughout this area.

There is, however, little evidence of such measures in the city itself. Tehrān has acquired an aspect similar to that of Western cities, but it still lacks any system of organized building. Nor do the heights of its buildings seem particularly Western. Tehrān is very spread out, and the houses are low—two storeys in the poorer quarters, three or four at most in the wealthier districts, where blocks of flats are to be found. In 1957–8 scarcely a dozen buildings in the whole city went to seven or eight storeys, and these towered up like veritable landmarks: such as the one situated in the great east–west business thoroughfare in the city centre, which proudly bears a miniature Eiffel Tower upon its terraced roof. The immense area that Rezā Shāh made available for building was certainly an important factor in the persistence of this low style of building. There was no shortage of space, and scarcely any incentive to build high. The Iranians' love of gardens, which they tend with the greatest care, might also have played its part in bringing about this state of affairs. But it must also be noted that buildings of average height (four or five storeys) are going up much more frequently in the residential areas than in the business centre, a fact which has led to the just remark that Tehrān is essentially a concave city, whereas European and American cities, having their highest buildings in the centre, tend to be convex.[3] This conformation, together with the broad avenues and low houses, remains typically Asiatic and "colonial".

---

[1] P. Vieille, Tehran.
[2] See a detailed study in De Planhol, Recherches, pp. 69–73.　　　[3] Bobek (1958), p. 21.

(*b*) *Activity and population. The city's zone of attraction*

For the city to grow at such a rapid rate there must have been good reasons for the influx of population. We have a reasonably reliable guide to the structure of the working population as it was in 1922, before the onset of modernization. Out of a total of 210,000 inhabitants, 18,000 were active in commerce and transport, and 12,000 in various trades.[1] And even today the life of Tehrān is based on industry to only a very slight degree. In 1958 the capital's industrial activity comprised a small number of textile factories; a variety of smaller workshops, which were closer to crafts than to industry proper; some factories devoted to food-stuffs (e.g. edible oil, margarine, pasteurization of milk, flour-milling); a mechanical sector represented principally by a large and complex mechanical construction enterprise (Arjuman); a relatively declining Skoda works; and a few other factories (including a glass-works) producing consumer goods. With the exception of brick manufacture and building, the development of industry in general has been seriously handicapped by the lack of water. During the last few years, soft-drink factories, breweries, a second establishment for the pasteurization of milk, two new mechanical enterprises, and some automobile assembly plants have been set up; but the principal industrial activity is still building. A few years ago, the number of workers engaged in modern industry, in the strict sense of the word, was estimated at between 20,000 and 25,000.[2] The figures for craftsmen and for building operatives now exceed this. In 1956, out of a working population of 750,000, the secondary sector accounted for only 25 per cent approximately, made up of 16 per cent industrial workers and artisans (no distinction was made between the two groups) and 8·4 per cent building workers.[3]

Two factors above all have contributed to the expansion of Tehrān. The development of political and administrative centralization has led to a tremendous increase in the numbers of civil servants and the staffs of public authorities. Then, too, the bulk of the provincial land-owning aristocracy and the wealthier classes have come to settle in Tehrān— for various reasons, ranging from the Russian occupation of the north-west during the Second World War, to a simple desire to enjoy the pleasures of the capital. These newcomers have been accompanied by large numbers of domestic servants. Overall, the tertiary sector accounts

[1] Bobek (1958), p. 22.
[3] Ahrens, *Die Entwicklung*, p. 33.
[2] *Ibid.* p. 24.

for 73 per cent of the working population, of which 29·3 per cent are domestic servants, 12·6 per cent governmental and public service employees, 14·5 per cent in private service, 11·3 per cent in commerce, and 5·6 per cent transport workers.[1]

Where do these new inhabitants come from? Our knowledge of the capital's field of attraction is still only fragmentary, but it seems that while the middle and upper classes have been drawn from all parts of the country, the lower classes are of predominantly local origin. Research carried out among the employees of a number of organizations and businesses has revealed that their places of origin are limited to the north and north-west of the country (the Caspian regions and Āzarbāī-jān), and to the oases of the Iranian plateau as far afield as Hamadān and Iṣfahān.[2] Few if any immigrants seem to have come from the Zagros or from the eastern and south-eastern parts of the country. Thus Tehrān is not yet completely fulfilling the function of a metro-polis: indeed, it is still handicapped by its geographical position. Within the zone of attraction, there seems to be a link between trades and professions and regions of origin. Persian-speakers from the plateau area and the Alburz are most readily to be found in domestic service, retail trading, and in jobs requiring a certain skill; while the Āzarīs are engaged in unskilled work, especially in the building trade, and make up the bulk of the temporary labour migrating to the city during the building season.

(c) *Site, water, and wind. Topographical and social evolution*

Though happily situated with regard to communications, and stimu-lated in its growth by deliberate political choice, Tehrānis in no way particularly favoured in its site. Lying at some little distance from the foot of the main Alburz, but between the two chief rivers of the region, the Karaj and the Jājī Rūd; and sufficiently far from the mountain to be out of reach of the perennial streams, the city belongs to the least favoured group of foothill oases, in having to rely for its water exclu-sively on subterranean resources. As these are too deep beneath the city to be tapped directly (or at least they were in ancient times), Tehrān is still fed by qanāts, and its whole life is traditionally linked with these long underground conduits, so difficult to construct and maintain. The regular slope of the plain on which the city is situated, to the south of the undulating foothills, has enabled flow from the mouths of the

---

[1] Ahrens, *op cit.*   [2] De Planhol, *Recherches*, fig. 24, p. 74.

tunnels to be maintained by means of gravity. These conditions, so favourable to the growth of a city of medium size, together with a location that is in no way different from those of many other towns in Iran, have weighed heavily upon the later development of the great metropolis.

When it was the capital of the Qājārs, Tehrān was supplied entirely by qanāts. The number of these gradually increased throughout the nineteenth century, though the quantity of water carried occasionally decreased, as a result of the progressive deterioration of the tunnels. Today there are thirty-four qanāts, giving a total output of approximately 1·3 cubic metres per second. Twenty-six of them are privately owned (some belong to foreign embassies), and eight supplying a total of about 240 litres (52 gallons) per second, are *vaqf* (=religiously endowed) property. The length of each is usually between five and ten km, but it can be as much as twenty-four km. At the outlets of the qanāts, the purer water is extracted for drinking purposes and distributed, at an average rate of four litres per head per day, by means of carts. The remainder of the water flows freely through the town in a network of open jūbs which by tradition remained uncemented for a long time; they are from 10 to 70 cm wide and from 30 to 40 cm deep, according to the breadth of the street, and are bordered by plane trees and poplars. The water, directed to different quarters of the town in turn, runs for two successive days. It is first allowed to run for a good while in order to clear out all impurities which may have gathered in the canals; then, when it is running clear, steps are taken to fill the tanks of private houses (these tanks are generally underground) and the public reservoirs.

The city's great extension under the Pahlavī dynasty has not been accompanied by any really fundamental change in the water situation. For more than a quarter of a century efforts have been directed towards finding new sources of water that might be added to the already existing system of distribution. It was because of this that the waters of the Karaj were brought to Tehrān. A channel had been built in 1845, and later abandoned; but a modern canal (20 km covered, 32 km open), and ending in the north-western part of the town, was constructed between 1927 and 1930 to carry the new water. This now supplies just less than 1·3 cubic metres per second, or almost as much as all the qanāts put together. More recently, wells have been sunk in the south of the town and in the north, 30 m and 80 m respectively in depth, so as to draw water from underground by means of mechanical pumps. Borings carried out during the reign of Naṣir al-Dīn S̲h̲āh were unsuccessful, and it was only in 1950 that renewed attempts were made. In 1954 thirty-five wells were already operating, yielding a total of 1·4 cubic metres per second. These new resources have taken their place alongside the qanāts, but, except for part of the well-water, they flow as always through the vast network of jūbs, from which the inhabitants of Tehrān get almost all their washing water and sometimes, in the poorer quarters, their drinking water, too. It was only in 1952 that a slow start was made on the installation of underground watermains, but this initiative is still far from keeping pace with the expansion of the city.

Until these new methods of supply and distribution are put into operation on a large scale, and at a rate of development that matches the growth of the population, Tehrān will continue to live—as it has done ever since the end of the Qājār period, and especially since the dramatic increase in the number of her inhabitants—under the shadow of an increasing shortage of water. In the 1920s, thanks to an almost completely developed system of qanāts delivering some 1·3 cubic metres per second, the 200,000 inhabitants had approximately 500 litres (100 gallons) of water per head each day. By 1956 the Karaj canal and numerous wells had been constructed. Yet Tehrān, with about 1,500,000 inhabitants and a water supply of four cubic metres per second, had available scarcely 250 litres per head per day—and that in an arid climate, with countless gardens crying out for water, and with a system of distribution whose wastage increased with every expansion of the city.

Since 1961 things have taken a turn for the better, with the construction of the great dam in the Karaj valley, which has a capacity of 184,000,000 cubic metres. Meanwhile the city has been growing steadily drier and dustier: a development accentuated as early as 1930 by the cementing of the jūbs. This measure, sound enough in principle, has prevented water from infiltrating into the adjacent ground, and since this led to the decline of numerous plane trees, it has been necessary in many places to break the cement in order to preserve the vegetation. The flow of water through the jūbs in the dry season is getting less and less frequent; at the height of summer, the interval between distributions can be as much as twenty days.

The extension of the surface area of the city has also led to a noticeable falling off in the quality of the water. Extensive building operations in the northern part of the city, above the final stretches of the qanāts, have greatly added to the risks of infiltration and pollution. Moreover, as the city has spread out towards the south, the distance the water must be carried by the jūbs has lengthened, and this, together with the increasing density of the population, has made the task of cleaning and maintaining the canals more difficult. Thus in present-day Tehrān there has come about a social and topographical division that springs directly from the city's position at the foot of the mountains, and from the surface conduction of its water. The poorer inhabitants are tending more and more to congregate in the southern parts of the city, where the water pollution continues to rise as the quantity supplied continues to fall; at the same time, the better-class residential areas move farther and farther north, towards purer water and deeper wells. This north-ward movement of the upper classes is already having its effect on the planning and life of the city, whose centre of gravity is shifting farther to the north, while the old nucleus of Ark (arg) and bāzār is now de-cidedly to the south.

This phenomenon was already perceptible in 1874, with the con-struction of Nāṣir al-Dīn's surrounding wall, but it has greatly in-creased since then, because the northern residential districts have taken up large areas with their numerous open spaces and gardens. This land development began between the two ramparts in the north-eastern sector, where most of the qanāts emerge into the light of day. But the aristocratic quarter which grew up in that area later gave way to more modest occupation, and the original large properties were split up into smaller units. From about 1929 to 1930, while the north-east was going into a decline, the better residential districts shifted over towards the north-west and those areas newly improved by the construction of the Karaj canal.

The expansion of the city has scrupulously adhered to the pattern of Rezā Shāh's checkerboard, whose north–south and east–west axes have gradually been extended into the new built-up areas. Another fact of nature, the direction of the prevailing winds over the Alburz foothill area, seems to have played a decisive role in ensuring the continuity of this symmetrical plan. Apart from occasional cyclonic depressions, the circulation of the air over Tehrān is dominated by currents moving alternately from the mountains, when the great mass of the Alburz is being heated, or from the valley, according to whether the great mass of the Alburz is absorbing or losing heat. Thus the most desirable orientation for a house is east–west, at right angles to the mountain breeze, which is essential for freshness in summer and must be allowed to pass freely through the dwelling at night. It is also preferable, on account of the winter cold, for the main façades of the houses to face south. Building-plots must therefore be orientated north–south, with the house built at the northern end facing the garden, which occupies the whole of the southern part. It follows that the roads should run from east to west (bordered on the south by the rear walls of houses and on the north by garden-gates), and be cut from north to south by the broad avenues that carry the principal irrigation channels. The orientation of the houses with regard to the winds, and the consequent shape of the plots, have thus confirmed the strict checkerboard pattern of the streets. Rezā Shāh's network, based originally on the limits of properties, which had been conditioned by natural circumstances, has therefore been extended with absolute regularity throughout all the newer sectors of the city.

But the desire for freshness has influenced more than the planning of the newer quarters: combined with the wish for a purer water supply, it has encouraged the northward migration. The ground rises gradually as one moves northward in the direction of the mountains, and the fresh breezes mean that summer temperatures are much less over-powering in those parts than elsewhere in the region. The northern suburbs have now met the old summer village-resorts at the foot of the Alburz; and Tajrish, Qulhak, and Shamīrān [Shimrān] are scarcely separated from the city. Shamīrān is in fact now more the name of a locality than a particular village. Remarkable expansion to the north of the town has brought about a great change in the summer life and habits of the population. The annual migration, which, even as late as 1930, used to take large numbers of the city's inhabitants out to the springs at the foot of the mountains, now plays a much less important part in the life of the capital. Changing residence for the summer has become comparatively rare nowadays, being limited to the sovereign, the embassies, and a small number of leading personages. The former summer resorts to the north have been adopted as permanent residences by the upper classes, whose daily participation in the life of the city has been facilitated by the country's large-scale importation of motor-cars.

(*d*) *New communal and professional sections*

The development of this social cleavage between northern and southern Tehrān has had important repercussions on the city's commercial organization. Under the Qājārs there was segregation of commerce in Tehrān as in other towns, and in the nineteenth century trade was rigidly confined to the bāzār. Today this quarter is extremely complex in its construction and bears the marks of long evolution, for innumerable extensions and alterations have been made necessary by the growth of the city. Its two main elements, business streets and caravansera, are inextricably mixed, and any reorganization consists basically in the construction of small, generally two-storeyed caravansera (= *timcheh*); these are built either by the vaqf administration, or by important property-owners or merchants. Here, as in a depot, a wholesaler will keep his stock, have his address, and operate a small shop-cum-office, which may be either on the ground floor or above. Building sites are still made available for these: for example, by the demolition of large houses which survive in the area prescribed for the bāzār's expansion. The business streets, for their part, clearly cannot be lengthened indefinitely. New ones have to be constructed, and a newly arrived tradesman or craftsman sometimes has to go into business a long way from the district normally reserved for his fellows.

Despite all its evident disarray, the bāzār in Tehrān reflects a development that was continuous at least until the early years of the Pahlavī period, and has gone on sporadically ever since then. The principal artery through the bāzār is entered by way of the road called *Bozarjomehri*, and in its northern section it does not reveal a complete segregation between goods, but merely a loose grouping of luxury articles, such as jewellery, cloth, and haberdashery. Farther to the south, the carpet-sellers are grouped together. But in general the principal streets contain a certain variety of merchandise. A road that might once have been traditionally reserved for, say, retailers of cloth has, during the past quarter of a century, been invaded by sellers of knick-knacks, hardware, and so on.

Segregation is much more strictly observed in the smaller streets: there is one for iron-workers, one for grocers, etc. In the early years of the Pahlavī period there was also religious segregation in the bāzār among traders belonging to the various minorities. There was a Guebre quarter, a Jewish quarter, and an Armenian quarter, each containing specialities of its particular minority. (In the Armenian quarter, for example, there was a street for sellers of wines and spirits, and a caravanserai devoted to musical instruments.) The departure of these "minority" traders for the new business streets in the north of the city has meant the disappearance of such distinctions and an influx of a great variety of new traders. For example, lamps are now sold in the former caravanserai of Armenian musical instruments.

The northward shift of the city has left the bāzār off-centre, towards the south; the creation of new residential areas, and Rezā Shāh's construction of broad avenues favourable to traffic and business mobility have all brought about a decline in the status of the bāzār. Strange though this may seem within a city whose recent growth has been so considerable, and where so many new needs have been created, certain areas of the bāzār are in process of being virtually abandoned. Moreover, the topographical evolution of the bāzār reflects that of the city as a whole. Being the farthest away from the new upper-class areas, as well as last in line for the continually more polluted water supply, the southern part of the bāzār is in particularly rapid decline, with some streets completely abandoned and others given over to dwellings of the lowest class; but there is still a certain amount of activity in the northern sector, where the vaqf administration continued to build timchehs until as recently as 1957.

A great part of the town's commercial activity now takes place outside the bāzār, and three features in particular characterize this change: a new commercial centre has grown up in the modern streets in the city centre, to the north of the old bāzār and therefore closer to the new upper-class residential districts; small and isolated patches of commerce are beginning to take shape in the northern suburbs; and the poorer districts to the south are being invaded by artisans.

The development of the new commercial centre has its roots deep in the past. By the end of the nineteenth century, the business quarter had already overflowed the bāzār to the north, and Lāleazār Street, between the two encircling walls, was rapidly attracting traders. Nowadays, however, the principal activity is to be found farther to the west, in Nādirī and Istāmbul streets, which are part of Rezā Shāh's checkerboard. The administrative buildings occupying the site of the ārg form a relatively quiet area between the new commercial centre and the bāzār, though these two are linked farther to the east by the shops lining such great north–south arteries as Firdausī Street and Nāsir-Khosrau Street.

457

To the west, the tranquillity of the ārg area continues into the zone occupied by the imperial palaces. The modern commercial centre also extends round to the east of the bāzār proper (east of Sirīūs Street), though here it is much less attractive. Recently, another commercial area has developed in the western part of the city, in the *Sal sabil* quarter, beyond Sīmetrī Avenue.

Very little religious segregation is to be found in these new quarters. The Armenians and Jews of the bāzār have almost all installed themselves here, but no separate grouping is apparent; there is, however, a section of Budālī Street (on the south side, opposite the Museum) where there seems to be an Armenian majority, while in the Sipah Square area, to the east of the municipal offices, one can observe a certain concentration of Sikh traders. Nor does the new commercial centre reveal any significant grouping by trade or profession. Luxury shops, jewellers, and drapers seem to prefer Lāleazār Street, while antique-dealers and carpet-sellers (some of them Jewish) favour Firdausī Street; there are also a few small and purely local groupings, such as that on the south side of Sipah Street, where seven drapers' shops stand side by side. In part, then, there has been a survival of that juxtaposition of rival businesses which is so deeply rooted in the commercial tradition of Islam; but this is evident only in occasional details of the contemporary urban scene. The only really powerful concentration in the new part of the city is that of garages, large numbers of which are to be found in Shīrāz Street, which is the main road to the wealthy quarters in the north of the town. Very much on the edge of the new commercial centre—indeed, located in the heart of the residential area—this concentration was clearly dictated by the garage owners' need to be in an area where traffic could circulate with reasonable freedom; this would not have been possible in the congested business centre or in the overcrowded working-class districts of the south. They were also anxious to establish themselves in those quarters where the majority of car-owners had their residence.

The wealthy residential area of the north, with its powerful appetite for goods and services, could not, in any case, be supplied entirely from the commercial centre. Consequently, small groups of shops have grown up actually within the residential suburbs, though they supply scarcely more than essential foodstuffs; here, too, are the homes of a small working class who are devoted to the cleaning and maintenance of the habitations of the rich. A few shops of a superior kind (furniture, bicycles, etc.) have also been set up, though in much smaller number than would be found in similar streets in Western cities. However, their appearance represents something far more complex than that of the local foodshops, which have always found a place in the residential quarters of Islamic towns. For the shops in the predominantly residential quarters are almost always found in groups, scarcely ever singly. They are like rudimentary commercial centres, bāzārs in miniature, always situated at crossroads, squares, or junctions, and separated from one another by long stretches containing nothing but the façades of dwelling-houses. As a rule, these little groups of shops owe their existence to the initiative of a private builder. Similar groups are being incorporated into the most recent housing developments; though the appearance of a supermarket in Ta<u>kh</u>t-i-Jam<u>sh</u>īd Avenue in 1961 might have foreshadowed a rather more westernized form of evolution.

The lower-class districts in the south of the city present quite a different picture. There the main streets are completely lined with shops, and one has to plunge into the maze of narrow kuchehs in order to have any impression of being in a residential zone. Moreover, the shops are occupied by craftsmen rather than traders. There are good reasons why shops and artisans should be so numerous in this part of the city. First, the high density of the population, not to mention the relatively low standard of living, demands the presence of great numbers of foodshops and technicians. And then, of course, crafts and small trades play an important part in the employment of labour in countries where there is little mechanized industry. The large numbers of artisans found here reflect the ease with which one can set up this kind of business with only a moderate capital investment; and it is natural that they should be found above all in the southern part of the town, close to their main source of labour and the bulk of their customers. Tinkers, cauldron-makers, mattress-makers, saddlers, cartwrights, and potters—the list of traditional crafts goes on and on, colourful and noisy. All the main avenues of the south seem more or less like extensions of the bāzār, especially when compared with the far more westernized commercial centre taking shape in the north. A notable effect of all this artisan activity is the relatively high cost of shop-frontage (so necessary for any trading activity) compared with land prices in general. This holds good throughout the southern part of the town, south of Sipeh Avenue.

The south also contains a number of genuine industrial areas. The city's brickworks, especially, are almost all to be found in the south.

The clay is dug from open pits in the plain, and when the excavations get too deep, kilns and equipment are simply moved on elsewhere. The brickfields are thus moving gradually farther to the south and east; in fact, many of the poorer quarters of the city are built in the abandoned quarries of old brickfields. These pits, filled with mud or water during the winter, are as much a part of the landscape as are the kiln chimneys of brickworks still in production.

(e) The problems of the southern quarters. Conclusion

The southern parts of the city—the poor quarters, where, more than anywhere else, the immigrants install themselves—present a problem of both sanitation and social inequality. Apart from a few residual diseases, of which smallpox is the most important, there is nothing "primitive" about public health in the city; indeed, the situation is typically European and normal. In the absence of mortality statistics, it nevertheless seems certain that for the southern parts of Tehrān there are more deaths in winter than in summer. This is in line with conditions in temperate countries, and quite contrary to those existing in nearby tropical India. The poor sanitary conditions of the southern part of the city, notably the lack of drains, seem to have no large-scale ill effects. In all parts of the city polluted waste is disposed of in cesspools sunk into the porous layer of foothill outwash constituting the subsoil. Through this, the waste matter filters away. As these cesspools are comparatively shallow (from ten to a maximum of twenty m), there remains sufficient space for filtration between them and the underlying layer of water. In the south of the town this layer is found at a minimum depth of thirty m. When one cesspool is full, another is dug.

In general, the city is reasonably salubrious. Indeed, the major health problem at the moment is partly of social origin. Tuberculosis, of which the country as a whole is free, has taken firm root in Tehrān, where it appears in seriously epidemic and galloping forms. Since its arrival in the city as a major feature twenty years ago, the dramatic forms of the disease have only served further to emphasize its spectacular rate of increase.

The fearful poverty of the southern quarters, together with the overwhelming social and topographical contrast existing between the two halves of the city, make up what seems to be the fundamental contradiction or paradox of present-day Tehrān. And herein lie the seeds of conflict—especially because the purely social differences are now accompanied by an ethno-cultural division, following the invasion of the southern quarters[1] by the relatively primitive Āzarīs, whose assimilation appears to be proceeding very slowly. It is still too early to know whether Tehrān will be able to sustain the role that should devolve upon her as Iran continues her evolution from an empire rent by internal forces, to a coherent and united nation. Far from being a point of fusion, the capital city of today all too often seems to accentuate differences and aggravate the contrasts that exist in other parts of the country. In Tehrān the difficulties attendant upon urban growth have been multiplied by hydrological and topographical factors, and the social-spatial segregation has been bilateral rather than concentric. The normal development of site utilization has led the city along a road fraught with difficulty.

NOTES ON HISTORICAL AND OTHER SOURCES FOR THE RECONSTRUCTION OF THE GEOGRAPHY OF IRAN

Sources for the study of historical geography are similar for many parts of the world, although their relative value and reliability obviously vary enormously. Such sources may be classified as:

(1) Descriptions by residents and visitors.

(2) Reports and official documents compiled either by municipal, local or national authorities.

(3) Maps, plans, engravings and photographs, either separate or with (1) and (2) above.

(4) Evidence in the present landscape and townscape.

The fallibility of sources, and various special considerations which must be applied in an Iranian or generally Middle Eastern setting became apparent as material is explored and analysed. One highly important point is that as regards Iran, and probably the Middle East generally, material relating to towns is much more readily available as compared with the countryside.

Most important simple sources—at least as regards volume—are the accounts of travellers who visited Tehrān, Iṣfahān and other Persian towns, and whose impressions and descriptions have been recorded in print. These include both Middle Eastern and European authors.

[1] Particularly in the industrial sections of the south-west.

Before the fourteenth century Arab and Persian historians and travellers
are the main source, since European accounts do not exist. As is the
case also with European medieval writings, however, these Oriental
accounts tend to be mixed with legends and popular beliefs, and are
often inexact in detail. Moreover, in the hand-written books of the
period diacritical marks could often be mis-read to give confusion. Such
is the case of al-Iṣṭakhrī's reference to a village called Behzān in the
vicinity of Ray in the tenth century. This has wrongly been claimed to
refer to Tehrān as it could be read thus without difficulty—تهران rather
than بهزان. Many writers were concerned primarily with history and
give most weight to the acts of kings and princes, though quite a
number often made extended reference to their own home province or
town. Hence any information on towns tends to be incidental, although
of course royal activities included building works, defence and fortifica-
tion; and there are accounts of the style and grandeur of court life. For
instance, Tehrān was noted as a large and pleasant village producing
excellent fruit; a halt in the progress north of a Saljuq sulṭān from Ray to
Māzandarān. Facts which can be derived from these sources include
first, the mere mention of a town or village as proof that it existed then,
and then possibly some indication of size—such as Ibn Rustah's comparison of Yahūdieh with Hamadān in area and population. Yahūdieh
was one of the twin-towns which constituted Iṣfahān in the ninth
century, the other being Jay, according to the same account, which was
half a league across and covering 600 acres, with four gates and a wall
containing a hundred towers. Exaggeration can often be rife, but even
two estimates of the numbers slaughtered by Tīmūr in Iṣfahān in the
late fourteenth century, of 70,000 and 200,000 serve to illustrate the
fact that Iṣfahān was then a town of some size and importance, at least
before the massacre. Other semi-fanciful accounts such as those of the
troglodyte dwellers of early Tehrān, living in underground burrows
like desert rats, and emerging to kill and rob cannot be totally dismissed,
since they are common to many writers, though they leave many
questions unanswered. In so far as these early Arab and Persian accounts
are the only sources for the study of medieval Persian cities they are
valuable, but they must be handled with great care in both translation
and interpretation.

Once European writers appear on the scene the Middle Eastern
authors fade in importance, not because they ceased writing—many
accounts such as Iskandar Munshī's *Tārīkh-i-ʿAbbāsī* and the *Tārīkh-i-*

Siāh contain valuable geographical and historical material—but because Europeans, with their eye for detail and insatiable quest for rarities and wonders, and because they wrote for Europeans who knew little of the east, produced information of much greater value to the historical geographer. On the other hand, of course, the English Sherley brothers could spend years at the Safavid court yet never describe Iṣfahān.

The first European to pass through Tehrān was Don Ruy di Clavijo, a Spanish Ambassador on his way to Tamerlane's court at Samarqand in 1404. Josafa Barbaro and Ambrosio Contarini, both Venetians, visited Iṣfahān in 1474, the one an ambassador and the other a merchant. From then on the motives of visitors were mainly diplomatic or commercial, or both; although from the early seventeenth century onwards, European religious houses were established in Iṣfahān from which the representatives sent regular reports.

Although these accounts vary very much as regards actual figures given (the length of the walls, number of houses, etc.), where a major urban feature is described, accounts are usually similar enough to allow reconstruction, especially if the feature has some surface expression in the present townscape, such as the Chahār Bāgh Avenue at Iṣfahān.

The seventeenth century was Iṣfahān's hey-day. Accounts in French, German, English and Latin are long and voluble regarding the glories of the Safavid capital, its palaces, gardens, mosques, squares, bāzārs and bridges. The very slight consideration of Tehrān at this period betokens its position as a small walled trading centre distinctly low in the urban hierarchy. After the flood of European visitors to the Safavid court comparatively little is known of the period characterized by Afghan invasions that started in 1722 with the fall of Iṣfahān. During a period of anarchy such as the Nādir Shāh and Zand periods trade is disrupted, diplomatic missions become pointless and conditions hazardous even for the most intrepid traveller. This results in gaps in knowledge at periods when much was happening to the towns, albeit with largely negative effects.

The re-establishment of law and order under the Qājārs in the late eighteenth century again encouraged foreign visitors, now with Tehrān as their principal destination. Diplomatic representatives and military advisors head the list, as Tehrān had little tradition of commerce or industry. Later, British civil servants passing to and from

India left valuable accounts, and in these both Tehrān and Iṣfahān are considered in detail. However in the case of Iṣfahān subjectivity is augmented by a certain amount of sentiment or even moralizing, as travellers bewail the town's fall from glory, and its ruin compared with past splendours. Thus it is often difficult to be certain as to what could be held to be facts and what amounts to aphorism reflecting the fashion of writing in a particular time. It may thus be difficult even to know which century the writer is speaking of. Accounts of Tehrān are also coloured with personal opinions usually of a derogatory nature. Whereas Iṣfahān was always compared favourably with the capitals of seventeenth-century Europe, Tehrān at first appeared as a village alongside the Victorian splendours of London or Paris. Attempts at westernization under Nāṣir-al-Dīn Shāh are usually decried as incongruous and inefficient mixtures of the east and the west, and anything which detracted from the picturesque orientalism of Persian towns, the chief aim of the traveller's quest, was naturally not approved of.

The twentieth century brought a succession of books concerned mostly with the political events in and concerning Persia. One contributing factor was the constitutional crisis of the early part of the century and another the two World Wars when Persia became a counter in the struggle for power between Russia, Germany and Britain. Far more Europeans have visited Persia in the twentieth century than ever before, but their contribution to the travel literature of the area is comparatively small and of low quality. Only a few texts, such as, for example, that of Sir Roger Stevens, former British Ambassador in Tehrān, can compare with the careful documentation of Chardin or Curzon.

The works of travellers may be summed up as being of great value to the historical geographer of Iran provided reservations are borne in mind as to the purpose of the work (whether intended to impress the general reader or set forth a serious view of the country), the author's length of stay and opportunities for study in Iran (including his knowledge of Persian) and the attitudes towards the Middle East prevailing in his country of origin at the time of his visit.

Official documentation on aspects of urban growth and development is regrettably lacking in Persia. Town government before the 1920s was vested in governors, who were often royal princes with little interest in the town except the collection of revenue (and, at lower levels of government, in local ward heads, guild officials and religious

464

leaders who rarely left written records even if they were literate). Royal decrees or "firmān" are useful in dating certain acts affecting the development of the cities, such as that of 1834 by Muḥammad Shāh granting the British representative jurisdiction over the village of Qulhak in the suburbs of Tehrān and preserved by the British Embassy, and those by Shāh 'Abbās I concerning the establishment and privileges of the Armenian community of Iṣfahān, now held in the Cathedral Museum at Julfā. Rarely, if ever, can statistics be obtained from official documents before the twentieth century. The first national census was not made until 1956. Before that only spot counts in certain cities had been carried out in the 1930s. "Official" population figures for Tehrān go back to 1890 but are admittedly unreliable. The same can be said for Zill-al Sulṭān's "census" of Iṣfahān about the same time. The Tehrān municipality was founded in 1920, and published population data which are often confusing and contradictory if birth, death and immigration rates are closely compared with total figures and estimates. Since the first census the Department of National Statistics has produced social and economic data concerning Persian towns on a modern basis but these are still imperfect owing to special local difficulties and lack of experience. In any case, it could be held that such figures, being entirely modern, have only very limited relevance to a historical study.

When this state of affairs is compared with the wealth of statistics and reports on all aspects of development available for many European towns, starting from medieval charters and land surveys and censuses, the problems of studying Iranian towns are clearly evident.

As regards maps, which are a principal tool of the geographer, the student of Iranian towns again discovers that he is at a disadvantage, as maps of many individual towns are unknown before the mid-nineteenth century. However, more general maps of Iran, or Middle Eastern countries including Iran, exist from the seventeenth century onwards, indicating by style of representation at least the comparative importance and size of the towns. The first map to show Tehrān as a small settlement north of the ruins of Ray was that of a Dutch cartographer dated 1720. At the same time Iṣfahān is depicted as a very large town equal to Constantinople, Damascus and Cairo, which were then the largest in the Middle East. The Hotz collection in the Royal Geographical Society of London has more examples of such maps.

Early writers often illustrated their works with engravings. These mainly illustrate individual buildings of note, street scenes and im-

465

portant personages, and are hence moderately useful. The more important ones, however, include panoramas of cities as a whole. Often these are stylized, such as for example the views of Struys and Olearius of Iṣfahān, showing the city with pitched roofs and battlemented walls like a European town. Some are especially valuable, like Kaempfer's planograph of the royal palace of Iṣfahān from which a reconstruction of the interior layout can be made. Again careful analysis is needed to sift truth from romantic fantasy in an age before the use of photographs was possible.

The first and only map of Iṣfahān prior to modern surveys is included in a folio of architectural drawings, "Monuments modernes de la Perse", by a Frenchman, Coste, compiled about 1840. This is little more than a reference-map locating the main monuments, but does outline the city wall giving names of various quarters and some indication of the number of inhabited houses in each ("inhabited" being a highly significant word in a period when two thirds of Iṣfahān was in ruins). Thus, although diffidently, a population distribution of a sort can be reconstructed.

In Tehrān Nāṣir-al-Dīn Shāh ordered the compilation of a map produced in 1858. Its outline is the walls of Āghā Muḥammad Khān which date from the 1790s, but inside this the street pattern, bāzārs, quarter names and principal religious buildings are marked, giving a valuable insight into mid-nineteenth century Tehrān. However the reading, translation and transliteration of names on this map present considerable difficulties, as decoration was as much a consideration as was legibility and the two are not always compatible. To the inexperienced eye Persian script can easily be mistaken for a sinuous street pattern. Another difficulty is the lack of information on the extent of extra-mural development, but this is compensated by a map of the same date by a Major Krziz of Tehrān and district showing gardens, yakhchāls (ice-factories) and caravansera just outside the walls. The same problems are encountered when studying the 1892 map of Tehrān. This shows the second walling carried out in the 1860s and the new areas thus enclosed, but otherwise provides similar information to that of the 1858 map. Tehrān and its surroundings are again illustrated by Stahl's map of 1900. These two maps however are excellent as a background for nineteenth-century accounts of Tehrān, when the city was establishing itself as capital, growing rapidly and acquiring the attributes of cityhood in the western sense. For the modern period post-

1926 maps are readily available for most towns, produced by military and municipal authorities, by the census department and more recently the National Cartographic Institute, which also has valuable air-photo coverage of major Iranian towns.

Finally, historical geography in Iran has its own approach to fieldwork. As all cities, those of Iran are a conglomeration of buildings, streets and open spaces including elements from the past, which if searched out and mapped, aid in tracing the town's development. For instance, many writers described the Ṭabarak citadel in Iṣfahān, but its site was unknown until the area was examined in detail with the aid of air-photos, and a deep ditch around three sides of a square discovered, which was all that remained of the fortress. The reconstruction of the palace quarter of Iṣfahān has also been mentioned. Some Safavid buildings still survive, often changed in appearance and use, which are of assistance in this task. The mapping of twelfth-century Saljuq remains in Iṣfahān gives an indication of the city's extent at that period. In Tehrān there is less scope for such fieldwork as the city contains few buildings of any antiquity. However, street patterns often follow the line of former walls, and the location of early nineteenth-century Armenian churches helps to fix the Armenian quarters of that date. Examples could be multiplied. Such approaches cannot rival in accuracy the detailed mapping or statistical surveying usually associated with research work in urban geography, but they are useful, indeed essential, to the study. It might be added that such types of survey entail considerable difficulties and can arouse what is natural suspicion and reserve on the part of the inhabitants. This is by no means confined to any one country. Such then are the sources available to the historical geographer in Iran, and it is hoped that the present note has given some indication of the methods found useful in their analysis and interpretation. These approaches sound tenuous, inaccurate, and unscientific to the student of modern towns where computer techniques are possible, but for the subject under study they are the only sources available. And it must also be borne in mind that in approaching the study of Middle Eastern towns, as opposed to European or American examples, special problems are encountered which can only be tackled with reference to their local context.

30-2

CHAPTER 14

POPULATION

According to the census taken in 1956, the total population of Iran was 18,944,821; it has increased since then at the rate of 2·4 to 2·5 per cent a year. Since Iran covers a vast territory of 628,000 square miles (1,648,000 sq. km), this means there is a fairly low numerical density:[1] 18·5 persons per square mile or 12 to the sq. km. Less than a third of the population live in the cities, the remainder being peasants and part- or full nomads. The birth rate is very high (about 45 per thousand), while the mortality rate is about 20 per thousand. It is a surprisingly youthful population, and the first census showed that 49 per cent of the inhabitants were under 20 years of age, with only 4 per cent aged 60 and over. Movements of population in and out of the country (i.e. external migration) are not of great importance. But, on the other hand, the rural exodus, the drift from the country to the towns, presents a highly intractable problem; and the seasonal migrations of nomads are also considerable.

VARIATIONS IN DENSITY

The Iranian plateau, whose altitude fluctuates between 1,000 and 2,000 m above sea-level, is crossed by three imposing mountain ranges: The Alburz runs southward from the Caucasus, follows the curve of the Caspian Sea, and crosses Khurāsān to join the Hindu Kush and the Himalayas. The Zagros, on the west, runs south-eastwards from the Caucasus, extending as far as the Persian Gulf, and the third major complex of ranges running from north-west to south-east, crosses the eastern interior of Iran. These ranges form an amphitheatre around the plateau, in the middle of which are the salt deserts (kavīrs). In sharp contrast, in the area south of the Caspian and north of the Persian Gulf, Iran is flanked by two flat strips.

[1] Provisional data from the Second Census of Iran taken in November 1966 gives a total population of 25,781,090. Density per square kilometre has increased from 18·5 to 25·2; urban population totals 9,820,922 persons and rural population 15,318,231. Fuller details are not yet available. Population growth as measured between the two censuses amounts to 3·1 per cent per annum; but Iranian research workers suggest that there could have been under-enumeration in the First Census, of the order of 250,000–400,000 persons. If adjustment is made to the First Census by an increase, for this possible under-enumeration, of 350,000, and the figures of the Second Census accepted as accurate, then the rate of growth comes to 2·9 per cent per annum.

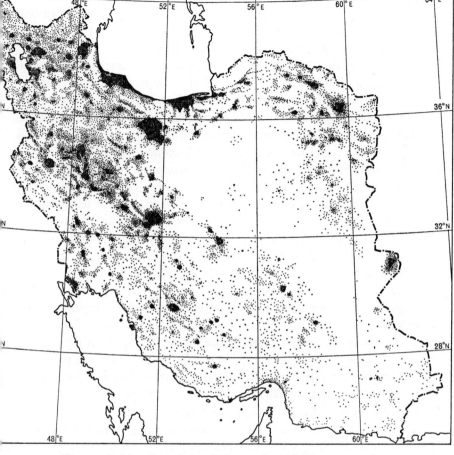

Fig. 105. Density of population. (After map issued by Department of Statistics, Ministry of the Interior, Tehrān.)

It is the disposition of relief which could be held mainly to determine the geographical distribution of the population. The centre of the country is largely empty and life has been driven either towards the exterior or towards the interior of the mountains, to the points where there is an adequate water-supply; people live among the foothills of all three mountain ranges, and each group has settled half in the plain and half on the mountain side. There are extraordinary variations in density: in the neighbourhood of Tehrān, 44 inhabitants per sq. km; on the shores of the Caspian, from 20 to 30; in Āzarbāījān 26, falling to 2 per

469

sq. km in some regions of the south. The centre is practically un-inhabited. Corresponding differences in density may be noted among the different cities: 253·2 to the sq. km in Tehrān; 170·5 in Ābādān; 51·6 in Tabrîz; 9·7 in Kāshān, and 4·2 in Kirmān.

By way of simplification, the most heavily populated areas may be classified as follows: the shores of the Caspian Sea; the watered mountain regions; the naturally watered or irrigated oases of the plateau. The elements which determine this distribution are the same that influence every dispersal of men throughout the world: natural factors and human factors (sociological, economic, and historical).

The most important natural factors affecting the population distribu-tion throughout Iran, as in a number of other developing countries (in the Middle East, North Africa, etc.), are water and temperature; and it is only by studying the hydrography, climate, and meteorology of these territories that it is possible to analyse the reasons for the striking variations in density from one region to another.

With certain exceptions, Iran appears as an arid zone with green islets scattered over it. The life of the plateau is dependent on the snowfall crowning the encircling mountains—indeed, regions which can support life are all to be found where the torrents swollen by melting snow rush down the mountains in the spring. The south of the country is scorched by the sun and swept by winds from the Arabian peninsula and from the interior of Asia. The northern region is well watered, owing to the mountain barrier of the Alburz; there is a sharp contrast between eastern Iran, which is desert, and western Iran, which is mountainous. The ranges of the Alburz and Zagros prevent the northerly winds from reaching the central plateau, and by this means they deter-mine the climates of two regions—one is humid, to the north and west; the other, in the interior and on the Persian Gulf coasts in the south, is dry. Apart from the region of the Caspian Sea with its high rainfall, Iran is very dry. The annual rainfall exceeds 400 mm over one third of the country only; it reaches 1,000 mm in the Māzandarān; but over half of the country it varies between 200 and 400 mm, and elsewhere it does not exceed 200 mm. The numerous rivers are small in volume; most of them flow at less than 300 cu. cm per second. Extreme aridity is therefore the main problem of agriculture—even of existence—in Iran.

In this parched country man has always been conscious of the need to make the soil fertile, if he is not to disappear from it by death or emigra-tion—hence the religious and traditional value of water, which has been

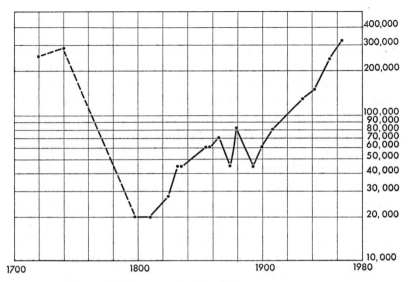

Fig. 106. Estimate growth of population, 1700–1963.

magnified in Zoroastrianism. The Iranians have had to use artificial irrigation, and their immense efforts in this sphere show to what extent the geographical distribution of the population is determined by hydrographical factors. Indeed, the maps of rainfall show closely similar patterns of distribution as compared with the location of the human population; and isopleths of population density come to resemble so exactly in their disposition the shape of rainfall maps that one might almost be justified in talking of superimposition.

URBAN AND RURAL POPULATIONS

According to the 1956 census, the urban population constitutes 30·1 per cent of the total population, and the rural population (including semi-nomads) 69·9 per cent. The population is distributed over 49,000 settled areas, of which 186 are towns (i.e. places with more than 5,000 inhabitants).[1]

[1] In the absence of reliable statistics regarding the nomads, this survey will be confined to the urban and peasant populations, and the reader is referred to separate historical and anthropological studies of the tribes of Iran. (See bibliography of "Geography of Settlement", pp. 754–6 below.)

Urban population

Cities, the constant elements of Iranian civilization, have always played a significant part in the history of the country. The larger ones, which originated with the need for centres of barter, are for the most part situated on the great international highways, and have always been rebuilt on the same sites. The history of many of them goes back three or four thousand years. Three routes have always been of fundamental importance: the northern one (the celebrated "Silk road"), which linked China with central Europe and the Scandinavian countries by way of Transoxiana, Nīshāpūr, Ray, Tabrīz, and Constantinople; the southern road running from Ray towards the Levant and Africa; and, finally, the sea route of the Persian Gulf, sustained by a chain of ports. In the past, not only were these routes important channels of trade, but they carried the civilization and ideas of the Far East into the West. Moreover it was along these two land routes that the great invasions of the Mongols and Tartars were launched.

Each city became a stopping place for caravans. At the centre were the caravansera and the castle of the local chieftain, which soon came to be surrounded by a citadel (*kuhandiz*); and around the caravansera were established meeting places, bāzārs, and living quarters (*shahristān*). Although they were threatened in the perpetual struggles among tribal marauders, local overlords, and foreign invaders, these mercantile cities put up a stout resistance. Throughout the centuries they existed as rich and prosperous islands among the mass of the peasantry, with whom they had few or no ties of interdependence. Before the nineteenth century no really new urban centres had emerged, for until this period the economic situation of Iran had not undergone any marked change; the capital shifted from one large town to another, but only in response to the political exigencies of the time. When the land routes of Iran were no longer used by intercontinental traffic however, the country was obliged to have a closed economy, and the towns came to resemble rural settlements. Similarly, a number of Iranian cities declined in importance after the opening, at the end of the last century, of the Suez Canal and the maritime route around Africa.

No longer able to play their part in international trade, and still lacking the industrial activity of modern cities, Iranian towns became exclusively centres of craftsmanship and of a very limited internal trade, while at the same time groups of villages, under pressure of a growing population, began to take on some of the features (i.e. numbers) of urban centres, without having any of the real functions and characteristics of cities.

Over the past fifty years the close and continuous communications with the West, the introduction of modern industry, and the rural exodus into the cities have all caused great changes in the appearance and the size of cities, as well as in the composition of the urban population. It was chiefly in the years between the two world wars and also during the last decade that manufacturing or industrial centres replaced the former towns living by craft trades; that "mushroom-towns" made their appearance (see below, pp. 475–6) and urban population increased to an astonishing degree. An analytical study of the country's urban population, according to the 1956 census, is not without interest. Of a total urban population over 5,500,000, the five leading cities (Tehrān, Tabrīz, Iṣfahān, Mashhad, Ābādān) contain nearly 3,000,000 inhabitants altogether and the other five centres of importance (Shīrāz, Ahvāz, Kirmānshāh, Rasht, Hamadān) account for 500,000, giving a total of 3,500,000; the remaining 2,000,000 are distributed among 103 towns.

TABLE 9. *Numerical grouping of most important cities according to size of population*

No. of inhabitants	Over 200,000	100,000–200,000	50,000–100,000	10,000–50,000	Less than 10,000
No. of cities	5	5	7	78	91

This distribution of the population, which is in itself singular, becomes even more striking when it is considered that the city of Tehrān alone, with 1,500,000 inhabitants, comprised half the total population of the five leading cities of the country; and that the population of the most important city after Tehrān (Tabrīz) did not exceed 290,000 inhabitants. These expressive figures show the degree of urbanization reached in one centre—the metropolis—of Iran.

The cities of Iran may be classified according to their size and functions as follows:

(*a*) The traditionally great cities mentioned above, have a brilliant history and are important at the present day as centres of provincial administration or even as manufacturing centres. In terms of their

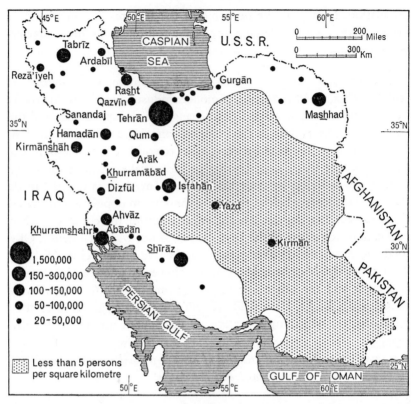

Fig. 107. Comparative population sizes in Iran, 1956. (After J. I. Clarke,
The Iranian City of Shiraz, 1963.)

number as well as their occupations, the inhabitants of these cities
have, since the distant past, constituted the truly urban population of
the country, which today comprises officials, merchants, landowners
living in the city, and, above all, craftsmen. These cities are the nerve-
centres of a vast country whose population is predominantly rural and
thinly scattered.

The merchants, in close association with the craftsmen, have retained
their original position in the cities: hence the astonishing importance
of that singular institution, the bāzār. Some sociologists have attempted
to trace a resemblance between the North African *Sūq* and the Iranian
bāzār, but any similarity appears fortuitous. The bāzār, indeed, does
not confine its activities to those of a market, but functions also as a
political and social force whose complexity and importance are com-

474

prehensible only to an integrated member of Iranian society. In a country where the political parties and syndicates play an insignificant part, this concentration of merchants and trader-craftsmen, living under the shelter of the brick vaults of the bāzār in complete unity and solidarity—without being officially organized for the purpose—is an essential element. Apart from the clergy, it is the only force that dares consistently to defy the governing classes and the landed proprietors. Under the threat of social and political insecurity created by the bāzār, the landed aristocracy have tended to sell their lands in order to buy city property instead; they invest their capital in the industrial and commercial sectors and thus constitute an influential class of urban society.

Over the past thirty years, three principal changes have occurred in the ancient cities. In the first place, the traditional manual and manufacturing industries have been superseded by modern processing industries (textiles, glass, chemical, and mechanical works), a change which has altered the country's professional structure and given rise to a working proletariat, with all its political, economic, and cultural consequences.

Second, the rural exodus or migration of the population from the secondary towns towards the principal cities, originally caused by economic stringency, today represents a psycho-sociological need. Those migrants who could not adapt to the still-embryonic industries of the cities have become part of a sub-proletariat, often inhabiting shanty-town areas and living at the worst by begging. "These rural populations thrown up against the cities are simply a mass of human beings encamped in the hope of work or of paid activity rather than groups constituting a true society."[1] They form an intermediate stage between the rural and urban populations, belonging to no definite community.

Finally, there is the growing importance of the middle classes (officials, members of the liberal professions, qualified craftsmen, etc.), who, by their activities and their ways of life, have engendered important changes. Moreover, there has grown up a westernized elite, an "intelligentsia" quite different from the aristocratic and religious elite of the traditional order.[2]

In these cities, where a relatively modern type of existence now

---

[1] Balandier, *Anthropologie des pays sous développés*, p. 78.
[2] E. Naraghi, *Les classes moyennes en Iran*.

prevails, there is evidence of the disintegration of traditional institutions, the disappearance of the patriarchal family—all the signs, in short, of a society in transition.

(*b*) A further segment of the urban population live in numerous smaller country towns, which cannot be compared with the cities of the first group. The inhabitants are chiefly farmers or people who still make a living by agriculture (an insignificant minority is occupied with skilled work and with trade); and according to existing information, their proportion to the increasing population remains fixed.

Such towns do not show the characteristics inherent in every true city, and this is apparent as much in their type of urbanism as in the way of life and the outlook of the inhabitants. For the most part they are nothing more than concentrations of human beings, fulfilling the function of a local market for the surrounding countryside and owing their promotion to the rank of "town" solely to their position as markets and administrative centres.

(*c*) In addition to these two urban groups, there has arisen here and there during the past thirty years a type of town that has no link with the past, but is simply an industrial settlement. Within this category may be listed the manufacturing centres of the north (Chālūs, Shāhī, Naushahr, and others), the mining centres of Khūzistān (Masjid-i-Sulaimān, etc.), and finally the oil-refinery town of Ābādān. These "mushroom-towns" which have grown too rapidly for proper organization, are teeming with life and producing an urban population of a different kind from those described above. Their inhabitants, who come from the most isolated and abandoned corners of the country without any experience of urban life, find themselves suddenly in contact with a twentieth-century industrial city. Thus the nomads of the Zagros and fishermen of the Persian Gulf made up the population of Ābādān without having lived through any prolonged phase of transition. These new elements which have so recently arrived on the demographic map of Iran, as on that of other underdeveloped countries, are the portents of fundamental changes in the Iranian society.

Rural population

According to the results of the 1956 Census, 69 per cent of the inhabitants of Iran live in the country. This figure includes the nomadic and semi-nomadic population; moreover, it is not clear exactly how to define the urban and consequently the rural population. An economic and sociological delimitation of the "village" must therefore be sought. The great majority of the rural population live in country settlements called "*deh*" (=villages), which are not only centres of habitation but also economic units of agricultural production and consumption. In a country whose economy is founded on agriculture, these villages produce the most important part of the national revenue.[1]

At the present day there are about 45,000 villages in Iran, each with a population of at least fifteen persons. (Hamlets and smaller rural communities are not included in this figure.) Two types of village may be noted in regard to the distribution of population: the scattered and the concentrated. The villages of the well-watered northern region are of the scattered type, while the concentrated type is to be found in those regions where water is scarce and people are obliged to draw together around a spring or a *qanāt*. In the north the dwelling takes the form of a house of one or two storeys, usually erected on wooden piles and roofed with dried rushes or with tiles. A concentrated settlement is sometimes in the form of a fort or *qalʿeh*, a term signifying not only the fort but also the village itself, which is surrounded by high walls containing dwellings and made of beaten earth, with round towers at the corners. Villages of this type are numerous over the whole of the Iranian plateau. (See "Geography of Settlement", pp. 425–8.)

Without embarking upon a study of the social and economic structure of the villages of Iran,[2] it is nevertheless possible to summarize the characteristics of a typical Iranian village:

1. The village constitutes an economic unit: i.e. it is a single enterprise often directed by a single promoter, who is the landlord.

2. It is solely devoted to agriculture.

3. It depends in large measure, often exclusively, on private ownership. This applies not merely to the fields and cultivated land, over which rights of private property are quite conceivable and legitimate, but also to the collections of human dwellings, the small cells of the social organization which are called villages and which in the view of many ought to be subject to the government and come under public ownership.

---

[1] It is estimated that 40 per cent of the national revenue comes from the agricultural sector, 10 per cent from petroleum exploitation and refining, 20 per cent from other industry, and the rest from a variety of other economic activities.

[2] See A. K. S. Lambton, *Landlord and Peasant in Persia*; and J. Behnam and S. Rassekh, *Introduction à la sociologie de l'Iran*.

4. Relations between peasants and landlords are regulated mostly by contracts of *métayage* (payment in kind), and in very rare cases by farm rent paid in money.

5. The village is a social unit, most frequently a group of related persons.

Within this general pattern it is possible to distinguish, broadly speaking, three kinds of villages:

(*a*) *Villages of the north.* Geographical conditions have an effect on the appearance of these villages and influence their mode of life as well as their juridical and economic structure. Here, unlike the other regions of Iran, rural settlement is dispersed over wide cultivated expanses. In the mountains, houses are single-storeyed and made of baked brick, with a terrace constructed from tree trunks; whereas along the Caspian shores and in the plain the houses are small and erected on piles to keep them dry. A generally adequate water supply has allowed the peasants some freedom of choice in what they grow and how they live, and the system of farm rent paid in money rather than in produce is widespread. It is the rural population of these provinces which forms the great majority of smallholding farmers in Iran. Since hydraulic installations are not necessary, the smallholders are able to maintain their independence in relation to the big estates. Existence in a favourable climate, among fields which bear abundant crops of rice, tea, and cotton, has given the rural population of the north, by and large, a cheerful temperament with a tendency to optimism.

(*b*) *Villages of the south and the south-west.* The life of these villages is quite different; the people are the poorest in the country and live in deplorable conditions, deriving their subsistence from a slender harvest of cereal crops. Water is scarce and each village is grouped around a well. Most houses are built of mud and matted grass (wattle and daub) and there are also huts made of mud and palm leaves. Landlordism is usual, and hence the land is cultivated solely under a system of *métayage*. Shortage of water drives the peasant from his village for long periods, and in some instances there are even mass migrations with the object of finding another source of water that will support a settlement. Some writers in describing this way of living have spoken of "itinerant villages".

(*c*) *Villages of the central plateau.* Although scarcity of water is also one of the main problems for the rural population of the central plateau, it is less acute for them than for the peasants of the south. Agriculture and human settlement have been made possible by various systems of irrigation, based on qanāts, wells or streams; these require collective undertakings, close co-operation and a certain amount of capital, and thus again they lead to concentrated settlement, large estates, and the system of *métayage*.

The peasants, who cultivate cereal crops, live in villages built of mud and crude brick. Two-roomed, poorly ventilated houses are huddled together, often forming the celebrated qal'eh which embraces within its walls both man and beast. The larger village is composed on average of some sixty families, usually totalling about 350 persons. Villages of a smaller size are more numerous, and these appear to have an average population of about 160.

All three types of village have a definite social structure. First, there are persons performing administrative functions, such as the mayor (*kadkhudā*); the *mīrāb*, or the distributor of water, who is nominated by the landowner; the rural policeman, tax collector, bailiff (*ẓābit, mubashir, sarkār*), and other minor officials. Then there are owners of oxen who lend out seed, oxen and ploughs, receiving a share of the harvest (*gāvband*) in return.[1] Persons in non-agricultural occupations (*pīlehvar*) include priests, carpenters, blacksmiths, barbers and pedlars. There are also fishermen and gleaners (*khūshehchīn*), as well as those who live in the village but have no settled occupation there. Finally, the people engaged in agriculture may be divided into cultivators of cereal crops, market-gardeners, fruit-growers, cattle-breeders, and so on.

As a result of recent agrarian reforms, the Iranian village is in a state of transition, and it is certain that the mode of life and methods of ownership and cultivation will undergo great changes in the future. These changes will necessarily affect the types of settlement and the composition of the rural population in terms of age and occupation.

MARRIAGE AND FERTILITY

The past half-century has seen a transformation in the Iranian family and the shattering of its traditional structure. For a long time marriage followed the strict rules imposed by religion and tradition, and within this conventional environment the "extensive family" and the authority,

[1] According to the "principle of the five factors", the landowner should provide land and water (two factors), while the peasant contributes the other three: seed, oxen, labour. The poverty of the peasants, however, allows undue privilege to accrue to the moneyed classes, who thus may become parasitic middlemen.

of the "father" were dominant. The extensive family was the foundation of the communities of related persons; the religion and the social position of the woman, and also the prevailing conventions, governed the choice of a spouse and the course of conjugal life. The size of the family made it possible for the children, even after marriage, to live close to their parents and to look to the family for help and protection. The family was founded on agnate relationship and on male predominance; it was characterized by a monarchical organization, including the rule of the father, the rights of the eldest son, and so on.

Contact with industrial civilization, the process of urbanization, and the fundamental transformation of the customary way of life have changed all this. On the one hand, conventions and legal or religious sanctions exist and are observed by the older generations; on the other hand, there is the impetus of a new generation that believes in a different scale of values and is obliged, under pressure of present social and economic changes, to destroy traditions and create a new existence for itself in an unconventional setting. Hence there are two types of behaviour, and the antagonism between native and foreign cultural practices heightens the friction between the generations.

The perceptible signs of transition from the extensive family towards the conjugal family are symbolic today of this period of flux, and changes in the conditions and the forms of marriage itself mark the first steps in this process. The former framework exists, but within it new forces are trying to bring about a break-up; and the elements of this "change from within" are becoming part of the characteristic features of present-day marriage in Iran. However, the principles that have traditionally governed marriage in Iranian society—"generality", "precocity" (i.e. early marriage), and "consanguinity"—are still very much alive in Iranian society today.

Generality

Society has always attached a paramount importance to marriage; according to Zoroaster, the Persian prophet, to plant a tree, to cultivate a field, and to engender children are three meritorious actions. Under the Sassanids, if a young man of marriageable age died a bachelor, his parents gave a dowry to a girl of their choice, arranged her marriage, and regarded her first-born son as one of their grandchildren. In Islam the celibate is regarded as "the worst of things" (Koran), and to marry in order to increase the numbers of the faithful is a religious duty.

Tradition and popular morals have always considered married life the state which is at once the most healthy and the most fruitful. No doubt urban conditions, with the attendant changes in the country's mode of living, have increased the difficulties and the responsibilities of the man in marriage; but in rural communities and among nomads the marriage rite is still dominated by the patriarchal spirit: marriage is a certainty, and practically all men and women marry sooner or later.

Another traditional reason for marrying is that women, being unable to hope for an independent life owing to their lack of emancipation, seek in marriage both prestige and, even more, a means of subsistence.

Few marriages are officially registered, which may not be surprising in a country where European law has not yet been assimilated among the most densely populated strata of the population. Religion still commands respect and therefore religious sanction in marriage is a substitute. Moreover, demographic migrations of some Iranians are not conducive to a system of up-to-date registration.

The marriage rate is generally higher among women than among men. This is because women marry earlier: only 10 per cent of women over fifteen years of age are unmarried, while for men this percentage is as high as 28. Further, many widowers remain without a partner. The number of married women at present exceeds by 78,671 the number of married men, a discrepancy which may be explained partly by polygamy.

The marriage rate also varies according to profession. It is much higher among workmen, skilled or unskilled, than among employees and officials. Statistics relating to civil servants as a whole show a percentage of 81·4 married men. However, there are great discrepancies among the officials themselves, and the most "intellectual" appear to be the least ready to marry. In the ranks of teachers, for example, the percentage of those married is 59 for men and 60 for women.

Precocity

Recent investigations have shown that early marriage is still the general rule, particularly in rural communities, and cases are not infrequent of motherhood at the age of fourteen or fifteen. Girls in the country districts or in the tribes are betrothed from birth and married when they attain puberty. Sociological changes of the last decades have, however, now tended to retard the age of marriage, chiefly among men in urban society. The causes of some of these changes are:

(*a*) The Civil Code, which has fixed the earliest age of marriage at

481

sixteen years for girls and eighteen years for boys. (This Code commands considerable respect, especially in the cities.)

(*b*) Military service.

(*c*) The increase of secondary and higher education, which also retards marriage.

(*d*) The desperate mass exodus of peasants towards the large urban centres, which retards marriage and reduces the number of young people in the villages. As mentioned above (p. 475) these near-destitute young people form groups of urban sub-proletariat; they live in camps and tend not to contemplate starting a family until they have some better prospects of regular employment.

(*e*) The increasing degree of freedom in the relations between the sexes in urban society.

(*f*) The wide range of amusements offered by the urban centres.

However there are still appreciable seasonal variations in the marriage rate, just as there have always been. The number of marriages at any time is closely linked with the cyclic fluctuations of economic life, which depends chiefly on conventional and religious factors. Thus rate is relatively low towards the end of the spring and throughout almost the whole of the summer, but it increases noticeably at the end of the summer (after the harvest) and maintains the same level during the autumn. This seasonal variation is also affected by the traditional distinctions between propitious days (21 March, New Year's Day, the anniversary of the birth of the Prophet, etc.) and the inauspicious days (a month of mourning, the anniversary of the death of the descendants of the Prophet).

Endogamy

Consanguinity and endogamy are among the characteristic features of marriage in Iran. Apart from considerations of convention (such as the very frequent marriages between first cousins), geographical and social-economic factors exert considerable influence. In Iran cross-marriages of cousins occur relatively frequently (the children of the brother marrying those of the sister, and vice versa), as do the marriages of direct cousins or ortho-cousins (the descendants of two brothers or of two sisters). According to the Swedish geneticist Dahlberg, author of the theory of the "isolate", an individual does not usually have the opportunity to marry outside certain geographical limits or outside a certain historical, economic, and social environment. The isolate is represented by Dahlberg as the zone of intermarriage, within which an individual may find a partner. For the villagers in an underdeveloped country, for example, the most important isolate is geographical, in view of the absence of means of communication, the closed economy of the villages, and the importance of the patriarchal family. The inhabitants of a village become more and more closely interconnected by marriage, and the matrimonial horizon of the young people does not extend beyond the few neighbouring villages. Isolates are not only geographical, however. An example of a religious isolate is to be found in the Zoroastrian minorities of Iran, which, having resisted Islamic infiltration and preserved their ancient religion, have lived for fourteen centuries according to their own traditions of consanguineous marriage. Historical surveys have shown that their numbers have diminished and today amount to only 10,000.

There is no doubt that increased contact between men and women in the factory, the office, and the university, in addition to public entertainments, have all helped to destroy the isolate. Consanguinity in marriage is on the decline, as demonstrated in part by the growing number of marriages between Iranians and foreigners.

CONCLUSIONS

The main demographic problems of Iran are: (a) the decrease in the death rate while the birth rate remains at its traditionally high level which means that the total population is expanding rapidly; (b) the youthfulness of the population; and (c) the rural exodus.

The "statistical period" of contemporary Iran extends only over the past three decades, during which time the state register has recorded a steady increase in the population. Although this increase is no doubt due partly to an improvement in methods of compilation of the statistics, it may also be regarded as symptomatic of a new era, which has been designated "the demographical revolution of the underdeveloped countries".

In about 1943 the total population of Iran was estimated at fifteen million. During the first years of the Second World War the population increased at the rate of 100,000 a year, but by 1944, however, when the war was nearly at an end, the annual increase averaged 300,000, and since that year there has been an overall annual increase of 2·4 to 2·5 per cent. As regards the figure which the population of Iran is likely to reach in the future, various prophecies may be mentioned, but with reserve: On the basis of either of two hypotheses, "eventual gradual reduction in fertility" or "immediate gradual reduction in fertility", it may be conjectured that the population could number respectively about 31·3 million or 30·5 million in 1970; and 43 million or 40·5 million in 1980.[1] According to another forecast, however, the Iranian population will reach a total of only 27,235,000 in 1971 and of 34,667,000 in 1981.[2]

Such obvious uncertainty with regard to the rate of increase makes it impossible to accept any of these figures unreservedly, but the estimates do emphasize the magnitude of the difficulties which must be faced in the future if the growth of the population is to be brought into line with economic development.

It has already been noted that 46–9 per cent of the Iranian population are under twenty years of age. This high proportion of young people results from the high birth rate, the high (though decreasing) death rate, and the short duration of middle age. The proportion of adults is relatively small: between 51·4 and 54 per cent of the total population. These figures may give some idea of the country's heavy financial liabilities for education and of the extent of necessary social expenditure.

The third demographic and social problem in Iran is the considerable rural exodus and the rapid increase in the population of certain cities. Since industrial development and the exodus do not proceed in step, and since the capacity of industry to provide employment is low, it often happens that unemployment or underemployment is simply transferred from the country to the town. Thus in the suburbs of the great cities, in industrial localities, and even in districts that are connected with the industrial centres by good transport facilities, a temporary population settles itself which is mostly male, and which often supports itself by menial work. Exodus does not bring to these people the assured subsistence for which they had hoped: since their previous experience has been limited to agriculture, the only employment available to them in the towns is unskilled labour, which is both uncertain as regards availability and irregular in duration.

Precise information on the extent of the rural exodus into the cities is lacking; nevertheless, from statistics relating to increases in urban population, a general idea may be formed of the astonishing extent of

[1] L. Tabah, *Revue Population*, no. 3 (1959).
[2] Setoudeh-Zand, *Population Growth in Iran*, pp. 15–18.

this migration. Since the natural rate of increase in urban zones is usually much lower than that in the rural areas, the cities' marked increase in numbers of people in relation to the total population must be explained by a heavy rural exodus.

In the light of these problems, it is clear that the replacement of an economy of subsistence by a monetary economy, the change in the material foundations of existence, and the infiltration of Western ideas have altered the traditional structure of society and are in process of destroying the hitherto existing equilibrium between numbers, resources, and ways of life. This maladjustment between the demographic and social-economic factors is tending to become progressively more severe, and a demographic balance within the framework of economic and social development must be achieved. The planners of Iran are aware of this state of affairs, and their aim is to apply effective remedies to the problems by carrying out a programme of economic development.

PART 3

ECONOMIC LIFE

CHAPTER 15

MINERALS

Tales from *The Arabian Nights*, told by such accomplished and, it seemed, reliable narrators as Sinbad the Sailor, implanted the idea in many a boyish mind that Iran was a realm with fabulously rich mines. Early prints showed the Shahs wearing crowns encrusted with precious stones, and their raiments were decorated with gems. Samples of both are preserved in museums, and privileged visitors to Tehrān may to this day view the well-guarded Crown jewels of the Shāhan Shāh. Brightly lit glass cases house dazzling heaps of diamonds, rubies, emeralds, sapphires, and pearls. Stacked amongst this galaxy are pillars of golden coins, magnificent and massive medallions that have been seen only by a few numismatists and hardly ever by the general public. Finally there are precious stones built into masterpieces of the jeweller's art. These exhibits give verisimilitude to the attractive fairy tales. Mines there must be, but so far no mines of Ophir, no placers of Klondyke or rubies of Burma, no diamonds of Kimberley have been discovered in Iran: even the hoards of pearls amongst the Crown jewels come mainly from the Arabian coasts of the Persian Gulf.

The treasures on display and the wealth of the Shah are one result of a long-enduring political fashion. When one Eastern potentate used to visit another he took with him presents, following the custom set by the Queen of Sheba when she captivated Solomon. The remoter the source of the specimen, the greater the virtue of the gift. Iran did have the monopoly of turquoise for many years, but except in the medieval East turquoise was regarded as only semi-precious. More recently nearly all the marketed turquoise has been produced by mines in the United States. Lately the tribes near Kirmānshāh entered the lists of gem-producers after finding veins with glittering crystals. But the crystals were calcite. The local expert had identified them as diamonds, which he later justified by pointing out that they would become diamonds though they were as yet unripe.

Old mine-workings have long been known in many provinces of Iran. Traces of gold in alluvium or quartz veins have been recorded, and minerals yielding silver, lead, zinc, and copper are widely but sparingly distributed. One of the earliest technical articles on the prospects of mining in Iran, written in 1879, began with the words "Mineral Riches". Such accounts stimulated and encouraged the hunt for concessions. Prospecting rights for minerals were occasionally granted, and sometimes a search was conscientiously carried out. Interest in the country's resources was also kept alive by the published observations of A. F. Stahl, the indefatigable director of the Persian Telegraph Company, who made many journeys through Iran between 1893 and 1911.

Following the chronic shortage of fuel in most of Iran at the beginning of this century, coal was dug from the mountains north of Tehrān. Petroleum in quantity was discovered in southern Iran in 1908, which gradually and impressively began to improve the mineral situation. By the end of the 1930s with Rezā Shāh firmly on the throne, foreign mining engineers were engaged to conduct a search for minerals of all kinds, and to provide the raw materials required to start industries and thereby strengthen the national economy. The general state of the country's affairs, cultural as well as economic, was brought home to Britons in January 1931, when the Persian Art Exhibition was held in London. And amongst the reviews published at that time, the one on minerals briefly listed localities where ores had been found and then discussed their prospects; in the list of metallic elements the article referred to showings of antimony, cobalt, copper, gold, iron, lead, mercury, nickel, and zinc, and it also drew attention to the potentialities of valuable non-metallic substances like coal, gypsum, marble, rocksalt, and sulphur. At that time the mining and sale of turquoise was bringing in about £10,000 a year to the country.

Government-sponsored surveys by Swiss and German specialists begun in the 1930s were pursued with great vigour after the outbreak of war in 1939, but this surge ended with the fall of Rezā Shāh in 1941. Some of the results were published in 1944 and 1945 in Switzerland, giving much of the available information regarding about 200 prospects. Some of the data resulted from actual examinations on the spot, while others reiterated and revised earlier records. Most of the descriptions dealing with the old workings are not precisely dated. The neighbouring villagers, however, refer to them as "very old", but they would be at a loss to name the decade, or perhaps even the century when work was done in them. Teams of German, Italian, and Swiss geologists have again been active in Iran for the last decade, and their studies have continued at least until 1961. Most of the country has been recon-

noitred, and in the Kirmān region studies of the mines have concentrated on those within the Ṭabas wedge, where many mines are
located. Some of the recent exploratory work up to 1962 has been published, but sundry other studies, mentioned in bibliographies that have
been printed in Iran, are not yet published.

COAL

Obtaining sufficient fuel has always been a difficult problem in Iran.
For centuries wood and charcoal, augmented by pats of stubble mixed
with dung and clay, were used to try to meet the demand, but were inadequate—and they are still being used in remote and thinly populated
parts. Charcoal was supplied by woodmen and charcoal-burners whose
activities laid waste the woodlands of the countryside. That woods once
existed on hills that are now treeless is shown by the survival of a few
trees which happened to be rooted within the stone circles marking
"holy ground"; these sanctuaries still exist and still provide protection
to anything left within them. During the 1920s plundering of the woodlands was accelerated with the increase in the number of motor roads.
Even distant woods came under the axe: for the authority of tribal
leaders, who had to some extent policed the woods against the in-
comers, was now weakened; and the charcoal-burner could deliver
his donkey-carried timber, to suitable points for loading onto trucks at
some roadside.

Coal is an obvious alternative to charcoal, and for a considerable
time coal has been dug in the mountains north of Tehrān. After its
discovery in south-west Iran in 1908, oil started slowly to compete as
fuel. Oil imported from Russia and also produced in southern Iran was
packed into four-gallon tins—tins which, subjected to the risks of the
journey, were wont to leak and lose their contents—and thus carried
laboriously by animals into the towns. Such were conditions in the
1920s. The improved motor roads in the next decade led to the introduction of tanker-trucks; these, and later the railway tank-wagons,
curtailed what had been huge transport losses. Finally by 1958 a few
pipelines had been built to link the producing fields with the large
centres of population; the construction and extension of pipelines
continues in 1967.

The need for fuel was most pressing during the half-century between
1900 and 1950, when new factories were about to start. At that time the

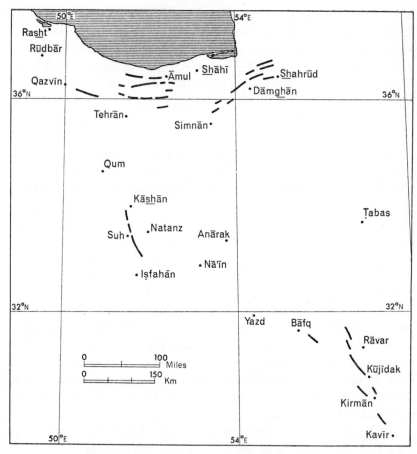

Fig. 108. Map of coal distribution. (After Böhne, 1932.)

distribution of oil for fuel was a growing business striving to overcome the difficulties of distance and terrain. That stage is now passed, and oil can be bought at innumerable rural as well as urban points. But in the 1930s coal was urgently needed and was therefore the object of particular research, especially as the Shāh was sponsoring an ambitious programme of industrialization. A useful review of the possibilities of coal was made by E. Bohne in 1932. As a result, coal measures of Lower and Middle Jurassic ages are now known to occur over a great Eurasian district that reaches from Hungary in the West through Turkey and Iran to Turkestan; from this last area it continues as far as Mongolia and China. Most of the coal in Iran exists in the north, in the Alburz mountains, but coal-fields are also known in the eastern part of the country near Kūjīdak, fifty miles north of Kirmān and mainly within the Ṭabas wedge.

Workable coal seams are known to occur for a distance of at least 300 miles along the Alburz mountains. Coal measures are exposed in the west at Rūdbār, south of Rasht, but although they continue along the strike to the east, they are sporadically covered by lava flows or associated ash-beds. A group of coal mines lies north of the road from Qazvīn to Tehrān, brought against volcanic rocks by a north-north-east fault near Ābīyak. The workings extend eastward for about twelve miles and are then covered up and hidden by alluvial fans, eventually disappearing east of Fashand. The most important group of mines is situated about twenty miles north of Tehrān between Karaj and the

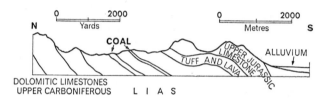

Fig. 109. Profile showing coal seams near Ābīyak. (After Böhne, 1932.)

Jājīrūd and Garmābdār valleys, near Shimshak and Lashārak. Individual seams tend to wedge out, so that one single coal bed can seldom be traced far along the strike. The coal itself forms only a small percentage of the measures, which are mostly barren shales, sandstones, grits, and quartzites, with which flows of andesite and basalt and sometimes their ashes are associated. Most of the coal seams that have been worked are less than two ft thick, but some thicker ones do occur.

In the Shimshak district large lenses of coal have been found known locally as *ambars* or lodes; some of them reach a thickness of forty ft but the same one never continues very far along the strike. Their origin is not clear. They may result from freakish conditions during accumulation, or they may be a result of imbrication following which the imbrics were packed together near the crest of the tight folds. Coal measures with sporadic seams persist up to, and are covered by, the volcanic rocks forming the peak of Damāvand. In the Alburz the Jurassic measures overlie the Carboniferous limestones unconformably; just above these limestones the coal contains a flora identified as Liassic, but some limestones interbedded at higher horizons contain

Bajocian fossils. The quality of the coal varies. Some is good coking coal even though much of it has been smashed in the process of folding. As a result, a high percentage of it is a carbonaceous grit with only a small residue surviving as lump-coal. The amount of carbon in fresh coal varies from 70 to 82 per cent; from 3 per cent upward is ash, and from 1 per cent upward sulphur. The resulting coke is mechanically strong and can serve metallurgical purposes. Calorific values range from less than 12,000 to more than 14,500 B.Th.U.s.

Coal was discovered long ago in the streams which flow into the Chālūs, Lār, and Harāz rivers on the northern slopes of the Alburz mountains. It was extracted in a small way locally, and on a larger scale near Zīrāb, which is about twenty miles south of Shāhī on the railway, and also at Gulandeh Rūd, forty-five miles west of Shāhī. Several coal

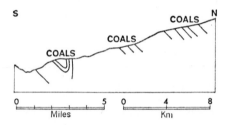

Fig. 110. Profile showing coal seams at Shimshak. (After Böhne, 1932.)

seams were encountered during the surveys preceding construction of the railway, and others were discovered during the actual cuttings. On the northern slopes of the Alburz occur the clay-ironstone bed and clay-ironstone concretions which supplied the easily reduced ore used formerly in the Māzandarān iron industry. Whilst the Jurassic between Fīrūzkūh and Simnān does not contain coal, there are many districts lying east of Simnān (e.g. Dāmghān, Shāhrūd) and farther east towards Mashhad where coal, although often thin, has been noted and is locally worked.

Before considering the more promising coal seams in the region north and north-west of Kirmān, we must mention a small deposit of coal near the Russian frontier in the valley of the Araxes, where the coal is Upper Jurassic—namely, Purbeckian—in age. Another, much younger, patch of coal in northern Iran is known close to Tabrīz. This is a Tertiary "brown" coal, and its age has been determined as Miocene.

494

The coal in southern and central Iran was reported on in 1912 when the Kirmān–Anārak region was rather inaccessible and remote. As a result of surveys since 1955, much more about the distribution of coal in the region is known, and the transport position has altered for the better. The Jurassic coal measures in the eastern part of central Iran overlie the beds below with apparent conformity. A series of dolomitic limestones follow upon the Upper Carboniferous and continue up to the Triassic. Then comes a group formed by beds of

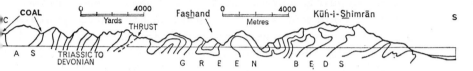

Fig. 111. Profile showing coal in the Lias in South Alburz. (After Böhne, 1932.)

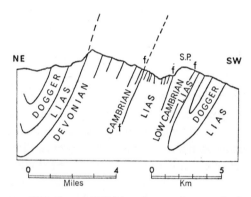

Fig. 112. Profile near Khānūk and Kūjīdak, where coals occur in the Lias and Dogger series in strongly folded country. (After Huckriede, Kursten and Venzlaff, 1962.)

bauxite, each up to forty ft thick, interbedded with sands and shales; while the Liassic coal measures, containing the usual flora, rest upon them. This Lias contains three groups of coal seams, and in the higher levels they are interbedded with a few limestones which have yielded a Bajocian fauna. Another group of coals appears above them.

The whole sequence of coal measures above the bauxite bed reaches a maximum thickness of over 6,000 ft near Zarand, but elsewhere it is sometimes much less. The coal is well developed and better preserved in a synclinal area near Kūjīdak about forty miles north of Kirmān. The measures extend for 100 miles north-westward, and farther on near Suh, north of Iṣfahān, a faulted patch of coal measures with some seams is present. The Kūjīdak area is one where there is strong folding and the coal seams crop out intermittently. Under such circumstances estimated reserves are not likely to be very trustworthy, for the coal is liable to have been smeared out and removed tectonically over most of the anticlinal areas. Huber and Stöcklin have suggested a figure of near forty million tons for the reserves, while Beckett has drawn attention to the strong lenticularity of the seams, as if to caution readers that it is easy to overestimate. It is recorded that 45,000 tons of coal had been mined from the Kūjīdak area by the end of 1958. Besides the faulted field near Suh in the north-west, a small synclinal field has been recognized at Bād 'Amū, twenty-four miles north-west of Kirmān. The Kūjīdak coal, like that in the Alburz, is largely reduced to a carbonaceous grit on account of folding and faulting. Only about 10 per cent of lumpcoal is preserved; this is a coking coal and contains 60 per cent fixed carbon.

IRON

Iron ore, especially the conspicuous red ochre, has been known since the early days of exploration in Iran. A Government plan to seek more specific information about the occurrence of iron was begun in 1935. Since then exploration has kept going by fits and starts, and much more is now known than formerly about the prospects of iron ore in Iran. As fig. 113 shows, iron ore deposits have been observed in many parts of the country, most of them between the southern slopes of the Alburz system and the Volcanic belt, especially somewhat north-east of the limits of the Volcanic belt. A couple of workings lie north and south of Tabrīz; and others occur along a strip of country running north-west and south-east, a few miles west of Zanjān, where in 1942 reserves were estimated at one and a half million tons. This ore contains, as well as magnetite, siderite and limonite associated with marbles and shales, themselves intruded by quartz porphyry.

Reports have been made about other prospects between Zanjān and Tehrān, all of them within easy reach of a blast-furnace erected in Karaj in 1941. The ore in these deposits is emplaced in limestone that has been cut by neighbouring acid volcanics. Reserves in the early 1940s were given as 60,000 tons. A deposit farther east, north of Simnān, was then of great short-term importance to the economy of the Karaj smelter, and had a total potential of two million tons. Granite intrusions are near the ore. The Lias near Dāvar contains a bed of

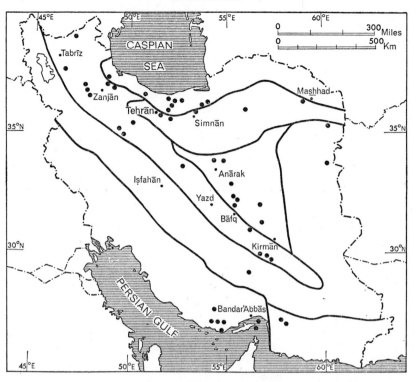

Fig. 113. Sketch-map showing iron mines or prospects in Iran. (After Ladame, 1945.)

chamosite, a mineral common in the Lias of Yorkshire but unusual in Iran. An iron mine producing clay-ironstone has been worked at Āmul on the northern slopes of the Alburz, where a primitive iron metallurgy was once practised. Farther east, south of Mashhad at Rīvjān, reserves of ore have been estimated at about half a million tons. Iron is also found distributed east and south-east of Isfahān—at Suhail for instance (on the road to Nā'īn), where ore bodies are located not far from a granite that is intruding limestone.

What seems to be the most important iron region in Iran occupies a strip running about sixty miles north–south, and about fifteen miles across, with Bāfq at its south-western and Saghand at its north-western corner. The ore bodies are composed mainly of magnetite, but haematite and goethite also occur. The iron ore is always associated with a carbonate—limestone, dolomite, or siderite—and is seldom far from a granitic or granodioritic intrusion. The ore is found along joints

32   497

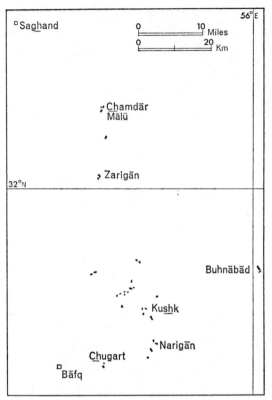

Fig. 114. Sketch-map showing the iron ore deposits north of Bāfq. (After Huckriede, Kursten and Venzlaff, 1962.)

in the carbonate rocks, and in most cases replaces much of the limestone or dolomite. But unaltered blocks of the carbonate rocks do survive sporadically within bodies of ore, and the ore itself still retains within itself structures which mark the original bedding. Much of the ore is titaniferous, and individual ore bodies contain, besides silica and sulphur, a small percentage of phosphorus or manganese. Some skarn—metamorphosed carbonate—occurs, and there are veins of quartz and calcite. In some places crystals of apatite are numerous.

Several geological parties have examined and described the iron deposits, but they differ in the deductions made about their age. Some regard them as old and belonging to the Lower Palaeozoic. Others see them as Mesozoic within the Trias or Cretaceous; still others regard them as Tertiary. The latest arguments support the view that the iron ore is old. The largest single ore body, Chugart, lies a few miles north-east of Bāfq and is reputed to contain thirteen million tons of ore, of which 65 per cent is iron and 0·3 per cent phosphorus. Another substantial block of ore, with 64 per cent iron and just under 0·2 per cent phosphorus, was described at Kūshk. South of it at Narāgān two massive slabs of ore, containing 37 and 44 per cent of iron respectively, follow the contact between a dolerite dyke cutting dolomite. If the more optimistic estimates are true, the total ore reserve in these four

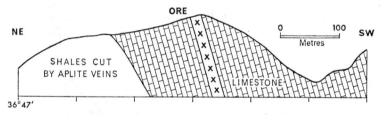

Fig. 115. Profile near Khān Qalʻeh Dasht, where dolomitic limestone rests unconformably on shales with aplite veins. Bodies of haematite occur along the bedding in the limestone. (After Ladame, 1945.)

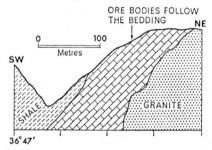

Fig. 116. Profile near Galījibulāgh, where granite intrudes the dolomite limestone. Haematite bodies have developed in the upper part of the limestone. (After Ladame, 1945.)

bodies is much over 100 million tons. Taking a more cautious view more than ten million tons can probably be easily worked; but the region is remote, the availability of sufficient suitable fuel doubtful, and the reduction of titanium-bearing ore difficult.

Red ochre is present in small quantities in many of the salt domes in south-western Iran. Flakes and crystals of specular haematite spangle the exposures of Lower Cambrian wherever they appear in the south-west. The island of Hurmuz is much more liberally endowed with ochre; the quarries here have been worked for many years before and after World War I, and the exported iron is used for making "red oxide" pigment.

32-2

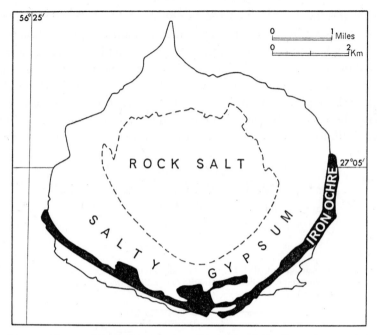

Fig. 117. Hurmuz Island. (After Gansser, *V. d. Naturf. Ges. Zur.* vol. CV, 1960.)

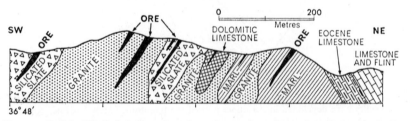

Fig. 118. Guljūk. Silicified shales and marls cut by granite and containing haematite bodies are overlain unconformably by Eocene limestones. (After Ladame, 1945.)

Iron localities:

Khān Qal'eh Dasht	36° N.	47° E.	Bīvehjān	36° N.	59° E.
Galijibulāgh	36° N.	47° E.	Kūh-i-Rūd	33° N.	51° E.
Guljūk	36° N.	47° E.	Suhail	33° N.	53° E.
Masīleh	37° N.	48° E.	Kharānaq	32° N.	54° E.
Bāshkhāl	36° N.	49° E.	Saghand	32° N.	55° E.
Mu'askarābād	35° N.	51° E.	Narāgān	31° N.	55° E.
Āmul	36° N.	52° E.	Firdaus	33° N.	58° E.
Simnān	35° N.	53° E.	Hurmuz	27° N.	56° E.

MANGANESE

Some of the iron ore deposits—for example, those at Simnān and near Bāfq—contain a small percentage of manganese. A vein with pyrolusite has been prospected near Ribāṭkarīm and was traced for nearly a quarter of a mile along the strike; it is up to twenty-five ft wide. This vein may contain 15,000 tons of ore averaging about 45 per cent manganese. Another prospect at Sargaz is confined to a vein six ft wide, of which 35 per cent is manganese.

Localities: Robatkarim 35° N. 51° E.   Sargaz 28° N. 57° E.

COPPER

Small veins with vestiges of copper minerals are numerous in central and northern Iran, but it is doubtful if there is even one large copper mine in the whole country. Of the prospects which have been investigated, and they are many, most are situated in the Volcanic belt, although a few lie outside it along the southern fringe of the Alburz system or within the limits of the Ṭabas wedge. Most of the "mines" in the Volcanic belt are associated with lava flows or their ashes, the rocks being porphyritic andesites and basalts. Some of the copper occurs as chalcopyrite in quartz veins, and pyrite is common in the lava. Secondary minerals, such as cuprite, malachite, and azurite, are present in greater or less amounts: indeed, it is these minerals which are most conspicuous in the veins. As a result, mining has gone on over the centuries and the ores have been reduced by the practice of simple metallurgy.

The volcanic rocks range in age from Upper Cretaceous to Recent, and the igneous activity culminated in Eocene or Lower Eocene times. Some of the ore is found in joint-planes in the lavas and some in the amygdales, suggesting that the copper mineralization may have followed the eruption of the lavas after only a short interval. The ore produced so far comes from the weathered and oxidized upper part of the lavas; no lower zone showing secondary enrichment has been recognized. The old abandoned workings are numerous and still attract attention. At least they provide evidence of the pertinaceous industry of people who were compelled to eke out an existence in the deserts.

Figure 119 shows the distribution of copper minerals, both unexplored prospects and old workings. Catalogues covering the whole country

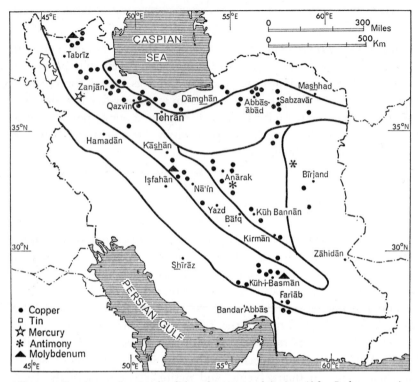

Fig. 119. Sketch-map showing localities of copper exploitation. (After Ladame, 1945.)

have been made by Diehl (1944) and Ladame (1945). In addition, several papers deal with the potentialities of the Kirmān province. Starting with Āzarbāījān in the north-west of Iran, half a dozen workings are known north of Tabrīz, and as many more westward of Zanjān. Two lie east of Zanjān on the way to Qazvīn, with five more between Zanjān and Tehrān; and two old sites are recorded east of the capital. Two other workings lie about thirty miles south of the south-eastern shores of the Caspian Sea, and fifty miles east of them. The village of 'Abbāsābād is situated here, near extensive but un-economic outcrops of copper minerals.

Still farther east, near Sabzavār, three other old workings are known. To the south, within sixty miles of Sabzavār, occur three more "mines". Others have been encountered between Kāshān and Yazd, and to the north-east of this line in the neighbourhood of Anārak. A trail of prospects is strung out between Yazd and Bam, along a line that is

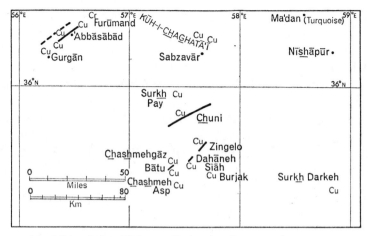

Fig. 120. The 'Abbāsābād and Sabzavār district, showing areas of copper mineralization and the turquoise mines. (After Ladame, 1945.)

oriented north-west and south-east, passing about fifty miles to the south-west of Kirmān. Some mineralized localities are known within the triangle formed by Bāfq, Kūh Bannān, and Kirmān, where shows of copper minerals are found associated with sandstones of Triassic, Liassic, and Dogger (Bathonian) ages. These are not directly connected with known igneous rocks. Three other prospects are situated farther south, near the village of Farīyāb, thirty miles north-east of the Strait of Hurmuz. Throughout Iran the old mines tend to be indicated by heaps of green- and blue-coloured spoil, some containing pieces of slag and charcoal at the particular sites where smelting has been undertaken. In spite of several international re-examinations of the "mines" since 1935, none has led to the discovery of substantial reserves of ore. Matters have not changed much since 1940, when Ladame reported that the output of copper ore, resulting from mining followed by hand-sorting, was only just sufficient to provide for the costs of keeping the plant at Ghanīābād working to its full monthly capacity of 150 tons.

In Āzarbāījān the prospects between Tabrīz and Russia are associated with intrusive granodiorites which have cut limestones and produced some contact metamorphism. At Sungūn, for example, quartz veins which carry pyrites, chalcopyrite, and chalcocite can be traced for half a mile through altered rocks containing garnet and epidote; part of the vein assayed about 1·5 per cent copper. A very little amount of gold is associated with copper in this district. Mines near Zanjān, south-west of Ra<u>sh</u>t, have also provided a complex ore containing lead and zinc as well as copper and a trace of gold. The largest area of copper minerals is in the 'Abbāsābād neighbourhood, where the "ore" is associated with intermediate and basic lavas which are overlain by Eocene and Oligocene shales. The old workings are extensive, but impregnation was uneven and the minerals include cuprite, malachite, azurite, chrysocolla, chalcosite, bornite, and covelline. The lodes run north-east and south-west for a few hundred yards, and the lavas carry zeolites and chalcedony. Similar conditions obtain at Bātu, Dāmaneh, Jalh, and Ma'dan Buzurg.

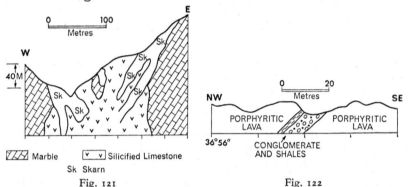

Fig. 121   Fig. 122

Fig. 121. Part of the copper mine at Sungūn. Limestone intruded by granodiorite altered to marble and skarn. (After Ladame, 1945.)

Fig. 122. Profile through <u>Ch</u>ugandarsar, south-west of 'Abbāsābād. Lavas above and below Eocene sediments are mineralized with copper. (After Ladame, 1945.)

The copper minerals in the mines north of Sabzavār occur at the contact between lavas and serpentine in the <u>Ch</u>a<u>gh</u>atā'ī hills. Anārak, about forty miles north-east of Nā'īn, stands in a mineralized district which was classed as important when the campaign of exploration started in 1935. At that time two prospects were examined at Talmesī and Miskānī. These stand about five miles apart, one on the north and one on the south limb of a syncline filled with young Tertiary red beds which are underlain by conglomerates resting upon a thick mass of andesite. The feldspars of the syncline are extremely decomposed, although its dark minerals biotite and pyroxene are still fresh; the andesite is underlain by Cretaceous conglomerate, and this rests unconformably on schist. The copper minerals fill a network of joints affecting the volcanic rocks. The ore is again a complex one, for it contains not only copper sulphides but traces of cobalt and nickel minerals carrying minute quantities of silver and gold; the separation process is difficult but can be accomplished by jigging and a flotation process. Nearly 100 miles south of Kirmān, a body of lavas and ashes in the Baḥrāsmān hills is cut by dykes and is therefore mineralized. Opinions differ as to its value, however, and it is still a controversial prospect.

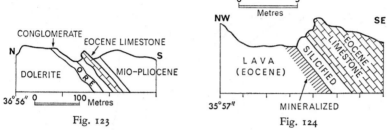

Fig. 123   Fig. 124

Fig. 123. Conditions at Dāmaneh, north of 'Abbāsābād. Copper impregnates the top of the dolerite and a conglomerate above it. Eocene sandstone, limestone and shale follow unconfirmably above. (After Ladame, 1945.)

Fig. 124. Chashmegāz copper mine. (After Ladame, 1945.)

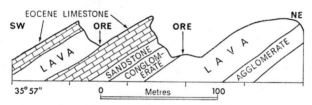

Fig. 125. Old working at Bātu, south of Sabzavār. Eocene limestone, sandstone and agglomerate with lavas mineralized at lava-sediment contacts. (After Ladame, 1945.)

Localities:

Sungūn	39° N.	47° E.	Zargān	36° N. 58° E.
Qareh Bulāgh	37° N.	48° E.	Kūh-i-Sarangī	35° N. 57° E.
Hisār	37° N.	49° E.	Kūh Bannān	31° N. 56° E.
Imāmzādeh Dā'ūd	36° N.	51° E.	Kūhrūn	30° N. 55° E.
'Abbāsābād	36° N.	57° E.	Kūh Baḥrāsmān	29° N. 57° E.

LEAD–ZINC

Lead and zinc prospects are recorded from several places in Iran, north-east of the zone of normal folding. Some mines occur within the Volcanic belt and others are beyond it, in the Ṭabas wedge and along the edge of the "foredeep". Many of the mineralized areas have been worked since ancient times. Lead, being an element with a radioactive

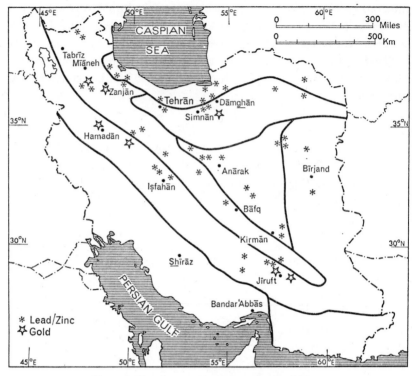

Fig. 126. Sketch-map of lead–zinc prospects in Iran.

history, lends itself to geochemical methods of dating, and results obtained suggest that Palaeozoic ores from Zargan and Kushk, not far from Bāfq, are much older than others in which the ore is emplaced in limestones that are Mesozoic or younger. One ore body near Kirmān occupies fissures in rudist limestone and is therefore certainly post-Cretaceous. The lead is argentiferous, some of it containing about 100 oz of silver to the ton of lead concentrate. Much of the lead–zinc ore impregnates shatter-bands in limestones or dolomites, and the bands are from Upper Carboniferous to Triassic in age. In these circumstances the carbonate rock within and adjoining the fracture zone is silicified but not otherwise altered. On the other hand some volcanic rocks include intruded schists and dolomite, and in the skarn produced by the resulting metamorphism, carbonates have gone to marble with garnets. Some of the ore is contained in quartz veins associated with the intruding rocks, which may be diorite or granodiorite. Besides quartz some veins contain calcite, barytes, and fluorspar: an assemblage not unlike that in the lead mines of Derbyshire. Crush zones are sometimes stained by the limonite produced by oxidation of pyrites, and such colouring may indicate the habitat of a lead–zinc ore body. Galena is the principal lead mineral and it is often accompanied by cerussite, a lead carbonate. Zinc

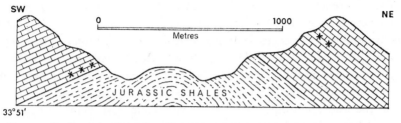

Fig. 127. Profile of the Kūh-i-Kunsik area, in which cretaceous limestone with veins of calcite contains galena in veins and pockets. (After Ladame, 1945.)

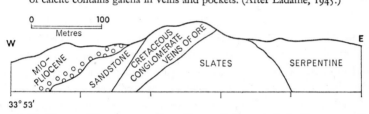

Fig. 128. Profile near Sibarz, twenty-five miles north from Anārak. Here, serpentine is faulted over slate and lies unconformably below conglomerate, which with the feruginous sandstone above it is Cretaceous. Mio-Pliocene series on top. The ore contains copper, nickel, lead and zinc. (After Ladame, 1945.)

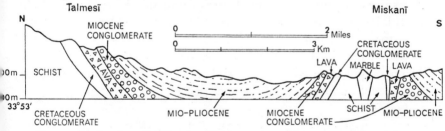

Fig. 129. Section through Talmesī and Miskanī mines with copper, cobalt, galena and sphalerite. (After Ladame, 1945.)

is found mainly as zinc blende or sphalerite, and with it is associated the mineral calamine. Pyrites and chalcopyrite are not uncommon and are likely to be tinted by the carbonates malachite and azurite.

Many of the lead–zinc localities are shown on the sketch map (fig. 126), but only a few need be given as examples since numerous individual "mines" have been described by Diehl and Ladame. Sungūn, situated between Tabrīz and Russia, has a complicated mineral content and structural setting. Lead, zinc, and copper occur with quartz veins in skarn, the metamorphic rocks having formed near the contact of a diorite mass intruded into impure dolomitic limestone. Farther south (at Zanjādeh thirty miles north of Miāneh), volcanic tuff forming part of the Eocene "Green beds" are cut by quartz veins carrying galena and zinc blende. The Government survey in 1942 demonstrated that considerable ore reserves were then available in this vicinity. A prospect at Mikhās between Qazvīn and Tehrān has yielded galena in veins bearing quartz, calcite, and fluorspar. Farther east the close connexion between ore bodies and intruded volcanic rocks is less apparent, and it is here that the lead–zinc minerals fill shear zones and gash veins in country that is rust-coloured from its content of limonite.

Other mines are encountered to the east of Tehrān, near Simnān Dāmghān, and in the region around 'Abbāsābād, from all of which lead and zinc have been won; the same may be said of old workings near Anārak. A review of mines in the Kirmān province was made in 1959 by Barfield and Clarke, who refer especially to the Zargan–Kushk district because further reserves of ore were determined there during recent mining. This ore occurs in a ferruginous Jurassic limestone folded into a syncline. Both limbs of the fold are mineralized and are stated to be ore-bearing for some miles along the trend. A shear zone stained with limonite disturbs metamorphic rocks at Zargan and gives rise to fissures containing lenses of cerussite. Mineralization near Kushk includes the emplacement of galena and zinc blende in Triassic limestones. Similar minerals fill veins following faults in the Cretaceous limestone near Jalāliyeh. Nearly 15,000 tons of galena were reported to be the output from Iran in 1961, and according to figures for 1958 the zinc blende removed was of the same order.

Localities:

Āzarbāïjān	Sungūn	38° N.	46° E.
Miāneh	Zanjādeh	37° N.	48° E.
Sāva–Tehrān	Pasqa'leh	35° N.	51° E.
Khurāsān	Ārsak	36° N.	54° E.
Kāshān–Iṣfahān	Kunsik	33° N.	51° E.
Anārak	Anārak	33° N.	54° E.
	Zargan	32° N.	55° E.
	Kushk	32° N.	56° E.
	Jalāliyeh	29° N.	55° E.

CHROMITE

The search for minerals in Iran was intensified when war broke out in 1939, and because of the demand for chromite in Europe the search for it was given high priority in Iran. Turkey was already an important producer, and it was known that chromite there was associated with peridotite. Large areas of peridotite and serpentine are distributed through Iran between Turkey and Balūchistān. As a result of investigations about this time, chromite was discovered in connexion with a serpentine strip at Farīmeh lying north of Sabzavār. Again, to the south of Mashhad, on the road to Turbat-i-Ḥaidarī, chromite occurs with a massive periodotite at Rubāṭ-i-Safīd. The largest body yet known in Iran was discovered at Isfand Āqeh about 100 miles south of Kirmān, from which some 150,000 tons were mined between 1940 and 1958. Other finds of chromite have been made in Iranian Balūchistān at Sardāgh and Rūdān.

Chromite is a component of dunite, an olivine-rich peridotite that readily alters to dark-green serpentine. Much of the ore occurs in lens-shaped masses many of which are bounded by faults, the fault-surfaces being polished or slickensided. One of the largest ore bodies found was lens-shaped: 1,300 ft long and reaching thirty ft wide; it has been followed underground to a depth of sixty ft. The reserves are hard to assess on account of impersistent as well as faulted lodes. The ore contains from 10 to 50 per cent of chromite. In 1958 the Isfand Āqeh mine was credited with perhaps 60,000 tons in reserve. In this region magnesite veins cut the serpentine and form conspicuous white streaks across the sombre brown country which the weathered serpentine produces. The output credited to Iran in 1961 was 49,000 tons of chrome ore, or approximately 24,000 tons of chromite.

Localities:

Fārūmad	36° N.	56° E.	Sardāgh	26° N.	57° E.
Ribāṭ-i-Safīd	35° N.	59° E.	Rūdān	26° N.	59° E.
Isfand Āqeh	29° N.	57° E.			

BAUXITE

An extensive deposit of bauxite was discovered and described in the course of a survey by Huckriede, Kursten and Venzlaff in the district between Kirmān and Saghand. The deposit reaches a thickness of the order of forty ft, including beds containing some impurities near Bulbulū, lat. 30° 10′ N.; long. 57° 10′ E., fifteen miles south-east of Kirmān. The presence of grains of bauxite in the sandstone at about the same horizon to the north suggests the lateral extension of the beds to cover an area at present undetermined. The bauxite rests upon a surface of Triassic limestone or dolomite that has been subjected to solution and thus etched into a complex of pillars and pits: the latter are partly filled with deposited bauxite, whilst the pillars tend to project. Overlying the bauxite deposit, after a zone in which sandy shales are mingled with bauxite, shales occur reddened along their joint planes. These shales are covered in turn by marly, grey-green, knobbly limestones inter-bedded with dark shales; and above them there is a yellow-brown fossiliferous limestone determined as Rhaetic. At Bulbulū the main bauxite is reddish brown in colour, pisolitic and lumpy in structure. The part that is mainly bauxite is about twenty-five ft thick, while that with only a little bauxite amounts to another fifteen ft. The bauxite is partly diaspore, partly bochmite; the iron impurity is largely goethite, and there is an admixture of sand.

It is doubtful whether such a remote deposit lying in a country of low rainfall will encourage exploitation in the near future.

MOLYBDENUM

Molybdenum occurs sparingly in Iran. It is always found associated with veins of quartz or pegmatite in a granite that may have been fractured, and the molybdenite is sometimes accompanied by chalcopyrite. One of its localities is within six miles of the Russian frontier at Gūlan Chai, near a copper prospect. Contiguous granite is thought to be pre-Tertiary, and veins of quartz and pegmatite contain molybdenite, chalcopyrite, pyrites, and traces of other copper minerals. At best molybdenite in the veins amounts to 0·8 per cent. A second occurrence lies at Qal'eh Kāfī, twenty miles east of Anārak, where veins of quartz up to one ft wide yield a mixture of copper, lead, and iron minerals, including a little molybdenite and wulfenite (lead molybdate). The veins are in a fracture zone in light-coloured granite regarded as Mesozoic in age. A similar setting of quartz veins in granite, with associated wulfenite and galena, is reported from Zargan near Bāfq, and from Lahrīgīneh about forty miles north of Iṣfahān. Another find of veins with molybdenum was made at Dahu Rāmūn, 100 miles south

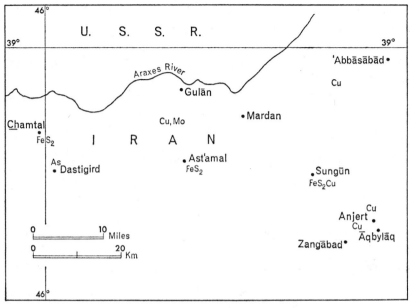

Fig. 130. Sketch-map of the Araxes River, with copper, pyrites, molybdenum and arsenic prospects in north-west Iran. (After Ladame, 1945.)

of Kirmān, in which the pegmatite veins occur in fractured granite. Molybdenum in Iran appears to be without economic importance at present.

Localities:

Gūlan Chai	38° N.	46° E.	Lahgrīgineh	33° N.	51° E.
Qal'eh Kāfī	33° N.	55° E.	Dahu Rāmūn	29° N.	57° E.
Zargan	31° N.	55° E.			

ARSENIC

Arsenic occurs in the Takht-i-Sulaimān mountains to the west of Zahjān at Zireh Shūrān, where the mineralization can be followed along a dolerite dyke that is crushed. Realgar (AsS) is found both massive and in veins in the decomposed dyke, the country rock it cuts being schist. From these mountains about 400 tons of arsenic ore have been mined per year, used largely for the production of insecticides. Farther north in Āzarbāijān, at Siāh Rūd on the Araxes river, orpiment (As_2S_3) has been found along a fault-plane cutting a conglomerate. Orpiment has also been deposited to the east of Tabrīz along a zone of

contact between conglomerate below and a lava above. Both the conglomerate and the lava are late Tertiary in age. Far to the east in
Khurāsān near Tārīk Darreh, in the contact zone between a porphyrite
and thin-bedded Liassic limestone, veins have been found carrying
mispickel (FeAsS) and also a complicated copper ore.

Besides forming the base of insecticides, the native arsenic is used
as a depilatory.

Localities:

Sīāh Rūd 38° N. 46° E. Zireh Shūrān 36° N. 47° E.
Tārīk Darreh 35° N. 60° E.

ANTIMONY

Antimony is found in small quantities in three mines in Iran. Two of
these, Patyār and Turkmanī, are situated respectively seven miles east
and twenty-five miles south-east of Anārak. The third is located farther

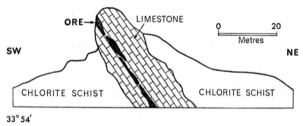

Fig. 131. At Turkmanī near Anārak the antimony ore bodies of stibnite and quartz occur
in dark limestone veined with calcite. (After Ladame, 1945.)

east, about 100 miles north-west of Bīrjand. The workings at Patyār
follow vertical quartz veins that cut a complex of chlorite and graphitic
schists interbedded with limestones of undetermined age. The veins at
Turkmanī which vary from six in. to four ft in thickness, carry calcite
as well as quartz. The mineralization is irregular. At Shūrāb the veins
follow a contact between a quartz porphyry dyke and the limestone it
cuts. The ore, stibnite (Sb_2S_3), is patchy: some of it occurs as large
crystals intergrown with quartz, and some of it is finely crystallized and
disseminated. Individual veins have been traced for about one quarter
of a mile. The fine-grained ore is not easy to concentrate economically,
but the coarse-grained ore can be effectively enriched by hand-sorting,
after which the concentrate is taken to a government refinery near
Tehrān, where it is sublimated. The main reserves are envisaged to be

at Shūrāb, though the present output there has been only a few tons per year.

Localities:

Patyār	33° N. 53° E.	Turkmanī	33° N. 54° E.
Shūrāb	33° N. 58° E.		

MERCURY

A little cinnabar (HgS), has been yielded by a Tertiary sandstone at Zireh Shūrān, one of the sites of gold in Iran, located south-south-east of Tabrīz.

Locality: Zireh Shūrān 36° N. 47° E.

BORATES

A mixture of borates occurs in a small basin at Khātūnābād, about 140 miles south of Yazd, but reserves are thought to be small.

BRICKS

Brick-making (mainly of sun-dried bricks) is done in a small way as a village industry, while burnt bricks are made on a larger scale near many towns: e.g. there are many brickfields south of Tehrān. Brick-making on a large scale has also been carried out near Ābādān and Ahvāz, where new towns have been built.

CEMENT

Cement-works function in Tehrān and Iṣfahān and cope with the national demand.

COBALT

Cobalt and nickel are found together at a few localities in Iran; nickel also occurs independently. The cobalt has been sought and worked for many years, as it provides the source of the blue glaze so familiar on tiles in Iran. The two elements are contained in ores occurring at Imāmzādeh Dā'ūd, north-west of Tehrān; at Kamsar, twenty miles south-west of Kāshān; and at Miskanī and Talmesī, both twenty miles west of Anārak. The ore near the capital is small and unimportant. Kamsar, however, has long been the principal mine yielding cobalt minerals in Iran. These minerals are asbolite, an earthy mass containing cobalt sulphide and hydroxides of iron; together with copper, nickel, and erythrite, a cobalt arsenate mixed with iron and nickel oxides and lime. The ores fill cracks and fissures in massive dolomitic limestones which have been cut by porphyry dykes. The iron and copper minerals occurring with the cobalt can be separated by hand-sorting, and a useful cobalt by-product thereby obtained. Not far from the mines the region is intruded by a granite that may be involved in the formation of the ore body.

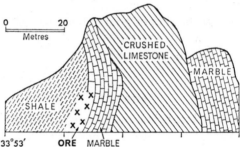

Fig. 132. Conditions at Chashmeh Āb-i-Shūr, showing the position of nickel-bearing marbles in a sequence of shales and shattered limestones. (After Ladame, 1945.)

A variety of cobalt arsenic and sulphur minerals accompanies chalcopyrite and pyrite at Miskanī and Talmesī. Here the country rock is schist overlain by a Lower Cretaceous conglomerate, which in turn is covered by a bed of decomposed igneous rock. This underlies a Tertiary conglomerate that passes up into a thick series of gypsiferous red sandstones, shales, and marls of the Upper Tertiary; these have been folded into a syncline and the volcanic rocks are mineralized at the surface. The values fall off, however, below 150 ft below ground. The ore here is concentrated by flotation and hand-sorting; once again nickel is present with the cobalt, copper, and iron. Small amounts of nickel minerals have been reported from Birinjiki in Balūchistān.

Localities:

Imāmzādeh Dāūd	36° N.	51° E.	Miskanī	33° N.	51° E.
Kamsar	34° N.	51° E.	Birinjīkī	27° N.	57° E.

GOLD

Gold in very small amounts is known to occur at seven places in Iran. At Zireh Shūrān, near Zanjān, about 180 miles west of Tehrān, it was found in the alluvium. A second locality, Kawand, a few miles south-east

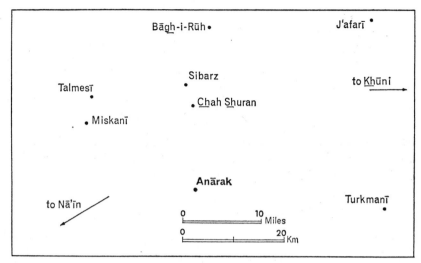

Fig. 133. Sketch-maps of nickel "mines" near Anārak, where there is a folded complex of slates, limestones and basic igneous rocks. General strike is N.W.–S.E. except near J'afarī in the north-east, where strike is N.E.–S.W.

of Zanjān, has yielded a little free gold associated with iron ochre in cavities within a siliceous limestone. A third auriferous site lies to the east of Tehrān, near Dāmghān, where a little gold has been washed from the gravels and sands lying at the skirts of *Kūh-i-Zar*, the "hill of gold"; but any chance of exploitation here is foiled by the lack of water, which would be needed in far greater amount than is available to work a placer deposit. West of Tehrān the mountain Kūh-i-Alvand stands overlooking Hamadān. Inquiry here has shown that quartz veins—near the junction between the granodiorite, which makes the bulk of the mountain, and the neighbouring schist—carry colours of gold and chalcopyrite.

The fifth site lies to the south-east of Hamadān, near Burūjird, where colours of gold are associated with the aureole in schists around a granodiorite body. Far to the south-east old workings at Khūnī, near Anārak, have been examined and shown to contain relics of a complicated ore whose elements include copper, lead, molybdenum, and gold. This same kind of complicated ore from the Bahrāsmān hills may have given rise to the gold found in alluvium in the Jīruft district, 120 miles south-south-east of Kirmān. Here gold occurs only in tantalizingly small quantities, and the only generalization that may be true is that chalcopyrite is present wherever primary gold is found.

Localities:

Zireh Shūrān	36° N.	47° E.	Burūjird	33° N.	49° E.
Kawand	36° N.	49° E.	Khūnī	33° N.	53° E.
Kūh-i-Zar	35° N.	54° E.	Jīruft	28° N.	58° E.
Kūh-i-Alvand	35° N.	50° E.			

MAGNESITE

Sporadic veins of magnesite cut some of the peridotite intrusions in the Isfand Āqeh district and also farther south near the northern end of Kūh-i-Zindān. They may have potential value.

Localities:
Isfand Āqeh 29° N. 57° E. North Zindān 28° N. 57°E.

BARYTES AND CELESTITE

Barytes is said to occur with copper workings in the Anārak and Kirmān districts. In addition, there are six veins at Talkeh and several at Chārī. No exploitation has taken place. In the oilfield district in south-west Iran veins of celestite are sometimes encountered.

Locality: Chārī 29° N. 57° E.

FLUORSPAR

References to fluorspar are made in the record of some of the lead–zinc workings, such as the one at Mīkhāṣ near Qazvīn where quartz, calcite and fluor are vein minerals. In Kūh-i-Kunsik near Iṣfahān the old lead mine provides exposures of barytes, fluor, and quartz. A considerable tonnage of fluorspar exists near lead workings at Darband, about 100 miles north of Kirmān.

Localities:
Mīkhāṣ	36° N.	51° E.	Kūh-i-Kunsik	33° N. 51° E.
Darband	31° N.	57° E.		

MARBLE

Yellow marble and also a white variety are worked about 100 miles south-south-east of Yazd, yielding a production of about 500 tons per year.

Localities: Ḥusainābād 30° N. 55° E. Rūdkhāneh Shūr 30° N. 55° E.

CHAPTER 16

INDUSTRIAL ACTIVITIES

Sugar-refining may be regarded as one of mankind's first large-scale industrial activities to employ more than a handful of workers and to use substantial quantities of fuel. Although it originally developed in the Iranian province of K͟hūzistān in the first centuries A.D., neither it nor any of the other early industrial activities (metal-working, textiles, dyes) survived into the nineteenth century. Even arts and crafts, normally a source of skill for industrial development, had decayed by then and could not be used as a nucleus for industrial growth. For this reason all the factors required for the building up of modern Iranian industries—management, skilled and semi-skilled labour, as well as capital—had to be imported from abroad. All that the country could supply in the first stages of modern industrial development were natural resources, and to this day exploitation of resources, especially petroleum, dominates the Iranian industrial economy.

Only at a later stage did there emerge modern industries such as textiles, which were not based on the exploitation of local resources. These industries began operation between the two world wars and grew rapidly during World War II and thereafter, relying on foreign machinery and instruction; however, most of the capital was provided from within the country. To some extent these newer industries are related to the re-emergence of arts and crafts, especially carpet-making. Based on traditional skills and patterns, and carried out and financed entirely by Iranians, arts and crafts began to reappear at the end of the nineteenth century, when foreigners were starting to take an interest in Iranian resources; and until recently, these activities owed their growth to markets abroad rather than in Iran. The following sections describe the evolution of the geographical distribution of modern industries and arts and crafts together with their effect on the regions and cities of Iran.

THE PETROLEUM INDUSTRY

Iran's resources began to attract the attention of Europeans, and to a much less extent of Americans, during the second half of the nineteenth century. The first major concession for exploitation of these resources was granted in 1872 to Baron de Reuter, a British subject, who received the right to mine minerals as well as to construct railways and establish a bank. This comprehensive concession was regarded as necessary by experts, since Iran, like most underdeveloped countries at that time, was unable to provide transport and the other services required in the development of its resources. However, the wide scope of the concession evoked opposition from within Iran, and diplomatic pressure against it from the Russians, while on a state visit to England in 1873 the Shāh was surprised to discover that it was only luke-warmly received by the City of London. Hence, the concession was cancelled by unilateral action on the part of the Shāh's government. In 1889 another, more limited, concession for oil exploration and banking, was granted to a son of Baron de Reuter, and drilling was undertaken at Dālakī [Daleki], inland from the Persian Gulf port of Bushire. Here the firm of Hotz and Company had, under a very limited concession of their own, earlier conducted a search for oil. De Reuter's team also drilled on the island of Qishm [Qeshm] near the entrance to the Persian Gulf. All these efforts were unsuccessful, and this concession, like the previous one of Hotz, was cancelled, except for the provision of banking services. In 1901 an entirely new concession for petroleum production covering all of Iran except the northernmost provinces adjoining Russia, was granted to William Knox D'Arcy, a Briton, who had made a fortune in Australian gold mining. D'Arcy's exploitation company later became known as the Anglo-Persian Oil Company; it changed its name in 1935 to the Anglo-Iranian Oil Company; after nationalization of its Iranian properties in 1951–4 it became the British Petroleum Company.

Although D'Arcy[1] had no accurate geological records to guide him, he believed that evidence of oil- and gas-seepages, historically affirmed in connexion with the locations of Zoroastrian fire temples and in other ancient sources, pointed to the existence of substantial petroleum reserves near ground level. Most of the then-known seepages were

[1] It should be noted at the outset that D'Arcy himself never set foot in Iran, initiating and directing his undertakings in that country from London.

Fig. 134. Oil operations areas.

located in the western foothills of the Zagros mountains of southern
Iran, and thus within easy reach of the Persian Gulf and accessible to
water transport up the Shaṭṭ al-ʿArab estuary and thence on either the
river Tigris or the river Kārūn. From points along these rivers most of
the seepages inland could be reached after only a few days' travel.
Although petroleum has subsequently been discovered elsewhere in
Iran, the ease of access from the Persian Gulf (now aided by railway
and motor transport) continues to be important, and though in more
recent times exploration for oil has spread to other areas in Iran,
to this day the south-western part of the country continues to be the
main centre of Iranian petroleum exploitation. Accessibility to the
Persian Gulf in D'Arcy's time was a factor inhibiting exploration for
oil beyond the Zagros range, and areas included in D'Arcy's original
concession farther away from the Gulf were in fact gradually abandoned.

D'Arcy drilled first near the well-known seepages of Chiah-Surkh, close to the main route from Baghdad to Tehrān and not far from the border between Iran and what was then Mesopotamia. Thus drilling equipment could be brought by water to Baghdad and taken from there by mule-drawn wagon to the drilling site. Oil was discovered in two wells during 1903 and 1904; but the quantities (about twenty-five barrels a day from each well)[1] were not sufficient to warrant commercial production, which would have entailed construction of pipelines to either Baghdad or the Persian Gulf. D'Arcy therefore abandoned drilling in the Chiah-Surkh area. In 1914 this area was part of the Turkish Ottoman empire; after 1918, it became part of Iraq. Commercial quantities of oil were finally discovered in the vicinity of the seepages in 1923, and extension of this oil field across the Iranian border was proved in 1932. The Iranian portion of the oil field is called Naft-i-Shāh (the Iraqi portion is called Naft Khana); it began production in 1935 after a 101 mile pipeline had been completed across one of the main ridges of the Zagros mountains to the town of Kirmānshāh. Here a refinery was built (the output of this field and of the refinery remains small, up to 3,500 b/d); but until recently it satisfied most of the demand of west-central Iran, and during the shut-down of most Iranian oil production in 1951–4, Iranians were able to keep the field and refinery in operation. Both are now entirely operated by the National Iranian Oil Company (NIOC).

The costly and disappointing operations at Chiah Surkh had used up so much of D'Arcy's capital that he was unable to continue his quest unaided. As his belief in the potentialities of his concession remained unshaken, he approached a number of financiers and companies. He achieved no success, however, until he succeeded in coming to terms with the Burmah Oil Company. This company provided funds for renewing the operations by means of the Concessions Syndicate, which was under the joint control of the Burmah Oil Company and D'Arcy. It was then decided to transfer operations to the province of Khūzistān, at the head of the Persian Gulf. Here the Kārūn river permitted inland movement from ports on the Shaṭṭ al-'Arab to the outer foothills of

---

[1] Production of wells or oil fields, or the capacity of oil refineries, is usually measured in barrels per day (abbreviated b/d). These are measurement barrels each equivalent to forty-two American gallons. Many countries now measure in tons per year. For an approximate conversion of barrels per day into tons per year, the number of barrels per day is multiplied by fifty. This approximate conversion rate can be used for metric as well as long tons. For conversion into cubic metres per year, which are sometimes also used, specific gravity has to be allowed for.

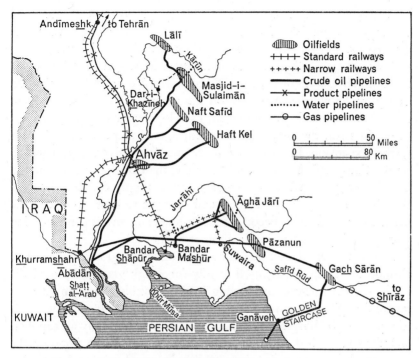

Fig. 135. Khūzistān.

the Zagros mountains and exclusively through Iranian territory. Steamship transport on the Kārūn had been established by a British firm in 1887 and several seepages could be reached in a few days' travel by mule or camel from landing stages on the river above the town of Ahvāz. After several failures and the absorbtion of most of his capital, when D'Arcy was almost ready to abandon the enterprise, large quantities of oil were finally discovered in 1908 near the seepages of Masjid-i-Sulaimān, at a depth of 1,180 ft in a layer of rock that was subsequently termed Asmari limestone.

The drilling site, originally known as Maidān-i-Naftūn ("the oily field"), lies near the ancient building known as the Masjid-i-Sulaimān ("Soloman's mosque") which, whilst long thought to have been a fire temple, was probably a gathering place for the local tribes; though the history and origin of this structure are still problematical. The quantities of oil were sufficient to warrant a properly organized transport system both for the inbound shipment of supplies and outbound delivery of oil. No development on such a scale as had now to be undertaken in

521

undeveloped, rugged, semi-desert country had ever been attempted before: considerable capital had to be invested over many years before the first drop of oil could be sold and profits begin to accrue.

It was in 1909, when success was assured at Masjid-i-Sulaimān, that the Burmah Oil Company and D'Arcy formed the Anglo-Persian Oil Company, by which the concession was taken over and all subsequent operations in Iran itself conducted. Development was greatly assisted when, in 1914, the British government agreed to provide capital for further expansion. In return the government was given representation on the Company's board. Simultaneously, the British government and the Company signed an agreement for the supply of fuel oil to the British Navy. Thus geographical and strategic reasons persuaded the British government to become a stock holder in an oil company that was exploiting a concession in another country.

The area where the oil was discovered lies in a region of hills of low altitude but steep slopes, used mainly for rough grazing by nomadic Bakhtīārī tribesmen; some sowing is also possible except in years of severe drought, though the area cannot be regarded as climatically or topographically hospitable to man.[1] Before 1918 virtually all supplies, including food, had to be imported from overseas. To improve the food supply the concessionaire established several dairy and vegetable farms in the oil region, but despite the economic development of Iran and particularly of Khūzistān since then, the position so far as food and luxury supplies are concerned still necessitates special arrangements and a measure of special imports. Until 1923 inbound supplies were brought by ocean-going ships to the port of Khurramshahr (formerly called Muhammareh) at the mouth of the Kārūn in the Shaṭṭ al-'Arab estuary. From there barges carried supplies 114 miles up the river Kārūn to the Ahvāz where they had to be unloaded for a portage of about one mile to circumvent rapids occasioned by parallel ridges of rock lying across the river bed. This portage was in the early days by wagons, but these were soon replaced by a narrow gauge railway. Smaller barges continued the journey for another ninety miles up river to Dar-i-Khazīneh. From Dar-i-Khazīneh supplies were carried another thirty-five miles by mule-drawn wagons through steep and tortuous valleys to Masjid-i-Sulaimān. This last part of the journey took two days and was usually accomplished at

[1] For a geological description of this and other oil fields, see "Oil and Gas in South-western Asia", Area Simposium de Petroleo y Gas.

night in the hot weather to avoid the intense heat of the day. Teams of mules, sixteen in each, hauled most of the drilling equipment, and the whole journey from Khurramshahr required about five days, after a sea journey of at least four weeks from north-western Europe, where most of the supplies came from. Many thousands of tons of steel for wells, pipelines, as well as other equipment were imported in this way. The construction of a narrow-gauge railway from Dar-i-Khazīneh to Masjid-i-Sulaimān was delayed until 1923 through shortage of equipment before and after World War I. With the railway the last leg of the journey was reduced to one day.

In the early days of oil development urgent messages had to be sent by horsemen, and with frequent changes of horses Masjid-i-Sulaimān was reachable from Khurramshahr in one day. By 1912, however, telephone and telegraph lines made communication much easier, and by then the area was also connected to the Indo-European telegraph system at Shustar. To facilitate the unloading of cargoes at Khurramshahr, in 1914, the Iranian government exchanged Chiah Surkh and other border territory farther north for about three square miles of Turkish territorial waters in the Shaṭṭ al-'Arab at the Kārūn.[1] Here the new part of Khurramshahr developed, at first to cater almost entirely for the requirements of the oil industry, and later to become the largest Iranian port for general cargo.

With the help of these transport facilities a pipeline 135 miles long was constructed from Masjid-i-Sulaimān to the Shaṭṭ al-'Arab, together with four pumping stations (later reduced to three). The salinity of the soil in the lowland region near the river made it impossible for the pipeline to be buried as it would have been corroded, so that it had to be placed on supports or an embankment above the ground, while considerable study of corrosion factors became a concommitant of pipeline operation in this area. It goes without saying that this method of construction facilitated sabotage of the pipeline, such as occurred in the early days of the First World War, necessitating repairs which took three months because replacement pipes had to be transported to the area by sea and by mule. On the Shaṭṭ al-'Arab the pipeline and tanker terminal as well as a refinery were built on a virtually uninhabited island to the south of Khurramshahr. A site of about one

---

[1] Since the Treaty of Erzerum (1847), the boundary had been located on the Iranian side of the Shaṭṭ al-'Arab. By this territorial exchange Iran obtained a midstream boundary in the Shaṭṭ al-'Arab, from a point about one mile below the mouth of the Kārūn to a point about four miles above it.

square mile (today extended to about five square miles), safe from the highest floods (it was untouched by the serious 1938 flood) and near sufficiently deep water to berth 20,000 ton tankers, was selected for the terminals and refinery. The refinery area, the town that developed adjacent to the refinery, and the island itself have all become known as Ābādān (a transliteration representing the present-day accepted pronunciation), and in 1962 their total population was over 226,683, of which just under 12,000 persons were employed in the refinery. Today, in area and potential, still the world's largest refinery, with a capacity of 500,000 b/d, it began operation in 1912 with a capacity of about 6,000 b/d. Within a few years Iran became one of the world's biggest suppliers of oil and today it is sixth in rank among the world's oil-producing countries.

To drill the wells and construct and operate the many installations, geologists, engineers (including experts on pipeline corrosion), drillers and administrative staff were brought to Khūzistān from all over the world. Many gained their experience in America, the Caucasus and Burma. Among skilled personnel the British predominated; but drillers from the Polish oil fields (then in the Austrian Empire) were conspicuous in the team before 1914 and they are remembered in Masjid-i-Sulaimān by a district known as "Poland". Other drillers came from Canada. Many skilled and most of the semi-skilled workers in the first instance came from India, some of them with oil experience in Burma. At the beginning local Iranians worked primarily as unskilled labourers and guards. Gradually, however, they advanced in employment, especially after immigrants from adjacent provinces in Iran (notably Iṣfahān), joined their ranks in the 1920s. By the early 1930s almost all Indians had been replaced by Iranians, and in 1962 only 478 foreigners, all of them highly skilled, remained at work in the former concession area; of these, 261 worked in the Ābādān refinery.

One oil field with one pipeline and one refinery supplied world markets until 1928. By that time demand for petroleum products—in its markets in Europe, in southern and eastern Asia, as well as in Australia —had considerably increased, whilst production at Masjid-i-Sulaimān was expected to decline in a few years. The concessionaire had been searching elsewhere in Khūzistān for over ten years. No discovery was made until 1928, when oil was found at a depth of over 2,000 ft, again in Asmari limestone, this time at Haft Kel, about thirty-five miles south-west of Masjid-i-Sulaimān and in the same rugged country. As early as the year of its discovery, Haft Kel was joined to the existing pipeline system and its production soon outstripped that of Masjid-i-Sulaimān. In 1965 it produced 104,000 b/d and ranked fourth of the Iranian oil fields, whereas Masjid-i-Sulaimān had by this time declined to 34,000 b/d. In 1928, however, Masjid-i-Sulaimān still produced a maximum of 118,000 b/d. Automotive transport assisted in bringing Haft Kel so rapidly into production. It also permitted a more rapid repair and improvement of existing facilities, and made further search for oil much easier.

After construction of a road, somewhat ruefully called the Golden Staircase, through the extremely difficult though picturesque country from Ganāveh on the Persian Gulf to a point in south-eastern Khūzistān, oil was discovered at this point, Gach Sārān, in 1928. Due to the slightly higher rainfall at Gach Sārān, the local tribesmen, among them Turkish-speaking Qashghai, still practise agriculture and fruit growing in the vicinity of this oil field. Here again oil was found in Asmari lime-stone at depths of over 2,500 ft; and as is the case throughout all the producing oil fields in Iran, gas dissolved in the oil under great pressure drives the oil up the wells, and even higher, without any pumping being necessary.

In 1934 oil was also discovered at Naft Safīd, ten miles north-west of Haft Kel; in 1937 at Āghā Jārī, sixty miles south-east of Haft Kel, and in 1938 at Lālī, about twenty miles north of Masjid-i-Sulaimān.

In all these fields the upper oil horizon is Asmari limestone at a minimum depth of 3,000 ft (Āghā Jārī, 4,500 ft); their topography resembles that of Masjid-i-Sulaimān—except for Lālī, a smaller field where the walls of the valleys tend to be higher and steeper and the area in fact mainly comprises high plateau land bisected by a deep and twisting gorge through which the river Kārūn turbulently flows. Because of the large volume of oil available from Haft Kel, and the repercussions on world markets occasioned by the depression be-tween the wars, neither the Āghā Jārī nor the Lālī field came into pro-duction before World War II. However, during the period 1928–39 Masjid-i-Sulaimān was fully developed as the supply centre for oil operations in Khūzistān, and a small topping plant was built there to cover local demand and to remove from the oil being pumped at Ābādān any products that were rendered unprocessable or unsaleable by the fall in general consumption and demand during the depression.

In connexion with the problem of the disposal of these products and surpluses in general arising as a result of the depression, the Company's technicians introduced into the operations in Iran the practice known as "recycling". This term is applied to the practice of pumping back into the natural reservoir any partly refined products which may, due to a variety of factors, be rendered, temporarily or otherwise, surplus to marketing requirements. This process did in fact represent a technical advance of considerable importance, for not only was it a useful conservation measure, but by it the productive life of the reservoir rock was increased; and hence the flow of oil in future years.

At Masjid-i-Sulaimān a bāzār, several housing areas, and a complex water-supply system, using water from the upper Kārūn, were constructed by the concessionaire. Thus by 1962 Masjid-i-Sulaimān had a population approaching 20,000, of whom a little under 3,000 were permanently employed in the oil industry. So much for the centre of the oil fields and the production area; likewise in the period before the Second World War great expansion took place in the Ābādān refinery, which reached a capacity of 240,000 b/d, with new and specialized equipment being added to the plant. This development of the oil fields and the refinery was, however, limited to the area between the Persian Gulf and the western Zagros mountains, for, as has already been intimated, the Company abandoned its concessionary rights in territorial areas beyond this region, a step which was taken in 1933. Thus the Company reduced its concessionary area to an aggregate of 100,000 square miles. This is a matter to be studied in connexion with the history of oil agreements generally. What may be said here is that study of the factors compelling a concessionaire to modify the size of his concessionary operational areas should contribute to an understanding of how considerations both technical and commercial gradually proved what could be the workable optimum in meeting the obligations of a concession; and, in the case in point, a generous concession, ambitiously undertaken.

Completion of the Trans-Iranian Railway in 1938 as far as Bandar Shāpūr, a new port on the Khūr Mūsa, which is an inlet on the Persian Gulf, did not have much direct effect on oil production until World War II. The railway did, however, facilitate transport of petroleum products to the interior of Iran, where the concessionaire established a distribution system which included all the provinces of Iran except those bordering Russia. In these provinces products imported mainly from the Russian oil field Baku across the Caspian were distributed by other companies; elsewhere products were distributed from the southern oil concessionaire's wholesale depots.

According to agreements between the Iranian government and the concessionaire, the wholesale price of petroleum products delivered for Iranian consumption at Ābādān equalled the lowest price regularly quoted for similar oil elsewhere in the world. Almost always prices prevailing on the Gulf coast of the United States determined those at Ābādān, although on some occasions Rumanian prices were also taken into consideration. Freight from Ābādān to the point of delivery inside the country was added to the Ābādān price in the determination of local prices.[1] The Iranian market absorbed only a small fraction of Iranian production.

During the first years of the Second World War a shortage of tankers for export shipments caused a substantial cut back in output. Although Gach Sārān had begun production in 1940, after completion of a 165 mile pipeline to Ābādān, the flow of its wells had to be stopped in the same year, when the fall of France reduced Iranian exports even further. Due to tribal unrest the isolated area of Gach Sārān was often in danger of being, or actually was, cut off during the rest of the war years, and its wells remained sealed. In other fields output began again to expand after Iran was occupied by British, Indian and Russian forces. An increasing flow of oil then had urgently to be directed northward to supply the Russian war machine. With the Trans-Iranian Railway heavily overburdened with other military supplies for Russia, in order to reduce traffic on the railway a petroleum-product pipeline was built from Ābādān to the railway centre of Andīmeshk, well inland at the foot of the Zagros mountains on the main route from Tehrān to the north. This pipeline crossed the river Kārūn on the Trans-Iranian Railway bridge at Ahvāz. From Andīmeshk, the products were loaded to continue their journey northward either by rail or in tanker lorries. However the expansion in sales which thus came about failed to compensate completely for the loss of sea-borne exports, until the last stages of the war in the Pacific resulted in very heavy requirements both for aviation spirit and fuel-oil bunkers. The Ābādān refinery was enlarged to 500,000 b/d to provide for this demand, so that it became the world's largest refinery by a wide margin. In addition, a gas field discovered in 1937 at Pāzanun, on the pipeline route from Gach Sārān

[1] For details of the pricing mechanism see A. Melamid, "Geography of the World Petroleum Price Structure", *Economic Geography* (October 1962).

to Ābādān, was developed in 1943 to produce a petrol condensate required as an ingredient in aviation spirit. The shut-down pipeline from Gach Sārān was now brought into use to transport this condensate from Pāzanun to Ābādān.

Additional quantities of fuel oil were obtained from the recently inaugurated field at Āghā Jārī. While crude oil from most other Iranian oil fields is of relatively light density, yielding much petrol and kerosene in the refining process, that from Āghā Jārī is a heavier medium grade yielding more fuel-oil and less petrol and other light fractions. To speed Āghā Jārī's development the railway from Dar-i-Khazīneh to Masjid-i-Sulaimān was dismantled and its components used to build a new line connecting the Trans-Iranian Railway port of Bandar Shāpūr with Āghā Jārī. Houses in this virtually uninhabited area were constructed, and water obtained by means of a ten mile pipeline from a tributary of the river Jarrāhī. In 1962 Āghā Jārī employed nearly 1,200 oil-workers but not many other persons were attracted to live on this barren and relatively remote site. A pipeline to Ābādān was also built, and late in 1944 the Āghā Jārī wells began flowing at an initial rate of 57,000 b/d—a larger output than the entire Iranian production in 1921. Subsequently Āghā Jārī has become the most prolific Iranian oil field, producing 863,000 b/d in 1964, or about 52 per cent of the total Iranian production for that year. In 1954 a beginning was also made in the feeding of Naft Safīd oil into the pipeline system leading from the Masjid-i-Sulaimān and Haft Kel areas to Ābādān; and in 1948 oil from Lālī was added to the same system. Neither the Naft Safīd nor the Lālī field, especially in comparison with Āghā Jārī with its slightly different kind of product, have become major producers.

Because of the distance from Gach Sārān and Āghā Jārī to Ābādān, the Khūr Mūsa sea inlet proved convenient for construction of another tanker terminal, a project whose investigation began as early as 1938–9. A suitable site about ten miles above the railway port of Bandar Shāpūr was discovered, but the combination of low ground and high tides (the highest spring tides are twenty ft; average neaps are twelve ft) would have necessitated much embanking (up to twenty-five ft) for any use of the surface area adjacent to the jetties; and in any event the outbreak of World War II prevented the execution of these plans. When the end of hostilities brought no reduction in the demand for oil, this terminal was constructed, with the necessary link to the already existing Āghā Jārī railway. The terminal, now called Bandar

Māhshahr (a Persianization, meaning "Moon City", of the original Bandar Maʿshūr, literally "Salt Water Port") and equipped to handle tankers up to 40,000 tons, was opened in 1948. Housing and a supply of drinking water from the lower river Jarrāhī were also provided for nearly one thousand employees and their families as well as for the servicing of ships. A refinery, originally planned at an adjacent site, was not built, for in modern refinery operations it has been found generally more economical to process crude oil in the area where its product is marketed.[1]

Already in 1946 another, smaller tanker terminal had been constructed at Khusraubād (often spelt Khosrowbād), seventeen miles downstream from Ābādān, to boost the export of Āghā Jārī crude oil until the Bandar Māhshahr terminal could be completed. Khusraubād has never been developed into an oil terminal of permanent importance, though doubtless it could always be considered available as a secondary terminal in case of need.

With the end of the Second World War, operations at Pāzanun had to be suspended, but by 1950 Gach Sārān was brought back into production and its pipeline into full use. By this time Iran had three definable geographical groups of oil fields and pipeline systems: the northernmost field of Naft-i-Shāh feeding the Kirmānshāh refinery; the northern Khūzistān fields surrounding Masjid-i-Sulaimān and connected by pipeline with Ābādān; and the southern fields of Āghā Jārī and Gach Sārān, each feeding into both Ābādān and the tanker terminal at Bandar Māhshahr. During the war the Trans-Iranian Railway had been extended to the port of Khurramshahr, so that the river Kārūn was abandoned by the concessionaire for inbound water transport in 1950, in favour of exclusive use of road and rail transport. Aircraft became widely used for passenger and some freight services from Ābādān to the oil fields and Bandar Māhshahr, as well as to Tehrān and the outside world.

In March 1951 Iran nationalized its oil industry and the Anglo-Iranian Oil Company was forced to withdraw, leaving its Iranian former employees working for the newly created National Iranian Oil Company, to operate its installations.

The Anglo-Iranian Oil Company let it be known that it would take proceedings against any purchasers of Iranian oil which it maintained was its property. Iran found virtually no export outlet for its oil and the

---

[1] For an analysis of the economics of refinery location, see A. Melamid, "Geographical Distribution of Petroleum Refining Capacities", *Economic Geography* (April 1955).

installations were shut down partially or completely until, following the signing of an agreement between Iran and a consortium of British Dutch, American and French oil companies on 29 October 1954 after protracted negotiations, oil started to flow abroad again.

Under the new Agreement the Consortium's concession area was limited to 100,000 square miles which specifically included an "offshore" three mile belt in the Persian Gulf and a similar belt round certain islands. The Naft-i-Shāh field and Kirmānshāh refinery and distribution of products throughout Iran were retained by the National Iranian Oil Company and the Consortium undertook to hand over progressively to NIOC all "non-basic" services such as health, housing and welfare, required in support of its operations, this arrangement being completed in 1961.

The Agreement was for twenty-five years, the Consortium having the right to extend its life by three periods of five years each thereafter, subject to relinquishment of 20 per cent of the current agreement area on each extension. All existing fixed assets remained the property of NIOC as also became all subsequent installations, the initial cost of which was to be met by the Consortium, with subsequent repayment without interest over ten years as operating costs.

The Consortium member companies formed two companies, Iraanse Aardolie Exploratie en Productie Maatschappij (Iranian Oil Exploration and Producing Co.) N.V., and Iraanse Aardolie Raffinage Maatschappij (Iranian Oil Refining Co.) N.V., known collectively as the Iranian Oil Operating Companies incorporated under the laws of the Netherlands, registered in Iran, with their head Office in Tehrān and their operational headquarters at Masjid-i-Sulaimān and Ābādān respectively. The sole shareholder in these companies was Iranian Oil Participants Limited with its head office in London. Shareholders in I.O.P. Ltd. were the Consortium member companies.

It was not the function of the Operating Companies to buy or sell oil, their income being derived from operational fees payable to them by the Trading Companies which each Consortium member company set up and registered in Iran. These Trading Companies, acting individually and independently of one another would buy from NIOC at well-head the crude oil produced in the Agreement Area and re-sell it for export or have it refined at Ābādān and sell the products for export.

The basis of payments to Iran would be the "posted prices" published by each Trading Company. Each Trading Company would pay NIOC a stated payment at the rate of 12½ per cent of the applicable posted price for the crude oil it bought. Each Trading Company and the Operating Companies would pay tax to the government at the rate of 50 per cent on its net income, less, in the cases of Trading Companies, the stated payments made to NIOC, but under a Supplemental Agreement made in 1964 stated payments became accountable as expenses and were no longer deducted from tax on net income.

TABLE 10. *Total Iranian oil production, average daily rate in thousands of barrels*

1912	2·5	1940	180·9
1913	5·1	1941	139·0
1914	8·0	1942	208·2
1915	9·9	1943	208·2
1916	12·2	1944	278·7
1917	19·6	1945	352·0
1918	23·6	1946	400·0
1919	27·8	1947	472·0
1920	33·4	1948	551·0
1921	45·7	1949	598·0
1922	61·0	1950	718·0
1923	69·1	1951	650·0
1924	88·5	(based on first six
1925	96·0	months' production)
1926	98·2	1952	21·0
1927	108·7	1953	26·0
1928	118·7	1954	39·0
1929	115·5	1955	331·0
1930	125·6	1956	539·0
1931	121·6	1957	721·0
1932	135·2	1958	826·0
1933	149·0	1959	928·0
1934	158·5	1960	1,053·0
1935	156·9	1961	1,182·0
1936	171·4	1962	1,321·0
1937	213·2	1963	1,474·0
1938	214·7	1964	1,690·0
1939	214·1	1965	1,886·0

NIOC was entitled to take oil in kind in lieu of stated payment but with this exception, the Consortium had the exclusive right to export crude oil or refined products from the Agreement Area.

In what remained of 1954, 1·4 million long tons of crude oil were produced. By the end of 1957 yearly production passed the pre-nationalization total of 32 million tons a year and, steadily rising, exceeded 88 million million long tons in 1965.

Because, in accordance with changes in the world pattern of refining, an increasing number of refineries had been built in consumer countries during 1951–4, the output of Ābādān refinery did not reach previous levels. In 1965 it was 18,300,000 tons or 376,000 b/d, whereas in 1951 it had been operating at 25,000,000 tons/year.

However, the growth of Europe's oil consumption and the needs of new refineries steadily increased the demand for Āghā Jārī crude oil, so that additional pipelines to Bandar Māhshahr soon had to be constructed and the tanker terminal also required continuous enlargement by the building of additional loading jetties.

Renewal of production from Gach Sārān, potentially the largest field in Iran, was deferred until 1965; then large-scale development began. As there was little room for further expansion at Bandar Māhshahr, where the depth of the water was inadequate for the new "super tankers", it was necessary to build a new terminal elsewhere. The shallow coastal waters of the east side of the Persian Gulf were unsuitable for loading large tankers and Khārg Island, some three miles out to sea, was therefore chosen as the new terminal site.

The pipeline from Gach Sārān to Khārg Island runs for seventy-five miles over some very difficult terrain to Ganāveh on the coast, thence for twenty-one miles under the sea to the little island of Khārgu which it crosses before continuing for three more miles under the sea to Khārg. As Gach Sārān is about 2,200 ft above sea level, the oil flows by gravity throughout to a tank farm on high ground on the island, and thence by gravity again to a 2,000 ft loading jetty approached by a causeway and pier nearly 4,000 ft long and capable of accommodating four tankers (including one of 100,000 tons dead-weight) at a time, there being sixty ft of water at low tide.

When completed in 1960 the Gach Sārān–Khārg pipeline had a capacity of 390,000 b/d but in 1964 a second pipe was laid, increasing the capacity to 500,000 b/d.

In the meantime, a further expansion of export facilities had been put in hand, by which Khārg Island would become the Consortium's sole crude oil exporting terminal. The first phase of this undertaking, completed in 1966, involved the laying of a 42 in. pipeline 106 miles from Āghā Jārī to the coast at Ganāveh (at the time, the largest crude oil delivery pipeline in the world) and two more 30 in. submarine lines to Khārg Island, expansion of the tank farm on the island to give a storage capacity of 7,767,000 barrels (in the eleven new 500,000 barrel capacity tanks alone, enough oil could be stored to provide every man, woman and child in Europe and North America with a litre of oil each), and extension of the loading jetty to 6,000 ft to provide berths for ten tankers (five of them 100,000 dead weight tons and over), making it the largest single-structure crude oil facility in the world oil industry at that time. "Super tankers" of 200,000 tons can be accommodated, and loading rates are in excess of 10,000 tons per hour. The investment required to develop the terminal with its pipelines bringing heavy crude from Ga_ch Sārān and light crude from Āg_hā Jārī, with a throughput capacity of over two million barrels per day without boosting, was more than £65 million over a period of seven years.

With the cessation of crude oil shipments from Bandar Māh_shahr, work began on the second phase of the big expansion scheme: the conversion of that port into the export terminal for the products of Ābādān refinery; a conversion scheduled to be completed in 1967. These products were formerly shipped from Ābādān down the predominantly Iraqi waters of the Shaṭṭ al-ʿArab, which imposed a limit of about 25,000 dead-weight on the size of tankers that could be used.

This phase involved the laying of new pipelines from Ābādān to Bandar Māh_shahr (one of them a heated line for the movement of fuel oil during the cooler winter months) and provision of increased storage facilities at Bandar Māh_shahr.

In the meantime, the Consortium had been active in the discovery of new fields. In 1958 oil was discovered near Ahvāz and commercial production began there in 1960. In 1965 production from twenty wells was 60·7 million barrels. Oil from Ahvāz feeds into the northern K_hūzistān pipeline system and more than offsets losses of output in the older oilfields, particularly Masjid-i-Sulaimān, Naft Safīd and Lālī.

Other new fields were Pāzanun (1961) which, having first been activated in 1937, was brought into oil production in 1963 and gave 6·6 million barrels in 1965; K_hārg (1962), being that part of the Darius field covered by the island and its three mile off-shore concession belt, commissioned in 1964, produced three million barrels in 1965; Bībī Hakīmeh (1962) producing since 1964, gave fourteen million barrels in 1965; Rām_shīr (1963) on production since July 1966 was flowing at 8,000 barrels per day in August of that year; Mārūn (1964) commissioned on New Year's Eve 1965 gave 7·7 million barrels in its first eight months as a producer; and Kāranj (1963) was the fifth largest producer in 1965 at 78,000 barrels per day.

Oil was also found at Bīnak (1960), Mansūrī (1962), Bushgān (1963), Gulkhārī (1963), Rāgh-i-Safīd (1964), Fāris (1964), Kūpāl (1965) and Mullasāī (1966) later, with Mārūn, known as Mārūn Kārūn. Drilling in eight other localities failed to find oil in commercial quantity.

From October 1954 until the end of 1965 the Consortium produced nearly 574 million long tons of crude oil, resulting in revenue to Iran of £1,169,166,757 (£183·3 million in 1965). Revenue per barrel rose annually from 74·4 cents in 1962 to 82·8 cents in 1965. In the ten years from 1956 to 1965, £222·7 million were disbursed in salaries and wages, £19·2 million in employee benefits (Social Insurance, Pensions, Savings Schemes) and £59 million in local purchases and payments to local contractors; and in the same period £262·7 million of foreign exchange was brought into Iran by the Consortium. Capital investment by the Consortium in the eleven years up to the end of 1965 was some £228 million, of which £67 million was spent on exploration and drilling.

At the end of 1965 the Consortium Operating Companies employed 29,657 persons of whom producing operations accounted for 11,557, refining operations 17,465 and the head office in Tehrān 635. Of these 372 or 1·3 per cent were non-Iranian. The overall total also included 11,603 employees of NIOC who were engaged on "non-basic" operations in support of the Operating Companies and at those Companies' expense.

Operations other than finding and exporting oil were necessarily carried on under the aegis of the Consortium. Roads, bridges, airfields and water and electricity supplies, for instance, tangibly extended the industry's benefits beyond its own immediate sphere. Schools, hospitals and medical services, baths and sewage systems, shops and sports facilities have been provided. Some 6,600 houses for employees were built from 1954 to 1965, many of them for sale under home-ownership schemes. Apart from training in technical and artisan schools, the Companies' career development system led to more than five hundred overseas training assignments, ranging from a few weeks to several years by the end of 1966. With the rapid development of new industries in the 1960s the Operating Companies became a source of trained men for key positions in other enterprises.

Another contribution to industrial development outside the oil industry was the setting up, by the Consortium in 1966, of the Iranian Investment Corporation with £2 million capital subscribed by the Consortium Member Companies to promote productive enterprises in

TABLE 11. *Iranian oilfields*

Name of field	Year of discovery	Production began	Surface area (acres)	No. of producing wells (Dec. 1965)	Production 1965 (b/d)	Geological formation	Remarks
Masjid-i-Sulaimān	1908	1911	28,400	32	34,000	Asmari and Eocene	—
Haft Kel	1928	1929	21,000	15	104,000	Asmari	—
Gach Sārān	1928	1940	117,000	22	509,000	Asmari and Cretaceous	—
Naft Safīd	1935	1945	23,000	16	23,000	Asmari and Cretaceous	—
Naft-i-Shāh	1935	—	—	—	8,000	—	Information incomplete
Lālī (Asmari)	1938	1949	28,000 }	3	5,000	{ Asmari	—
Lālī (Cretaceous)	1949	—	12,400 }			Cretaceous	—
Āghā Jārī	1938	1944	61,000	42	833,000	Asmari and Cretaceous	—
Alburz	1956	—	—	—	—	—	Information incomplete; 16 wells shut in
Ahvāz	1958	1959	73,000	20	167,000	Asmari	—
Pāzanun	1961	1963	90,000	4	18,000	Asmari	Discovered as gas field in 1936
Khārg	1962	1964	20,000	4	8,000	Khami	Same field as Darius
Bībī Hakimeh	1962	1964	91,000	3	38,000	Asmari, Eocene and Cretaceous	—
Kāranj	1963	1964	38,000	3	69,000	Asmari	—
Rāmshīr	1963	1966	—	—	—	Asmari and Cretaceous	Production began in 1966
Mārūn	1964	1965	105,000	—	—	Asmari	Production began Dec. 1965
Rāgh-i-Safīd	1964	—	—	—	—	Asmari	—
Fāris	1964	—	—	—	—	Asmari	—
Kūpāl	1965	—	—	—	—	Asmari	—
Bahrigānsar	1960	1962	—	7	24,000	—	Offshore field
							Information incomplete
Darius	1961	1963	—	—	46,000	—	Offshore field
							Information incomplete
Cyrus	1962	—	—	—	—	—	Offshore field
							Information incomplete
					1,886,000		

535

the private enterprise sector by means of assistance in the fields of management techniques, credit and industrial expertise, and in the same year the Member Companies made an interest-free loan of £6 million to NIOC for carrying out certain development projects in Khūzistān.

As a result of the 1954 agreement with the Consortium, NIOC, which is owned entirely by the Iranian government, took over all the areas outside the "Agreement Area". It also operates in the northern provinces, which were excluded from D'Arcy's original grant and have at various times been claimed by other, mainly Russian, companies. Unassigned off-shore areas up to the three mile limit and as far as the boundary of Iran's claims of off-shore jurisdiction are also in the territories of NIOC activities. Their national headquarters are in Tehrān. Their field headquarters are at Khurramshahr, and teletype communications connect the two places with all major areas of operation, while, in accordance with its needs aircraft are available for NIOC to hire. As has been indicated, NIOC furnishes the Consortium with all those services not directly related to petrol production and refining: for example, medical assistance. Due to the remarkable increase in Consortium production since 1957, there has been a great deal of rapid new construction in Ābādān, Gach Sārān, Āghā Jārī, and Khārg. NIOC has also taken over from the former concessionaire and from others all the marketing of petroleum products within Iran itself, with the exception of imported petroleum specialities such as waxes and some lubricants. In this connexion, NIOC now operates the Naft-i-Shāh oil fields and the refinery linked with it at Kirmānshāh, whose capacity has been expanded since 1960. The pipeline constructed during the war from Ābādān to Andīmeshk to relieve the burden on the railway is also now operated by NIOC and has since 1955 been extended, first across the Zagros mountains to Tehrān, subsequently from Tehrān to Qazvīn, and finally to Rasht near the Caspian Sea. Other extensions of this line have been built from Tehrān to Mashhad in Khurāsān and from Aznā in central Iran to Iṣfahān. The total length in 1956 of pipeline system operated by the NIOC, if the more recently doubled Ahvāz–Tehrān line is counted as one, was 1,610 miles. Distribution of products in Iran have been improved and expanded by the construction of additional wholesale installations. The special domestic-price arrangements already mentioned as being related to the lowest quotations elsewhere in the world have been continued, except that on most products the cost of freightage from Ābādān is now absorbed by the NIOC.

After 1954 the NIOC began exploration for additional oil in its own area. In 1956 oil was discovered near Qum at a drilling site known as Alburz, about eighty-five miles south of Tehrān. The discovery well caught fire and so development of this field was delayed. Originally it was planned to export the oil through a 1,600 mile pipeline to the Turkish port of Iskanderun. However, these and other export plans had to be relinquished, for Alburz oil solidifies at a temperature below 70° F, which makes pumping across the Iranian plateau and the mountains on the Irano-Turkish border impossible in winter. Also in connexion with the Alburz Field, plans were envisaged of laying a pipeline from the field to a refinery to be established at Tehrān, scheduled for completion in 1967; but owing to the difficult nature of the Alburz Field, the Trans-Iranian pipeline from Ahvāz to Tehrān was doubled in 1966 to bring crude oil from the Agreement Area to meet the new Tehrān refinery's needs. Meanwhile, after eleven wells had been drilled, the potential of the Alburz Field gave the impression of being limited.

In 1958 the NIOC discovered an important gas field at Sarājeh, about ninety miles to the south of Tehrān. Drilling elsewhere—for example, near the Caspian Sea—has produced further indications of oil, but no commercial discoveries had been reported up to 1966. Throughout its areas of operations NIOC has made geological surveys covering the possible presence of oil; a number of foreign experts have assisted the NIOC in these surveying operations, while experienced drillers from abroad have been recruited and careful consultation with foreign production experts has always been maintained.

According to its Statutes, the National Iranian Oil Company may also assign permission to search and mine for oil to other foreign companies. It is thus that the NIOC has embarked upon several international arrangements, notably that in 1957 with the AGIP–Mineraria, a subsidiary of the Italian government-owned Ente Nationale Industria (E.N.I.); and the contract of 1958 with the Pan American Petroleum Corporation, an American company associated with the Standard Oil Company of Indiana. These were the first of what are known as the "Seventy-five/Twenty-five Agreements", under which, after the Government has received 50 per cent of the profits in income tax, NIOC, as an equal partner with a foreign company, shares the residue. Of parallel significance in the matter of bettering the financial return for Iran was the fact that the Government through its national oil company acquired a real share in the control of operations. The joint

Iranian–Italian company, Société Irano-Italienne des Petroles (SIRIP), was formed to exploit three areas, covering about 8,000 square miles: an inland area of about 4,000 square miles, east of Masjid-i-Sulaimān; another area of about 2,000 square miles, off-shore near the head of the Persian Gulf and beyond the three miles of territorial waters assigned to the Consortium; and a third area on the coast of Makrān on the Gulf of Oman, which includes the territorial water area. In 1960 oil was discovered by SIRIP off-shore in the Persian Gulf, and the field, called Baḥrgān Sar, which came into production in 1962, was producing 24,000 b/d by 1965 while late in 1966 there has been a promising discovery at Seh Dihistān, a site in the 4,000 square mile concession inland.

Pan-American Petroleum received two off-shore sections beyond the three mile limit, near the head of the Persian Gulf. These sections total about 5,000 square miles and are separated from each other by the SIRIP off-shore concession; they also exclude Khārg and other islands, together with their surrounding areas of territorial waters. Two oil fields, named Cyrus and Darius, were discovered in 1961 in the southern section of this petroleum concession area to the west of Khārg Island, which, as already hinted, has in recent times sprung into considerable prominence and where Pan-American Petroleum has constructed an important tanker terminal. The Darius field started production in 1963 and produced 46,000 b/d in 1965. As for the Cyrus field, which is farther away from Khārg, by November 1966 it was still not in production, nor had a pipeline to Khārg been built. NIOC also assigned an inland area to a Canadian company, but for lack of results this assignment had to be cancelled; the possibility of litigation between the Iranian government and the assignee was reported early in December 1966.

Off-shore oil production in the Iranian portion of the Persian Gulf was complicated by the boundary disputes with Iraq, Kuwait and Saudi Arabia. These boundaries appear never to have been satisfactorily defined among the states concerned, and interpretations of the various claims involved differ. One of the more serious aspects of the problems thus posed is a claim lodged by Kuwait to off-shore areas co-terminous with or overlapping part of the Cyrus oilfield. Another problem presented itself, this time in connexion with inshore areas. The frontier with Iraq is located on the eastern shore of the Shaṭṭ al-'Arab, thus greatly hampering access by water to the port of Ābādān, with consequent detriment to oil exports. An agreement to relocate the boundary in midstream (similar to changes already effected by the nearby port of Khurramshahr) had in fact been arrived at in 1937, but never implemented. Consequently, differences over pilotage and related dues arose, but with the switching of refined product exports from Ābādān to Bandar Māhshahr in 1957, the difficulties thus occasioned have been satisfactorily resolved.[1]

In 1962 Iran announced that 14,400 square miles beyond the three mile limit in the Persian Gulf would be put on offer. Before these off-shore concessions were put up for bidding no less than thirty-one companies, individually or in groups, participated in the cost of a joint marine seismic survey of the whole area. Of these, five groups and one individual company were subsequently successful bidders and comprised American, French, German, Indian, Italian and Anglo-Dutch interests. NIOC had a 50 per cent interest in each of the six new joint-structure companies formed to exploit the concessions and Iran received nearly £68 million in cash bonuses on signature of the agreements which provided for a further £18 million once commercial production reached stated figures. But up to mid-1966 the results in terms of oil found were disappointing, only the Lavan Company (NIOC Atlantic Refining Company, Murphy Oil Corporation, Sun Oil Company and Union Oil Company of California) having by that time struck oil in commercial quantity.

In 1966 Iran once again made oil agreement history when it entered into an arrangement with the French group of companies, Entreprise de Recherches et d'Activités Petrolières (ERAP) under which three land and one off-shore concession areas were to be explored at the French group's expense. Under this agreement NIOC had full control of all operations, from exploration to production, to export and marketing, the position of the other party being that of a contractor working on NIOC's behalf. In the event of oil being discovered in commercial quantity, 50 per cent of the proven reserves would be retained by NIOC as "national reserves". The contractor would provide all necessary capital for exploration and development, considered as a loan to NIOC, to be amortized in fifteen years after commencement of production or by discounting at the rate of ten cents per barrel. Movable and un-movable property and all crude oil at well head would be the property of NIOC, but ERAP would have the right to

[1] Bases for agreement between Iran and Saudi Arabia were laid during King Faisal's visit to Tehrān in December 1965, when oil boundaries in the Gulf area figured prominently. [Ed.]

buy between 35 and 45 per cent of discovered oil for a period of twenty-five years at cost plus 2 per cent. NIOC's share of revenue would be from 89 to 91½ per cent. During the first five years of commercial production ERAP would be obliged, if so required by NIOC to sell three million tons per annum of NIOC's share of oil, on 2 per cent commission, and similarly four million tons during the second five years.

As in all Middle East countries the flaring of potentially valuable gas produced with crude oil but for which there was little local outlet was a cause of dissatisfaction to Iran. The Consortium Operating Companies used some gas in their own operations (75,573,000 cu. ft per day were delivered to Ābādān refinery in September 1966) and in 1961 NIOC completed a 239 mile gas line from Ga<u>ch</u> Sārān to <u>Sh</u>īrāz, where it is used by a cement plant, two sugar factories and a power station, and to a new fertilizer factory at Marvda<u>sh</u>t (13,187,000 cu. ft per day in September 1966); but great quantities continued to be flared.

However, in the 1960s the world was becoming increasingly interested in gas as a source of energy and at the same time the problems of processing and transporting gas were becoming better understood. Thus 1966 saw the signing of an agreement between Iran and U.S.S.R., under which Iran contracted to supply the latter country with seven billion cu. m of gas per year commencing 1970, to be increased to ten billion cu. m by 1975 until 1985 when arrangements would be renewable. The gas would come from the Consortium Agreement Area through a 1,200 mile pipeline the cost of which would be met by a Soviet loan repayable in gas. Supplies of gas would also repay the U.S.S.R. for the cost of a big steel plant near Iṣfahān. The pipeline would, at the same time, form the main artery of a supply system to Iranian cities and would tap, also, NIOC's Sarājeh field.

Concurrently talks were going on between NIOC and the Consortium regarding the export of gas by tanker and internal supply of feed-stock to the newly formed National Petrochemical Company, an offshoot of NIOC, formed in 1964.

The National Petrochemical Company's initial programme included the construction of a PVC and detergent plant at Ābādān, an ammonia and fertilizer plant at Bandar <u>Sh</u>āpūr and two sulphur plants, at Masjid-i-Sulaimān and on <u>Kh</u>ārg Island. By entering into partnership agreements with B. F. Goodrich (74%/26%) (Abadan Petrochemical

Company), Allied Chemical Company (Canada) Limited (50%/50%) (Shapur Chemical Products Limited) and Pan-American (50%/50%), Iran ensured that it would have all the "know-how" required and an overseas marketing organization from the beginning of production from these plants.

Meanwhile, with encouragement from the Government, NIOC's Board of Directors has been actively seeking to enlarge the presence of NIOC in the world oil industry with the avowed object that NIOC should become one of the major completely integrated international oil companies, expanding into all the down-stream phases of the industry— transportation, refining, overseas distribution and marketing.

In pursuit of this objective, NIOC signed an agreement in 1965 to supply 50,000 b/d of crude oil to the Indian government's Madras refinery (in which NIOC had a 13 per cent stake) beginning in 1967. The Indian government guaranteed to import 40,000 tons of crude oil from the Iran Pan-American Oil Company (IPAC) over twenty years beginning in 1967.

This was followed by two further agreements in 1966. The first was with the Argentinian government for 350,000 cu. m of Iranian crude oil against the delivery of Argentinian wheat to Iran. The second was with the Rumanian government whereby Iran was to deliver 10,000,000 tons of crude oil over a ten-year period against the supply of Rumanian tractors and industrial equipment.

Earlier (1963 and 1964) NIOC had entered into an agreement with Afghanistan to supply refined products, especially aviation fuel, and to carry out re-fuelling operations at Kabul Airport.

In 1960 the Western oil companies operating in the Middle East announced reductions in posted prices, and this was largely instrumental in bringing the major Middle East producing countries together (with Venezuela) to form the Organization of Petroleum Exporting Countries (OPEC). Iran was a founder member of this organization and from the first, as the Middle East member with by far the longest experience of the oil industry, played a leading part.

The reduction in posted prices was symptomatic of the world oil situation at that time, in which the rate of production was increasing more rapidly than world demand. In these conditions realized prices were falling short of the posted prices on which income tax to host countries was based, and the so-called 50/50 agreements were becoming unbalanced to the companies' disadvantage, a situation which continued despite the posted price reductions. On the other hand, OPEC members were united in their eagerness for increased revenue per barrel and increased production.

Iran, with striking programmes of industrial agricultural and social development well under way, and a much larger population than her oil-producing neighbours, was understandably anxious for greater returns from her oil wealth, and put the Consortium under particularly heavy pressure in 1966 to speed up the rate of increase of production. But the amount of oil which companies take from their production sources is naturally determined by their estimates of what they can sell in world markets, and the member companies of the Consortium could only accelerate their rate of increase of production from Iran at the expense of their offtake from other Middle East countries with one or more of which nearly every one of these companies was under agreement.

Iran demanded an annual increase in production of 17 per cent. The Consortium, while unable to meet this request, made alternative proposals designed to give Iran in the region of a 17 per cent increase in oil revenue, and agreement was reached at the end of 1966, the Consortium undertaking to deliver to NIOC under very favourable terms over the period 1967–71 20 million tons of crude oil which NIOC would be at liberty to trade with certain East European countries where such sales would be unlikely to compete with any by Consortium Member Companies.

At the same time the Consortium voluntarily relinquished 25 per cent of the Agreement Area, although under the 1954 Agreement no relinquishment was called for until 1979; and while not committing themselves to a specified rate of increase, undertook that the Member Companies would take practical steps to increase the rate of growth of their oil offtake exclusive of the quantities being made available to NIOC.

OTHER MINING INDUSTRIES

Other mining and processing activities are far less important in the economy of Iran than the petroleum industry. This could in some limited degree be the result of the available geological surveys—while the search for oil received most thorough attention, other minerals were somewhat neglected. But the principal fact remains: available surveys so far point to the conclusion that these mineral deposits are not of a magnitude comparable in value to the petroleum resources. It has become evident that most of the known deposits are small, widely scattered geographically, and not conveniently located for commercial exploitation. (See Chapter 15.)

Coal is found in the southern Alburz mountains north and north-west of Tehrān, and also in the northern Alburz of the eastern Caspian region. Largely bituminous, it is not very good in quality, and most of the deposits are high up in the mountains and not easily accessible. Mining began during World War I and approached 100,000 tons per year at the time of the opening of the Trans-Iranian Railway to Tehrān in 1938. Completion of that railway permitted the inexpensive import of petroleum fuels from Khūzistān, and coal-mining did not expand at a high rate thereafter. However, shortages of petroleum-product transport facilities during World War II raised coal production to 150,000 tons per year after the end of hostilities, and in 1965 it reached 230,000 tons. Most of the coal is used for brick-making and in small-scale industries in the region of the mines.

Iron-ore deposits have been discovered in Kirmān; in the eastern Alburz mountains; near Isfahān and Yazd, and on the island of Hurmuz at the entrance of the Persian Gulf. The most important mining activities take place on Hurmuz, where red oxide iron ore is mined. In recent years as many as 45,000 tons yearly were exported from there to Europe; an additional 15,000 tons annually are mined elsewhere. Scrap iron is processed in several small plants, mostly in Tehrān and Ahvāz. A plan to construct an integrated steel mill near Tehrān, relying mainly on local supplies of raw material, has not been carried out, because of the size of the Iranian market so far does not make it economical to run such a plant at full capacity.[1] Due to growth of the petroleum and other industries in Khūzistān, there would, however, seem to be better prospects for the location of an integrated steel mill at Ahvāz. Small-scale steel processing, shaping, and stamping (e.g. of building components) take place in Tehrān, Rasht, Tabrīz and Ahvāz.

Lead and zinc ore are mined near Yazd (85,000 and 27,000 tons, respectively, in 1962); and since World War II, up to 45,000 tons of lead ore per year were sometimes exported to the Soviet Union. Copper ore is found in the eastern Alburz mountains and near Zanjān, adjacent to the south-western Alburz. A copper refinery at Zanjān built before

---

[1] It is, however, in the provisions of the Agreement for Economic and Technical Co-operation, concluded between Iran and the U.S.S.R. in January 1966, that Soviet experts assist in establishing a steel foundry. [Ed.]

World War II is closed down now, and ore production in 1960 did not exceed 5,000 tons. Chrome ore is found in many deposits throughout the Alburz mountains: its production reached 74,000 tons in 1962. Antimony is now mined near Hamadān, but no production figures are yet available. Turquoise and emeralds were mined on a small scale up to about World War II; since then production has sunk to very low levels.

Rock-salt, clay, limestone, gypsum, and similar materials have been mined since immemorial. Cement is made from limestone in several centres, e.g. near Tehrān and Shīrāz; there has been a recent expansion of cement production (over one million tons in 1965), and Iran no longer imports this important building material. Bricks are made outside almost every town: a large concentration of brick plants is found for instance, on the southern outskirts of Tehrān. From 1960 onwards rock-salt output throughout the country reached over 80,000 tons, and crude-gypsum production exceeded one million tons. Further growth of the Iranian economy could be expected to increase production substantially in certain minerals (e.g. cement); but since 1962 there has been a crisis in production of metallic minerals despite the occurrence of many known and widely dispersed deposits. In addition Iran's many salt lakes and swamps, like the Dead Sea of Israel and Jordan, offer large workable deposits of potash, borax and other minerals.

Most mines are operated by private Iranian companies who have their offices in Tehrān; some lead and zinc companies have their offices in Yazd, and the antimony mine companies have offices in Hamadān. The cement plants and associated quarries, as well as a few other mines, are operated by government-owned companies.

ELECTRICITY GENERATION

One of the major obstacles to Iran's economic development has been the shortage of cheap electric power. As recently as 1961, demand for electricity in Tehrān was estimated to be twice or three times as large as the existing generating and distributing capacity. Although the generation of electric power began over thirty years ago, the main expansion took place after World War II. Total generating capacity in the early 1930s was only 600 kW; in 1956 it was 253,000 kW, and in 1966 it reached 1,000,000,000 kW. The major plants are in

Tehrān, which consumes about half the electricity of the country; all other cities today have generating plants, though in smaller towns and villages electricity is rare. In Ābādān and a few other cities, electricity generation is the by-product of other industrial activities. Diesel engines usually provide the energy except in Ābādān and a few other towns that use steam turbines. Shustar relies partly on water power. The completion of the Diz dam in Khūzistān, the Karaj dam near Tehrān and the Safīd Rūd dam between Qazvīn and Rasht will change this pattern of energy supply by providing more hydro-electric power. And the provision of natural gas to Shīrāz and Tehrān will contribute another cheap form of energy for electricity generation. The beginning of a grid system of electricity-transmission lines is already visible in Khūzistān, and a similar system is now being evolved in the Tehrān region.

FOOD-PROCESSING AND OTHER RESOURCE-BASED INDUSTRIES

The next modern industry to develop after petroleum was the processing of food and other agricultural products. In the early 1920s an Iranian landowner built a sugar-beet refinery near Mashhad, using German machinery and engineers. This effort failed, but a few years later the government intervened and constructed near Tehrān the first large sugar refinery, which began operations in the 1930s. Upon completion of the Trans-Iranian Railway, other refineries were built alongside its tracks near the Caspian Sea, outside Tehrān, and at Arāk. When the railway was extended westward from Tehrān in 1940, another large plant was built at Karaj. Some smaller plants were built away from the railroad, at Shīrāz, at Kirmānshāh, near Lake Rezā'īyeh, and at Mashhad. The last two plants were reached by the railway after World War II. These refineries as well as the plant at Shīrāz have since been considerably enlarged. Total refined-sugar production in 1939 was under 30,000 tons, or about one third of the country's consumption. By 1959 production exceeded 83,000 tons, yet due to the increased population and higher living standards of living, an additional 260,000 tons had to be imported. Most of the refineries process sugar-beet only. For long there was no commercial sugar production in Khūzistān, where the industry originally developed; it disappeared from there over 1,500 years ago as the result of warfare, the decay of irrigation, and increased salinity of the soil. With the completion of new irrigation works, a restoration of the sugar industry in Khūzistān is now in progress. Total internal production of sugar has now reached 330,000 tons.

Another old industry, the extraction of vegetable oil from sesame and other seeds, was reintroduced after World War I. Although one ancient, gigantic wooden press is still in operation in the bāzār of Iṣfahān, almost all the other equipment in the country is new, and today it also processes cotton seed. Modern plants are located in areas of seed production in the vicinity of Iṣfahān, Tabrīz, Tehrān, and along the Caspian seashore near Bābol. Output of vegetable oil totalled 27,000 tons in 1960, but another 7,000 tons had to be imported—the country now produces 50,000 tons. Iranian slaughter-houses added another 24,000 tons of processed animal fats and oils to these supplies; only large slaughter-houses in the big cities manufacture these by-products.

Wheat milling takes place on a small scale throughout the farming area; in the 1930s larger mechanical plants were built adjacent to the government silos at Ahvāz, Tehrān, and a few other large towns. When harvests are insufficient, as for example in 1961, additional wheat is imported from overseas and milled in the large government installations. In 1966 production of wheat was thirty-five million tons. Modern rice mills are located in the rice-growing western Caspian Sea region. Fruit-preserving by means of canning was established at Mashhad shortly before World War II: a speciality of this plant is the canning of the famous Mashhad peaches. Other fruit canneries have since been built in the Caspian Sea area, as well as near Shīrāz and elsewhere.

The industrial processing of tobacco began after World War I, and the first cigarette factories were built by Greek experts at Tehrān and Tabrīz. Virginia-type cigarettes began to be made shortly before World War II. As the manufacture and sale of tobacco products are a government monopoly, the location of new plants in other tobacco-growing districts is severely controlled.

The introduction of tea cultivation to the Caspian region meant that selection, drying, and fermentation plants had to be built; and these factories are widely dispersed throughout the tea-growing region, to prevent spoilage of the tea-leaves after picking. With the advice of British experts, teas are produced which equal in quality the best Himalayan grades. Output reached 8,000 tons in 1965, but tea-drinking Iran has to import as much again to satisfy its thirst.[1] German-style

[1] Iranians drink weak tea without milk but with sugar, and sometimes they add lemon or lime juice.

beer is brewed in Tehrān, and several northern towns produce vodka and various sweet liqueurs. A large modern vodka distillery is also located at Ahvāz. Wine—made in Shīrāz, Qazvīn and Iṣfahān—is a modern European introduction, and entirely unrelated to the industry Iran had in medieval times. Relatively sweet "Rhine" wines and burgundy are now produced. Another traditional industry, revived in many small, widely scattered plants, is the drying of fruit (grapes for raisins; dates apricots, etc.). Nearly 200,000 tons are normally processed, of which about one third is exported.

Until 1952 very little fish was industrially preserved in Iran. In that year the Irano-Russian Fishing Agreement was abrogated by mutual consent. This agreement had reserved the processing of all caviar in Caspian waters to the Soviet Union; since the abrogation, however, the government-owned Iranian Fisheries Company has processed caviar at Bandar Pahlavī and at Bābol Sar.[1] Iranian caviar production reached 184 tons in 1965–6, of which one third was exported to the Soviet Union. Other fish products are now also made in the Caspian Sea ports, and since 1961 the Iranian Fisheries Company has extended its activities to the Persian Gulf.

Altogether Iranian food-processing industries now employ about 25,000 workers. This number can be expected to grow further with the extension of irrigation in Khūzistān and central Iran, and the increase of cultivation in the Caspian Sea region. Also, the anticipated increase of cash cropping and modern animal husbandry will boost employment in the food-processing industries. Except for sugar-refining and tobacco processing, most of these industries are owned by Iranian companies or Iranian individuals.

Forests cover 11 per cent of the land surface of Iran. Most of the forests outside the Caspian region consist of thin stands which cannot be used industrially except for charcoal-burning. The Caspian forests contain a dense growth of temperate and subtropical woods, much of which is inaccessible on very steep slopes. Despite this serious handicap, sawing, milling, and wood-treating have developed in this region in order to supply building-timber, as well as wood for furniture and barrels. Plywood and railroad ties are also manufactured. More persons are employed in charcoal-making than in any other form of wood-processing. Charcoal kilns are widely dispersed throughout the forests,

---

[1] The best caviar comes from a variety of sturgeon that lives only in the Caspian Sea. Sturgeon elsewhere produces a roe that is qualitatively inferior, though extensively used.

although more recently locations near highways have been preferred. After the exhaustion of local wood supplies, the kilns are abandoned and new ones established elsewhere. Due to soil erosion following the indiscriminate cutting of trees for charcoal-making, severe restrictions on the location of new kilns can be expected to reduce production within a few years.

OTHER INDUSTRIES

Following the growth of industries based upon, and located on or near, mineral and agricultural resources, there have developed other industries, whose location is determined primarily by the availability of local markets. Raw materials might be produced locally, but usually this is economically unimportant: market-located industries tend to obtain their raw materials from a number of regions, or from abroad. Typical among these industries in Iran are textiles: although some of the wool or cotton used is produced locally, the bulk of supplies comes from the other, more distant producing regions of the country; and special yarns, chemicals, etc., required in the industrial process are imported from overseas. Other typical market-located industries are the manufacture of ice, ice-cream, the assembly of automobiles or other machinery from imported parts, and the bottling of soft drinks. Throughout the world the trend to locate industries in markets rather than in resource areas is very marked, and is generally regarded as a sign of advanced modern industrialization. As was shown before, even oil refineries tend today to be located in consuming areas rather than in or near oilfields. In Iran the location of the refinery at Kirmānshāh in 1935 was a development of this nature, and the building of a refinery in Tehrān continues the trend. Overall, Tehrān has benefited most from this development, which is least marked in the south-east of the country.

Apart from a few exceptions, such as an ice plant in Ābādān built about 1912, market-located industries did not emerge in Iran until the 1930s. Among the first large plants of this type was a government-owned textile plant near Tehrān, producing cloth for uniforms and other military supplies; other government-owned and private plants were built at the same time or during and after World War II. Today the main cotton textile plants are located in or near Tehrān, Iṣfahān Tabrīz, Yazd, Shīrāz, and in several towns of the Caspian region. The major wool textile plants are found in Iṣfahān, Tabrīz, Arāk, Tehrān, and Yazd. Wool carpets are also manufactured industrially in Tabrīz

548

and Arāk. Of the textile plants located in the area of their raw-material production, neither is economical or working at full capacity. These are a natural-silk factory suffering from the competition of synthetic material, and a jute-processing plant whose production fluctuates substantially from year to year. Both are located in Rasht. Leather is produced on a small scale in most cities; however, the major industrial centre for leather production is in Tabrīz. Total employment in textile and allied industries exceeds 88,000 workers, which is now more than double those employed in the petroleum industry. Textile plants are owned by the government, by private companies, or by individuals. Other market-located industries have been mainly established since World War II. Outstanding among these are the assembly of refrigerators, radios, and other electrical equipment; motor-cars and other machinery and the manufacture of some of their parts, such as tyres. Most of these new industries are located in Tehrān, where the bulk of their Iranian market is concentrated. Ahvāz, the centre of the oil region, has also attracted a few of these plants. Assembly plants tend to be owned by foreign companies, frequently in association with Iranians. For lack of a railway connexion, Iṣfahān for long failed to attract any of the heavier assembly industries; instead it continued to specialize in textile manufacture and textile accessories. In January 1966 it was however announced that agreement had been reached with the U.S.S.R. to build a steel plant and machine tool manufacturing plant at Iṣfahān, using natural gas and fuel. The plant is planned to be completed by 1971, and to have an output of 1,200,000 tons of raw steel per annum.

Shīrāz has also largely found itself isolated from major industrial development, but has a fertilizer plant based on natural gas received by an NIOC pipeline from Gach Sārān. Now benefiting from the completion of the railway to Tehrān and the south, Tabrīz can expect more industries (especially assembly plants for imported parts) when the railway connexion to Turkey and thus to Europe is completed. Mashhad and Yazd, though they are also connected to the Trans-Iranian Railway, are located too far from the main centres of population to attract assembly plants. However, all large Iranian cities now have printing, paint, ice and softdrink-bottling plants; Tehrān also has photographic-processing and other chemical industries.

ARTS AND CRAFTS

Although the traditional arts and crafts never completely died out, they were no longer significant in the eighteenth and early nineteenth centuries. At that time the main trade channel to Europe was still the old caravan route from Tabrīz to Trabzon (then called Trebizond) on the Turkish coast of the Black Sea, and then by the ship the rest of the way. Merchants in Tabrīz used this route to export many, if not most, of the old carpets. But in the 1880s a shortage of carpets developed, and these merchants began to invest some of their profits in commissioning the manufacture of new carpets in bāzārs and homes. Gradually the ancient craft revived, and works of both good and inferior quality were produced under this system. In the beginning the new craft was concentrated in Tabrīz, but in a few years it spread to other districts and became a type of "cottage industry", even nomadic tribes participated. The growth of other economic opportunities, as well as prohibitions against the employment of child labour, later halted the geographical dispersal of the craft, which today is mainly concentrated in Tabrīz, Arāk, Kirmān, Hamadān, and Mashhad. Partially or completely machine-made carpets are also produced in Tabrīz. The designs for the new carpets were determined primarily by the demand in Europe and later also in the United States. Merchants commissioned carpets accordingly, and regional design specialization therefore declined; for example, a Kāshān design or even Bukhara design from Russian Turkistan might now be made in Arāk. During recent decades the internal market for handmade carpets has also become significant, and for this market more conventional patterns are used. Although natural dyes are still used, most of the production since World War I has relied on imported synthetic colouring material.

The making of decorative tiles, pottery, and jewellery by craftsmen has also been revitalized, mainly during the last forty years. The ancient Iranian art of painting on wood and ivory was revived similarly, mainly as the result of European interest. Main centre of these arts and crafts is Iṣfahān, although other cities, among them Shīrāz, also produce excellent work. No statistics for employment in arts and crafts are available, as these data are included with other industrial employment.

INDUSTRIAL GROWTH

As in most other countries—for example, the United States of America— Iran's industrial activities have changed over the years from mere resource exploitation to increasing manufacture for local markets. Nevertheless the industries based on resources will probably continue to expand. Industries based on minerals other than petroleum will benefit substantially from improvements in geological surveys as well as in transport services. A very important factor is the availability of natural gas, now fed in increasing quantities through a developing national "grid" northwards from the oil fields to the larger towns of the centre and the north. The extension of the railway from Yazd to the Pakistan border will assist mineral developments in south-eastern Iran; highway improvements between central Iran and the shore of the Persian Gulf east of Khūzistān and in south-eastern Iran will also be important. In addition, these new transport facilities, all in the planning or building stage, will probably attract to eastern cities more of the industries that are not based on indigenous natural resources.

Over the last thirty years trade with the Soviet Union has tended to decline in comparison with trade with other countries, and this decline has slowed the growth of Tabrīz, Mashhad, and Caspian seaports. But within the very last few years there has been a reversal, with, since 1960, marked increase, especially in Soviet purchases from Iran: the U.S.S.R. currently ranks as fifth most important buyer of Iranian goods, and twelfth in order of suppliers. If trade with Russia reaches its former importance, and with the 1966 agreement to export natural gas to Russia as part of the Steel Mill project then new industries, especially assembly industries, could be attracted to these towns.

Air transport has had so far little or no effect on the location of industries and little change can be expected in the near future. The extension of irrigation in Khūzistān will probably more than counter-balance any of its loss of industries following the development of Tabrīz and of other cities which are likely to benefit from the new trade routes to the west and north. To what extent this geographical spread of industries will reduce their present centralization in Tehrān remains to be seen. Overall employment in market-located industries can be expected to increase much more than employment in resource-located industries.

CHAPTER 17

COMMUNICATIONS, TRANSPORT, RETAIL TRADE AND SERVICES

Up to the last decades of the nineteenth century, trails and caravan routes were the only means of communications with Iran. Marked relief, particularly near boundaries and seacoasts, together with limited commercial activities, had discouraged the construction of highways and railways. Exports consisted mainly of carpets, which could travel by pack-horse or camel; and imports were handled in the same manner. Wheeled traffic was rare and limited to local transport within a few towns and oases. Retail trade in bāzārs and by pedlars included very few imported goods: most of these were traded second-hand. Only Tabrīz, Rasht, and Tehrān in the north, and Bushire [Būshahr] and Bandar 'Abbās in the south, traded regularly with foreign countries. Other towns and villages were almost entirely self-sufficient, and pilgrims provided their major contact with other parts of the country and with the holy places of the Muslim world. Modern medical and other services were available only at foreign missions, both governmental and private, and then only sporadically.

This position began to change in the late 1880s with the gradual introduction of new means of transport. Both Great Britain and Russia participated in these developments, which immediately increased the scope and volume first of internal trade and later of services. In most towns bāzārs began to expand. Change was rather slow, however, until the introduction of the motor-car during World War I; and the speed of change further increased during the 1930s by the construction of the Trans-Iranian Railway. As a result, local self-sufficiency was reduced considerably, causing a substantial urban growth. Many Iranians were encouraged to train in professions and to supply their services to the growing cities. A new pattern of living emerged, in which the cities and regions of Iran were economically much more closely integrated, and trade with foreign countries became more important than before. This new pattern encouraged further growth of the retail trade and services after World War II.

However, despite the large number of professionally trained Iranians now available, more foreigners are required today to provide specialized services—for example, in hotel management and aircraft maintenance. Moreover, large areas of the country located away from highways and railways are still virtually self-sufficient, and poverty elsewhere has substantially reduced participation in the retail trade and services.

INLAND TRANSPORT AND THE GROWTH OF RETAIL TRADE AND SERVICES

As in the United States of America, modern transport in Iran was first established on a navigable river. There is only one, the Kārūn, which, since it flows from the Zagros mountains through the plains of Khūzistān into the Shaṭṭ al-'Arab and the Persian Gulf, contains a sufficient volume of water to permit navigation throughout the year. In 1887 a British entrepreneur established a steamship service on the Kārūn from Khurramshahr (then called Muhammareh) on the Shaṭṭ al-'Arab to Ahvāz, a distance of over 100 miles. At Ahvāz a brief portage around rapids was necessary; and from there, a few years later, smaller steamers continued the journey another 100 miles to Shustar. Beyond Shustar, traffic had to continue by caravan until about 1914. This steamship service increased Shustar in size and function: it became the major retail centre of south-western Iran, and its population was 28,000 before the completion of the Trans-Iranian Railway in 1938. Khurramshahr meanwhile was developing as the port of south-western Iran; here, too, foreign consulates and a customs post (which until World War I was supervised by a foreign expert) were established. Subsequently with the development of the oil industry and the connexion to the Trans-Iranian Railway, made during World War II, Khurramshahr became Iran's largest dry-cargo port.[1] Today its population is over 50,000.

During the last decades of the nineteenth century, as British interests gradually pushed the construction of a road towards Shīrāz and Iṣfahān, Bushire was increasingly used as a port for southern Iran, and thus it became a major trading centre. Bushire trading firms made the first attempts to exploit Iranian resources; although these efforts failed, they provided the initial training for Iranians in drilling techniques, engine maintenance, and other technical services. However, urban

---

[1] The liquid-cargo ports of Ābādān, Bandar Ma'shūr, and Khārg handle much greater tonnages of petroleum exports but virtually no imports. As a result, port employment in these towns is small, e.g. under 1,000 people at Khārg.

growth here has been limited, as the port is an open roadstead where ships have to discharge their cargoes into lighters over three miles from the shore; and the population today barely exceeds 20,000. Bandar 'Abbās, at the entrance of the Persian Gulf, has been used much less than Bushire for foreign trade, because the road connecting this port to Kirmān was not completed until nearly the end of World War I. Subsequently, and because the adjacent parts of Iran are the least developed portions of the country, Bandar 'Abbās has remained small: its population today is under 20,000.

Whilst transport and trade in the south were developed mainly by British interests, Russian endeavours helped to create similar changes in the north. Already by the end of the nineteenth century, wheeled traffic was able to reach Tabrīz from the Russian border. Due to the export of carpets, Tabrīz had for some time been the trade metropolis of Iran, and this position was reinforced by the early construction of roads. Whereas formerly almost all trade in Tabrīz had been in Iranian hands, increasing numbers of Russian as well as German traders now began to settle there. An American missionary school was established, which prepared Iranians for business and the professions. Repair services for vehicles, etc., were set up, mainly by Armenians and other Christian residents of the area. The bāzār was extended, and by 1900 was the largest in Iran. Most investments, such as hotels, were made by Russians.

The most outstanding Russian project, however, was the construction in the first years of this century of a road about 200 miles long, from Rasht, near the Caspian Sea, to Tehrān. This road—the shortest route from the Russian road and railway system via the Caspian Sea to the Iranian capital—replaced a narrow, dangerous trail which had previously deterred most travellers. From Rasht the road follows the Safīd river through a narrow gorge across the Alburz mountains, crossing a minor pass to Qazvīn and continuing along the southern foothills of Alberz to Tehrān. By post-chaise the trip from Rasht to Tehrān could be made within forty-eight hours; without changing horses, the trip took seven days. Russian hotels were built at Rasht, Qazvīn, and Tehrān. During the nineteenth century, Caspian ships were able to reach Rasht by travelling up a creek from the sea. Later, due to a drop in the level of the Caspian, ships had to terminate their journey at Bandar Pahlavī (then called Enzeli), and passengers and goods continued their journey by boat to Pīr Bāzār, six miles outside of Rasht, where the highway journey began. Before World War I a narrow-gauge railway (now abandoned) was built connecting Bandar Pahlavī directly with Rasht; and several Russian hotels were built at Bandar Pahlavī, which could be reached by an overnight steamer journey from Baku in Russia.

Completion of the road from Rasht immediately changed the economy of Tehrān. Whereas formerly the court and its services, as well as the foreign missions, had dominated the capital, now trade and manufacturing became increasingly important. Many foreigners—not only Russians but also Germans, Austrians, French, British, Americans, and others—moved there to trade or supply professional (including educational) services. As a result, Tabrīz lost some of its business to the capital, and traders from this city as well as from Iṣfahān and other towns began to settle in Tehrān and expand its bāzārs. Although immigrants from other regions and foreign countries contributed to the growth of Tehrān, Russian economic and cultural influences were paramount, as can be seen, for example, in the types of vehicles then used. Similarly, the Russian style of tea-drinking, since adopted by all classes of the population, was introduced in this period.

Shortly before World War I an Iranian entrepreneur built a third road to connect with the Russian transport system. This highway ran from Mashhad to the Russian border in Turkistan, where it joined a feeder road from the Trans-Caspian Railway between 'Ashqābād and Merv. Although this road has contributed to its growth (e.g. pilgrims from Russian Turkistan to Mashhad also use the road), Mashhad is located in dry eastern Iran and thus it has not had the development of Tabrīz or Tehrān. Very few foreigners came to trade and the bāzār remained relatively small.

Other roads were built to connect Tehrān with Iṣfahān, Qazvīn with Tabrīz, and Qazvīn with Hamadān, Kirmānshāh, and ultimately Baghdad. All these roads, completed either shortly before or during World War I, assisted the development of trade and increased the significance of Tehrān as the commercial centre of the country. Iṣfahān also benefited from its direct connexion with the capital, for this restored some of its former trade. Altogether, by the time of World War I, Iran had acquired the rudiments of a transport system. Some of these highways had been financed by the collection of tolls, others were free; in general the collection of tolls was stopped by events during World War I. Overall, travel was still very slow; for example, in 1914 the journey from Khurramshahr to Tehrān took three weeks to a month, and personnel of the oil company in Khūzistān discovered that it was quicker and much more convenient to travel by boat from Khurramshahr via the Suez canal and Istanbul to the Russian Black Sea port of Batum, from there by railway to Baku, and then by ship across the Caspian to Bandar Pahlavī, and finally by road to Tehrān. Rapid communication by telegraph, however, had been available for some time before World War I. A major line, the Indo-European telephone and telegraph system, crossed western and southern Iran; and its station at Shustar, for example, could dispatch telegrams from south-western Iran, including the oilfields, to both Europe and India. By 1914 all major cities were connected to this telegraph system, and telephone services were linking the oilfield at Masjid-i-Sulaimān with Shustar, Khurramshahr, and Ābādān.

Although the first motor-car appeared in the streets of Ahvāz in 1912, and one or more cars made the trip from the Persian Gulf to Iṣfahān and Tehrān during the next year, serious use of the automobile for long-distance transport did not begin until after the outbreak of World War I. After Turkish provocation on Iranian territory, Russian troops advanced through Āzarbāījān in 1915 to attack the Turkish fortress of Ruwāndiz, in what is now north-eastern Iraq. For this purpose the Russians used a broad-gauge railway from their border on the Araxes river to Tabrīz, which they had completed shortly before the beginning of the war. Westward extensions of this railway were then constructed towards the Turkish border. All of these extensions were later abandoned, except for a line to Lake Reżā'īyeh (then called Lake Urumīyeh). Due to difficulties of transport west of the lake, the Russians were unable to advance beyond Ruwāndiz and they retired to Iranian territory, where railways as well as wagons and a limited number of automobiles could be used to supply their forces.

In the meantime German agents had induced some of the tribes of southern Iran to take up arms on their behalf. These tribes succeeded in blowing up parts of the British-owned pipeline from Masjid-i-Sulaimān to Ābādān,[1] and threatened to interrupt all communications between Russia and the British-patrolled Persian Gulf. British and British-Indian troops intervened, and a few automobiles were used to transport their supplies. In this way the first cars made the trip from Bandar 'Abbās to Kirmān, and to other relatively isolated towns. Later,

[1] See the chapter on "Industrial Activities", p. 523.

regular motor-car trips were made from the Persian Gulf and the Indian border (now the border of Pakistan) to Tehrān and Ma<u>sh</u>had. Towards the end of the war and shortly thereafter, automotive transport was used to carry troops and supplies from the Persian Gulf to the Caspian in an effort to halt a Soviet advance into the Caucasus and northern Iran. Although Iran suffered much damage in these campaigns, it also benefited by additional road and telegraph construction and the improvement of some existing roads. Even more important was the training many Iranians received in road construction, as well as in driving and servicing vehicles. These trained men provided a nucleus of manpower for the development of Iranian industries, as well as for the many services required in the subsequent growth of motor transport. After 1917, refugees from the Soviet revolution provided additional training for Iranians as well as their own skilled services—mainly in Tehrān, but also in Tabrīz and Ma<u>sh</u>had. The presence of foreign troops also encouraged a marked further growth in retailing and other services.

When additional numbers of motor-cars began to reach Iran during the 1920s and 1930s the country possessed both roads and services. None of the roads were originally more than tracks suitable for cars and lorries, but most of the important stretches were improved gradually by the provision of better bridges and generally better maintenance. Additional long-distance and feeder roads were built throughout the period between the two wars. Outstanding among these was a connexion from Tabrīz to Mosul (Iraq) through the mountains of Kurdistān, which had so effectively stopped the Russian advance in 1915. Of the several roads built across the Alburz mountains, the most important is the <u>Ch</u>ālūs road, which crosses the Alburz at an elevation of over 9,000 ft; a tunnel carries the road under the crest of the pass. Another road, which required much bridge construction in the Caspian lowlands, connects Tabrīz with Āstārā on the Caspian Sea, then follows the shore of the Caspian a few miles inland from Āstārā to Ra<u>sh</u>t, <u>Ch</u>ālūs, Bābol, Gurgān, and finally inland to Ma<u>sh</u>had. Roads were also built into Luristān from Hamadān, and south-east and east from Iṣfahān. It has now become possible to reach all major boundary points within a two-day car trip from Tehrān. In addition, these new means of communications considerably tightened governmental administration and eliminated local autonomy, which until then had prevailed in parts of the country distant from Tehrān: for example, in <u>Kh</u>ūzistān.

From about 1925, trade with the Soviet Union began to decline. Decreased use of the routes to Russia affected the growth of Tabrīz, Rasht, and Mashhad, whose retail trade and services became relatively stagnant. In contrast, southern cities like Hamadān, Iṣfahān, and Shīrāz, now easily accessible by motor-car, grew considerably. Kirmān developed relatively less, although it was now lying on the major automobile route from Europe and the Middle East to India; only very few cars made this trip before World War II, when the journey was still very strenuous.

Even before World War I the construction of a railway from Europe to India, roughly along the same route through southern Iran (Hamadān, Iṣfahān, Kirmān), had been discussed. This railway was to connect with either the Turkish or Russian railroad system, or both. As nothing was done to implement these plans, Rezā Shāh, then ruler of Iran, decided to build an 886 mile standard-gauge, north–south railway to connect the Persian Gulf with Tehrān and the Caspian Sea. Construction of this "Trans-Iranian Railway" began in 1927 and was completed in 1938, by several associations of contractors from many foreign countries. Its construction entailed much tunnelling and bridging to cross both the Zagros and Alburz mountains, and as a result the Trans-Iranian is one of the world's most spectacular railways. The line starts at the port of Bandar Shāpūr, on an inlet of the Persian Gulf in Khūzistān; from there it crosses the Kārūn river at Ahvāz and by-passes Shustar, Hamadān, and Iṣfahān on its way to Tehrān. As a result of the railway construction, Ahvāz grew into a sizable town (there are over 150,000 inhabitants today), and thus usurped the position of Shustar as the main retail and service centre of south-western Iran. Shustar's population therefore declined from about 28,000 to 15,000 today. The effect of the railway on both Hamadān and Iṣfahān was not quite so marked, though there is no doubt that the growth rate of both towns was reduced. On the other hand Arāk, located on the railway between Hamadān and Iṣfahān, developed as an industrial and retail trade centre. On the Caspian Sea a new port, Bandar Shāh, was built at the terminus of the railway; due to shallow water and lack of trade with Russia, Bandar Shāh never grew into a trading centre.

Tehrān was again the major beneficiary of the new transport system. More trading, manufacturing, and services concentrated here, and the city began handling nearly half the retail trade turnover of imported merchandise in the country. As almost all imports now enter from the

Persian Gulf, the great bulk of all freight is carried from its ports to Tehrān. Freight-cars returning to Gulf ports carry less cargo than to Tehrān, and relatively little traffic is carried between Tehrān and Bandar Shāh.

British occupation during World War II, together with the presence of American transport experts, again proved to be beneficial to Iranian transport, the retail trade, and services. There was virtually no war damage, and despite heavy use both railways and roads were improved. Moreover, additional numbers of Iranians were trained for transport and other services, providing again a nucleus for post-war expansion. Severe shortages reduced local self-sufficiency and thus affected Iranians much more than did similar shortages during World War I; nevertheless retail trade and services benefited from the money spent by occupying troops. Expansion of bāzār trade was most marked in Khūzistān, but it affected all towns on the railway and on north–south roads. The growth in the number of tea-houses (chāīkhānehs) along major routes was quite marked. But north of a line drawn through Tehrān, Iran was occupied by Russian troops and benefited very little or not at all. Experiences of the Russian occupation during and after the war caused a substantial exodus of retailers and services personnel from Āzarbāījān and other northern provinces to Tehrān. During the same period retailers from Iṣfahān and Hamadān migrated in lesser numbers to Khūzistān and Tehrān.

When the shortages disappeared after World War II, the present pattern of Iranian living emerged. Railways today provide the basic freight-transport service from Persian Gulf ports to Tehrān and the eastern Caspian Sea region. Branch lines have been extended to Tabrīz and Mashhad, mitigating to a high degree the relative decline of these cities since 1925. A 120 mile westward extension of the railway line from Tabrīz, now being built under the sponsorship of the Central Treaty Organization, will connect the Iranian and Turkish railways.[1] An eastward extension from Qum, south of Tehrān, is now complete as far as Yazd and will ultimately connect with the Pakistan railway system in Balūchistān. During World War I a line of this system (then part of India) was extended as far as Zāhidān in Iran, a short distance from the border. Service to Zāhidān is provided by Pakistan National Railways, but there is no regular schedule.

The Iranian railways, which are operated by the government-owned

[1] It was completed between Tehrān and Tabrīz by 1960.

Iranian State Railway Company, have in all about 2,300 miles of routes. Rolling stock in 1959 comprised 120 steam and 252 diesel locomotives, 378 passenger coaches, 27 dining-cars, and 5,762 freight-cars of all types. Employees numbered over 36,000; the total volume of freight carried was 334,000 tons, and there were about four and a half million passengers. (Another line, of narrow gauge and not operated by this company, supplies the oilfield Āghā Jārī from Bandar Shāpūr.) The country's railway service is supplemented by, and at the same time suffers severe competition from, road transport, though there are considerable restrictions on the types of cargoes lorries may carry on the routes running parallel with the railway. Railway freight traffic also suffered from the construction of petroleum-product pipelines from Khūzistān to Tehrān and Mashhad, which eliminated its most important cargoes; and the completion of a refinery in Tehrān in 1966 has removed most of the railway's transport of fuel-oil.[1]

Altogether Iran had in 1962 over 18,000 miles of roads; of these, only 1,988 miles were paved; an additional 6,000 miles are being improved by reconstruction or paving, and new roads are being built or completed: for example, another road across the Alburz from Shāhrūd, on the highway from Tehrān to Mashhad, which goes to Shāhpasand in the Caspian lowlands. Most paved or improved roads are in the Khūzistān oilfields or in the vicinity of Tehrān. In 1962 all these roads were used by about 131,000 automotive vehicles; of these, about 80,000 were passenger cars, over 30,000 were lorries, and nearly 10,000 were buses; the rest were motorcycles. As local self-sufficiency has been further reduced, retail trade and services have again expanded considerably. Most retail trade still takes place in the traditional bāzārs, though westernized shops have emerged in all larger cities and especially in Tehrān and Ābādān. The growth of retail trade has permitted the personnel of oil companies to reduce their dependence on company stores (commissaries). The growing cities also offer much greater opportunity for the supply of services. Increasing numbers of Iranians have been trained as doctors, lawyers, architects, etc., either within the country or abroad; and other services include pharmacy, photography, advertising, and accounting. Provision of these services is most significant in Tehrān, but has also spread to the other cities.

As a result of all these developments, Tehrān now has a population approaching two million. Within the city there is much omnibus

[1] For details on petroleum transport and refineries, see "Industrial Activities", pp. 527–33.

transport, which also extends to its growing suburbs in the foothills of the Alburz mountains. Taxis replaced the Russian droskies after 1945; they are frequently rented or shared for long-distance trips. Due to the centralization in Tehrān of governmental and other services, of retail trade, and of manufacturing, the other cities are much smaller. Estimates for 1967 are: Tabrīz and Iṣfahān about 370,000 each; Mashhad about 230,000, and Rasht, Hamadān, and Shīrāz about 170,000 each. The expansion of transport and a general increase of wealth among the growing upper and middle classes have made travelling fairly common, and hotels and associated services are now provided, not only in all major cities, but also along the Caspian coast and in the mountains near Tehrān and Hamadān. Hotels set up mainly for foreign tourists have also been built at Tehrān, Iṣfahān, and Shīrāz.

SEA AND AIR TRANSPORT

At the beginning of this century a regular weekly steamship service was available from Bushire and Khurramshahr to India. Additional direct sailings from these ports to Europe were available about twice monthly. Monthly shipping services to the United States and Japan were added after World War I; and before the war, direct connexions to Russian Black Sea ports were occasionally provided. This pattern, except for services to Black Sea ports, persists to this day. The frequency of shipping services has not increased, but bigger ships are now used, which can carry substantially larger cargoes. In addition to these regular services, more and larger tankers carry crude oil and oil products from the specialized petroleum ports of Ābādān, Bandar Ma'shūr,[1] and Kharg.[2] Khurramshahr is today the foremost port and can handle ships up to 20,000 tons. It offers storage space for over 800,000 tons of cargo, and permits unloading of ships directly into railway freight-cars and lorries. Bandar Shāpūr, the original terminus of the Trans-Iranian Railway, handles today a much smaller volume of cargo than it once did. Bushire and Bandar 'Abbās are still open road-steads and handle little traffic today. These ports, together with Ganāveh and Lingeh, are also used by dhows which sail to Kuwait, Sharjah (on the Trucial coast), and other Persian Gulf ports.

[1] Bandar Ma'shūr: the name has recently been Persianized to Bandar Māhshahr, see "Industrial Activities", p. 529.
[2] For details, see "Industrial Activities", pp. 532–3.

One privately owned Iranian line, which operates six ships, now provides service to Red Sea, Mediterranean, and West European ports. Caspian Sea transport was and is provided only by Russian ships. Before World War I there were several sailings per week from Baku to Bandar Pahlavī, but during the 1930s and 1920s these sailings were gradually reduced to one per week without an increase in the size of vessels: the same ships, built in the nineteenth century in British or German yards and assembled in Caspian ports, still provided this service. After World War II the number of sailings was reduced; e.g. during 1957 there were only two or three sailings per month, and no passengers were carried.

Passenger services on Persian Gulf lines have also declined. This is partly due to the increased volume of passengers travelling by car or bus across Iran's frontiers into Iraq, Turkey, Pakistan, Afghanistan, and further destinations. Permission to cross the borders of the Soviet Union by car or bus is only rarely granted. Instead, travellers to and from Russia may walk now across the boundary bridge that spans the Araxes river; from the Russian side of the river, a railway service to Tiflis and beyond is available once a week. But passenger services to foreign countries have been even more affected by the growth of air transport. Irregular commercial air services were established as early as the 1920s, but did not develop much until World War II, due to disputes over routes and fees. Since then, air traffic has grown very rapidly. In 1953 regular air services carried 11,000 persons; this figure increased to about 90,000 in 1957 and exceeded 100,000 in 1962. Tehrān's international airport Mihrābād is now the eastern terminus of several trans-European airlines that serve the Middle East. It is also a port of call for many lines operating from Europe and the Middle East to southern and eastern Asia and Australia; one line flies to East and South Africa, and an Iranian line flies to Kuwait and Mecca. As a result, Tehrān has several daily flights to Europe, and several weekly flights to eastern and southern destinations. Ābādān is another port of call on several flights per week from Europe to eastern destinations. There are no regular flights from Iran to the Soviet Union; passengers between the two countries usually change airplanes in Western Europe. Flying to and through Iran is encouraged by the relatively low price of aviation fuel in Iran.[1] In the regular internal flights by Iranian Airways (an Iranian government airline managed by American experts), thirty to

---

[1] For a discussion of Iranian petroleum-product pricing, see pp. 541-2.

forty passenger-aircraft connect Mihrābād airport with Tabrīz, Mashhad, Iṣfahān, Shīrāz, Ābādān, and other cities. Due to the improvement of roads across the Alburz mountains, air services from Tehrān to points in the Caspian lowlands have been suspended. Regular daily flights by oil-company planes connect the oilfields and tanker terminals with Ābādān and Ahvāz.

TELEGRAPH, TELEPHONE, RADIO, AND TELEVISION

The Iranian government telegraph system, which evolved from the Indo-European telegraph line built well before World War I, spans Iran from the Russian border at Julfā to Zāhidān on the border of Pakistan, and it also has a branch line to the Persian Gulf. Because of the extensions from this system, there are today over 12,000 miles of lines which reach all parts of the country. Radio telegraph facilities have been added, so that today Iran is linked to almost all countries. And a Telex system has been installed in Tehrān, which provides written communications via Germany and London with over 60,000 subscribers in fifty-five countries. Ābādān and the oilfields are also connected to the Telex system.

Telephone trunk lines built during World War II connect Tehrān with Basra and Baghdad, and these lines are linked to local exchanges. Although there are now over 70,000 telephones in the country, the local facilities are generally insufficient, except within the oil region, which has an automatic system to which about 1,000 telephones are connected.

Radio Tehrān, today the major broadcasting station in the country, operates on medium and short wavelengths. Other radio stations are located in Rasht, Tabrīz, Mashhad, Kirmānshāh, Hamadān, Iṣfahān, Shīrāz, Ahvāz, and Ābādān. Both Tehrān and Ābādān broadcast regularly in foreign languages; stations in Iraq, Saudi Arabia, and Soviet Russia are also regularly heard. In 1961 the number of radio receivers in the country was estimated at about one million; since many radios are heard in public places, the total listening audience was estimated to be about ten million. Tehrān also has two television stations. One privately owned station was opened in 1958 and telecasts five to six hours per day to about 30,000 receivers and 250,000 viewers (1960 estimate). In addition, the United States Armed Forces Radio and Television Service offers daily transmissions of programmes of American origin.

A third television station, in Ābādān, opened in 1959 reaches the Iranian oil region as well as southern Iraq and Kuwait. Overall it was estimated that in 1960 there were about 70,000 television receivers in the country and about 400,000 viewers.

CONCLUSION

Despite its geographical handicaps, Iran now has a satisfactory communications system. Completion of the east–west railway links and extensions will complement the already developed north–south system. However, this railway will not remove the communication handicaps of Hamadān and Iṣfahān; instead it will further centralize the national economy and thus stimulate more growth in Tehrān. This is not an unusual geographical pattern of economic development: it is also found in France and many other countries.

Retail trade and services have expanded in accord with the growth of communications and the resulting reduction in local self-sufficiency. After the completion of the transport-construction programme, any further growth in retail trade and services will be largely a function of an increase in the standard of living. Changes of this nature will in their turn increase other communication services, particularly television, which today is limited to the most affluent parts of the country.

CHAPTER 18

AGRICULTURE

The economy of our nation is based primarily on agriculture. The majority of our people are engaged in agricultural activities. The backwardness of farming methods and the great deprivations suffered by the masses of farmers have made agricultural development and land reform a critical economic and social question.

This extract from a major speech by Dr 'Alī Amīnī in 1961 is no simple political asseveration but is supported by all the facts available.

The finances of the Iranian state depend heavily on agriculture. In spite of being the sixth largest petroleum producer in the world Iran still derives between 23[1] and 30 per cent[2] of her gross national income from farming. Of exports other than oil approximately 97 per cent by value are of agricultural products of which only one quarter—carpets—are fully processed. Even in the case of internal revenue agriculture is of key importance. In the budget for 1342 (1963–4), a not atypical year, of the total estimated revenue, 23 per cent was derived from the sales of agricultural products and services by state monopolies and organizations[3] as compared with 29 per cent from the government share of oil revenues and petrol tax and with 21 per cent from direct and indirect taxation.

Thus Iranian financial stability clearly rests on two founts of wealth, oil and agriculture. The strength of the former, as noted elsewhere, depends on global circumstances, and is evanescent; the latter is primarily a matter of internal organization of the exploitation of territorial resources and can be permanent.

More than finance however is involved. Between "75 per cent and 80 per cent of the Iranian population lives on farming"[4] and "except for the population of Tehrān, and of five other important cities, which

[1] *Studies of Economic Problems of Farming in Iran.* Economic Research Bureau. Tehrān, 1962.
[2] Annual Report of the Agricultural Bank. Tehrān, 1965.
[3] Note: Government purchasing departments exist for grain, cotton, tea, sugar, olives and tobacco and associated monopolies, and, together with chemical, seeds, animal husbandry and other departments of the Ministry of Agriculture, have trading profits which accrue to General and Special Revenues.
[4] *Bulletin of the High Economic Council* (1962).

number about three million, the remaining urban residents also are indirectly involved in agriculture".[1] Moreover, as Professor Lambton has noted[2] and as elsewhere in this volume is emphasized,[3] even in the populations of the great cities the more powerful and wealthy still obtain most of their power and wealth from recent or present land ownership, and their psychological links with the country remain extraordinarily strong. The "thousand families", not yet defunct, together with many lesser landowners, have closer physical and mental relationships with the land and the peasants than the term "absentee landlord" would imply to Western ears. A truly urban bourgeoisie and technocracy remote from rural ways is only now beginning to appear.

This social and economic pre-eminence of agriculture and agricultural problems is of course by no means peculiar to Iran. The distinctiveness of the situation lies in the especial regional interrelationships between economic, social, biotic and edaphic elements, interrelationships developed in time and involving specific physical forces and particular peoples. First, then, the general situation as it appears in statistically mensurable terms.

The resources used and usable for agriculture are severely limited as is illustrated in the following table:

TABLE 12. *Land utilization in Iran*[4]

		Million hectares	Per cent
Total land area		163·6	100·0
Cropland under annual and perennial crops		6·0	3·7
Fallow cropland		12·0	7·4
Pasture and woodland of villages		1·3	0·8
Potentially cultivable (*sic*) wasteland	31·5 ⎫	113·1	69·1
Desert and other wasteland	81·6 ⎭		
Forest and rangeland		28·0	17·1

Thus on the 12 per cent of the land area which can be regarded as productive under sedentary agriculture, some nineteen million hectares of which less than one third is under cultivation at any one time, there

[1] *Studies of Economic Problems of Farming in Iran.*
[2] Ann K. S. Lambton, *Landlord and Peasant in Persia* (Oxford, 1953).
[3] See chapter 12, "Early Man in Iran".
[4] *Review of the Second Seven Year Plan Program of Iran* (1960).

depend directly for their livelihood more than eighteen million people, more than 75 per cent of the total population.

The classification and enumeration in this table are necessarily fairly crude approximations and considerable regional variations are obscured, as in the contrast between the Tenth Ustan in central Iran around Iṣfahān and Yazd where considerably more than 50 per cent of cropland as defined above was in temporary fallow at the time of the last census of agriculture,[1] and the Caspian region stretching from S̲h̲āhsavār to Gurgān on the other hand where less than 3 per cent of cropland is normally fallow. More important is that the potential resource wealth implied in the table above should not be exaggerated.

The correlation of field observation and statistics makes it quite certain that the largeness of the area shown as "potentially cultivable wasteland" is illusory. Much land could hypothetically be brought into use but only on the assumption that high cost techniques, capital installations and land use expertise were available or could be made available in the foreseeable future. Indeed it would be ecologically unsound to bring much more dry-farmed and steep-slope land into production. Moreover against any possible gain must be set the thousands of hectares of land now tilled and grazed which should be retired from use, also for sound ecological reasons.

The area classified as desert and other wasteland is indeed intractable while much of the range-land, roughly equivalent to the Spanish "pastos y montes", is of very low carrying capacity and capable of only limited improvement. Forest includes both high forest and degraded scrub woodland, almost entirely in the public domain, most of it once Crown land but now donated to the nation, and needing protection against encroachment rather than providing a reserve of arable or pastureland.

In general it can be assumed that the areal extent of land available for agricultural production cannot be increased by any significant amount although the regional balance, as noted later, may well be altered. Indeed the present cultivated area is largely the product of an extensive rather than an intensive approach to land use; and unused land has only remained in such a condition because of either extremely obdurate physical characteristics or, more rarely, some complex socio-economic hindrances to development.

As with all statistics in this sector, those appertaining to the use of

[1] First National Census of Agriculture, Department of Public Statistics. Tehrān, 1960.

agricultural land must be used with great caution. Nevertheless some salient points are clear. By far the greatest area of arable land is devoted to two staple grains. Of the little over five million hectares of cropland not under fruit and nuts, 3¼ million are under wheat and another 1½ million under barley. These cereals, constituting the bulk of the food supply of the rural population are, in general terms, grown as subsistence crops, and, in spite of the considerable acreage devoted to them, are only marginally sufficient to supply domestic consumption. Rice, grown on some 330,000 hectares, is the only staple food product of which there is an exportable surplus, and this results only from the biotic restriction of production to a few regions and the relatively high prices obtainable for rice in the world markets.

Both tea and sugar, essential ingredients of village diet, are not produced in sufficient quantities for national self-sufficiency, although vigorous efforts are being made to expand production, particularly of the latter. Cotton is the sole industrial crop of any significance, and while approximately half of the crop is exported as lint this is more a measure of low internal demand for manufacturing than of real profitability.

As might be expected with a very small cultivated area devoted to fodder crops and a preponderance of range and unimproved land used for grazing, the most important livestock are sheep and goats, some twenty-seven million of the former, thirteen million of the latter, as compared with five million cows and oxen.

From these few figures alone, the general pattern of agriculture begins to emerge, that of a large rural population confined to a small area of cultivated land, using that land mainly for annual cereals and relying heavily on waste and range-land feeding sheep and goats. The remaining statistically measurable elements complete this first general picture.

Although approximately one third of all cultivated land is irrigated, wheat yields are on average less than one metric ton per hectare (c. eight cwt an acre), about 40 per cent of the average Australian yield, and less than 23 per cent of yields in Denmark. Most cultivators, both before and during the implementation of present Land Reform policies, work and live on small plots of land, rarely exceeding 50 hectares, and usually less than 10 hectares in extent, only part of which land is carrying crops at any one time. Since, as a recent survey[1] shows, the financial

[1] *Cost and Return Ratios for Major Agricultural Products*, CENTO, 1964.

return to labour per day on wheat cultivation in central Iran may be less than two American cents ($1\frac{1}{4}d$.) per acre, it is not surprising that poverty in kind and in cash is normal.

As noted later, there are considerable regional variations on the socio-economic plane corresponding generally to geographical differences between regions. However, the predominant situation approximates to the average.

Of the Iranian population of some 21·6 million in 1961, a sociological study conducted by the University of Tehrān[1] estimated that 82 per cent of the whole population had a per capita income of less than 625 rials (£2. 10s.) a month. A Bank Melli survey[2] of the same period suggested that the rural per capita income was on average between 140 and 500 rials a month (12s. to £2). Together with low gross income is found a low subsistence diet. While there are no official figures available which meet F.A.O. standards, the generally quoted estimate of an average per capita daily intake of 1,700 calories is probably not wildly inaccurate. This low calory diet, between 50 and 60 per cent of that normal in Western Europe and North America, is also associated with a very low level of protein intake.

Added to paucity of land resources and rural poverty there is also, as might be expected, ignorance. Some 85 per cent of the total population (an even higher proportion in the villages) is illiterate,[3] and in the field of agricultural technology peasant "rule of thumb" husbandry is only now being challenged. As relative political and economic stability enables the development of social welfare services, so also the rate of population increase rises and problems of education and training of the young are made more difficult. The number of children reaching school age as a percentage of the total population was 8 per cent in 1962/63 and will rise to 14 per cent in 1972/73.[4] This is not merely a matter of increased strain on resources. There are some 45,000 villages with populations of less than 5,000. In these rural centres educational opportunities range from meagre to nil and yet without education and training the peasantry cannot successfully grapple with the usually harsh environment let alone develop sophisticated approaches to economic organization such as those envisaged in the Land Reform proposals for village co-operatives.

[1] *Income in Iran, Institute of Social Research and Studies*, Univ. of Tehrān, 1961.
[2] Review of the Bank Melli, Tehrān, 1961.
[3] *Monthly Bulletins of the Ministry of Education*, no. 1. 1961.
[4] *Ibid.*

The limitations imposed on agricultural production by physical factors are clearly of great importance and require examination. South and east from Āzarbāïjān run the great mountain zones of the Zagros and the Alburz enclosing between them and the Makrān and Afghan mountains a central region of high basins and ranges. Recent orogenesis and structural contortion together with prolonged erosion and detrital accumulation have produced ruggedness and steep slopes on the one hand and low-gradient basins on the other. The resulting landscape with its preponderance of abrupt angular junctions is frequently picturesquely impressive but has obvious difficulties for farming.

As noted in chapter 5, Iran is the meeting point of air masses of varying characteristics. The outward facing masses of the northern and western mountains receive, by orographic action, some winter precipitation from the weak and variable frontal activity arriving from the west and from the slowly moving cold air drifting south from Central Asia. Upper atmosphere convergence produces some winter precipitation on the central basins and ranges.

Except for the Gulf littoral, the Makrān coast and the Caspian coastlands this precipitation falls on mountains and high plateau basins where altitude reinforces the winter drop in temperature. The season of maximum precipitation over highland Iran is therefore relatively or absolutely bleak. Agricultural activity is reduced to a minimum; and of the seasonal water-balance surplus in the mountains much is lost either in direct runoff or in rapid snow-melt runoff in spring. Relative winter harshness also serves to restrict the crop-range, although this general pattern is broken up by the multitude of differing micro-climates produced by variations of altitude, slope and aspect in the more dissected regions. Along the Caspian shore the shelter provided by the Alburz and the thermally stabilizing effect of the Caspian Sea together result in generally humid and mild conditions which nevertheless even here are periodically broken by cold air incursions.

In summer the Zagros, central and southern Alburz and the central area have general air-mass stability, but land heating turbulence can produce violent changes in temperature and precipitation very similar to those experienced on the Spanish Meseta. The northern Alburz and Caspian receive orographic precipitation from the frequent movements of humid air from the Caspian lowlands, while Makrān and the Gulf experience generally weak but sometimes catastrophic monsoonal effects.

The climates of Iran are clearly restrictive of farming. Everywhere except in a few areas along the Caspian shore very definite seasonal rhythms tend to encourage reliance on annual crops, particularly of grains which require vernalization and which have short growing seasons. Violence and variability particularly affecting precipitation are also climatic factors of great significance.

Supremely important of course is the availability of water for plant, animal and human life. For Iran, as for the Middle East as a whole, the Qur'anic "We made from water every living thing",[1] is as true today as ever.

Rain-fed agriculture, as can be deduced from the brief statement above and from the preceding study of climate,[2] is poorly productive and hazardous in all regions. In central Iran the reported yields of dry-farmed wheat,[3] on about 30 per cent of the tilled area, vary between 290 and 360 kg per hectare (c. 2–2½ cwt per acre) as compared with between 850 and 1,900 kg per hectare (c. 6–13 cwt per acre) on irrigated land. In arid Sīstān and Balūchistān the yields of dry-farmed grain are so low and variable that practically none is produced except in some small favoured mountain areas.

The relatively pluvious regions of Āzarbāījān and Kurdistān, and the Caspian littoral have a smaller proportion of irrigated arable land, generally c. 20 per cent, but the differences in yield between dry and irrigation farming remain considerable. In these regions, as in the semi-arid east, centre and south, precipitation variability is great. Fluctuations in time, type and quantity are all significant, and when thermal seasonality, so often exaggerated by altitude and aspect, also produces critical conditions for crop plant germination and maturation, then precipitation variability can make dry-farming extremely hazardous. Even in near-tropical Khūzistān, killing frosts can occur as late as April.

Reliance on wasteland grazing under such climatic conditions is catastrophically dangerous. The only available estimates suggest that, on average, during one year in every five a total of between 800,000 and one million head of sheep and goats perish in drought conditions. The greatest losses are suffered by the nomadic pastoralists of the southern Zagros and Balūchistān, many of whom are periodically reduced to destitution by the not infrequent decimation of their flocks. In 1962 and

[1] The Qur'ān xxi, 31.   [2] Chapter 5, "Climate".
[3] First National Census of Agriculture, *op. cit.*

1963, thousands of once-proud Balūchi tribesmen were forced away from their mountains to meagre relief and begging in Zāhidān and Zābul, and spread as de-tribalized migrant casual labourers throughout eastern Iran, producing in their wake dislocation of the labour market and secondary poverty—this following a four-year absolute drought between April 1958 and April 1962.

The direct consequences to agriculture of climatic harshness and hazard are equalled by the indirect effects operating through the whole hydrological, edaphic and biotic complex. The most extreme conditions are found south and east of Kirmān, where the total average rainfall for between two and four years (8–24 in.) not infrequently falls in one or two days of violent storms.[1] Occurrences less extreme only in degree are recorded regularly in all parts of Iran. Under such conditions and associated also with great diurnal and seasonal temperature conditions, weathering produces on all slopes a preponderance of coarse detrital matter *in situ* together with graded concentrations of fine sand and silt in the lower basins of interior drainage. Runoff rates become extremely high on all sloping land, and water holding capacity (in any case low on the thin and slowly formed soils) has been dangerously reduced by encroachments on forest and scrub by the plough and livestock. Flood damage in the plains is estimated at more than one million U.S. dollars annually.[2] Downstream siltation adversely affects groundwater and drainage conditions, water-supply installations and soil formation. Upstream in the catchment areas the effectiveness of precipitation is reduced in some cases to 10 per cent of the actual fall, and land which in the absence of cultivation and grazing possessed a dry forest or mountain steppe ecological stability is often reduced to pebble-desert or gullied badland.

Biotic conditions for agriculture may then be summarized as follows. As water balance studies show[3] (fig. 136), the regions of moderate mean water surplus are restricted to the Zagros and Alburz mountains, the Caspian littoral, the highlands of Khurāsān and the isolated mountains of the interior. Even here the lower lands such as those in the Lake Rezā'īyeh [Urumīyeh] basin and the valleys of the Araxes [Aras] and

[1] Khuzistān Regional Development Programme, Eleventh Quarterly Review, June 1960.
[2] *Multi-Purpose River Basin Development*, Flood Control Series, no. 18, U.N. Publication 61.II.F.8.
[3] Thornthwaite, Mather and Carter, "Three Water Balance Maps of South-west Asia", Publications in Climatology, vol. XI, no. 1. Centerton, New Jersey, 1962.

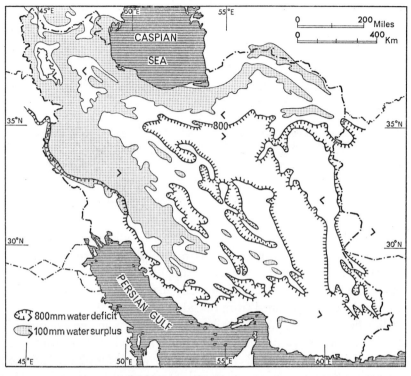

Fig. 136. Mean annual water balance. (After Thornthwaite, Mather and Carter.)

upper Safīd Rūd are areas of deficit. The mean surplus, such as it is, everywhere "occurs in one season alone".[1]

In these regions and on their peripheries are found the best potential edaphic conditions for cultivation—relatively deep forest soils and considerable expanses of fairly mature alluvial material, and also the least ephemeral natural grazing.

Even so, winters are frequently thermally harsh and snow common. Seasonal summer aridity, particularly when associated with high day temperatures results in a precarious ecological balance for natural climax tree growth. On the steep slopes of predominantly impermeable rocks this balance is very easily destroyed by even the most cautious intrusion of agriculture as any traveller in the Persian highlands can observe in the contrasts between controlled forest land and the ruined soils and degenerate flora of grazing and ploughed land.

[1] *Ibid.*

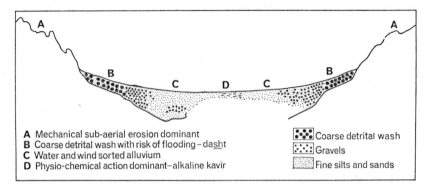

A Mechanical sub-aerial erosion dominant
B Coarse detrital wash with risk of flooding – da<u>sh</u>t
C Water and wind sorted alluvium
D Physio-chemical action dominant–alkaline kavir

[•••] Coarse detrital wash
[∴∵] Gravels
[⬚] Fine silts and sands

Fig. 137. Schematic section of an Endoreic basin.

In all other areas the mean water deficit is medium to high. "The production of grasses for grazing is not reliable...Virtually all the water required for agriculture must be supplied artificially; almost none is available from precipitation; practically all the water used in the zone of great deficits is obtained from outside the region."[1]

Climatic, ecological and hydrological conditions in the regions of seasonal water surplus impose stringent controls on the use of such water in the deficit zones. As noted elsewhere, river volume is highly variable and surface flow most often ephemeral. Storage and control of flow is made even more difficult and costly by the heavy load of solids carried by streams in spate. Since most surface water flows into interior drainage basins geomorphological processes normal under these conditions have produced since late Tertiary times a near-ubiquitous type of complex physiographic feature which is of common enough occurrence in semi-arid regions, but which is of especial importance to Iranian agriculture (fig. 137).

The basic elements are (*A*) steep fringing hill sides with the characteristics described above, (*B*) wide or narrow pediment shelves covered for the most part by overlapping fans of coarse boulder and pebble detritus deposited by inflowing streams. The central basins, usually tectonically structural in origin are infilled by finer material ranging from (*C*) gravel at the edges to silt and clay sediments at the hydrological centre (*D*). Wind erosion and sorting have reduced the degree of superficial textural uniformity while the length period over which these

[1] Thornthwaite, Mather and Carter, "Three Water Balance Maps of South-west Asia", Publications in Climatology, vol. XI, no. 1. Centerton, New Jersey, 1962.

processes have operated has allowed the non-coincidental superimposition of material of different kinds and grades.

Surface water flowing into such depressions usually percolates into the coarser colluvium and follows tortuous subterranean paths, only reappearing periodically in ephemeral lakes or marshes in the lowest parts of the basins when local or general saturation is reached.

Most inflowing water is more or less heavily charged with soluble salts, and high rates of surface evaporation during summer produce and have produced general or local concentrations of heavily charged groundwater. As a result there occur, areally and in depth, great variations in salinity and alkalinity which bear little clear correspondence to the texture of surface soils.

The environment in which both the upland and plain dwelling agriculturalist has to operate is thus extraordinarily limiting. Dry-farming is clearly climatically hazardous and tends to be only of importance in the relatively pluvious mountains and hill-lands which have their own special problems arising from the enforced use of frequently immature, steep slope soils of mechanical and chemical instability The only exceptional region is that including Māzandarān and Gurgān, the former as a result of relative climatic benignity[1] the latter because of the special characteristics of deep löss soils.[2] Here annual, perennial and forage crops give good returns even without irrigation; and for an explanation of the present less than maximum exploitation of land in Māzandarān and Gurgān one must turn attention away from simple physical controls.

Irrigation farming can only be carried out successfully under some stringent conditions. On the valley terraces and floodplains in the seasonally pluvious mountains one finds the following general situation:

Mountain rivulets and streams provide water for irrigation, being deviated by canals to both sides of the valleys. In these higher zones the density of cultivated lands relative to available land is much higher than in the lower plain or piedmont zones. Complicated water works conduct the water to minute fields and terraced agriculture is often of an ingenious kind. The work of generations has shaped the sedentary agricultural landscape and crop diversification exists together with an important fruit growing complex. These zones suffer most from shortage of land and the distance to market centres.[3]

---

[1] "Irrigation Project—Mazanderan." Preliminary and Full Reports to Plan Organization of Iran by Sir Alexander Gibb and Partners, 1958.

[2] "Amenagement de la Rivière Gorgan." Report to Plan Organization of Iran by E.T.C.O., 1959. In particular the "Etude pédologique et agronomique".

[3] "A study for the Modernization of Peasant Life and Animal Husbandry in the Zagros." Memorandum to Plan Organization of Iran by Italconsult, 1960.

In the high valleys and terraces of the northern Zagros and Alburz ranges, in the isolated central mountains at Tezerjān[1] and on Kūh-i-Taftān in Balūchistān,[2] as everywhere in the highlands of the Middle East, lushness and fertility seem to dwell, accentuated by contrast with the low plains. It is important however that the visual impact made by the rows of poplar, the groves of almonds and apricot and the steps of terraced fields with their variety of pulses, legumes and vegetables should not deceive the traveller into believing that rustic plenty abounds. Even that intensity of production which exists has been developed only by strenuous uncosted manual labour which has to be expended more and more prodigally as growing populations impose increasing strains on the inexorably restricted resources of topographically usable land. Here lies the paradox of apparent plenty and real poverty.

The 1960 Agricultural Census presented the position statistically in the following way for a typical region, the Ustān of Kurdistān. Of all agricultural land 48·5 per cent was under annual crops, 50·2 per cent fallow and only 1·3 per cent carried the eye-catching trees, perennial crops and fodders. Of the productive arable land over 95 per cent was under wheat and barley (of which in turn only some 12 per cent was irrigated). Thus the illusion of fertility which deceives even many Iranians is created by the little over 6 per cent of utilized land available for perennial and multi-cropping. To sustain even this the holdings, 82 per cent of which were share-cropped, have become diminished in size and fragmented. Forty-five per cent of all holdings have less than five hectares of land and are each composed of an average number of three parcels, usually non-contiguous. Another 23 per cent of holdings were between five and ten hectares in size, divided on average into 7·4 parcels. The typical worked plot, whatever the holding size, averaged 1·4 hectares.

In regions such as this are to be found the most desperate ecological, economic and social conditions. As in many analogous areas to be found in the Old World subtropical belt extending from Atlantic Iberia eastward to Japan, the Persian peasants of the mountain valleys, no longer as strictly numerically controlled by disease and disaster as traditionally they were, are presented with few alternatives to dependence on local agricultural resources, and increasingly compete for land and once plentiful water. Further intensification of rudimentary

---

[1] Chapter 12, "Early Man".

[2] "Socio-Economic Development for the South-Eastern Region." Preliminary Report, Agricultural Survey. Report to Plan Organization of Iran by Italconsult, 1959.

production techniques[1] can only mean a greater and more constant expenditure of human energy with an ever-decreasing prospect of a breakthrough to the social and economic opportunities of which improved communications inform the villagers. The brutal fact remains that a multitude of tiny regions of this kind are rurally over-populated except on the basis of a low standard peasant way of life. No adjustments of tenure or technological improvements can significantly ameliorate this situation in which the range of choice is confined to three possibilities. The first is that of migration to the towns, a practice which is steadily increasing as recent studies have evinced.[2] The second possibility is essentially static, of allowing local pressure on land resources by sedentary cultivators to spill over on to more and more range and forest land. The evil ecological consequences to mountains and plains alike of such a course are amply documented in many of the U.N. Arid Zone Research Series.[3] The Iran range-lands require more careful management and a diminution rather than an increase of encroachment.[4] Present efforts to encourage sedenterization of nomadic tribes in the central Zagros would be seriously hindered by any extension of simple hill farming, and even the recently established sedentarization of the type found in the Dasht-i-Mughān region[5] might be imperilled. Any increased dependence on mountain dry-farming, with its consequent diminution of the socio-economic territorial stability which is implied in irrigation farming, is also bound to increase the importance of sheep and goats as an economic reserve. Since pastoral traditions die hard, as can be seen from studies in Turkey and Āzarbāījān,[6] such a rekindling of ancient flames is severely to be avoided.

The third possibility is that of the deliberate development in the

[1] See Frederik Barth, *Principles of Social Organization in Southern Kurdistan*, Universitets Etnografiske Museum (Oslo, 1953); and "Réseau du Barrage de Sefid Roud; Mise en Valeur de la plaine du Guilan, Livre 1. Situation Actuelle." Report by Société Grenobloise d'Etudes et d'Application Hydrauliques to Plan Organization of Iran 1958.

[2] Xavier de Planhol, *Tehran*. Institute of Social Studies and Research, Univ. of Tehrān, 1962; and "Du Piémont Teherannais à la Caspienne." *Bulletin de l'Association de Géographes Français* (1959).

[3] See in particular "A History of Land Use in Arid Regions", UNESCO, *Arid Zone Research No. XVII*, 1961, and "The Problems of the Arid Zone", UNESCO, *Arid Zone Research No. XVIII*, 1962.

[4] "Report of Range Management Experts", CENTO. Unclassified Note EC/13/AG/D5, July 1964.

[5] C. op't Land, "The Permanent Settlements of the Dachte-Moghan", *Problems of the Sedenterization of Pastoralists No. 5*, Institute of Social Studies and Research, Univ. of Tehrān, 1961.

[6] Xavier de Planhol, "La vie de montagne dans le Sahend", *Bulletin de L'Association de Geographes Français* (1958).

valley regions of commercial specialization for regional or distant markets. Such a policy would have the advantage of producing incentives for those considerable improvements in quantity and quality which are feasible, while at the same time increasing cash income and creating new employment opportunities in trade, transport and processing which would to some extent relieve direct employment pressure on agricultural resources. Attractive though this may sound, experience in neighbouring countries discourages facile optimism. The creation of sophisticated commercial and market-orientated economies is in fact one of the most difficult policies to implement, as has been exemplified in Malta where many conditions for such development were theoretically near optimal.[1] In Iran the first prerequisite for such development, a large and relatively wealthy urban market, does not as yet exist.

Ironically enough it would appear then that the relatively well watered and traditionally desirable upland valleys, the gardens of Iran, have less potential not only for development but even for maintaining present standards than have the superficially less attractive basins, plains and lowlands which now require examination.

Both in area and in economic significance the Tertiary/Quaternary basin units already schematically described are of the greatest importance. Ranging from the complex units of the Great Kavīr and the Lūṭ each covering an area of between 30,000 and 50,000 square miles down to the 120 square miles of the oasis of Shīrāz, all these basins have certain common characteristics of vital importance to agriculture. Practically all surface water entering them from the surrounding hills percolates into the sedimentary infill. Only very rarely and in the smallest units is there any simple water-body development; almost invariably aquiferous sands and gravels are found in lenticular bodies and ancient water-courses. Even so, gravitational movement tends to produce a series, frequently discontinuous, of graded water-tables. The essential features of all irrigation systems in physiographic units of this kind logically follow. The water must be obtained near to the basin edge where its content of solubles is low, but it can only be utilized further downslope where coarse detritus is succeeded by cultivable silts. Both in enclosed basins and where exoreic drainage is impeded by structure, lithology or low gradient, the lowest land with the gravity-

[1] H. Bowen-Jones, J. C. Dewdney and W. B. Fisher, *Malta: Background for Development*, University of Durham, 1961.

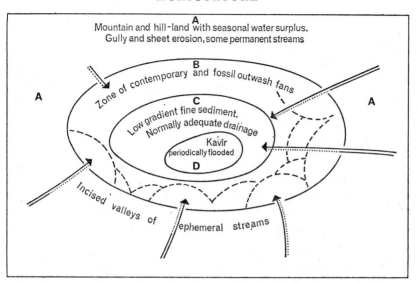

Fig. 138. Schematic plan of an Endoreic basin.

sorted finest silts is rendered unusable by the high concentration of soluble salts resulting from constant inflow and high evaporation—this is the *Kavīr*. Schematically therefore cultivable land occupies an annular zone on the intermediate slopes of each basin unit (fig. 138, Zone *C*) compressed between the fluctuating margins of the sterile Kavīr (Zone *D*) and the periodically storm-flooded coarse colluvium of the piedmont (Zone *B*).

In reality structural, physiographic and hydrographic variations distort this simple pattern. The basins of the Great Kavīr and the Lūṭ are composed of many central and peripheral, incomplete and whole units of this kind,[1] and even the smaller regions such as that centred on the plain of Juvain possess considerable complexity.[2] Moreover, in most places simple concentricity has been further destroyed by the peripheral siting of settlements either in the main piedmont zone as in the case of Hamadān or near minor hill features as exemplified by Kirmān.[3] The need for defensive sites, the attraction of natural routeways, the presence of potable spring water together with many other

[1] Hans Bobek, "Features and Formation of the Great Kavir and Masileh", Arid Zone Research Centre. Tehrān, 1959.
[2] Brian Spooner, "Arghiyan. The Area of Jajarm in Western Khuresan", *Iran*, vol. III. London, 1965.
[3] P. H. T. Beckett, "Agriculture in Central Persia", *Agriculture*, vol. XXXIV, no. 1. Jan. 1957.

factors have influenced the siting of nucleated settlement quite independently of strictly agricultural requirements.

In turn, the growth of settlements by creating new market opportunities and raising land values has permitted extensions of cultivation
which would not have been called into being by purely rural subsistence
requirements. The changing historical patterns of land use which
accompanied the varying fortunes of Iṣfahān illustrate this very clearly.[1]

Nevertheless the basic elements of the basin-unit-type, viz. the
"dead heart", the utilizable zone surrounding the centre and the relatively
repellent periphery, remain dominant agricultural controls. Unlike the
Konya basin of Turkey, in which the physical characteristics are otherwise
analogous, very few Iranian basins receive a sufficient and regular volume
of surface river water to allow gravity irrigation by canal. The few areas
in which this is possible, such as the Iṣfahān basin watered in particular
by the Zāyandeh Rūd, are notable for their agricultural prosperity.

For the most part the smaller basins of the arid centre and south-east,
together with less well-defined fringes of the Great Kavīr, receive
incoming water mainly by piedmont seepage of many small ephemeral
streams, and the traditional method of tapping this subsurface wealth
is by the *Kāriẓ* (better known in the Arabic qanāt) system. This system,
described in many studies (and see chapter 19), essentially consisting
of infiltration galleries graded from their surface outlets in the intermediate cultivable zone, Zone *C* (fig. 138), to their deep origins in
Zone *B*, represents an admirable technical response to physical conditions but has important implications for agricultural organization and
practice. The alignment and digging out of these galleries, already an
established technique even in Sassanian times, requires a considerable
amount of specialized knowledge and experience. The employment of
expert *muqannī* (qanāt diggers) for the months or even years necessary
for galleries frequently ten miles in length and sometimes much longer,
imposes formidable demands on capital. There have also developed
many customary and codified laws governing the construction of and
distance between qanāts and the need for controlling the distribution
of water further imposes some requirement of formal organization.[2]
(See Chapter 19.)

[1] Judith Brown, "The Historical Evolution of the Cities of Tehrān and Iṣfahān".
Unpublished thesis, Univ. of Durham, 1966.
[2] "Water laws in Moslem countries", F.A.O. Development Paper No. 43, 1954; and
Farhad Ghahraman, "Water Rights in Iran", Seminar Paper UNESCO Institute of Social
Studies. Tehrān, 1963.

Wherever such long-established irrigation systems exist, they have required that some type of controlling body either emerge or be imposed. In Valencia one finds the centuries-old communal "grass-root" organization of the "Tribunal de los Aguas"; in India, particularly from the fourteenth century onward, there appeared first royal and later imperial initiative and control.

In Persia, central authority, when strong, more or less confined its attention to Khūzistān and Turkistān, while, when weak, allowed economic as well as political disintegration. For the same reasons which account for the historical evolution of a strong and powerful group of landowners no individual member of which possessed much greater security than did the members of the Afghan or Mogul aristocracy, the ownership of water became concentrated in much the same hands. Whilst large-scale ownership units of low capacity dry-farmed land is in many ways, technical, social and economic, a logical development, in the case of qanāt irrigation justification rests almost entirely on the absence of available capital other than in the hands of the landowner and on the virtual absence of any authority other than his. Techniques other than the traditional have in fact hardly ever been improved and in this sector of agriculture, as also in others, one of the most serious deficiencies of the traditional tenurial system is that only very rarely did any technological lead come from the landowners, a situation similar to that existing in pre-Revolutionary France and in complete contrast to English historical experience.

At this point it becomes necessary to consider, in the context of agricultural geography, one particular aspect of Persian society which is dealt with in its own right elsewhere in this volume. This is the relationship between landlord and peasant, a relationship which, as Professor Lambton has emphasized, has been until recently one of the few dominant factors in Iranian life and which, although changing rapidly, will continue to be of great importance.

The Persian land system was "basically a bureaucratic, not a feudal, system".[1] One of Professor Lambton's great contributions to scholarship has been her clear elucidation of the administrative logic which, under Persian conditions, led to the growth of a land assignment system by which "the functions of the provincial governor, the provincial military commander, the tax collector, the tax farmer, and the man

---

[1] A. K. S. Lambton, "Some Reflections on the Question of Rural Development and Land Reform in Iran", CENTO Symposium, Tehrān, 1963.

to whom the land assignment was made tended to be combined in one person. This led to the emergence of large landed properties virtually independent of the central government."[1]

As an institutional development this system can be found in analogous forms elsewhere, for example in Moghul India and in the Spanish New World,[2] but in Iran it must also be seen as frequently possessing some particular environmental rationale. Where the carrying capacity of land is low in terms of the prevailing technology then concentrations of wealth can only accrue from the exploitation of large areas. The closest analogy to the Iranian situation then becomes not Bengal of the Settlement but of parts of pre-reform Italian Calabria.

Before the technological revolution of the 1850s any areally large-scale non-pastoral exploitation was necessarily associated, everywhere in the world, with large-scale labour application. We find, from Solon to Stolypin, the inequalities which derive from the low-productivity poverty of the many individual cultivators on the one hand and on the other the wealth inevitably resulting from the accumulation in some few hands of the small surpluses derived from the many. The crude logic of the situation in many cases is that between the two extremes there can be no simple intermediate situation. In the case of Iran, by far the greatest area of cultivable land, both traditionally and today, is only capable of giving such low yields that any process of revenue collection must be based on an almost universal low per capita levy; a discrepancy of scale between these small indivisible units and the accumulated totality of such units becomes inevitable. Moreover, when land productivity, potential as well as actual, is low then land capability becomes a fixed element and any variability in the institutional arrangement of production or ownership tends rationally to group around extensiveness rather than intensity. This is the real difficulty in Iran; large-scale private ownership is not merely a "historical accident" but is in part at least a product of the same rational resource-appraisal processes which operate in communist Russia and capitalist North America. This basic fact must be remembered even when one also notes that large-scale cultivation is only economically justifiable in terms of suitable technology.

The cultivation of staple grains on semi-arid marginal land can best be carried out, on the basis of low yields per acre and high yields per

[1] A. K. S. Lambton, "Some Reflections on the Question of Rural Development and Land Reform in Iran", CENTO Symposium, Tehrān, 1963.
[2] J. H. Parry, *The Audiencia of New Galicia* (Cambridge, 1948).

capita, by the sophisticated use of capital equipment in mechanized farming on a large scale. Anything less than this leads to land/labour ratios below optimum, as discussed by Tuma[1] and others, manifesting themselves in rural underemployment[2] and poverty. In the words of Italconsult: "for as long as economic activity relies upon the vicissitudes of annual rainfall it may be expected that a self-sufficient and stagnant agriculture will persist."[3]

When, on the other hand, an attempt is made to increase the intensity of land use through irrigation then we also find the necessity for the deployment of relatively or absolutely large masses of capital. Even qanāts are expensive: Beckett has noted[4] that near Kirmān capital costs for one qanāt capable of irrigating 130–200 acres amounted to some £30,000. Only in the case of small stream-diversion schemes in the pluviose mountain valleys can irrigation intensification be carried out by uncosted self-employed peasant labour.

These comments are in no way a defence of landlordism of the "encomienda" type but rather are an insistence that over much of Iran the environment demands that the agricultural response should be on a large working scale. Partly in order to replace the landlord as an institution, partly in order to introduce some positive social and economic benefits, rural co-operatives are now being founded and officially supported. This is an acknowledgement of the need for some institution on a larger than farm scale. However, as long as the effective pressure of rural population on apparently limited land resources remains high and the physical opportunities for production are limited then the farms themselves will remain small and returns to labour and capital will rise but slowly. The farmers themselves therefore have none of the sophistication necessary for rapid growth of co-operatives. The pilot-project for small-scale mechanization through primary co-operatives in Marāgheh is of especial interest.[5]

It is of course also true that large-scale land ownership is also found in areas where small-scale cultivation on an individual or small group basis is environmentally suitable. In Māzandarān and in many of the

---

[1] Elias H. Tuma, *Twenty-six Centuries of Agrarian Reform* (London, 1965).
[2] Carl K. Eicher and Lawrence W. Witt (see e.g. part 3), *Agriculture in Economic Development* (New York, 1964).
[3] "A Preliminary Assessment of Potential Resources in Khorasan Province." Prepared for Italconsult. Tehrān, 1963.
[4] P. H. T. Becket, "Qanats around Kerman", *Jl R. Cent. Asian Soc.* XL (1953).
[5] A. H. Amir Parviz, "Use of Cooperatives", CENTO Symposium, Tehrān, 1963.

valley lands in the Alburz and Kurdistān individual peasant initiative has been vitiated rather than aided by the superstructure of larger-scale land ownership.

From what has already been noted it will have become apparent that methods of and attitudes to husbandry are in part the products of normal practical responses to local resource conditions, but also are in part by-products of social and economic processes remote from the realities of agriculture.

Technologically, Iran is in a transition stage. The main tillage implement is the animal-drawn *ard* or wooden plough. Here, in or near its place of origin some six millenia ago, this tool is still dominant in one or other of its variant forms, all of which are characterized by the absence of a sod-inverting mould-board and the leaving of an uneven mulched rather than furrowed surface. Today in Iran, the *khīsh* as it is most generally called, tends to be regarded as primitive and inefficient and is being replaced relatively rapidly by the mould-board, or disc plough, usually tractor drawn. Unfortunately, under Iranian conditions this replacement is ecologically hazardous. The mould-board plough was developed for soils and climates where rapid sward recrudescence, in Fitzherbert's words, necessitated: "the turning up moche molde, and to lay it flat, that it rere not on edge. For if it rere on edge, the grasse and mosse wyll not rotte."[1] In environments of sub-tropical aridity not only do such conditions not occur but inversion of the top-soil (which is usually severely degraded in any case), encourages oxidation of the slight humus content and presents a vulnerable surface to the erosive forces of wind and rain. Disc ploughing and other means of producing a fine tilth only exacerbate the situation. For over a century the virtues of a stubble-mulch surface under semi-arid conditions have been academically accepted but still today that aspect of farm mechanization most readily acceptable to countries such as Iran is tractor plough-ing by mould-board and disc even although the various types of stubble cultivator, such as the Graham plough, functionally similar to the khīsh, are obtainable.[2]

Perhaps even more serious is that the main advantages of tractor tillage—the saving of time and effort—can, as in the case of neighbour-ing Turkey, encourage the expansion of cultivation without necessitating any improvement in ecological understanding. In Turkey, virtually the

---

[1] Master Fitzherbert, *The Book of Husbandry* (London, 1534).
[2] See e.g. *U.S.D.A. Yearbook for 1943–47* (Washington, 1948).

whole of the 60 per cent increase in cereal production since 1928 has come from an expansion in arable acreage and practically none from increased yields. The ecologically damaging results are everywhere apparent. In Iran the consequences of a similar response would be catastrophic.

In the technological sector here then is the type problem of how can the best of contemporary technical knowledge be utilized under ecologically hazardous conditions by a generally illiterate peasantry with limited experience?

The other implements in general use are of traditional type, the sledge or roller animal-drawn thresher, the wooden levellers and pseudo-harrows, the hand sickle, and the long-handled spade. The replacement of these by time and energy saving modern analogues depends mainly on the scale and profitability of operations. Cotton growing in Turkistān, sugar-beet in Khurāsān, are cash crops grown on a commercial scale for commercial markets. It is therefore not surprising that mechanization in these regions proceeds apace. Sugar-cane production in Khūzistān and tea growing in the Caspian region on the other hand still require considerable use both of hand labour and modern capital equipment.

Since cattle are for the most part dual-purpose beasts for draft and food products, and since sheep and goats are mainly associated either with nomadic pastoralism or with the utilization of uncultivable village wasteland, fallow and scrub-forest, livestock husbandry is ill-developed. Many of the local breeds such as the Khurāsānī Zebu cattle would seem to have breeding-development potential, but feeding and veterinary standards are so low and the drought hazards to grazing so great that the net return in meat, milk, wool, hair and hides is uniformly poor. Only in a few cases of urban fringe farming, as in south Tehrān, is there any commercial specialization and even this is of a primitive type.

The production of traditional perennial crops is distinguished in the main by the great number of varieties grown of each species, by the small scale of cultivation and by the absence of selective specialization. Thus small citrus gardens at Bam (fig. 139) contain so many natural and degenerate hybrids that in order to say more than that the four species orange, lime, lemon and citron are represented would require serious taxonomic research. This is an extreme case, and in the more recent Caspian plantations things are better ordered but in general the pome, stone and citrus fruits exist in countless varieties not all of which are

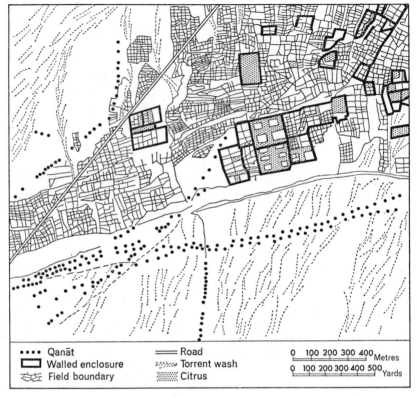

•••• Qanāt	═══ Road	0 100 200 300 400 Metres
☐ Walled enclosure	Torrent wash	0 100 200 300 400 500 Yards
⬚⬚ Field boundary	▦ Citrus	

Fig. 139. Land use: Central Highlands oasis type—Bam.

genetically stable. As is to be expected a considerable amount of tradition based care is expended on most of these crops, but pests and diseases are rife. Very considerable economic possibilities potentially exist, but quality grading and marketing can hardly develop spontaneously given the small size of the sophisticated consumer market.

For the most part therefore agricultural practices are dominated by environment with the peasantry responding in a biotic rather than an economic sense. Almost everywhere the staple grains are the first concern; after these come those other crops which it is physically possible to grow. Where water is available for summer irrigation then vegetables, including a great range of cucurbits, are dominant. In most areas other than the south and east, perennial food crops are limited to the winter hardy fruits and the vine. Only during the last fifteen years or so has this simple pattern, based on the overwhelming nature of subsistence or local demand become broken down by the encouragement of cash cropping for the national market. This situation is reflected not only in the material aspects of husbandry but also in rural concepts. It is no accident, for example, that land area is very difficult to define. Thus the Land Reform Law of January 1962, Section Two, stated that the maximum area to be held by a single individual was to be a village of six *dang* or parts of several villages in total to be equivalent to six *dang*. The *dang* however has no absolute areal value and varies in significance from village to village and region to region. So too with lesser measurements. In the Garmsīr region,[1] the unit of land in terms of which farming operations are conducted is the *Kharvār*—the area of land on which can be sown one donkey load of seed, approximately 2¼ hectares, the average farmer operating between one and three kharvār. In Khūzistān the unit is known as the *Khīsh*—the area of land which a farmer with the traditional khīsh plough and two oxen can handle, in this case approximately 6 hectares.[2] In the Caspian provinces the *Jarīb*, and elsewhere the *Juft* and the *Gīn* variously represent some relationship between area and either sowing capacity or tillage capability.

The importance of these terms lies not merely in their variability; until very recently, customary acres showed similar variations in Britain. In Iran very few farmers even think in terms of absolute area. Thus yields are generally thought of as gross quantities or as an approximate ratio of returns on seed. Irrigated land is most frequently discussed in terms of minutes or hours of water application, in much the same way that distances are mainly conceived of in time units. These points are unimportant in themselves, but together with the physical and technical characteristics of Persian agriculture, are symptomatic of parochial peasant attitudes which in turn are reinforced by the nature of the farmers' environments.

Without water land is a meaningless abstraction to a cultivator whose survival depends largely on his own efforts and traditional local experience. In the absence of strong market orientation distance is only really meaningful in terms of nomadic marches or the time it takes to reach cultivated or grazing land. The great arterial routes which for millennia

[1] O. T. Osgood, Kumaris Maghul and Fatolah Raji, "Report of the Agricultural and Water Economy in the Garmsar Area". Independent Irrigation Corp. of Iran and FAO. Tehrān, 1960.

[2] C. C. Spence, in *The Development of Land and Water Resources in Khuzistan*, Section 9. FAO. Rome, 1956.

have converged on northern K̲h̲urāsān or have traversed the piedmonts of the Alburz and the Central ranges are remote from the farmers' experience. The relative isolation imposed on each small pocket of reasonable and watered land by the great intervening stretches of salt pan, desert and mountain, has tended to produce a separatism which has regularly triumphed over the periodic imperial centralizations. Within each region and sub-region therefore local variations in re-source availability at one level and political and even religious parti-cularism on another have been normal.

It is in this context of fragmentation that we must set the changes which, as a result of great effort, are now affecting agriculture. A new infrastructure of communications, governmental social and economic agencies and law enforcement, armed with the power of modern technology is affecting profoundly albeit slowly all the attitudes and values. The effects of the mobility afforded to the peasantry by the simple motor-bus is manifest to any traveller. The potential for change which accompanies the establishment of markets for new crops is well illustrated by the effect of the introduction of sugar beet and processing factories to the Mas̲h̲had region.[1] In the Diz development area the avidity with which intensive mixed farming techniques are being adopted is impressive.[2] In many of the oasis basins the implementation of new appraisals of potential of a kind similar to those now being adopted around Iṣfahān[3] is equally possible.

It is necessary however to enter a caveat against facile development optimism. As noted elsewhere, the urban population of Iran is numeri-cally small and in terms of demand for agricultural products is qualita-tively minute. As yet most of the cash crop innovations have been in the nature of import-substitutions, and the scope for further extension is not unlimited. A great deal of future development will have to be locally generated and for local needs. Per capita income and purchasing power will have to rise considerably before the emphasis on subsistence is weakened, and the matching of needs with resources can be neither easy nor nationally even.

In this short study, emphasis has been laid on the characteristics of

[1] D. J. Flower, "The Agricultural Geography of the Mas̲h̲had Region." Unpublished thesis, Univ. of Durham, 1966.
[2] See Development and Resources Corporation, New York, Reports to Plan Organiza-tion of Iran, 1959– .
[3] Xavier de Planhol, "Les Tendances Nouvelles de l'Agriculture Irriguée dans l'Oasis d'Isfahan", Révue Géographique de l'Est, IV (1964).

sedentary agriculture to the near-exclusion from consideration of pastoralism and nomadism. Given the changing nature of Iranian society and economy such a course can be defended; indeed, in Iran as in other parts of the Middle East, state policy has been directed towards the sedenterization of pastoralists and the elimination of nomads.

Nevertheless some points need to be made concerning the position of nomadism and pastoralism as it affects agriculture. In the first place there is the matter of differences in social organization between the nomads and the settled peasantry. Nomadic pastoralists are invariably tribally organized, owing their allegiances through families and clans to their tribal chiefs and, while there is here a considerable complexity involving both economic and social status, in general this tends to lessen the authority of the central government not only on the politico-legal plane but also in the field of economic development and land use policy. Between 1922 and 1932 the strong Qashghai tribe was in bitter conflict with the central government essentially over matters of socio-political status, while since 1962 the measures taken by the state have been more concerned with the enforcement of economic sedenteriza-tion and land reform. The reasons for this change in emphasis essen-tially derive from the facts of the distribution of the nomadic pastoralists.

It has been estimated that about 18 per cent of the populaton of Iran is composed of tribal groups of which, although estimates vary widely, about one million are still nomadic pastoralists inhabiting the Zagros, Afghan–Balūchī and Alburz mountains in that order of importance. The Kurds of the central Zagros, the Lori speakers of Luristān and the southern Zagros, and the Qashghai of Fārs are the dominant groups, but the Balūchī, Türkmen and Arab tribes are also of significance.

In their highland territories bordering on and frequently lapping over state frontiers these nomadic groups have for millennia been a source of political and military danger to settled cultures, while through the territories they inhabit pass all the land routes which connect Iran with her neighbours. Also in these territories, as already noted, lie the main water and forest resources of the country, and in which the pressure on land by settled cultivators is the greatest. These highland areas are the key regions for ecological conservation in that any further deterioration of the hydrological balance in them would imperil the utilized lands of the basins and plains.

Hitherto nomadic pastoralism based on transhumance over consi-derable distances has not too severely impinged on the life of villages,

589

which in many areas are also dependent on transhumant movement of village flocks.[1] Indeed it has been shown that the socio-economic links between nomad and village are now almost essential to the survival of tribal nomadic life.[2] However as the ecological balance of the highlands becomes recognized to be a vital factor in Persian agriculture so at the same time demographic pressure in the highlands has been increasing. Under traditional conditions Malthusian checks prevented imbalance from growing too quickly, simply because "unless techniques for the storage of fodder are developed, absolute population size is limited by the carrying capacity of the pastures in the *least* productive period of the year".[3] In recent years the checks imposed by morbidity have weakened and ecological deterioration has accelerated.[4] As in all the semi-arid regions of the Old World, and as, for example, in Jordan today, one finds on one hand the tribally organized and linguistically distinct nomadic groups with a traditional ethos that has been unchanged for millennia, and on the other relatively modern concepts of range management based on scientific thinking and powered by national economic need.[5]

There can be no simple outcome of this confrontation because the facts of environment and of man's present relationship with it are in themselves complex.[6] In the highland regions pastoralism cannot simply be replaced by cultivation; as already noted, conditions of considerable seasonal climatic change from hot arid to cold bleak impose great restrictions on all activity and make arable farming hazardous economically and ecologically. Nomadism is itself a response to low permanent carrying capacity and any settled range-farming has to be based on low stocking rates and to be economical must be operated by a tithe of the present pastoral population. The resettlement of any displaced group is a difficult operation involving as it does the enforced re-orientation of an integrated way of life and in any case presupposes the existence of other economic opportunities.

In this sector, therefore, as with all sectors of agriculture, one is

[1] Xavier de Planhol, "La vie de montagne dans le Sahend", *op. cit.*
[2] F. Barth, *Nomads of S. Persia* (London, 1961).
[3] F. Barth, "The Land Use Pattern of Migratory Tribes of South Persia", *Norsk geogr. Tidsskr.* XVII, 1–4 (1959–60).
[4] L. Krader, "Ecology of Central Asian Pastoralism", *South-western Journal of Anthropology*, XI (1955). [5] "Range management", CENTO Seminar, 1964.
[6] "Nomadic Pastoralism as a Method of Land Use." General Symposium on Arid Zone Problems, Paper No. 17, UNESCO NS/AZ/526. Paris, 1960; and F. Barth 'Nomadism in the Mountain and Plateau Areas of South-west Asia', *ibid.* Paper No. 16.

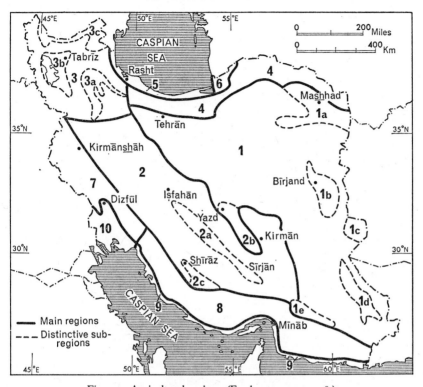

Fig. 140. Agricultural regions. (For key see pp. 592–8.)

faced in Iran with the seeming paradox that the future of farming depends on the speed with which the present overwhelming predominance of agriculture can be diminished. In less epigrammatical terms this is to say that because of the limited resource opportunities, the ecological hazards, and the nature of the socio-economic responses peculiar to Iranian communities, agricultural development must be approximately in phase with evolution in, and the sectoral balance of, other aspects of economic and social life: the factors of production, distribution and trade as they affect manufacturing and farming, and the trend to urbanization.

In conclusion the basic regional characteristics of Iranian agriculture should be noted. Figure 140 illustrates these in general, and reference is made to other illustrations of some aspects of the varied land use patterns which may be observed.

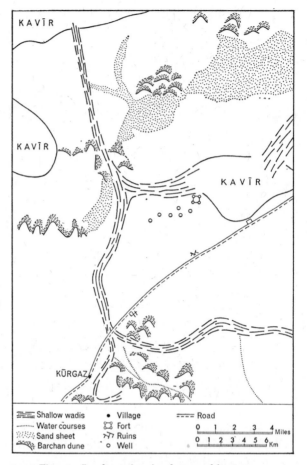

Fig. 141. Land use: interior desert and kavīr type.

1. *Central Basin and Range Region.* Marked water deficiency, extreme temperature range. Includes the Lūṭ with kavīr flats, sand and gravel dunes, and the Great Kavīr with alkaline flats, fig. 141. Pastoralism almost excluded; cultivation, mainly of annuals, dependent on peripheral and endoreic mountain streams, fig. 142.

Sub-regions: 1*a*. Mashhad basin. Thermally mild, with extensive alluvial valleys well supplied with water from Khurāsān hills which carry livestock on upland pasture. Well-developed commercial agriculture with recent emphasis on sugar-beet.

1*b*. Bīrjand highlands. Less-marked water deficiency with good pasture in mountains, irrigated agriculture in intermontane tracts.

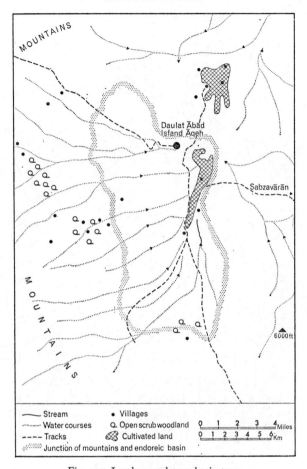

Fig. 142. Land use: plateau basin type.

1*c.* Sīstān basin. Alluvial plain surrounding Hāmūn-i-Helmand. Seasonal grazing on periodically inundated lake shores, cultivation on high-water table and irrigated interfluves. Potential depends on agreement with Afghanistan over use of Helmand River water.

1*d.* Kūh-i-Taftān highland. High orographic precipitation giving mountain pasture and valley cultivation. Culturally a refuge area.

1*e.* Jāz Murīān basin. Arid structural basin but with considerable total of sub-surface water. Very high summer temperatures. Tree-crops important in oases.

2. *Zagros and Central Highlands.* High ranges with relatively high orographic rainfall diminishing to south and east, winter snow cover.

593

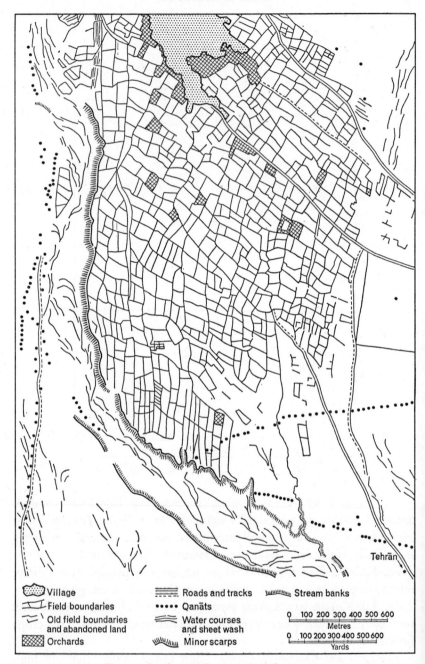

Village
Field boundaries
Old field boundaries
and abandoned land
Orchards

Roads and tracks
Qanāts
Water courses
and sheet wash
Minor scarps

Stream banks

0   100 200 300 400 500 600
Metres
0   100 200 300 400 500 600
Yards

Fig. 143. Land use: Alburz south piedmont type.

594

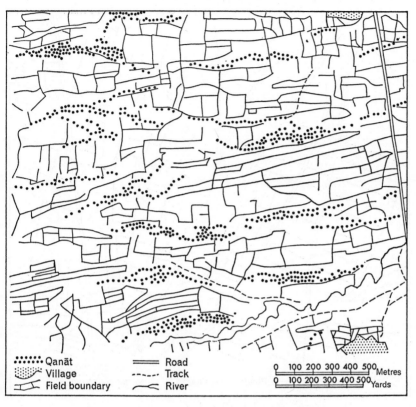

Qanāt   **Road**

Village   **Track**

Field boundary   **River**

0 100 200 300 400 500 Metres
0 100 200 300 400 500 Yards

Fig. 144. Land use: Caspian coast type—Māzandarān.

Annual precipitation in balance or slight surplus. Natural climax vegetation of forest very largely cleared. Nomadic pastoralism dominant with cultivation in valleys and peripheral basins. Tribal hill societies with urbanized oases. Standard crop range of grains, vegetables, subtropical fruits.

Basin sub-regions: 2*a*. Iṣfahān–Sīrjān basin. Intensive cultivation in northern area utilizing Zayandeh Rūd water. Important north–south routeway. Highland pasturage and high valley cultivation linked to basin settlements.

2*b*. Yazd–Kirmān basin. Discontinuous series of basin edge irrigated oases. Highland-basin links as in 2*a*. Routeway.

2*c*. Shīrāz basin. Stream irrigated oasis small in scale but regionally important.

3. *Āzarbāījān.* Dissected pluvious highland with great ecological

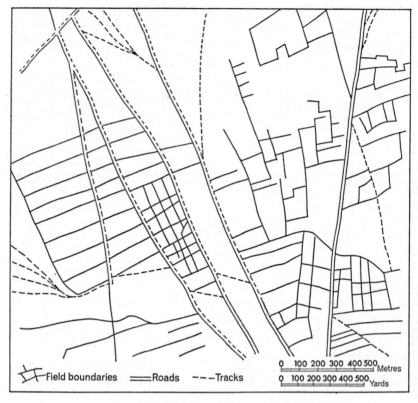

Fig. 145. Land use: Türkmen Plain type—Gunbad-i-Qābūs.

and ethnic diversity. Cold winters with prolonged snow cover on mountains, rain-shadow hot summer basins. Forest climax almost entirely cleared, with nomadic and village pastoralism dominant in mountains.

Basin sub-regions: 3 *a*. Qizil Uzūn valley lands. Underdeveloped irrigable alluvial lowlands with empty surrounding hill lands.

3 *b*. Lake Rezā'īyeh [Urumīyeh] Basin. Saline lake in lacustrine and alluvial plain watered by mountain streams. Intensive agriculture of standard crop range plus cotton, rice and tobacco.

3 *c*. Aras valley. Irrigated cash crops, e.g. cotton and tobacco, with normal crop range. Nomadic sedenterization in a politically delicate frontier zone.

4. *Alburz and Tālish Highlands*. Marked climatic divide with high year-round precipitation on northern slopes and drier southern slopes,

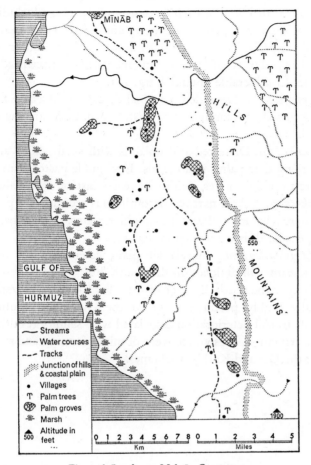

Fig. 146. Land use: Makrān Coast type.

with winter concentration of precipitation. Severe and prolonged winters in general with terrain controlled diversity of micro-climates. Moisture surplus diminishes from north-west to south-east. Degraded forest soils. Mixed cultivation in valleys grain on medium altitude benches and scrub forest grazing to upper limits of steppe. Southern piedmont watered by highland streams with agriculture dominated by needs of Tehrān, fig. 143. Less nomadic pastoralism than in Zagros.

5. *Caspian coastlands.* Humid sub-tropical climate most pluvious in central region. Range of terrain from coastal lagoons through lacustrine levels and outwash plains to Alburz foothills. Densely but discontinuously populated. Diversity of cultivation from commercial

plantations to smallholdings with extensive crop range including rice, cotton, tea, sugar-cane, citrus, mulberry and tobacco, fig. 144.

6. *Türkmen plain.* Löss steppe with nomad sedenterization well advanced. Large farms of recent settlement with specialized cotton cultivation. Considerable potential, fig. 145.

7. *Zagros foothills.* Degraded marginal forest on dissected hill-lands thinly populated and dominated by pastoralism. Low carrying capacity rangeland.

8. *Makrān hills.* Dissected arid uplands with small valley and well-oases carrying date palms and cereals. Low-grade pastoralism in poor scrub forest on high ridges. Aridity increases eastwards to Balūchistān.

9. *Makrān coast.* Arid narrow discontinuous sedimentary plain with oases watered by intermittent mountain streams. Mīnāb basin with highly specialized date production, fig. 146.

10. *Khūzistān lowlands.* Alluvial silt plain watered by five large permanent streams, ill-drained in the south but potentially of great productivity in the north. Prosperous base for Elamite civilization, and periodically highly productive up to the eighteenth century A.D. Vulnerable to soil deterioration associated with salinity resulting from inefficient irrigation. Present recovery of mixed farming and sugar cane based on the Diz and Karkheh schemes.

CHAPTER 19

WATER USE IN NORTH-EAST IRAN

A Persian proverb claims that "everything is alive by water"[1] and in Iran, particularly to the south of the Alburz mountains, water is indeed the most precious of commodities. A common complaint among all concerned with agriculture and the land is the shortage and limitation of water supply. With more water there could be more food, and the area of fertility extended, even into present sandy and stony desert.

In this essay it is proposed to examine in some detail conditions of water supply and irrigation in one small area of Iran—the rural zone surrounding Mashhad. Here, there are three types of water supply— from wells, and from qanāts and direct from rivers and streams. By this somewhat closer study of actual methods and practices it is hoped to throw light on conditions in a region which in many ways can be held to be characteristic of Iran generally. Comprising fairly extensive lowland and piedmont expanses, the area impinges on what could be described as desert margins and also includes a number of upland or mountain ridges. In fig. 147 the three principal sources of water

Supply by

QANĀTS	WELLS	RIVERS
Kāshif	Qalāt-i-ʿAlī	Murghānān
Qāsimābād	Bīd-i-Bīd	(irrigation)
Naṣrabābād	Qalāt-i-Shaikhha	Gulistān
Murdakishān	(irrigation)	(irrigation)
Hājjīābād	Tel-i-Gird	
Chahār Burjeh	Mahdīābād	
Naushahr	Khīābān	
Bīldār	(part only)	
Dehnau		
Shahr-i-Hashak		
Pīānī		
Āb-i-Shūr		
Khīābān (part only)		
Gulistān (domestic)		
Qalāt-i-Shaikhha (domestic)		
Murghānān (domestic)		

[1] Based on the Qur'ān xxi, 31: "We made everything from water."

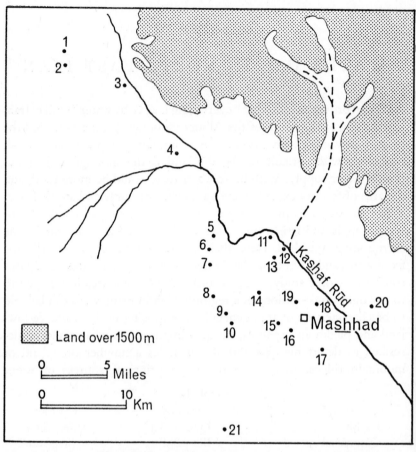

Fig. 147. Location of the settlements mentioned. 1, Qalāt-i-Shaikhha; 2, Bīd-i-Bīd; 3, Qalāt-i-'Alī; 4, Kāshif; 5, Shahr-i-Hashak; 6, Piānī; 7, Dehnau; 8, Bīldār; 9, Naushahr; 10, Gulistān; 11, Chahār Burjeh; 12, Murdakishān; 13, Hāj'jābād; 14, Qāsimābād; 15, Naṣrabābād; 16, Maḥdīābād; 17, Khiābān; 18, Tel-i-Gird; 19, Āb-i-Shūr; 20, Murghānān; 21, Khānrūd.

supply can be categorized by village as above. This short survey is hence intended as a simple case-study illustrative of the broad aspects of water-use within Iran. The area actually involved is shown in fig. 147.

It should of course be remarked that the assignment to a particular category, as in the above list, is in no sense totally absolute. Drinking water tends very largely to be obtained so far as possible from qanāts, since these tend often to provide water that is least contaminated, and quantities will therefore be carried quite a distance. Moreover, as will be observed from the list above, some villages use more than one means of supply. The most unusual and, in a way, most impressive form of irrigation is perhaps from the qanāt (see lower part of fig. 18, p. 71)—a construction which fascinated *inter alia* the authors of *Blind White Fish in Persia*. The exact method of locating an area to dig the starting or "mother" well can sometimes at least appear to be a guarded secret, but in the area investigated villagers showed no reticence in revealing how the construction of qanāt was carried out. The fullest explanation of qanāt construction was obtained at Bīldār, where the village was built at the exit point of the underground tunnel, the "mazhar-e-qanāt".

In the example now quoted—from Bīldār—the first well was dug to a depth of 80 m, when a source of water was tapped. Then at a distance of approximately 100 m lower down the slope away from the first shaft a second well was dug and once these two basic sources for ventilation by fresh air had been opened and lined with circular sun-dried supports of mud, then the first section of the underground connecting tunnel could be dug between the two vertical shafts. This main tunnel slopes very gently downwards so as to allow free flow of water—an essential for proper functioning of the qanāt. This process was repeated each time until the tunnel was completed, but as the vertical air shafts became shallower then the horizontal distance between them was reduced, from 100 m to about 30 m. These vertical shafts are necessary to provide both fresh air and later access for the qanāt builders and repairers. The point where the qanāt emerges at the surface is called the "mazhar-e-qanāt" and it is from this point onwards into the plain that a settlement often grows up. Villages can however also make use of a qanāt which passes beneath. An example of this is at Marghānān where the qanāt is located below the south-west corner of the settlement. South of the village itself there is a steep descent to reach the qanāt. A shaft with fifty to sixty steps reaches down to the qanāt and at the bottom an enlarged space provides room for three or four women to wash clothes, dishes or themselves.

The qanāt systems serving the two villages of Bīldār and Pīānī, have been mapped by the Department of Irrigation in Mashhad, with further information regarding source and use of the water. At the village of Bīldār, the qanāt water is led first into a reservoir by the side of the village and then into the irrigation ditches where its flow is controlled by a foreman who regulates supply according to the needs of the various fields and crops. The bulk of the water is supplied from a spring underground, and the foreman in charge at Bīldār stated that there was much seasonal fluctuation, with a considerable reduction in the supply during the dry period of summer and autumn: hence the need for a storage device in the form of a reservoir, in order to even out supplies from the qanāt. At the time when Bīldār was visited by the writer there was an abundant supply of water—so much so that the foreman was attempting to find another village which might buy water from Bīldār. Eventually an arrangement was arrived at with Pīānī, where the qanāt is considerably less constant in its supply of water. Here the foreman in charge claimed that it was essential only for gardens to be kept watered, but not the remainder of the land; therefore, if there was not sufficient water available from the qanāt the inhabitants of Pīānī would either reduce their area of cropland, or buy water if it happened to be available from elsewhere. In fact, the previous year they had been able to buy excess water from Bīldār at the rate of 300 tomans for 24 hours' supply measured along the main connecting channel. The qanāt at Pīānī is looked after by the villagers themselves, whereas at Bīldār it is tended and repaired by an expert employed by the Holy Shrine of Mashhad.

An example of a somewhat more elaborate method of controlling and organizing the water supply from a qanāt system occurs at Kāshif. Here the landlord actively endeavours to make the optimum use of the available water supply, by careful regulation of supply and mode of exploitation. The villagers of Kāshif irrigate the whole 134 hectares which are under cultivation in a rotation of 16 days, so that for irrigation purposes the watered area is divided into 16 areas/days. The qanāt which supplies the water to the village extends some 6 km from the north-west and is again owned by the Holy Shrine; but since the whole farm area is rented from the Holy Shrine the qanāt system is also included in the agreement. Flow of water in the qanāt is fairly constant throughout the year but it is only in summer that day and night irrigation is carried on: this means that during the spring evenings it is necessary to store the water in a special reservoir or tank which has been built by the present landlord. Prior to the construction of this tank the water was allowed to flow away unchecked, often causing considerable surface erosion. The tank itself (fig. 148) has an area of 400 sq. m and the flow of water is arranged as shown in the diagram, so that it can either be admitted directly to the main irrigation channels, or diverted into the storage tank. By this means the effectiveness of the qanāt has been greatly increased.

The qanāt system at Kāshif, although belonging legally to the land-lord is nevertheless maintained by the Holy Shrine, and as in the case of Bīldār, specialists from the local villages are employed directly by the Holy Shrine to clear the qanāts and keep them in good repair. This means that the farmers themselves in the village give little or no concern to the maintenance of the qanāts. The landlord, on the other hand, is in frequent, even daily touch with the Holy Shrine so that the qanāts can be kept in good repair. Sharing out of the water is actually arranged and controlled by the foreman. The landlord at Kāshif held the opinion

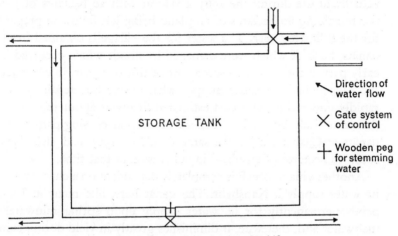

Fig. 148. Detail of irrigation scheme at Kāshif.

that irrigation of wheat and sugar-beet entails a much greater loss through evaporation since the area exposed is much greater than in the trench-type irrigation used for melon plots. When the supply of water is very limited, irrigation can thus be much less effective for wheat and sugar-beet than for melons and other trench-watered crops.

The qanāt irrigation systems at Bīldār and Kāshif could be held to be generally characteristic of conditions elsewhere in the region, and probably for Iran as a whole. However, it is interesting to note certain minor differences and variations occurring in other villages of the Mashhad region, and these must now be mentioned.

Murdakishān village has a single yet very good and well-kept qanāt as its only source of regular water supply. All the cultivated land belonging to the village can be watered by qanāt, and the crops are usually watered once in every 12 days as compared with once per 16 days at

Kāshif. The foreman at Murdakishān believed that for the first two months, that is during the period of initial germination the sugar-beet needs no water at all and it is only subsequent to this that it receives a regular supply one day in twelve. This practice of leaving the beet for two months without water is clearly very much a matter of individual decision since in other areas some watering of the crop is practised.

At Chahār Burjeh, the next village to Murdakishān, only 100 hectares of total 180 hectares of cultivated land are watered each year. Analysis of these figures shows that 80 hectares of cropland were actually in use during the 1963–4 season with 20 hectares of garden, the remaining 80 hectares of cropland being left fallow in preparation for the following year. The water for the village is obtained from two qanāts, both of which were damaged by floods which occurred in the early part of the year. For some part of this one year, in consequence, the village had no water supply whatsoever, but repair work was rapidly undertaken, at a cost estimated finally as about 50,000 tomans (borne entirely by the landowner). As well as causing damage to the qanāts at Chahār Burjeh the same floods of 1963 had also damaged some 50 hectares of cropland in cultivation at that time.

Another village which is completely dependent on a qanāt system for its water supply is Nanshahr. The qanāt here, like many in Iran, depends permanently for its water supply upon spring rainwater and meltwater and, therefore, it diminishes greatly in yield during summer when the need is greatest. The actual date when irrigation commences depends to a great extent upon the amount of rain that has fallen during the winter and spring months. Obviously the more rain that falls in spring the longer it is possible to delay the actual irrigation, and the available water supply may therefore last throughout the growing season. When irrigation is started then it is practised normally once every 16 days, as in Kāshif. Unfortunately the mother well of the qanāt has now reached hard bedrock, which means that it is useless to dig any deeper. Hence there has developed a definite and recurring shortage of water making this particular village especially vulnerable during cycles of drought.

In the earlier reference to Pīānī, the necessity of having to buy water was mentioned; and another village which has a similar water problem is Shahr-i-Hashak. This village has one qanāt providing its water supply and since the amount available is small in relation to demand it is necessary to purchase water from outside. One area from which water could be obtained is Naushahr, which however has its own problems of supply as well. An arrangement gives the landowner at Shahr-i-Hashak the possibility of having a 24 hr supply of water for limited periods from Naushahr but this clearly reflects personal interest and financial strength of the landowner concerned. In Shahr-i-Hashak it was hoped to construct a deep well in order to obviate the awkward (and expensive) arrangement with Naushahr. Surveys by water engineers have established that whilst it will be possible to construct a well in the village with water at 70 m depth the shaft will need to be another 30 m deep in order to tap an assured and uncontaminated supply of water. Construction of such a well will obviously prove extremely costly, and the economics of the project are still further complicated by the fact of land reform. The best answer to the situation would undoubtedly be for governmental action to sink the well, with later and gradual amortization of part, or whole of the cost by those likely to benefit. Possibly a single landlord might also feel able to undertake the entire cost if he were sure of continuing as sole owner. On the other hand, a group of newly invested peasant owners might well find joint action much more difficult, not only as a personal matter with their neighbours, but also in that the burden of a heavy extra capital investment could be too great in the initial stages of exploitation.

Two more brief studies should confirm the fact that it is very difficult to generalize on matters of irrigation, since marked differences can be found within very small areas. Gulistān is one of the larger villages of the Mashhad area, and it receives its water supply from three qanāts and also from a river. Because the villagers can use river water without legal restriction there have occurred several acrimonious discussions as to the exact sharing out of the supply, since up-stream users tend to ignore those lower down. In contrast to use of surface water, the qanāt water is shared equally and in a well-organized manner. The Irrigation Department in Mashhad has complete records of the qanāt systems and the amount of water flowing in each, hence the supply to each individual can be allocated closely according to the amount of land which each has, and it is measured in hours of supply. This basically ensures that fair dealing occurs and eliminates many of the difficulties involved in the use of surface streams.

Finally in this outline of the qanāt system of irrigation, the village of Āb-i-Shūr shows yet another pattern of water use. Here the qanāt extends over 60 km, but, instead of flowing through earth-lined tunnels, metal pipes have recently been used as an experiment, ensuring more safety in times of heavy rain. At Āb-i-Shūr the method of allocation of water is by basing the unit of supply on the number of pairs of cows owned by each individual—a total of forty-two animals in all.

The second major method of irrigation in this area around Mashhad is by obtaining water from deep wells. This method of supply is considered to be so far under-utilized; and with the newer mechanized methods of construction and the use of motor pumps, there is much thought among landowners, foremen and some peasant farmers about the possibilities of constructing wells and the comparative costs of keeping them working constantly. Several of these deep wells already

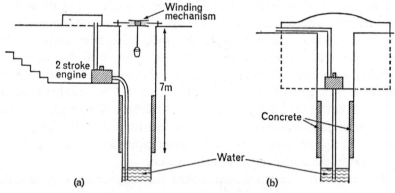

Fig. 149. The pumped well at Qalāt-i-'Alī.

exist around Mashhad and the methods employed in their actual construction may now be considered (fig. 149).

At Qalāt-i-'Alī a deep well was previously dug to a depth of 12 m, although water had been found at 7 m. At the start of construction a small two-stroke petrol-driven pump was first installed on a little platform by the side of the well some 3 m below the surface in order to drain water as quickly as possible. Further digging of the well-shaft was aided by a hand hoist located on planks above the mouth of the well, by which rock waste could be extracted. Seven men were employed on the digging of the well, at a wage of four tomans per day. For a height of about 2 m just above the water level, the sides of the well were supported by concrete: this was necessary because clay topsoil became sandier and more friable with depth and therefore increasingly liable to subsidence. On completion a more powerful engine was installed as a permanent fixture.

At Bīd-i-Bīd a landowner constructed two deep wells during the period 1959–63. From these all the area of land under crops at Bīd-i-Bīd could be irrigated but, despite the innovation of power pumping, the traditional rotation of irrigation as used for hand-watered crops was still followed: first wheat, then potatoes, peas, beans and finally sugar-beet. The actual irrigation period of the various crops varies very slightly, the wheat being watered once every 15 days and the other crops once every 12 days. Prior to about 1957 the irrigated area was very small indeed, and yields were meagre. The arrival of an active landowner resulted, as has already been described, in the sinking of two large wells with mechanical pumps that have a total maximum capacity of 500 cu. m of water per hour. During the spring season the pumps are hardly needed, since rainfall is adequate for crop needs; but during the remaining eight months of the year the pumps run continuously. The costs of this watering system are of interest. One pump running on petrol consumes 400 litres of fuel per day at a total cost of approximately 1,000 rials; the other consumes 15 litres of diesel oil at a cost of 300 rials, but for a smaller output of water. Further items such as maintenance, depreciation and renewals of the plant when set against the value of the extra produce obtained make motor pump irrigation an uncertain and even marginal proposition in some areas—at least, in strictly economic terms. In human returns, however, the value of a greater supply of foodstuffs is far less debatable.

In an effort to minimize costs, the use of electrical power for irrigation pumps is becoming more widely used, since electricity can in certain localities prove cheaper than oil fuel. This is the case of Tel-i-Gird, where a well has been sunk to a depth of 80 m and a German-made electrical pump is installed. As a result, a market-gardening area has grown up in the village, with outlets in Mashhad.

A somewhat more complex water scheme serves five major villages, namely Khiābān, Shafi', Gārijangān, Kadarbāgh and Sakhtamān. The water for these five villages comes from Chashmak Gīlās by *jūb* (open ditch) extending about 80 km to the north-east, and sixteen men have the task of maintaining the canal and its supplies. Some two thirds of the original volume led from Chashmak Gīlās are lost by evaporation and by use for flour milling. The system costs in maintenance alone some 15,000 tomans each year. Each one of these villages takes an appropriate share of water that comes from Chashmak Gīlās, calculated, as has been described above, on the pair of cows as a basic unit—one pair of cows confers the right to use one *juft* of water. Khīābān with its 20 pairs of cows thus takes 20 *jufts* daily, within a fixed and allotted period. Khīābān village covers a relatively large area lying near to the sources of the water in the Chashmak Gīlās and is crossed by several qanāts and jūbs, some of which do not directly supply Khīābān itself. Land in the immediate vicinity of these qanāts and jūbs cannot be cultivated, otherwise there would be little or no water available for the other four villages. These latter, however, are required to pay a sum calculated as the equivalent yield from the unused land in Khīābān based on an area some 20 m deep on each side of the jūb or qanāt.

Within the last ten years, the improvements due to a progressive landlord have resulted in the sinking of four deep wells in the area of the five villages. Altogether, surveys have indicated that another ten wells could be dug, but uncertainties over land reform have curtailed further developments for the present. To dig a well of the required depth of 9 or 10 m has taken about three years, and cost 120,000 tomans. From this well about 7 hectares of land can be watered for an expenditure of about 350 tomans per day in oil fuel. The situation in Khīābān and its neighbours highlights the general problem that arises because of growing unreliability of flow by qanāt partly due to the greater human use (as population increases), partly to greater use upstream for agriculture to the detriment of areas lower down, and partly due to fluctuation in rainfall. But capital cost is an insuperable obstacle to the smallholder, especially as he may be struggling to establish himself as the new owner, with inexperience in marketing, and no capital to fall back on in bad seasons. Co-operation at village level, in the absence of such previous tradition, is not at first easy; and thus the gap ought to be filled by governmental action. But here the absence of trained personnel is a limiting factor even granted the desire on the part of central authority to undertake the provision of wells and the framework of financial and technical support that are necessary.

The remaining major source of irrigation water not so far mentioned is that from rivers and streams. As can be imagined, water supply from surface flow is often more unreliable than that obtained through qanāts since the flow of water down many Iranian rivers tends to be highly erratic and very seasonal. One village which obtains some of its water supply from a river has already been mentioned; Gulistān makes use of both qanāts and the river, the one supplementing the other. The most detailed example, however, could be held to be Murghānān, where water for irrigation is brought direct from the Kā<u>sh</u>if Rūd, which lies at a short distance to the south of the village, whilst the drinking water and water for washing are obtained from a qanāt which flows under the village. The water is diverted along a channel, when needed, by means of a small mud dam across the river, until it reaches a concrete device. Here canals lead off to two villages, Mur<u>gh</u>ānān with a population of about 175, and Sanābīs with 6,000 inhabitants. Allocation is on a basis of one seventh to the former village, and six sevenths to Sanābīs. As far as Mur<u>gh</u>ānān is concerned this means that water is in relatively ample supply with little or none of the careful system of allocation that is normal for Iran. Small concrete constructions on the inflow channels prevent constant flow from the river, and also retain excess flow on the fields, as a kind of basin. Floodwater can be retained or blocked off from the fields to a limited extent; but the great difficulty is always spring flooding. Until land reform both Mur<u>gh</u>ānān and Kā<u>sh</u>if, which is irrigated totally by qanāt, were owned by one landlord, whose opinion was that there could be relatively little to choose between the yields and cost of the two irrigation systems. This is unusual in that access to relatively abundant free-flowing water usable for agriculture is not widespread in Iran. Skill in using the water, even when available and abundant, is highly important. At one village, Bīd-i-Bīd, already discussed, it was held that wheat ought to be irrigated even in spring, since at this season it is late in maturity and has a deep root system. Sugar-beet however is less developed at this season, and as we have noted above, can rely to a greater extent on the limited seasonal rainfall—hence it needs irrigation in quantity later in the year only. These are relatively commonplace matters, but they illustrate the point that in Iran, agricultural practice has adapted itself very closely to prevailing natural conditions and is slow to change from established routines. Alteration or augmentation in the sources of water supply will not automatically, therefore, always necessarily produce an increased agricultural yield: some degree of education and change in techniques will be a necessary concomitant. The effects of land reform on capitalization of improvements such as deep wells must also be studied. Conditions in Iran are complex and not immediately susceptible to rapid alteration. Improvement and reform are highly necessary—vital—but their achievement will not be a simple or straightforward matter.

As in West Pakistan, a key to future development lies in the provision of deep wells. Cost will however remain a highly important factor, and actual use of the water when obtained will also be a critical matter. Nothing so far has been said regarding soil salinity, but one major penalty in this part of the world that attaches to misuse of available water is the probability of increased salinity. Consequently a partnership is necessary: on the one hand governmental activity providing both wells and the training in the new methods to make effective use of them. On the other, there is implied enlightened appreciation by the local populations of the need for co-operative exploitation of water resources and the development of an intelligent, enlightened pattern of husbandry to match the expanded supply.

CHAPTER 20

PASTORALISM, NOMADISM AND THE SOCIAL ANTHROPOLOGY OF IRAN

As a modern state, Iran exerts unitary governmental and political control within its boundaries. Yet practically all nation states throughout the world contain, either relatively easily or else with difficulty, certain disparate elements which refuse wholly to conform to the wishes of the central government, however constituted, and which choose for some purposes to be in control of their own affairs and in charge of their own destinies. In this respect, Iran is no exception.

Because of aridity and the rugged nature of the terrain, Iran, despite its large size, is discontinuously occupied and utilized by its people. This in itself might well be expected to produce a certain particularism: it is difficult to imagine close bonds existing between Balūchī tribesmen in the south-east and Turkish speaking groups of cultivators in the north-west for instance, separated as they are by vast and comparatively empty areas. Both groups occupy niches within one body politic, but linguistically as well as in more general cultural terms, they show considerable differences. Again, for some purposes there could be said to be a great social chasm dividing the nomadic tribesmen of Fārs and the sophisticated urbanites of Tehrān. The oil installation workers on the Persian Gulf are far removed socially from the peasantry of the central Iranian plateau; there exists between them a substantial technological and ideological gap which is difficult to bridge.

Yet, within the country, there also exists a certain social mobility which, though its advent might possibly be dated to the arrival of Islam in the seventh century A.D., increases in volume and accelerates with the passing years. Such mobility poses problems of varying kinds: those arising from the difficulties of nomads who become sedentary, of peasants who become urbanites, and of peasants who give up their traditional agricultural activities in favour of newly available employment requiring industrial, technological skills. All these conceivably culminate in the supremely testing process of imposing the will of the central government on each of these, and also other, diverse elements. This is the Iran of today; a land which shares with so many others a rapid sequence of social changes and which hence has to cope with the passing of traditional society (or at least with large segments of it), and with the creation of a new society, now imbued with ideas that partly incorporate the old, but are sometimes desirous of renouncing the past altogether.

Social change, seemingly in order to secure social advance, has moreover to be undertaken in a land of considerable geographical difficulty. For instance, it has been estimated that some five eighths of the country are quite uncultivable, that one eighth is cultivable and that the remainder consists of forests and pastures. Because of aridity over much of the Iranian plateau proper, most of the cultivation in the country depends on obtaining water from the high areas, either in rivers flowing from them or else in *qanāts* (= wells). These devices are of course widespread, and fundamental in the Middle East,[1] and Marx[2] wrote of the Asiatic type of society as one which had an agricultural economy based on small units of production with at the same time a centralized state and bureaucracy whose power rested upon its regulation of water supplies. He wrote of the prime necessity of an economical and common use of water. Weber[3] also shows the crucial importance of irrigation in western Asia, and there are frequent references to the irrigation civilizations and "hydraulic" societies of the Asian continent. In much of Iran it is clearly evident that organized group activity is required in order to secure an adequate water supply, usually from qanāts, which are frequently capable of supporting an entire village community. Such qanāts require a great deal of maintenance, and access to them is obtained through vertical shafts which occur at variously spaced intervals. Some qanāts are very long, extending for many tens of miles and the water table may be reached at a point several hundred feet below the surface.

On many of the arid plateau areas of Iran, qanāts often constitute the unique means whereby community life is rendered possible, since surface water is frequently absent or inadequate, and deep wells often provide only brackish or highly saline water. One may therefore with some cogency argue that water supply is the primary factor in site location for villages, and settlements of this form are usual in much of

---

[1] G. B. Cressey, "Qanats, Karez, and Foggaras", *Geogr. Rev.* vol. XLVIII (1958), pp. 27–44.

[2] K. Marx, "The British Rule in India", *New York Daily Tribune*, 25 June 1853. Quoted in T. B. Bottomore, *Sociology* (Allen and Unwin; London, 1962), p. 118.

[3] M. Weber, *General Economic History* (English translation, 1950), pp. 321–2. Quoted in T. B. Bottomore, *op. cit.* (1962), p. 118.

the country, each separated more or less distantly from other villages according to the quantity of water in the ground which may be tapped by the one village without adversely affecting the supply of the others. Of course, other factors such as defensibility, ease of access, salubriousness, and the like may also be important, but, in most instances, water availability is singularly crucial and overrides other considerations.

The rural community is a small social unit, living within a defined area and drawing its livelihood from working this territory in a more or less closed economy. This community, with its social, economic, and at times legal organization and its system of ethical values, forms a whole capable of ensuring the continuity of the group, and the sustenance, both material and moral, of its members. Arensberg defines communities as "structural units allowing of organization and of cultural and social transmission".[1] Again, Rioux, referring particularly to rural groups writes "The term community implies a given territorial area, a very large number of personal relationships and contacts among the members of the group, and homogeneity of interest and culture".[2]

The tempo of peasant life is generally slow. "Although many rural communities have become conscious of the speeding up of history in our time, residual structures, whether ecological or mental continue to hinder their evolution."[3] The bond of co-residence, the bond of locality, is strong in such communities, though it is not the only organizational principle. Other factors include the role of the family system, and particularly of agnatic kin, though extensive agnatic descent groups are not often found and some stress is placed on social relations with matrilineal and affinal kin. Also important are personal friendships, non-family sub-units of the rural community, and various principles governing the organization of local authority and the group's relationship with larger socio-cultural systems. Non-family sub-units of the rural community tend to subdivide the community further, but they are also complementary forms of solidarity against centrifugal forces. Unchecked they could lead to a fundamental division of the community into antagonistic groups, whose conflicting interests

[1] C. M. Arensberg, "The Community Study Method", *Am. J. Sociol.* vol. LX, no. 2 (1954), p. 109.
[2] M. Rioux, *Description de la culture de l'Ile Verte* (Ottowa: Minis. of Northern Affairs and Nat. Resour., 1954). Nat. Mus. of Canada. Bull. no. 133. Anthrop. Ser. no. 55.
[3] I. Chiva, "Rural Communities. Problems, Methods and Types of Research", *Reports and Papers in the Social Sciences* (UNESCO, no. 10, 1958), p. 15.

might be irreconcilable, thus making an ordered social life difficult if not impossible. Such divisions may become very important during and after a transition from a fairly self-sufficient economy to marked involvement in a money exchange economy. The inequality of wealth developed in the new profit economy is reflected in the formation of antagonistic socio-economic groups, amounting to real and distinctive social classes at village level. In this way, the community structure is impaired, institutions are modified and social life becomes more or less sectionalized.

One example of a local community is Tezerjān (Tizirjān; Tezerjūn), located in the high mountain areas south-west of Yazd and known to the writer as a result of a period of two months of field investigation carried out there. For some purposes at least it will serve to exemplify certain features characteristic of Iranian villages generally. In Tezerjān, as in much of Iran, water availability is the great limiting factor in any increase or intensification of agricultural activity. This has of course been said of many parts of the country, as for instance by Spooner[1] of the area around Jājarm. As in so many regions of Iran, land is plentiful and only the water required for irrigation is in unfortunately short supply. The ownership and control of water resources is therefore of great social significance. In Tezerjān water diversion channels are found throughout the area occupied by the village. Those which lead directly from the streams draining the contiguous high mountain slopes are simple open ditches; whilst the longer channels leading water to more distant cultivated areas, and frequently going underground in the process, are of necessity much more elaborately constructed and often stone-lined. Their construction must have required much labour and commensurate organization; the utilization of the water they bear also requires social co-ordination. Though locally termed qanāts they in no way resemble the qanāts described as typical of much of the Iranian plateau since they tap surface water rather than underground sources. The irrigation system in Tezerjān is entirely gravitational, and no water raising devices are constructed by the villagers.

In much of Iran, rights to water and to land are held conjointly, but in this respect Tezerjān is exceptional for, as Lambton writes, "In the Yazd area . . . ownership of land and water is separate".[2] In Tezerjān water is owned by a few wealthy men who may not necessarily have

---

[1] B. J. Spooner, Unpublished manuscript, 1963, p. 16.
[2] A. K. S. Lambton, *Landlord and Peasant in Persia* (Oxford, 1953), p. 220.

caused the qanāts to be built. Water is supplied in rotation to the various cultivated plots, the needs of fruit trees (a lasting source of income for a number of years) often taking precedence over the shorter-term needs of wheat and similar crops. Again, water is allocated according to its total availability; that is, the cycle of rotation varies as more or less water becomes available. Discrepancies between supply and demand can and do cause conflict, and satisfactory means of water allocation are an essential requirement for social harmony. Usually when a rotational change is necessary, the village men congregate in the presence of the headman together with, at need, a gendarme who may have to be imported from elsewhere for the purpose. The likely needs of each person are considered, and after much debate detailed rotations are agreed upon, in theory at least by mutual consent. This method appears to be satisfactory whenever water is fairly adequate in quantity. In times of scarcity however agreement is very difficult to attain, and social conflict is much in evidence. Nowadays the outside authority of the gendarmerie is available to assist in resolving difficulties. Inevitably in dry periods only a minority of gardens can be adequately watered, and others must lie untilled with their owners possibly unable to grow anything like an adequate supply of foodstuffs. For a peasant owner this is naturally an extremely serious matter; and in theory the situation is alleviated by the unwritten agreement that all those able to have an allocation of water and so to cultivate should give part of their produce to their less fortunate neighbours who may be kinsmen or friends. The extent to which this is practised is unknown, but it is probably an ideal rather than a totally practical solution of the difficulty. There appears to be little recognition in Tezerjān and elsewhere of extended kin groups, among whose members aid of this kind might be distributed. Thus, many people, who in recent years have experienced agricultural difficulty owing to inadequate water supply have tended to leave villages like Tezerjān. One informant said "If there is no water, there are no tree crops and no wheat, the people have nothing to eat and they go away".

Social mobility of this kind becomes progressively more feasible as internal national security and economic opportunities increase. Tenant farmers who may need to leave because of natural disasters such as drought are sometimes transferred to their landlords' other properties, possibly in distant parts of Iran. This is usually arranged for highly valued, reliable tenants, who may be transferred either alone for a period of time, or else accompanied by their families. However, the main exodus is urban-orientated and periods of water scarcity serve to reinforce such a movement of people who are in any case attracted by the enhanced economic and social opportunities of city life. Movements of this kind may be sporadic and unsystematized although the departure of a few individuals who successfully adapt themselves to city conditions may well induce others to follow them. Consequently throughout Iran the urban population may expand rapidly, to some extent as a result of natural increase but largely also because of this exodus from the villages by individuals who have experienced social difficulties and economic distress. These latter migrate partly as the result of geographical realities and partly because of social limitations in village life. Once in the urban centres the immigrants, of necessity, look for new work, and in Yazd many who once lived in the surrounding villages are employed in cloth-making factories. If unable to find employment in the nearest city, villagers will migrate farther afield particularly to the Persian Gulf area and to Tehrān.

In some parts of Iran, including the Yazd region, water shortage has been marked for a decade and has caused much social difficulty. The mutual trust and interdependence which facilitates social activity is in large part eroded and there is less respect than there was formerly for authority, wherever vested, since the person with authority has much to do with water allocation which obviously can never be undertaken to the satisfaction of the whole community in times of water scarcity. During periods of more adequate water supply it is simpler for villagers to concur in the decisions taken with regard to the water allocation cycles. When water is scarce, while individuals may publicly agree to abide by the decisions taken, privately they may take matters into their own hands. Thus some individuals may divert the water illicitly at night onto their own plots, and tenants may be required to sleep in the open near the qanāts in order to secure their landlords' water supply. Much of this nocturnal activity is publicly denied by villagers. It would appear that in Tezerjān, as must surely be the case in so many Iranian villages, the circumstances contingent upon a shortage of water have provoked, in this field of action, a system of double values among the villagers.

A social group may be defined as being a distinct unit such that those outside it can appreciate that it is a unit and those inside it feel themselves to be members of it, interacting with others inside it more than with individuals outside it and having common values and common systems and standards of conduct.[1] If such criteria are applied to the behaviour of villagers when faced with a shortage of water it is found that in some fields of action they no longer act as members of a group, but as if the standards of the group did not exist. Those who remain in the village do not interact with one another as frequently, since they have come to doubt whether the others hold the same values as themselves, while the people who have left the village have, of course, ceased to interact at all. The majority of the former have some economic resources which reinforce their wish to remain in the village with their kin and friends but for the latter, economic necessity has overruled their ties of affection and caused them to leave, thereby further weakening the structure which they have left behind. In fact it can be argued that natural calamities such as drought are able markedly to undermine social solidarity at village level. Other factors tend to bring about the same result and will be considered later.

Very many Iranian villages are small and a large number contain fewer than a hundred inhabitants. These usually live in a cluster of houses built of one basic material, sun-baked mud, though in styles which vary regionally within the country. The houses, often grouped around a small open area or square referred to as a "maidān", are small, and usually consist of one or two rooms, possibly with an additional kitchen-alcove and with a small yard surrounded by a high mud wall. The furnishings in such dwellings are few and generally consist of bedding, cooking, and eating utensils, a lamp, some baskets, a container for glowing charcoal, and a tin trunk containing specially prized items. These houses may occasionally and of necessity also be utilized by livestock. Although Iranian villages are very dependent on cultivation, livestock is also important. The animals most frequently found are goats, sheep, chickens, and a few cows, together with donkeys for transport. Most households own a few animals which may be grazed near the house on untilled land or else in herds collectively looked after by a number of small boys on the surrounding uncultivated areas. Animal products are altogether a useful supplementaty economic asset. Tenants may care for animals on behalf of their landlord, the two individuals sharing the produce under a variety of agreements.[2]

A house is normally occupied by a monogamous family. In Tezerjān,

[1] W. J. H. Sprott, *Human Groups* (Penguin Books; London, 1958), pp. 11 *et seq.*
[2] A. K. S. Lambton, *op. cit.* p. 351.

617

dwelling units can be classed as belonging to one of two categories. Inside the larger gardens, where much of the cultivated land is found, the dwelling unit is a single large house. The other type of dwelling unit appears to be a cluster of small houses having some walls in common. Their gardens are usually minute and untilled. These houses belong to the landowners and the peasants respectively—to the townsmen of Yazd and to villagers. So it is that a certain cleavage in Iranian society is visible here at village level, if only, in the present context, in terms of dwellings. The social dichotomy noted as existing in this village is widespread in Iranian villages generally but is accentuated here by the fact that the landlord element is large, since the Yazd middle classes live in Tezerjān and other high altitude villages nearby for much of the hotter part of the year in order to escape from the dreadful heat in Yazd itself. A winter-time population of some 2,000 or so expands to approximately 7,000 in the summer months. The social consequences of such an influx to the village, though not witnessed by the author, must be considerable.

In order to cope with these people the means of transport, buses and cars (taxis), increase enormously in number, both within the village and on the Tezerjān–Yazd route. The Tezerjān–Yazd telephone line is much used, a newspaper appears for sale, radios and privately owned cars are found. There is constant coming and going both within the village and from it to other villages and to Yazd. The population increase causes a more than equivalent increase in the number and variety of services available in the village, fostered and accentuated by the greater needs and demands of the summer-time residents compared with an equal number of villagers. Of eighty-five shops open in summer, only fourteen remain open in winter. Doctors appear in summer, so do gendarmes. The kadkhudā (see p. 628) spends the summer in Tezerjān, the winter in Yazd. No effort is spared in the attempt to re-create in the village the middle-class pattern of life of the town. But once this outside stimulus to all manner of social activity is removed, which happens in the non-summer months, very little corporate activity continues among the villagers. During winter the village group is acephalous, and non-corporate in function.

Villagers' diet consists essentially of bread, *māst* (buttermilk or yoghourt), and tea, with occasional rice, eggs, meat, and fruits. Despite its organizational simplicity the village as a unit is by no means isolated. Thus, economically speaking, there are certain commodities which villagers need to buy, usually in towns, and this requires the use of cash and systematized economic relationships. Although it may be true to say that little cash is used by a village family (which is fairly obviously so since the total annual income of a household is variously estimated as £40–£120, including the value of the share of the crops that the peasant consumes himself), nonetheless the monetary economic system is well established here. Money does not however act as a medium of exchange for all purposes, and this markedly cuts down the number of impersonal transactions since barter or exchange rest mostly on personal relationships. The cash which is available is used to acquire essentials such as articles of clothing, utensils and various foodstuffs, especially tea and sugar. Much of this money is spent in towns; consequently the economic ties of villages and towns are frequently of much greater importance than those of villages with one another.

In parts of Iran, as in the high mountains south-west of Yazd for example, the villages are not compact and nucleated but straggle along mountain streams whose water is used for irrigation (fig. 150). In this instance, streams radiate from the perennial snows of Kūh-i-Barf which is some 12,800 ft above sea-level. Along the flanks of the high gorges, long narrow areas of inhabited and cultivated land occur. These generally become wider and more extensive downstream, but become progressively desiccated at lower altitudes, eventually passing into unkempt land. In order to maintain and to extend the fairly level areas available for cultivation, particularly by gravitational irrigation, a considerable amount of time and effort are expended by groups of men in repairing and constructing retaining-walls for the cultivated plots of land. This results in the creation of terraces whose dry stone retaining-walls may be as much as twenty feet high. Soil and animal manure are then transported in panniers on donkeys' backs to these plots. In recent years fewer individuals or groups seem prepared to exert themselves strenuously in order to maintain these terraces, and as a result many terraces have ruined retaining-walls, with the plots of land quite derelict so that the water cannot be used to full advantage on them. Plots of land tend to be small, numerous, and irregularly shaped and some have high mud walls built around them. Beyond the area of cultivated land, which also contains the sporadically distributed houses, there is a periphery of marginal land which may be cultivated in years of extraordinarily plentiful water supply. However, most of the land contiguous with the cultivated areas consists of bare rocky slopes. Few, if

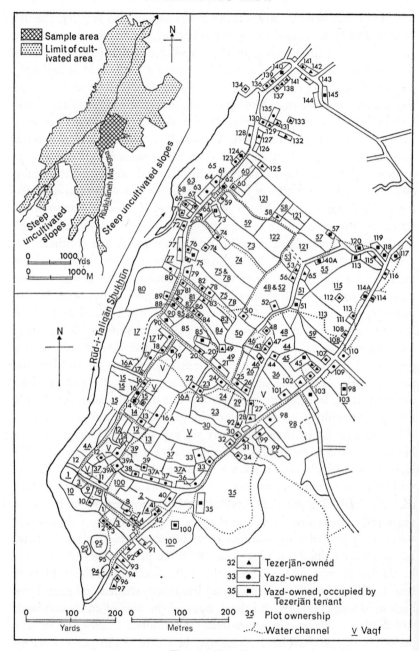

Fig. 150. Tezerjān.

any of the houses are located outside the area of cultivation, so that even a straggling village such as Tezerjān has a certain compactness in the context of its setting within a large-scale wilderness.

The main source of livelihood in Iranian villages is in the growing of cereals, particularly wheat, and the labour involved in cereal growing constitutes the main task of the peasants. This work is organized in an unending cycle of ploughing, sowing, and harvesting, with, in many areas outside Āzarbāïjān and the adjacent west-Caspian provinces, irrigation. Ploughs of many kinds, though usually the wooden nail plough, are used in Iran though in some parts of the country, as in the villages in the vicinity of Yazd, all the cultivation is by long-handled spades and no ploughs are used, even in the 1960s. The simplicity of the agricultural implements used requires considerable human effort in order to get adequate returns from the land. It seems strange that technological innovations in agriculture should not have been introduced to many villages such as Tezerjān, especially as the wealthier inhabitants of Yazd are often widely travelled both in Iran and to a lesser extent abroad. They are acquainted with fairly wide social horizons and with the social and technological advances going on in so much of the country. As a group they constitute the landlords of these villages, and in order to increase efficiency and to obtain better yields and greater income, they could introduce technological innovations which were in their view both appealing and even necessary. The reasons underlying present attitudes might well be examined: labour is very cheap, but the price of innovation, especially if technological, is by comparison high; and innovation, which must disrupt the present satisfactory social situation (at least as far as the landlords are concerned), is considered cautiously. The landlord–peasant relationship in Iran has a considerable antiquity, and is not discarded easily or spontaneously.

Of the cultivated land in Tezerjān, very little does not contain fruit trees, either planted on the plots or along their margins. The fruit trees include apples, pears, cherries, mulberries, walnuts, apricots and plums. Wheat, the most important crop, is usually grown on comparatively treeless terraces. Wherever the trees are abundant, the ground crops more usually comprise potatoes and turnips. Poplars, grown for their timber, are very frequently found near any adequate water supply.

Both here and in many other Persian villages fruit, in particular, is grown for marketing. On the other hand, commercial considerations seem to be of lesser importance with regard to the other crops grown.

The cultivation process undertaken by the peasants is more or less regularly supervised by the landlords, and this supervision may be done personally during periodic visits throughout the year or else by agents. In recent years, government-sponsored and -organized land reform has been in progress in many parts of Iran. Yet, certainly until recently —and even today—the land cultivated by the peasants in much of the country is owned by landlords who allocate their property piecemeal among the tenants for this purpose.

Lambton has shown that the landownership system in Iran is to be understood both in terms of historical development as well as of geographical conditions. For many centuries landowners have held much of the land, from which, to varying extents, they obtained the produce as well as the taxes from the peasants who cultivated for them. Lambton demonstrates the fixity and rigidity inherent in such a system since the greater the taxation, the more dependent on the landowners the poor peasants become, and hence the more tied to the land. A dichotomy in the social situation was therefore clearly established many centuries ago. Recently, the S̲h̲āh has attempted to break up many of these large land holdings and to ensure that parcels of land are handed over to peasant owners. However, in Tezerjān as well as in many other villages in the country, the traditional system still operates. The S̲h̲āh writes[1] that approximatately one half of the arable land of Iran is owned by private landlords, many of whom may possess from two or three to a dozen villages, and some may even own more.

In Tezerjān, of 191 individually owned properties in a sample part of the village, 117 (61·3 per cent) were owned by non-villagers, mostly from the Yazd middle class, while the remaining 74 (38·7 per cent) were owned by the peasants. Moreover the best-quality arable land is mostly owned by absentee landlords. This is understandable since although some landlords simply utilize their property as summer residences, many of them aim to cultivate for profit, with or without hired help, so as to supplement their town incomes. This type of ownership, as Lambton points out,[2] is frequently found in villages located near towns, as in Tezerjān, where the village land is not held by a single proprietor but is divided among a large number of owners, each of whom controls a small share of the total. These owners may cultivate their own land, but usually the cultivation is done by tenants who,

---

[1] Mohammad Reza S̲h̲āh Pahlavī, *Mission for My Country* (Hutchinson; London, 1960).
[2] A. K. S. Lambton, *op cit.* p. 281.

since they own comparatively little of the village land, must obtain much of their income from tenancy as such. Sometimes these tenants own some land, and also supplement their incomes by crafts or else by casual labour as it becomes available. As regards Tezerjān, this is most likely during the summer.

Thus for both landlord and peasant, the land as such constitutes only a part of his total resources, though it is of very different relative importance for the two. For an owner in Yazd, even if his market-garden produce is considerable in absolute terms, it constitutes but a small fraction of his total income, and crop failure will be hardly more than an inconvenience. For the peasant, the land is much more relevantly the main source of income and a bad year may cause privation or starvation, and to such an extent as to induce the man to move. As social mobility is now quite feasible, much use is made of this possibility.

We have noted that the present nature of the tenancy system is to be understood partly in terms of the historical development of the system and partly in terms of the environment in which it operates. Maximizing the areas on well-built terraces simultaneously maximizes efficiency. However, in the absence of any significant mechanization, this situation requires control of a large labour force in order to function efficiently. Without such a labour force, efficiency is obviously greatly reduced, just as it is on small terraces built and worked by a few peasant-labourers. Control over large-scale water resources is likewise advantageous.

For these reasons Lambton writes "The natural conditions under which agriculture is caried out would seem on the whole to favour large landed proprietorship",[1] involving of course both landlord and peasant. The landlord's control over his property and over the peasants who cultivate the land for him is complete, and the latter have little actual responsibility beyond doing exactly as the landlord directs and wishes. It would appear that the disintegration of this long-established landlord–peasant relationship must lead to social and economic difficulty, whether or not it be justifiable on grounds of social equity.

Whether the land in one village is owned by a single landlord or by a number may make very little difference to the lot of the peasants, except that, given harsh usage by one of them, the peasants might find a choice of masters something of an advantage. Frequently, the land allotted to a single family is very limited but this is in some areas

[1] *Ibid.* p. 280.

slightly outweighed by the communal use of draught animals and of equipment such as ploughs. In any event, in view of the simple and crude agricultural techniques practised, there is a pronounced limit to the area of land with which any one family can in fact cope.

There is in Iran a widespread practice of considering the necessities of agricultural production under five headings, namely, land, water, seed, oxen or other animals, and labour; and of allotting or sharing the crop yield according to the supplier of each of the five items listed. Thus, for instance, a landlord providing land, water, and seed and a peasant providing oxen and labour would share the crops in the ratio of $3:2$. Quite evidently the poorer peasants who were in a position of only being able to provide their own labour might receive merely one fifth of the total produce and so remain abysmally poor. Such poverty is so marked that in some parts of the country the peasants receive allocations of grain in advance from their landlords, so that a system of permanent indebtedness exists, tying the peasants firmly to the land in order to fulfil their obligations. In traditional society it must have been extraordinarily difficult for any peasant to divorce himself from such an economic situation. The diversification of the Iranian economy with the multitude of alternative forms of employment that it contains, together with the land reform programme, should serve to ameliorate the lot of the peasants in this unenviable position.

Actual crop sharing of this kind, though widespread in Iran, is not found, for instance, in the Yazd region. As with so many social phenomena in Iran it is difficult to generalize for the country as a whole. In Tezerjān, the tenant is, as it were, employed and is paid a wage for his labour roughly according to the number of days of work which he has completed, with the entire produce going to the owner. Few, even extra-conscientious tenants will do any more than those things strictly required by the landlord. Wages are not high, at least if one may judge by living standards. Again some specialist agricultural work might be done by particularly skilled men called in for the purpose and paid accordingly.

Besides cash, the tenant may receive additional payment as perquisites. He may, for example, be allowed to use part of the landlord's house in winter; he may receive gifts of clothing and perhaps other gifts as on the occasion of the birth of a child. Moreover, at the discretion of the landlord, the tenant may be given a share of the crops grown, particularly fruit, over and above the quantities laid down in any

contractual agreement. Then there may well be more intangible rewards for services rendered; even today in Iran some administration is
conducted in terms of personal connexions and influence, and a powerful landlord may well be able to procure benefits for his tenants which,
without his interest in them, they could never hope to achieve. A "good"
landlord may therefore be a patron and protector of his tenants and
disposed to assist them on occasions of difficulty. Thus in years of crop
failure, the landlord may present the tenant with sufficient means to
tide him over until the following year. Tenants are therefore, in times
of difficulty especially, rather better placed than the small owners who
cultivate their land themselves. They are far more secure and it is not
difficult to understand why in fact "The vast majority of the peasant
population in Persia is...composed not of peasant proprietors, who
are a small minority, but of crop sharing peasants or tenants and 'landless' labourers".[1] Yet it should be noted that some areas are in this
respect atypical. Moreover, everywhere in Iran changes are taking place
in traditional village organization, changes which seem likely to
accelerate in the coming years.

Landlordism in Iran is often equated with a feudal system. It has,
as an institution, a considerable antiquity, but in Iran no landed
aristocracy transmitting land from one generation to the next has ever
emerged. This may be due in part to the inevitable fragmentation of the
estates according to Islamic demands which state that when a man who
owns land dies, his estates are divided among his sons. This is virtually
obligatory. Again dynastic changes with accompanying instability and
warfare have effected the same end of breaking up large estates by
alienation and appropriation. In fact many large landholdings today
only date back to the nineteenth century. Land is therefore frequently
regarded as a source of direct gain to be profitably utilized and not as
property involving in its utilization various moral obligations and a
definite way of life. This is especially true in the case of landowners who
are primarily concerned with some other economic activity such as
trading, and for whom landowning may be of subsidiary importance.

In Iran, landholding became in relatively recent times a means of
investment of wealth with associations of social prestige and political
power attached. In terms of prestige, landholding still ranks high, even
though the monetary return from other forms of investment is now
probably much higher. It is a fact that certainly until a short time ago

[1] A. K. S. Lambton, *op. cit.* p. 295.

the larger the area of land owned by an individual, irrespective of its quality, the greater was his social prestige likely to be. Examples of important landowning families are to be found in Bīrjand, Gīlān, and Fārs. The importance attached to the areal extent of land owned may at least partly explain the reluctance on the part of certain landlords to allow the fragmentation or alienation of their estates under the terms of the land reform policy. Alternative status symbols are as yet not totally accepted. This factor complicates the situation to a greater extent than do the financial consequences of the land reform programme.

The major landowning families, often called "The Thousand Families", intermarry a good deal, but they are by no means all reactionary and opposed to political, economic and social reform. Many have foreign educated members (chiefly, but not always, sons) who become progressively more important in economic planning and in government generally. That is, they contain members who are far from totally dedicated to preserving the status quo.

Their large landed estates are, of course, cared for by tenants who may have had a long enduring tenancy relationship with a landlord for much if not all of their lifetimes, as their respective forefathers might also have had. Yet the enduring quality of the relationship does not seem to alter its fundamental characteristics, namely formality and, for the tenant, social restraint. There is no development of the relationship in personal terms. The two classes are separated by what in some respects could be termed a social chasm bridged effectively only by their depersonalized economic relationship and by religious affinities in so far as these may now be held to be important. One, possibly extreme view is stated as "in no sense is there a spirit of co-operation or a feeling of being engaged in a mutual enterprise".[1] The roles played by individuals of both classes are quite characteristic.

There are factors which foster a certain social restraint and which mitigate any incipient harshness in the landlord's attitude towards his peasant tenants. Too severe a treatment of the tenants would be nonsensical; a certain humanitarianism based partly on Islamic principles fosters some concern for the welfare of the tenants. Thus, although the living standard of the tenants is by any assessment low, they are very rarely destitute.

Traditionally, tenants would have accepted this social situation as immutable. Nowadays the acceptance tends to be more and more

[1] A. K. S. Lambton, *op. cit.* p. 263.

partial. Whilst fully aware that his material condition could be worse, the peasant is also quite aware that it could be better, even in tenancy. There would hence appear to be a mounting dissatisfaction with the conditions of tenancy. Western and urban influences have affected the landlords far more intensively than the peasant tenants, and this process has further widened the gap between the two classes. The same ultimately western-inspired innovations in the Iranian economy have also presented the peasants with perfectly realizable alternatives to the traditional way of life. The former fatalistic acceptance of social reality is no longer as firmly entrenched as it used to be: there is now a more or less felt and expressed wish to improve matters affecting the individual's circumstances. Even a fairly well provided for tenant may be critical of his landlord's disdainful attitude towards him, and he may be progressively more inclined to emulate fellow villagers who have escaped from the traditional local social organization in which landlordism is such an important element by moving to a town or city. A number of peasants, possibly only a minority, hope that the land reform programme, closely identified with a paternalistic monarch, might soon be implemented in their villages, seeing in this eventuality the panacea for all social and personal ills. This hope may be illusory since small-scale ownership of the land cultivated may well prove to be a far less efficient means of utilizing that resource than the present system provides. Yet in the opinion of some, the programme provides the solution to current social and economic difficulty at the local level, and many peasants remain in the villages awaiting its fulfilment.

Full-scale traditionally organized landlordism appears therefore to be becoming a thing of the past in Iran, and the peasants hope to gain by the amelioration and modification of the system. Those at present dissatisfied with the nature of or the rate of change evade the unsatisfactory social situation of tenancy in villages and move to other, urban communities where social life is ordered along different principles. Nonetheless, despite the rapid rate of population growth in Iranian towns and cities, largely due to immigration, the tenant cultivator at present still constitutes a very considerable segment of Iranian society, and the process of effectively integrating this element into the conditions of the modern world is both far from complete, and fraught with difficulty. The passing of traditional society is inevitably only slowly achieved.

Landlords are not usually very active in village life, and as a rule they are absentees, at any rate for a significant part of the year. Hence, on a personal level temporary absence could contribute to a formality and even chasm in social relations when landlords were in fact present. The estates are usually administered on their behalf by employees, referred to as agents, bailiffs, headmen, or kadkhudā. The kadkhudā is a man in the difficult position of representing the landlord and, to a lesser degree, of presenting the views of the peasants to the landlord, and again, particularly in more recent years, of representing the authority of the central government in the village. Thus, in his person, the kadkhudā might unofficially represent the local organized community, the village, to a bigger "outside" social world of landlords and ultimately the agencies of the central government of the country; but far more effectively he embodies supra-village authority at village level. In some of the larger villages, governmental authority may be delegated to one or two gendarmes, or an advisory official who is concerned, for instance, with matters such as public health, and there may also be a village schoolmaster. All this may be interpreted as the means of progressively integrating the local village community into the widely ramifying network of associations within the state of Iran.

In the first instance disputes at village level may be settled, if at all possible, by the older members of the families directly concerned. Should this fail an approach is made either to the headman or, in his absence, his deputy, the medical assistant, or the mullā, with the request that the individual concerned might attempt to settle the dispute. Villagers prefer to settle their disputes among themselves, and only if the internal village mechanisms fail are the gendarmerie called in from the nearest place where they are permanently to be found, in the case of Tezerjān, from a village located some fifteen miles distant, or else from Yazd. The gendarme enforces the law; and since his authority ultimately derives from the Iranian government and because his decisions are final, he can settle quarrels and arbitrate in quasi-legal disputes. Apart from periodic visits for purposes of this kind, he has little direct contact with village affairs, unless during a more prolonged period of residence in summer. However, other than in water disputes which do not occur with any frequency or intensity except in abnormally dry periods, the gendarmerie is not normally required. The village, in Iran, has its own mechanisms for effecting social control: it is usually in this respect both self-regulating and autonomous.

Should the presence of the gendarme be required, he is usually summoned by the kad<u>kh</u>udā or his depty. The position and role of the kad<u>kh</u>udā is defined in a law of December 1935 which is given in outline by Lambton.[1] The kad<u>kh</u>udā of a village is appointed by the landlords who own most of the particular village and there is no provision for allowing villagers to express their preference in this matter. This man's prerequisites are as follows: "Persian nationality, a clean record, a reputation for honest dealing, trustworthiness and capability, residence in one of the villages in the area over which he is to be appointed, and that he should carry out some cultivation in the area."[2] In addition to representing the landowners he is "responsible for the execution of laws and regulations referred to him by the government". More particularly he is to "oversee agricultural affairs in accordance with the orders of the landowners. He can decide minor cases in the villages involving up to fifty rials. He is to prevent disputes breaking out among the people: if and when they break out he must settle them, as far as possible, by conciliation." His primary function is to serve the purposes of the landowner and to protect his interests, and he could hardly be described as the official representative of the people as a collective unit.

From the villager's viewpoint, the principal role of the kad<u>kh</u>udā is to conduct the necessary relations, on his behalf, with the authorities of the "outside" world. The kad<u>kh</u>udā will speak for a villager, the more fluently perhaps if given a financial inducement, and main topics tend to be water disputes, serious crimes or recruitment for military service.

In Iran all young men aged from eighteen to thirty years must in theory conclude two years of full-time military service. However, individuals may delay performing this necessary period of service if domestic situations require it. Men may be excused from year to year by the recruiting personnel provided that the reasons given by the men are sufficiently cogent. The presentation of the case to the recruiting staff on behalf of a young man may be made by an aged father or some such relative personally or else by the kad<u>kh</u>udā. The effectiveness of the appeal may again be reinforced by monetary inducements.

Thus the gendarme, the kad<u>kh</u>udā, and his deputy all have formal legal authority and yet they are not community leaders in the sense of having much power in the daily life of the villagers, partly since they may only periodically reside in the village and partly because the

[1] A. K. S. Lambton, *op. cit.* p. 190.   [2] *Ibid.* p. 190.

formal legal authority which they do represent is alien to the internal structure of the village society.

It may well be therefore that the place of the "village leader" is filled by some other figure, who may have no formal legal authority vested in him. In Tezerjān the medical assistant provided such a leader. His higher status was partly derived from the nature of his work and partly from the fact that both as a medical man and as a person in his own right he was well known to, and respected by, virtually everyone in the community. By village standards he lives well and has a number of well-appointed houses, and he also happens to be a descendant of the Prophet, as his green turban clearly indicates. He is a devout Muslim, literate, and intelligent. This man in a multitude of roles wields great influence in village affairs of all kinds; and his authority, when invoked, was particularly efficacious in settling serious disputes, one of which occurred in the village during the period of field work spent there.

Traditionally in many Iranian villages, some social life clusters around the communal bath, though as for example in the Dasht-i-Mughān villages along the Aras river this is not always found. Again tea houses, though renowned, are only found in villages located along major routeways and they cater mainly for travellers. Family events—weddings, births, deaths, and the like—are of great importance. These are accompanied by traditional ceremonies and group activities, which have survived from past times. Social organization in the villages is such that the major patterns of personal relations are defined in terms of co-residence and kinship.

The typical household, living in a single dwelling, is the nuclear family with an occasional addition such as an aged parent or an unmarried sibling. There is a great intricacy of kinship interconnexions in Tezerjān, with many related individuals living close together in the village. Yet kinship relationships need not lead to a proliferation of actual social interactions among kin. Kinship serves to identify, and possibly to reassure, the individual. It places the individual in the community and the community embraces the individual, defined in kinship terms, within itself, and also partially rejects and excludes others undefinable in such terms. It is probably true to say that the greater the number of kin which an individual has, the more difficult will it be for him to divorce himself from them, either within the village or else by moving to the comparatively depersonalized world lying outside the village. Those in the village who are not much related to other villagers are partially prepared by this situation for the comparatively kinship-less society of towns and cities. By their moving out, the remainder of the villagers are progressively more interrelated and might be said to exhibit a certain organic unity.

Islam of course permits polygyny, but Salim writing of ech-Chibayish in Iraq (the subject of a detailed study that might also be held to be representative of conditions in much of Iran) states that of 118 men, "85 of them (72 per cent) were monogamous and the rest, 33 (28 per cent), were polygamous".[1] In Tezerjān no such high frequency of polygamous marriages is found. Only three men had two wives and no man had a greater number. In certain Dasht-i-Mughān villages, of thirty-four married men, thirty-one were reported to be monogamous and three men had two wives each. In Iranian villages virtually every adult is married (with the exception of the mentally defective), usually at the age of 15–19 years for females and during the early twenties for men. Divorce, though fairly rare, does occur. Most marriages are arranged, and occur within the village itself. The marriage ceremonies in a Persian village are described by Najafi and Hinckley.[2] No significance seems to be attached to widely ramifying kinship-based relationships. There are no unilineal descent groups and few preferential marriages within the terms of the kinship system. This may not of course be universally true and it is difficult here, as in so many other respects, to generalize regarding Iranian village life.

Barth (1953) has reported that in some groups in southern (Iraqi) Kurdistān, cousin marriage may attain a frequency of 57 per cent; family endogamy 71 per cent and village endogamy 80 per cent. The two former figures are quite unrepresentative of a village like Tezerjān, and no figures even approaching those quoted are to be found there. The village endogamy rate does however appear to be of a similarly high order. Again in southern Kurdistān, the preferred spouse is unequivocally the father's brother's daughter and considerable social effort and pressure makes this marriage a frequent form. Again, no high cousin marriage rate is universally found in Iranian villages. In Dasht-i-Mughān, for example, Op't Land[3] reports that of forty recorded

---

[1] S. M. Salim, *Marsh Dwellers of the Euphrates Delta* (Univ. of London Press, 1962), p. 57.
[2] N. Najafi and H. Hinckley, *Reveille for a Persian Village* (Gollancz; 3rd imp.,1960), pp.82–8.
[3] C. A. Op't Land, *The Permanent Settlements of the Dachte Moghan Area. Problems around the Sedentarization of Pastoralists* (Paper no. 5. Inst. for Social Studies and Research, Univ. of Tehrān, 1961), p. 21.

marriages only four were between blood relatives. Two were of a man with his father's brother's daughter, one of a man with his mother's sister's daughter, and the other of a man and his mother's father's brother's daughter. That is, there is a very low parallel cousin marriage rate. There were five cases of village endogamy and also nine marriages with women of the same ṭā'ifeh, all of which might be expected in these communities composed of newly sedentarized nomads. Moreover, there were five marriages with women from the regional market place.

Iranian villages are defined by a high degree of particularism and group consciousness, although there is an observable tendency towards intra-village marriage related possibly to greater ease of communication and better transport facilities which foster all manner of involvements in wider relationship networks.

Participation in the beliefs and practices of formal religion, generally a sect of Islam, is highly valued in the villages, although precise knowledge of the actual content of the faith is both limited and un-sophisticated, and all manner of extra-orthodox accretions effect con-siderable regional variation. Moreover, in the villages there are usually present religious personages termed Sayyid, Ḥājjī, Karbalā'ī and Mashhadī. The former is, or claims to be a descendant of the Prophet and demonstrates the fact by wearing a green turban; the others have, in order, performed pilgrimages to Mecca, Karbala and Mashhad.

" The peasants continue to consider their village as an entity pecu-liarly their own. This point of view is derived from a strong set of personal sentiments interwoven with the feeling that the village affords the best guarantee of security, although this security is not necessarily based primarily on economic factors but on the allegiance of person to person. The close bonds of kin . . . establish a fabric wherein the individual at all times is certain of some form of aid and assistance."[1]

In the present decade especially, sincere attempts have been made by the government to reform much of the social, political, and econo-mic structure of the country. One of the major means of effecting such changes—giving over possession of land to the peasants and share-croppers—directly affects a very numerous section of the population. As we have seen, this policy has been implemented largely as a result of mounting pressure within the country. Owing to great regional varia-

[1] A. H. Fuller, *Buarij. Portrait of a Lebanese Village* (Harvard Middle East Monograph Series, 1961), p. 97.

tions in the tenurial system, generalization is difficult, but there appears to have been little security of tenure in the past either for the landlords or, therefore, for the peasants. Many estates were looked after by agents selected by the landowners and these agents were very exacting in their demands on the peasantry who had no institutionalized means of resisting their excessive demands. Peasants were traditionally very ignorant both of agricultural techniques and of land management beyond the traditional framework, and neither they nor the agents could be effective factors in introducing agricultural reforms and increasing efficiency. Iranian peasant villages are variously estimated to number from 40,000 to 60,000, the lower figure probably being the more realistic. Yet more than half the cultivated land was owned by a minute fraction of the population—landlords, the Crown, the State, religious foundations and the like. The peasants themselves probably owned only some 10 per cent of the cultivated land.

The land reform programme put into effect in this decade could be held to be the culmination of demands for such action from the early years of this century, partly stimulated by European precepts among the politically active intellectuals. Little change in this respect was effected under Rezā Shāh though some land was allocated to peasants in Āzarbāījān and Sīstān for instance, and the crown acquired additional estates. After the Second World War while many landowners were opposed to land reform, some of the more progressive, western-trained intellectuals, mainly non-landowning, advocated it. Eventually the Land Reform Law in its first form was implemented in 1962–3 and, in certain parts of the country, this confirmed the peasant in the ownership of land which he had previously share-cropped or upon which he had laboured. Moreover, water traditionally used for certain areas of land was to be transferred to the new (peasant) landowner. Both the maximal and the minimal area of land to be owned by one individual were fixed, and large-scale accumulation of landholdings by individuals were thereby disallowed, as was excessive fragmentation among heirs on the death of the owner. In those areas of the country unaffected by the land transference the contractual relationship of landlord and sharecropper was legally defined. The sharecropper was given security of tenure and the landowner required, by legal sanctions, to carry out his obligations to the village community, as in the provision of an adequate water supply. A greater share of the produce was everywhere guaranteed to sharecroppers. The original 1962 law, however, was to affect some 8,000 villages only. A pilot scheme at Marāgheh in Āzar-bāijān proved very successful and partly led to changes in the law later promulgated in 1963. Landlords were permitted to lease, sell, or divide their land and so bring their holding below the maximal landholding limits prescribed for different parts of the country. Over 33,000 villages were to be affected by this later legislation, frequently referred to as Phase Two.

This was, in turn, amended in 1964, somewhat to the advantage of the landowners. Thus, large estates were allowed under certain con-ditions, as when a man reclaimed for agricultural use land which had hitherto been unutilized for this purpose, and so, presumably intending to introduce modern farming techniques. With this exception, maxi-mum limits of landholding were again stipulated.

Originally, the land reform programme aimed at breaking the social and the political power of the landowning class by removing the economic foundation of that power. This clear-cut intention was some-what obscured by modifications of the reform developments. The modifications were partly the result of active opposition to reform by landowners, religious groups, and students, particularly in Tehrān. Yet, by and large, the reforms were successfully applied, due partly to the support of the Shāh, devoted government personnel, the use of mass media to popularize the intention, and the success which the new peasant owners achieved in the good agricultural season of 1963–4. In most cases the condition of the peasants has been much improved by this programme of reform and the peasant groups have been more effectively drawn into wider social relationships than ever before, since they now have to order their own dealings with governmental and financial agencies rather than leave such matters in the hands of the landlord's agent. The programme of reform has already achieved much in rural Iran, most of the changes being seemingly for the better.

PASTORAL SOCIETY

The peasants of Iran, cultivating small patches of land and living usually in compact villages constitute some three quarters of the country's population. But in the absence of readily available and constant water supplies at fixed places on much of the central plateau, there is little possibility of sedentary life over great expanses of it and the alternative human response therefore on parts of this plateau is pastoralism. A certain form of pastoral exploitation is found associated with villages since the village sheep and goats in particular are grazed on the forage available in an extensive area surrounding the villages, usually cared for by the young boys. However, this is of subsidiary importance to the predominant interest in cultivation, though it is of some economic significance.

The extensive form of the pastoral adaptation is virtually always practised by tribally organized groups, often nomadic. Sub-tribes are often referred to as *ṭāʾifeh*, *tīreh*, *dasteh*, and so on. Tribal leaders are frequently styled K̲h̲āns, and sub-tribe leaders as Kalāntars. Other terms, such as Beg, for instance, are also used. The romantic connotations of the nomadic life coupled with the practical difficulty of maintaining political control over nomads within the nation state have together combined to focus much attention upon nomads in Iran just as in other parts of the Middle East. Of a total Iranian population of some twenty millions, the tribal groups are estimated to number from one to two millions. Some tribally organized groups are sedentary, as in many parts of Kurdistān; other groups remain nomadic or semi-nomadic continuing a way of life in some respects little changed from that of their forebears.

They are of much greater significance within Iran than their numbers alone might suggest since they constitute well-organized and disciplined, economic, social, and even political units within the state, and for certain vital purposes hold themselves aloof from the activity of the central political authority to which they are all in theory subject.

The major tribal groups of Kurds (fig. 151) numbering somewhat fewer than one million people in Iran, are located mainly in the Zagros Mountains. Although the majority of them are now sedentary, they still appear to be well organized on a tribal basis. They have compatriots in both Iraq and Turkey but the Kurdish nationalist movement which is powerful, especially in Iraq, does not flourish to anything like the same extent in Iran.[1] They are linguistically distinct and the majority of Kurds, unlike most Iranians, are Sunnī by religion. Leach[2] and Barth[3] provide more detailed analyses of Kurdish tribes, though both worked among Iraqi groups.

[1] D. Kinnane, *The Kurds and Kurdistan*. Inst. of Race Relations. London (Oxford, 1964).
[2] E. R. Leach, *Social and Economic Organization of the Rowanduz Kurds* (Univ. of London Press, 1940).
[3] F. Barth, "Principles of Social Organization in Southern Kurdistan", *Univ. Etnografiske Mus. Bull.* no. 7 (Oslo, 1953).

Fig. 151. Approximate distribution of major tribal groups in Iran.

South of the Kurds and speaking dialects closely related to Kurdish, are the Lur and Ba<u>kh</u>tiārī peoples. All three languages basically resemble Persian itself. The Lur and Ba<u>kh</u>tiārī together number some 500,000 individuals. Tribal organization still exists and the Ba<u>kh</u>tiārī continue to migrate to and from their summer areas near Iṣfahān and their winter quarters in <u>Kh</u>ūzistān.

In the province of Fārs one finds the Turkish speaking Qa<u>shgh</u>ai, as well as the various tribes of the <u>Kh</u>amseh Confederation who speak a variety of languages including Persian, Turkish, and Arabic. These two major tribal groups have frequently been rivals and enemies and have both, on occasion (as have the other tribes mentioned), had serious encounters with the state authorities, culminating in physical violence, even in the present decade.

Arabic-speaking tribes are found in <u>Kh</u>ūzistān, and the oil industry has done much to sedentarize these nomads, having attracted them away from the traditional pursuits of nomadic pastoralists. The Turkish-speaking Afshārs live in Kirmān province, while Balūchī tribes, mainly Sunnī, live in south-east Iran. Again some Hazāra and the Brāhūīs are found along the eastern frontier of the country. In Khurāsān, the once feared Türkmen are now very largely settled. Kurds are also settled here, having been sent to the area by Shāh 'Abbās in the early seventeenth century as part of his policy of mixing the distinctive elements of the population of his realm, and for the strategic reason of establishing march wardens on the Khurāsān frontier. The pastoral Shāh Savan tribe is located in Āzarbāījān.

It would therefore appear that some of the tribes in Iran are nowadays sedentary and, as such, they constitute more manageable entities as far as the central government's authority is concerned. At least they are static and therefore may be more systematically found and dealt with than are the nomadic tribes proper. The tribes in Fārs, namely the Qashghai and Khamseh, may be taken as representative of the latter type; the others live a life little differentiated in many respects from that of sedentary villagers.

Barth has described[1] the response of the nomads in Fārs to ecological conditions. It is clear that conditions favourable for the pastoral adaptation are only found periodically in parts of the total territory occupied during a year by the tribes. Thus the high areas of the Zagros which have long severe winters are at that time uninhabited by tribesfolk, who utilize the winter grazing areas in lower lands to the south which, in turn, are fiercely scorched and arid during the long summer season. Thus the tribal territory would appear to be large but it should be remembered that only part of it is occupied by the tribe at any one period. The migratory routes are followed annually so that the most advantageous conditions for the animals are achieved. Such routes lie alongside and through the lands of sedentary communities which have economic relationships with the tribes. These latter, though thereby economically integrated with other social units are nonetheless, politically, to a certain degree distinctive and autonomous.

Power held by the tribal leaders stems both from their tribal followers and also from the land which they own. Their land in the villages is cultivated by peasants who give dues to the Khāns, usually in the form of crops produced. Moreover, the Khān's wealth may be further

[1] F. Barth, "The Land Use Pattern of Migratory Tribes of South Persia", *Norsk Geogr. Tidsskr.* XVII (1959–60), pp. 1–11.

augmented by the collection of levies from tribesfolk. The relative importance of the dual income sources of the K̲h̲āns varies both spatially and temporally. Among the sedentary tribes the K̲h̲āns are hardly, if at all, distinguishable from the large-landed proprietors.

Among the nomads each tribe follows a customary, well defined route during its migration. Sub-groups of the tribe, termed *tīreh*, have the traditional right to pass through certain parts of the tribal area. This area is known in Fārs as the tribal *ravāl*. The rights to move in this way are usually customary and there are few precise grants or leases. Quite evidently, so long as the route lies through open, sparsely settled country, there are few difficulties, but where the route of migration approaches or passes through cultivated areas, then, unless there is very strict control of movements by the tribal leaders themselves, considerable damage may be inflicted to the crops of the sedentary population. There is therefore a vital, necessary interrelation of interests which links the nomadic and sedentary populations. Occasionally in the past, in times of weak state authority, the nomads could not be held at bay and they assaulted villagers with impunity. There can be little doubt that villages in many parts of Iran suffered on occasion as a result of tribal depredations. There is, for instance, full documentation by travellers from Europe of Türkmen depredations in K̲h̲urāsān. However, in many parts of Iran, violent actions of this kind were kept in check by other forms of more peaceful interrelationships between settled and nomadic groups, these principally taking the form of economic exchanges. Since the village community is not economically self-sufficient and since this is also true for the tribes, then the way is clear for a mutually advantageous economic link-up whereby pastoral produce may be exchanged for village commodities.

Nowadays the migration routes do not simply depend on customary procedures, because governmental agencies are also involved. For instance, when the Īlī (Arab) section of the K̲h̲amseh confederation migrates, the route is decided upon by the tribal leaders in consultation with local government authorities. Along this route each group and sub-group have their own recognized camps and pasturage areas, and their rights to these are traditionally founded. Should other tribes or groups impinge upon these rights then difficulties are sure to occur. Such infringement is likely to take place if many groups have to pass through a limited area in a short space of time. The time-tabling requires to be very exact or else several groups simultaneously require to use a single small area for pasturage whilst in transit. This situation can and does cause difficulty as in the Marv-i-Dasht area east of Shīrāz, as recorded by Barth.[1]

Where two hostile tribal groups such as the Qashghai and the Khamseh both require to use certain pastures at a particular time then much difficulty arises. This could occasionally be settled by parleying but has been more usually resolved by force of arms. More recently, government officials, supported by soldiers, assist in regulating migrations so as to minimize the possibility of conflicts of this kind. Such methods are probably successful in achieving the required purpose but, on the other hand, the tribes traditionally resent what they term governmental interference in their own affairs, as they conceive these to be, and violent reactions to such interference have repeatedly occurred, with much loss of life.

Lambton[2] has said that the tribal pastures in some parts of Iran, such as Fārs in particular, belong legally to tribal leaders in whose names they are registered. In other areas, such as Āzarbāījān, they are *Khāliseh*, that is, they are government controlled, and the government either levies a pasture due or else lets the pasture. Again, in other areas, the pastures are the property of settled groups who either lease them to the tribes for a lump sum or else levy pasture dues. Among the Qashghai, different sections and individuals of the tribe seem to have traditional rights to pasture lands owned by the Khāns. Such rights are neither registered nor absolute, though they are occasionally based on documentary evidence. The practice is for the Khāns to allot these pastures to their followers annually, and in fact a person is usually given the same pastures yearly. Even so, the formality of allotment is carried out every year, so that tribesmen cannot acquire undisputed title to land, and in order that the holder can be removed if he is insubordinate or otherwise difficult. It was formerly customary to exact payment when the pastures were re-allotted, but it is said that this practice has now been abandoned by the Qashghai.

Thus we find the traditional form of nomad organization in Fārs to be largely based on Khāns and Kalāntars who wield enormous authority within the tribe, partly because of their birthright and ensuing status as members of noble lineages, and partly because of their powers of allotting and of withdrawing rights to use pastures to and from

---

[1] F. Barth, *Nomads of South Persia* (Allen and Unwin; London, 1961), p. 5.
[2] A. K. S. Lambton, *op cit.* p. 284.

persons and sections of the tribes. Moreover, they fix the times and routes of migration and they represent the tribes in their external relations.

The social organization of these tribes has been described by Barth.[1] Individual tents are grouped in common herding units, with two to five tents to a unit. During some winter months these also constitute disparate camps. At all other times of the year several such groups form a common camp consisting usually of some thirty to sixty tents or some 200 to 400 individuals. These camps have a recognized leader, in some cases invested as sub-chief or Kadkhudā by the chief but, more usually, several camps are grouped administratively under one sub-chief. These sub-chiefs are directly responsible to the chief, who is assisted by a small number of specialized functionaries who are also herd owners. Among the Bāsirī with a total population expressed as 3,000 tents by Barth, there were thirty-two chiefs under a tribal chief. The highest echelon of the confederacy administration is not mobilized in the normal routine of seasonal migrations. Because of the universal acquaintance of the nomads with the details of the *īl rāh* and the place of each camping group in this scheme, as well as the universal recognition of the supreme authority of the chief, no more elaborate administrative hierarchy is necessary.

It has already been said that economic factors link the nomadic and sedentary groups together, and it is apposite to consider in more detail the interrelationships of these two elements in Iran, both in economic and political terms and also socially in the widest sense. There is no doubt that the towns and cities of Iran have a magnetic effect upon the rural populace in that annually they attract large numbers of people to themselves; whilst there is usually no balancing movement in the other direction. Again, the settled communities in villages along the migration routes of nomadic tribes have a certain facility for attracting nomads to their way of life. The attractiveness of village life is, from the nomad's point of view, partly voluntary and partly involuntary. In times of difficulty due to drought and epidemics, for instance, the pastoral adaptation is, as a way of life, less attractive and less secure than during most other periods. Given such conditions, the relatively more secure life in villages may become attractive to nomads. During periods of good rainfall there is little movement in the opposite direction since the necessary number of animals for sup-

---

[1] F. Barth (1959–60), *op. cit*. p. 10. See also: F. Barth (1961), *op. cit*.

porting a nomadic family cannot at once be accumulated. On the other hand, in times of harsh treatment by the central government amounting even to exploitation, it may be that the villagers are induced to leave their villages and endeavour to resume a nomadic existence and so minimize effective contact with the agencies of the government. This course of action is far from easy, since it is socially difficult for tribal units to integrate individuals who own few or no animals into their structure. Yet it does appear that despite this difficulty the nomadic and sedentary groups are not mutually exclusive, nor, as we have seen, can they really be so. A certain social mobility has enabled individuals and groups to change their mode of living and to move from one category to the other, although the principal movement has been from the nomadic to the settled communities. Moreover, owing to the difficulties in the relationships existing between the government and the nomadic tribes, this sedentarization movement has occasionally in the past been reinforced by government imposition and direction. It would therefore appear that the sedentarization of nomads, as an ideal solution to the nomadic, tribal "problem" frequently advocated by Iranian governments, may be explained in terms of factors inherent in the economic and social organization of nomadic society, coupled with government action to encourage or even to enforce such a solution.

In the twentieth century, the most dramatic attempt at enforced mass transition of this kind was instigated by Rezā Shāh (1925–41), but this was by no means the first attempt to sedentarize Iranian nomads. Rezā Shāh saw the tribes as a potential threat to the security of the settled majority in the country, and also considered that no integrated Iranian state was possible whilst the nomadic tribes literally formed states within the state. Again, the tribes were viewed as an anachronism in the modern Iran for which Rezā Shāh strove. He would not tolerate their remaining a law unto themselves, ruled by hereditary leaders and owing little but nominal allegiance to the central government of the country.

The impact of the West on Iran was both material and non-material, and in the early days of westernization these two elements were not clearly differentiated, as they were to be later with the growth of Iranian nationalism. During the Rezā Shāh period, emphasis was placed on adopting the technology and other material achievements of the West. The ideology that inspired the ambitious programme of material reforms was an intense nationalism, itself a product of the West.

"This nationalism was inspired by the example of cohesive, autarchic European states and fanned by the frustration of being coerced and exploited by those states."[1] Early manifestations of nationalism had been expressed in religious terms; those of the Rezā Shāh period were inspired by the concept of the omnipotent secular state. The earlier phase had also been more spontaneous but less productive of effects. As a result of this strongly aroused feeling of nationalism, Rezā Shāh was able to achieve a great deal and by firm autocratic, centralized control, many changes were implemented. This autocratic control was of extraordinary importance as a means of effecting the westernization of Iran. The regime glorified the past, there was much industrialization, there was active imitation of western society and a desire to become an important power. In the effort to achieve the Western-inspired goals, the loss of Iranian society's cultural traditions seemed a small price to pay and few, according to Banani, lamented the loss. Yet, later, during the Second World War, after Rezā Shāh's abdication, "the strain of hasty westernization upon the fabric of traditional society was held responsible for the state of flux and tension in Iran".[2]

In his pursuit of the ideals innate in westernizing and modernizing the country, Rezā Shāh dealt severely with the tribes. Many tribal leaders were either executed or imprisoned and the vitally essential migrations were either forbidden or else greatly curtailed, with consequent hardship brought about by the considerable loss of livestock. Tribal social life, dependent as it was on ordered migrations throughout the year, was generally disorganized, as Rezā Shāh intended. Again, whenever possible, numbers of tribesfolk were transferred in groups to areas distant from their tribal territory and many attempts were made forcibly to settle nomads in villages newly built for this purpose. This deliberate policy was pursued as a matter of considerable urgency as part of the process of creating the modern Iranian state—which was not to have approximately one ninth of its population consciously holding itself aloof from the remainder.

Despite the fact that Rezā Shāh's sedentarization policy had the support of the majority of non-tribal Persians, who thus took the opportunity to retaliate for past tribal depredations, the enforced settlement of tribesfolk in villages was an inadequate solution which left many outstanding problems. The policy was in fact instigated and

[1] A. Banani, *The Modernization of Iran, 1921–41* (Stanford Univ. Press, 1961), p. 146.
[2] *Ibid.* p. 151.

pursued with inadequate preparation. No detailed surveys of the possibilities and difficulties of sedentarization were attempted. Moreover, the general implications of destroying tribal economic systems were not objectively examined. Tribal groups which were forced to become sedentary were often settled in areas quite unsuitable for the required and necessary agricultural pursuits, and inadequate provision was made for health services, educational facilities, agricultural training, and the supplying of agricultural guidance and implements. Quite evidently the transition from pastoral to agricultural or from nomadic to sedentary life was fraught with difficulty.

According to Lambton, Rezā Shāh's tribal policy was "ill-conceived and badly executed"[1] and it led to great loss of livestock, the impoverishment of the nomadic tribes, and a marked reduction in their numbers. In national terms it might have been politically expedient, but it was economically disastrous. The environmental conditions found in Iran—the terrain, soils, climate, and water supply—are outlined elsewhere in this volume, and it would appear that in view of the ecological conditions existing in much of the country, the nomadic-pastoral way of life is an admirable human response over extensive areas, and that there can be in these parts no other equally satisfactory economic activity, and associated tribal social organization. In the absence of plentiful supplies of water for irrigation schemes, it is difficult to envisage alternative human response to these ecological conditions which would more satisfactorily allow the full utilization of natural resources and at the same time sustain the complex social life and well-being of large communities. Such considerations seem not to have affected Rezā Shāh's earlier tribal policies. However, as a result of these policies, the Iranian economy suffered. The all-important tribal sources of pastoral produce no longer functioned satisfactorily. The effects of this situation within the country became so critical that in the latter years of Rezā Shāh's reign, the policy was modified and limited tribal migrations were once more allowed. Nomadism, geographically a splendid adaptation to the conditions found in much of Iran but involving social and economic difficulties when viewed within the national context, was partially reinstated; and after the 1941 abdication, many more forcibly sedentarized tribal groups returned to the nomadic way of life which they seemingly valued and loved. Thus were restored the tribal entities that had been partly in abeyance for two decades; and

[1] A. K. S. Lambton, *op. cit.* p. 286.

41-2

they rapidly resumed their participation within the national economic system and, moreover, again showed their political distinctiveness by refusing to submit altogether to the authority of the Tehrān government. In fact, since 1941, there has been a tendency for certain tribal leaders to increase their power, to such a level that in at least some areas, the government has been obliged to reverse Rezā Shāh's policy and entrust public order and security to the tribal leaders.

Thus it would seem that despite Rezā Shāh's attempt to solve the tribal "problem", it nevertheless remains. More recent attempts directed to the same end, as implemented in parts of Āzarbāījān for instance, try to effect sedentarization by the provision of water for cultivation on a large scale, and by providing technological assistance. to effect sedentarization by the provision of water for cultivation on a large scale, and by providing technological assistance.

Sedentarization of a sizeable population was the main objective of the Dasht-i-Mughān project in Āzarbāījān; and in order to make this possible, large-scale technological developments, especially an irrigation system, were obvious prerequisites. The sedentarization was fully planned and guided in accord with information concerning matters such as rural consumption patterns, budget studies, and rural demography. That is, social information was regarded as a necessary adjunct of technological innovation.

This project concerns the sedentarization of the Turkish-speaking Shāh Savan nomadic pastoralists of the Aras River region near the Iran–U.S.S.R. frontier. In economic terms it was argued that pastoralism and irrigation projects are incompatible since the capital outlay for the latter requires an intensive and more productive type of land use than the more casual utilization possible with nomadic pastoralism. Consequently, with the introduction of a costly irrigation scheme, pastoralism must give way to a regular and continuous form of land utilization such as agriculture or intensive animal husbandry. Sedentarization therefore became a necessary concomitant of the irrigation scheme, and the newly introduced sedentary population had to learn modern, sophisticated farming techniques, in order to make adequate use of the considerable capital investment, and to overcome the difficulties of peripheral location in the state, far away from main consumption centres—Tehrān, for example, is some 600 miles away. It is estimated that between 1,000 and 1,100 Shāh Savan families have lost their winter pasturages to the irrigation project. Over seventy qishlāq (winter quarters) have become agricultural land; and one *qi_s_hlāq* on average had a grazing capacity for fifteen family herds.

In addition to the pastoral-sedentary social mobility just described, there is in some regions, such as the Da_s_ht-i-Mu_g_hān area, high inter-village mobility: that is, movement entirely within the sedentary population itself. This has been interpreted as "betraying social insecurity and marginal conditions of existence".[1] In the Mu_g_hān region some villages have been in existence for more than forty years, but official, planned settlements of the Development Area are of far more recent origin. In the early 1960s the government department responsible for sedentarization decided to build permanent model villages where individuals could rent houses and each have some twelve hectares of land to farm. There is some doubt as to the suitability of the location of the twelve settlements set up by the plan (one of which is intended to grow into a small township), and it is not known what sort of living standards may be attained on the basis of the twelve hectares of farmland, especially as the area allocated to each farmer pays no heed to the geographically variable soil conditions.

Each model village will contain approximately ninety-four residences for tenant farmers, each consisting of two rooms, a hall, and a kitchen. Each village will have also a health centre, a public bath, a primary school, a water distribution system, and possibly a mosque. Op't Land (1961) has argued that the accommodation provided is inadequate, that the villages insufficiently cater for the needs of non-cultivators such as shopkeepers and administrators, that there are too few social amenities such as meeting halls, and that the projected capacity of the villages is below requirements. Be this as it may, a sustained attempt at planning has been made, and the experiment should provide useful guidance for the implementation of further schemes elsewhere in the country. In Da_s_ht-i-Mu_g_hān, the model villages are already established and may perhaps be modified in the light of experience.

In this planned sedentarization, to date, the people seem to adhere, at least in some respects, to their original tribal organization. Bessaignet[2] says "their traditional organization has been carried over" and that they will impose it on the new society of the Mu_g_hān whether one likes it or not. Some continuation of the traditional organization is inevitable; but its total imposition on the new society is hardly to be credited.

---

[1] C. A. Op't Land, *op. cit.* p. 15.   [2] P. Bessaignet, quoted in Op't Land, *op. cit.* p. 49.

Over the years, the traditional tribal organization had become well adapted to the pastoral activities pursued, and it allowed full utilization of natural resources. The grazing unit, the *oubeh*, moved as necessary and not when ordered to do so. Authority was decentralized; the chief delegated his power, of necessity, knowing that were he not to do so then petty leaders would be impelled to usurp his power.

When several *oubeh* become sedentary, living together and cultivating together in one settlement, the situation is quite different. Here there is a concentration and stabilization of authority, and it need not be delegated. Such groups of *oubeh* or a single *oubeh* usually become sedentary as a result of impoverishment. They claim to have been originally " '*adam*", that is, composed of the completely destitute social elements.

Any tribal authority remaining among the settled communities is therefore vestigial. New settlers are not felt to be entitled to positions of authority in the communities which they join. Even with time, the emergence of new leaders from among their numbers is difficult, since there are no mechanisms for the formulation of common opinions, or plans of action, or for the election of suitable candidates for office from among themselves. The pastoral S̲h̲āh Savan society was, according to Op't Land, patriarchial. Only the imperious character could establish himself as an authority, and only then provided the odds were not too heavily against him. He had to be a man of wealth, and of a family in which wealth had been hereditary. He had also to be demonstrably more successful than others so that men should follow him. Obviously, among the destitute " '*adam*" such people were rarely found, and in any event might be unsuitable to wield the new kind of authority in the villages. Here, the newly arrived man as well as the traditional chief might well feel at a loss. One agrees with Op't Land[1] that "when the hereditary authorities fail to find the right solution for the reconstitution of the power hierarchy, fail to make the correct adaptations, the old tribal organization will disappear...", though perhaps not "without a trace" as Op't Land claims.

Other individuals from the tribes are unable to make the effort required in assuming the role of leader since they are unacceptable in terms of tribal traditions. Therefore, during the initial stages of sedentarization there will be no organized power hierarchy, but a semblance of order remains since people are still bound by most of the

[1] C. A. Op't Land, *op. cit.* p. 50.

rules of their old traditions. Yet some leader vested with enough power to regulate social activity is required. In the early days of the scheme no kadkhudā had been elected by the people, nor had one assumed office by virtue of his own strength. All the village headmen had in fact been appointed by the government in the absence of defined means of selecting such men, either in terms of tribal social life or of the new sedentary life. Similarly, among the pastoral Shāh Savan, the chiefs are invested by the central government, though, in keeping with the tribal rules of inheritance and succession, the eldest son of the late Beg is normally nominated. Here too the chiefs claim to be indisputably paramount because of their appointments by a greater, higher, non-tribal authority.

Even so, individuals vested with authority, however derived, are not automatically accepted. Leaders must prove themselves, always a difficult task in newly established settlements where novel social situations and unfamiliar behaviour patterns pertain. It means that the function of the kadkhudā is largely conditioned by the personality of the office holder, by his charisma, but the kadkhudā is generally ineffective since he is, in this new situation, unsure of his supposed purpose, and has neither the formal approval of the local population nor the traditional support. Any limited success in getting things done is due to persuasive capability or to the assistance of a personal retinue of dependants (as defined in economic or kinship terms). There are no institutionalized means of assisting him to resolve disputes or to arrive at common opinion. Frequently, therefore, he is accused of favouritism or, alternatively, of inertia.

Authority is differently based in tribal pastoral communities. Individuals gained power among the nomadic Shāh Savan, for example, by directing the grazing programme. Evidently in settled villages such bases for authority are quite obsolete, and most of the traditional pastoral-orientated organization has gone, including the effective Beg, Āq Saqāl, and the camp chiefs. So have the *tireh* and the *oubeh* gone. Village chiefs are most often selected without reference to tribal authorities, and so there is little continuity in the pattern of administrative functions.

One tribal feature which is to some extent retained in the villages is the name of the ta'ifeh from which the individual is descended—though the fact has no real significance in the new environment. Second generation settlers are simply accepted as native villagers who make no attempt to stress their origins among the pastoral Shāh Savan. It is argued that since they have neither the livestock nor, apparently, the wish to resume a pastoral existence, why should they lay claim to rights which they cannot utilize and by so doing demonstrate their detachment from the village where they wish to reside? Since they wish to cultivate village lands they will use all means to identify themselves with the village community. Some claims to the right to use village land are based on older claims to the use of winter pastures which lay where the villages are now located, that is, where villages are built on former *qishlāq*. To squatters, this claim is about the only certainty left them.

So it is that some people quickly disclaim tribal origins, while others advertise them simply in order to claim ground on former *qishlāq*. Both situations are found. Very few people desire to return to pastoralism. Bessaignet(1961) pictures the settler as "still a nomad within his soul . . .", but this view does not appear to be corroborated by Op't Land's data. As previously stated, one thing is certain, and that is that economic practicalities make a return to pastoral nomadism impossible for the vast majority of the people. This is not to deny the fact that circumstances may force certain farmers back to pastoralism against their will and against their better judgment. Men are unlikely to rush into a new activity like farming, throwing all caution to the winds. The advantages of farming compared with those of pastoralism are not yet fully demonstrated to this population in the Project Area and thus the economic advantages of animal keeping are still borne in mind. Agriculture will become of greater importance when pastoralism is singularly unrewarding, as in times of herd disasters such as occurred in this area during the years 1960–61.

This newly settled group has the possibility of becoming a community of expert, modern-style farmers well served by a large number of non-agrarian specialists. These latter will be concentrated in service centres in villages and particularly in the single, much larger village there. Moreover, the agrarians will also live in villages located as closely as possible to the fields which they will work, so as to minimize the distance between their homes and their work. Too great a distance from the fields tends to detach the peasant from the land. Yet, on the whole, it is advantageous to locate the peasant homesteads in villages and not to scatter them individually in and among the fields. Iranian peasants are traditionally village dwellers and a greater feeling of community may be more quickly engendered in a village group than in a dispersed settlement.

Sedentarization using technical aid may be quite feasible and may well have a fair measure of success since, as we shall see, nomadic groups appear to lose certain of their members to village communities particularly in times of economic difficulty. However, it is surely not easy to envisage large-scale voluntary sedentarization occurring as it were overnight since, other practicalities apart, the value systems of nomads and peasants are in so many respects utterly different. There would appear to be a great deal more to the sedentarization process than simply renouncing pastoralism in favour of cultivating. The much vaunted freedom, the urge to move to new areas, the whole organization of social life based on movement and fluidity are impossible in a small village. The Petlū community in the Shāh Savan region of Āzarbāījān is in process of becoming sedentary. This group relies for its existence partly on agriculture, partly on pastoralism, and as an index of "pastoral intent" it is noteworthy that the people have camels but no cows in Petlū, whilst true villagers invariably have cows but no camels. It is difficult to assess the relative contributions of the two main types of occupation to the total income of the group, and to use these as an index of the degree to which pastoralism has been renounced. In terms of mental attitudes the sedentarization process seems not to be very advanced. In 1953 the group took to agriculture, though without totally renouncing pastoralism, and the settlement became permanent. Yet most people (in 1961) still had tents, and families still lived in them. The nomad mentality is also suggested by the extraordinary distances which separated dwellings and by the absence of compounds. In fact Petlū "village" still resembled in layout a Shāh Savan *oubeh* except that most of the tents had been replaced by mud houses.

Petlū men still preferred to marry females of other Shāh Savan ta'ifeh, and maintained few contacts with people in the new Development Area villages. However, since it is no more self-sufficient than any other village settlement it is of necessity linked for economic purposes with Pārsābād, the main centre of the region. Once included in the Development Programme, Petlū will pose a problem. It could be liquidated, and its people put into another village. Alternatively, it could remain where it is now, and its twelve or thirteen families would have newcomers added to them so as to make the settlement viable. Both proposals would effect the breakdown of the old *tīreh* unity, and "the traditional tribal organization will remain nothing but a name and a recollection".[1]

[1] C. A. Op't Land, *op. cit.* p. 38.

Moreover, it is difficult to believe that there is an unequivocal wish for the nomads to disappear completely from the Iranian scene. It is more than idle curiosity which prompts one to ask how else it is envisaged to utilize adequately the resources of the arid, semi-desert areas of Iran, other than by extensive pastoral nomadism. It would appear that both for economic reasons and for gratifying their wishes, the nomads should be allowed a place in the new Iranian state.

Currently, of course, the nomadic tribes are very much in existence, and in this decade there has been much conflict between the central government and tribal groups in south-west Iran. Conflicting social, political, and economic interests have still to be satisfactorily reconciled, and at present no clear-cut solution seems to present itself. It is possible to understand sedentarization as a process of deliberate political policy by the central government. Moreover, as has already been stated, there are indisputably both social and economic conditions which, if found among nomadic groups must inevitably lead to sedentarization, either of individual families or else of considerably larger tribal sections.

Thus, whilst it is true that for many purposes the nomads may be considered as distinct from the majority of Iranians who are settled cultivators, they are, as groups, closely interrelated for certain purposes. The two elements are in social contact periodically and of necessity there must be ordered mechanisms for controlling their relationships on these occasions. It should not be accepted that the much-publicized hostility occasionally manifest in such contact is the rule. The most important meeting place in Iran, as in other similarly constituted populations, is the market place. When viewing the political situation, the tribe as a political entity has systematized contact with the larger-scale Iranian society via the tribal leader, the chief, or Khān, and this may be thought of as a corporate relationship through the tribal leader. On the other hand, economic contact is of a different order. Nomads have individually established relationships with men in the sedentary communities along the migration routes. Such individual relationships, stemming from the independent nature of the nomadic household within the tribe in economic terms (Barth[1]), are of course invariably numerous, since it is in fact necessary for each household to have relationships of this kind. The total result has been described as an "enmeshing effect" by Barth,[2] whereby the tribe as a whole, is eventually, closely related to

[1] F. Barth (1961), *op. cit.* p. 20. See also F. Barth (1953), *op. cit.* p. 24.
[2] *Ibid.* p. 97.

the various sedentary communities which it encounters. The economic factor is seemingly of paramount importance in establishing and maintaining these individual relationships.

Tribesmen buy and sell commodities in the bāzārs of villages and towns and they establish credit relationships with personal trading partners in these places. This involves a measure of trust, particularly on the part of the villager, since the nomad may be far away from the locality of the village for many months and must be trusted to return in due course and to settle his debts. So it is that each of these independent nomadic households has dealings with the extra-tribal marketing facilities described here. It is within these relationships that some clues as to the nature of the sedentarization process may be found, as Barth has described for the Bāsiri.[1]

Among nomadic tribes, the herds of certain individuals, given good fortune and careful management, will increase in number fairly regularly over a period of years. In addition, the owner's personal supervision of the herds is progressively less complete and effective and more and more herding is performed by hired men who, in the absence of strict supervision, tend to absorb ever more of the animal produce. Moreover, large concentrated herds invite disaster in the event of natural calamities, though this may be minimized by scattering the herd over a large area under the control of a number of herdsmen. It is fully realized that exceedingly large herds are imprudent assets; and in consequence there is a tendency for many owners to convert at least part of this wealth into imperishables such as carpets and jewellery, though limiting their conversion since those commodities, whilst aesthetically satisfying and very evident in the household, give no direct economic return. This, partly at any rate, accounts for the focusing of attention on land as the outstandingly important alternative form of imperishable wealth. Rich nomads often buy land along the migration routes in places, usually near villages, where water is available, and subsequently they let portions of it to villagers under a variety of agreement, the whole system being controlled and supervised by the appointed agent of the landowner. Rents are most frequently paid in kind, and evidently the situation is economically very advantageous for the rich nomad. So it is that the nomadic-village link of this type is initially based upon economic factors, and the rich nomad has no conscious thought of settling down.

[1] *Ibid.*

However, as a result of this a sequence of inexorable events has been set in motion. Landowners among the nomads have a substantial income in agricultural produce with the result that during many years, if not always, their herds can remain more or less untouched because very few animals need to be sold in order that their owner might buy necessary agricultural produce. In the absence of natural calamities the herds continue to increase and the nomad, becoming even wealthier, is able to buy additional land which may eventually constitute a very important proportion of his total wealth. As the relative importance of landholdings increases, so is there an even greater need to supervise adequately the utilization of this resource, with the result that the rich landowner among the nomads is partly divorced from pastoral interests and is inexorably drawn into the set of activities characteristic of sedentary landlords. At this stage there is both economic and social integration, and the landowner's interests are largely focused upon the world of the sedentary farmer and his concerns. Such a process belies the importance of the emotional attachment to nomadism as a way of life. Once the predominance of the landed interests is established, any herd disasters which occur can only serve to diminish, or even end, the landowner's close bonds with pastoral activity, and in this way the process of sedentarization (due to the increasing affluence of the individual) is completed.

There can be little doubt that such a process takes place among nomads in many parts of the country and that the tribes are constantly drained of this rich element, which their way of life produces. The rate of loss will depend partly on natural conditions and partly on the social conditions of the period. Equally, factors exist which prevent this from becoming a dominant social pattern, and thus ensure the continued existence of nomadic tribes.

Thus, according to Barth,[1] sons among the Bāsirī are given their patrimony when they marry, so that when a man has adult sons, in his own middle age, the fragmentation of his herd begins as soon as those sons marry. A poor man with sons will endeavour to postpone their marriages until they are thirty to forty years old, since otherwise there would be economic difficulty for both father and sons: adequate herds would not be available for both of them to be able to support their own households. A rich man who, as described, might become sedentary has both family and community pressure exerted upon him to arrange

---

[1] F. Barth (1961), *op. cit.* p. 106. See also F. Barth (1953), *op. cit.* p. 24.

his sons' marriages when they are approximately twenty years old. This of course leads to early herd fragmentation and delays the amassing of sufficient wealth for the instigation or the completion of the process of sedentarization. The more numerous a man's sons, the more adequate his labour force for herding and the more rapidly will his flocks tend to increase as a result. However, given such a situation, the shorter is the available period of growth for the flock number before the sons marry and remove their shares of the parental herd in order to set up their own economically independent households. It appears therefore that if a man is to become sedentary, he has approximately twenty years in a normally fertile marriage in which to complete the process. Childless men, or men who have daughters only, might expect that their herds should increase throughout their lifetime, but, in the absence of sons to act as herdsmen, such growth in animal numbers is somewhat improbable.

Sedentarization in Iran may therefore be the result of individual affluence, but far more often it may also be caused by the impoverishment of the individual owing to herd reduction. Such reduction may be due to a variety of factors including calamities, such as epidemics and drought, and mismanagement or overtaxing the herds in order to satisfy personal needs or to cancel long-standing debts. It should again be pointed out that economic risks of this kind are borne by the independent households of many nomadic tribes, and extended kinship groupings appear to be socially irrelevant in this context. Each household has its own herd, and without it, or with only a small herd, the nomadic way of life becomes impossible. Thus, serious losses of stock almost invariably cause sedentarization to occur.

This type of sedentarization might be expected to occur most regularly and frequently in areas of considerable ecological difficulty for pastoralism, as, for example, in parts of Balūchistān, unless the difficulty is counterbalanced by factors such as extended kin group solidarity and assistance in time of difficulty. There is little doubt that impoverishment and consequent sedentarization are grimly real possibilities for poorer households in the Iranian tribes. In many instances the process of impoverishment is gradual and, because of its undesired consequences as well as its own unpleasantness, great efforts are made to halt it. One means of delaying the process is by carrying over large debts from year to year, providing that the consent and co-operation of sedentary trading partners is forthcoming. The greater the debt, the greater the probability, even with good herding, careful management, and minimal consumption by the householders themselves, that most of it will remain unpaid in the following year. Again, if the debt is paid by selling stock which is the sole productive capital, then impoverishment is far more in evidence and the downward spiral progresses further, despite the preventative measures taken. In this case sedentarization presents itself as the most feasible means of resolving the problem.

Barth[1] estimated that among the Bāsirī nomads sixty animals represented the minimum number for a herd if sedentarization was to be avoided. One means used by the Bāsirī to stop the sequence of events as outlined is for the head of the household to become a herdsman for a richer household. This, in turn, may not be simply achieved, particularly when the difficulties in the one household are due to natural calamities which may have affected many herds and consequently many other households. If that is the case, then there is little demand for extra herdsmen. Herding for others in this way is in fact only possible if one or a few herds have been markedly reduced in number owing to factors which most herds have escaped.

However, it is certainly true that all households with seriously diminished stock numbers will seek to augment their income by temporary expedients, but virtually all the means of doing so are intimately linked with the sedentary communities, including seasonal occupations such as harvesting, guarding winter crops, acting as village shepherds, and the like. These resorts tend to multiply and to strengthen the bonds with villagers, and such types of occupation tend to accelerate the herd reduction rate, since the normal migratory cycle, so necessary for the well-being of the animals, is either abandoned or only partly followed, or else the animals may be cared for during migration by men who demand payment for the work involved. In general, the consequence is a further loss of animals. Moreover, if the migratory cycle is not followed there is loss of significant contact with the appropriate tent group. Also there must be increased dependence on village sources of income, and eventually the impoverished individuals are integrated into the settled communities as property-less villagers. The process of sedentarization by impoverishment, everywhere in Iran the predominant form of the phenomenon, is then complete.

Thus, in addition to the primary economic interdependence of the nomadic and sedentary elements in the population, there is social

---

[1] F. Barth (1961), *op. cit.* p. 109. See also F. Barth (1953), *op. cit.* p. 24.

assimilation, the preponderant direction of population movement being from the tribes to the sedentary groups in villages, towns, and cities. When the tribal economic system is incapable of sustaining the individual and his household, then economic and social opportunities are sought in the settled communities of the country. It appears that given certain conditions the sedentarization rate may actually exceed the tribes' fertility rate, with the result that the tribes disappear as organized social units. Barth[1] states that in the Khamseh confederacy, the Ainālū "vanished" in the 1870–80 period and the Bahārlū around the turn of the century.

The settled populace of Fārs, as of virtually all Iran, was, and continues to be, poor. People are ill-nourished and readily succumb to all manner of illness. Malaria was endemic in many parts of the country and resulted in a loss of labour efficiency and, together with secondary, partly consequential diseases, probably caused much loss of life. Trachoma was widespread and infant mortality was high. Moreover sporadic outbreaks of other diverse diseases often took heavy toll of life in Iranian villages, in the absence of adequate medical care. Reproductive rates in villages are low. In terms of population fitness, that is, both reproductive and survival fitness, the nomadic group is the more favourably endowed. In the recent past many sedentary populations have not been self-reproducing, and the consequent depopulation of the areas which they occupied increased the possibility of settlement by nomads.

In the surveyed area of the village of Tezerjān there were 102 families with an average of 3·1 children per family. In recent years, the establishment of a government-sponsored health centre here, as in many other Iranian villages, has markedly improved the survival chances of children, as well as generally improving health conditions. Moreover, powdered milk provided by the government was distributed to village children who attended school, and this again contributed to the same end. However, located in a healthy, high mountain valley, with a good constant supply of water, at least for personal consumption, the population in this village may be atypical of Iranian villages, and the reproductive fitness and survival chances of the population must in fact be above average.

Thus, in general, the sedentary population was continually replenished by accretions from the nomadic tribes; a process which was in turn essential for the survival of nomadic groups, and for nomadic society as such to persist. A continuing accumulation of population

[1] *Ibid.* p. 119.

in the nomadic tribes would overtax the pastures since progressively larger flocks would be kept and there would certainly be both economic and social organizational difficulties.

It would therefore appear that the two alternative human adaptations in Iran which have been described coexist in a state of equilibrium, an equilibrium which might be expected to persist in the absence of interference by other agencies, particularly the central government. One group performs social functions vital for the continuing existence of the other. Therefore any attempt to modify the one way of life must have repercussions in the other.

Sedentarization proceeds in Iran partly as a consequence of internal social factors in nomadic society, partly as a result of government action intended to effect social integration largely for socio-political reasons. Nomads are considered to be incompatible with a centralized state organization. The government-inspired attempt at sedentarization is however not an altogether violent process. As was stated, the government hopes that by large-scale technological projects, and especially by irrigation schemes in areas not previously utilized for agriculture, nomads may be induced to settle. This type of provision of water does make both cultivation and a sedentary way of life possible but nomadic attitudes are not as quickly adapted to the social needs, values, and demands of the new situation. Nonetheless the major settlement schemes, as in the Dasht-i-Mughān in Āzarbāijān, appear in fact to be having a certain measure of success.

More insidiously, other government-inspired agencies cause tribal sedentarization and also village depopulation to occur. State-provided education at all levels is now widely available in Iran, particularly for boys. Young men are conscripted into the Iranian army, in which further education, not entirely military, is provided. Young men are employed as technicians and skilled operatives at Ābādān and other industrial centres in the country. These media collectively serve to divorce many of these young men from close identification with the interests and aspirations of traditional society, either nomadic or in villages. Thus, for instance, Narāghī has written that "Schools create an 'acquired' authority, that of knowledge, which saps the natural, sometimes moral and sometimes intellectual authority of the father".[1] It appears that in Iran, as in so much of the underdeveloped world now

[1] E. Narāghī, *Social Consequences of Economic and Technological Development in Iran* (Univ. of Tehrān, n.d.), p. 7.

undergoing rapid social change, there is a wide chasm separating the social ideals of fathers and sons. "This eternal conflict between generations takes on all the more scope in Iranian society because the transition between traditional family stability and the westernization of morals has been abrupt."[1] In a survey conducted in Tehrān, Narāghī found that many cases of neurosis appeared among individuals aged 16–25 years in the middle class. "The cause was the general spread of feelings of frustration, guilt and anxiety, due to uprooting, to the transition from one politico-economic age to another, from one environment to another, and to an inability to reconcile different systems of values."[2]

URBAN SOCIETY

At this point we are involved with a third significant element of the social scene in Iran today, namely, the urban group. Towns and cities have, of course, a considerable antiquity in Iran, and they have long contained groups having a complex social organization. It has been argued that, to some extent, the growth of towns was a natural result of the impact of nomadic migrations on communities which originally settled in villages and clustered together behind walls for purposes of mutual defence and security, and which were later to outgrow and to overspill the walls. Initially within the walls, the cities evolved from the village originals, having a main central square around which were grouped the principal buildings and the homes of the more important inhabitants. The bāzār was also located near the central square. Basically a market, the bāzār was also to become the social and political hub of the city's life, the habitat of the middle class—a feature unknown in the villages—and hence wielding great influence in the affairs of the country as a whole. Thus it is that, traditionally, the city and its people have exerted considerable influence on places and people more or less distant from it, including particularly the surrounding countryside—so much so that the way of life in the countryside cannot be understood without reference to the city. Nor is the converse possible. The rush to the towns of Iran from the countryside, so conspicuous a feature of the current social scene, is an accelerated continuation of a long-established tendency based upon the intimate economic and social associations of the two throughout the centuries. Anthropologists have traditionally defined and studied primitive

[1] *Ibid.* p. 7. [2] *Ibid.* p. 8.

isolates, which have been termed academic abstractions with which reality may usefully be compared. This may constitute a valuable and worthwhile procedure, particularly as regards many tribally organized peoples, since abstraction and reality here have sufficient resemblance to make the more or less unconscious comparisons valuable. Theoretical developments in the subject are largely geared to dealing with situations of this type. A marked departure from the primitive isolate is, however, found in more complex societies such as exist in Iran, and in this case it may be argued that an integrative approach is required whereby the "isolate", be it a town, village, or tribe, is systematically viewed and understood as a social unit in terms of its interrelationships with other socially defined groups.

If the nomadic groups are for the moment left out of the picture, one sees the towns and their inhabitants as contrasted with the countryside and its people; we have in fact an approximation to a certain polarity of social life, town- and country-based respectively. Robert Redfield wrote extensively upon the topic of the folk or peasant ideal type as contrasted with the urban societal type, and he sought to explain diversity in social organization in terms of a folk-urban continuum. Redfield made the initial, tentative formulation of the folk concept in his study of Tepoztlán,[1] a village in Mexico, and this has since been critically re-studied by Oscar Lewis.[2]

This scheme of Redfield's defines an ideal type, the folk society, as the polar opposite of urban society. The ideal type is a mental construct and no known society precisely corresponds to it. It is therefore an aid to the understanding of social reality in that it may indicate the aspects of real societies which require study; and it can ultimately suggest hypotheses as to what, under certain defined conditions, may be generally true about society.

Integrative studies are therefore essential for the present purpose, and in this context it is appropriate to quote from Pitt River's introduction to *Mediterranean Countrymen* which states that the central theme of the book is examining "the relation between the social structure of the local community and the wider society of which it is a part . . ."[3]

[1] R. Redfield, *Tepoztlán, A Mexican Village. A Study of Folk Life* (Univ. of Chicago Press, 1930).

[2] O. Lewis, *Life in a Mexican Village; Tepoztlán re-studied* (University of Illinois Press, 1951). See also: O. Lewis, *Tepoztlán Restudied: a Critique of the Folk-urban Conceptualization of Social Change* (Rural Sociol. 18, 1953), pp. 121–34.

[3] J. Pitt Rivers, ed., *Mediterranean Countrymen* (Mouton, 1963), p. 17.

Both the degree and the mode of the integration of the local community into the national structure is variable, but everywhere—and Iran is in this respect no exception—"the solidarity of the community, the kinship group and the extended family as social, economic and juridical entities has suffered during the last two centuries at the hands of national integration".[1] An accelerated rate of national integration and the effectiveness of the means employed to secure it have been increasingly apparent in Iran, especially in the twentieth century.

According to Redfield,[2] the folk society is characterized as small, isolated, non-literate, and homogeneous, with a strong sense of group solidarity. The ways of living are conventionalized into that coherent system which may be termed "a culture". Behaviour is traditional, spontaneous, uncritical, and personal. There is no legislation, nor is there a habit of experiment and reflexion for intellectual ends. Kinship, its relationships and institutions, are the type categories of experience and the familial group is the unit of action. The sacred prevails over the secular; the economy is one of status rather than of markets. Redfield devotes much effort in fact to defining and describing the "folk" pole of the continuum, and one presumes that the definitive qualities of the urban type are logically the opposite of the folk characteristics. This opposite pole is often referred to as "modern urbanized society" or some such phrase. There is an implicit use of this pole of the continuum as an ideal type; and it is taken as standing for urbanized society in general. Modernized, westernized urban society simply represents the specific case most closely approximating the polar category "Urban society".

Redfield suggests that loss of isolation and increasing heterogeneity are causes of disorganization, secularization, and individualization. Whether this seems to be so or not, it does not of course follow that these are the only causes of such effects, and that these are the only causal relationships to be discovered in the same data. In fact, Redfield's final conclusion is that there is no single necessary cause for secularization and individualization.

It is probably true to say that the rural communities of Iran may be thought of as occupying various positions intermediately located between the two poles. Communities of this kind appear to support the

---

[1] *Ibid.* p. 17.

[2] R. Redfield, *The Little Community* (Univ. of Chicago Press, 1955); and R. Redfield, *Peasant Society and Culture* (Univ. of Chicago Press, 1956).

42-2

view that as the folk-like community loses its isolation through contact with the city, now much more systematically than formerly owing to improved communications, it becomes more heterogeneous, a market economy develops, and evidence of disorganization appears.

Narāghī writes that "the countryside, suddenly brought into contact with urban structures, has lost sight of its own manner of living and is still seeking something to replace it".[1] It is possible to view the new routes of communications, the educational programme in the countryside, and the extension of the use of a monetary system as emanations of the urban way of living in particular, and if this is so, then much of the change evident in the folk culture can be explained in terms of this new confrontation. Traditional social life appears to disintegrate when faced with the new needs and demands introduced by these urban influences. Many individuals in the villages, once they are educated, and once they catch a glimpse of new and broader social horizons, are so ill-content with their traditional social niches that they join the flood of people who migrate from the countryside to the towns where no socio-economic framework is provided for them, with consequent difficulty for the would-be urbanites as well as for those in the towns who have to cope with the presence of newcomers. Again, "the settlement of nomads accustomed to the cohesion of tribal life, patriarchal authority, the clan spirit and subtle hierarchization has had the paradoxical effect of disintegrating apparently solid personalities and wearing away the old group morale. The tent and the steppe, though synonymous with instability and wandering, would appear to have been better capable than villages or towns of ensuring the stability of the 'home' and the solidity of 'roots'".[2]

All this does not appear necessarily to be directly the result of so called westernization. Miner's work in Timbuctoo[3] shows that lack of isolation, together with marked population density and heterogeneity seem to be accompanied by disorganization, secularization, and impersonalization, even in the absence of western influences.

One is aware that there have been many criticisms of Redfield's theory. Thus, Lewis maintains that the folk-urban concept of social change focuses attention primarily on the city as a source of change, to the exclusion of, or to the comparative neglect of, other factors, either internal or external. Again he states that the folk-urban dichotomy

[1] E. Narāghī, *op. cit.* p. 6.　　[2] *Ibid.* p. 6.
[3] H. Miner, *The Primitive City of Timbuctoo* (Princeton Univ. Press, 1953).

as used by Redfield is a system of value judgments which contains the old Rousseauan notion of primitive people as noble savages and the corollary that with civilization came the fall of man. It is assumed that all folk societies are integrated, while urban societies are a great disorganizing force.

Yet it would appear that in Iran many of the social changes which are so dramatically occurring in the villages may be satisfactorily explained and understood at least partly in terms of such a concept of a dichotomous continuum. Administration, marketing, all manner of new social services, landlordism, radical new ideas which conflict with traditionalism—all seem to emanate from towns or else are based upon towns, and they constitute in their entirety a very real source of change which seems to be of far greater significance than those causes of change which are innate in the social structure of the rural communities themselves. Having suggested that this may be so, it would be interesting to have precise, detailed studies of the actual mechanisms involved in such social change in Iran. How do the great tradition and the little tradition of Redfield's terminology interact in Iran? Redfield wrote "In a civilization there is a great tradition of the reflective few, and there is a little tradition of the largely unreflective many. The great tradition is cultivated in schools or temples; the little tradition works itself out and keeps itself going in the lives of the unlettered in their village communities. The tradition of the philosopher, theologian and literary man is a tradition consciously cultivated and handed down; that of the little people is for the most part taken for granted and not submitted to much scrutiny or considered refinement and improvement."[1]

Thus peasant society has been defined as a "part" society but the question: part of exactly what, and how related to that of which it is a part remains largely obscure; while, according to Pitt Rivers[2] the temporal dimension of this relationship remains obscurer still. It is however necessary to consider the problem of the structural relationship between the local community and the region, city, and state—in fact, with the outside world. Quite evidently the community's relationship to outside forces is significant in determining its internal structure, and it is surely true that as the little community's relationship with the external world changes, so does its internal structure. This is exemplified, for instance, by Barth[3] for part of Iraqi Southern Kurdistān.

---

[1] R. Redfield (1956), *op. cit.* p. 70.   [2] J. Pitt Rivers, ed., *op. cit.* p. 10.
[3] F. Barth (1953), *op. cit.*

In recent years in Iran, as elsewhere, state-controlled functions which impinge upon the local community have increased both in number and in importance. Thus, responsibility for law and order is no longer in the hands of kinship-based groups such as lineages for instance. Communications and economic organization have vastly extended both conceptually and also territorially. Increased functions of this kind have fostered the desire to impose a greater uniformity of law within the national territory; that is, to have a single system of law applicable to all. To date, as we have seen, this is not completely effected. Again, it is reported that there is, in many Iranian cities, a good deal of juvenile delinquency—a problem which is partly left in the hands of the families involved and partly dealt with by government agencies. The problem itself is not of course peculiar to Iran; however, as Narāghī puts it, "It is . . . all the more apparent in societies like that of Iran, where public institutions have not yet been able to make up for family and tribal inadequacy".[1] As the traditional methods of social control disintegrate and become less effectual, then alternative methods of effecting the same ends are obviously highly desirable but, as yet anyway, not satisfactorily established.

Again, the concept of individual ownership, though long recognized, has grown at the expense of that of collective ownership of property. The passage from relatively autonomous communities to component units within an integrated state necessarily involves the breakdown of pristine collectivities in favour of individual rights. This process is accelerated by economic factors, particularly in the vicinity of towns and cities, where individual trading for cash becomes increasingly important. The crops grown may be sold for cash to an ever more significant extent as the urban population grows, largely as a result of the movement of rural dwellers into towns and cities, and the areas affected by this commercialization increase as communications improve. The population of Tehrān alone doubled in the 1940–50 decade to over one million, and there is every indication that this growth rate has continued since, with progressively more demands made on the agricultural capacity of many parts of the country, particularly regions near the capital itself. Writing in 1958, Lerner states that "these urban migrants in Iran...encounter unemployment, undercompensation, and the miserable conditions of slum life. For there are few signs of a growth phase in the Iranian economy.

[1] E. Narāghī, *op. cit.* p. 10.

Without industrial expansion, the movement of discontented and deprived thousands to cities augurs not economic growth but political instability."[1]

The breakdown of collectivities of a traditional kind fosters the flourishing of individualism. The individual is someone with whom the modern state can have dealings. His responsibility towards the state can be defined by the national law; he can simultaneously belong both to the national and to the local communities. He suffers little or none of the tremendous strain involved in the conflict of loyalties to the local community and to the larger community—the state—to which the former pertains. Conversely, the state cannot deal with a village collectivity or with the patrilineal descent group in an altogether satisfactory manner. It is well known from African as well as other tribal material that the growth of centralized state control spelled the doom of kinship-based local groups, even, in some instances in East Africa, before the coming of Europeans. The process is not simply, therefore, to be understood in terms of the impact of European institutions on social life in Iran. The demands of the state and of the kinship group upon the individual cannot be reconciled; and the larger, more powerful social unit thrives at the expense of the lesser. The consequent integration into the national system, politically, economically, and socially, involves adopting its standards and its techniques. Currency, contractual freedom, wage labour, and investment thrive, all of which are incompatible with customary law and social processes which rely upon and maintain the cohesion of collectivities.

A balanced participation in collectivities implies a certain egalitarianism, certainly in economic matters. Once this balance is destroyed or impaired, individual ownership is paramount, and this sooner or later leads to increased economic inequalities. This, in turn, makes possible a system of patronage based on economic power, and through this the local community may be controlled in a manner quite new to it and quite unlike the control founded upon hereditary allegiances or traditional leadership. Individual ownership, to the exclusion of all other forms of ownership, appears then as a function of political and economic centralization, and the process is strikingly evident in Iran today.

The association of the sedentary and nomadic rural world on the

[1] D. Lerner, *The Passing of Traditional Society; Modernizing the Middle East* (Free Press, Glencoe, 1958), p. 361.

one hand, with the urban monetary system on the other, is depriving the rural economy of its comparative social independence. A subsistence economy where speculation with the meagre fruits of the land was inconceivable (even on account) is being replaced by a system based on money. Inevitably, speculation is then a consequence. The land is not utilized in a manner calculated to satisfy consumer needs immediately and directly, but in accordance with rumours from the city about the presumed values of the produce to be expected from the countryside. The traditional balance has been upset; a new balance, involving a realistic idea of the speculative values which, for example, prospects of foreign trade may offer, has yet to be found. On coming into contact with the city, the countryside adopted its tastes in a speculative spirit.

In Iran, "the population is dispersed around the vast desert, in villages isolated by inadequate or non-existent communications. They remain locked in the ancient round of daily life, eking from their old soil with their antique tools (some antedating the Christian era) their immemorial produce. Regarding the new world stage, on which their national drama now unfolds, they are uninformed and uninvolved."[1] This, however, is only part of the tale. There is no doubt that changes, largely inspired by and originating in cities, are occurring in the Iranian countryside. However, in contrast to the comparatively uninformed and inarticulate peasants, there is a small but growing group or urbanites with a profound personal involvement in national affairs. "These persons care deeply about public affairs, vibrating to the day's headlines with the intense affectivity of a farmer hearing news of his sick calf or a mother of her soldier son."[2] This deep concern with public issues further causes them to wish to change existing conditions, whenever possible, for the better. Lerner has called this "agitational disposition" a "distinctive mark of revolutionary extremism". Whether this be so or not, it is perhaps significant that although the land reform programme most directly affects the large group of peasants in the country, a good deal of the public agitation concerning it has been conducted in cities.

The urban population is economically involved in trade, processing industries, political administration, and the provision of specialized personal services such as medical and legal facilities. Both trade and processing are owned and organized partly by individuals, partly by

[1] D. Lerner, *op. cit.* p. 361. [2] *Ibid.* p. 362.

kin groups. Such occupational co-ordination as exists is effected by syndicates, unions, and guilds. Moreover, the processing industries, unless under direct western control or influence, have continued to operate in many instances on a pre-industrial technological level. Now, there is an enormous amount of technological innovation, largely as a result of importation of machinery and the necessity for new industrial and agricultural techniques. But despite a programme of vocational education it is evident that the training of sufficient men to utilize the innovations will be a long and difficult part of the programme.

In the urban centres, there is pronounced economic stratification; a very small and extremely wealthy upper class, a small, emerging middle class, and a very large and economically depressed lower class. The dominant upper class exists in pockets in this underdeveloped land at grips with problems provoked by rapid economic and social change. By and large, political administration is not directly responsible to majority popular opinion, even though certain steps in this direction have been taken; it is rather of a directive nature and it is very much urban orientated. It is staffed at decision-making levels by members of the upper class together with some middle class individuals, or else by army personnel. In Iran, as in much of the Middle East, the army is one generally effective means of achieving upward socio-political mobility.

As among the non-urban population, social organization in towns and cities involves some basic reference to kinship both in the ascrip-tion of social and political status and in the definition of economic opportunity. However, there is even less explicit allocation of dif-ferential functions in the extended family and lineage, and more interest is evinced in maternal and affinal kin. Spatial location is less signi-ficant in the current definition of reciprocal obligations, except as established along economic or religious lines. Again as a function of economic heterogeneity, occupational associations emerge as import-ant groupings.

To some extent towns are becoming synonymous with the middle-man class, representing, as Narāghī puts it, "The triumph of specula-tion over production".[1] New urban dwellers just arrived from the countryside provide many heterogeneous elements for urban society, and it is often reported that a certain uneasiness, symptomatic of difficulties of adjustment, exists among the newcomers, who tend mainly

---

[1] E. Narāghī, *op. cit.* p. 5.

to congregate in certain parts of the cities. The traditional well-organized life, of the smaller provincial cities as well as the countryside, does not exist in the larger cities, and perhaps least of all in Tehrān. Village life and the structured interrelationships of village households minimized and even eliminated risk, as, too, did tribal life. Village and tribal institutions provided social security at the domestic level. The tribe and the village simultaneously provided collective education for children, leisure, religious observances, and an adequate social life generally. These known bases for social behaviour, learned and understood from childhood are largely irrelevant in the cities. Urban centres have created anonymity and introduced the element of risk.

Yet it is, in general, perhaps an over-simplification to state that a transition from the countryside to the city necessarily involves a loss or a breakdown of the organic solidarity so characteristic of the peasant way of life. It is surely correct to state that many people positively welcome their new surroundings and are not very prone to find fault with them nor to wish themselves back in traditionally organized social units. The misfits of the small-scale societies have here new social opportunities which, however imperfectly grasped and however difficult to manage, are at least available and make present adversity bearable in view of possible future promise.

Again, the integration of the disparate parts of the nation has been remarked upon and it is necessary to bear in mind that city and country people alike do ultimately form part of a single Iranian society, so that the peasant newly arrived in the town from the countryside need not necessarily suffer a profound cultural shock as a result of the transition. The present population of Iran reflects the many movements of peoples into the region in the past, and discrete residues from these movements remain. Yet there is also a basis for national unity and consciousness in the overwhelming adherence to the Shīʿa sect of Islam, and in the all-pervading influence of Persian literature, culture, manners, and customs. Moreover, Benet has stated that "It is one of the tenets of Islam that the good life can really only be conducted in an urban setting...".[1] If this is so then the migrant is not necessarily confronted with a personal moral loss.

Benet (1963) goes on to explain that the city may be "cushioned" for the arrival of newcomers from the countryside, in so far as certain parts

[1] F. Benet, *Sociology Uncertain: the Ideology of the Rural-urban Continuum* (Comparative Studies in Society and History, VI, 1963), p. 9.

of the city might tend to contain individuals from geographically distinct parts of the country with each ward or similar urban unit becoming a projection of its occupants' native social habitat, tribal or village. It is then possible in these urban areas to lead a full neighbourhood life without too abrupt a change. Old established residents may actively assist the newcomers; the newcomers may emulate the forerunners and may in fact become active inventors of urban social institutions. Thus do the wards or similarly constituted units manifest a "cushioning" effect against the impersonal relationships characteristic of city life. Some traditional institutions may adapt themselves very well to urban conditions. However, in Iran, it is in some respects as yet unclear whether the transition from the village to the city has a profoundly disturbing and disruptive effect upon institutions and personalities. A careful investigation of the process is required to ascertain whether or not the operative mechanisms are comparable here to those suggested by Benet and known to be relevant in this context in other parts of the Middle East.

In the cities the profession of a religion remains normative, but actual participation in religious observances by individuals varies from nil to complete. Among most Persian communities the established religion is Ja'farī Shī'a, although the people of certain areas such as parts of Kurdistān and of Balūchistān are Sunnī. Spooner travelled extensively in Iran in order to observe the practice of the established religion in many areas, though not in cities or large towns, since it is implied that innovations in the religious sphere are most likely to originate in towns. "The intention was to study the majority religion in its own community as unaffected as possible by foreign and modern influences and alien contacts, that is, in conditions where it was not self-conscious."[1] He concludes that there is an official religion, fed and taught in the countryside by men and ideas originating in urban centres. Various acts are required of believers, such as ritual praying, fasting, celebration, mourning, and other aspects of general conduct. In so far as attitudes are evoked in the believer by the performance of such actions, they involve an awareness of the unchanging, omnipotent, separate unity of God who is responsible for everything other than the decisions attained in terms of man's free will. Furthermore, they involve a feeling of equality with, and independence of, one's fellows before God. According to Spooner "this feeling of detachment . . .

[1] B. J. Spooner, "The Function of Religion in Persian Society", (*Iran*, IV, 1966), p. 83.

from one's fellow men is an integral part of the social order, whether that social order be viewed as a religio-social equality before God, or a politico-social equality before the Shāh".[1]

Iran contains many diverse religious groups within its boundaries. Yet, 98 per cent of the population is Muslim, of which 93 per cent is Shī'a, the remainder being Sunnī. There are some 50,000 Armenians, mainly in Āzarbāijān and in towns elsewhere, some 30,000 Nestorian Christians, a number of Jewish groups, probably about 100,000 Bahāī, and also certain Zoroastrian or Parsi communities. For the non-Islamic minorities such as the Zoroastrians of Yazd and Kirmān, the Christian sects, and the Muslims in situations evoking opposition to western, equated with Christian, influences, a religious stance is often only symbolic of a perception of threat to the total cultural configuration, of which religion is but a part.

It is in the cities and particularly in Tehrān that one sees most clearly the conflict of social groups which have evolved differently and correspond approximately to the "westernized" and the "traditionalist" classes. The latter contains both the unthinking, accepting element and the consciously traditionalist type of person who sees in innovation a threat to the social situation in which his own role and social situation are clearly defined and acceptable. Tehrān provides a splendid example of a dichotomy in these terms. The city consists of a westernized northern part and an "old fashioned" southern part. "The bonds between the inhabitants of these areas grow weaker; the north despises the south, and the south mocks, envies or hates the north. Antagonism between old and new values sometimes takes on the strongest forms: violent outbursts of the old spirit then serve to remind those who govern of this tribe which is, so to speak, camping outside the gates of a brand new city."[2]

According to Narāghī, Ābādān is a less characteristic instance of the urbanization process. While Tehrān is concerned with trade and politics, Ābādān lives on petroleum. "This mono-industrialization was deliberately accentuated by local authorities who wish to create an independent economic and social unit—for example, self-sufficient sociability (clubs), food supplies (co-operatives), employment centres (working class 'dynasties' in the petroleum industry)."[3]

Given, therefore, that in Iran there is a tripartite division of the

[1] B.J. Spooner, *op. cit.* p. 94.   [2] E. Narāghī, *op. cit.* p. 5.
[3] *Ibid.* pp. 5–6.

population into nomadic tribes, urban dwellers, and peasants, there is a somewhat complex social situation best understood, partly in terms of a scheme such as the folk-urban continuum provides, and partly in terms of the integrative mechanisms which hold the various components together within the state unit. One thing is certain, namely, the great need for effective integrative structures in so diverse a land which has only recently launched the endeavour of creating a nation state in the full modern sense, out of the great variety of peoples and groups which its boundaries contain. Frye[1] has pointed out that there is a long history not only of internal disunity and strong individualism, but also of solidarity in the face of the foreigner. "Indeed it is primarily the influence of Persian culture which has triumphed over the great physical and geographical obstacles to weld the various groups of Iran into one nation." Despite the diversity of the social groups in the country, it is noteworthy, as Wilber[2] has pointed out, that none of the constituent elements feels driven to attempt to detach itself from Iran. This is true of the Iranian Kurds, though their counterparts in both Turkey and Iraq are actively secessionists. Again, the Shi'a Āzar-bāijānī Turks have long been accustomed to regard the Sunni Turks of Anatolia with strong aversion, and to identify themselves politically with the Shi'a Persians. Again in the fast-growing Iranian towns such distinctions are being replaced by an urban outlook which often has no relationship with local origins. Yet "factional strife and community isolation remained as factors inimical to communal solidarity and national unity".[3] Wilber writes that few Iranians have a good word for people in other parts of the country. The villagers who have seen little of the country, beyond their own community, view most towns-people with distrust and have them categorized with epithets which are often uncomplimentary.

This account has, for purposes of description and understanding, categorized the social reality of Iran into city, tribal, and village units. Such a categorization accords with the usual anthropological approach of comparing the self-contained community isolate abstraction with reality. Any one of these units has customarily been considered a sufficient unit and an appropriate one for anthropological study. A certain comprehensive inclusiveness and breadth of view at a "primitive level"

[1] R. N. Frye, *Iran* (Allen and Unwin; London, 1960), p. 11.
[2] D. N. Wilber, *Contemporary Iran* (Praeger; New York, 1963), p. 13.
[3] *Ibid.* p. 45.

may result in a limitation of focus in the examination of more complex social groups. Quite evidently, in any part of the world, given certain conditions, any one of these units may function, at least for a time and for some purpose, in a comparatively independent manner and distinct from other units similarly defined. In situations of this type, "society" or the effective social group for the individual, within which he is significant, is composed of people who occupy a series of immediately contiguous places, geographically and socially: fellow tribesmen, neighbours in a village or group of villages, or else people in the city or some part of it. In any event, the social horizons are manifestly circumscribed. However, each unit of this kind must always have had some more or less systematic interrelations with other similarly constituted and defined groups, and the situation in modern Iran may in fact be regarded as a culmination of such processes of interaction over many years. Such interactions may be either hostile or friendly, distrustful or otherwise, co-operative or exploitative, but all have the common factor of expressing, inducing, and effecting a certain interrelatedness.

The larger cultural entities to which rural communities belong may or may not be institutionalized, and may or may not be formed on a hierarchical system. Among the non-institutionalized types are what are often called the cultural areas: linguistic, religious, "racial", technological. On the other hand, tribal societies, peasant federations, graded societies of the feudal type, and modern states are institutional entities to which the villages belong. "The closeness of the tie can be estimated by the number of social functions of all kinds, vital to the group, which are assumed by the higher entity."[1] Between the local community and the supra-local society of hierarchical type, there is a range of complex cultural situations in which it becomes difficult to say whether the territorial bond of community or the wider structural bond is the more important.

The development of village communities has become increasingly affected by the spread of the phenomena of modern civilization, such as industrialization, urbanization, and the extension of the money exchange economy. The institutions of modern-type states exercise various influences on these small social units. There is an observable tendency towards their integration into the state complexes, with an inevitable weakening of village structures. Under such influences, a local peasant community becomes less effective as a collective techni-

[1] I. Chiva, *op. cit.* p. 20.

cal agent, a setting for economic activity, a corporate body, and a source of law and social control.

In the past in Iran, whenever the central political authority was weak, then conditions were usually appropriate for the exploitation of peasant communities by urbanites and by pastoral raiders. Raiding of this kind was reputedly most prevalent among certain Kurdish tribes in the west and by Türkmen tribes in Khurāsān. Many nineteenth-century travellers from Europe have reported on the devastation caused by raiders in the latter area. Again, urban centres were attacked by both peasants and the tribes and in turn, the peasants dealt violently with any small and vulnerable numbers of pastoralists or urbanites who might come their way. Yet at all times these elements were interlocked with varying degrees of effectiveness in a larger politico-cultural and social configuration. Within such a configuration as the Iranian state of today, the long-established habitual distrust among villagers, urbanites, and nomads remains significant in the value systems and fraught with emotional connotations, and is expressed, for instance, in reciprocal terms of contempt or denigration, even in the context of relatively long-term peaceful political, economic, and social integration. Thus in Iran, as in much of the Middle East, an understanding of social reality may be achieved by assessing the various constituent elements in contexts of interrelationships, patterned by integrative structures which link units of various types on a regional basis and effect diverse types of subdivisions within the overall cultural configuration. The principal integrative mechanisms have an economic, political, religious and linguistic nature, and of these the first is always of some significance in linking the constituents, even in times of almost total breakdown of the other structures of integration.

In the long term, the peasantry is least dependent on external trading for its survival though it is very vulnerable to depredation. Even here however it is noteworthy that, as a result of depredation, a year's crop may be lost but the land itself and the basic means of future production remain. Depredation among pastoral nomads may have far more drastic consequences since there may be total destruction or removal of the means of production. However, depredation of peasant communities is far more usual, as has been abundantly testified by travellers in Iran in recent centuries; and the peasants may be driven into economic relationships outside the village, such as in sharecropping, or due to loss of landownership to urban landlords, as a consequence of economic failure and/or the search for protection of some kind. Again, viewed in economic terms, there is a perpetual demand by the peasant communities for some fundametally important foodstuffs which must be imported as, for example, sugar, salt, and processed goods such as metal objects, tools, and cloth, since local resources and skills cannot adequately provide all of these. The total annual needs for such commodities in a peasant household is small when assessed in monetary terms. This has been clearly demonstrated by Op't Land (1961) in the Dasht-i-Mughān. Nonetheless the needs of this kind which must be satisfied are of the utmost importance in the households and they constitute an effectual economic basis for social interactions.

Villages and tribes are the producers of foodstuffs which are essential for the non-producing town populations. Urban wealth is therefore partly utilized to obtain such commodities through middlemen who organize extra-urban and intra-urban trade. In extreme instances, the urban authority may resort to seizure of foodstuffs from rural populations and various forms of wealth from other urban units, should the normal arrangements break down.

Pastoralists specializing in animal production and growing few crops must obtain agricultural produce from sedentary communities and manufactured equipment from urban-based specialists. This is customarily done by trading, although raiding and brigandage occasionally provide an alternative solution. The latter is only effective in the short run, unless the areas exploited are perpetually changed. Trading is the only effective long-term solution. Barth[1] has described how the Hamawands entered southern Iraqi Kurdistān from Iran as nomadic herdsmen and they now live in areas just inside Iraq. "They entered on a career of brigandage, looting the caravans that passed between Persia and Iraq." The Hamawands reported that "For more than a generation we reaped our daily bread with our gun barrels". It is significant that they are atypical even in Kurdistān—so frequently renowned for its brigands, and also that their activity involved widely separated areas. Such considerations must always have applied to similarly constituted groups in adjacent areas of Iraq, as well as in Iran.

Given, therefore, that economic practices and trading are the prime means of integration, then the focal point of the process must be in the city or town where the urban traders, peasants, and pastoralists meet in the markets. As an extension of the marketing system, urban-based

[1] F. Barth (1953), op. cit. p. 45.

brokers and their agents travel into the countryside to buy all kinds of farm produce. The role of the village shopkeepers and itinerant merchants in the total pattern of economic exchange appears to be of secondary importance. As reported for the Dasht-i-Mughān for instance, the monetary turnover in a shop may be extremely low. Thus in the village of 'Alī Rezābād in that region eleven shops had annual turnovers of 728,000, 182,000, 130,000, 208,000, 78,000, 416,000, 187,000, 520,000, 36,500, 36,500, 54,800, and 182,000 rials. An auxiliary economic activity of some kind would appear to be necessary for many shopkeepers in order to sustain an adequate standard of living.

Political systems are, historically, the most variable of the integrative structures. They are characterized by always having been urban-based, and orientated towards furthering the interests of urban populations. Moreover, even in many contemporary situations, such systems have been regarded by their elites as being almost solely devices for the exploitation of rural and tribal areas for manpower and goods. They have tended to operate within fixed economic limits, focusing upon the control of hinterlands from defensible urban centres and, because of the difficulties inherent in mounting effective action against mobile pastoralists, have only recently approached any real physical control over tribal herders, a control which is still disputed by the tribes, particularly in Fārs. For Iran, the nation state itself may be taken as the maximal unit of regional integration, and there is little concern with supranational integration such as appears to interest various Arab states in the Middle East.

A religion may nominally be the ultimate reference for a great range of social sanctions operative among its adherents; it may be utilized as a general symbol of political solidarity and various cultural traits may fortuitously be attached to it. This frequently seems to prevent the precise categorization and analysis of religious phenomena. Thus Muslims, whilst praying, are engaged in a purely religious act. A man giving alms to the poor is engaged in an act which, whilst having religious connotations, may correctly be viewed in economic terms as a means of effecting a redistribution of wealth.

The integrative role of religion may be viewed as supranational in the Middle East. Historical evidence in the area suggests that religion as an integrative structure there defines in-groups in a basically negative fashion, and that such definition is only a secondary reflexion of primary definitions established in economic, political, and linguistic terms.

Since the initial expansion of Islam, at which time the interests deriving from all these various bases coincided, religious identification has tended to be associated with general ethnic and special economic and political interests, as is amply exemplified by the rise of sectarian divisions. Originally Islam had great success in integrating the political life of its adherents "in the formation of the *ummah* or Islamic community, which, while it had a religious basis, was also a political body".[1]

The religious heterogeneity of Iran, as of much of the Middle East, can perhaps best be considered by differentiating religion from the secular aspects of cultural activity. Nowadays the facts belie generalizations based on the concept of overriding allegiance to religious communities, and in fact serious behavioural studies of religious institutions and their function as integrative mechanisms are few in number.

Shī'ism, as such, may be regarded as a Persian phenomenon. "The Shī'ites, to begin with at least, were giving an Islamic form to the old South Arabian tradition of a kingdom with a semi-divine king."[2] Watt (1961) states that the Shī'ite movement was, in essence, a group of men, who found significance and security in being the followers of a charismatic leader. It attempted to supply Islam with that infallible actual authority which all religions seek and require. The Shī'ites placed that authority in a man, often regarded as a man-god. This is the central feature of the Shī'a faith, accompanied by innumerable subordinate ideas involving sacrifice, the atonement made at Karbala for the sins of mankind, the holding of the world as a dowry by Fatimah, the bearing aloft of 'Alī on the sinless shoulders of the Prophet during the iconoclastic raid on the Ka'aba, and many others. The whole complex of beliefs and ideas was not, of course, held simultaneously by all Shī'ites. However the belief system is frequently conceived of as being co-terminous with Iran, where it is today the official religion and as such may be considered as an efficient integrative mechanism—though perhaps of lesser contemporary relevance than formerly. If the definition of an entity is partly to be established by its distinctiveness when compared with another similarly constituted entity, then Shī'ism may well be distinct from Sunnism. In this way, integrative achievement by means of a religious polarity is attained. Nowadays it may be of less importance in this religious context than as a manifestation of distinctive Iranian identity recognizably separate from components of the non-Islamic world which impinge upon it.

[1] W. M. Watt, *Islam and the Integration of Society* (Routledge and Kegan Paul; London, 1961), p. 174.   [2] *Ibid.* p. 106.

Another major integrative structure is provided by language. National affiliation is reinforced by, and finds primary symbolic representation in, a highly emotional and explicit valuation of the national language, Farsi, by its primary speakers. There is, of course, nothing peculiar to Iran in this situation of linguistic identification, but a long history of complex population movements together with periods of comparative isolation of sub-groups has resulted in a pattern of some linguistic heterogeneity within the state frontiers. In spite of this, since the pattern of heterogeneity, defined linguistically, does not coincide with heterogeneity defined in other terms, the language situation may clearly be assumed to be an effective integrating factor. It cuts across economic divides, it overlaps religious divisions, and it intersects the nomadic–village–urban trilogy. Moreover the Persian language is now dominant in Iran, and either it, or else its forerunners, have been spoken in this region for some thousands of years. Kurdish, Pashtu, and Balūchī are closely related forms. Nevertheless there are numerous groups speaking quite different languages in Iran, particularly Turkish and Arabic.

Thus, whether viewed in cultural or in social-structural terms, or analysed on a basis of institutional interaction, it would appear that the crux of the current anthropological situation in Iran emerges through consideration of integrative mechanisms. The disparate parts of the social reality in modern Iran are in some respects isolated from one another, but this is merely because of our academically orientated way, now sanctioned by tradition, of looking at that reality. In fact, by means of a whole series of mechanisms, the isolate, for so long the unit of anthropological study, is being inexorably integrated into ever larger units. Quite evidently, analysis of an integrative process and of an integrated structure of the kind discussed for Iran is difficult. It is certainly more complex and more difficult to handle than is the particular, discrete and fairly homogeneous community whether pastoral or peasant, or the "majority culture" as defined either in terms of the numerically predominant religious sect, or else through casual generalization achieved by ignoring (or else being ignorant of) socio-cultural diversity.

The notion of social change in Iran is both expressed and implied in much of this article. Change occurs in all societies; it is really only the rate of change which varies from one society to another. Social pressures for change may always be present within a particular system, but if these pressures are markedly increased by the impinging of a new social pattern upon the old, there will inevitably ensue an acceleration of change, through the medium of social institutions. A society, however organized, allows a certain measure of choice for its individual members. The total social system may make it very difficult for individuals to depart far from traditional norms and behaviour patterns; and yet, individuals are able, and are allowed, to choose among a number of permissible courses of social action. What western influences have done in Iran, as in so much of the underdeveloped world, is to increase the range of choices available for the individual, and so to speed the rate of change since more and more courses of action become acceptable. Some individuals will choose to remain within the traditional scheme of things. Writing of the village of Balgat near Ankara, Lerner considers the village chief and the grocer. In a situation of social change such as may currently be found in so much of the Middle East, "the Chief...desires to be, and usually is, a vibrant sound box through which echo the traditional Turkish virtues". From his "parochial fund of traditional virtues, the Chief drew equally his opinions of great men, nations, issues".[1] On the other hand the grocer has departed from this traditionally orientated world. "He lives in a different world, an expansive world, populated more actively with imaginings and fantasies—hungering for whatever is different and unfamiliar." He said "I want better things. I would have liked to have a bigger grocery shop in the city, have a nice house there, dress in nice civilian clothes." All the dreams are not yet realized, but the desires are there and simply await their fulfilment in course of time and in the not-too-distant future. These prototypes exist very widely in the Middle East countries though in different proportions from place to place.

New social situations have to be assessed by individuals involved in them, a choice has to be made with regard to the differential socio-economic potential which they offer, and an estimation as to the value of the new as compared with the old. The advantages or gains implied in the various situations may be gauged in terms of prestige, wealth, power, and so on. Evidently, all these factors are differentially significant and important to various personalities in these social situations involving conscious choice and decision.

The actual innovations which induce change may be of many kinds.

[1] D. Lerner, *op. cit.* p. 23.

Daryll Forde observes that "the impact of new techniques often leads to socially destructive individualism and conflicts of loyalties".[1] Again, among the Marsh Arabs "the impact of the market economy has greatly disturbed the former relation between economic and social standing. It also reflects the existence side by side in the same society of two opposed sets of values, the mercantile and the tribal."[2] In Iran, social changes often stem from economic considerations, but there is, as is dramatically evident in Iraqi Kurdistan also, social change due to the impinging of an external administration on the indigenous tribal or village administrative system as the case may be. Socially organized semi-autonomous groups of a tribal and non-tribal kind cannot comfortably exist within one political entity. Any attempt at coexistence may lead to political instability in the larger unit and social difficulty in both.

It has also been argued that there is an inherent instability in societies where the overwhelming majority of the population is organized on the basis of peasant village communities. Parsons suggests that "one of the reasons for this is the fact that the village community as a primary force of solidarity can only within very narrow limits be an effective unit for the organization of the use of force. It is, in the face of any more extensive organization, not a defensible unit. Hence, there must always be a 'superstructure' over a peasant society which, among other things, organizes and stabilizes the use of force. The question is how far such a superstructure is, as it were, 'organically' integrated with the self-contained village communities, and often the level of integration is not high."[3] Any inherent instability in the Iranian setting to which the quotation could be referred is progressively and more efficiently counteracted by the integration achieved by the political superstructure, reinforced as it is by economic and other, social factors.

Social change is very evident in the nature of institutionalized activity, and in the behaviour of individuals. Novel characteristic patterns of behaviour emerge during periods of social change. That is, the defined relationships, appropriate among members of society, are altered, and this may be as the result of any one of a great variety of factors, though frequently these are technological. Changes of this kind are everywhere evident in Iran, most of all, perhaps, among the large numbers of newcomers to the towns. There, the traditional role and status with

[1] C. D. Forde and R. Scott, *The Native Economies of Nigeria* (Faber; London, 1946), p. 30.
[2] S. M. Salim, *op. cit.* p. 143.
[3] T. Parsons, *The Social System* (Tavistock Publ. Ltd; London, 1952), pp. 162–3.

which they are familiar are no longer fully effective means of regulating social behaviour. In particular, role and status dependent upon kinship may be quite inappropriate, and the new relationships into which a person enters depend on quite different criteria according to personal attributes and ambition, as, for example, in marriage or occupation. Marriage becomes less an arranged matter in the hands of kin groups than a matter of choice by the individuals directly involved. Again, with the minimized importance of kin groups, various claims on services made upon kin and rewards for services rendered become very different. The whole idea of hiring labour, though known in peasant society, is mainly operative in villager–external landlord relationships and not in intra-village relationships. Whilst entirely pre-commercial, Iranian villages are usually no more than partially organized in accordance with commercial principles.

We have seen that production in Iran is frequently organized on a small scale and that the peasant communities are for many purposes self-contained units. In fact Redfield distinguishes the wholly self-contained "folk community" from the peasant community which is a population living on the land, but linked to a town where produce is marketed, some necessities obtained, and from which it is governed by locally resident officials. Even so, despite the essential relations between town and country, for the peasants nearly all the crucial events of life are village-centred and other events, focusing upon extra-village life, are of marginal significance to the community which the village contains.

Both the nature and the scale of the processing and producing techniques used in peasant societies are comparatively simple and crude compared with those of the "advanced" societies and can serve as a basic means of distinguishing the two. It appears that, voluntarily or otherwise, westernization, particularly in the form of technical advance as a means of raising living standards, is desirable and wished for by many Iranian peasants and especially by those outside the village communities who have their welfare in view. The introduction of technological advances appears by far the surest means of inducing social changes in peasant groups. Westernization causes far more noticeable economic changes than political changes in Iranian village communities. This is very evident since economic changes in such small-scale social groups must affect all the individuals in those units. They are too small for the social isolation of the non-conformist individual to be effective.

Modern farming techniques, the growth of new crops, the sale of the crops grown for cash, and the method of organizing the agricultural cycle must all surely affect every member of the community whether actively participating in the novel activity or not. This process of change has been under way in Iran and adjacent areas for some time. Leach, writing of the Ruwāndiz Kurds, observes that "owing to the increased trading contacts opened up since the coming of the road, and the need to satisfy newly developed wants for imported 'luxury' goods, the whole structure of the economic organization of these hill people is undergoing very rapid change and readjustment".[1]

It may be more generally stated that an increase in the importance attached to a monetary economy and, on a national scale, industrialization will inevitably produce striking changes in many aspects of the social structure of the affected group. Economic changes induce subsequent changes in social relationships. "The wider relationships involved in large scale commerce and industry are focused in the urban centres which new developments have either created or greatly enlarged, and it is there that the new social groups which they have called into being are growing up. The social structure of these towns is affected only a little by the rural background of their new populations, and it is better discussed by itself as something which is being created rather than experiencing change."[2]

The terms used to denote changes of this kind are many and varied. It may be useful to quote from Dr Mair's work—"Acculturation was officially described by Linton, Redfield and Herskovitz in 1936 as comprehending 'those phenomena which result when groups of individuals having different cultures come into continuous first-hand contact, with subsequent changes in the original culture patterns of either or both groups'. It is a narrower term than 'culture change', which would include internally generated change, and wider than 'assimilation', which may be 'a phase of acculturation'."[3]

Most British anthropologists consider society or social relations as their main theme of study, and would agree with Fortes when he wrote "Culture contact is a process of the same order as other processes of social interaction, both in the literate societies of Europe, America and Asia and in the pre-literate societies of other parts of the world", and

---

[1] E. R. Leach, *op. cit.* p. 33.
[2] L. Mair, *New Nations* (Weidenfeld and Nicolson; London, 1963), p. 32.
[3] *Ibid.* p. 199.

"the anthropologist must work with communities rather than customs. His unit of observation must be . . . a unit of common participation in the everyday political, economic and social life."[1] As we have seen, the structure of society is not immutable. Normative patterns of behaviour are required by all societies of their members. Equally, these patterns, however validated and enforced, are by no means accepted unquestioningly by all. This being so, the feasibility of change occurring is evident. Socially constructed and defined rules and laws which seek to limit and to control individual behaviour are nevertheless transgressed and the frequency of the transgressions may be taken as an index of the need felt for social change. A chasm between normative and actual behaviour patterns presupposes changes in value systems. Evidently when many social rules are simultaneously contravened, social difficulty and chaos ensue. This may occasionally be disastrous as far as the previous social order is concerned, but in all known instances there eventually emerges a new social order. Thus the diversity of social organization among the world's peoples today can be expressed in terms of differential social changes in the past. Total social integration of individuals is unknown anywhere, and so conflict between individuals and the social system is always found, and herein lies a fundamental cause of social change. Conflict presupposes a dissatisfaction with at least a significant part of the current social reality and a desire, possibly ill-expressed, to change it. Given this desire for change among a large group, then the change will surely occur. The effect of the West impinging upon traditional Iranian society was, as elsewhere, simply to accelerate the rate of change and to pose novel questions of adjustment to new social conditions for the people involved. Mair has cogently argued that whereas in the advanced, western countries, technological advance has been gradual and continuous, in a society such as that of Iran this is not so, with the result that its sudden introduction (as a thing complete in itself) has produced a wide gap between the old society and that which is sought for and emulated today, that is, western-type society. The adoption of western-originated technical advances here as elsewhere increase man's control over his environment and makes "it possible to link wider circles of people in continuing social relationships to which recognized norms of conduct apply. Some inventions, in weapons and communications, have increased the possible

[1] M. Fortes, "Culture Contact as a Dynamic Process", *Methods of Study of Culture Contact in Africa* (Int. Af. Inst. Memo. xv, 1938).

range of governmental control; the most recent have increased the possible range of material comforts, and made it necessary for people who wish to enjoy these comforts to be organized for economic co-operation on a scale undreamt of two centuries ago."[1]

Consequently, in Iran, many of the challenges to the persistence, or very gradual change of past social patterns, have originated from the impact of the West upon the country. Modern Iran, looking at the West, became increasingly aware of superior military strength, economic power, material prosperity, democratic institutions, and well-organized systems of law, education, and administration. Iranians felt peculiar mixtures of frustration, jealousy, resentment, and even hatred. Some eminent individuals advocated copying the West; others sought refuge and solace in ancient traditions and particularly in religion, whilst others attempted and advocated the implementation of social and political reforms that might eventually lead to success in competition and coexistence with the West.

As the twentieth century wore on, a new generation in Iran increasingly repudiated the formalism and authoritarianism of Iranian society. Some of this group have questioned the necessity for allegiance to the monarchy, Islam, traditional ethics, and the structure of society. They queried the nature and the necessity for their required allegiance to the family, and later to many other forms of established social patterns. They actively sought new allegiances and novel standards and, finding difficulty in discovering them remained "... suspended between two alien worlds—that of the older Iran and that of an unknown future".[2] Some placed their faith in humanism, but more in materialism, especially in order to find security within a society where insecurity seemed widespread. Financial security was in fact sought not by persistent application to one business but by speculation in land, housing and the like. As they prospered, so were they attracted by western-style consumption patterns, social behaviour, and other attributes and they withdrew from the cultural interests of previous generations of the privileged elite. Many felt no real allegiance to a society from which they felt progressively divorced.

It has been noted that changes occur in all societies: in Iran, there has been a marked acceleration in the rate of change during recent years. Thus, tribal society no longer provides all that is considered necessary by many tribal people for an adequately full life. Among

[1] L. Mair, *op. cit.* p. 215. [2] D. N. Wilber, *op. cit.* p. 56.

681

members of the young and the educated groups in particular, traditional allegiance to agnatic descent groups, to those who carry out their herding together, to tribal chiefs with their ascribed rather than achieved status, all seem ever less relevant. In addition, there is increasing economic and social identification with non-tribal society, a process frequently equated with "progress". Even so, the tribal "problem" remains, since there are groups still organized on a tribal basis, utilizing the natural resources of the Iranian mountains and plateau very much along traditional lines and, in so doing, maintaining a certain independence of action which still occasionally conflicts with the Iranian national government. This way of life, though economically viable, is politically unsatisfactory.

Equally, however, progress is evident in the peasant communities and is often considered desirable by these comparatively uninformed people since they believe that progress will bring in its train a certain ease, contentment, medical care and so good health, and prosperity, all with minimal effort on their part. In particular, it will be the means of ending the backbreaking toil necessitated by their present crude agricultural techniques. It is paradoxical that, despite the wish for progress, traditionalism is still very powerful and there is "very little room for variation from the village-ratified and validated norms of behaviour and response".[1] The social situations which arise in the traditional village allow predictable individual responses to occur. However, one innovation in such a context may lead to many others. "Empirical data have demonstrated that one single innovation, if accepted and incorporated into a social order, can bring about an ever-increasing degree of innovation and change."[2]

Thus the comparatively self-sufficient village communities in Iran change, partly as a result of the impinging of outside factors, and partly as a result of active volition and initiative by the villagers. But in either event more and more non-conformists appear who disregard traditionalism, at least in some respects, and who are able to cope successfully with unfamiliar social demands, to accept alien value systems, and to adopt new technological skills.

Changes of this kind are most pronounced in the urban centres and, from these, new ideas and skills penetrate the countryside. The standards of the towns and cities constitute goals desired by many rural people

[1] R. H. Nolte, ed., *The Modern Middle East* (Atherton Press; New York, 1963), p. 115.
[2] *Ibid.* p. 122.

who hope there to find social fulfilment by means of their own achievements, irrespective of their traditional role and status in the villages. The intellectual elite, business specialists, and governmental agencies all have urban bases and from these they would appear to intend to continue the process of social change now operative through most of Iranian society. In this way one could envisage an ultimate integration of the heterogeneous elements within the country into one viable entity.

CHAPTER 21

LAND REFORM IN IRAN

Within the period of 1962–4, the Shāh and his Council of Ministers promulgated a series of decrees aimed at fundamental reform of the social, political, and economic structure of Iran. These reforms have become generally known as the "Six-point Reform" or the "Shāh's revolution". The most significant measures in this reform programme are those concerned with agriculture and the system of land holding. Resulting transfer of large areas of agricultural land from the hands of a small group of proprietors to the mass of share-croppers will inevitably do much to alter the pattern of economic and social life within the country. In the following discussion, the legislative basis of the land reform, the background to its implementation, and the observable results arising from it will be examined in turn.

The speed with which land reform is currently being implemented has surprised opinion both within and outside the country. The need for some kind of reform had long been recognized, and as early as 1906 there was open advocacy of the re-distribution of landlord estates to the cultivating peasants during the Constitutional Movement of 1906–21. Yet, apart from tentative and largely unsuccessful attempts to distribute *khāliseh* (Domain Land) in Sīstān and Khūzistān, the land problem remained and the situation appeared highly intractable even to the most optimistic observer, who saw that "A wide-spread conservatism is . . . an obstacle to change: there has always been an endeavour on the part of the government and the landowners to maintain the status quo; a tendency in which, it must be admitted, the peasants largely acquiesce".[1] As late as 1951, an informed observer could remark that "the same deterrents to reform which have existed for generations are still in evidence today". Nonetheless, the steadily increasing pressure for change and agricultural development witnessed in other parts of the Middle East has not been without its counterpart in Iran, and it is to the credit of the present Shāh that he has harnessed these pressures to help overcome the impasse surrounding landownership and tenure.

The condition of rural Iran before land reform has been well docu-

[1] A. K. S. Lambton, *Landlord and Peasant in Persia* (R.I.I.A. 1953).

684

mented by Professor Lambton. Wide variations in tenurial and physical characteristics from village to village make meaningful generalization impossible, but the basic forces underpinning the land system may be usefully isolated as a preliminary to discussion of the changes wrought in it by recent land reform legislation. The *iqtaʿ* (land assignment institution), which underlies the present landholding situation was used as an administrative and financial device and thus was bureaucratic in conception, rather than a feudal system on the West European model. The assignee was expected to act as the agent and regional representative of central authority in all its many aspects, from tax collection to military control. Consequently, the power of the large landholders tended to be absolute and become more so with distance from the seat of central government.

Curtailment of the powers of the landlords could be brought about usually only by violent displacement either by force of arms or by political intrigue. This in turn has led to insecurity of tenure and the growth of a tradition whereby most landlords undertook only minor short-term improvements in their lands and sought to amass the maximum amount of profit in the shortest time in order to buttress their political and military position. Even in modern times, insecurity of tenure has continued to be an important influence, with relatively large land areas being forcibly moved from private hands into the Crown Domain in the period of Reza Shāh's rule.

Insecurity, whilst afflicting the actual owners of land, also affected the peasant class to a greater or lesser extent, depending on local practices of share-cropping. In most areas of the country, the peasants were liable to be expelled at the discretion of the landlord. While this right was in practice rarely used by the landlords, the mere existence of the threat and its maintenance in custom through annual land redistribution and other landlord tactics designed to preclude peasants acquiring permanent right in land was sufficient to create an atmosphere of insecurity, and discourage long-term interest on the part of the peasant cultivator.

The majority of large landowners in Iran were neither willing nor, in many cases, able even with the best intentions to play a personal role in the running of their estates. Thus, day-to-day administration of large areas of the country was left to the care of landlords' bailiffs or contractors. It might be argued that the landlord class had a traditional, if pecuniary, interest in looking to the welfare of the peasants, but this could not be said of the bailiffs. Even more than the landlord, the bailiff, holding a temporary position and having little feeling of obligation, identity, or patronage interest towards his villagers, was prepared to exact high returns from both land and people. Furthermore, since the bailiff was often of peasant stock himself, he was equally unaware as the villagers of any opportunities for agricultural improvement and, in consequence, rarely contributed significantly to advance in the use of seeds, tools, or methods.

Lack of leadership from the landowner and his agent in the technical field was but infrequently compensated by the peasants themselves. Until comparatively modern times, with the notable exception of the Birjand region, the peasantry were isolated by lack of training and educational facilities from knowledge of management and agricultural improvement. Similarly, the peasant had access only to limited and expensive sources of unorganized credit, while, under the prevailing tenurial and tax conditions, by which as much as 85 to 90 per cent of the government's tax revenue could come from indirect taxation, his opportunities for accumulating capital were very restricted.

These were some of the salient elements of and features arising from the situation in Iran before the implementation of the Land Reform Law and Additional Articles to it of 1962 and 1963: ownership of large areas of land based on military and fiscal expediency, insecurity of tenure at both the landlord and the peasant level, an absence of incentive for agricultural improvement, and isolation of the peasantry from knowledge of conditions prevailing in other areas and countries.

There are discrepancies between the available figures for the distribution of landownership, largely because of the inadequate census data and variations in the definition of the basic village unit. Estimates of the number of villages in Iran range from 42,000 to 58,000, but it is now generally accepted for land reform purposes that there are 48,592 villages in the country. Distribution of ownership in terms of area cannot, however, be calculated from the arbitrary village unit, and thus it is difficult to gauge the pre-reform situation in this important dimension.

The overall position of landownership in the country before implementation of the 1962 Land Reform Law is illustrated in table 13. From these figures, it may be seen that observers attribute varying values to each ownership group discernible in Iran. Nevertheless, available statistics indicate clearly that about 56 per cent of cultivated land was owned by 1 per cent of the population. About one third of the total agricultural land held by these large proprietors was controlled by 0·2 per cent of the agricultural population. Small-holders and peasant owners are estimated to have had between 10 and 12 per cent of the total cultivated land.

TABLE 13. *Estimates of the distribution of landownership in the period before the Land Reform Law of January 1962*

Type of ownership	Per cent of all land owned	Number of villages	Per cent of all villages
Large proprietors	56·0[a,b,d]	13,569[c]	34·43
(of whom those owning over 100 ha)	33·8[d]	—	—
Small proprietors	10–12[d]	16,522[c]	41·93
Royal Domain	10–13[d]	812[c,e]	2·06
Religious endowment	1–2[d,f]	713[c]	1·81
Tribal holdings	13·0[d]	—	—
Public Domain	3–4[g]	1,444[c,g]	3·67
Other holdings	—	6,346	16·10

Notes

[a] G. Hadary (1951) suggests that 56·0 per cent of all land owned is in the hands of 100,000 proprietors.

[b] This figure is supported by Eng. Dehbud, Deputy Director of the Land Reform Organization, who quotes 55 per cent of land belonging to large proprietors.

[c] Latest official estimates by the Land Reform Organization, quoted by D. Homāyūn, (1963).

[d] G. Scarcia (1962).

[e] Official statistics, Administration of Crown Estates (*Idāreh-ye Amlāk*).

[f] Dehbud (1963) quotes 15 per cent for charitable endowments as a likely figure. Hadary (1951) suggests 25 per cent as the total area of *vaqf*.

[g] Some 1,800 villages were Public Domain in 1951. Dehbud (1963) quotes 1,754 villages in the Public Domain in 1963. The difference in these figures and the official figures noted in the table above is due to the inclusion of farmstead settlements in the former calculations.

Quite apart from the private owners of agricultural land, large estates were also held in the hands of the State, Crown, and administrators of religious endowments. Hadary (1951) contended that "the largest single owner of land is the government, which actively controls from nine to thirteen million acres of land", a claim which is supported by consideration of the number and percentage importance of Public Domain villages. The figures in table 13 further show that according to the Agricultural Census 1,444 villages fall officially into the category of Public Domain, accounting from some 3·67 per cent of total villages in Iran. In the period previous to the distribution of Crown

Domains, these accounted for some 10 to 13 per cent of all lands owned. In fact, 812 villages remained in the Crown Domain at the time of the Agricultural Census in 1957, accounting for 2·06 per cent of total villages. Of the large surface area included in the Crown Domains, it is estimated that some 80 per cent was forest and range land. In the period 1951 to 1957, the Administration of Crown Lands estimates that 120,000 hectares had been distributed among the peasants.

The religious endowment lands referred to in table 13 account only for those villages which are designated for public charitable works, *vaqf-i ʿamm*, i.e. lands endowed for public charities such as schools and shrines, and do not include those constituted for private use, *vaqf-i khās*, i.e. lands endowed for the personal benefit of the benefactor's successors. Of the 713 villages entirely devoted to charitable *vaqf*, some 466 are dedicated to the Shrine of the Imām Riẓā at Mashhad, with 430 of these actually located in Khurāsān Province. The total area of *awqāf* holdings, which is made up of innumerable tiny fragments of land (representing as little as $\frac{2}{91}$ of the village ploughlands in the case of one village in Turbat-i-Ḥaidarī) in addition to the entire villages noted above, is variously estimated. The Land Reform Organization suggests that some 15 per cent of cultivated land is "private endowment, public endowment or a combination of these", whilst other sources put the total at as much as one quarter of the total cultivated land. Scarcia (1962) puts the figure for *vaqf* as low as 1 to 2 per cent. It is clear whichever way one regards the situation, that *awqāf* land still represents a large element in the Iranian landholding system, especially in Khurāsān.

Radical changes in the landowning hierarchy are not new to Iran. Financial and political expediency had periodically forced the ruling groups to interfere with and reorganize the distribution of land-ownership and the systems of land tenure with a view to increasing the State revenues through agricultural and land taxation. As late as Qājār times, changes of this kind were effected in the agrarian structure.

During the twentieth century, continuing pressure for financial reform and the growing need for modernization in the face of the technical and political advance of the Western World brought about a limited demand for reform of landholding. Concepts of social justice and egalitarianism also tended to influence the politically active intellectuals who had studied and travelled in Europe, particularly France. These various formative pressures had opportunity for expression during the period of the Constitution of 1906–21, when the Democratic Party championed the appropriation of large landed estates and the distribution of land to working peasants. During this period, certain measures for reform of landholding were put into effect, e.g. abolition of the *tuyūl* (land assignant) in 1907, but these had relatively little impact because of the general spread of lawlessness at that time throughout the country and the interference—for reasons other than land reform —of interested foreign powers, mainly Russia and Britain.

The rule of Rezā Shāh brought little change in the agricultural sector and throughout his reign the land system remained intact, though the pattern of ownership was changed somewhat with the movement of several large estates, expropriated by the Shāh, into the Crown Domain. In the later years of Rezā Shāh's reign, an attempt was made to control and improve the conditions of the landless and share-cropping peasants by legislation. The first enactment of November 1937 was designed to ensure that landlords, especially non-resident landlords, would keep their lands in a productive state by taking more personal interest in exploitation and maintenance of sources of water supply. Since the Act was intended to operate at the local level through the regional governors, who were in most cases of the landlord class, its provisions were hardly ever enforced. A second attempt to improve rural conditions by legislation was tried in September 1939. On this occasion, the Majlis empowered select committees from the Ministry of Agriculture and the Ministry of Justice to re-examine the question of land division between landlord and peasant and report their findings and recommendations to the Assembly. With the outbreak of war, the proposal was not followed by the necessary rules of procedure (*āīnnāmeh*) and was thus never implemented.

The issue of agricultural reform was not reopened until 1946, when the Council of Ministers approved a bill which stipulated that landlords increase the crop-share of peasants and share-croppers by 15 per cent. The bill was enforced in some areas, but, since it was valid for only one year, it lapsed in the face of the united opposition of the landlords, who in 1947 constituted a conference to review the effects of the law and recommended its discontinuance. This situation, of opposition to land reform from the landlord groups both within and outside the Majlis, countered by a demand for such reform from the more progressive elements amongst western-trained intellectuals and the non-landowning classes, continued as an underlying factor in the political

44   689

activities of the period. In fact, the political power of the landlords, expressed mainly through the Majlis, two thirds of whose members were landowners, continued to prevail until the new Land Reform Law was implemented in the years 1962–3.

In the post-1945 period, land reform became an established part of the policies of many political parties in the Middle East and, in the hands of the emergent revolutionary governments, had developed into a social, economic, and political weapon. Land reforms of varying effectiveness were passed and implemented in Egypt in 1952, Syria and Iraq in 1958, with Turkey committed to a less radical but more carefully considered programme of agrarian reform from 1945 onwards. In consequence, the inequalities of landholding and corresponding maldistribution of income among rural classes in Iran were made to seem all the worse by comparison with progress achieved in neighbouring countries. Through travel abroad, propaganda broadcasts from Egypt, Iraq, and the U.S.S.R., and receipt of left-wing newspapers published outside Iran, students, intellectuals, and other politically conscious groups were informed of reform activity in other countries and of Iran's increasing agrarian backwardness relative to its close neighbours.

Within the country, the gathering movement for reform, together with increasing foreign pressure upon the administration to put its house in order, persuaded the Shāh to attempt land reform once again through direct constitutional channels. Iran's allies in the West were especially concerned at this time that weaknesses in the agrarian structure would reduce the country's power to resist Communist penetration and possible social and political revolution. In May 1960 a bill, drafted rather inadequately by or under the influence of foreign advisers, was presented to the Majlis proposing among other provisions that the maximum individual landholding should be limited to 400 hectares of irrigated land, 800 hectares of dry land, or a combination of these. Generous provision was made for the regulated transfer of land within the landowning families. Although the bill was passed by the Majlis on 16 May, it provoked the opposition of the leading *mujtahid*, Āyātullāh Burūjirdī, who proclaimed the law contrary to both the Shari'a and the constitution. No attempt was made to implement this law, which in any case suffered considerable modification to the benefit of the landlords during its passage through the assembly.

The early history of the reform of Crown and Public Domain lands was slightly happier than that of privately owned lands. First steps in the distribution of Public Domain lands were taken during the years 1932 and 1933, when Rezā Shāh obtained the approval of the Majlis for the transfer of Public Domain lands to cultivating peasants in the regions of Luristān, Kirmānshāh and the Dasht-i-Mughān. In fact, the area of land actually transferred to private hands was very small, and Luristān was entirely unaffected by the implementation of the Act. The Sīstān region was subject to the provisions of a 1937 Act for the distribution of the Sīstān Domain lands, but as a result of misappropriation and mismanagement, particularly the failure to provide adequate credit facilities for the new peasant proprietors, land moved into the ownership of merchants and large proprietors.

In the post-1945 era, after an abortive attempt at reform of the Public Domains in 1949, further sales of Public Domain took place under the provisions of the 1955 law for the distribution of Public Domains. Implementation of the law began in 1958, when Public Domains throughout the country were made available to peasants and share-croppers actually cultivating them, to a maximum of ten hectares on irrigated land and fifteen hectares on dry land. In the period up to the promulgation of the Additional Articles to the Land Reform Law in January 1963, it is estimated that some 157 villages of the Public Domain were distributed amongst 8,366 families.

By the Amended Law for the sale of the Public Domain lands, passed by decree in February 1963, the previous system and rate of disposal of lands was abandoned and replaced by the provisions of the Additional Articles to the Reform Law of the same year. Under the original law for the sale of Public Domain lands, each property had been surveyed and divided into blocks of ten to fifteen hectares, and later distributed to peasants and share-croppers. This process, although allowing holdings to be divided evenly among the peasants, was both slow and costly in operation. While some 157 villages had been distributed in the period 1958 to 1963 (end of January), no less than 318 villages were distributed under the terms of the amended law within the period from February to September 1963.

Reform of the Crown Domains began in 1951. Before that time, the Crown Domains had been subject to vicissitudes mainly as a result of the doubtful circumstances under which a section of them—*amlāki vā guzārī* or the Ceded Properties (see Lambton, 1953, p. 257)—had been acquired by Rezā Shāh. In fact, the Ceded Properties were made up of lands appropriated, forcibly purchased, or compulsorily exchanged for other estates during the reign of Rezā Shāh. On the accession to the throne of Moḥammad Rezā Shāh in 1941, the Ceded Properties were transferred to the State under a royal decree and, in the following year, a law was promulgated providing for the return of the estates to their former owners through the *Idāreh Amlāk*. Although some areas were returned to their owners by the *Idāreh Amlāk*, the bulk was retained and, in July 1949, converted into *vaqf* for the Pahlavī family with the income allotted for charitable purposes to the Imperial Organization of Social Services. Partly to set an example to other landed proprietors and partly, no doubt, in his own interests, the Shāh issued a decree in January 1951 enacting a law for the sale of the Ceded Properties to the cultivating peasants. Despite the fact that the Ceded Properties then constituted *vaqf* and were thus inalienable under the Civil Code, the legality of the decree has not been challenged.

Within the decade 1953–62, some 517 villages are reported to have been distributed among resident cultivators totalling 42,203 farm families. In the period January to September 1963 a further 289 villages of the crown estate were sold to the peasants.

Reform of the Public and Crown Domains was clearly seen to produce striking political results favourable to the Shāh. Land reform activities could be of considerable propaganda value both within Iran itself and also abroad, particularly in Europe and the United States of America. From the accumulated experience of these limited reforms, it was apparent that the peasants were capable of managing their own farms when given the opportunity to do so together with a minimum of support services—especially credit facilities. These factors helped to augment the pressures for land reform from other sources, and thus from this situation arose later general reform of the agrarian structure.

The law governing the first phase of land reform was drawn up and approved by the Council of Ministers and the Shāh in the absence of the Majlis after its prorogation in 1961. Previous experience of the treatment of land reform legislation by the landlord-dominated Majlis had indicated with no lack of clarity that effective measures could be drafted and implemented only by the direct authority of the Crown. In an attempt to keep within the word of the constitution, the Land Reform Law of 1962 was treated as an amendment to the existing Land Reform Act of 1960 rather than as a new directive from the Crown.

Article 38 of the Act provided that the decree be subject to confirmation by the next Majlis. The 1962 law remains the basis of land reform throughout the country up to the present time, and all changes in the reform appear as additions to or revised regulations for the 1962 law.

The Land Reform Law of 9 January 1962 contains a total of nine chapters dealing with a multitude of aspects of the reform, from transfer of ownership to the provision of agricultural services. Chapter Two lays down that the maximum land area to be held in absolute ownership by one person is to be one village of six *dang*,[1] or parts of various villages to a total of six *dang*. All landlords holding more than six *dang* are required to transfer ownership of their excess lands to the peasants working the area, or to sell these lands to the government, which will itself arrange distribution of land to the occupying peasants. In the case of lands being endowed for private use, the limit of one village for each beneficiary is again applicable, the excess being subject to sale.

The limit of six *dang* of land held by one owner applies only to share-cropping areas under field crops. Additionally, a person may retain lands under orchards, tea plantations, or woodland where he holds sole rights in both land and water. Again, land utilized for mechanized cultivation entailing the employment of fixed, daily-paid labour is left in the hands of individual owners, in addition to the one village maximum stipulated in the Law.

All lands which are uncultivated and which lie outside the service area of existing village water supplies are liable to expropriation by the State for the purpose of land distribution.

Chapter Three of the Land Reform Law lays down the means and the methods to be used in purchase and expropriation of the lands defined in Chapter Two. The supreme body responsible for supervising and controlling purchase and expropriation is the Land Reform Council, made up of the Minister of Agriculture, the Director of the Land Reform Organization, and four other high-ranking members of the Ministry of Agriculture. Actual implementation of land acquisition policies determined by the Land Reform Council is delegated to the Land Reform Organization, the Director of which is to be recommended by the Minister of Agriculture and the appointment confirmed by the Crown. Final sanction for the decisions of the Land Reform Council

---

[1] Iranian villages are normally divided into six parts (*dang*). The *dang* has no absolute areal value and varies from village to village depending on the amount of cultivated land each village has.

and, by implication, of the Land Reform Organization itself is to be with the Council of Ministers.

The Land Reform Organization is bound to notify all landlords twice that they must declare their holdings, including those which are above the maximum limits prescribed by Chapter Two. Landlords are allowed one month in which to make their returns of total holdings to the local Land Reform Organization Department. Stringent penalties are provided for use against intransigent landlords who fail to comply with or seek to evade the law.

Landlords who comply with the demand to declare their properties are to be compensated for those lands adjudged to be in excess of the limits defined by Chapter Two. Chapter Four stipulates that the purchase price of estates thus bought by the government is to be reached by establishing an index for land values in any given region, and then multiplying this index by the land tax pertaining to the particular estate in question. In effect, the so-called index is a mean value of sample villages in any given region, averaging out variations in income accruing to the landlords as a result of location, utilized resources, and traditional practices in dividing the crop between landlord and peasant. Where the application of average values for a region to a particular estate is felt to be unfavourable, the owner may appeal to a reviewing committee independent of the Land Reform Organization, although it is specifically stated that such appeals will not hinder the process of land acquisition in any way.

Once the price of an estate or fragment of land to be purchased by the State has been settled, the sum is to be paid to the ex-landlord in ten annual instalments by the Agricultural Bank, the first payment being due on the date of purchase. Later legislation extended the repayment period to fifteen years.

The redistribution of land purchased under the foregoing regulations is to be governed by the provisions of Chapter Five of the law. Here, it is stipulated that lands taken over by the Ministry of Agriculture are to be redistributed forthwith to suitable applicants at a cost of the purchase price from the ex-landlord together with a service charge not exceeding 10 per cent. This price is to be repaid to the Agricultural Bank over a period of fifteen years.

For the purposes of the law, suitable applicants are those engaged in agricultural production in the area of each village or part of a village to be redistributed, but who do not own land of their own. Specifically, this is designed to make land available to share-croppers, though the definition is framed in such a way that local officials of the Land Reform Organization may also grant land to other local residents where this is feasible and desirable. It is further laid down that land may be sold only to those who join the village co-operative society. Provision is made in Chapter Nine of the same law for the establishment of village co-operative societies.

In order to effect physical distribution of the cultivated lands among the landless operators without undertaking a land survey of each village, the Land Reform Law utilizes existing traditional practices of division among individual farmers current in each village.[1] In effect then, the law merely confirms the share-cropper in ownership of lands which he is currently farming (i.e. in the year the reform is implemented in that area). As with the use of the purely arbitrary village unit, the choice of *nasaq* to implement division between individual farmers keeps down the costs by avoiding re-survey and permits immediate action to carry out distribution. Similarly, it is decreed that the water supply traditionally provided for any plot of land should be transferred to the ownership of the person taking over that land.

The limitations on rights of ownership specified for the lands distributed under the Land Reform Law are embodied within the framework of Chapter Two of the law in respect of maximum areas and in Chapter Six in respect of minimum areas. The maximum area to be held by one person either as a result of or subsequent to the Land Reform Law is not to exceed one village, and distributed holdings are not to be fragmented below limits to be fixed by the local Land Reform Organization. The heirs to land owned by a farmer benefiting by the land reform programme are obliged by the terms of the Act not to fragment the original holding below the established limits of the reform. Where heirs cannot agree on the disposal of the land, the Land Reform Organization is authorized to adjudicate between the parties involved. These restrictions on absolute ownership are guaranteed by the fact that title to the distributed lands remains with the Land Reform Organization until the full price of the land is paid (i.e. for a maximum of fifteen years).

---

[1] *Nasaq*, the pattern of land utilization and exploitation in the Iranian village, is based on a complex of land plots each capable of being worked by a team of oxen. Share-croppers have an allotted number of plots lying within the cultivated area either on a permanent or annual basis. Share-croppers are confirmed in ownership of those plots within the *nasaq* which they are currently farming.

After dealing with the transfer of lands from the landlords to the peasants and share-croppers, the law goes on to reform the contractual relationship between landlord and peasant in those regions not affected by actual land division and transfer. According to official statistics, this area includes more than 80 per cent of Iranian villages. The key provisions confirm existing conditions pertaining to the upkeep of water supplies and administration in the village, and are designed in many ways to ensure that the landlord fulfils his obligations through legal sanction rather than because of traditional practice. Share-croppers are granted security of tenure, since the landlords are denied the right of arbitrary dismissal of share-croppers working their lands.

Reform of the traditional scheme of crop division under the share-cropping system is effected by the stipulation of a universal increase in the share-croppers' right to their produce of 5 per cent on irrigated land and 10 per cent on dry land. Similar increases are provided for agricultural workers, whether they receive their wages in cash or kind. Further security and social welfare measures are contained in the law by provisions confirming rights to peasants in non-reformed villages in such matters as land for houses, schools, public baths, and other civic amenities, to be provided by the landlord without cost.

Chapter Eight of the law places financial responsibility for the repayment of the landlords with the Agricultural Bank, which, in turn, has legal resort to the State budget. This Chapter also provides that peasants holding distributed land who fail in three consecutive years to pay their due instalments are to be dispossessed at the discretion of the Land Reform Organization.

In the final Chapter of the Land Reform Law, it is laid down that the government shall provide agricultural support for the areas involved in reform by way of credit facilities, rural extension services and marketing control. Communal affairs are to be dealt with by a local village co-operatve society. In its references both to national and to local support, the Chapter is vaguely framed and open to wide, even divergent interpretation.

Following the implementation of the Land Reform Law at Marāgheh in Āzarbāījān, the law was amplified and extended by some eleven further decrees and directives. Among these, the most important single provision was that landlords might voluntarily sell their lands to the Land Reform Organization even where such lands were not included in the land acquisition programme.

The apparent success of the early implementation of the Reform Law at Marāgheh and the political aims of the Minister of Agriculture, Dr Arsanjānī, gave rise to a more far-reaching plan for land reform embodied in the Additional Articles to the Land Reform Law issued on 17 January 1963. The Additional Articles became generally known as Phase Two. In essence, while the 1962 law affected only those landlords owning more than one village, Phase Two affected all owners with landholdings of one village or less; at the same time, in terms of impact of the reform programme, it is expected that the 8,000 villages involved under the 1962 law will now ultimately be increased to a minimum of 33,000 villages.

Phase Two offers the landlords three ways of reducing the area of land they cultivate: by lease, sale, or land division. In the case of landlords opting to lease their lands, they are required to offer to the peasants who are actually cultivating the land a lease calculated on an annual rental equal to the average revenue gained during the three preceding years multiplied by the regional coefficient of land values established by the local Land Reform Organization. Rentals established in this way are to be scrutinized by the Land Reform Organization to ensure just treatment for the tenants. The period of lease is to be fixed at thirty years, with a limiting clause that the terms of the contract may be revised at five-yearly intervals to cater for any possible changes in economic circumstances.

The second option permits landowners to sell their cultivated lands to the peasants currently working the soil. It is left to the landlord and peasant to find mutually acceptable prices for the land to be sold. In fact, since the landowner is under duress to dispose of his lands and the market value of land is now depressed by the direct effects of the Land Reform Laws, it was felt that the peasants would be in a good bargaining position *vis-à-vis* the landlords.

The third course open to landlords under the Additional Articles of 1963 is for them to divide their village or equivalent land area, selling land to the peasants and share-croppers in the same ratio that is traditional in the share-cropping system. Thus, a village in which the peasants normally retain two fifths of the crop will be divided between peasant and landlord in the ratio two to three. Throughout the country, peasants receiving land under this option will repay the ex-landlord two fifths of the value of the village land (even where they receive less than this amount in areal terms) over a period of ten years, though

697

in practice there appears to be greater flexibility in the period of repayment. Under the 1964 regulations for the Additional Articles, the landlord may take as much as four fifths or more of the village lands depending on traditional practices of crop division under the old share-cropping tenancy, whereas, under Dr Arsanjānī's proposals for Phase Two outlined in the Additional Articles of 1963, the area to be held by landlords was circumscribed by rigid maximum ceilings. In normal circumstances, since the peasant must give his agreement to his participation in this option, the peasant has not generally suffered from its existence; at the same time, it is on record that some landlords have taken advantage of the peasants by manipulating the terms of the law with the connivance of local land reform officials.

Lands held under charitable endowment (*vaqf-i 'amm*), which are affected only by the Articles dealing with the 5 and 10 per cent increases in workers' and share-croppers' wages and shares under the law of 1962, are subject to more radical, but nonetheless tactful, treatment under the conditions of Phase Two. It is provided that land charitably endowed should be let to the cultivating peasants and share-croppers on a 99-year lease, to be revised every five years if necessary. It is further stipulated that all such leases are to be on a cash basis and not in kind. By this means, it is expected that the condition of agriculture and the welfare of the farmers on these lands will be raised from the prevailing depressed state.

Privately endowed lands (*vaqf-i khās*) are subject to more severe treatment by the Additional Articles of 1963. It is provided that such lands should be available for purchase by the State for redistribution where this may be deemed necessary. The condition of privately endowed lands is generally poor, especially where there is more than one beneficiary and the village is administered through agents. The purpose of the law in this matter is to ensure that private beneficiaries will take a more personal interest in their lands and in the farmers working them; or, alternatively, the lands may be transferred to the peasants by the Land Reform Organization. An interesting case example of the effects of this provision is the village of Gāīsur in east-central Khurāsān, where one of the beneficiaries has recently allocated a portion of the income accruing from the endowment to a village improvement fund, which is to finance maintenance of the *qanāt* system, housing, and other public utilities such as street building and garden cultivation. All lands in private endowment are to be let on a thirty-year lease to the peasants on the same terms as those applying to charitable endowments.

A further provision of the Additional Articles of 1963 is that payment of the purchase price for lands taken over by the State under the law is to be extended from ten to fifteen years (though landlords affected by the reform before the enactment of Phase Two are disputing the change). Thus, most landlords are to be compensated at the same rate as that fixed for the repayments by the peasants to the State, thereby spreading out the weight of the burden on the State budget.

Phase Two of land reform was not implemented immediately upon enactment, but was scheduled to begin only when the 1962 law had been effected in the villages subject to its provisions. The Land Reform Organization was at that time under-staffed and was fully engaged in the work of distributing the villages expropriated from the large landlords. In fact, implementation of the 1962 law was completed officially in October 1963, although the final distribution of lands in the politically and militarily insecure areas of Fārs was not effected until later. As late as September 1964 there were reports of unreformed enclaves in the Varāmīn and Garmsīr areas.

Shortly after Phase Two had been announced as a statement of future policy rather than a programme for immediate action, Dr Arsanjānī resigned from the Ministry. There was a feeling in the more conservative government circles that, under Dr Arsanjānī's direction, the Phase Two reforms would be pushed ahead with undue haste and corresponding inefficiency, while, more importantly, there was some misgiving on the part of the Shāh that Dr Arsanjānī's interest in land reform and mobilization of popular support for his programme might take on unwelcome, longer-term connotations. Phase Two was postponed for a further six months after the official close of Phase One, a decision which was approved by the new Majlis, many members of which were ex-land reform officials and supporters of the Shāh's general reform policies. In the interim period between phases One and Two there was an increasingly strong belief that Phase Two would never be implemented.

Shortly after the government of Mr Hassan 'Alī Mansūr came to power, the regulations for the Additional Articles governing Phase Two of land reform were presented to the Majlis on 19 May 1964, but revised regulations were eventually issued on 25 July of the same year. The Additional Articles of 1963 are modified in several significant ways in the regulations of 1964, mainly, it would seem, to the advantage of the landlords, though the original provisions for the share-croppers are left intact. Whereas the Additional Articles of 1963 appeared to pursue the political objective of destroying the landowning class root-and-branch, the regulations for Phase Two tend to be more constructively phrased and leave scope for large-scale landownership within certain well-defined conditions.

According to the regulations of 25 July 1964, estates can be disposed of by the landlords in conformity with one of the three options provided for in the Additional Articles (Article One) of 1963—lease, sale, or land division. Additionally, the 1964 regulations permit a fourth option under which lands may be exploited by landlord and peasant through a joint agricultural unit established by mutual consent. It was expected that poorer villages, in areas where natural conditions are particularly harsh, would benefit from this option, whereby the landlord's function as economic risk-bearer and social leader could be retained. In fact, this fourth option, which originally caused considerable controversy, has proved to be of minor importance, since less than 1 per cent of villages affected by land reform up to January 1966 had made use of it.

The regulations for Phase Two re-state the principle that a landlord may come to an agreement with his share-croppers for the purchase of the peasants' rights to cultivation (*haqq-i rīsheh*), though maximum ceilings are provided on the areas of such holdings:

Province	Maximum area (ha.)
Gīlān and Māzandarān (rice growing regions)	20
Gīlān and Māzandarān (other lands)	40
Tehrān, Southern Māzandarān, Shahr Ray and Karaj	30
Gurgān, Gunbad-i-Qābūs and Dasht	40
Sīstān and Balūchistān	150
Other areas	100

In its final form, Phase Two also contains an interesting clause which permits landlords to retain their orchards and woodlands.

In the regulations, the government lays down the procedure to be followed by landlords in disposing of their lands. Of some importance regarding the future development of co-operative societies, it is permitted that landlords may effect land disposal by direct negotiations with the peasants individually, or with the village co-operative acting for all the peasants benefiting from the law. If the peasants so decide, the landlord is bound to deal with the co-operative, in which case the co-operative is given further benefit from a 2 per cent commission on rents and payments transacted. On lands disposed of by lease, the Additional Articles of 1963 allow rents to be paid in kind where this is mutually acceptable to landlord and tenant.

Lands disposed of by sale are subject to the conditions laid down in the Additional Articles, but under the regulations of 1964, it is provided that the Agricultural Bank will be given a direct grant of 1,000 million rials[1] annually with which to finance loans to farmers purchasing land, though such loans are paid to the landlords. Loans to individual farmers are to be on the scale of up to one third of the value of the land purchased at 3 per cent interest repayable over fifteen years commencing five years after the completion of the transaction.

From the experience of implementing the 1962 law and as a means of expediting the Phase Two reform, the Additional Articles contain both incentive and mildly coercive measures for the landlords affected. Those landlords disposing of their excess lands in the period November 1963–November 1964 were guaranteed payment in cash. In the case of land valued at less than 500,000 rials, 5 per cent of the purchase price was to be paid on completion of the transaction, with the balance to follow in fourteen annual instalments. Lands valued at more than 500,000 rials were to be bought by an initial payment of 5,000 rials with the balance following in fourteen annual instalments. On the other hand, landlords not transferring their lands before November 1964 were to receive promissory notes from the purchaser which may be realized only against an equivalent value of shares in State-owned factories. It is relevant to note here that during the period of the Third State Plan, government policy was to sell shares in State-owned factories to the public with the ultimate aim of entire disposal of its industrial holdings.

Lands utilized for mechanized farming (i.e. "where ploughing, at least, is done mechanically") are subject to special conditions. The 1964 regulations confirm that the surface area of mechanized farms on the established cultivated lands is to be restricted to a maximum holding of 500 hectares. However, where it can be shown that land under mechanized farming was previously uncultivated, or where subsequent to the land reform programme virgin lands are put under the plough using mechanized-farming techniques and fixed, daily-paid

[1] In 1964 the rial was officially valued against the pound sterling at 209 and against the U.S. dollar at 75.

agricultural labour, landlords are not subject to any restriction on the total size of holding, provided that the regional office of the Land Reform Organization gives its approval. In effect, the 1964 regulations are designed to halt the movement of capital and entrepreneurial talent away from the agricultural sector, and provide an incentive for them to move into agricultural reclamation of the vast unutilized areas of the country.

The regulations of 1964 specify that the government must begin issuing notice of implementation on 23 October 1964 (1 Ābān 1343). In fact, Phase Two was begun a month earlier than this during September 1964 in Kurdistān Province.

Thus, the final draft of Phase Two of land reform in Iran was very differently constituted, and deviated considerably in spirit from the original conception of its author, Dr Arsanjānī, who had aimed at destroying the political and social power of the small and large proprietors by removing the economic basis for their strength. In place of a so-called "feudal", landlord-and-peasant agrarian system, he had hoped to establish a new structure founded on small peasant proprietors organized locally through village co-operatives and centrally through the Organization of Co-operatives. It had further been a stated policy of the Arsanjānī programme to dispose of the State-owned factories and thus finance the land reforms cheaply by forcing all landowners to accept shares in these factories as compensation for the expropriated land. It does not follow that either of these aims will necessarily be realized by the land reform legislation actually enacted. From the foregoing outline of the Land Reform Law, the Additional Articles, and the regulations pursuant to them, it will be apparent that large landed proprietorship is specifically encouraged where it might contribute effectively to modernization of the agricultural sector and offers promise of increased crop production. Under the terms of the Phase Two regulations, only recalcitrant landlords are subject to forcible compensation by shares in State-owned factories. True peasant proprietorship will be established only in those villages distributed under Phase One legislation. Under Phase Two of the land reform programme, most villages are being distributed in accordance with the 1964 regulations for the lease option and, in consequence, the majority of beneficiaries under the reform as a whole will become tenant farmers.

As noted earlier, the Land Reform Law of 1962 was first implemented in the Marāgheh region of Āzarbāijān. Although the administration had some experience of the problems of land distribution in its dealings with Public and Crown Domains, and in spite of the expressed need to expedite the land reform programme, it was felt that the entirely new concepts embodied in the law and the large-scale nature of operations required a regional and even piecemeal approach in its implementation. Further, it was apparent that opposition to the programme could be more easily countered within a small area during the initial stages and that once the reforms had been effected in this area, later opposition during the broader application of the programme would be less resolute. Āzarbāïjān was chosen as the best region in which to begin operations, since it was predominantly a province of large landed proprietors and was also adjacent to Russian Āzarbāïjān, from whence came much of the Russian propaganda directed against the "feudal" landlord system of Iran generally and of Āzarbāïjān in particular. Also, the landlords in this area were less entrenched since they were temporarily dispossessed during the Pishevārī period, 1945–6.

The value of the Marāgheh experiment was threefold. In the first place, the time period allowed Dr Arsanjānī opportunity to concentrate his propaganda efforts against a small group of landlords while simultaneously utilizing all the material and human resources to support the relatively small number of peasants who were to take over the landlord estates. Second, the project gave a chance for the officials in the field to be trained for later leadership in other regions. Finally, during the Marāgheh project, the hastily formulated and ill-defined legislation governing land reform was re-cast where necessary and made a more effective medium for use in field implementation of the land reform. The need for more financial and administrative support for the co-operative organization was particularly apparent; although this was to have little effect on practice during later application of the law throughout the country.

Landlords in Marāgheh region submitted to the provisions of the law after a short period of active opposition and sporadic violence in certain rural areas. The first estate was volunteered to the State on 1 March 1962, and thereafter the Marāgheh land purchase and subsequent division amongst the peasants was accomplished rapidly.

The pattern established in Āzarbāïjān was repeated, with minor variations arising from environmental and structural differences in other regions. In the early period of application of the Land Reform Law to other areas, the order of priority was determined by the degree of co-operation forthcoming from the local landlords. Thus, those areas where landlords voluntarily handed over their estates to the Land Reform Organization before the official date of implementation of the law were dealt with first. Gīlān and Qazvīn, geographically close to Āzarbāïjān and the Marāgheh, offering no problems of military insecurity, and having a substantial portion of landlords volunteering their lands for division, were subject to land reform immediately following the completion of the Marāgheh area. In more difficult areas, where landlord obstruction and opposition was more prolonged and intense, the Land Reform Law was applied slightly later and was brought more slowly to a conclusion. The province of Fārs presented considerable problems of civil disorder and landlord opposition and, in consequence, was only reformed over limited areas as late as September 1963, when land purchase and re-distribution had already been completed in Gīlān.

Over much of the country, the Land Reform Law was implemented honestly and with what might be termed unusual efficiency for a government department. Under Dr Arsanjānī's leadership the newly formed Land Reform Organization developed a remarkable *esprit de corps* and sense of dedication to the land reform ideal, which helped considerably in overcoming the administrative limitations arising from an inefficient bureaucracy, subject to various adverse pressures from a variety of sources. In those areas where the terms of the law were not strictly adhered to, the reasons were often political advantage rather than personal gain. Thus, in the Qazvīn area, for example, one of the major landowners had large areas of land expropriated without legal warning as provided for in the Reform Law. In this case, the usurpation was intended to act as an example to others who might feel that resistance was possible. After the completion of land distribution in the area, the landlord was permitted to contest this expropriation, several villages being returned to the family in question. The delayed implementation of Phase Two of the land reform had an unfavourable effect on the regional strength of the Land Reform Organization, especially since some of the most experienced cadres were withdrawn to take seats in the Majlis,[1] but it was generally assumed that recruitment of further young cadres would off-set these losses.

---

[1] Members of the Land Reform Organization were nominated as candidates for the Majlis election in September 1963. It was felt by the administration that they would form a strong lobby to ensure confirmation of the Land Reform Decrees.

TABLE 14. *Regional distribution of villages (whole and part) purchased by the Land Reform Organization in the period up to September 1963*

Area	Total number of villages	Villages purchased	
		Number	Percentage of total
Arāk	479	291	61
Balūchistān and Sīstān	1,283	2	1
Central Regions	2,311	337	15
Eastern Āzarbāījān	3,960	1,184	30
Iṣfahān	1,709	284	17
Fārs	2,779	989	36
Gīlān and Shāhsavār	2,284	305	14
Hamadān	655	196	30
Kirmān	5,457	359	7
Kirmānshāh	2,765	631	23
Khurāsān	6,716	1,133	17
Khūzistān	1,825	459	25
Kurdistān	1,681	325	20
Māzandarān	2,331	261	11
Oman Coast	754	16	2
Persian Gulf Coast	451	58	13
Qazvīn	820	159	20
Salmās Shahristāns	599	129	22
Tehrān	4,052	240	6
Western Āzarbāījān	2,710	285	11
Yazd	2,000	—	—
Zanjān	971	399	41
Total	48,592	8,042	16·5

SOURCE: Abstract of Statistics, Land Reform Organization, Tehrān, 1342 (1963–4).

Land distribution arising from the implementation of the 1962 Land Reform Law is shown in table 14 by the various land reform districts of the country. The effect of land reform obviously varied in different areas depending on the incidence of large estates. Generally, the incidence of reformed villages coincides with the distribution of regional concentrations of large properties as elucidated by Professor Lambton.[1] There are, however, some notable exceptions to this, particularly in the Kirmān area, where local problems of water rights and the high cost of *qanāt* maintenance precluded the application of land reform in spite of the preponderance of large proprietors in the region. It had been expected that a larger proportion of villages would have been affected by the provisions of the Land Reform Law than the 8,042

[1] Lambton (1953), pp. 259–74.

complete and part villages actually reformed[1] by September 1963. Official estimates of the number of villages to fall under the terms of the 1962 law are 13,904 of which 3,788 are complete villages and 10,116 part villages. It is probable that in the absence of reliable statistics, the original estimate regarding villages owned by large landlords holding more than one village was slightly inflated for political reasons. It is even more likely that far-sighted landlords took the opportunity to transfer lands to their relatives before and after the abortive Land Reform Law of 1960. However, the number of villages concerned in Phase One of land reform ceased to be of importance after the announcement of 19 May 1964, that Phase Two would be implemented and thus most villages brought within the scope of general reform.

The cost of land reform activities to the economy as a whole is difficult to estimate. The disbursements and operating costs of the Land Reform Organization in the different regions for the official period of Phase One are known, however, and are shown in table 15. The budget of the Organization for the months March 1962 to March 1963 was 115 million rials, while a further 650 million rials was made available for the purchase of land. This budget was 200,000 rials above that for the previous twelve months. Costs had risen considerably by the Iranian year 1343 (March 1964 to March 1965), when 1,441 million rials were allotted for agrarian reform purposes, representing a third of the total agricultural budget. The cumulative value of land purchased by the Land Reform Organization reached 6,293 million rials, of which 988 million rials had been paid to landlords as compensation by the end of 1343.

The low cost of implementation of the law of 1962 is attributable to two major factors. First, the prices paid by the State to the dispossessed landlords were not equivalent to pre-reform values. Based on a tax schedule which tended to under-assess real values and a regional co-efficient of land values arbitrarily established by the local Land Reform Organization, the compensation to the ex-landlords was correspondingly low.[2] In the second place, the use of traditional operating units existing in the agrarian structure proved very economical. The village

---

[1] Official figures of the Land Reform Organization for the period up to September 1963 indicate that of the 8,042 villages reformed, only 6,000 had at that time been transferred to the peasants.

[2] The same technique was used in the Egyptian land reforms. However, it should be noted that in some areas the index worked to the benefit of many landlords, who have received a good price for their land (e.g. Āzarbāījān).

unit had established boundaries known to all. Within the village, each worker or share-cropper was temporarily confirmed in ownership of the area defined by the customary *nasaq* which he had been farming in the year land reform was executed. The actual title received by each peasant gave him no absolute right to any defined piece of land, but merely a share of the total land being distributed in his village. Thus, at both the village and individual holding level, distribution rarely required the use of ground survey, with a consequent saving in cost.[1]

TABLE 15. *Disbursements for land purchase and distribution effected by the Land Reform Organization in the period up to September 1963 (in rials)*

Area	Disbursements for land purchase price per village or part of village	Disbursements for land distribution cost per village or part of village
Arāk	638,753	13,541
Bālūchistān and Sīstān	659,045	823,240
Central Regions	320,306	16,256
Eastern Āzarbāïjān	1,284,705	11,660
Iṣfahān	291,278	21,548
Fārs	364,804	16,053
Gīlān and Shāhsavār	1,051,027	30,834
Hamadān	789,180	11,051
Kirmān	368,153	18,811
Kirmānshāh	450,412	7,759
Khurāsān	213,226	—
Khūzistān	188,191	16,900
Kurdistān	357,641	13,794
Māzandarān	844,071	32,123
Oman Coast	265,405	140,411
Persian Gulf Coast	472,321	72,327
Qazvīn	912,401	26,201
Salmās Shahristāns	859,792	36,869
Tehrān	657,115	46,690
Western Āzarbāïjān	427,342	21,854
Yazd	—	—
Zanjān	819,118	9,673

SOURCE: Abstract of Statistics, Land Reform Organization, Tehrān, 1342 (1963–4).

Unfortunately, the fact of the system of land distribution's being itself based on the customary units gave rise to one of the most serious problems affecting the implementation of the land reform. Both the surface area and the population of Iranian villages vary very considerably: there is not necessarily any correlation between population

[1] Dr Arsanjānī estimated that the cost of survey would have been 4,800 million rials and that survey would have taken twenty-five years to complete.

and the cultivated area of any village. Within a village, the allotment of shares of land in the *nasaq* was rarely on an equal basis, and varied from operator to operator, depending on the means of production at his disposal, his farming skill and, often, on his relations with the landlord or his bailiff. Obviously, the ratio of land per person was different as between any two villages, depending on population numbers and availability of water supplies for irrigation. In consequence of these appreciable variations within the individual village and from village to village, there were inequalities in the allotment of land to farmers. Much of the Land Reform Organization's work has been to persuade peasants to accept these inequalities, at least on a temporary basis or in attempting to even them out. Where the influence of the Organization was weak, inter-peasant strife delayed settlement of the land reform and caused considerable unrest. This was a feature especially in the Fārs and Arāk regions.

The lack of adequately trained staff in the Ministry of Agriculture, Agricultural Bank, and the Land Reform Organization for the implementation of land reform may be accounted responsible for some of the failures of the land reform programme. The enthusiasm and diligence of the small staff of the Land Reform Organization was sufficient to execute satisfactorily the process of land acquisition and distribution. However, the necessary provision of support services for credit and management guidance was not widely undertaken because of the lack of staff.[1] This was particularly apparent in the case of the newly founded village co-operative societies which, apart from Marāgheh and Varāmīn projects, were largely left without expert guidance. Some 1,184 administrative and field staff were responsible for the creation and operation of a total of 8,042 village co-operatives. Many staff were tied to office duties in Tehrān and the provincial towns, which left little scope for adequate supervision of co-operatives. Yet, it was in this very sector of support service that any lasting success of the land reform was to be achieved. Intense official and unofficial propaganda against the landlords had led to a widely held belief that all landlords were absentee, acquisitive, and parasitic. Whilst this was true of some landlords, many of their number fulfilled a useful if expensive function as the providers of credit, management, and social welfare facilities. It was intended that after land reform these functions would be taken

---

[1] A. Salur states that the Land Reform Organization had less than twenty staff at its inception, a number which had reached 1,184 by September 1963.

over by the village co-operatives, but the underestimation of the part played by the landlords, the lack of experience in co-operative organization, and the shortage of trained staff resulted in a situation where these facilities were no longer adequately provided.

It had been expected that the greatest problem to be faced by the implementation of the land reform would be political and even military opposition from those groups with a vested interest in maintaining the status quo in landholding and distribution of economic power. In fact, overt political opposition was shortlived. An attempt to re-establish the Landlords' Association, which had so effectively blocked the reforms of 1946 and 1960, was countered by a warning to its leadership that prompt action would be taken against it if there were any attempt to interfere in the operation of the land reform. A rival Farmers' Congress was held in Tehrān in the summer of 1963 to demonstrate the solidarity of the peasants behind the land reform, an act which further reduced the fading power of the landlords. Disturbances, both political and military, continued throughout the reform period, but these were, generally speaking, isolated incidents.

Several of the major landlords in Āzarbāījān proposed military resistance to the work of the land reform officials, but were dissuaded from this by reinforcement of the Gendarmerie. The only major incident in the first year of implementation was the shooting and killing of a land reform official in the Shīrāz area, allegedly in the course of his work for the Land Reform Organization. The incident provided the government with an opportunity to take even stronger measures against unco-operative landlords. Dr Arsanjānī was also able to use the Fārs murder as a further instance of the unbridled power of the landlords in their villages, and as a justification for a demand for their elimination.

The announcement of the Land Reform Law was the occasion of student riots in Tehrān in June 1962. More serious, the provisions of Phase Two in respect of religious endowment lands were not acceptable to the religious leaders in spite of the generous terms in which they were couched. Resentment, fanned by the extended group of landlords now liable to the Land Reform Law, was expressed in a prolonged period of rioting in early June 1963, which coincided with the end of the Muharram festival. Order was restored only after the imposition of a curfew and use of the military.[1] Although the student riots of 1962

---

[1] It was officially announced that 97 persons were killed by government troops, but unofficial estimates put the figure much higher.

and the general riots of 1963 were occasioned by the Land Reform Decrees, there is every reason to believe that they were also caused by deeper resentments which existed for other causes. In Professor Lambton's view, the 1963 riots were "the culmination of a movement of resistance to the exercise of arbitrary power by the government which by the summer of 1963 was felt to be intolerable" (*Studia Islamica*, fasc. xx, 1964). The absence of a Majlis was a point emphasized by rioting students. Economic misery of the poorer classes following the end of the economic boom in 1961 must also be accounted an important factor in the June riots of 1963.

That the implementation of the Land Reform Laws was successful in spite of the various opposition groups they provoked, may be attributed to several factors. It is certain that no reform would have been possible without the support of the Shāh. For whatever reasons, the Shāh was convinced that land reform was necessary and throughout the period he used those political and military means at his disposal to ensure its execution at both the legislative and implementation levels. In this he was aided by his selection of able and dedicated ministers, particularly Dr Amīnī and also Dr Arsanjānī, who as Minister of Agriculture formulated the Reform Law of January 1962 and began its implementation. Dr Amīnī was himself a large proprietor in Gīlān and was amongst the first to volunteer land for distribution; whilst Dr Arsanjānī was important to the success of land reform in three major spheres, the first being his political management of the landlord class by uniting the mass of the peasantry behind the Shāh through the Farmers' Congress and the Six-Point Referendum. Secondly, the personal presence of Dr Arsanjānī in the more difficult land reform areas also contributed to the solution of local problems in a very material way. Thirdly, the unique character of the Land Reform Organization, with its strong *esprit de corps* and single-minded efficiency was in many ways Dr Arsanjānī's personal creation.

During the land reform programme, the government made clever use of the radio to propagate its ideas and policies. All local stations in Iran maintained a close coverage of land reform activities for the benefit of the rural population and ensured that the official government view was widely understood. While the broadcast propaganda in favour of land reform fulfilled a useful function in the early period, when it was necessary to counteract the influence of the landlords, the inflated claims made for land reform later caused considerable misunderstanding amongst the peasants. In Fārs, for example, there were several incidents in which peasants attempted to seize landlord property outside the terms of the law.

The visible results of land reform legislation covering the period January 1962 to January 1966 are so far confined mainly to those emerging from the Land Reform Law of 1962. Of all villages in Iran, only 18 per cent were affected by land distribution.[1] Thus, the results of Phase One cannot be assessed directly in terms of the mere physical area encompassed. In fact, the land reform under Phase One regulations is to be appraised from its overall success in the political and social spheres. Purchase of the large estates has at least begun to weaken the political power of the landowning families by undermining the regional basis for their influence, particularly their ability to control the election of candidates for the Majlis. This process has affected social and political conditions throughout the country and is in no way limited to the areas falling directly under the provisions of the land distribution programme.

The radical diminution of the landlords' power at village level left an economic and social void in those areas from which they withdrew. For the reformed villages, the absence of the landlord meant an end to a long-established dependence of the villagers on his capital and managerial resources, and this observation will no doubt hold true for villages concerned in Phase Two of the programme. Although the Land Reform Organization had hoped that the institution of a system of village co-operatives would replace the landlords' functions, as already noted, lack of trained staff and adequate credits made this ineffective in many villages. In most villages, the co-operatives only function well when outside pressures such as the Agricultural Bank or a sugar beet factory require all operators in the village to act commercially as a single unit through the medium of the co-operative. Otherwise, the farmers tend to operate in small groups, often in conflict with one another.

It has proved very difficult for the administration to train manpower with which to service co-operatives on the scale made necessary by the rapid implementation of the reform programme, especially since the beginning of Phase Two. The short-comings of the co-operative effort are illustrated clearly in the returns of the Land Reform Organization,

[1] The total number of villages affected is 13,904, of which 3,788 are fully liable and 10,116 partially liable for division. Assuming each partially affected village as half a village, the overall proportion of villages involved to the extent of their total area works out as 18 per cent of the whole number. See H. Mahdavī (1964), p. 140.

which show that only 3,846 co-operative societies had been established in the period January 1962 to March 1965. In the same period, some 8,478 villages had been purchased wholly or in part, all of which required the services of a co-operative; though it should be noted that some co-operatives served more than one village or part of a village. Some 644,926 farmers were officially listed as members of co-operatives at the end of March 1965.

In reformed villages, the position of the peasant has nevertheless improved despite the short-comings of the co-operative organizations. In most villages, the amount of money now paid each year for the instalments on the mortgage held by the Agricultural Bank is less than the amount formerly paid to the landlord in the pre-reform era. On the other hand, income has risen sharply, since the difference between the amount formerly paid to the landlord and the amount of the annual repayment on the mortgage accrues to the peasant. The peasant is now freed from the responsibility of providing traditional dues and servitudes to the landlord. Moreover, the peasant himself is tending to work harder than in the days of landlord control, with a consequent increase in productivity. Socially, the peasant is freer than in the pre-reform period, since he has no longer to submit to attendance on the landlord and bow to his political opinion. The breadth of social contact has expanded significantly in recent years. Peasant representatives have now to deal directly with the town offices of the Ministry of Agriculture, the Agricultural Bank, the Ministry of Justice, the urban merchants, and the factories using agricultural raw materials. In spite of his lack of education and training, the peasant is gradually "finding his feet" in this new environment and to an increasing extent is able to get a hearing for his case.

Phase Two of land reform has now emerged as a constructive programme for agrarian development. The provisions of Phase Two allow as much scope for the existence of large landed properties as peasant holdings, provided that the share-cropping system is avoided, the means of exploitation mechanized, and the land reclaimed from wasteland outside the traditional cultivated area.

Implementation of Phase Two is currently being pressed forward rapidly and successfully, with no less than 1,293 villages purchased and redistributed during the period September 1964 to April 1965. Officially, the phase was completed in January 1967, though in an estimated 2 per cent of villages reform had still to be carried out. Most of the lessons of

Phase One have been learnt, and, particularly, due attention has been given to the provision of credits for owners and tenants receiving land under the reform. In the year March 1963 to March 1964, credits worth 3,427 million rials were extended to farmers, while in the following year 4,132 million rials were made available in the form of small loans. These allotments for credit compare most favourably with the original level of allocations for agricultural credit under the Third Plan, which were set at 1,235 million rials each year. At the same time, greater attention has been paid to the organization of extension services and it is intended to develop educational and health facilities in rural areas, where, it must be added, they are desperately needed. While it might be acknowledged that the co-operative movement has still to prove that it can emerge as an effective medium for the articulation of agricultural leadership, on balance, it appears that there is every reason to suppose that the Shāh's planned revolution can be brought about.

Nonetheless, it will be necessary to demonstrate clearly that once the reform is complete, no further radical changes in landownership will be introduced, so that in both peasant and landlord areas development can take place in an atmosphere of confidence without the feeling that land reform could be no more than a further temporary upheaval in the long and disturbed history of landed property in Iran. The announcement of a Phase Three reform in January 1966, by which programmes for tribal resettlement, large-scale mechanization of agriculture, the strengthening of rural co-operative organization and the conservation of water resources will be introduced, should do much to convince both peasant owners and tenants and the large landowners that the government has a long-term interest in the welfare of the rural population and in the continuing improvement of agricultural production.

PART 4

CONCLUSION

CHAPTER 22

THE PERSONALITY OF
IRAN

Certain regions of the world are distinguishable as being associated
with a particular human culture pattern, which is at once distinctive in
character and also sufficiently strong to have survived as a readily
identifiable entity over many centuries. Such geographical regions—e.g.
China, Egypt, and France, to take a few only—can be said to be the
home of a human group that each possesses a high degree of social
cohesion, which in turn fosters a sustained though possibly fluctuating
political identity, a characteristic way of life, and a material culture
which can be recognized as individual and is capable of affecting other
cultures to a varying degree. China has remained a significant political
unit over several millennia, with its artistic and commercial products
esteemed in Europe by Romans and moderns alike; Egypt, despite
recurrent invasion and temporary subjection, has remained one of the
focal areas of the eastern Mediterranean since biblical times at least;
and there is no need to emphasize for the modern period the pervasive
intellectual, political, and artistic influence of France.

In the designation of such human groups, association with a particular territory is implied. Use of the term "association" is deliberate,
and invites the question: how much, if anything at all, of human
activities, political groupings, and cultural efflorescence can be said
to derive from the geographical location in which they develop?
Could the city-states of classical Greece have evolved as they did if
Athens had been located within the forests of Hercynian Europe;
or is it reasonable to believe that Sung pottery might equally have been
produced on the banks of the Zambezi? For many, such questions will
be totally irrelevant, since it is possible to hold that the evolution of
human society is a function of human will, wholly controlled by
human impulse and predilection, with no or at most only incidental
relationship to non-human agencies. One must explain a Napoleon, a
Gladstone, or a Hitler in terms strictly of personality and individual
action within the human circumstances of a particular epoch. Many

millions lived under exactly the same physical conditions of terrain, climate, and resource availability, but no one else responded in the same way to the situation of the time.

The opposite idea, that the nature and variety of civilization are to a large degree conditioned by a particular geographical environment, is of long standing, though possibly less generally accepted. Traceable as far back as Herodotus, its modern expression first emerges in certain of the seventeeth- and eighteenth-century rationalists: De Bos, St Evremond, Rousseau, and especially Montesquieu, for whom "natural influences" in the evolution of human society were sufficiently developed and widespread to be an all-important determinant.

Involved in this general question are two fundamentally opposing ideas. On the one hand, man's evolution can be held to be subject to general laws and conditions that influence and are applicable to all equally. On the other hand, an analysis of human society could pursue an empiricist approach that takes into account the various aspects of reality facet by facet and with separate weight to each. If we accept the former, we are immediately brought up against a universalist concept that postulates human development as, in the widest view, a pattern of rational, orderly progression towards definite objectives. If one is an optimist, these objectives are likely to spell betterment, even a near-ideal condition, for society; moreover, they are to be regarded as part of a broad design constructed by a power outside and above man, who may therefore not be able fully to comprehend its nature. Logically pursued, and given an all-wise Creator, this system of thought means that unalterable and inexorable rules order man's existence.

It may be suggested that this point of view has three main attractions for man in his attempts to explain society. First, it requires rigorously logical relationships capable of interpretation by rational analysis; and second, patient accumulation of knowledge, together with efforts towards its interpretation, must inevitably lead to full understanding or at least considerable comprehension of the real pattern of human behaviour—just as a jig-saw puzzle can gradually be made, by assiduity and diligence, to adumbrate a total picture. Third, provided that one assumes a beneficent rather than a neutral or malevolent purpose in creation, the evolution of human society as a whole is likely to involve progress and improvement for most people, if not for everyone. Given diligence, close study, and above all, the application of enlightened rational thought, the principles guiding human society will one day emerge ineluctable and clear.

Such reasoning has obvious dangers, and one in particular has special relevance here: the temptation to fit an individual human society into a neat pattern, the outlines of which have been set up from data and ideas acquired in another context, and extrapolated as part of a universalist theory. Thus it becomes necessary to consider the alternative approach, that of empiricist observation. It may never be possible for the human mind to comprehend the total nature of reality; and in dealing with the human species the use of absolute terms may be arbitrary and highly misleading. Man is infinitely complex: his society therefore may reflect many influences and impulses rather than a few major controls arising from the possible existence of a rational plan that gives an assigned function to every individual in the universe. We ought, therefore, at least to envisage the fluctuating influence of a range of factors, some related to or deriving from man himself, others external to him and not necessarily connected directly with his existence.

According to some thinkers, one of these influences is the natural environment in which man lives: the landscape, using the word in its German sense (*Landschaft*) to mean the sum of natural elements—physiography, climate, and resources—that make up a particular regional pattern. It is the view of most, if not all, geographers that landscape thus defined is a powerful contributing factor in the elaboration and development of human society. As, however, human occupancy becomes established in a particular locality, then man's activities in turn can greatly alter and vary the original natural environment. A highly complex situation of cross-influence and mutual involvement thus develops: in a wider sense we have a repetition of the situation, "The plant builds its cells, but the cell builds the plant".

With the ideas so far stated almost all geographers, with very few exceptions indeed, would be in accord; but there is considerable divergence when the notions of universalist or of empiricist approaches are applied in detail to the problem of the geographical environment. Undoubtedly the most distinguished geographer to hold at least partially universalist views was Emmanuel Kant, who held a Chair of Physical Geography at Königsberg during a large part of his academic career. While accepting that reality in human experience could be said to derive from *a priori* laws, Kant nevertheless held that man as a social being had need of external direction, and would not easily advance without such direction. Part of this direction could be given by an earthly human ruler; part might arise from general human circumstances of the time (e.g. Reformation or Age of Enlightenment); and part might develop from the influence of place, i.e. the controls exercised by the facts of geography.

A contemporary of Kant's, J. G. Herder, stated the problem in a somewhat different way. Human existence, in his view, is part of a natural unity formed by a symbiosis between geographical environment and the forces of human growth and movement. These latter, originating from man himself, consequently alter and evolve, and must therefore be analysed separately at different times and in different places. If one refuses to believe that human existence is swayed by general and absolute principles, and thus forms part of a wider design, then the opposite approach must enter in—that of empiricism and consideration on a smaller scale—that is to say, of regionalism. Hence for each community we must trace the various influences upon its development; and certainly some of these influences, possibly the greater number, will be unique to a given society.

This brings us to the question of whether any one group may be said to have "progressed" or "improved", which in turn leads to the necessity for some sort of evaluation or qualitative judgment. If we regard all human societies as part of a single universal pattern and bound by laws or principles common to all, then the idea of quality may not have great importance. But if every human group is to be regarded as special in itself and unrelated to others, then it becomes very difficult not to apply some sort of judgment or common standard, with an implication of superior and inferior achievement. Carried a little further, these latter ideas can give rise to the nationalist and racialist concepts of which we are only too painfully aware at the present time.

Herder, however, was greatly concerned to justify a process of qualitative assessment, and yet to prevent it from evolving in this undesirable direction (which is the direction it in fact took in the hands of such writers as Fichte, Nietsche, and H. S. Chamberlain). Thus he insisted that although communities varied in their ways of life, they were each wholly justifiable in themselves, and could not be evaluated by direct comparison one with another. Such relative evaluation is wholly inappropriate, according to Herder, because different cultures and human groups have differing values, and are to be assessed as communities only within their own context, for "each is a harmonious lyre, and one must have the ear to hear its melodies". Support for this viewpoint could be said to come from the apparent fact that "primitives" appear to be no less personally content in their normal way of life than we do in ours; indeed, whilst many might say that Western urbanized civilization of the present-day "developed" nations is superior to that of, say, peasant India or Africa, yet the proportion of those wishing to leave their civilization, by suicide, is far greater in Western society than among less "advanced" groups. If each people is to be evaluated as an entity in itself, within its own environment, there is need for a regional approach. Communities are to be studied as disparate units, and not through any synoptic view of the pattern of mankind as a whole.

The idea that the community is a more appropriate subject of historical study than are the actions and influence of particular individuals, has over the last two or three centuries become a commonplace: Vico, Hume, and Montesquieu gave especial significance to it. What is distinctly less frequent, however, is the view that each community arises from the interaction between purely human ideas and personal predilections on the one hand, and the influences of natural circumstance—time, and especially place—on the other. The importance of human initiative has been examined intensively from many standpoints: some have held that individual action is predestined and part of a universal design; others have felt it could be best explained in terms of either nineteenth-century Romanticism, or of its later developments, existentialism and the ascription of human progress to the influence of a superman, *élan vital*, hero, or even to the force of a negative. Possibly because man's self-esteem tends thereby to be enhanced, he may be considerably attracted to the idea that human society is entirely motivated and controlled by human will, individual or collective, with a social organization that reflects purely human experience and decision. Yet the facts of man's existence provide considerable evidence of other influences, which are at least partly derived from the environment, and are wholly external, in their origin, at least to man himself. To say that such influences profoundly modify human existence and the evolution of society might be a less congenial philosophical system than one that postulates man to be the total measure of his social circumstances; nevertheless, in the opinion of this writer, this does in fact seem to offer a closer and more valid explanation of reality.

The average member of a particular community will have before him a restricted number of possibilities of a livelihood. The native of New England or Yorkshire, for example, is far more likely to become an industrial worker or a clerk than is, say, an inhabitant of Arabia or India. We must of course restrict our statement of "likely", since, given more than average initiative and money, an Indian could migrate to Bradford or, with rather more difficulty, to Boston. Such circumstances of unusual pertinacity and individual possibilities of migration could for a small number nullify the inherent differences posed by the geographical environment—but this is a partial limitation applicable only to a minority, and alongside it one must consider the situation as this exists for most people. For example, we can say that rice-growing would never commend itself as a basic activity to a Yorkshire farmer, or fishing to a native of inner Arabia. In other words, a general situation can be said to obtain for the majority, and this derives closely from the society's particular geographical setting.

Literature, and historical studies that attempt through literary forms to elucidate the circumstances of man's past, have overwhelmingly emphasized the central importance of the human individual as a determinant in the historical process; but in order to arrive at a truer interpretation it may be salutary and even necessary to consider the part also played by external circumstances—however limiting this may be to the concept of man as the arbiter of social evolution.

From time to time, theories of history have been put forward in which the geographical environment is regarded as an important influence. It was stated by Herder (though of course not original to him) that because the earth's axis is inclined at 23° or 24° from the vertical, then human experience differs significantly from one region of the world to another. Stemming from this simple proposition there have been a number of sustained attempts to demonstrate closer causality between geography and the course of history; such attempts have been made by Montesquieu, Kant, Buckle, and in our own time by Toynbee.

Though one may dispute in detail certain of the statements made by Toynbee in his *Study of History*, it is difficult in the present author's view to dissent from what could be regarded as Toynbee's fundamental theme: that the course of history is influenced by environmental factors, many of which are of a human kind, such as the prevailing historical situation, while others derive ultimately from changes in the natural geographical background that, on occasion produce a "crisis" or "stimulus". Toynbee's views can be criticized *inter alia* for their over-simplified correlation of what might certainly seem at a first examination to be similar geographical environments, and for the use of such superficial correlations as a basis for general deductions. To take two well-known examples of Toynbee's approach: the pampas of South America and the steppes of inner Asia may appear to have undoubted similarities in respect of topography, climate, and vegetation, and this led him to say that these two regions could be regarded as environmentally identical. But geographical location is a distinguishing factor: the steppes, unlike the pampas, lay in close proximity on east, west, and south to three of the most active centres of human development, and were traversed by routes (such as the Silk Road) that maintained an importance over several thousand years.

Similarly, as a basis for argument, Toynbee assumes geographical conditions in the Jordan valley to be closely similar to those of the lower Nile, both being deeply cut troughs crossing arid territory. In fact, however, the Nile waters are fresh, and hence a source of life and development for plants and humans throughout its length, whilst the lower Jordan is not only saline and unusable for irrigation in its lower reaches, but also deeply cut well below the level of its main valley floor, and thus even less usable for farming.

Over-simplified assessments of particular geographical circumstances do not invalidate Toynbee's argument that most human society has developed and evolved because of special pressure or stimulus applied to particular human communities. In the present writer's opinion (though not in Toynbee's) part of this pressure comes from the direct influence of the geographical environment. Human situations obviously exert strong pressure, but neither element alone can consistently provide a full and adequate explanation of the growth of a society. We must believe that both enter in, to varying degrees. As a wholly "human" situation, the influence of Revolutionary France and of Napoleon upon the course of history in nineteenth-century Europe was very considerable but not absolute; and possibly it is no more than equal in significance to the emergence of the prairies of the New World as suppliers of food to industrial Europe. On the other hand, however one regards matters, desiccation of the North African steppes at the end of the Quaternary must be held as the principal cause of man's development of settled agriculture.

Toynbee is concerned to demonstrate extensive similarity and even parallelism among various regions of the world; but it is truer to suggest that in geographical endowment no single area of the world exactly resembles another. The idea that the earth possesses a fundamental symmetry, regularity, and order is once again more psychologically attractive, and since the time of the Greeks at least, there have been diligent attempts to erect systems or models of the distribution of geographical elements that would demonstrate balance, and even local congruence. Yet the obstinate fact remains that the earth is not totally symmetrical even in overall shape. It is not set "upright" in relation to its elliptic; it moves with slight but measurable irregularities; and only in the most limited possible degree can the distribution of land and sea on its surface be regarded as conforming to a pattern; Lothian Green saw here a tetrahedron with water dominant in the centre of the four faces, but few would push this interpretation very far. Irregular disposition far transcends any detail that might fleetingly imply order, balance, and symmetry.

This is not to suggest that no orderly classification of geographical elements is possible. A systematic study of the earth is certainly feasible, provided it is recognized that what we distinguish as a geographical region represents a unity composed of many disparate elements, each of which may or may not be repeated elsewhere, but always in a differing formula or relationship. For many years geographers have endeavoured to construct a system that will give logical and universal expression to this situation; but they are ultimately forced back to the stubborn fact that no one region can totally resemble another, and is therefore special to itself. We have already implied that after the primary major irregularities inherent in the disposition of land and ocean and altitude, the second factor leading to geographical distinctiveness is location: for if the whole pattern of land and sea is irregular, then there can be no true congruence of siting, and location must be a factor making for variability. This is all the more significant when we consider the effect that a predominating irregularity has upon the distribution of living things—floral, faunal, and human. Why, for instance, in the two major islands of New Zealand, was there not a development of human society broadly similar to that in Great Britain? Differences in mineral endowment are one answer, but the major cause lies in the 1,200 miles that separate New Zealand from the nearest large land mass, that of Australia. Moreover, this land mass itself is partly arid, and devoid of native domesticable animal and plants— which is also in part a result of its location and its general climate.

When we come to consider human activity as an influence on geographical distribution then there arises further ground for debate. If we are willing to accept the idea of progress among human societies, then some sort of judgment or assessment of various groups must be made, with eventual arrangement in a qualitative hierarchy: group A is advanced, group B is static, group C has regressed. In other words some communities appear to have done "well"—they have a "superior" level of material living and of culture, and are to be termed more progressive or civilized than the average of mankind. According to Toynbee, there have been twenty-three such movements within human society, which have given rise to recognizable "civilizations" associated with a particular people and a particular geographical locality. Other groups, however, are more static—"backward", therefore, to a varying degree. Once again we become involved in a question of principle: we must grant that the series of changes that have supervened between the Old Stone Age and the present day are, for the urbanized and industrial societies of Europe and North America, on the whole an "improvement". Over such a wide range some form of judgment is easy and, most people would feel, also valid. But can similar estimations be applied in the short run to the various societies existing at the present day? How far would it be right to suggest that, say, the Spaniards, Scots, and Swedes are more "evolved", "developed", "civilized" (whatever term commends itself) in comparison with the Poles, Pakistanis, or Portuguese? Those who would uphold the concept of a world and human society progressing generally under fixed and universal laws towards an ultimate predetermined destiny will find distinctly easier the process of ascribing to a particular community a "rating" or defined place on a differential, qualitative scale.

But there are those who have passionately denounced any attempt by one or a few groups to arrogate to themselves the right to establish standards of judgment which are then applied to others. Inherently, judgments can and must only apply to themselves. According to this view, Nature does not make certain nations or peoples intrinsically superior, nor is it possible to say more than that individuals and societies are merely good and valid in themselves, and also ends in themselves—not stages to something different, or better. Here we reach the concept of a multiplicity of values arising from dissimilar, and hence incommensurable, cultures. It is only for a German to assess the merits of Germanic life: since full knowledge can only come from within and by participation, only a German can entirely weigh these merits.

Acceptance of either principle—that of stages of progress or that of the uniqueness of every culture—can ultimately, if carried rigorously to extremes, come to involve contradiction. If some societies "fail", or even die out, as did the various divergent subhuman species of the pre-Palaeolithic, as well as the Carthaginians, and the Tasmanians, one can only regard their having existed at all either as a form of blind experimentation without foreknowledge of the result; or else, involving what would seem to be injustice, and one could say that such peoples were not "designated" for advancement. According to some, the extinction of these peoples is a negation of the view that all cultures are good in themselves.

In consequence, one tends to fall back on the answer so frequently occurring in sociological analysis: "somewhere in between", the Socratic "moderation" and "mean", with one particular instance tending more closely to demonstrate the first principle, and another suggesting validity of the latter. Whilst it would strain credulity to suggest that Palaeolithic man's community and personal life were as rewarding as those of modern man, it would be equally impossible to ascribe closely relative values to nations and communities of the present day.

We are, however, left with some useful common ground. It could hardly be argued that change in human society takes place equally at all periods and in all places. Mankind does not alter by regular stages on a single broad front, but rather by sudden irregular spurts, comparable in the broadest possible way with the processes of biological mutation, or even with the random unpredictable form of movement postulated in quantum mechanics. The proponents of the idea that there is swifter progression among certain peoples, and the defenders of the validity of all cultures agree that there is variation regionally: at any one time, peoples and cultures are not the same. We may accept this without necessarily including in the concept any qualitative evaluation.

We therefore have two acceptable concepts springing from regional variation: that such variation is the essential characteristic of physiographic environment, and that it can be a principal distinguishing feature among human societies. Herein lies the major justification for the study of regions as such. Considerations of this sort have led many geographers to regard the identification and delimitation of regions as the principal aim of geography: E. W. Gilbert has even gone so far as to assert that geography as a whole could be defined as the art of regional delineation.

It might be attractive to rest our argument at this point in the safe haven of regionalism. But one cannot feel wholly satisfied that sufficient weight has been accorded to the overall view, both of the world and of mankind. Gilbert is content with a regional conclusion, but Vidal de la Blache, believes that the prime consideration in geographical study is not to sunder what Nature has created as one; there is, in other words, a totality that is greater than the sum of the regional parts. To take an example, it is customary to regard France as possessing a distinctive overall geographical unity; one expression of this is the notion commonly put forward, over several centuries, of the "natural boundaries" of France. Yet another generally accepted view is that the country is composed of strongly defined local regions that exhibit marked diversity on a small scale: though recognized as a unitary area, France exhibits a remarkable juxtaposition of fertile water-meadow, barren upland, sterile *causse*, and lush plain, over which three distinctive climatic regimes can be discerned. This terrain, characterized by small-scale variation as in a mosaic or oil painting, composes a powerful unity, recognized universally for its physical distinctiveness, its political cohesion, and cultural strength.

The notion of unity arising from local geographical diversity has especial relevance to conditions in the Middle East. This area, defined as lying between the Indus basin, the Black Sea, tropical Africa, and the Atlantic, cannot be delineated accurately as one simple geographical region, since in certain respects it contains pronounced diversity. Nevertheless, from this area there have arisen several strong and pervasive cultures—Jewish, Christian, and Moslem—each of which is still concerned to demonstrate that its roots or fundamental origins lie in a specific territory of the Middle East. Zionism has overcome the Diaspora; Christ is still set against the background of Galilee and Judea; and pilgrimage to Islamic holy cities is enjoined on all true Moslems. Of the three, however, it is the Islamic pattern of life which has come to be most characteristic of the Middle East, and has provided one of the main bases for cultural unity within the area.

Alongside its theology, Islam has endeavoured to provide guidance in mundane matters of life, to a degree that distinguishes it sharply from other religious systems of the area. Muslim thought and observance are closely rooted in everyday ways of living, and these in turn are largely conditioned by the environment, which in many respects is unusual within the world. Climate could properly be held to be the most important element of the environment, not only by its own nature, but for its effects upon plant growth and thus in turn upon human life through farming routines. Over most of the world, the heaviest rainfall tends to occur at the time of greatest heating from the sun; while clouds reduce the direct incidence of heat below the theoretical maximum. But in the Middle East the greatest heat coincides with the driest time of the year: clouds are few or largely absent, and insolation is relatively uninterrupted, producing maximum daily temperatures far in excess of those experienced at any time near the equator; hence these temperatures are among the highest in the world. In winter, rainfall is largely of the instability type, closely affected by the abrupt relief, and this means heavy onset but limited duration. Consequently skies soon become relatively clear, which causes much heat loss, particularly in regions of high altitude, and also considerable contrast in total amounts of rainfall from one local region to another.

We thus have a climate which can be regarded as unique, in that it imposes a "resting" season on most plants (and some animals) during the hot season, with major growth at other times of the year. Plants native to the Middle East exhibit this tendency to a remarkable degree, and their cultivation requires human routines very different from those in the rest of the world. This special "Mediterranean" climatic regime occurs in very small areas of other continents, but the Middle East and other Mediterranean countries make up at least 85 per cent of its total world area.

Because this climate exacts special techniques in agriculture, there has grown up a distinctively Middle Eastern way of life. This is basically seen in the habit of winter and spring cultivation, with high summer regarded as the most difficult time of the year, particularly where animals and pasture are involved. Development of irrigation has since allowed a break away from this long-established cycle, and has made possible the introduction of plants that are native to regions where summer rainfall is normal: e.g. cotton, maize, millet, rice, ground-nuts, and sugar. Irrigation therefore means not only a supplement to pre-existing levels of production, but a major change in agricultural routine and habit of life. For example, several large communities have grown up which depend entirely upon irrigation from major rivers. These "hydraulic" cultures present special features of their own: a highly developed sense of co-operation in order to allow the functioning of intricate irrigation schemes; acceptance of closely organized and demanding annual routines, with particular methods of cultivation; participation in large-scale social units often showing strongly hierarchical organization; and extreme vulnerability to pressures from outside. Such conditions are to be found elsewhere in the world where large-scale irrigation is practised, but they are at their most developed in the Middle East.

It is instructive to follow out in further detail the possible influence of climate upon human activity in this part of the world. Largely conditioned by scantiness of effective rainfall (even where temporarily heavy rain may disperse quickly as a flash-flood), and also by extremes of temperature, which in turn are affected by variations in altitude, Middle Eastern people have made special responses to their environment. Measures to conserve water, style of clothing, and housing as protection both against heat and cold; simple measures to promote sanitation and better health in a territory greatly liable to animal and human disease; adaptation to widely differing amounts of rainfall, and to agriculture under irrigation—all these, when regarded as a function of climatic control, stand out as characteristics of human life in the Middle East, and confer upon it a special cultural pattern. As has been explained earlier, diversities may arise because of regional differences in the environment; but we can be clear that the various peoples of the Middle East follow a way of life and exhibit a culture, material and non-material, that is highly distinct compared with those of neighbouring lands in Further Asia, Equatorial Africa, or Europe. This means that an Arab, Turk, or Iranian can readily adapt himself in all parts of the Middle East with relatively few problems of cultural assimilation.

Another characteristic feature of Middle Eastern life is the intimate association between settled cultivators and those pastoralists who practise some form of annual migration. In most parts of the world, animal-rearing is integrated (usually to a considerable extent) with settled farming. Alternatively, if migration occurs, it has been by small groups of transient importance. But until quite recently, nomadic and transhumant peoples have been relatively numerous in the Middle East, and their high degree of social cohesion has enabled them to maintain considerable social parity with settled communities. The uneasy relations between the desert and the village have for centuries been a fundamental element in Middle East social affairs; and the strength of the nomads—unusually great here as compared with elsewhere—has meant that the two groups were probably more nearly matched.

Another element creating the individual response characteristic of the Middle East is its geographical location as the junction between the major land masses of the Old World. Deeply penetrated by arms of the sea, the Middle East is a massive isthmus, a bridge between wider territories, yet large enough to have an individuality of its own. This has produced extensive intercontinental traffic; and thus, whilst profiting from this traditional long-distance trade, the region has now added its own resources, principally in oil. Hence a second aspect emerges: a profound mercantile tradition, stemming basically from a wealthy trading community, but also affecting others: those directly employed in some form of transport, and those upon whom currents of trade impinge indirectly, such as pastoral nomads through whose territory caravans pass, and agricultural peoples engaged in supplying goods for trade. Pragmatism, an awareness of world-wide relations and of the necessity to look beyond the immediate territory to more distant regions of potential supply and demand, have produced a characteristic attitude among these people. Merchants from the Middle East have appeared over and over again in most parts of the Old World—Syrians have been known alike in Merovingian France, medieval India, and contemporary Tropical Africa; Arabian traders have been active to the east since before the birth of Christ; and there is no need to emphasize the important commercial role of Armenians and Jews since the Middle Ages.

It is therefore hardly accidental that the inhabitants of the Middle East should have exhibited sustained interest in other lands, and that one of their strongest intellectual contributions should be in the sphere of regional description. Travel was at first a commercial activity; and then, with developments of an "imperial" nature under Islam's aegis, it became an administrative matter. Today, in the form of pilgrimages, it has come to be an integral part of Islamic observance, and is a powerful unifying factor among Moslems.

Growth of commercial activities in medieval Europe led to the emergence, in the south and west at least, of a powerful self-confident bourgeoisie that fostered local civic government; as a larger number of self-ruling urban units grew up each came to act as the undisputed dominant element in an entire local region. Such an evolution occurred only in a more attenuated form over much of the Middle East. Merchants were often of great wealth and personal influence, but their impact and scale of activity tended in some areas to remain at an individual level. Relatively fewer permanent and powerful corporations comparable with the medieval European guilds or city councils emerged as capable of taking over the entire function of city government in the Middle East. Down to our own time, administration, in certain aspects at least, tended to remain largely in the hands of a central authority that delegated government to a nominated official, aristocratic or plebeian, with mercantile and bourgeois interests only partially represented. A characteristic figure has often been a military governor, who has tended to encourage the migration of non-local groups into the towns, partly to offset local pressures.

Hence, whilst a city can frequently develop greatly in power and wealth, it may at the same time attain only an incomplete relationship with the immediately surrounding rural area. Mercantile attention might be focused on through trade routes involving distant regions and urban centres; but less attention has been given to the geographically immediate problems of economic and social environment, and thus the rural population has sometimes been inhibited from developing full relations with the city. Immigrant rulers, officials, or traders might employ a language different from that spoken by the rural people; and this tendency towards differentiation might be reinforced by a separate cultural development. For instance, new religions developed and propagated themselves in the towns; different racial groups could form; and even though the wealthy might own rural estates, their habit of residing permanently in the towns, leaving their estates to be run by overseers, could further emphasize what could sometimes be called the gap between town and country.

Such an evolution, described by Weulersse as typical of the cities of the Levant, is also characteristic of some other neighbouring areas. However, in Iran and in lands which during earlier times came under Persian rule (e.g. the oasis cities of Central Asia such as Bukhārā and Samarqand) a different pattern occurs. P. W. Avery has drawn attention to the distinction between towns lying on international trade routes, and associated with the ancient Silk road, and a second-order, interior group, which lack major long-distance trade activities and thus tend to function not always, however, completely as a local centre. In this, as P. English has shown, Iran displays a special character which tends to differentiate it from areas farther west.

As regards material culture one may discern certain influences that stem once again from the geographical environment. The raw materials for textiles—cotton, wool, silk, mohair, camel's hair, and flax—have long been traditional products of the Middle East, and textiles ranging from fine muslin to carpets probably afford the widest spectrum of Middle Eastern handiwork. Persian carpets, increasingly sought after in our own day as supreme examples of Middle Eastern craftsmanship, are probably the most appreciated art form of this region, since they command steadily rising prices in many parts of the world.

The absence of extensive supplies of good building stone is a marked feature of the Middle East. Much of the surface strata of the region contains deposits of clays, sands, and alluvium, frequently underlain (especially in the south) by intractable igneous and metamorphic rocks, chiefly granites. Limestone, though abundant, is often too coarse or too fissured for effective use in building, and rocks such as basalt do not easily lend themselves to elaborate ornamental construction. On the other hand, clay, which is very abundant, and limestone used as a raw material of cement, are both important in ceramics—and this is the second significant art form in the Middle East. Tiles are extensively used as ornament on the otherwise plain style of building; tile-work both for floors and as a major architectural decoration is therefore highly developed; and domestic pottery-working is another minor, but far from insignificant, art form.

Various metallic ores have been found on a small scale in certain areas of the Middle East, and have been conducive to metal-working. This reached high artistic and technical levels in past centuries, but it is now, with minor exceptions, somewhat less successful. Hardly any contemporary product is comparable in esteem to early Damascene steel or silver. Nevertheless, some work of a high order is still characteristic of a few regions—notably Iranian and Amara silverware.

Painting and sculpture are much less developed. In the case of sculpture one might invoke the operation of a minor control due to intractable material, though it is more correct to see here the effect of human predilection. The climate is against painting on cloth; on the other hand, carpets can be shaken to rid them of insects, and their fading with age even becomes a commercial advantage, whilst paintings survive much less satisfactorily in the climate. Miniature painting on ivory, paper, or stone is one response to the situation, but generally speaking one may best explain matters by citing the strong Islamic reluctance to portray natural forms—though in so doing one may again be involved in a circular argument.

Music could be said to have only a limited part in Middle Eastern life. Muslim observance relies upon it far less than do other religions of the world; and extremes of temperature and humidity are often against the elaboration of finely tuned string instruments. Percussion and fairly small wind instruments are therefore most characteristic of Middle Eastern music generally, with the human voice taking an important share, often alone (since accompaniment by percussion and wind is not always effective), or in alternation with another voice or orchestral group. Although singing reaches a high level, with much delicacy and expertise in performances, this is nearly always confined to unison and solo performance, so that part-singing and canon are uncommon. Greek Orthodox congregations are almost the only people who use this latter form of expression.

Middle Eastern literature could be said to show distinctive qualities that are related to environment. A marked feature of the Middle Eastern landscape are the rapid changes from harsh, oppressive terrain— desert, salt marsh, or bare mountain, all experiencing extremes of climate—to the opposite of abundance and amenity, where living is pleasant. Also, there can be dramatic reversals of fortune, with poverty giving way to riches, and the opposite. A single disastrous season may reduce rich and powerful nomads to physical destitution; a prosperous farmer or merchant may be ruined by arbitrary commercial laws or boundary changes, and a comfortably placed individual may suddenly find himself a destitute refugee. On the other hand, "boom" conditions have also occurred, making the fortunes of at least some. Among a population whose majority have had only low standards of life, this theme of violent alteration in mode of life has come to be a common theme of literature. The economic changes of the past thirty years have heightened disparities rather than levelled them out. An Arab monarch recently rewarded an exceptionally agile scramble up the Great Pyramid with the equivalent of thirty or forty years' income at fellah level; and one need only compare today's living conditions on the coast near Beirut with those a mere twenty-five years ago to realize the scope for reversal of fortune.

This is why the theme of oscillating fortune has long been popular in Middle Eastern literature, and why the harsh realities experienced by so many in their daily lives stimulate ideas of sensual ease and gratification at a later stage, possibly on earth but far more likely in an afterlife. Changes over the past thirty years have also given rise to a recurrent but much more modern theme—dissatisfaction with the social order, a questioning of the hitherto accepted bases of society, and a profound desire for some sort of evolution and change, with a sense that the present represents failure. Characteristic of many but by no means all the younger writers, this spirit of *Angst* and repudiation is becoming an increasingly significant aspect of modern Middle Eastern literature, alongside more traditional themes. T. E. Lawrence observed that the mind of the Arab appears "at ease only in extremes", and since his time economic and social conditions have served to heighten this situation.

It has probably been observed, and with mounting surprise, that so far in this discussion little or no reference has been made directly to Iran. The writer has been concerned to establish at some length, first, that environmental factors can be held to exert an influence upon the nature and evolution of society; next, the significance of the specific regional unit within a more general environmental framework; and third, the special characteristics which may be partly responsible for giving the societies of the Middle East their distinctive quality. It now remains to consider specifically the population of Iran within its general setting; its Muslim culture and its geographical location within the Middle East. We shall also try to show that, whilst its overall features make it part of this wider unity, Iranian society also occupies a unique situation within the Middle East.

At the start of this essay, it was suggested that certain regions of the world possess a special geographical character and historical tradition. Of these regions, Iran is certainly one, since the country fulfils in a remarkable way the criteria of a recognizable human unit with a culture that has been distinctive for many centuries.

The simplest fact about Iran is its pronounced physiography. An outer ring of mountain chains, reinforced to north and south by arms of the sea and by regions of pronounced climatic difficulty (winter temperature contrasts of the west, aridity on the east), together form a definitive unity that has relatively few counterparts elsewhere in the world. It is rare to be able to trace such a precise geographical boundary as that between Mesopotamian plain and Iranian mountain. Most geographical boundaries are in reality zones, though for convenience and clarity they are drawn on a map as lines, but in the case of Iran these zones happen to be extremely sharp and narrow, as Didalus Siculus pointed out centuries ago.

Human settlement in Iran is concentrated on the interior piedmont slopes of the north and west, and it extends through the outer Alburz piedmont to include the southern Caspian coastlands. Juxtaposition of mountain and plain, with the former an almost continuous periphery around Iran, has conferred upon the country the physical cohesion which, it has been argued, is an important requisite for the growth of a national unit. The early American states, located on a somewhat similar piedmont, developed a conscious national feeling when they were closely bounded by the mountain rim of the Appalachians on one side and the Atlantic on the other. An opposite case may be cited from Europe. It has been the frequently expressed regret of many German historians and geopolitical thinkers that the natural environment of Germany is relatively formless: German geography shows transition rather than distinctive change, and the land forms continue outside the area of German speech and culture. Whilst many Middle Eastern states are defined by arbitrary boundaries drawn between determined points (as in Saudi Arabia, Jordan, Kuwait, Libya, and even Egypt), Iran has an indisputable and clearly defined territorial unity. Shape of national territory can be of importance to political cohesion: a long, narrow morphology, for example, can prove a handicap, as in ancient Egypt, with its Upper Middle and Lower, kingdoms, or in modern Czecho-slovakia and Indonesia.

Climatically, whilst it is fundamentally part of the general Middle Eastern regime, Iran has wider extremes than are experienced in many other countries of that region. The Sahara and inner Arabia are equally as arid as the driest parts of Iran, but their winter cold is less intense; districts of Lebanon and Turkey have as much rainfall as the wettest parts of Iran, but they do not experience the same high summer temperatures. In Iran it is as if all the main features of climate were exaggerated: great heat, enormous unreliability of rainfall, bitter cold, alternating calms and sustained windiness, regions with extremely wide seasonal fluctuations, and the unusual aberrant of the Caspian coastland with its almost monsoonal warmth and dampness.

The fact that Iran has few large rivers—and of those of any great size all flow either totally or in part outward into non-Iranian territory—is of considerable importance. There is no scope for the elaboration of a large-scale civilization or way of life based on control and utilization of a major waterway, either as a source of irrigation or as an avenue of commerce. The pattern of existence sometimes termed "the great hydraulic civilization" has no place in Iran. Yet the scope and need for water management remains, and are achieved through relatively small-scale, local efforts by means of *qanāt*. Such a usage of natural water supplies produces a garden-like pattern of cultivation with very few of the larger-scale units that characterize many other irrigated parts of the world. Observers have frequently commented that Iran conveys the overall impression of a cluster of gardens, with pockets of local richness set as it were in a matrix of harsher, less tractable territory. Characteristic of Iran is the qanāt, with its associated small network of irrigation channels, and the possibility of setting aside a few corners for pleasure and ornament within the sterner realities of subsistence cropping. This contrasts with the lands "watered by the foot" in the great alluvial valleys of Egypt and Mesopotamia, where large canals predominate, the scale of cultivation is greater and qanāts very few.

Besides the settled communities there are important groups of nomads and semi-nomads in Iran. Over much of the Middle East this situation creates a dichotomy; but in Iran it is sometimes less easy to draw sharp distinctions between the two groups, since certain sections of a community may be migratory with a mixed pastoral economy, while other sections of the same communities are more closely identified with settled agricultural routines. As we have seen in the articles by De Planhol and Sunderland (pp. 409–67, and 611–83, above), such situations are especially common in the Alburz and parts of the Zagros regions.

Handicraft has also linked together groups of varied ways of life, both in the past and again at the present. For not only does this activity create a single market for raw materials (chiefly wool), but finished products made by pastoralists and their families find their way into the towns, and even abroad. Here is a considerable contrast with a country like Egypt, where the spread of artisan activity does not occur to the same extent among the rural population. This fairly close association between rural and urban groups through handicrafts is probably less technologically efficient than the specialization and division of labour now characteristic of Egypt and to some extent Turkey; but it lends a special flavour to Iranian life, and could be regarded as one useful element preventing the disintegration of local society (especially of the pastoral and nomadic elements) that is now so prominent a feature elsewhere in the Middle East.

A moderate abundance of various natural resources, together with the presence of numerous and often sophisticated skilled workers, have provided the mechanism for an enhanced degree of productivity in Iran. This is one important area of the Middle East where, in relation to human numbers, there has usually been a small but recurring surplus of food and raw materials which could provide the basis of social and political advance. A material and intellectual culture and complex social institutions can only develop from some surplus in material productivity, and Iran has emerged as one significant area where there has been scope for such efflorescence. Other such seminal regions have appeared in Egypt, round the Aegean, and to a somewhat less degree in the Mesopotamian valley, and in the Levant coastlands as far inland as Aleppo, Damascus, and Jerusalem. Throughout history, the impact of Persian styles, ideas, and methods of rule, along with those of the Ottomans at a later period, have been major consistent influences in the Middle East. Centuries ago, Iran conquered Egypt, represented a recurring menace to the Greeks, set a decisive limit to Roman and Ottoman expansion, and in later years profoundly influenced India. Though liable to temporary phases of administrative weakness and decline—such as happened during the time of Alexander the Great when Iran was occupied by Hellenistic invaders—Iran has stood out as a highly significant polity of vigour and distinctiveness.

Iran has also been drawn into European political calculations, a process that during the last century and a half produced a decline which reached a nadir some fifty years ago. Yet intrinsic cohesion and toughness as an organic unit allowed Iran to remain a major influence within Asia, even when threatened from without latterly, the effects of petroleum exploitation have redressed the situation, largely re-established the country's international position, and given impetus to internal economic development.

It might be argued that prior to exploitation of oil, it was the location of Iran with respect to strategic and commercial routes within Asia generally that drew down upon the country the predatory interest of outside powers. In more recent times cupidity aroused by Iran's richness in petroleum made this richness a political liability rather than an asset. Whatever cause the invasions of Iran can be ascribed to, the resilience of Iranians has made the process a two-way one. New resources, material and temperamental, and even a long and not infrequently tried special technique for dealing with initially successful invaders, may be seen to have given rise to forces ultimately deterrent to outside interference.

As we have said, geographical location is a partial explanation of the somewhat separate cultural and historical evolution that Iran has experienced. In the first place, her predominant language is of the Aryan family, suggesting links with Europe and India. Semitic speech, like Turkic, is confined to a number of small minority groups. As well, Iran is the major area of the world where Shī'a observances predominate. And whilst this brings Iran clearly within the Muslim Middle East, it also distinguishes her from other countries where, except for the Yemen, Shī'a adherents tend to form a minority among larger Sunnī groups. Moreover, the Iranians are very far from being late entrants within a pre-existing social and political system, as were the Ottoman Turks in Anatolia and Byzantium. Consequently, whilst Turkish life now exhibits something of an amalgam of several major elements— Turkic speech, Semitic religion, and certain Byzantine social traditions —Iran is more properly to be regarded as a wholly indigenous society which has developed, by accretion, into an already existing and firmly based system. Society in Iran has always been strong enough to absorb. Nor are there the recurring difficulties of the sort that arise in Egypt, where a long, very narrow and vulnerable valley can be quickly overrun from the surrounding desert, and must therefore be defended at a distance in the outer arid zones, where the terrain is hostile to both attacker and defender.

As we have seen, there has always been sufficient resource-wealth within Iran to support a moderately large population capable of achieving a high cultural level. The favourable zones—regions of increment—are, however, surrounded by harsher or intractable areas where communications are inevitably restricted to a small number of well-defined routes. In consequence, the towns situated on such routes, or lying in a nodal position within a small productive region, have exerted the same functions over many centuries: the currents of human activity cannot easily take alternative routes or sites. Places like Iṣfahān, Shīrāz, Kirmān, and Tabrīz, to name only a few, are the obvious centres for their region, and have had no rivals. We have also noted earlier in this chapter the differentiation in function and hence in sociology between towns that are chiefly long-distance trading centres, and those that are local capitals for a region. For some of the trading cities the changes in external geographical relationships have had important repercussions. When political and economic supremacy was exerted by Mesopotamia, by the Nile valley or the Levant states, the west and south-west of Iran tended to hold greater importance than other sections. Now, emphasis is more on the north and north-west of Iran, partly because of the ascendancy of Russia in Asian affairs. This is well seen by the changing capital cities of Iran. Were the country uniformly productive and well endowed, the geometric centre would appear as the obvious site for a capital. But the presence of desert and *kavīr* inhibits such a development, and the capital must lie somewhat away from the centre. In fact, the importance of external relations is shown by the manner in which the capital has altered: in early days, it was mainly in the west, though occasionally east; and then it moved decisively north. This periodic shift in centre of gravity within Iran is by no means unknown in the world—Germany offers something of a parallel, as also does Turkey—but the air of newness, almost accident, about Tehrān gives a special quality to the city. It could be added that the migratory days would now seem to be over, and that Tehrān is now too far developed ever to lose its metropolitan function.

The uniqueness of Iran amounts to far more than a few outstanding textile designs, a cluster of medieval buildings, and volumes of lyric poetry. The visitor to Iran, if he is in any degree perceptive, soon becomes aware of an evolving yet firmly rooted pattern of life which, in its continuity with the past, retains much depth of tradition. Some countries and societies impress mainly by a newness of their institutions: a historical and sociological "unconformity", if one may adapt a geological expression, divides them sharply from the past—as, for example, in Amman, which has been a continuously inhabited site for only eighty years.

With Iran, however, one can recognize a clearly defined unitary response over many centuries to prevailing natural conditions. The continuity of this response could in itself be interpreted as proof of the sustained influences exerted by the geographical environment. And through maintaining its own identity, Iran has been able to reach out to influence other lands. Some countries, as historians interpret matters, have come into existence and are held together by virtue of a specific "mission": i.e. they developed in response to the exigencies of a particular human situation. Austria defended Western European values first against the Ottomans, then, less successfully, against the Slavs; Spain resisted Islamic penetration through Africa; medieval

Rome functioned as residuary legatee of Imperial Rome. Other territories, however, have never had such an explicit mission or role; their virtue and qualification rest in their being, and in what they themselves are. It is not possible or desirable, even, to assess or compare them one with another: they exist in themselves, and that is enough.

In no sense could Iran be regarded as merely a smaller or attenuate version of another stronger cultural or political area. Rather, it should be considered as an integral unit with its own institutions that contribute in a major way to the character and hence broader unity of the Middle East. The fact that the Iranian state can contemplate at the present time the celebration of 2,500 years of monarchy is a remarkable index of its resilience, and to this the clearly defined physiography of the country makes a strong contribution. If we seek to define Iran's function as a state and as a human grouping in terms of a "personality", then the country can be said to generate, to receive and transmogrify, and to re-transmit.

BIBLIOGRAPHY

Volume Editor's Note

The bibliographies printed below are selective and incomplete. Their purpose is not to list all publications that bear directly or indirectly on the subject, but to enable readers to carry further the study of selected topics. A later volume in this series (vol. VIII) will present at much greater length a systematic bibliography. As a rule, books and articles superseded by later publications have not been included, and references to general treatises not directly relevant to the subject-matter of individual chapters have been reduced to a minimum. Since the principal aim of the volume is to supply interpretations and summaries of knowledge already available in secondary literature, references to original sources have either been omitted altogether, or have been confined to the most essential classes of evidence.

Within the limits set by these principles, contributors were free to compile bibliographies as they thought best. The "layout" of the lists, therefore, varies from chapter to chapter. The editor did not even find it desirable to produce a uniform method of abbreviating references to learned periodicals. Form of presentation is, therefore, the decision of the individual author.

Chapters 6 ("Soils") and 19 ("Water Resources in North-East Iran") are based almost entirely upon work in the field and personal observation. For this reason, and also because of the paucity of general studies, no bibliographies are given. Readers are, however, referred to volumes cited in this Bibliography for other chapters, as some of these have a general bearing on chapters 6 and 19.

CHAPTER I

Admiralty, Naval Intelligence Division. *Persia*. London, 1945.

Argand, E. *La Tectonique de l'Asie*. Brussels, 1924.

Blanchard, R. "Asie Occidentale." *Géogr. Universelle*, vol. VIII. Paris, 1929.

Bakher, A. J. "River Discharges in Iran." *UNESCO Symposium on Salinity Problems in Arid Zones*. Tehrān, 1958.

Bobek, H. "Forschungen in Persien, 1958/9." *Mitt. Öst. Geog. Ges.*, 1959.

Bout, P., Derruau, M., Dresch, J. and Peguy, P. "Observations de Géographie Physique en Iran septentrional." *Edns. du Centre Nat. de la Recherche Sci.* VIII, 1946.

Brüning, K. *Asien*. Frankfurt, 1954.

Butzer, K. *Quaternary Stratigraphy and Climate in the Near East*. Bonn, 1958.

Clapp, F. G. "The Geology of Eastern Iran." *Bull. geol. Soc. Am.* vol. LI, 1940.

Curzon of Kedleston, G. N. (Lord). *Persia and the Persian Question*. London, 1892.

Furon, R. "La Géologie du Plateau Iranien." *Mém. Mus. d'Hist. Nat. Paris*, 1941.

Gabriel, A. "The Southern Lut and Iranian Baluchistan." *Geogr. J.* vol. XCII, 1938.

—— *Im Weltfernen Orient*. Munich, 1929.

Gansser, A. "New Aspects of the Geology of Central Iran." *Proc. 4th Wld Petr. Congr.* sect. I A, no. 5. Rome, 1955.

Goblot, H. *Les Problèmes de l'Eau en Iran*. Tehrān, 1960.

Harrison, J. V. "The Bakhtiari Country, South West Persia." *Geogr. J.* vol. LXXX, 1932.

—— "Coastal Makran." *Geogr. J.* vol. XCVII, 1941.

—— "The Jaz Murian Depression, Persian Baluchistan." *Geogr. J.* vol. CI, 1943.

—— "South-west Persia, a survey of Pish-i-Kuh in Luristan." *Geogr. J.* vol. CVIII, 1946.

Lees, G. M. "Persia." In *Science of Petroleum*, vol. VI, part 1. Oxford, 1953.

Lees, G. M. and Falcon, N. L. "The geographical history of the Mesopotamian Plains." *Geogr. J.* vol. CVIII, 1952.

Lees, G. M. and Richardson, F. D. S. "The Geology of the Oilfield Belt of South-west Iran." *Geol. Mag.* vol. LXXVII, 1940.

Morgan, J. de. *Mission Scientifique en Perse*. Paris, 1905.

Planhol, X. de. *See under* chapter 13.

Rieben, H. *Notes sur la Géologie de l'Iran*. Lausanne, 1942.

—— *Notes Préliminaires sur les terrains alluviaux de Tehéran*. Lausanne, 1953.

Scharlau, K. "Iran." *Westermanns Lexicon der Geographie*. Braunschweig, 1963.

Skrine, C. P. "The Highlands of Persian Baluchistan." *Geogr. J.* vol. LXXVIII, 1931.

Wilson, A. T. *A Bibliography of Persia*. Oxford, 1930.

CHAPTER 2

Baier, E. "Ein Beitrag zum Thema Zwischengebirge." *Zentbl. Miner. Geol. Paläont.* Abt. B, 1938, pp. 385–99.

Bailey, E. B., Jones, R. C. B. and Asfia, S. "Notes on the geology of the Elburz mountains north east of Tehran, Iran." *Q. Jl geol. Soc. Lond.* vol. CIV, 1948, pp. 1–42.

Blanford, W. T. "Note on geological formations seen along the coast of Baluchistan and Persia from Karachi to the head of the Persian Gulf, and some of the Gulf Islands." *Geol. Surv. India,* vol. V, 1872, pp. 41–5.

Bobek, H. "Reise in Nordwest Persien." *Z. Ges. Erdk. Berl.* no. 9/10, 1934, pp. 359–69.

De Böckh, H., Lees, G. M. and Richardson, F. D. S. *The Structure of Asia.* Ed. J. W. Gregory. London, 1929.

British Petroleum Ltd. *Geological maps and sections of south-west Persia.* 20th Int. geol. Congr. Mexico, 1956.

—— *Notes to accompany* 1 : 250,000 *geological maps of south-west Iran.* 22nd Int. geol. Congr. Delhi, 1964.

Clapp, F. G. "The geology of eastern Iran." *Bull. geol. Soc. Am.* vol. LI, 1940, pp. 1–102.

Dietrich, W. O. "Ordovic in Nordwest-Iran." *Zentbl. Miner. Geol. Paläont.* Abt. B, 1937, pp. 401–4.

Dozy, J. J. "A sketch of post-Cretaceous vulcanism in central Iran." *Leid. geol. Meded.* vol. XX, 1955.

Elles, G. L. "The geology of salt plugs in Laristan." *Q. Jl geol. Soc. Lond.* vol. LXXXVI, 1930.

Falcon, N. L. "The position of the oil fields of south-west Iran with respect to relevant sedimentary basins." *Habitat of Oil.* American Association of Petroleum Geologists, 1958, pp. 1279–93.

—— "The geology of the north-east margin of the Arabian Shield." *Advancement of Science,* vol. XXIV, 1967–8. (Presidential address delivered to Section C (Geology), 4 Sept. 1967 in Leeds.)

Flugel, H. "*Receptaculites neptuni* Defr." *Bull. Iran Petrol. Inst.* no. 4, 1961, pp. 75–81.

Furon, R. "Géologie du plateau iranien." *Mém. Mus. Natn. Hist. nat. Paris,* vol. VII, n.s., 1941, fasc. 2, pp. 177–414.

Furrer, M. A. and Soder, P. A. "The Oligo-Miocene marine formation in the Qum region (central Iran)." *Proc. 4th Wld Petrol. Congr.* Sect. 1A, no. 5. Rome, 1955.

Gabriel, A. *Im Weltfernen Orient.* Munich, Berlin, 1929.

Gansser, A. "New aspects of the geology in central Iran." *Proc. 4th Wld Petrol. Congr.* Sect. 1A, no. 5. Rome, 1955.

—— "Ausser Alpine Ophiolithprobleme." *Eclog. geol. Helv.* vol. LII, 1959, pp. 659–80.

——— "Über Schlammvulkans und Salzdome." *Vjschr. naturf. Ges. Zurich*, vol. CV, no. 1, 1960, pp. 1–46.

——— and Huber, H. "Geological observations in the central Elburz, Iran." *Schweiz. Miner. Petrogr. Mitt.* vol. XLII, 1962, pp. 583–630.

Gray, K. W. "A tectonic window in south-western Iran." *Q. Jl geol. Soc. Lond.* vol. CV, 1950, pp. 189–223.

Gregory, J. W. *The Structure of Asia*. London, 1929.

Harrison, J. V. "The geology of some salt-plugs in Laristan, south Persia." *Q. Jl geol. Soc. Lond.* vol. LXXXVI, 1930.

——— and Falcon, N. L. "Gravity collapse structures and mountain ranges as exemplified in south-western Iran." *Q. Jl geol. Soc. Lond.* vol. XCII, 1936, pp. 463–552.

——— ——— "An ancient landslip at Saidmarreh in south-western Iran." *J. Geol.* vol. XLVI, 1938, pp. 296–309.

Henson, F. R. S. "Observations on the geology and petroleum occurrence of the Middle East." *Proc. 3rd Wld Petrol. Congr.* Sect. 1. The Hague, 1951, pp. 141–61.

Hirschi, H. "Über Persiens Salzstöcke." *Schweiz. Miner. Petrogr. Mitt.* vol. XXIV, 1944.

Huckriede, R., Kürsten, M. and Venzlaff, H. "Zur Geologie des Gebietes zwischen Kerman und Sagand (Iran)." *Beib. geol. Jb.* vol. LI, Bundesanstalt für Bodenforschung. Hannover, 1962.

Ion, D. C., Elder, S. and Pedder, A. E. "The Agha Jari oilfield, southwestern Persia." *Proc. 3rd Wld Petrol. Congr.* Sect. 1. The Hague, 1951, pp. 162–86.

Kent, P. E. "Recent studies of south Persian salt plugs." *Bull. Am. Ass. Petrol. Geol.* vol. XLII, 1958, pp. 2951–72.

——— Slinger, F. C. and Thomas, A. N. "Stratigraphical exploration surveys in south-west Persia." *Proc. 3rd Wld Petrol. Congr.* Sect. 1. The Hague, 1950, pp. 141–61.

Lees, G. M. "Persia", in *Science of Petroleum*, vol. VI, pt. 1. Oxford, 1953.

——— and Falcon, N. L. "The geographical history of the Mesopotamian plains." *Geogr. J.* vol. CXVIII, 1952.

Loftus, W. T. "On the geology of portions of the Turco-Persian frontier." *Q. Jl geol. Soc. Lond.* vol. XI, 1855, pp. 247–344.

Mitchell-Thomé, R. C. "Reconnaissance, structural and tectonic studies of part of northern Iraq." *Proc. 21st Int. Geol. Congr.* pt. 18, 1960, pp. 149–66.

De Morgan, J. *Mission Scientifique en Perse*, vol. III, pt. 1, 1905.

Mustofi, B. and Frei, E. "The main sedimentary basins of Iran and their oil possibilities." *Proc. 5th Wld Petrol. Congr.* Sect. 1, no. 17, 1959.

Naqīb, A. "Geological observations in the Mizūrī Bālā area, northern Iraq." *Proc. 21st Int. Geol. Congr.* pt. 18, 1960, pp. 167–81.

Oberlander, T. *Zagros Streams*. Syracuse, N.Y., 1965.

O'Brien, C. A. E. "Salt diapirism in south Persia." *Geologie en Mijn.* vol. XIX, n.s., 1957, pp. 357–76.

Rivière, A. "Contribution à l'étude géologique de l'Elbourz." *Révue Géogr. Phys. et Géologie Dyn.* vol. VII, 1934.

Schroeder, J. W. "Essai sur la structure de l'Iran." *Eclog. geol. Helv.* vol. XXXVII, 1944, pp. 37–81.

Seward, A. G. "A Persian Sigillaria." *Phil. Trans. R. Soc. London,* vol. CCXXI, ser. B, 1938.

Stahl, A. F. "Zur Geologie von Persien." *Petr. Mitt. Erg.* vol. CXXII, 1897.

—— "Persien." *Handb. Reg. Geol.* vol. V, Heft 8. Heidelberg, 1911.

Stöcklin, J. "Lagunare Formationen und Salzdome in Ostiran." *Eclog. geol. Helv.* vol. LIV, 1961, pp. 1–27.

—— Eftekharj, K. and Huishmandzadeh, H. "Geology of the Shotori Range (Tabas Area, East Iran)." *Geol. Surv. Iran,* Rept. 3. Tehrān, 1965.

—— Nabavi, M. and Samini, M. "Geology and Mineral Resources of the Soltanish Mountains (N.W. Iran)." *Geol. Surv. Iran,* Rept. 2. Tehrān, 1965.

—— Ruttner, A. and Nabavī, M. "New data on the Lower Palaeozoic and Pre-Cambrian of north Iran." *Geol. Surv. Iran,* Rept. 1. Tehrān, 1964, pp. 1–29.

Thomas, A. N. "The Asmari Limestone of South-West Iran." *Proc. 18th Int. geol. Congr.* pt. 6, 1950, pp. 35–44.

CHAPTER 3

Bobek, H. "Die Landschaftsgestaltung des südkaspischen Küstentieflandes." *Festschr. f. Norbert Krebs.* Stuttgart, 1936.

—— "Klima und Landschaft Irans in vor- und frühgeschichtlicher Zeit." *Geogr. Jber. Öst.* vol. XXV, 1959.

—— "Forschungen in Persien, 1958/59." *Mitt. Öst. Geogr. Ges.* 1959.

—— *Features and formation of the Great Kavir and Masileh.* Arid Zone Research centre pub. II. Univ. of Tehrān, 1959.

—— "Die Salzwüsten Irans als Klimazeugen." *Anz. phil.-hist. Klasse Öst.* Akad. Wissenschaften, 1961.

Bonnard, E. G. "Contribution à la connaissance géologique du Nord-Est de l'Iran (Environ de Mésched)." *Eclog. geol. Helv.* vol. XXXVII, 1944.

Bout, P., Derruau, M., Dresch, J. and Peguy, P. "Observations de géographie physique en Iran septentrional." *Editions du centre national de la recherche scientifique,* vol. VIII. Paris, 1961.

Falcon, N. L. "The evidence for a former glaciation in the S.W. Persian Mountain belt." *Geogr. J.* vol. CVII, 1946.

Furon, R. "Sur l'existence d'une axe ouralien, déterminant de la structure du plateau iranien." *C.R. Acad. d. Sc.* vol. CCIII. Paris, 1936.

Gabriel, A. "Beobachtungen im Wüstengürtel Innerpersiens." *Mitt. geogr. Ges. Wien,* 1934.

—— "The southern Lut and Iranian Baluchistan." *Geogr. J.* vol. XCII, 1938.

—— *Ein Beitrag zur Gliederung und Landschaftskunde des innerpersischen Wüstengürtels.* Festschr. Hundertjahrfeier Geogr. Ges. Vienna, 1957.

—— "Zur Oberflächengestaltung der Pfannen in den Trockenräumen Zentralpersiens." *Mitt. geogr. Ges. Wien,* 1957.

Harrison, J. V. "Coastal Makran." *Geogr. J.* vol. XCVII, 1941.

—— "The Jaz Murian Depression, Persian Baluchistan." *Geogr. J.* vols. CI–CII, 1943.

—— "The Bakhtiari country, S.W. Persia." *Geogr. J.* vol. LXXX, 1932.

—— and Falcon, N. L. "The Saidmarreh landslip, south-west Iran." *Geogr. J.* vol. LXXXIX, 1937.

Hedin, S. von. *Zu Land nach Indien, durch Persien, Seistan, Belutschistan.* 1910.

Hövermann, J. "Uber Strukturböden im Elburs (Iran) und zur Frage des Verlaufs der Strukturbodengrenze." *Z. Geomorph.* 1960.

Kaehne, K. "Physische Geographie des Urmija-Beckens." *Z. Ges. Erdkunde Berlin,* 1940.

Scharlau, K. "Zum Problem der Pluvialzeiten in NE-Iran." *Z. Geomorph.* no. 2, 1958.

—— "Klimamorphologie und Luftbildauswertung im Hochland von Iran." *Z. Geomorph.* 1958.

—— "Das Nordost-iranische Gebirgsland und das Becken von Mesched." *Z. Geomorph.* 1963.

Stahl, A. F. "Die orographischen und hydrographischen Verhältnisse des Elbursgebirges in Persien." *Petermanns geogr. Mitt.,* 1927.

Stratil-Sauer, G. "Geographische Forschungen in Ostpersien: I. Die ostpersische Meridionalstrasse." *Abh. geogr. Ges. Wien,* vol. XVII, nos. 2, 3, 1953. "II. Routen durch die Wüste Lut und ihre Randgebiete." *Abh. geogr. Ges. Wien,* vol. XX, 1956.

—— *Forschungen in der Wüste Lut.* Wiss. Z. Martin Luther Univ., V. Halle-Wittenberg, 1956.

—— *Die pleistozänen Ablagerungen im Innern der Wüste Lut.* Festschr. z. Hundertjahrfeier Geogr. Ges. Wien, 1957.

CHAPTERS 4 AND 7

Adams, R. M. "Agriculture and Urban Life in Early Southwestern Iran." *Science,* vol. CXXXVI, no. 3511, 1962, pp. 109–22.

Carter, D. B., Thornthwaite, C. W. and Mather, J. R. "Three Water Balance Maps of Southwest Asia." *Publications in Climatology.* Laboratory of Climatology, Centerton, New Jersey, vol. XI, no. 1, 1958, 57 pp.

Development and Resources Corporation. *The Unified Development of the Natural Resources of the Khuzestan Region.* New York, 1959, 162 pp.

Oberlander, T. M. *The Zagros Streams.* Syracuse, New York: Syracuse University Press, 1965, 168 pp.

Pirnia, H. "Experience in the Integrated Development of a River Basin." Excerpt from an Economic Report on the Conservation and Utilization of the Natural Resources of Iran (with reference to the Iranian Seven-Year Plan for Reconstruction and Development). Proceedings,

United Nations Scientific Conference on the Conservation and Utilization of Resources, vol. IV, *Water Resources*. New York: U.N. Dept. Economic Affairs, 1951, pp. 162–5.

CHAPTER 5

Adle, A. H. *Climats de l'Iran*. Tehrān, 1960.
—— *Régions Climatiques et vegetation en Iran*. Tehrān, 1960.
Peterson, A. D. *Bibliography on the Climate of Iran*. Washington, 1957.
Weight, M. L. and Gold, H. K. *An Annotated Bibliography of Climatic Maps of Iran*. U.S. Weather Bureau.
Iran Almanac, 1961, 1962, 1963, 1965, 1966. *Echo of Iran Institute*, Tehrān.
Publications of the Meteorological Institute, Tehrān.

CHAPTER 7

See under chapter 4.

CHAPTER 8

(A complete bibliography can be found in the book by
M. Zohary cited below)

Adle, A. H. "Regions climatiques et vegetation en Iran." *Pub. Univ. de Teheran*, no. 626. 1960 (in Persian, with a French summary).
Bobek, H. *Die Verbreitung des Regenfeldbaues in Iran*. Vienna, 1951.
—— "Die natürlichen Wälder und Gehölzfluren Irans." *Bonn. geogr. Abh.* no. 8. 1951.
—— "Beiträge zur Klima-ökologischen Gliederung Irans." *Erdkunde Jg.* vol. VI. 1952.
—— "Klima und Landschaft Irans in vor- und frühgeschichtlicher Zeit." *Geogr. Jber. Öst.* vol. XXV. 1953–4.
—— "Vegetationsverwüstung und Bodenerschöpfung in Persien und ihr Zusammenhang mit dem Niedergang älterer Zivilisationen." *Int. Un. Conserv. Nat. nat. Resour.*, 7th Tech. Meet., vol. I. Athens, 1958; Brussels, 1959.
—— "Nature and implications of quaternary climatic changes in Iran." *UNESCO and WMO Symp. on Changes of Climate, Rome 1961*. UNESCO, 1963, pp. 403–13.
Dewan, M. L. *Soil map of Iran*. 1:2,500,000. Soil Dept. FAO, Tehrān, 1961.
Linchevski, A. J. and Prozorovski, A. V. "Basic principles of the distribution of the vegetation of Afghanistan." Trans. H. K. Airy-Shaw. *Kew Bull.* no. 2. 1949.
Zeist, W. van. "Preliminary palynological study of sediments from lake Merivan, S.W. Iran." (MS courtesy of the author.)
Zohary, M. "On the geobotanical structure of Iran." *Bull. of the Research Council of Israel*, Sec. D, Botany suppl. to vol. XI, D. 1963.

CHAPTER 9

Blanford, W. T. "The Zoology of Persia." In *Eastern Persia*, Persian Boundary Commission, vol. II, London, 1876.

Harrison, D. L. *The Mammals of Arabia*. I. *Insectivora, Chiroptera, Primates*. London, 1964.

Heptner, W. G. "Fauna der Gerbillidae Persiens und die tiergeographischen Eigenheiten der kleinasiatisch-irano-afghanischen Länden. *N. Mem. Soc. Nat. Moscou*, vol. XX, 1940, pp. 5–7.

Kullmann, E. "Die Säugetiere Afghanistans. I. Carnivora, Artiodactyla, Primates." *Science, Quart. J. Fac. Sci. Kabul*, 1965, pp. 1–17.

Misonne, X. "Analyse zoogeographique des Mammifères de l'Iran." *Mem. Inst. R. Sci. Nat. Belg.* vol. LIX, 1959, pp. 1–157.

Niethammer, J. "Die Säugetiere Afghanistans. II. Insectivora, Rodentia, Lagomorpha." *Science, Quart. J. Fac. Sci. Kabul*, 1965, pp. 18–41.

Petter, F. "Répartition géographique et Ecologie des rongeurs désertiques du Sahara occidental à l'Iran oriental." *Mammalia*, vol. XXV, 1961, pp. 1–222.

CHAPTER 10

Note: Anyone concerned with the geographic problems in South-west Asia should be familiar with the Henry Field bibliographies and indexes. A comprehensive bibliography for the herpetology of Iran will be found in Anderson (1963).

Anderson, 1963. "Amphibians and reptiles from Iran." *Proc. California Acad. Sci.* ser. 4, vol. XXXI, pp. 417–98.

—— 1966a. "A substitute name for *Agama persica* Blanford." *Herpetologica*, vol. XXII, p. 230.

—— 1966b. "The lectotype of *Agama isolepis* Boulenger." *Herpetologica*, vol. XXII, pp. 230–1.

—— 1966c. The Turtles, Lizards, and Amphisbaenians of Iran. Unpublished doctoral dissertation, Stanford University.

Anderson, S. C. and Leviton, A. E. 1966a. "A new species of *Eublepharis* from south-western Iran (Reptilia: Gekkonidae)." *Occ. Pap. California Acad. Sci.* no. 53, 5 pp., 2 figs.

—— 1966b. "A review of the genus *Ophiomorus*." *Proc. California Acad. Sci.* ser. 4, vol. XXXIII, pp. 499–534.

Banta, B. H. 1961. "Herbivorous Feeding of *Phrynosoma platyrhinos* on southern Nevada." *Herpetologica*, vol. XVII, pp. 136–7.

Blanford, W. T. 1876. *Eastern Persia, an Account of the Journeys of the Persian Boundary Commission, 1870–1872*, vol. II. *The Zoology and Geology*. London (Macmillan), 516 pp., 28 pls.

Bobek, H. 1951. "Die natürlichen Wälder und Gehölzfluren Irans." *Bonn. Geog. Abh.* vol. VIII, pp. 1–62.

Bobek, H. 1952. "Beiträge zur Klima-ökologischen Gliederung Irans." *Erdkunde*, vol. vi, pp. 65–84, map suppl.

—— 1963. "Nature and implications of Quaternary climatic changes in Iran." *In*: UNESCO. *Changes of climate; Proceedings of the Rome Symposium organized by UNESCO and the World Meteorological Organization. Arid Zone Res.* vol. xx, pp. 403–13.

Böckh, H. de, Lees, G. M. and Richardson, F. D. S. 1929. "Contribution to the stratigraphy and tectonics of the Iranian ranges." *In*: J. W. Gregory (ed.), *The Structure of Asia*. London (Methuen), pp. 58–177.

Bodenheimer, F. S. 1937a. "The zoogeography of the Sinai Peninsula." *Comptes Rendus XII Congrés International Zoologie*, Lisbonne 1935, vol. ii, pp. 1138–64.

—— 1937b. "Prodromus Faunae Palaestinae. Essai sur les éléments zoogeographiques et historiques du sudouest du sous-regne paléarctiques." *Mém. Inst. Egypt*, vol. xxxiii, 286 pp.

—— 1938. "On the presence of an Irano-Turanian relic fauna in North Africa." *Mém. Soc. Biogeographie*, vol. vi, pp. 67–79.

Butzer, K. W. 1956. "Late glacial and postglacial climatic variation in the Near East." *Erdkunde*, vol. xi, pp. 21–34.

Butzer, K. W. 1958a. "Quaternary stratigraphy and climate in the Near East." *Bonner Geogr. Abh.* 157 pp., 4 maps.

Cowles, R. B. and Bogert, C. M. 1944. "A preliminary study of the thermal requirements of desert reptiles." *Bull. American Mus. Nat. Hist.* vol. lxxxiii, pp. 265–96.

Furon, R. 1941. "Géologie du plateau iranien." *Mém. Mus. Hist. Nat., Paris*, n.s., vol. vii, pp. 177–414, 8 pls., 1 col. map.

Haas, G. 1952a. "Remarks on the origin of the herpetofauna of Palestine." *Rev. Fac. Sci. Univ. Istanbul*, ser. B, vol. xvii, pp. 95–105.

—— 1957. "Amphibians and reptiles from Arabia." *Proc. California Acad. Sci.* ser. iv, vol. xxix, pp. 47–86.

Heptner, W. G. 1945. "Desert and steppe fauna of palearctic region and centres of its development." *Bull. Soc. Nat. Moscou, Sect. Biol.* vol. l, pp. 17–38.

James, G. A. and Wynd, J. G. 1965. "Stratigraphic nomenclature of the Iranian Oil Consortium Agreement Area." *Bull. American Assoc. Petr. Geol.* vol. xlix, pp. 2182–245.

Kraus, E. B. 1958. "Meteorological aspects of desert locust control." *In: Climatology and Micro-climatology. Proceedings of the Canberra Symposium*, UNESCO, pp. 211–16.

Lay, D. M. 1966. *A Study of the Mammals of Iran resulting from the Street Expedition of 1962–63*. Fieldiana: Zoology (in Press).

Loveridge, A. and Ernest E. W. 1957. "Revision of the African tortoises and turtles of the suborder Cryptodira." *Bull. Mus. Comp. Zool., Harvard*, vol. cxv, pp. 163–557, pls. 1–18.

Mason, K. (ed.). 1945. *Persia*. Geographical Handbook Series, B.R. 525, xix + 638 pp.

Mayhew, W. W. 1963. "Temperature preferences of *Sceloporus orcutti*." *Herpetologica*, vol. XVIII, pp. 217–33.

—— 1964. "Photoperiodic responses in three species of the lizard genus *Uma*." *Pan-Pacific Engomologist*, vol. XL, and reprinted in *Herpetologica*, vol. XX, pp. 95–113.

—— 1965 a. "Growth response to photoperiodic stimulation in the lizard *Dipsosaurus dorsalis*." *Comp. Biochem. Physiol.* vol. XIV, pp. 209–16.

—— 1965 a. "Hibernation in the horned lizard, *Phrynosoma m'calli*." *Comp. Biochem. Physiol.* vol. XVI, pp. 103–19.

Merterns, Robert. 1952. "Amphibien und Reptilien aus Türkei." *Rev. Fac. Sci. Univ. Istanbul*, vol. XVIIB, pp. 41–75.

Minton, Sherman A., Jr. 1962. "An annotated key to the amphibians and reptiles of Sind and Las Bela, West Pakistan." *American Mus. Novitates*, no. 2081, pp. 1–60.

Minton, Sherman A., Anderson, S. C. and Anderson, J. A. "Remarks on some geckoes from South-west Asia, with descriptions of two new forms." *Occ. Pap. California Acad. Sci.* (in Press).

Misonne, X. 1959. "Analyse zoogéographique des mammiféres de l'Iran." *Mém. Inst. Roy. Sci. Nat. Belgique*, ser. II, no. 59, 157 pp., 3 pls., 97 maps following text.

Murray, J. A. 1884. *The Vertebrate Zoology of Sind*. London and Bombay, 423 pp., woodcuts and pls. (not seen).

Nairn, A. E. N. (ed.). 1961. *Descriptive Palaeoclimatology*. New York (Interscience Publishers), xi + 380 pp.

Rechinger, K. H. 1951. "Grundzüge der Pflanzenverbreitung im Iran." *Verh. zool.-boot. Ges. Wien*, vol. XCII, pp. 181–8.

Romer, A. S. 1956. *Osteology of the Reptiles*. Chicago, xxi + 772 pp.

Schmidt-Nielsen, K. 1959. "The physiology of the camel." *Scientific American*, vol. CCI, pp. 140–51.

Schwarzbach, M. 1963. *Climates of the Past*. (D. Van Nostrand) London, xii + 328 pp. (translated and edited by Richard O. Muir).

Shapley, H. (ed.). 1953. *Climatic Change*. (Harvard University Press) Cambridge, xii + 318 pp.

Sobolevskii, N. I. 1929. "The herpetofauna of the Talysh and of the Lenkoran lowland." *Mém. Soc. Amis Sci. Nat. Anthrop. Ethnog., Sec. Zool.* vol. V, pp. 1–141. (In Russian, English summary.)

Stamp, L. Dudley (ed.). 1961. *A History of Land Use in Arid Regions*. UNESCO, Paris, 388 pp.

Taylor, E. H. 1935. "A taxonomic study of the cosmopolitan scincoid genus *Eumeces*." *Univ. Kansas Sci. Bull.* vol. XXIII, pp. 1–643, pls. 1–43.

Walter, H. and Lieth H. 1960. *Klimadiagram—Weltatlas*. Gustav Fischer, Jena. (Looseleaf, pages issued at irregular intervals.)

Wettstein, O. von. 1951. "Ergebnisse der Österreichischen Iran-Expedition 1949/1950, Amphibien und Reptilien. Versuch einer tiergeographischen Gliederung Irans auf Grund der Reptilienverbreitung." *Sitzb. Österr. Akad. Wiss. Wien. Math.-naturw.* vol. CLX, pp. 427–48.

Wilson, Sir A. T. 1932. *Persia*. London, xvi + 400 pp.

Zeuner, F. E. 1959. *The Pleistocene Period*. London (Hutchinson and Co. Ltd), xviii + 447 pp.

CHAPTER 11

Allouse, B. E. *The Avifauna of Iraq*. 1953.

Beldi, Graf Gregor. "Ornithologische Notizen aus West Persien und Mesopotamien." *Aquila*, xxv, p. 91.

Berlioz, J. "Etude d'une Collection d'Oiseaux d'Iran." *Bull. Mus. Hist. Nat. Paris*, xxix, 1957.

Blandford, W. T. *Eastern Persia*, vol. ii. 1870–2.

Boswell, C. and Moore, H. J. *Field Observations on Birds of Iraq*. Baghdad, 1956.

Buxton, P. A. "Notes on birds from N. and W. Persia." *J.B.N.H.S.* 1921.

Capito, C. E. "Some birds from N.W. Fars, Persia." *J.B.N.H.S.* 1931.

Dahl, S. K. "The Vertebrate Fauna of Armenia." *Erevan*, 1954.

Dementiev, G. P. "Falco Jugger in Turkestan." *Ibis*, lxxxix, 1947.

—— and Gladkov, N. A. *Birds of the Soviet Union*.

Diesselhorst, A. *Stuttgarter Beitrage zur Naturkunde*, no. 86.

Isakov, J. A. and Vorobiev, K. A. *Wintering Birds and Migration on the South Coast of the Caspian Sea*. 1940.

Jervis-Read, S. H. *Check List of the Birds of Iran*. Teheran Univ. 1957.

—— "Notes from the Tuslo Gol, Central Iran." *Ibis*, 1958.

Loppenthin, B. "Sea birds of the Persian Gulf." *Proc. X Inter. Ornith. Cong.*

Ludlow, F. "Notes on the bird life of Ahwaz." *J.B.N.H.S.* vol. xxv, p. 303.

Meiklejohn, M. F. M. "Summer notes on the birds of Teheran and the Elburz Mountains." *Ibis*, xc, 1948.

Meinertzhagen, R. *Birds of Arabia*. London, 1954.

Misonne, X. "Les Grands Quartiers d'Hiver dans le Sud-Ouest de la Mer Caspienne." *Gerfaut*, 1953.

—— "Notes Complementaire sur les Oiseaux de la Cote Caspienne." *Gerfaut*, xliv, 1954.

—— "Note sur les Oiseaux de la Syrie et de l'Iran." *Gerfaut*, xlvi, 1956.

—— "La Migration d'Automne dans le Kurdistan Oriental." *Gerfaut*, 1955.

Norton, W. "Notes on birds in the Elburz Mountains of N. Persia." *Ibis*, 1958.

Paludan, K. "Zur Ornis des Zagrossgebietes W. Iran." *J. für Orn.* 1938.

—— *Danish Scientific Investigations in Iran*, pt. ii, 1940.

—— *On the Birds of Afghanistan*. 1959.

Passburg, R. E. "Birds Notes from N. Iran." *Ibis*, ci, no. 2, 1959.

Phillott, D. C. *Baz-Nama-i-Nasiri: A Persian Treatise on Falconry*. London, 1908.

Schuz, E. "Von Fruhjahrs Durchzug der Motacilla Flava." *Vogelwarte*, vol. xviii, Dec. 1956.

—— "Vogel-Erhebnisse bei Bandar-Schah." *Beitrage zur Vogelkunde*, vol. vi, 1957.

BIBLIOGRAPHY

—— "Ein Vergleich der Vogelwelt vom Elburzgebirge und Alpen." *Orn. Beob.* vol. LVII, 1957.

—— "Vögel von Teheran und Bagdad." *Vogelwelt*, LXXVIII, 1957.

—— *Die Vogelwelt des Sud-Kaspischen Tieflandes.* Stuttgart, 1959.

Stresemann. "Die Vögel des Elburz Expedition 1927." *J. Ornith.* 1928.

Ticehurst, C. B. "Birds of Mesopotamia." *J.B.N.H.S.* 1922.

—— "Birds of the Persian Gulf Islands." *J.B.N.H.S.* vol. XXX, no. 4, 1925.

Troff, A. C. "Notes on birds seen in the Lar valley in 1943 and 1944." *Ibis*, LXXXIX, 1947.

Vaurie, C. *The Birds of the Palaearctic Fauna*, vol. I. London, 1959.

Whistler, H. *Popular Handbook of Indian Birds* (4th edn.). 1940.

Witherby, H. "Ornithological journey in Fars, S.W. Persia." *Ibis*, 1903.

—— "On a collection of birds from W. Iran." *Ibis*, 1907.

—— "On a collection of birds from the S. Coast of the Caspian Sea and the Elburz Mountains." *Ibis*, 1910.

—— *et al. Handbook of British Birds.*

Zarudny, N. *Ornithological Results of the 1898 Expedition to E. Iran.* St Petersburg, 1903.

—— "Verzeichnis der Vögel Persiens." *J. Ornith.* 1911.

—— and Harms, M. "Bemerkung über einige Vögel Persiens." *J. Ornith.* 1912.

—— —— "Die Sperlinge Persiens." *J. Ornith.* LXI, 1913, p. 630.

—— —— "Die Steinschmatzer Persiens." *J. Ornith.* LXXIV, 1926, p. 1.

CHAPTER 12

Angel, J. L. "The human remains from Hotu Cave, Iran." *P.A.P.S.*, vol. XCVI, no. 3. 1952.

Braidwood, R. J., Howe, B. and Reed, C. A. "The Iranian prehistoric project." *Science*, vol. CXXXIII, no. 3469. 1961.

Le Gros Clark, W. E. *The Fossil Evidence for Human Evolution.* Chicago, 1955.

Coon, C. S. "Cave explorations in Iran, 1949." *U.P.M.M.* no. 1. 1949.

—— "Excavations in Hotu Cave, Iran, 1951; a preliminary report." *P.A.P.S.* vol. XCVI, no. 3. 1952.

—— "The excavations at Hotu Cave." *T.N.Y.A.S.* ser. ii, no. 14. 1952.

—— *Seven Caves.* London, 1957.

—— *The Origin of Races.* London, 1963.

Coon, C. S. and Ralph, E. K. "Radiocarbon dates for Kara Kamar, Afghanistan. Univ. of Penn. II." *Science*, vol. CXXII, no. 3176. 1955.

Dupree, L. "The Pleistocene artifacts of Hotu Cave, Mazanderan, Iran." *P.A.P.S.* vol. XCIII, no. 3. 1952.

Field, H. "Contributions to the anthropology of Iran." *F.M.N.H.* Anthrop. ser., 29. 1939.

—— "The Iranian plateau race." *Asia*, vol. XL, no. 4. 1940.

—— "Reconnaissance in south west Asia." *S.J.A.* vol. VII, no. 1. 1951.

Field, H. "Caves and rock shelters in south western Asia." *B.N.S.S.* no. XIII. 1951.

—— "Mountain peoples of Iran and Iraq." *A.J.P.A.* vol. IX, no. 1. 1951.

—— "Contributions to the anthropology of the Caucasus." *P.M.P.* vol. XLVIII, no. 1. 1953.

—— *Bibliography on South Western Asia.* 3 vols. Univ. of Miami, 1953–6.

—— "An anthropological reconnaissance in the Near East, 1950." *P.M.P.* vol. XLVIII, no. 2. 1956.

—— *Ancient and Modern Man in South Western Asia.* Univ. of Miami, 1956.

Howell, F. C. "Upper Pleistocene stratigraphy and early man in the Levant." *P.A.P.S.* vol. CIII, no. 1. 1959.

Krogman, W. M. "The peoples of early Iran and their ethnic affiliations." *A.J.P.A.* vol. XXVI. 1940.

Nesturkh, M. *The Origin of Man.* Moscow, 1959.

Ralph, E. K. "University of Pennsylvania radiocarbon dates I." *Science*, vol. CXXI, no. 3136. 1955.

Senyürek, M. S. "A short preliminary report on the two fossil teeth from the cave of Karain." *Belleten*, vol. XIII, no. 52. 1949.

—— "The skeleton of the fossil infant found in Shanidar cave, Northern Iraq, preliminary report." *Anatolia*, vol. II. 1957.

—— "A further note on the Palaeolithic Shanidar Infant." *Anatolia*, vol. II. 1957.

—— and Bostanci, E. "The excavation of a cave near the village of Magracik in the Vilayet of the Hatay, preliminary notice." *Anatolia*, vol. I. 1956.

Solecki, R. "Shanidar Cave, a Palaeolithic site in northern Iraq." *Smithsonian A. Rep. for 1954*. Washington, 1955.

—— "Three adult Neanderthal skeletons from Shanidar cave, northern Iraq." *S.R.P.* no. 4414. 1959–60.

Stewart, T. D. "First views on the restored Shanidar I skull." *Sumer*. vol. XIV, nos. 1–2. 1958.

—— "Restoration and study of the Shanidar I Neanderthal Skeleton in Baghdad, Iraq." *Y.A.P.S.* vol. CII. 1958.

—— "The restored Shanidar I skull." *S.R.P.* no. 4369. 1958.

—— "Form of the pubic bone in Neanderthal Man." *Science*, vol. CXXXI, no. 3411. 1960.

Welker, J. E. "Neanderthal Man and Homo sapiens." *A.A.* vol. LVI, no. 6. 1954.

CHAPTER 13

(Modern works only; primary sources, whenever used, are acknowledged in the notes.)

Aubin, J. "Références pour Lar médiévale." *J. asiat.* vol. CCXLIII. 1955.

Balsan, F. *La colline mystérieuse.* Paris, 1957.

Barth, F. "The land use pattern of migratory tribes of south Persia." *Norsk geogr. Tidsskr.* vol. XVII, nos. 1–4. 1959–60.

——— *Nomads of South Persia: the Basseri Tribe of the Khamseh Confederacy.* Oslo, 1961.

Bobek, H. "Die natürlichen Wälder und Gehölzfluren Irans." *Bonn. geogr. Abh.* vol. VIII. 1951.

——— "Die Verbreitung des Regenfeldbaues in Iran." *Festschrift J. Sölch.* 1951.

——— "Beiträge zur klima-ökologischen Gliederung Irans." *Erdkunde,* vol. VI. 1952.

——— "Die klima-ökologische Gliederung von Iran." *Proc. 17th Int. geogr. Congr.* 1952.

——— "Klima und Landschaft Irans in vor- und frühgeschichtlichen Zeit." *Geogr. Jber. Öst.* vol. XXXV. 1953–4.

——— "Teheran." *Geogr. Forschungen, Festschrift H. Kinzl.* Innsbruck, 1958.

Castiglioni, G. B. "Appunti geografici sul Balucistan Iraniano." *Riv. geogr. Ital.,* vol. LXVII, nos. 2, 3. 1960.

Clapp, F. C. "Tehran and the Elburz." *Geogr. Rev.* vol. XX. 1930.

Clarke, J. I. "The Iranian city of Shiraz." Research Papers Series no. 7. Dept. of Geogr., Univ. of Durham, 1963.

Collin-Delavaud, C. "Trois types de terroirs dans les provinces caspiennes d'Iran." *Mémoires et Documents du Centre de Documentation Cartographique et Géographique,* vol. VIII. C.N.R.S. Paris, 1961.

Coon, C. S. *Caravan, the Story of the Middle East.* London, 1952.

Dillemann, L. *Haute Mésopotamie Orientale et pays adjacents.* Paris, 1962.

Feilberg, C. G. *Les Papis.* Nationalmuseetsskrifter, Etnografisk Roekke, IV. Copenhagen, 1952.

Ferdinand, K. "The Baluchistan barrel-vaulted tent and its affinities." *Folk,* vol. I. 1959.

——— "The Baluchistan barrel-vaulted tent, supplementary material." *Folk,* vol. II. 1960.

Field, H. *Contributions to the Anthropology of Iran.* 2 vols. Chicago Anthrop. Ser., Field Mus. of Nat. Hist. Chicago, 1939.

Frye, R. W. "Remarks on Baluchi History." *Central Asiatic Journal,* vol. 6. 1961.

Gabriel, A. *Die Erforschung Persiens.* Vienna, 1952.

Gershevitch, I. "Travels in Bashkardia." *R. cent. Asian Soc.* vol. XLVI, no. ii. 1959.

Herzfeld, E. "Eine Reise durch Luristan, Arabistan und Fars." *Petermanns Mitt.,* vol. LIII. 1907.

——— *Iran in the Ancient East.* Archaeological Studies presented in the Lowell Lectures at Boston. O.U.P., New York, 1941.

Lambton, A. K. S. *Landlord and Peasant in Persia.* London, 1953.

Lindberg, K. *Voyage dans le Sud de l'Iran.* Lund, 1955.

Lockhart, L. *Persian Cities.* London, 1960.

Melgunof, G. *Das südliche Ufer des Kaspischen Meeres oder die Nordprovinzen Persiens.* Leipzig, 1868.

Minorsky, V. Article on Teheran, *Encycl. de l'Islam,* vol. IV. 1934.

Pabot, H. *Rapport au Khuzistan Development Service sur la végétation naturelle et son écologie dans les bassins versants du Khouzistan.* Tehrān, Ahwaz, 1960.

Pakravan, E. *Vieux Téhéran.* Institut Franco-Iranien. Tehrān, 1951.

Planhol, X. de. *Le Monde Islamique, essai de géographie réligieuse.* Paris, 1957.

—— "La vie de montagne dans le Sahend (Azerbaidjan iranien)." *Bull. Ass. Géogr. fr.* 1958.

—— "Les villages fortifiés en Iran et en Asie Centrale." *Annals Géogr.* 1958.

—— "Observations sur la géographie humaine de l'Iran Septentrional." *Bull. Ass. Géogr. fr.* 1959.

—— "Pressione demografice et vita di montagna nella Persia settentrionale." *Boll. Soc. geogr. Ital.* 1960.

—— "Un village de montagne de l'Azerbaidjan iranien, Lighwan (versant Nord du Sahend)." *Revue Géogr. Lyon.* 1960.

—— "Caractères généraux de la vie montagnarde dans le Proche-Orient et l'Afrique du Nord." *Annls Géogr.* 1962.

—— "Traits généraux de l'utilisation du sol dans l'Iran aride." *Act. Symp. d'Heraklion.* U.N.E.S.C.O. 1962.

—— "Recherches sur la Géographie Humaine de l'Iran Septentrional." *Mem. Docums. Cent. Docum. cartogr. géogr.* vol. IX. C.N.R.S. Paris, 1963.

Rabino, H. L. "Les provinces caspiennes de la Perse." *Revue du Monde Musulman*, vol. XX. le Guilân, Paris, 1917 (and as a separate pamphlet).

Rosenfeld, A. Z. "The Qal'a, the Iranian fortified village" (in Russian), *Sov. étnogr.* vol. I. 1951.

Scharlau, K. "Moderne Umgestaltungen im Grundriss iranischer Städte." *Erdkunde*, vol. XV. 1961.

Schwarz, P. *Iran im Mittelalter.* 9 vols. Leipzig, Stuttgart, 1896–1935.

Stein, A. *Old Routes of Western Iran.* London, 1940.

Stratil-Sauer, G. *Meschhed.* Leipzig, 1937.

—— "Birdjand, eine ostpersische Stadt." *Mitt. geogr. Ges. Wien*, vol. XCII. 1958.

—— *Geographische Forschungen in Ostpersien.* I. *Die ostpersische meridional-strasse*; II. *Route durch die Wüste Lut und ihre Randgebiete.* Abh. geogr. Ges. Wien, vol. XVII, nos. 2, 3, 1953–6.

Sykes, P. M. *Ten Thousand Miles in Persia.* London, 1902.

Tolstov, S. P. *Villages with "Habitable Walls"* (in Russian). Kratk. Soobshch. Inst. Istorii Materialnoï Kultury, 1947.

Vieille, P. *Tehrān: les prix, le marché des terrains et la société urbaine.* Section de Sociologie Urbaine, Institut d'Etudes et de Recherches Sociales, Univ. de Tehrān, 1961.

Wilber, D. N. *Persian Gardens and Garden Pavilions.* Rutland and Tokyo, 1962.

CHAPTER 14

Ministry of the Interior, Public Statistics Department. *National and Province Statistics of the First Census of Iran*, 2 volumes. Tehrān, 1956.

Regional Co-operation for Development (Iran, Pakistan, Turkey). *Seminar on Population Growth.* Ankara, 1966.

CHAPTER 15

Beckett, P. H. T. "Coal deposits near Kirman, south Persia." *Econ. Geol.* vol. LI.

Böhne, E. "Die Steinkohlenvorkommen Persiens." *Z. Prakt. Geol.* vol. XL. 1932.

Diehl, E. "Beitrag zur Kenntnis der Erzfundstellen Irans." *Schweiz Miner. Petrogr. Mitt.* vol. XXIV. 1944.

Huckriede, R., Kürsten, M. and Venzlaff, H. "Zur Geologie des Gebietes zwischen Kerman und Sagand (Iran)." *Beih. geol. Jb.* vol. LI. 1962.

Ladame, G. "Les resources metallifères de l'Iran." *Schweiz. Miner. Petrogr. Mitt.* vol. XXV. 1945.

Overseas Geol. Survey, Min. Resources Division. *Statist. Summ. Miner. Ind.* 1955–1960. London, 1962.

Stahl, A. F. *Persien Handb. reg. Geol.* vol. VI, no. 8, 1911.

Tipper, G. H. "Geology and mineral resources of eastern Persia." *Rec. geol. Surv. India*, vol. LIII. 1928.

Walther, H. W. "Orogen-Structur und Metalverteilung im östlichen Zagros (Sudost-Iran)." *Geol. Rdsch.* vol. L. 1960.

—— and Wirtz, D. "Geologie und Lagerstätten in sudost Iran." *Z. dt. geol. Ges.* vol. III. 1960.

CHAPTER 16

Ebtehaj, G. H. *A Guide to Iran.* Tehrān, 1956.

Elwell-Sutton, L. P. *Modern Iran.* London, 1941.

Fisher, W. B. *The Middle East.* London, 1956.

Grunwald, K. *Industrialization in the Middle East.* New York, 1960.

Issawi, C. *Economics of Middle East Oil.* New York, 1962.

Lockhart, L. "The causes of the Anglo-Persian oil dispute." *J. R. Cent. Asian Soc.* vol. XL. London, 1953.

—— "Şan'at-i-Naft", *Īrānshahr*, Tehrān, 1964, vol. II, pp. 1888–1917.

Longrigg, S. H. *Oil in the Middle East.* London, 1955.

Melamid, A. "Geographical Pattern of Iranian Oil Development." *Econ. Geogr.* vol. XXXV, no. 3, July 1959.

Nakhai, M. *Le Pétrole en Iran.* Brussels, 1938.

Royal Institute of International Affairs. *The Middle East.* London, 1958.

Stevens, R. *The Land of the Great Sophy.* London, 1962.

Twentieth International Congress of Geology. *Simposium Sobre Yacimientos de Petróleo y Gas.* Mexico, 1956 (in English).

United States Government, Dept. of Commerce. *Basic Data on the Economy of Iran.* Washington, 1962; and *Economic Developments in Iran* 1962. Washington, 1963.

Wilber, D. N. *Contemporary Iran.* New York, 1963.

Wilson, A. T. Persia. London, 1932.

—— *South-west Persia.* London, 1941.

CHAPTER 17

Ebtehaj, G. H. *A Guide to Iran.* Tehrān, 1956.
Elwell-Sutton, L. P. *Modern Iran.* London, 1960.
Fisher, W. B. *The Middle East.* London, 1956.
Hamilton, A. M. *Road through Kurdistan.* London, 1958.
Melamid, A. "The Russian-Iranian Boundary." *Econ. Geogr.* vol. XLIV, no. 1. Jan. 1959.
Skrine, C. *World War in Iran.* London, 1962.
Stevens, R. *The Land of the Great Sophy.* London, 1962.
United States Government, Dept. of Commerce. *Basic Data on the Economy of Iran.* Washington, 1962.
Wilson, A. T. *Persia.* London, 1932.
—— *South-west Persia.* London, 1941.

CHAPTER 18

Amir Parviz, A. H. "Use of Cooperatives." *CENTO Symposium on Rural Development.* Tehrān, 1963.
Agricultural Bank of Iran. *Annual Reports.* Tehrān.
Bank Melli Reviews. Tehrān.
Barth, Frederik. *Nomads of South Persia.* London, 1961.
—— *Principles of Social Organisation in Southern Kurdistan,* Universetets Etnografiske Museum. Oslo, 1953.
—— "The Land Use Pattern of Migratory Tribes of South Persia." *Norsk Geografisk Tidsskrift,* XVII, 1–4, 1959–60.
Beckett, P. H. T. "Agriculture in Central Persia." *Agriculture,* vol. XXXIV, no. 1, 1957.
—— and Gordon, E. D. "Land Use and Settlement round Kerman in Southern Iran." *Geogr. J.* vol. CXXXII, pt. 4, 1966.
Bobek, Hans. *Features and Formation of the Great Kavir and Masileh.* Arid Zone Research centre pub. II. University of Tehrān, 1959.
Brown, Judith. "The Historical Evolution of the Cities of Tehran and Isfahan." Unpublished Thesis, University of Durham, 1965.
C.E.N.T.O. *Cost and Return Ratios for Major Agricultural Products,* 1964.
—— *Report of Range Management Exports.* Unclassified Note EC/13/AG/D5, 1964.
—— *Range Management.* 1964.
de Planhol, Xavier. "Du Piemont Teherannais à la Caspienne." *Bull. Ass. Géogr. fr.* 1959.
—— "La vie de Montagne dans le Sahend." *Bull. Ass. Géogr. fr.* 1958.
—— "Les Tendances Nouvelles de L'Agriculture Irriguée dans L'Oasis D'Isfahan." *Revue Géogr. L'Est,* IV, 1964.
—— *Tehran.* Institute of Social Studies and Research. Tehrān, 1962.
Department of Public Statistics. *First National Census of Agriculture.* Tehrān, 1960.

BIBLIOGRAPHY

Economic Research Bureau. *Studies of Economic Problems of Farming in Iran.* Tehrān, 1962.

Eicher, C. K. and Witt, L. W. *Agriculture in Economic Development.* New York, 1964.

F.A.O. *The Development of Land and Water Resources in Khuzistan.* Rome, 1956.

—— *Water Laws in Moslem Countries.* Development Paper No. 43, 1954.

—— and Independent Irrigation Corporation of Iran. *Report of the Agricultural and Water Economy in the Garmsar Area.* Tehrān, 1960.

Farhad Ghahraman. "Water Rights in Iran." *CENTO Symposium on Rural Development.* Tehrān, 1963.

Fitzherbert, Master. *The Book of Husbandry.* London, 1534.

Flower, D. "The Agricultural Geography of the Mashad Region." Unpublished thesis, University of Durham, 1966.

High Economic Council of Iran. *Annual Bulletins.* Tehrān.

Institute of Social Research and Studies, University of Tehrān. *Income in Iran.* Tehrān, 1961.

Khuzestan Regional Development Authority. *Quarterly Reviews.* Tehrān.

Krader, L. "Ecology of Central Asian Pastoralism." *Southwestern J. Anthrop.* XI, 1955.

Lambton, Ann K. S. *Landlord and Peasant in Persia.* Oxford, 1953.

—— "Some Reflections on the Question of Rural Development and Land Reform in Iran." *CENTO Symposium on Rural Development.* Tehrān, 1963.

Ministry of Education of Iran. *Monthly Bulletins.* Tehrān.

Op't Land, C. *The Permanent Settlements of the Dachte-Moghan.* Institute of Social Studies and Research. Tehrān, 1961.

Plan Organisation of Iran, Reports by:

E.T.C.O. *Aménagement de la Rivière Gorgan.* 1959.

Development and Resources Corporation, Khuzestan. 1959–63.

Gibb, Sir Alexander and Partners. *Irrigation Project-Mazanderan.* 1958.

Italconsult. "Socio-Economic Development Plan for the South Eastern Region." *Preliminary Report Agricultural Survey.* 1959.

Italconsult. *A Preliminary Assessment of Potential Resources in Khurasan Province.* 1963.

Societé Grenoblaise d'Etudes et d'Application Hydrauliques. *Réseau du Barrage de Safid Roud; Mise en Valeur de la plaine du Guilan.* 1958.

Spooner, B. "Arghiyān. The Area of Jājarm in Western Khorassan." *Iran,* vol. III, 1965.

Thornthwaite, Mather and Carter. "Three Water Balance Maps of Southwest Asia." *Climatology,* vol. XI, no. 1. Centerton, New Jersey, 1962.

UN. *Multi-Purpose River Basin Development.* Flood Control Series no. 18. 61.II.F.8.

UNESCO. *A History of Land Use in Arid Regions.* Arid Zone Research no. XVII, 1961.

—— *The Problems of the Arid Zone.* Arid Zone Research no. XVIII, 1962.

759

UNESCO. *Nomadism in the Mountain and Plateau Areas of South West Asia*, Paper no. 16.
—— *Nomadic Pastoralism as a Method of Land Use*, Paper no. 17.
—— *General Symposium on Arid Zone Problems* NS/AZ/526. Paris, 1960.

CHAPTER 20

Alberts, R. C. "Social Structure and Culture change in an Iranian Village." Ph.D. Dissertation. University of Wisconsin, 1963.
Arasteh, A. R. *Education and Social Awakening in Iran*. Leiden, 1912.
—— *Man and Society in Iran*. Leiden, 1964.
Arberry, A. J. *Sufism. An Account of the Mystics of Islam*. London, 1950.
—— (ed.). *The Legacy of Persia*. Oxford, 1953.
Arensberg, C. M. "The community study method." *Am. J. Sociol.* LX, no. 2, 1954, pp. 109 *et seq.*
Avery, P. *Modern Iran*. London, 1965.
Banani, A. *The Modernization of Iran, 1921–1941*. Stanford, 1961.
Barnett, H. G. *Innovation: The Basis of Cultural Change*. New York, 1953.
Barth, F. "Principles of social organization in Southern Kurdistan." *Universitetets Etnografiske Museum Bull.* no. 7. Oslo, 1953.
—— "FaBrDa marriage in Kurdistan." *Southwestern J. Anthrop.* X, 1954, pp. 164–71.
—— "The land use pattern of migratory tribes of South Persia." *Norsk Geografisk Tidsskrift.* XVII, 1959–60, pp. 1–11.
—— "Nomadism in the mountain and plateau areas of South West Asia." *UNESCO Symposium on Arid Zone Problems*, XVI, 1960.
—— *Nomads of South Persia*. London, 1961.
Beckett, P. H. T. and Gordon, E. D. "Land use and settlement round Kerman in Southern Iran." *Geogr. J.* CXXXII, pt. 4, 1966, pp. 476–90.
Benet, F. "Muhammad and the Mountain." (Typescript.) Paper presented at 2nd Int. Ec. Hist. Conf., Aix-en-Provence. 1962.
—— "Sociology uncertain: the ideology of the rural-urban continuum." *Comp. Studies in Society and History*, VI, 1963, pp. 1–23.
Childe, V. G. *Social Evolution*. London, 1950.
Chiva, I. *Rural Communities. Problems, Methods and Types of Research*. Reports and Papers in the Social Sciences. UNESCO, no. 10, 1958.
Coon, C. S. *Caravan. The Story of the Middle East*. New York, 1961.
Cressey, G. B. "Qanats, Karez and Hoggaras." *Geogr. Rev.* XLVIII, no. 1, 1958, pp. 27–44.
Elwell-Sutton, L. P. *A Guide to Iranian Area Study*. Ann Arbor, 1952.
Forde, C. D. and Scott, R. *The Native Economies of Nigeria*. London, 1946.
Fortes, M. "Culture contact as a dynamic process." In *Methods of Study of Culture in Africa*. Int. African Inst. Memo. XV, 1938.
Foster, G. M. "What is folk culture?" *Am. Anth.* LV, 2, pt. 1, 1953, pp. 157–73.
—— *Traditional Cultures and the Impact of Technological Change*. New York, 1962.

Friedl, E. "Studies in peasant life." In *Biennial Review of Anthropology*, ed. by B. J. Siegel. Stanford, 1963.

Frye, R. N. *Iran*. London, 2nd ed. 1960.

Fuller, A. H. *Buarij. Portrait of a Lebanese Village*. Harvard Middle East Monograph Series, no. 6, 1961.

Garrod, O. "The nomadic tribes of Persia today." *J. Roy. Cent. As. Soc.* XXXIII, pt. 1, 1946, pp. 32–46.

—— "The Qashqai tribe of Fars." *J. Roy. Cent. As. Soc.* XXXIII, pts. 3 and 4, 1946, pp. 293–306.

Geertz, C. "Studies in peasant life: community and society." In *Biennial Review of Anthropology*, ed. by B. J. Siegel. Stanford, 1961.

Gibb, H. A. R. and Bowen, H. *Islamic Society and the West. A Study of the Impact of Western Civilization on Moslem Culture in the Near East*. Oxford, 1950 (vol. I, pt. 1); 1957 (vol. I, pt. 2).

Grunebaum, G. E. von. *Muhammadan Festivals*. London, 1951.

—— "The structure of the Muslim town." In *Islam: Essays in the Nature and Growth of a Cultural Tradition*. London, 1955.

—— "The problem: unity in diversity." In *Unity and Variety in Muslim Civilization*, ed. by G. E. von Grunebaum. Chicago, 1955.

Hadary, G. "The agrarian reform problem in Iran." *Mid. East J.* V, 1951, pp. 181–96.

Hayden, L. J. "Living standards in rural Iran. A case study." *Mid. East J.* III, 1949, pp. 140–50.

Ivanow, W. "Notes on the ethnology of Khurasan." *Geogr. J.* LXVII, 1926, pp. 143–58.

Kinnane, D. *The Kurds and Kurdistan*. Inst. of Race Relations. Oxford, 1964.

Lambton, A. K. S. *Landlord and Peasant in Persia*. Oxford, 1953.

—— "Impact of the West on Iran." *Int. Affairs, London*. XXXIII, 1957, pp. 12–25.

Leach, E. R. *Social and Economic Organization of the Rowanduz Kurds*. London, 1940.

Lerner, D. *The Passing of Traditional Society; Modernizing the Middle East*. Glencoe, Ill., 1958.

Levy, R. *The Social Structure of Islam*. Cambridge, 1957.

Lewis, O. *Life in a Mexican Village; Tepoztlán restudied*. Univ. of Illinois Press, 1951.

—— "Tepoztlán restudied: a critique of the folk-urban conceptualization of social change." *Rural Sociol.* XVIII, 1953, pp. 121–34.

Mair, L. *New Nations*. London, 1963.

Marx, K. "The British rule in India." *New York Daily Tribune*. 25 June 1853. Quoted in T. B. Bottomore, *Sociology*. London, 1962, p. 118.

Masse, H. *Persian Beliefs and Customs*. Hum. Rel. Area Files. New Haven. Conn., 1954.

Miner, H. "The folk-urban continuum." *Am. Sociol. Rev.* XVII, no. 5, 1952, pp. 529–37.

—— *The Primitive City of Timbuctoo*. Princeton, 1953.

Minorsky, V. "The tribes of western Iran." *J. Roy. Anthrop. Inst.* LXXV, 1945, pp. 73–80.

Mohammed Reza Shah Pahlevi. *Mission for My Country.* London, 1960.

Najafi, N. and Hinckley, H. *Reveille for a Persian Village.* London, 1960.

Narāghī, E. *Les classes moyennes en Iran.* Cahiers International de Sociologie, XXII, 1957.

—— "Social consequences of economic and technological development in Iran." Univ. of Teheran. (Typescript.)

Naval Intelligence Division. *Persia.* Geographical Handbook Series, 1945.

Nikitine, B. *Les Kurdes: Étude sociologique et historique.* Paris, 1956.

Nolte, R. H. (ed.). *The Modern Middle East.* New York, 1963.

Op't Land, C. A. *The Permanent Settlements of the Dachte Moghan Area. Problems around the Sedentarization of Pastoralists,* Paper no. 5. Inst. of Social Studies and Research. Univ. of Teherān, 1961.

—— "Land reform in Iran." *Persica.* Annuaire de la Société Néerlando-Iranienne, pp. 80–122, 1965–6.

Parsons, T. *The Social System.* London, 1952.

Pitt-Rivers, J. (ed.). *Mediterranean Countrymen.* Paris, 1963.

Planhol, X. de. "Recherches sur la géographie humaine de l'Iran septentrional." *Mémoires et Documents du Centre de Documentation Cartographique et Géographique,* Tome 9, Fasc. 4. Éditions du Centre de la Recherche Scientifique. Paris, 1964.

—— "Aspects of mountain life in Anatolia and Iran." In *Geography as Human Ecology,* ed. S. R. Eyre and G. R. J. Jones. London, 1966.

Redfield, E. *Tepoztlán, a Mexican Village. A Study of Folk Life.* Chicago, 1930.

—— *The Folk Culture of Yucatan.* Chicago, 1941.

—— *The Primitive World and its Transformations.* Cornell, 1953.

—— *The Little Community.* Chicago, 1955.

—— *Peasant Society and Culture.* Chicago, 1956.

Rioux, M. "Description de la culture de l'Ile Verte." *Ottawa Nat. Mus. of Canada Bull.* no. 133. Anthrop. Series, no. 55, 1954.

Safrastian, A. *Kurds and Kurdistan.* London, 1948.

Salim, S. M. *Marsh Dwellers of the Euphrates Delta.* London, 1962.

Sjoberg, G. *The Preindustrial City, Past and Present.* Glencoe, Ill., 1960.

Spooner, B. "The function of religion in Persian society." *Iran,* I, 1963, pp. 83–95.

—— "Iranian kinship and marriage." *Iran,* IV, 1966, pp. 51–9.

Sprott, W. J. H. *Human Groups.* Harmondsworth, 1958.

Stirling, P. "Structural changes in Middle East Society." In *Tensions in the Middle East,* ed. P. W. Thayer. Baltimore, 1958.

—— *Turkish Village.* London, 1965.

Tolstov, S. P. (ed.). *Narody Perednei Azii.* Moscow, 1957, pp. 53–308.

Ullens de Schooten, M. *Lords of the Mountains: Southern Persia and the Kashkai Tribe.* London, 1956.

Upton, J. *The History of Modern Iran: an Interpretation.* Harvard Mid. East Monograph Series. Harvard, 1960.

Vreeland, H. H. (ed.). *Iran*. Human Rel.'Area Files. New Haven, Conn., 1957.
Watt, W. M. *Islam and the Integration of Society*. London, 1961.
Weber, M. *General Economic History*. Glencoe, Ill., 1950.
—— *The City*, trans. and ed. by D. Martindale and G. Neuwirth. New York, 1962.
Wilber, D. N. (ed.). *Iran: Past and Present*. Princeton, 1958.
—— *Contemporary Iran*. New York, 1963.
Wittfogel, K. A. "The hydraulic civilizations." In *Man's Role in Changing the Face of the Earth*, ed. by W. L. Thomas. Chicago, 1956.
Wolf, E. R. *Peasants*. New York, 1966.
Young, T. C. "The problem of westernization in Modern Iran." *Mid. East J.* II, 1948, pp. 47–59.

CHAPTER 21

Arfa, H. "Land reform in Iran." *Royal Central Asian J.* vol. L, part II, April 1963, pp. 132–8.
Alam, A. "Land situation in Iran." In *Proceedings of the International Conference on Land Tenure and Related Problems in World Agriculture*. Madison, Wisconsin, 1951.
Dehbud, A. "Land ownership and use conditions in Iran." *Symposium on Rural Development*. Cento, 1963.
Elm, M. *The Need for Institutional Changes in Iran's Agricultural System*. UNESCO/Tehrān University, S.S/Tehrān Sem./103, undated.
Hadary, G. "The agrarian reform problem in Iran." *Middle East J.* vol. V, no. 2, Spring 1951.
Homayun, D. "Land reform in Iran." *Tahqiqat-i Eqtesadi*. University of Tehrān, vol. II, nos. 5 and 6, September 1963.
Iran Almanac, 1963, 1965 and 1966. Tehrān.
Lambton, A. K. S. "A reconsideration of the position of the marja' al-taqlid and the religious institution." *Studia Islamica*, Fasc. xx, Paris, 1964.
—— *Landlord and Peasant in Persia*. R.I.I.A. 1953.
—— "Reflections on the iqta." *Arabic and Islamic Studies in Honour of Hamilton Gibb*. Leiden, 1965.
—— "Some reflections on the question of rural development and land reform in Iran." *Symposium on Rural Development*. Cento, 1963.
Land Reform Organization. *Abstracts of Statistics*. Tehrān, 1963–5.
Mahdavi, H. "A review of the statistics of the first stage of land reform." *Tahqiqat-i Eqtesadi*, University of Tehrān, vol. II, nos. 7 and 8, March 1964.
—— "The coming crisis in Iran." *Foreign Affairs*, October 1965.
Millspaugh, A. C. *Financial and Economic Situation of Persia*. New York, 1926.
Ministry of Interior, Department of Statistics. *Agricultural Census*, 1339.
Salur, A. "Land reform activities in Iran." *Symposium on Rural Development*. Cento, 1963.
Satur, A. *The Operation of Land Reform in Iran*. Tehrān, 1965.

Scarcia, G. *Aspects of Land Reform in Iran*. Tehrān, 1966.
—— "Governo, riforma agraria e opposizione in Persia." *Oriente Moderno*, Anno XLII, n. 10–11, 1962, pp. 731–801.
Warriner, Doreen. *Land Reform and Development in the Middle East*. R.I.I.A. 1962.

CHAPTER 22

Anuchin, V. A. *Teoreticheskiye Problemi Geografi*. Moscow, 1960.
Avery, P. W. *Modern Iran*. London, 1966.
Gilbert, E. W. *Geography as a Humane Study*. Oxford, 1954.
—— *Seven Lamps of Geography*. London, 1951.
Hartshorne, R. *The Nature of Geography*. Lancaster, Penn., 1939.
Herder, J. G. *Geographischen Geschichte*. Berlin, 1795.
Hettner, A. *Die Geographie, ihr Wesen und ihr Methoden*. Breslau, 1927.
Isard, W. *et al. Methods of Regional Analysis*. New York, 1960.
Lösch, A. *The Economics of Location*. New Haven, Conn., 1954.
Toynbee, A. J. *A Study of History*, 6 volumes. Oxford, 1934– .
Vidal de la Blache, P. *Tableau de la Géographie de la France*. Paris, 1908.
Weulersse, J. *Paysans de Syrie et du Proche Orient*. Tours, 1946.

CONVERSION TABLES

metres to feet

1	3·281
2	6·56
3	9·84
4	13·12
5	16·40
6	19·68
7	22·97
8	26·25
9	29·53
10	32·81
100	328·1
1000	3281

feet to metres

1	0·305
2	0·61
3	0·91
4	1·22
5	1·52
6	1·83
7	2·13
8	2·44
9	2·74
10	3·05
100	30·5
1000	3048

km. to miles

1	0·621
2	1·24
3	1·86
4	2·49
5	3·11
6	3·73
7	4·35
8	4·97
9	5·59
10	6·21
100	62·1
1000	621

miles to km.

1	1·609
2	3·22
3	4·83
4	6·44
5	8·05
6	9·66
7	11·27
8	12·88
9	14·48
10	16·09
100	160·9
1000	1609

hectares to acres

1	2·471
2	4·94
3	7·41
4	9·88
5	12·36
6	14·63
7	17·30
8	19·77
9	22·24
10	24·71
100	247·1
1000	2471

acres to hectares

1	0·405
2	0·81
3	1·21
4	1·62
5	2·02
6	2·43
7	2·83
8	3·24
9	3·64
10	4·05
100	40·47
1000	405

CONVERSION TABLES

sq. km. to sq. mile			sq. mile to sq. km.	
I	0·386		I	2·590
2	0·77		2	5·18
3	1·16		3	7·77
4	1·54		4	10·36
5	1·93		5	12·95
6	2·32		6	15·54
7	2·70		7	18·13
8	3·09		8	20·72
9	3·48		9	23·31
10	3·86		10	25·90
100	38·61		100	259·0
1000	386		1000	2590

Temperature °C and °F

5° C on scale = 9° F

°C	°F		°C	°F
100	212		15	59
60	140		10	50
55	131		5	41
50	122		0	32
45	113		− 5	23
40	104		− 10	14
35	95		− 15	+ 5
30	86		− 20	− 4
25	77		− 25	− 13
20	68			

INDEX